Anthony ~~~~~~~~
          12/16

→ Megan UL

SHADOW WARS

Also by Christopher Davidson

After the Sheikhs: The Coming Collapse of the Gulf Monarchies

Power and Politics in the Persian Gulf Monarchies (as Editor)

The Persian Gulf and Pacific Asia: From Indifference to Interdependence

Abu Dhabi: Oil and Beyond

Higher Education in the Gulf: Shaping Economies, Politics and Culture (as Editor)

Dubai: The Vulnerability of Success

The United Arab Emirates: A Study in Survival

SHADOW WARS

The Secret Struggle
for the Middle East

Christopher
Davidson

ONEWORLD

A Oneworld Book

First published by Oneworld Publications Ltd, 2016

Copyright © Christopher Davidson 2016

ISBN 978-1-78607-001-2
eISBN 978-1-78607-002-9

Printed and bound in Great Britain by
Clays Ltd, St Ives plc

Oneworld Publications Ltd
10 Bloomsbury Street, London WC1B 3SR, England

CONTENTS

CONTENTS

CONTENTS

CONTENTS

CONTENTS

INTRODUCTION

S wept along on a tidal wave of euphoria, many people had cautiously begun to believe that the Arab uprisings of 2011 heralded the dawn of a new era in which more progressive, secular, and perhaps even democratic states could finally be built from the ruins of tyranny. But hopes were dashed almost as soon as they were raised, and any remaining optimism quickly gave way to shock and dismay as resurgent religious politics, bloody counter-revolutions, and sectarian wars began to take hold. To make matters worse, not only were the ideals of the so-called 'Arab Spring' left lying in tatters, but its failures somehow seemed responsible for the rise of ever more repressive dictatorships, along with some of the most brutal incarnations of Islamic extremism the world has ever seen.

Forlorn, dispirited, and resigned to an Arab world doomed to fail, activists and scholars inevitably began to ask, 'What went wrong?' After all, if parts of Europe, Latin America, and even Africa once managed to cut the shackles of authoritarianism, then why not the Arabs? Moreover, and more urgently, many have asked why the region's predominant and essentially peace-promoting Islamic faith had once again proven so vulnerable to co-option and subversion by powerful fanatics, even in the twenty-first century. All are important questions demanding a response and explanations, not only because an honest and thorough post-mortem of the Arab Spring is needed, but because those who aspire to a brighter future for the region must be better prepared to identify the real root causes behind its perennial afflictions.

Beginning at the beginning, the answers put forward in this book first require a little time travel, not only to establish the causes of the Arab Spring, but also to help understand how it sits in history. Demonstrating that the events of 2011 and the subsequent counter-revolutions were in many ways nothing new, it shows how important elements of each have frequently surfaced in what is best understood as a centuries-old and worldwide pattern of popular challenges and autocratic reactions. Importantly, these struggles were rarely limited to just one country or a region's elites and their opponents, but instead were often a function of the inextricably interlinked interests of influential foreign powers and their local clients. In some cases, when threats to the status quo were especially severe, this even led to multinational counter-revolutionary coalitions involving volatile mixes of competing empires allied to on-the-ground despots, feudal dynasties, and conservative clerics. Tragically for the resource-rich and strategically vital Middle East, such efforts have been particularly pronounced, especially in the wake of its first major oil exports – crucial to global energy supplies – and its subsequent centrality to Cold War proxy power struggles.

With the stakes getting ever higher, and arguably now still greater than in any other part of the developing world, it is a little easier to appreciate the considerable lengths taken by those both inside and outside the region to protect their positions and their unfettered access to its wealth. In some cases, the familiar fingerprints from covert campaigns littered across the twentieth century, from Malaya to Iran to Nicaragua, can easily be found in the Arab world today. In others, however, there are signs of older and much darker strategies having been rekindled, including those that have enlisted and wilfully cultivated the most fundamentalist religious forces so as to suppress progressive movements and reverse efforts to found independent nations more capable of controlling their own resources and destinies.

In this context, the book's most forceful argument, and the one that will prove most unsettling for citizens of the Western world, is that the primary blame for not only the failure of the Arab Spring, but also the dramatic and well-funded rise of Islamic extremist organizations since the late twentieth century – including the deadly al-Qaeda and now the blood-curdling 'Islamic State' – must rest with the long-running policies of successive imperial and 'advanced-capitalist' administrations and their ongoing manipulations of an elaborate network of powerful national and transnational actors across both the Arab and Islamic worlds. As the final chapters will attest, the threat to present-day Western states and their constituent corporations from self-determining 2011-style Arab nations has not only been foiled, but has also been covertly redirected into a pretext for striking at their other enemies. Meanwhile, hidden behind ever more carefully layered veils of agents and intermediaries, the same powers that have distantly ruled the region for hundreds of years are now making sure their grip gets even tighter.

1

COUNTER-REVOLUTION –
A PATTERN EMERGES

LESSONS FROM THE PAST – NOTHING IS NEW

N amed after their mascot, King James II, the Jacobite nobles of Britain and Ireland are often touted as good early examples of 'counter-revolutionaries'.[1] Seeking the restoration of James and his Catholic House of Stuart, their goal was the reversal of the 'Glorious Revolution' of 1688 that led to the coronation of James' Protestant son-in-law.[2] Also intending for James to resume the 'divine right of kings' and continue efforts to weaken parliament, their plan was to realign the country with the Pope, in Rome, and the King of France. Put simply, the Jacobites were backing an old, absolutist regime buttressed by distant powers and underpinned by conservative religious forces that sought to roll back political freedoms and return Britain to a more medieval system of rule.[3]

But fast-forwarding to the late eighteenth century, it was the intensifying resistance to the French Revolution of 1789 that started to give a taste of how displaced European *ancien régimes* would really begin to fight back against both progressive forces and mass uprisings. In Paris itself, the 'Thermidorian Reaction' of 1794 – named after the new revolutionary calendar's warm summer month of *Thermidor* – saw the forcible ousting of Maximilien Robespierre and other leading politicians from the National Convention, the first French parliament to be elected by universal male suffrage.[4] Outlawed, hunted down, and then executed, Robespierre and the proponents of the new revolutionary constitution gave way to a reactionary regime which set about creating a dual-chamber English-style parliament in an effort to protect the interests of the wealthy and powerful.[5]

In parallel, the nascent revolutionary republic came under attack in the countryside too, with a full-scale rebellion in France's western Vendée province blamed on exiled noblemen and a clergy that sought to spark peasant unrest and dissuade parishioners from joining the national army.[6] With another clear alliance in place between sidelined aristocrats and traditional religious powers, Antoine-François Momoro – the originator of the phrase *'Liberté, Égalité, Fraternité'* – described how 'criminal priests, taking advantage of the credulity of the inhabitants of the country, remained hidden behind a screen, as did the former nobles who crowded into the region from the four corners of France; they waited for the favourable moment to appear and put themselves at the head of the rebellious peasants.'[7]

Meanwhile, as the effects of the Thermidorian and Vendée counter-revolutions began to reverberate beyond France's borders, any hope of spreading new political ideas or – as they have been described – 'radical republican agitations' was being firmly nipped in the bud back in Britain. Severe legal repression and the banning of influential texts such as Thomas Paine's *Rights of Man* was soon followed by the looting and burning of houses belonging to 'radicals and dissenters'. England had become a country 'covered with a network of barracks', with restive industrial areas 'treated almost as a conquered country in the hands of an army of occupation.'[8]

In Catholic Italy, as it was for the Vendée nobles and Jacobites before them, the Vatican became an important ally for those opposed to a new republic that sought to bring democracy to Naples and rekindle the ideals of the region's ancient Greek colony of Parthenope.[9] With priests, bishops, and even cardinals mobilizing peasants, and with the help of a British naval blockade, a branch of the old ruling Bourbon dynasty was violently restored and an absolutist 'Kingdom of Naples' re-established in 1799.[10] For the first four weeks of his return, King Ferdinand IV kept his headquarters offshore as a guest of British rear admiral Horatio Nelson on *HMS Foudroyant*, and it was from there that he set about ordering the executions of over a hundred political prisoners including poets, scientists, and constitution writers. Complete with public beheadings, an era of debilitating censorship and the suppression of all political movements duly began.[11]

Attempting much the same strategy, the Spanish 'Carlists' who fought for the installation of another Bourbon, Carlos V, were backed by both displaced feudal landowners and the Pope in their efforts to reinstate the divine right of kings on the Iberian peninsula. Finally attacking in 1833, their forces may not have been successful, but they did much to weaken a fledgling Spanish state which, twenty years earlier, had introduced arguably the most modern and liberal constitution in the world, complete with land reform laws, universal male suffrage, and guarantees for freedom of the press.[12]

Despite the many setbacks and the hardening of counter-revolutionary fronts, the people of Europe were nonetheless still on the move, and by 1848 the 'Spring of Nations' or 'Springtime of the People' blossomed across the continent. Only days after Karl Marx and Friedrich Engels published their *Communist Manifesto*, euphoric crowds took to the streets of France to demand a new republic, while worried monarchs in Sweden, Denmark, and the Netherlands quickly made concessions as demonstrations swept through their cities.[13] Seemingly unassailable, with a mass popular mandate, the new French government introduced sweeping new employment rules and other social reforms, along with restoring the original revolutionary goal of universal male suffrage. But in a careful manoeuvre, this time not co-opting religious forces and instead just claiming to 'restore order', the old monarchists and other conservatives engineered the appointment of a military general as head of the new state, who in turn paved the way for the election of Louis-Napoléon Bonaparte as president by the end of the year. As the strongman nephew of Napoléon I, who had morphed France into an empire earlier in the century, Louis-Napoléon's security-focused strategies – *Bonapartism* – were enough to hold the spirit of 1848 in check. Within three years he and his supporters were then able to launch a 'self-coup' that abolished the National Assembly outright and initiated the second French Empire, with Louis crowned Emperor Napoléon III.[14]

More than a thousand miles to the east, Russia's absolutist and corrupt Romanov dynasty was weathering repeated uprisings and even full-blown rebellions, but by the turn of the twentieth century its more than ninety million subjects were ripe for their own revolution.[15] With the Marx-inspired Bolshevik or 'Majority' faction of the Russian Social Democratic Party rising to the fore in the wake of Tsar Nicholas II's eventual ouster in 1917, the movement was poised to burst its Russian banks with a threat to 'furnish the new proletarian society in Russia with a suitable parallel environment in other European and extra-European countries'.[16] The inevitable reaction across Europe, and indeed the world, is important to understand as it involved not only collaborations between worried royals and other old regimes, but also new states with supposedly progressive agendas but which were increasingly being underwritten by capitalist modes of production and were thus equally alarmed at the prospect of an international workers-led movement reaching their own territories. After all, the Bolsheviks had not only supplanted a tsar, but, as historian William Blum describes, had also displayed the 'audacity of overthrowing a capitalist-feudal system and proclaiming the first socialist state in the history of the world'. As such it became 'a virus that had to be eradicated'.[17]

For it to succeed, any counter-revolutionary campaign therefore had to go far beyond the old methods of co-opting religion, reinvigorating aristocrats, or launching military coups. After all, the indigenous resistance, known as the 'White Movement', was a poorly performing loose confederation of monarchists, non-socialist republicans, peasants, and even conscripts from Ukraine.[18] Conducting pogroms against ancient Jewish communities and being rolled back on the battlefield, it stood no chance of winning on its own, but its potential usefulness had nevertheless caught the attention of the young British minister for war and air, Winston Churchill, whose stated aim was to 'strangle at birth' the new Russian socialist republic.[19]

Forming a global coalition to back the White Movement, Churchill also sought to insert foreign troops into an increasingly chaotic and destabilizing 'civil war'. Using the pretext of rescuing a stranded Czechoslovak legion in Russia, Britain and France requested help for their expeditionary forces from the similarly concerned United States, which duly dispatched five thousand soldiers to the northern coastline while a further eight thousand disembarked on the Pacific coastline near Vladivostok. With foreign counter-revolutionaries soon outnumbering actual Russians, troops from Canada, Australia, India, and Japan joined the fray, while Italy, Greece, Romania, and several other countries also eventually made a contribution.[20]

Disturbingly, Britain also sent officers to Central Asia to lead and recruit forces for a campaign by Turkmen tribes against secular Russia. Requiring that its 'officers should be accompanied, if possible, by persona qualified to conduct Muhammadan propaganda in favour of the allies', Britain was knowingly entering into a relationship with an anti-Bolshevik force committed to founding 'an Islamic emirate with sharia law courts'. Although the British-led Turkmen troops were officially withdrawn in 1919, camel caravans of weapons and supplies continued to flow to large numbers of these Islamic guerrilla fighters. Described by Moscow as *basmachi* or 'bandits', their religious-political campaign had by then spread to Tajik and Kazakh territories.[21]

Despite its size and the dozens of states involved, the massive alliance ultimately failed. Poor morale and wariness of another world war had seemingly combined with real fears of revolt in the backyards of the reactionary powers. The German revolution of 1918–19 may have failed to transfer power to Russian-style people's assemblies, due to the violence of *Freikorps* nationalist militias and the hesitancy of the Social Democratic Party to exclude fully old elites, but as Leon Trotsky observed, 'the only reason the Austro-German military powers did not carry their attack upon Soviet Russia through to the end was that they felt behind their back the hot breath of the revolution.' Similarly, the French sailors' revolt in the Black Sea in 1919 undoubtedly obliged Paris to call off its attacks on Russia, while London withdrew its forces from northern Russia the same year due to pressure from British workers' movements.[22]

The emergence of the *Freikorps* had, however, already heralded the birth of a new counter-revolutionary front across Europe. In Italy's case the *Bienno Rosso* – a two-year-long 'red movement' that had begun in 1919 – was violently confronted by 'black shirt' militias and eventually defeated in 1922 after the 'March on Rome' by Benito Mussolini's National Fascist Party. Having sparked workers' strikes and promoted Moscow-like worker-led councils in both factories and the countryside, the *Bienno Rosso* had led to Italy's trade union membership swelling to several hundred thousand, but with Mussolini in power its work was quickly undone, with a sort of corporate-friendly nationalism putting Italy on a very different path. Adopting many of the more popular ideas of the socialist and communist revolutionaries of the previous decade, and having clearly recognized the need for a new type of society, Mussolini had seemingly succeeded in creating a form of state-led capitalist organization with much tighter restrictions on labour and workers' movements.[23]

LESSONS FROM THE PAST – THE PREVENTIVE COUNTER-REVOLUTIONS

Witnessing the ongoing rise of the fascists in the 1930s, the German theoretician Karl Korsch saw it as evidence of a 'preventive counter-revolution' and a 'dangerous new international alliance'. With the Russian Revolution and the resulting socialist republic as their doomsday scenario, Europe's old ruling and business elites – or at least those that had survived the First World War – had quickly found common ground, however uncomfortable, with those who could not only summon nationalist mobs but could also safeguard at least some capitalist structures and, so it seemed, offer protection for the status quo. In this sense, fascism became a 'counter-revolution against a revolution that never took place' at a time when the common goal of most European heads of state – whether the elected leaders of Britain and France or the dictator of Italy – was to 'create conditions which will make impossible any independent movement of the European working class for a long time to come'.[24]

Adolf Hitler's divisive policies were thus supported or appeased by many in London. Warning parliament in 1934 against condemning the National Socialist German Workers' Party, former prime minister David Lloyd-George reasoned that Hitler and 'the Nazis' were 'destined to be the most reliable bulwark against communism in Europe'.[25] In a 1936 interview with the *Washington Post* he went further, rationalizing that Hitler's attacks on trade unions and freedom of expression were justifiable on the grounds that Germans were an order-loving and 'highly disciplined people', and thus the situation could not be compared with anything in Britain or elsewhere.[26] In a follow-up article in the *Daily Express*, he even declared Hitler 'as immune from criticism as a king in a monarchical country. He is something more. He is the George Washington of Germany.'[27]

In the early stages of the Second World War, senior US politicians, like future president Harry Truman, were delighted at first by Germany's

COUNTER-REVOLUTION – A PATTERN EMERGES

invasion of the Soviet Union: Truman remarked that 'if Russia is winning, we ought to help Germany, and that way let them kill as many as possible, although I don't want to see Hitler victorious in any circumstance.' But long before the war itself, the perceived strategic usefulness of a fascist Berlin–Rome axis was readily apparent. Beginning in 1936, the Spanish Civil War saw almost all of the old European counter-revolutionary strategies deployed with vigour and ruthlessness against the republic of Spain. With its progressive 1931 constitution, and with both its heads of state and government democratically elected, the new 'free' Spain was considered a product of both mass mobilization and the successful dismantling of an old political order representing traditional elites.[28] Still on the scene, the Carlists were pushing for a restoration of the monarchy and unsurprisingly had the support of clergymen agitated by the new state's secular legislation. But this time their alliance was much stronger as it included the Spanish nationalists – the *Falange* – who were backed by the new transnational network of corporate-authoritarian regimes taking root across Europe.[29] Most dramatically, and in a throwback to the hordes of foreign fighters that fought alongside the Russian White Movement, more than a hundred thousand Moroccan mercenaries were airlifted over to Spain, many of them by Nazi Germany's Luftwaffe, to serve the nationalists as the 'Army of Africa'.[30]

Clearly identifying the war as a fascist counter-revolution, and fearful of the demise of the hope-bringing Spanish republic, people all over Europe volunteered to fight and to bring weapons and aid with them. Although officially neutral, the British government made it a criminal offence for its citizens to travel to Spain, and Foreign Secretary Anthony Eden testified that his government preferred a nationalist victory to a republican one.[31] Meanwhile, Britain had not only permitted the nationalists to set up a signals base on Gibraltar but also granted overfly rights for the German–Moroccan mercenary supply route. The German chargé d'affaires in Madrid even reported back to Berlin that Britain was supplying ammunition to the nationalists.[32] Although the US Congress had passed a resolution banning the export of arms to Spain, this did not stop several of its major automotive corporations sending over twelve thousand trucks to support the nationalists. When the war was over the new undersecretary of the Spanish foreign ministry claimed that 'without American petroleum and American trucks, and American credit, we could never have won the civil war.'[33]

With Moscow widely considered to have been outplayed in Spain by Hitler and Mussolini, the spectre of a mighty Soviet Union spreading its revolution across the continent seemed to have finally faded. But in many ways this line of thinking obscured important developments within Russia itself. Having only barely achieved Marx's baseline of 'low communism', and still being what Trotsky would call a 'transitional regime', Moscow by this stage was increasingly being dominated by an army and bureaucracy that had 'grown into a hitherto unheard of apparatus of compulsion'. The bureaucracy had turned into an 'uncontrolled force dominating the masses' while the army had 'not been replaced by an armed people ... and had given birth to a privileged officers' caste, crowned with marshals'. Going further, Trotsky reasoned that the Russia now headed by General Secretary Joseph Stalin was wholly incompatible with the workers' state envisioned by Marx, Engels, and Lenin, and in many ways was just as anti-revolutionary as the Thermidorian regime.[34]

Korsch similarly believed that the Soviet Union by then had already 'abandoned its original revolutionary and proletarian features at home' and this meant that on an international level it was increasingly participating in 'the game of imperialistic politics, in military alliances with certain groups of bourgeois states against other groups of bourgeois states'. It also meant that Moscow, like the fascist powers, was 'contributing its full share to what in the highly deceptive language of modern bourgeois diplomacy is called a furtherance of peace and collective security'.[35] Indeed, as per Lenin's earlier warnings of 'reactionary utopias' and Trotsky's 'pacifist illusions', Stalin's Kremlin was soon engaging with Geneva's courts of arbitration, and the Western powers' various disarmament programmes.[36] Joining the League of Nations in 1934, Stalin himself described the imperialist nations that underpinned it as 'friends of peace'.[37]

In this sense the once revolutionary Soviet Union, ever more dominated by its 'cult of bureaucratic elites', was now closely resembling its purported European enemies. Those Russians who began to speak of the need for the 'state' to come to an end, as the Bolsheviks originally proposed, were soon deemed 'counter-revolutionary'.[38] Meanwhile, Moscow's foreign policy had, in Trotsky's words, 'liberated itself from the programme of

international revolution' and, with reference to the global workers' movement, 'the Communist International [became] a completely submissive
apparatus in the service of Soviet foreign policy, ready at any time for any
zigzag whatever'.[39]

With Russia gripped by its own internal counter-revolution, it is not
surprising that the Spanish republic was left to flounder. Some Soviet aid
certainly did arrive, but it was limited in scope, and if anything, as historian Anthony Beevor describes, Moscow was actually hostile to many of
Madrid's reforms, including its efforts to set up Bolshevik-like workers'
assemblies to run factories and farming collectives.[40] Beyond Spain, the
Kremlin even seemed willing to deal directly with the fascist powers, having
played an 'equivocal role' in the Italo-Abyssinian War of 1935–6, so as not
to harm its valuable Italian trade links, and of course with its foreign minister, Vyacheslav Molotov, signing a non-aggression pact with his German
counterpart, Joachim von Ribbentrop, in 1939. In a betrayal of the people
of Eastern Europe and the Baltics, the deadly secret protocol agreed to
carve up Poland, Romania, Lithuania, Latvia, Estonia, and Finland into
German and Soviet 'spheres of influence' before eventual new 'territorial
and political arrangements' could be put in place.[41]

BRITAIN'S HUNGRY EMPIRE

Having limped through the Second World War as technical victors, but
still licking their wounds from the blowback of unbridled fascism and
the devastation wrought by their adversaries' armies, the surviving global
empires of Britain and France were in full-scale retreat. With repeated
uprisings and national liberation movements chipping away at overseas
possessions, their officials and planners were already expert in devising
strategies aimed at blocking or reversing indigenous challenges. But with
increasingly resource-intensive heavy industries based on new technologies requiring vast imports of basic materials at a cheap and stable price
from their remaining colonies and protectorates, such imperial counter-
revolutionary efforts had to become much more focused on what was now
the greatest threat of all: economic nationalism. For Britain in particular,
the enemy insurgents it was facing by the mid-twentieth century were no

longer being measured by their ideology, religion, or barbarity, but quite clearly by their capacity to nationalize resources and industries or, at the very least, build states capable of demanding greater stakes in the local production of wealth.

Erupting in 1948, the twelve-year-long 'emergency' in British-controlled Malaya vividly illustrates this important shift. With South-East Asia already identified by the Foreign Office as a 'substantial economic asset and a net earner of dollars', and with the colony of Malaya alone estimated to be worth an enormous $145 million annual surplus, its ongoing stability was unquestionably vital for British industry. Giving plenty of detail, a Colonial Office report from 1950 noted that Malaya's rubber and tin industries were in fact Britain's biggest earners of foreign currency across the whole empire, with seventy percent of the rubber estates owned by British and other European companies.[42] In 1952 Lord Ogmore told the House of Lords that Malaya's resources 'have very largely supported the standard of living of the people [of Britain] and the sterling area ever since the war ended; what we should do without Malaya, and its earnings in tin and rubber, I do not know.' Although he argued for the need to diversify Malaya's economy further, he only envisaged 'more and diverse cash crops, such as cocoa, palm oil and the rest'.[43]

As for Britain's response to the uprising, the Colonial Office was quick to brand it a 'war against bandits [that] is very much a war in defence of the rubber industry'.[44] Meanwhile, British officials on the ground referred to their enemies as 'communist terrorists' or 'CTs' for short.[45] In reality of course, those supporting the Malayan People's Liberation Army had far more deep-rooted grievances, as much of Malaya's ethnically Chinese population felt greatly exploited and discriminated against, especially as they made up a significant portion of the low-paid labour force, and because many had earlier fought alongside Britain against Japan. Although a rights-protecting constitution had been drafted by the colonial authorities when the war was over, Britain's local client rulers – the hereditary Malay sultans – objected on the grounds it gave 'too many rights to the immigrants' and that it allowed the Malayan Communist Party, which was mostly but not entirely made up of ethnic Chinese, to become a legal entity. As a former British official describes, the sultans displayed their displeasure in a variety of ways, including symbolic no-shows at airport greeting ceremonies. Extensively reworked, the constitution eventually introduced by the Colonial Office in 1948 thus became an explosive act of appeasement as it permanently consigned all of the Chinese along with other immigrants to second-class or even non-citizen status underneath the more compliant, pro-British Malay community. Moreover, following a full ban on the Communist Party and a crackdown on trade unions, all such organizations were described at British-led meetings as 'subversive'.[46]

With the fuse lit, the Liberation Army was able to recruit widely, and by 1949, with the ascendant and nearby People's Republic of China catalysing the insurgency, its numbers swelled massively. Initially considering co-opting the local Malay chapter of the Kuomintang nationalists to fight on their behalf, British officials quickly dropped the idea on the grounds that they were just too 'corrupt and vicious'.[47] Instead, the now classic counter-revolutionary strategy of bringing in foreign fighters was adopted, with troops arriving from Australia, Fiji, Rhodesia, and other parts of the empire.[48] In parallel, efforts were made to stem the tide of young men joining the rebel movement by providing 'large cash payments' to 'highly productive agents' working within the Chinese community, along with the creation of 'strategic hamlets' or 'new villages' on the periphery of cities, which were then kept under close surveillance and curfew. Serving as de facto refugee camps, the idea was that rural populations coming under British bombardment would have little choice but to flee to these areas, thus 'isolating the insurgency, both physically and politically from the population' and helping to stop the passing of food from sympathizers to the opposition.[49] Put another way, in the words of a British official involved in the strategy, the aim was to 'deny the CTs support from the communities they had intimidated'.[50] In contrast to the flattened countryside, the central district of Malacca was declared a 'white area' and was thus exempt from curfews, food controls, and 'other inconveniences of the emergency' on the grounds that the citizens of the area were cooperating so loyally.[51]

In an apparent reference to the ongoing supremacy of British businesses in Malaya, British officials who served during the emergency have since described how their victory in South-East Asia was unique because 'we stayed to help our friends after independence.'[52] But an extensive 1960s Amnesty International report was less forgiving, concluding that the British campaign involved 'opponents being unreasonably denied the right of full expression and arbitrarily detained.'[53] Even greater, it seems, was criticism of the conflict within parliament itself, with MPs repeatedly questioning the veracity of the government's claims about the actions of the insurgents, including supposed acts of murder and sabotage.[54] Furthermore, according to a former official based in Malaya, 'parliamentarians were critical of [the high commissioner's] dictatorial ways, and would have been more critical had they known of the speed with which the colonial administrators, with the support of the state war executive committees, could make decisions.'[55]

With striking similarities, but with an arguably even more violent response, a concurrent British crackdown in the 1950s against the Kenya Land and Freedom Army, known as the *Mau Mau*, led to many thousands of deaths along with an estimated ninety thousand imprisoned and the confiscation of land from over ten thousand families.[56] With its valuable agricultural land, most of which was owned and farmed by European settlers, the colony of Kenya had become a veritable breadbasket for the British Empire. Tensions were understandably running high, with an earlier British East Africa Commission report noting that the 'treatment of tribes [from the coastal regions] was very bad ... [they were] moved backwards and forwards so as to secure for the Crown areas which could be granted to Europeans.'[57]

Recently declassified official documents demonstrate that the state of emergency – sparked by the killing of a European woman in 1952 – and Britain's scapegoating of the *Mau Mau* were in fact 'covers for halting the rise of popular, nationalist forces that threatened control of [Britain's] colony'. Justifying this, the attorney-general of the colony had privately portrayed the *Mau Mau* as a 'secret underground nationalistic organization which is virulently anti-European'. In reality, as senior British academic David Maughan-Brown has shown, the rebellion was primarily against economic exploitation and administrative repression under colonial rule and, in particular, years of British refusal to listen to requests for land or constitutional reform. Problematically, however, the British government was unable to link convincingly the *Mau Mau*'s land nationalization ambitions to international communism, with the Colonial Office admitting, 'There is no evidence that communism or communist agents have had any direct or indirect part in the organization.'[58]

Instead officials had to depict the *Mau Mau* as 'gangsters who indulged in cannibalism, witchcraft, devil worship and sexual orgies and who terrorized white settlers and mutilated women and children'.[59] Others similarly tried to describe the movement as being based on 'perverted tribalism'.[60] Writing in much the same sort of racist and one-sided terms was Ian Henderson, the Scottish colonial police officer credited with resolving the emergency by capturing the *Mau Mau*'s leader. Awarded the George Medal for his acts of civilian bravery, his book *Man Hunt in Kenya* received an unusually favourable review from the CIA's historical department, which described it as 'a fascinating and well-written book'.[61]

As an important epilogue to the conflict, a recent legal battle in Britain involving representatives and descendants of the *Mau Mau*, seeking compensation for the losses and the denigration of their ancestors, led to the rediscovery of formerly 'lost' Colonial Office archival material. Known as the 'migrated archives', their contents revealed the full extent of British human rights abuses over the course of the eight-year-long counter-insurgency, including multiple instances of torture, rape, and execution.[62] In 2011, the *Guardian* suggested that 'the documents [had been] hidden away to protect the guilty', while *The Times* noted that 'thirteen boxes of top secret files are still missing.'[63] Given the weight of evidence, in 2012, the High Court in London ruled that the elderly Kenyan survivors were entitled to sue the British government for damages.[64]

THE THREAT FROM ARAB NATIONALISM

Since its secret Sykes–Picot agreement with France that effectively carved up the territories of the crumbling Ottoman Empire in the wake of the First World War, Britain's grip over much of the Middle East and its resources had been more or less uncontested. But by the 1950s, and certainly the 1960s, a potent pan-Arab movement was threatening to unseat remaining British client rulers in the region and jeopardize lucrative trade arrangements and control over valuable natural resources. With 'classic nationalism [having become] impotent' in the Middle East, as veteran correspondent Patrick Seale described, many of the new 'Arab nationalist' revolts were effectively military operations, often led by army officers intent on forcibly removing foreign influences from their countries. Described by some as 'armed plotters waiting in the wings, legitimized by a third world discourse',[65] the Arab nationalist uprisings and revolutions may have had little in common with the progressive movements of mid-nineteenth-century Europe, but, as illiberal as they were, they nonetheless represented one of the most organized and potent challenges to imperial structures Britain had ever faced.

The gravity of the situation was not lost on London: Foreign Office reports warned of Middle Eastern ruling elites 'losing their authority to reformist or revolutionary movements which might reject the connexion with Britain'; official references were made to the dangers of 'ultra-nationalist maladies'; and the cabinet secretary informed the prime minister in no uncertain terms that 'we are fighting a losing battle propping up these reactionary regimes.'[66] According to a particularly candid 1952 Foreign Office study entitled *The problem of nationalism*, there were two strains to watch out for. The first was 'intelligent and satisfied nationalism' which was not very well defined but seemed to involve Britain being able to divert inevitable nationalist sentiments into regimes that would 'minimize losses to Britain'. The other, however, was likely to be very harmful to British interests as it would lead to new governments that would 'insist on managing their own affairs ... including the dismissing of British advisers, the appropriation of British assets, unilateral denunciation of treaties with Britain, and claims on British possessions'.[67] Declassified documents from 1961 have shown that British officials were even wary of the 'force of liberalism' in such countries for much the same reason.[68]

Egypt, the most populous Arab state and the centre of the region's cultural production due to most publishing and print houses being based there, was where the cost of losing influence was undoubtedly the greatest. Having weathered a rebellion in 1919, in which more than eight hundred predominantly non-violent street protestors were killed by British troops, and having ended its formal protectorate three years later, Britain had since been ruling by proxy through two descendants of Muhammad Ali – the former Ottoman governor or *pasha* of Egypt. Upgraded from sultan to king in 1922, the first of these was Fuad I, who was then succeeded by his son Farouk in 1936.[69] When it launched its revolution in 1952 the 'Free Officers' movement led by Muhammad

14

Naguib and, more prominently, Gamal Abdel Nasser was thus quick to abolish the monarchy and establish a republic. As feared, it was also committed to the speedy nationalization of resources and assets, mostly at the expense of British and other European companies. Although Arab Marxists such as Samir Amin have questioned the true revolutionary credentials of the 'Nasserists' on the basis that army officers and bourgeois were at the forefront, with no significant participation from the masses, others have noted that the Nasserists were nonetheless the first of a wave of Arab nationalist movements that 'propelled into power leaders ideologically committed to building the state as the primary instrument for reforming society and achieving [both] national and pan-Arab goals'.[70] Moreover, as literary theorist Ahmad Aijaz argues, 'The Nasserists introduced fundamental systemic shifts very swiftly through such measures as abolishing the monarchy as well as feudal privileges, redistributing landholdings, restructuring foreign alignments ... building a public sector and adopting a whole host of policies that favoured the poorer and the lower middle classes.'[71]

Even more troublingly for London, courtesy of 'agents, political support, the powerful voice of radio in Cairo, and by virtue of his charismatic appeal', Nasser soon became the effective leader of a region-wide independence movement.[72] Moreover, after statements made in 1955 at a conference in Bandung, Indonesia, his version of Arab nationalism became an explicitly anti-imperialist project.[73] Thus, unlike the narrowly focused national liberation movements British planners had had to contend with before, there was a growing concern that Nasser might try to form some sort of Arab superstate, especially if he was able to unify Egypt with other Arab states and perhaps even spark revolt in the Gulf sheikhdoms. Such a nightmare scenario would have led to a manpower- and resource-rich greater Arab republic or, as US president Dwight Eisenhower warned, Nasser would become the head of an 'enormous Muslim confederation'.[74]

As with the *Mau Mau*, it proved difficult to link Nasser to a global communist plot as he himself 'suppressed the Egyptian left and the various communist parties vigorously'.[75] Even the Foreign Office internally decided Nasser was 'avowedly anti-Communist [and] unfortunately ... strongly neutralist'.[76] According to subsequent Foreign Office documents, this was a serious problem as it meant that Nasser's 'neutralist position fits in with the desire of the regime to show that Egypt can stand up to Western powers on equal terms'.[77] Even worse, Nasser was proving to be quite an adept administrator, with Britain's ambassador admitting that the new government was 'as good as any previous ... and in one respect better than any, in that it is trying to do something for the people of Egypt rather than merely talk about it'.[78] Eisenhower's public comments notwithstanding, elements of the US government also seemed to have formed a favourable impression, with declassified reports having revealed fairly close relations with Nasser's government, at least in the early days.[79]

Britain's need for a counter-revolution nevertheless soon took on a great urgency, as the safety of shipping routes through the Suez Canal and access to its remaining interests in the region were deemed to be at risk. As early as 1953 Prime Minister Anthony Eden reportedly considered a British-sponsored coup d'état, with Nasser's colleague Naguib identified as a possible frontman.[80] Referred to by the *New York Times* as 'Kerensky with a Fez' in reference to his potential role as an Arab equivalent of the prominent anti-Bolshevik leader Alexander Kerensky, and with Nasser branded 'Egypt's Lenin', the stage seemed set. Eden even told a Foreign Office minister that in the event of Nasser's removal, 'I don't give a damn if there's anarchy and chaos in Egypt.'[81]

Importantly, in another parallel with the White Movement and the co-opting of the Turkmen Islamists, Britain also sought to manipulate Naguib's connections to the Muslim Brotherhood, as Nasser was seemingly reliant on his co-leader's not-so-secular background to appease the increasingly powerful Islamist organization.[82] The relationship between Britain and the Brotherhood was of course nothing new, as ever since its formal founding in 1928 it had been identified as primarily an anti-nationalist and anti-liberal vehicle rather than a pro-democracy movement, even though its most prominent ideologue, Hassan al-Banna, publicly endorsed the parliamentary system and constitutionalism.[83] Its chief rival before Nasser had been the anti-British nationalist Wafd Party, and on this basis the building of the Ismailia mosque, which was to become the Brotherhood's first headquarters, was even funded by the Anglo-French Suez Canal Company.[84]

For London, this fitted well within a broader existing strategy for North-East Africa to ensure the loyalty of religious conservatives, with

Britain concurrently supporting Sayyid Abd al-Rahman, the Mahdist leader in Sudan and the son of Muhammad Ahmad bin Abd Allah, who had proclaimed himself the messianic redeemer of the Islamic faith in the late nineteenth century.[85] By the 1930s the Brotherhood was already proving useful to Britain, with its paramilitary 'rovers' enlisted to provide security at King Farouk's coronation. It enjoyed growing support from conservative army officers and, according to Richard Mitchell's definitive study of the organization, most Egyptian landowners regarded it as an ally.[86] As investigative journalist Robert Dreyfuss notes, the Brotherhood's dedication to founding an Islamic state should not on paper have been compatible with collaborating so closely with foreign imperial powers, but given its well-documented relations with both the royal palace and British officials, its leaders were in practice quite comfortable being 'double-dealers and agents'.[87]

Although the Brotherhood's activities during the Second World War greatly strained the relationship, Britain still managed to keep the connection alive, with the Islamists' immense long-term strategic value continuing to outweigh any concerns. At one point, for example, Brotherhood leaders appeared to have found common ground with German agents, with former CIA officer Miles Copeland having described the organization as 'virtually a German intelligence unit', while others claimed German officers were helping to set up its military wing. In 1941 elements within British intelligence regarded the Brotherhood as the biggest danger to the security of their position in Egypt, a view which seemed well founded after several subsequent assassinations, including those of a police chief and a cabinet minister. Bomb attacks in the late 1940s against British troops in the Suez Canal Zone were also linked to the Brotherhood, as was the discovery of a substantial cache of weapons and a plot to overthrow the monarchy in 1948. Although then officially dissolved, the Brotherhood still claimed responsibility for the assassination of Egypt's prime minister later in the year while – in an apparent tit-for-tat – al-Banna himself was killed in 1949.[88] With a retrospective MI6 report confirming that the latter's 'murder was inspired by the government, with palace approval', it was apparently justified on the grounds that 'so long as he was at liberty, he was likely to prove an embarrassment to the [Egyptian] government.'[89]

With relations inevitably at an all-time low, some Brotherhood supporters even began to endorse the Free Officers' revolution when it began, with members taking part in 'Cairo burning' anti-British riots, and its leaders 'lending the revolutionary leaders important domestic support'.[90] Nonetheless, despite the manifold dangers of continued collaboration, Britain was quick to rehabilitate most of the Brotherhood's members, including Nazi sympathizers and those who had incited anti-Zionist and anti-British riots in Jerusalem.[91] In 1954 both MI6 and the CIA began considering a plan to assassinate Nasser with Brotherhood assistance, with a CIA telegram to London stating that they had 'been in contact with suitable elements in Egypt and in the rest of the Arab World'.[92] The US ambassador in Cairo had also been holding secret meetings with the Brotherhood's senior leadership, who had told him they would 'be glad to see several of the Free Officers eliminated'.[93] According to one former CIA agent, 'the Agency was involved in a covert operation – a very inept one I might add – relying on members of the *ancien régime* who could overthrow him, mostly figures tied to the old regime – landowners, industrialists, and other old enemies of Nasser's. It was a futile project'.[94] Another former CIA agent has described how these plots could co-opt the Muslim Brotherhood on the basis that 'if Allah decided political assassination was permissible, that was fine … so long as no one talked about it in polite company … Like any other truly effective covert action, this one was strictly off the books … All the White House had to do was give a wink and a nod to countries harbouring the Muslim Brothers, like Saudi Arabia and Jordan.'[95]

Rather far-sightedly, when Nasser eventually began to crack down on the Brotherhood in 1954 and sought to marginalize Naguib after a number of Islamist attacks on secular students at Cairo University, the government decree that banned the organization was justified on the grounds that 'the revolution will never allow reactionary corruption to recur in the name of religion.' In October that year, however, a Brotherhood member managed to fire eight shots at Nasser.[96] Although some suggest this attempt was stage managed, providing a pretext for Nasser to finish off Naguib, who was promptly placed under house arrest, there seems little doubt Nasser was by then a heavily marked man, especially given the long list of further assassination attempts. Despite Prime Minister Winston Churchill sending Nasser a message after one such Brotherhood plot saying, 'I congratulate you on your escape from the dastardly attack made on your life,' Britain was in fact directly involved in a number of attempts of its own, ranging from the use of poisoned darts and coffee to even poisoned chocolates.[97] More complex were its efforts to enlist regional proxies, including bribes paid to Bedouin tribesmen in Jordan to kill Nasser when he entered the country, and an assassination plot later revealed by the Syrian army chief that implicated a Syrian member of the Saudi king's court. The latter, it seemed, had received substantial payments so that he could organize the shooting down of Nasser's aircraft as it landed in Damascus.[98]

With Nasser still very much alive in 1956, Britain had to switch to a more drastic 'Plan B' with a full-blown military intervention. Despite having signed a legal agreement with the Egyptian government in 1954, which allowed Britain to retain military basing rights at the Suez Canal, London had begun conspiring with Paris and the infant Israeli state, while also renewing its discussions with the Brotherhood, which by this time had had to shift its headquarters to Geneva.[99] The complication in the scheme, which centred on forcibly taking control of the canal, was that the plot was too obviously an old-fashioned imperialist manoeuvre. To get around this, Israel was to go in first, seemingly independently, and would then later be backed up by Britain and France reacting to the 'unexpected' and fast-moving events.[100]

With the planned operation apparently too heavy-handed for the White House's liking, the US media reported fears that it would provoke a backlash across the whole Arab world that could play into the hands of the Soviet Union.[101] An alternative view, however, is that the US was privately willing to support the Anglo-French invasion, but only if it was done very quickly and did not aggravate rising Cold War tensions in Europe, and especially the situation in Budapest. According to correspondence between a US Department of State official and a CIA officer given the task of liaising with Britain, the former claimed, 'We'll back them up if they do it fast. [But] what we can't stand is their goddam hesitation, waltzing while Hungary is burning.'[102]

Surviving this spectrum of efforts to destroy it, the fledgling Egyptian republic proved resilient and was arguably stronger than ever by the time of Nasser's death from natural causes in 1970. Indeed, even its military defeat by Israel three years earlier had been carefully manipulated by Nasser into an opportunity to remove remaining military opponents from power.[103] Chosen to succeed by a trio of Nasser's closest advisers, Anwar Sadat was seen as the best temporary solution, but unsettlingly for many he had quickly begun to seek out his own allies, including semi-feudal elements of the old regime, who sought to regain their political and economic networks, and even the outlawed Brotherhood. That he considered the latter a powerful counterweight to both left-wing ideologues and Nasserist loyalists dominating the media and cultural institutions should have come as no surprise, as Sadat himself had been a Brotherhood sympathizer in the 1940s and had claimed it was 'the perfect organization'. Moreover, he had once praised al-Banna as a 'true Egyptian'.[104]

In a far cry from its confrontation with Nasser, who had eventually executed its leading member Sayyid Qutb in 1966 after the publication of the controversial *Milestones*, the Brotherhood's other leaders were quickly released from prison by Sadat on the condition that they publicly rejected Qutb's more extremist writings.[105] With Sadat then enshrining Islam in the constitution, releasing many more Brotherhood members from prison, and allowing exiles to return from Saudi Arabia,[106] the informal alliance continued to strengthen. Ending his speeches with a Qur'anic verse, regularly appearing on television praying in mosques, and even beginning to describe himself as the 'believer president', Sadat was clearly beginning to take on some of the mantle of Islamic caliph.[107]

With his religious conservative allies in place, Sadat's main purge took place in May 1971 when most Nasser-era officials were removed from office including several ministers and Nasser's old security chiefs. Despite himself having once lauded the 'men from the army whom we trust in their ability, their character and their patriotism', Sadat accused them of using 'inane socialist slogans' and claimed he needed to perform a 'second revolution'.[108] Predictably supported by the religious establishment and academia, Sadat even oversaw the prestigious Al-Azhar University entering into relations with Saudi Arabia in a move since described as its 'capture by the right once again, ending the role it had been developing as a more balanced, and non-fundamentalist, Islamic centre'. Soon after, and as something of a final stage, Sadat also undertook full government restructuring, with the creation of the post of deputy prime minister for religious affairs and the establishment of a new Supreme Committee for Introducing Legislation According to the Sharia.[109]

The extent and rapidity of Sadat's Islamist-assisted counter-revolution surprised even Moscow when in 1971 he expelled all Soviet personnel from Egypt, seemingly as part of a deal brokered by Saudi intelligence chief Kamal Adham who had promised aid to Cairo in return. As some suggest, Saudi Arabia may have also been offering to help get US support to facilitate the return to Egypt of land held by Israel.[110] After all, as the former US secretary of state Henry Kissinger notes, because the US had no embassy in Cairo during this period, Saudi Arabia was relied upon as the intermediary.[111] Either way, and even if it dismayed many of his Brotherhood backers, just seven years later Sadat was in a strong enough position to sign off on the Egypt–Israel Peace Treaty following his Camp David Accords with Israeli prime minister Menachem Begin and US president Jimmy Carter. An unthinkable prospect under the revolutionary Nasser administration, Sadat's increasingly Islamist and Saudi-aligned Egypt seemed to have joined the ranks of Western proxies in exchange for the promise of billions of dollars of annual aid for its military.[112]

TROUBLE ON THE ARABIAN PENINSULA – REVOLUTION REACHES YEMEN

As Britain feared, the rising star of Arab nationalism and the fast-spreading popularity of Nasser soon reached its strategically vital protectorates and colonies along the southern shores of the Arabian Peninsula. At stake was not only Yemen's natural harbour in Aden, but also control over a key shipping lane that passed from the Indian Ocean into the Red Sea through a twenty-mile-wide strait called the *Bab el-Mandeb* or 'Gate of Tears'. With a growing realization that organized nationalist movements could easily secure a foothold in such territories, Britain also faced the alarming prospect of a contagion effect into its other possessions on the Arabian Peninsula including the hitherto placid sheikhdoms of the Persian Gulf with which it had held peace treaties for more than a century.[113] Having allowed for a low-cost informal network of truce-based or 'Trucial' states, Britain had promised to fortify their dynastic ruling families from both external and internal threats in exchange for guarantees that pirates would not be harboured in their ports and, by the late nineteenth century, that all foreign relations would be conducted through British-appointed 'native agents'.[114] Stretching across most of the Arab littoral of the de facto 'British Lake', the unswerving loyalty of these pseudo-potentates gave Britain almost exclusive access to the island harbour of Bahrain, the water inlets of Dubai and Sharjah, and the Strait of Hormuz chokepoint at the mouth of the Persian Gulf.

Having ignored UN requests to withdraw its troops from Aden and allow self-determination, and after trying to merge the city's colonial government into an unpopular 'Federation of Southern Arabia' alongside various Yemeni sheikhdoms, sultanates, and other entities, by 1963 Britain's position was increasingly precarious. According to Amnesty International 'a significant section of the population of Aden state' bitterly opposed its forced federation, and conditions were ripe for the growth of both a new Marxist-Leninist inspired National Liberation Front and its rival, the Arab nationalist Front for the Liberation of Occupied South Yemen.[115] Initially bribing tribal elders and adopting a mixture of police-based counter-insurgency strategies, including many honed from its Malayan and Kenyan campaigns, Britain nonetheless soon went further by bombing rebellious villages to the west of Aden and launching a repressive crackdown in the city itself. The International Red Cross was repeatedly denied access to Aden for two years, and when Britain's Amnesty International delegate finally arrived in 1966 he claimed he was 'refused all facilities'. Sweden's Amnesty delegate had however managed to gain access and collected a large number of personal affidavits alleging widespread physical torture and degrading treatment, many of which were backed up by a range of respected Aden civil society organizations including the jurists' and teachers' associations. Disturbingly, in 'non-attributable comments' given to the British media by Whitehall officials, the Swede was described as being untrustworthy due to his Egyptian origin.[116] Nonetheless, with the situation deteriorating, criticism soon emerged from within Britain's own ranks when the chief justice of Aden, Sir Richard le Gallaise, claimed that detainees were being handed over to the much-reviled Sultanate of Fadhli – a constituent of the new federation and one of the main reasons why many of Aden's residents protested at their inclusion.[117]

To make matters worse, by the early 1960s the British-backed Imam Ahmad bin Yahya Hamidaddin, the ruler of mountainous northern Yemen and the spiritual leader of its Zaydi-Shia majority, was also coming under severe pressure. Not only poverty stricken and with minimal education and no basic women's rights, his religiously conservative fiefdom was also deeply sectarian with only a small number of aristocrats from within the Zaydi-Shia sect being able to access economic or political opportunities while most of the Sunni Muslim population were left marginalized.[118] Described by historian Joe Stork as a clear case of 'Britain following a policy [of] arming and subsidizing ruling families to preserve ... and perpetuate an archaic and decaying social order' so as to prevent Yemeni claims for sovereignty or the encroachment of other foreign powers, even Ahmad's own subjects referred to their country as *mutakhallif* or 'backwards'.[119]

With Ahmad ruling autocratically and with a reputation for brutality, campaigns had begun for at least some sort of reform. Heavily influenced by revolutionary ideologies and clearly inspired by Nasser, a number of army officers came to the fore in 1961 to lead a 'free Yemeni movement' and were even joined by some of Ahmad's relatives, including one of his brothers. Following some injudicious indirect criticism of Nasser from Ahmad, an assassination attempt was soon made, and in 1962 the battle lines began to be drawn. Even though Ahmad then died from natural causes and was suc-ceeded by his son Muhammad al-Badr Hamidaddin, who quickly declared an amnesty for nationalist sympathizers in the army, the family's palace came under tank fire within just a week and Muhammad was forced into a swift exile.[120] Political scientist Fred Halliday deemed this to have been a nationalist revolution on the basis that the ruling dynasty's land was then confiscated, and he also argued that North Yemen had become the only truly independent state on the Arabian Peninsula.[121] With some British officials grudgingly acknowledging that the new officer-led government was more popular and democratic than the oppressive old regime, even the US seemed to approve, with a chief aide to President John Kennedy warning that 'the House of Saud well knows it could be next'.[122]

Despite Washington's views and the UN's eventual recognition of the republic, Britain was far from ready to relinquish its long-running influ-ence in northern Yemen. With political solutions clearly a non-starter, London's counter-revolution quickly escalated into a full-blown campaign of air strikes. Most infamously, in March 1964, Royal Air Force aircraft that had flown up from Aden launched a bombing run over Fort Harib in the Marib province. Described by the *Sunday Times* as being 'virtually defenceless against 600 mph jets', twenty-five people were understood to have died in the fort including women and children. After stating that 'if they were civilian casualties they were either put into the fort or not removed from it despite the leaflet warning,' a Foreign Office minister then told parliament that 'we do not know how many casualties were suffered by Yemeni military personnel in Harib fort. We regret any loss of life which may have occurred despite the warning given by leaflet.'[123] It was reported, however, that only a fifteen-minute warning was given, and according to Durham University's Clive Jones, 'Many of the bundles failed to disperse on impact and it is doubtful if many could actually read the leaflets because of high levels of illiteracy.'[124]

By the end of the year the officers' republic was still standing, having been boosted by the arrival of senior Egyptian commanders and – at one point – close to seventy thousand Egyptian troops. As the conflict's international significance grew, and keen to bolster a new Arab nationalist republic, even Nasser visited the area on the basis that it had become a true struggle against 'reaction'.[125] Accused by British officials of using mustard gas and suspected of trying to link the northern revolution with the uprisings around Aden, the Egyptians' volatile presence soon provoked an even more intensive counter-revolutionary campaign. Mobilizing its Arab allies and clients, including the kingdoms of Jordan and Saudi Arabia, both of which were keen to curry favour with London, Britain was mindful of the need to avoid unwanted international attention and tried to ensure that as much of the work as possible was left in the hands of its proxies. Following purportedly Saudi-led air strikes and the heavy Saudi financing of village elders in the far north of Yemen, a number of irregular tribal militias duly began to rise up against the republic and quickly gained control over about half of northern Yemen's rugged highlands.[126]

As implausible as it sounds, Britain's role in assisting Saudi Arabia was initially denied, despite lurid accusations in the Arabic press that over three hundred British, French, and other fighters had been covertly deployed among the tribes. In July 1964, when things had really started to get going, Prime Minister Alec Douglas-Home stated in parliament that he had been assured by the high commissioner for Aden that the government was not aware of the involvement of British mercenaries. However, only the next day he sent a memorandum to Foreign Secretary Richard 'Rab' Butler in which he decreed that Britain 'should make life intolerable [for Nasser] with money and arms', and that this 'should be deniable if possible'. Based on this, a secret committee was formed to handle further British actions in northern Yemen.[127]

Published a few years later Halliday's study of the conflict provides perhaps the most detail, citing a former British SAS colonel who described the campaign and his role in it as being part of a 'deliberate attempt to overthrow a government of which Britain disapproved, but where Britain did not want to be seen to intervene directly'. Halliday also proves that pilots supplied by the British Aircraft Corporation to Saudi Arabia as support staff were those actually flying the Saudi jets on their operational missions across the Yemeni border.[128] According to British academic Stephen Dorril, MI6 was also providing logistical assistance to the Saudi-backed fighters while funds earmarked for Britain's overseas aid programme were being secretly redirected to support the war.[129]

As with Suez, Israel also appears to have played a significant part, with the British government having approached Mossad to provide instructors and trainers for the tribal militias, and with Israel's defence attaché in London having reportedly promised to supply Yemeni Jews who had earlier emigrated to Israel and who could 'pass themselves off as Arabs'. Understood to have been an opportunity that 'the Saudis eagerly grasped', Israel also began to furnish Riyadh with Soviet-made weapons it had earlier seized from conflicts of its own, and according to a former US official it used its air force to patrol the Red Sea so as to signal to Egypt to keep its distance from Saudi Arabia.[130] Less is known about US involvement, although US special forces may have had some sort of role, with a former US ambassador having claimed that during this period 'Kennedy was screwing around with all sorts of covert operations and the Green Berets in Arabia.'[131]

Flattening out into a long and exhausting stalemate, the conflict finally came to an inconclusive end in 1970 after a Saudi–Egyptian peace agreement was reached. Greatly damaged by several years of civil war, and exacerbated by the bloody and clandestine interventions of several foreign powers, the new Yemen Arab Republic that emerged was widely considered a 'deformed state'. Having reluctantly recognized that the northern nationalist revolutionaries were less of a threat than the increasingly powerful

Marxist National Liberation Front in the south of Yemen, which was already espousing the need to erase tribal hierarchies and other traditional political structures, Saudi Arabia – and by extension Britain – nonetheless continued to foment unrest in the north. Having come to power in 1974 as part of a 'corrective coup' within the military, and seeking to stamp out bribery, decadence, and remaining aristocratic privileges, President Ibrahim al-Hamdi was assassinated in 1977, most likely by Saudi agents.[132] As a Yemen Arab Republic minister put it, the murder was precipitated because of '[al-Hamdi's] trying to stop corruption, trying to curb tribalism, and trying to establish a state'.[133]

Meanwhile, in the south, even though the National Liberation Front had succeeded in setting up its own People's Democratic Republic of Yemen, it remained harassed by well-funded militias formed by former south Yemeni exiles who were flooding back across the border from Saudi Arabia.[134] More seriously, after changing its name to the Yemeni Socialist Party in 1978 and then openly aligning itself with the Soviet Union, the National Liberation Front faced an even more concerted campaign against it including covert operations aimed at destroying physical infrastructure and killing government officials.[135] While direct links between these attacks and Western intelligence agencies are hard to establish, both MI6 and the CIA are known to have trained small teams to blow up Yemeni bridges in the early 1980s, and in 1982 the Yemeni Socialist Party announced that an 'MI6–CIA plot' had been uncovered involving Yemenis who had been trained in Saudi Arabia and had been caught bringing explosives into the country. The *New York Times* and Reuters reported that 'the convicted men had brought explosives into southern Yemen as part of a plan to destroy economic installations in Aden' and, putting it bluntly, explained that the men were charged with 'engaging in sabotage with the complicity of the US'.[136]

THE CONTAGION SPREADS – THE SULTANATE OF OMAN

Heavily intertwined with the developments in Yemen, especially in the 1950s and 1960s, was a mounting challenge to Britain's indirect rule over Oman and the bustling trade hub of Muscat. With the London-registered

company Petroleum Development Oman as the country's primary source
of revenue, and with a British bank having held a monopoly over all of
Muscat's finances since 1948, the stability of Said bin Taimur al-Said's
sultanate was paramount to British commercial interests, even if most of
Oman languished in an impoverished state. In 1957 a small-scale uprising
in the mountainous Nizwa province had greatly rattled Said, even though,
as the British ministry for air claimed, it was only made up of 'simple
agricultural tribes'.[137] Moreover, given that its leader was a conservative
religious figure, Imam Ghalib bin Ali al-Hinai, who was even accused of
having nominal support from Saudi Arabia, many dismissed the unrest
as a disorganized feud between two reactionary camps rather than as
an attempted revolution. Nevertheless, the movement did call itself the
Omani Liberation Army, and according to Halliday most of its supporters
had joined up to fight against British imperialism.[138] Records also indicate
that the imam had been elected by some elements of the Nizwa region
and, according to descendants of those who fought in the conflict, religion
was never a central issue for the rebels.[139]

Already wary given the increasing agitation around Aden and in
northern Yemen, Britain was unwilling to take any chances and crushed
the imam's forces within two years. Fresh from their experiences in
Malaya, SAS counter-insurgency specialists were flown in and, to back
up Said's rudimentary army, systematic British airborne attacks were
launched against the restive mountain villages, their agricultural crops,
and even their livestock.[140] According to one Foreign Office memorandum
from 1957, three particularly troublesome hamlets had been 'warned
that unless they surrendered the ringleaders of the revolt, they would
be destroyed one by one by bombing'.[141] Britain's political resident in
Bahrain, its most senior official in the region, similarly recommended
bombing as a means of 'showing the population the power of weapons at
our disposal' and 'inflicting the maximum inconvenience on the population so that out of discomfort and boredom they will turn against the
rebel minority'.[142]

The truly brutal British operation against Nizwa's ill-equipped tribesmen, now mostly referred to as the 'Jebel Akhdar War', named after the
most prominent mountain in the province, earned stiff criticism from
the UN. Under the secretary-generalship of the increasingly outspoken

Swedish diplomat Dag Hammarskjöld, it stated in 1960 that the operation and the resulting deaths were the results of 'imperialistic policies and
foreign intervention', and in remarkably candid terms suggested that 'had
it not been for the possibility of oil being discovered in the interior, the
action taken by Britain might well have been less drastic and much damage,
destruction, human suffering and loss of life might have been avoided.' By
the end of the year the UN General Assembly had adopted a declaration
'on the granting of independence to colonial countries and peoples' and
had called for steps to be taken for powers to be transferred to people in all
'trust and non-self-governing territories.'[143] More specifically, a few years
later the General Assembly stated that Oman's right to self-determination
was being held back by Britain, and it asked Britain to withdraw.[144]

But with no intention of withdrawing given the stakes involved, Britain
and its client al-Said sultans soon entered into a decade-long fight for
Oman, following a much more extensive uprising in 1965 in the Dhofar
region. Soon organized into a proper revolutionary people's front, the threat
posed by this 'Monsoon Revolution' has been described as 'no backyard
police operation' and that 'far more than Vietnam it affected control of a
major economic asset of the capitalist world – Gulf oil.'[145] Its close proximity to Yemen also raised the prospect that it might ally with the various
revolutionary fronts across the border, and, according to Halliday, there
was concern it could receive assistance from the Arab nationalist republic
of Iraq and, soon after, even Muammar Gaddafi's revolutionary Libya.
Faced with this unsettling scenario, it is no surprise that Britain quickly
began to implement almost all of the counter-revolutionary strategies it
had been deploying and honing in Malaya, Kenya, Yemen, and elsewhere,
including the co-opting of traditional religious authorities, cash payments,
covert special operations kept hidden from parliament, and the crafting
of yet another international coalition of allied powers.[146]

As with northern Yemen, Nizwa, and most other parts of Oman,
Dhofar was similarly backward with 'no economic development of any
kind'. Most importantly its poverty and misery persisted even as Muscat
began to receive limited oil revenues and was fast becoming home to
hundreds of expatriates from Britain, the US, Germany, Japan, and Sudan.
Infrastructure building was becoming increasingly disproportionate and
'lopsided' with almost all of the new oil-financed amenities being built in

and around the capital. Aware that the Omani government was unlikely to alleviate their situation any time soon, Dhofar's new 'People's Front' took matters into its own hands, using its limited resources and basic taxes to build the region's very first schools and medical centres. Agricultural development became a priority with the People's Front focusing on 'nationalizing' water sources on the basis that they always used to cause disputes when left in the hands of government-appointed tribes.[147] In contrast, and notwithstanding the needs of the oil industry's Muscat-based employees, the sultan had been banning the import of medicine, the wearing of shoes and trousers by Omanis, and even talking in public for more than fifteen minutes at a time.[148]

Britain and Said held on to Dhofar at the beginning, partly by offering tribes 'material attractions' for dropping support for the Front, but also by burning villages and having corpses of rebels hung in public, while goats and cows were shot.[149] Leaflets were distributed after these attacks stating 'automatic weapons are out hunting for you … wherever you have crept, they will teach you a lesson, and in the end will kill you all.' As a good example of British false-flag operations, mines with Soviet markings were also left near watering holes frequented by tribes, so as to discredit the Front. Interestingly, and as an important precedent for further Western-sponsored counter-revolutions, the campaign also involved British-produced propaganda publications that criticized some of the Front's attempts at basic female emancipation and also vilified its efforts to limit men to having only one wife. These were followed up by leaflets 'written in bad Arabic by British intelligence officers' that promised Omani men that they could have four wives again, as per traditional rules, and others featuring defectors saying they had 'rallied to the cause of the sultan and Islam'. In further efforts to harness traditional religion for their purposes, Britain also encouraged Said's government to repaint all mosques and hire religious instructors to deploy to Dhofar.[150]

Officially denying its front-line involvement in the ground war, Britain claimed that the SAS were there only to 'seek out realistic training situations … but if fired upon, would fire back'.[151] Moreover, when replying to a concerned non-governmental organization, a Foreign Office official unequivocally stated: 'We do not accept your basic premise that Britain is assisting the Sultan of Oman "in his brutal attempt to crush all dissent in his country".[152] However, as government leaks from the period indicate, it is thought that the early phase of the war involved about a thousand clandestinely deployed special forces.[153] As Halliday explains, these were disguised as a 'British Army training team' while they were actually taking part in offensive operations and organizing a 'hearts and minds campaign' to wrestle tribal support away from the insurgents.[154]

By 1970, with the rebellion entering its fifth year, and with Said's legitimacy steadily eroding elsewhere in the country and even in the capital, the campaign began to enter a new and more overt phase. Exiling the unpopular sultan to London and replacing him with his son in a palace coup, British officials responded to media enquiries 'with amazement' at suggestions that Britain had had anything to do with it, while a public relations expert was engaged to fend off further queries.[155] Since then a number of memoirs have been published by British soldiers based in Oman at the time, including some with direct knowledge of Said's removal. In one particularly riveting account by Ray Kane, who was part of the team that actually entered the palace, the ensuing gun battle is colourfully described, along with the roles played by other British servicemen, some of whom went on to become long-serving advisers to the Omani ruling family.[156] Among these was intelligence officer Tim Landon, the 'White Sultan', who died in 2007 as one of Britain's wealthiest men.[157]

With the young and less tarnished Qaboos bin Said al-Said as their new figurehead, Britain soon did little to disguise its expanding war effort by ramping up the training of 'Dhofari irregulars' in camps erected in loyalist areas. With similarities to the Saudi-financed northern Yemeni tribesmen, these *Firqas* were recruited from exiles and deserters, as well as those who sought a salary to fight. One of their missions, it seems, was to undo the People's Front's efforts to centralize control over water by trying to reclaim water sources on behalf of specific tribes. One battalion was incongruously even named after Nasser, with the Sultan having been advised to try to claim at least some Arab nationalist credentials for himself. Bizarrely, the 1970 coup was even likened on state-controlled radio to the 1952 Egyptian revolution despite obviously having been engineered and carried out by a foreign power.[158]

The British-managed regular Omani army was soon supplemented by forces from elsewhere in the empire, notably Nepalese *Gurkha* regiments.[159]

Regional proxies and clients were again brought on board, playing an even greater role than in Yemen, with Saudi Arabia and the newly formed United Arab Emirates – the British-organized federation that subsumed seven of the Trucial States – sending troops to relieve the Omani forces from routine service in cities so as to free them up for battlefield duty.[160] Jordan meanwhile provided several thousand troops along with police and intelligence experts, while Shah Muhammad Reza Pahlavi's Iran dispatched four thousand soldiers, as well as thirty helicopters to help secure Dhofar's airspace. Smaller teams from India, Pakistan, and Sudan also arrived, as did a team from the US to provide additional expertise for what had become a truly multi-national counter-insurgency.[161]

A recent academic article on the Iranian deployment has made the argument that the Shah was acting unilaterally and deployed his troops without prior consultation with Britain or the US.[162] But given the heavy integration of the Iranian forces into the British strategy this seems unlikely. Indeed, the Shah's contingents in Oman were reportedly rotated every few months so that the army could receive British training in counter-insurgency, and there are credible accounts of how in 1975 Iranian naval forces fired fifteen hundred shells at a six-mile stretch of Omani coastline in order to force the population to seek sanctuary in government-held areas.[163] In effect these 'safe areas', complete with heavily surveilled refugee camps, were the latest incarnation of Britain's old Malayan 'strategic hamlets' system.

THE SMALLER SHEIKHDOMS – PREVENTIVE MEASURES

Elsewhere on the Arabian Peninsula the ruling families of the smaller sheikhdoms faced nowhere near the same potency of challenges from nationalists or other antagonistic forces, although there were instances of pushback from merchant communities and xenophobic citizens against British-controlled markets and the influx of expatriates.[164] Due to the greater geographic isolation of these sheikhdoms from the rest of the region and, so it seemed, their rapidly accelerating ability to channel new oil revenues to relatively small populations, conditions were far from ripe for the sort of mass rebellions witnessed in Yemen and Oman.[165] Nonetheless, as events unfolded Britain increasingly began to intervene in the domestic politics and affairs of these proto-states, mostly as part of a preventive strategy.

In Sharjah, for example, Saqr bin Sultan al-Qasimi was soon deemed problematic. Having ousted his father in 1951, he had begun to invite representatives of the Arab League to his fort, while later in the decade visitors described seeing portraits of Nasser hanging on the wall and overhearing him discuss the benefits of the 'great Arab nation'. Egyptian military officials were also thought to have been invited to Sharjah, and Saqr was understood to have discreetly visited Cairo and Damascus. In 1958 he had sought Arab League recognition for a new mini state made up of Sharjah and three other nearby Trucial States, and in 1964 – as a final straw, it seemed – he allowed the opening of an Arab League office in his sheikhdom. According to Britain's resident agent at the time, this led to 'dismay [as] Saqr had thrown down the first explicit challenge to Britain's position'. Summoned to the agent's office, Saqr was shown a document purportedly signed by his relatives calling for his dismissal before then being escorted out through the back door and flown into exile. His more malleable replacement, Khalid bin Muhammad al-Qasimi, was a paint-shop owner working next-door in Dubai.[166]

Further down the coast the ruler of Abu Dhabi was also being lined up for removal. Although there are no suggestions that Shakhbut bin Sultan al-Nahyan ever entertained subversive visitors or nationalist elements in his sheikhdom, his younger brother had nonetheless been waging a slow-burning campaign to discredit him in the eyes of British officials. Painting a picture of Shakhbut as an anachronistic figure incapable of judiciously spending Abu Dhabi's rising oil revenues, by 1966 Zayed bin Sultan al-Nahyan had persuaded Britain to engineer another Trucial States succession. As the British political resident in Bahrain claimed, '[Zayed] was consistently bitter about Shakhbut, and openly so ... he said that his brother had set his mind absolutely against development plans.' Furthermore, according to a member of the agency staff, Zayed had already told Shakhbut that 'you should not only seek but also take the advice of the [British] agent.' Although the circumstances remain murky, with differences in the historical accounts over exactly how smoothly the coup took place, all versions describe the arrival of British scouts and the de facto arrest and exiling of Shakhbut. With Zayed installed Britain had found a much more reliable client. After all, he had already told the agent that 'Britain should do to Cairo what the Russians have done to Budapest.'[167]

Much more precarious was the situation in Kuwait, not least due to its proximity to revolutionary Iraq and its much greater value to Britain at that time. By 1960, the sheikhdom was not only supplying Britain with forty percent of its crude oil imports but its exports were also accounting for around a third of total British sterling reserves. A Foreign Office report from the time explicitly stated the need to keep Kuwaiti investments flowing back to Britain and into sterling so as to 'avoid the necessity of sharing their oil wealth with their neighbours'.[168] On the cusp of achieving independence, its ruling al-Sabah family was well liked and trusted by London, but at the same time it was coming under pressure from powerful citizens who openly expressed sympathy with the Arab nationalist cause. The fear, put simply, was that the ruling family would quickly buckle after independence and would seek to cancel any sort of postcolonial British protection system.[169] Giving remarkable insight into official thinking at the time, a secret Foreign Office report from 1958 had already identified an urgent need to keep an independent Kuwait separate from other regional powers and region-wide ideologies, and had suggested upholding some sort of divide and rule strategy to keep the people of Iraq, Iran, Saudi Arabia, and the smaller Gulf sheikhdoms firmly apart. It stated: '[Britain's] interest lies in keeping Kuwait independent and separate, if we possibly can, in line with the idea of maintaining the four principal oil producing areas under separate political control.'[170]

Quite dramatically, just five days after Kuwait finally declared independence in June 1961, Iraq announced that it considered Kuwait to be part of its territory, and Kuwait's government was informed by Britain that Iraq was already in the advanced stages of preparing an invasion. Unsurprisingly, given its small armed forces, Kuwait immediately sent a formal request to London for help, with seven thousand British troops duly being deployed. In turn this led to the ratifying of a defence treaty that stated Britain would always come to Kuwait's defence if ever needed.[171] Britain maintained its defence force in Kuwait until October of that year, and although the Arab League then officially took over Kuwait's protection, Britain still kept some troops in place for a further decade which, it seemed, greatly strengthened the hand of the ruling al-Sabah family against its domestic opponents. Justifying the mission and basing its conclusions on a selective reading of British archival sources, the CIA later published a lengthy report detailing the various mechanisms of Britain's 'Operation Vantage' in Kuwait.[172]

The supposed Iraqi invasion threat was, however, almost certainly a fabrication, with declassified Foreign Office documents indicating that at the time Baghdad's bellicose statement was made, British officials had largely dismissed it as a 'spur of the moment' affair and had concluded that 'on present indicators it seems on the whole unlikely [that Iraq] will resort to military action'. Moreover, the British consulate in nearby Basra stated quite emphatically that 'no (repeat no) reliable information has been seen or heard of any unusual troop movements.' Similarly, the US had understood Iraq's threat to be little more than a 'postural move', with officials stating that 'they did not (repeat not) believe that [Iraq] intends further action.'[173]

But on the same day as the Basra consulate made its report, the British ambassador in more distant Baghdad claimed he had information 'revealing [Iraq's] intentions to build up in Basra a striking force suitable for an attack on Kuwait'. His assertion was then quickly repeated by the Foreign Office, which added references to a 'tank regiment' and claimed that 'the latest information shows [Iraq] to be making preparations which would enable [it] to make a very early military attack.' The Joint Intelligence Committee then duly produced a series of assessments that, according to the CIA narrative, 'convinced Whitehall the risk of invasion was high and Iraq might attack with virtually no warning'.[174]

As historian Mark Curtis has demonstrated, the new and much more alarmist information appears to have originated entirely from the Baghdad embassy, with no sources provided, and with no evidence supplied from the Royal Air Force's photo reconnaissance unit based in Bahrain. As he notes, even on the day after Kuwait's formal request for British help, and well after the Joint Intelligence Committee's assessments, the Basra consulate was still stating that 'evidence so far available does not (repeat not) indicate that an attack on Kuwait has been under preparation.' Similarly, a Ministry of Defence report, dated eleven days after the British deployment began, conceded that Iraqi tank movements to Basra were 'unlikely', and that, if anything, there had been an actual reduction in Iraqi military activities in the area so as not to create any misunderstanding.[175] Even Britain's political agent in Kuwait, upgraded to ambassador after independence, complained that the intelligence reports were 'too shallow and unclear' and argued that 'the Iraqis might verbally threaten Kuwait but they will not invade.'[176] Casting more light on the affair is a secret memorandum from October 1961 written by Edward Heath, then the lord privy seal. He wrote that Britain recognized its interests in Kuwait had been threatened and stated that planners were urged to 'continue to use the opportunities which our protective role will afford to ensure so far as we can that Kuwait does not materially upset the existing financial arrangements'.[177]

2

COLD WAR, OIL WAR – AMERICA TAKES OVER

D espite some muted discomfort over the imperialist practices of its British and French allies, the United States of the mid-twentieth century was rapidly waking up to the demands of its own resource-hungry industries and the realities of its Cold War stalemate with the Soviet Union. Seeking to ensure vacuums left in the wake of the retrenching European empires were not filled by antagonistic forces bent on nationalizing assets or – equally dangerously – liberation movements likely to align themselves with Soviet-sponsored international communism, the US government and its intelligence agencies soon found themselves at the very forefront of counter-revolutionary action. As Karl Korsch put it, the US may have been based on the ideals of revolutionary France, but by this stage it was fast losing its 'capitalist infancy'.[1] Certainly the need to sustain a ravenous economic system, combined with its inheritance of the old Western order from London and Paris, heralded a new era of unprecedented international interventions, meddling, and covert operations.

In words that could just as easily have flowed from the pen of a *fin de siècle* British Foreign Office official, a US National Security Council study from 1949 warned that the US needed to find ways of 'exerting economic pressures' on low- and middle-income countries that were not willingly accepting their role as suppliers of 'strategic commodities and other basic materials'.[2] Unsurprisingly, but rather hypocritically given its own recent history of isolationism, the US had also become wary of smaller states trying to maintain 'neutrality'. As Secretary of State John Foster Dulles argued in 1956, neutrality was 'increasingly becoming an obsolete conception, and except under very exceptional circumstances, it is an immoral and short-sighted conception'. On this basis any state anywhere in the world, not only a revolutionary state but also one that merely strived for middle ground or showed little interest in US aid, could find itself targeted.[3]

With the passing of the Mutual Security Act in 1955, which specified that all US aid recipients must not only contribute to 'the defensive strength of the free world' but must also 'encourage the efforts of other free nations … to foster private initiative and competition', the link between US-sponsored capitalism and the need for counter-insurgency strategies became more clearly defined.[4] Along with the carrots, however, also came the sticks, with President Dwight Eisenhower setting up a programme for the training of foreign police forces, before the John Kennedy administration massively expanded the operation and called it 'US counter-insurgency'. An international academy was even established in Washington to train members of approved foreign security services, with part of their curriculum focusing on 'internal security, counter subversive and counter-insurgency aspects of foreign police operations'.[5]

Bringing the Department of Defense together with the nascent Central Intelligence Agency, Washington also began to 'consider various areas where the implementation of our policy may require indigenous paramilitary force'. An important development, and in some ways a refinement of earlier British counter-insurgency operations, the recognized usefulness of local militias that could help disguise the identity of a campaign's true sponsor was to become the bedrock of most subsequent US covert operations. Facing some internal criticism, Kennedy's Overseas Internal Defense Policy of 1962 nonetheless firmly defended the use of such subversive tactics and described the 'pressures, hopes, and anxieties in the developing world that seem to justify violent action'. As a Department of State official later remarked, 'notably absent in the [policy] was any mention of human rights … despite the barbaric record of Third World security forces, [the] Department's repeated efforts to include human rights were rejected.'[6]

In practice, these and other such policies soon left the latter half of the century littered with US efforts to buttress the internal security of a range of reactionary, illiberal, and in many cases truly despotic regimes across the developing world. As long as these client governments were willing to ensure the smooth flow of resources out of their territories and were avowedly anti-communist, they invariably had the backing of the White House. Nationalists, neutralists, and all shades of domestic opponents were almost always slotted into the US's narrative, with regimes quick to brand them accomplices of 'international communism'. As historian Weldon Matthews argues, the counter-insurgency strategy effectively 'entailed US support for developing states in strengthening their repressive capabilities', while as Robert Dreyfuss describes, the enemy was never just the Soviet Union, or even communism, but rather any 'leaders who did not wholeheartedly sign on to the US agenda or who might challenge Western and in particular US hegemony. Ideas and ideologies that could inspire such leaders were suspect: nationalism, humanism, secularism, socialism.'[7]

AMERICA'S GLOBAL COUNTER-REVOLUTION

Getting an early taste of Britain's post-Second World War impotence, the US was almost immediately pressed into action to ensure that the newly liberated Greece did not fall into the wrong hands. With Prime Minister Winston Churchill and his successor, Clement Attlee, having duplicitously switched sides by beginning to arm former Nazi collaborators against communist guerrillas who had earlier fought alongside Allied special forces, their counter-insurgency was proving unsuccessful, with the war dragging on into 1947. With the White House justifying to Congress its need to intervene on the basis that Britain had complained it could no longer keep bankrolling Athens and that if Greece fell to communism then 'Turkey and the entire Middle East would fall as well,' the US soon launched a 'foreign internal defence mission' so as to counter the 'communist insurgency'. According to a declassified US military intelligence monograph, this involved 'economic and military aid, plus civilian and military advisers'.[8]

Meanwhile, much closer to home, the new capitalist-imperialist US had already begun to interfere in what it considered its own backyard. Backing a counter-revolution in Guatemala, a long series of covert US campaigns in Central and South America had begun. Ruled since 1931 by a US-backed dictator, Jorge Ubico, who sympathized with European fascist leaders and referred to the indigenous Mayan population in racist terms, Guatemala had also allowed the US to establish military bases on its territory and, more significantly it seems, for the US-incorporated United Fruit Company to operate more than forty percent of the country's arable farmland.[9] In 1944 a popular revolution involving 'free officers', students, and intellectuals had swept Ubico from power and democratic elections were held by the end of the year. The new president, Juan José Arévalo, set about introducing a range of social and political reforms including free education, universal suffrage, and minimum wages. Despite more than twenty coup attempts during his term in office, follow-up elections were successfully held in 1950, and were considered by international observers to have been fair.[10] With the country's new progressive constitution in place, presidential re-elections were not permitted, so Arévalo duly stepped aside. Continuing with his predecessor's agenda, Jacobo Árbenz began to introduce much-demanded land reforms, including the nationalization of unused United Fruit Company-owned land and handing it over to peasants.[11]

Duly lobbying the White House and hiring a leading public relations specialist, Edward Bernays – known as the 'father of PR' – the United Fruit Company launched an inflammatory anti-communist smear campaign against Guatemala's elected government.[12] With pressure building on the Department of State to protect US interests, an official warned that Árbenz's reforms had become a 'powerful propaganda weapon' while the 'broad social program of aiding workers and peasants in a victorious struggle against the upper classes and foreign enterprises' would have a strong appeal to neighbouring states such as Honduras and El Salvador 'where similar conditions prevail'.[13] As historian Nicholas Cullather has contended, CIA director Allen Dulles and his brother John Foster either mistook or wilfully misinterpreted the reforms as a sign of increasing Soviet encroachment in Central America as they claimed Guatemala had become a 'Soviet beachhead'.[14]

With the stage set for firmer action, a CIA-sponsored paramilitary invasion of Guatemala began in 1952.[15] Led by exiled Guatemalans who had been funded, trained, and equipped in Florida, the mercenary force's advance was supported by US air patrols which were violating Guatemala's airspace on the pretext of stopping 'communist weapons' arriving in the country.[16] By 1954, with a full US naval blockade in place, the exiles had reached the capital, overthrown the president, and installed a military dictator.[17] With Árbenz's 'new deal' reforms rolled back and Guatemala's 'Ten years of Spring' brought sharply to an end, the already problematic UN secretary general Dag Hammarskjöld stated that the US-sponsored operation had clearly contravened the UN charter.[18] Over the next few decades several subsequent attempts to restart the revolution were put down by a series of dictators, all of whom were products of the 1952 campaign. All were accused of human rights violations, including peasant massacres and the use of 'scorched earth' tactics against the indigenous Mayan population. Most opponents, as per the Mutual Security Act, were quickly branded communists.[19]

With a successful test case behind it, the US soon began to expand its secretive Central American campaign to other problem states. In Honduras, for example, veteran US diplomat John Negroponte recalls how 'the National Security Council [was] running operations off the books, with no findings.'[20] But most infamous, of course, were the efforts to unseat Cuba's Fidel Castro after his 1958 overthrow of the US-backed military dictator Fulgencio Batista. Having already allocated $13 million to fund a Cuban counter-revolution, Eisenhower had then passed the baton on to the Kennedy administration, which attempted to repeat the Guatemala invasion. Organizing Cuban exiles and channelling weapons to them through Rafael Trujillo, the military strongman in control of the Dominican Republic, the CIA had created 'Brigade 2506'.[21] As an indigenous paramilitary force, it was an important experiment for the eventual Overseas Internal Defense Policy, even if its total failure exposed multiple shortcomings in the strategy. From their launch pad in Guatemala, fourteen hundred of the CIA's fighters set sail for Cuba in April 1961. Although the US bombed Cuban airfields while the invaders were en route, Castro's forces were more than a match for them after their landing at the Bay of Pigs, and within just four days they were routed.[22] With Kennedy humiliated,

Castro's Argentinian sidekick Ernesto 'Che' Guevara sent a note to the White House that read 'thanks for [the Bay of Pigs]. Before the invasion, the revolution was weak. Now it's stronger than ever.'[23]

More complex was the concurrent situation in West Africa. As with the Greek operation, the US was required to pick up slack left by declining European powers and operate in territory with which it had little familiarity. With a multi-faction war of independence erupting in 1961 in the Portuguese overseas province of Angola, the US eventually found itself backing the 'UNITA' militias, who answered to the *União Nacional para a Independência Total de Angola* – a movement which had claimed to support capitalism.[24] Receiving aid from both the US and then later Saudi Arabia, the UNITA fighters were, with some assistance, launching their attacks from across the border in the Congo. With the stakes getting higher the longer opposing groups stood in the way of UNITA, and with many US and European companies keen to exploit the country's vast oil and diamond resources, it became imperative that a quick victory was achieved.[25]

A key problem had emerged, however, as the situation in the Congo itself was beginning to threaten US interests. Having gained independence from Belgium in 1960, the state's first democratic elections had been won by the *Mouvement National Congolais* led by Patrice Lumumba. With his commitment to replacing European military and administrative elites with Congolese, and to nationalizing resources in the country's wealthy outlying provinces, Lumumba was a growing problem. Described as having vast deposits of strategic minerals, including cobalt, the Congo's uranium mines had also earlier been labelled by the US's Manhattan Project as the 'most important deposits yet discovered in the world'.[26]

Sharing a usefully long and porous frontier with Angola, the Congolese province of Katanga was the first to declare its secession from Lumumba's new government.[27] Reportedly backed by both the Belgian and US governments, the Katangans were led by their army chief, Joseph Mobutu, and openly assisted by Belgian mercenaries. After Mobutu's forces reached the capital city and provoked a coup d'état, Lumumba was handed over to them, and he was tortured and executed in early 1961.[28] During the chaotic period that followed in the Congo, with no functioning central government, Dag Hammarskjöld tried to fly to Katanga to meet Mobutu to establish some sort of UN peace deal, but he died when his aircraft crashed while flying in British-controlled Northern Rhodesian airspace. Sparking great controversy, both the Northern Rhodesian and UN internal investigations concluded the plane had been flying too low. But in 2015 the UN reopened the investigation on the basis of new evidence, and following the conclusion of a 2013 UN panel which 'found that there was persuasive evidence that the aircraft was subjected to some form of attack or threat as it circled to land'. The evidence included testimonies of two former US intelligence officers who were working at listening posts and heard what seemed to be an in-flight strike on the plane, as well as one of the men's claim that 'Americans were somehow implicated'.[29] The 2013 panel's findings also appeared to corroborate portions of earlier documents produced by the South African Truth and Reconciliation Commission, which were revealed to the public by Archbishop Desmond Tutu in 1998. Implicating British, US, and South African agents, the commission was aware of meetings held between the three parties along with a South African military front company, and of the existence of plans to place explosives in the wheel bay of the aircraft.[30]

Following much further instability and no further peace efforts, Mobutu emerged as the Western-backed dictator and, as later described by the BBC, he managed to 'stash much of the country's economic output in European banks'. As the BBC also reported, the renamed state of Zaire then 'became the most notorious example of a country where state institutions came to be little more than a way of delivering money to the ruling elite'.[31] Meanwhile, back in Angola, the war finally came to an end, but only following a revolution in Portugal itself. In 1974 the 'Carnation Movement' – described by the British media as 'rebels seizing control' – brought to an end the corporate-authoritarian regime of the *Estado Novo*, which had been receiving anti-riot training from British police in London and Northern Ireland.[32] After winning free elections, the new Portuguese government immediately sued for peace in its remaining colonies and began a series of progressive social reforms along with the release of hundreds of political prisoners. However, given its commitment to nationalize sixty percent of the economy and initiate land reform, it soon found itself, even as a Western European democracy, as a threat to US interests. As the University of California's Ronald Chilcote has described, the CIA soon served as a conduit for covert funds to right-wing parties in Portugal and possibly for the financing of riots against the new government. Ingmar Oldmar has similarly claimed that such financing did take place and that 'the US reaction to the Portuguese revolution was to a great extent coloured by anxiety over the role and influence of the communists ... there was a certain penchant for repressive measures.'[33]

Over in South-East Asia, the Vietnam War was by then entering its twentieth year. Although at first glance seeming to have little in common with the US's covert counter-insurgency operations, especially given the hundreds of thousands of US troops that were eventually deployed, in many ways the roots of the conflict were much the same as those in Central America and West Africa. Certainly in the early days of the Vietnam conflict, most of the strategies outlined in the Overseas Internal Defense Policy were very much in evidence. Divided into two halves by the Geneva Agreement in 1954, the old French Indochina had in effect become the Far Eastern crucible of the Cold War, with the northern Democratic Republic of Vietnam being nominally backed by both China and the Soviet Union, while the south – the Republic of Vietnam – became home to fast-expanding Western embassies where a 'vast effort' was directed against the Vietnamese communists known as the 'Vietcong'.[34] Fearing a sweeping Vietcong incursion into the south and the complete ejection of all Western personnel, in 1962 the US adopted the old British strategic hamlets scheme – tried and tested in Malaya and later in Oman – in an effort to cut off links between potentially sympathetic South Vietnamese rural communities and the advancing insurgents.[35]

By the mid-1960s, the strategy seemed to be failing, despite the presence of a 17,000-strong US military advisory group and the US providing an estimated seventy-five percent of the South Vietnam government's funding. Whether due to unwavering support and steady supplies to the Vietcong from China and the Soviet Union or, as claimed by a former senior British intelligence official, the US's lack of experience in 'colonial control', the counter-insurgency had clearly reached a dead end. But as with Malaya, the stakes seemed too high to countenance withdrawal as US planners had long since identified Vietnam as potentially a 'most lucrative economy' given its abundance of iron ore, copper, gold, and coal. Thus, despite its public dismissal by President Lyndon Johnson as a 'raggedy-assed, little fourth-rate country', it was in fact nothing of the sort, with the

US government already seeking a mechanism through which to justify the deployment of even larger numbers of regular troops.[36]

In 1964, following a series of threats made by the US to the Democratic Republic of Vietnam, US destroyers clashed with North Vietnamese 'fast boats' in the Gulf of Tonkin. A number of US officials, CIA officers, and also crewmen aboard the destroyers have since suggested that the ships were sent into the Gulf as a deliberate act of provocation.[37] Moreover, despite Johnson's presidential address referring to the incident taking place on 'the high seas', which gave the US public the impression it had happened in international waters, the destroyers were later understood to have been only eight miles off the coast and just four miles from offshore islands belonging to the republic.[38] It has also been suggested that the incident was timed to coincide with US commando raids within the republic's territory, so as to plant the idea that the destroyers were directing these raids and thus making it more likely that they would be intercepted and attacked. Adding considerable weight to these views, formerly top-secret National Security Agency documents declassified in late 2005 include an in-house historian's description of how 'the agency's intelligence officers deliberately skewed the evidence passed on to policy makers and the public to falsely suggest that North Vietnamese ships had attacked [the] US destroyers.'[39]

Either way, with the *casus belli* established, full-blown war quickly ensued. Although most of the ground manoeuvres were conducted by US troops, including thousands of conscripts, the campaign also bore striking similarities to many of the Western-led multinational interventions before it, including the anti-Bolshevik campaign in Russia and the Dhofar operations in Oman. Contingents turned up from Britain, Australia, New Zealand, Sri Lanka, and Taiwan. Soldiers from Thailand and the Philippines also arrived, having received counter-insurgency training at the British-run Jungle Warfare School in Malaya. As with Dhofar, even Shah Muhammad Reza Pahlavi was keen to help, sending Iranian Phantom jets.[40] But caught off guard in 1968 by the Vietcong's massive Tet Offensive, which captured vast swathes of the country, reached the centre of Saigon, and was clearly facilitated by local support, the US intervention already seemed to have reached the 'beginning of the end'.[41]

Although defeated in Asia, the US was very soon embroiling itself again in the affairs of Central and South America, but this time with important lessons learned from the Vietnam experience and with some interesting innovations to its counter-revolutionary strategy. Democratically elected in 1970, Chilean president Salvador Allende was pushing forward his 'Chilean way to socialism' or *La vía chilena al socialismo*. Land reforms and even free milk for schoolchildren were being introduced, while the new government also attempted to nationalize Chile's lucrative copper mines, most of which were owned by US firms. Far from seizing such assets, by all accounts the foreign companies were well compensated by Allende, with the biggest among them – Kennecott and Anaconda – thought to have received much more than their book value due to years of excess profit-taking.[42]

In 2014 a series of declassified US documents, including Department of State reports and CIA annexes, revealed how President Richard Nixon's administration was running a 'cool and collected' campaign to destabilize Allende's government while simultaneously building up US ties with the Chilean military. A treasure trove of information, with the handwriting of Secretary of State Henry Kissinger and others appearing in the margins, the documents fully lay bare the US modus operandi at the time.[43] One section, for example, shows how the US copper companies in Chile had been complaining of increasing tax pressure and their worries over future nationalization. Anaconda, in particular, was understood by US officials to have 'an abrasive historical legacy' in Chile and 'symbolized to Chileans their inferiority and dependence on the US'. It was also admitted that Anaconda was considered by most Chileans to be a 'foreign state within a state'.[44] The primary US objective, according to the documents, was that Chile should not fall under communist control and then be able to influence the rest of South America. Among the other listed objectives was, unsurprisingly, the protection of US economic interests in the country, in an apparent reference to the copper industry.[45]

With a 'covert action budget' assigned, the CIA's operation was secretly described as a 'program to hamstring Allende and play for the breaks'. Most disturbingly, proposals for a more peaceful solution in Chile were rejected on the basis that 'only some kind of adversary strategy promises to contain or deter the adverse impact of Allende's policies [on US interests].'[46] The eventual military coup in 1973, representing the culmination of these efforts, was immediately endorsed by the US and paved the way for army chief Augusto Pinochet to take full control within a year and then launch a wave of brutal purges against remaining opponents.[47] Most interestingly, and signifying a growing awareness within the CIA of the need for sustained media campaigns, even after Pinochet's installation its operation continued, but with a shift in emphasis to help burnish the new junta's image at home and abroad.[48] Aware of the US's considerable difficulties in portraying the change of power in Chile as anything but a severely regressive development, the CIA co-produced a *White book of the change of government in Chile* which was then widely distributed in Washington, London, and other major international capitals.[49]

But it was further north in Nicaragua in the final decade of the Cold War that the US intelligence community embarked on its most clandestine and risky counter-revolutionary campaign. Ending forty-six years of dictator-ship, the Sandinista National Liberation Front, or Sandinistas – named after the 1920s Nicaraguan rebel leader, Augusto Sandino – had seized power in 1979 and formed a revolutionary government. Beginning a process of 'national reconstruction', they prioritized mass literacy, healthcare, and better gender equality, and announced that elections would be held within five years.[50] Concerned at the fall of the long-serving strongman Anastasio Somoza, who was famously quoted as saying, 'Since the Nicaraguan people are no more than oxen, they don't need schools,' Secretary of State George Shultz claimed that if the Sandinistas 'succeeded in consolidating their power ... then the [other] countries in Latin America, who all face serious internal economic problems, will see radical forces emboldened to exploit these problems'.[51]

With no Pinochet-like Nicaraguan military chief for the US to turn to, the situation seemed better suited to a reprise of the old Guatemalan and Cuban strategies of training up exiles and then inserting them back into their country to topple the new government. This time, the US-sponsored paramilitaries were to go down in history, as the *contrarrevolución* fight-ers that eventually emerged were soon to have their abbreviated nick-name – the 'contras' – used to describe all subsequent similar militias elsewhere in the world. Although numerous protests were made to the UN's International Court of Justice that the contras were a US creation, these were all rejected, while President Ronald Reagan's administration claimed they were merely 'democratic resistance'. Today there is of course overwhelming and incontrovertible evidence that proves the US's covert role, despite Congress having earlier banned such activities for US intelligence agencies.[52] Notably, the National Security Council is understood to have created a front organization called 'The Enterprise', which had its own Swiss bank accounts, its own aircraft, and had co-opted CIA staff from the region.[53] Third-party funds and assistance were also channelled to the contras from Argentinian intelligence and from the Saudi embassy in the US.[54] More controversially, funds are also believed to have been channelled from Muammar Gaddafi's Libya, despite his poor relations with the US, and even from the proceeds of US arms sales to the newly formed Islamic Republic of Iran (sales that violated the UN embargo on the supply of arms to participants in the ongoing Iran–Iraq War).[55]

Of perhaps even greater concern than the 'Iran–Contra' affair are the now well-documented CIA efforts to channel proceeds from drug-trafficking operations to the contras. According to a CIA internal investigation at the time, there was an awareness that some agents were working with traffickers, while a White House report from 1986 sought to downplay these 'contra-cocaine' connections claiming that 'we have evidence of a limited number of incidents in which known drug traffickers have tried to establish connections with Nicaraguan resistance groups.'[56] In 1989, however, a committee led by Senator John Kerry reported unambiguously that 'contra drug links included ... payments to drug traffickers by the Department of State of funds authorized by the Congress for humanitarian assistance to the contras.' Moreover, 'in some cases [this happened] after the traffickers had been indicted by federal law enforcement agencies on drug charges, in others while traffickers were under active investigation by these same agencies.' The report concluded that the Department of State had paid over $806,000 to known drug traffickers 'to carry humanitarian assistance' to the contras.[57]

AMERICA'S MIDDLE EAST – SPECIAL TREATMENT FOR A SPECIAL CASE

Soon advancing into the void left by Britain's retreat, and quickly overcoming their initial fence-sitting on Nasser's Egypt, by the mid-1950s US planners acknowledged that securing the Middle East, and especially the Persian Gulf region, was going to be vital to the future prosperity and stability of the Western states and, in turn, for holding the Soviet Union in check. As it was in the rest of the world, the extraction of natural resources was once again an obvious priority, so all indigenous attempts to nationalize economic assets – regardless of any progressive, liberal, or even democratic agendas – needed to be intimidated or destroyed by the US. In 1955, according to secret correspondence between British officials, President Dwight Eisenhower had even called for a 'high-class Machiavellian plan to achieve a situation in the Middle East favourable to our interests which could split the Arabs and defeat the aims of our enemies.'[58]

Just two years later the region got its own 'Eisenhower Doctrine'; an evolution of the earlier Truman and Monroe doctrines that had sought to secure US interests against international communism and foreign encroachment on the American continents.[59] Stating that 'the US regards as vital to the national interest and world peace the preservation of the independence and integrity of the nations of the Middle East,' Eisenhower effectively made the Middle East a special zone of US control. Moreover, as with Truman's more global declaration, Eisenhower sought to tie the Cold War to all threats to the Middle Eastern status quo by claiming he was 'prepared to use armed forces to assist [any Middle Eastern country] requesting assistance against armed aggression from any country controlled by international communism'.[60] He also proclaimed that 'the existing vacuum in the Middle East must be filled by the United States before it is filled by Russia.'[61]

The sudden special treatment of the Middle East at this time was, for the most part, due to the simultaneous deepening of US dependency on crude oil imports. Although still a net exporter at the end of the Second World War, by 1950 the US was importing a million barrels per day, and by the 1960s more than a third of the US's energy demands were being met by such imports, mostly from the Shah's Iran and the Gulf monarchies. US oil companies had already arrived on the Arabian Peninsula in 1933, eventually founding the Arabian American Oil Company – Aramco – in Saudi Arabia, and with President Franklin Roosevelt proclaiming in 1943 that 'the defence of Saudi Arabia is vital to the defence of the US.'[62] With Britain's oil needs also growing, its interests and relations in the region fell increasingly under the US shadow, with Whitehall planners admitting that Middle Eastern oil was 'a vital prize for any power interested in world influence or domination.'[63]

Despite some initial Anglo-American tension over how to divide up the region, a deal was eventually worked out after the White House told Britain's ambassador that 'Persian oil ... is yours. We share the oil of Kuwait and Iraq. As for Saudi Arabian oil, it's ours.'[64] Well aware of the awkward relationships the US would have to nurture with autocratic and reactionary monarchies at a time of rising Arab nationalist sentiments, the Department of State did acknowledge that 'among increasing numbers of Arabs there is ... a conviction that we are backing the corrupt governments in power, without regard for the welfare of the masses.'[65] But as US reliance on Gulf imports continued to grow, such voices were quickly crowded out as the defence of the oil-rich monarchies and the need to remove their rivals became increasingly intertwined with US national security and its very survival as a superpower.

In an originally top-secret but now declassified Department of State document from 1976, it was stated bluntly that the highest-priority policy objective for the US was the 'continued access to Saudi Arabian petroleum for the Western alliance and Japan'. US planners were told to keep persuading Saudi Arabia and the other Gulf monarchies that their long-term interests were parallel to those of the US and, somewhat pragmatically, were to caution Saudi Arabia that any shift to non-US technologies for its oil industry could lead to 'incompatibilities, inefficiencies, and even breakdowns'. It was also stated that Saudi Arabia should be made aware of the necessity to keep US citizens in key positions at Aramco.[66] Two years later another Department of State document explained that the nearby island emirate of Bahrain would have been of 'very little importance to the US were it not for its central location in the oil-rich Persian Gulf. The Western world needs continuing access to this region's oil.' The document's author also urged that for its own good the Bahraini government should integrate more closely with Saudi Arabia and purchase more US arms 'which would fit well within the role that the US government sees for Bahrain's small military'.[67]

By the late 1970s the tightening relationship was continuing to pay off for the US and Britain, with some of the monarchies, notably Saudi Arabia and the United Arab Emirates, having secretly circumvented the production quotas of the Iraq-based Organization of the Petroleum Exporting Countries cartel by supplying Britain with all the oil it needed to ease its own domestic energy crisis, and with Riyadh understood to have lobbied OPEC to set lower prices than Iraq and Iran had wanted, so as to suit the US economy's needs.[68] By the 1980s, according to a former CIA special assistant during the Reagan administration, Saudi Arabia had even been asked by CIA director Bill Casey to ramp up oil production so as to collapse deliberately the price of oil in an effort to weaken the Soviet Union's ability to earn foreign currency. With oil duly falling from $28 to $10 a barrel, the strategy has since been described by a former CIA chief of staff as a 'body blow to the Soviets. It was the equivalent of stepping on their oxygen tube.'[69]

After the Cold War ended, the safeguarding of the oil alliance naturally remained a top priority, as it was never just about defeating communism. With viable alternative energies a distant speck on the horizon, the leading academic journal Science revealed that nearly half of the US's total oil needs were still being met by foreign imports.[70] In many ways speaking for the entire US governmental and military-industrial complex, Norman Schwarzkopf, commander-in-chief of US Central Command (CENTCOM), put it best by explaining that 'Middle Eastern oil is the West's lifeblood. It fuels us today and … is going to fuel us when the rest of the world has run dry. It is estimated that within twenty to forty years the US will have virtually depleted its economically available oil reserves, while the Persian Gulf region will still have at least a hundred years of proven oil reserves.'[71]

REMOVING THE RIVALS – IRANIAN DEMOCRACY

The first big test for the US's new Middle East strategy came from one of the West's biggest oil suppliers when, in 1951, the democratic election of a new and progressive prime minister threatened to end the vast and lucrative monopoly held by a British company over Iran's most valuable resource. With Shah Muhammad Reza Pahlavi having gradually slid into accepting the role of constitutional monarch, Muhammad Mosaddegh had been able to win a large parliamentary majority. Having immediately advanced a number of social and political reforms including rent control and land reform, both of which sought to redistribute landlord profits so as to fund public amenities, Mosaddegh then began to discuss the possibility of half-nationalizing the Iranian oil industry, which had been controlled by the Anglo-Persian Oil Company since 1913, with a concession extending all the way up to 1993.[72] In 1948 alone, APOC had made profits of over £50 million and was described as the 'pride and joy of Britain's imperial assets, having gotten its start as the special project of Winston Churchill'.[73] According to one British official it was 'in effect an *imperium in imperio* in Persia' as it even had its own private intelligence agency, the Central Information Bureau.[74]

Troublingly for Mosaddegh and indeed the Iranian nation, Tehran was only earning between ten and twelve percent in royalties on APOC's net proceeds, which meant that the British government was making far more revenue from Iranian oil than the Iranian government.[75] To make matters worse, most of APOC's Iranian workers were poorly paid and housed in very bad conditions. As Stephen Dorril describes, the company effectively operated as though 'it was still the nineteenth century, regarding Iranians as merely wogs'.[76] Trying to defend the status quo, at least with regard to the tough revenue-sharing arrangement, the British ambassador to Iran argued that 'it is so important to prevent the Persians from destroying their main source of revenue ... by trying to run it themselves.' Meanwhile, as the British minister for fuel and power explained, it was one thing to say that Iran was 'morally entitled to a royalty ... [but to then say] they are morally entitled to fifty percent of enterprises to which they have made no contribution whatever, is bunk'.[77] Aware of these sentiments and, so it would seem, the dangers that lay ahead, Mosaddegh warned that his efforts to nationalize oil on behalf of the Iranian people would be 'opening a hidden treasure upon which lies a dragon'.[78]

Only after first trying an informal fifty-fifty offer and having this rejected by the British government did Mosaddegh then press forward in parliament with a full-blown nationalization act. But even then there were provisions to allow for twenty-five percent of oil profits to be set aside so as to compensate APOC for its losses and for job protection for all of APOC's British employees in Iran.[79] Despite the British government internally deeming the act to be legitimate in international law, its reaction was to deploy the Royal Navy and orchestrate a British-led naval blockade of Iran, while simultaneously freezing Iran's overseas assets. The aim, according to chiefs of staff committee documents, was 'to bankrupt Persia thus possibly leading to revolution'.[80]

In parallel, a more covert second strategy was already being implemented, with an exiled but pro-British former prime minister of the Shah's father being brought back to Tehran to help pro-APOC politicians mount a parliamentary challenge to Mosaddegh. Apparently on good terms with the Shah and with substantial funding behind him, it was hoped Britain's man could get re-installed as prime minister and, according to the Foreign Office, 'get a reasonable oil settlement with us'.[81] Put together, these British manoeuvrings helped confirm Mosaddegh's belief that London was 'evil but not incomprehensible' and that Britain had 'for centuries been manipulating Iran for British ends'.[82] But little did he know that an even more severe third strategy had also been on the table. Developed but not implemented, the plan was for British forces to seize territory near the main oil refinery in Abadan. It was a high-risk move that British foreign secretary Herbert Morrison believed 'might be expected to produce a salutary effect throughout the Middle East and elsewhere, as evidence that British interests could not be recklessly molested with impunity'.[83]

In any case, after its general election success in late 1951, the new British government seemed ready for action, with reinstalled prime minister Winston Churchill doing little to hide his contempt for the preceding Clement Attlee administration, which he accused of having 'scuttled and run from Abadan when a splutter of musketry would have ended the matter'.[84] Stating his preference for a full-blown coup d'état and the installation of a pliable new authoritarian Iranian regime, Churchill's view seemed to be shared by the British embassy in Tehran, with the ambassador calling for 'a dictator ... who would settle the oil question on reasonable terms'.[85]

Mindful of Britain's declining power, however, Churchill and Foreign Secretary Anthony Eden began to petition the White House to get US help in forcibly overthrowing Mosaddegh. Done secretly, this involved a Foreign Office cable being sent to the Department of State explaining that 'it is essential at all costs that [Britain] should avoid getting into a position where they could be represented as a capitalist power attacking a nationalist Persia.'[86] The first stumbling block for the plan unexpectedly came from the CIA, as its field officers reportedly quite liked Mosaddegh, while other CIA elements directly opposed US assistance on the grounds it would help perpetuate British colonialism. The Truman administration duly advised Britain to reach a compromise with Mosaddegh, but of course one in which Iran allowed other foreign companies – including those from the US – greater access to its oil. But with Eisenhower assuming office in 1953 and the Dulles brothers in control of both the Department of State and the CIA, the mood soon shifted as the Mosaddegh situation fell more firmly into line with the US's other global counter-insurgency operations. Believing Iran was 'too important to US strategic interests to be allowed self-determination', the new US administration duly began to suggest Mosaddegh was in league with communism.[87]

Problematically however, there was no hard evidence available that could prove Mosaddegh had any sort of affiliation with the *Tudeh*, Iran's Communist Party.[88] Even Britain's ambassador agreed that 'they have not been a major factor in the development of the Mosaddegh brand of nationalism,' while other British officials complained that 'the Americans would be more likely to work with us if they saw the problem as one of containing communism than restoring the position of APOC.'[89] Nonetheless, with inconvenient truths pushed to one side, a CIA propaganda campaign soon alleged that Mosaddegh's 'spy service' was funded by his land reform programme and never spied on the 'Soviet *Tudeh* Party'.[90] Meanwhile, in a further effort to divide Iran's parliament, a purported letter began to circulate claiming that Eisenhower had refused to offer Iran any US financial aid as long as Mosaddegh remained in power.[91]

Recently declassified documents from the period indicate that the CIA was also willing to 'expend money' on Iranian MPs to engineer a no-confidence vote on Mosaddegh and subvert his efforts to hold public referendums.[92] Moving beyond Britain's original frontman choice, the CIA also identified Fazlollah Zahedi as a potential new prime minister. The son of a wealthy landowner and a former chief of police with a reputation for ruthlessness, Zahedi was also endorsed by the Foreign Office and housed in the British embassy despite having been arrested by British forces in Palestine during the Second World War for engaging in pro-Nazi activities. Not all were convinced, however, with the Shah hesitant to act, and the

CIA reporting that even Zahedi himself was unwilling to commit 'political suicide' by being involved in 'extra-legal moves'.[93]

Nevertheless the CIA's Operation Ajax was launched in summer 1953 with John Foster Dulles informing colleagues that 'this is how we get rid of that madman Mosaddegh.'[94] A meeting, organized by Ajax coordinator Kermit Roosevelt,[95] was later described as involving surprisingly little discussion and, as one of its participants put it, he was 'morally certain that almost half of those present, if they had the courage to speak, would have opposed the undertaking'.[96] The controversy, it seemed, was that the CIA and MI6 had not only begun to approach military commanders in Tehran in preparation for their coup, but had also been hiring numerous mobs to serve as false flag *agents provocateurs*.[97]

Paid to protest, the thugs posed as communist *Tudeh* members and threatened religious leaders with murder if they didn't support Mosaddegh. In some cases, they even firebombed the houses of leading clerics. According to one former CIA agent, the men had no real ideology behind them and were 'more than just provocateurs, they were shock troops, who acted as if they were *Tudeh* people'. As another former agent described, the CIA gave 'serious attention' to issuing 'black propaganda in the name of the *Tudeh* Party', and countenanced threatening phone calls made to religious leaders, also in the name of the *Tudeh*. A former US general has also explained that everything from the guns used by the mobsters to the trucks they drove in was fully funded by the US, while the CIA planted stories about the situation in both the Iranian and the US press.[98]

Declassified files have shed more light on the operation, revealing that the men were organized into four bands, some of which were four hundred strong and described even by CIA officials as being 'ruffians'.[99] They were also reported to be 'acting as if they were *Tudeh* by throwing rocks at mosques and priests', presumably for the benefit of foreign journalists.[100] Kermit Roosevelt was a little more complimentary of his new employees, especially the team leaders, later claiming they were 'extremely competent professional organizers' who had no difficulty in buying a mob and handing out money as they went along.[101]

Supporting the narrative, being a CIA plant, or simply falling for the story, the *New York Times'* correspondent in Tehran seemed oblivious to his colleagues' earlier claims that Mosaddegh had 'acquired a reputation for being an honest patriot'. Instead he wrote that the protestors on the streets were in league with the prime minister and were '*Tudeh* partisans and nationalist extremists'.[102] Even the BBC was involved, using coded language on the World Service to help prove to the Shah that Kermit Roosevelt was indeed operating on behalf of US and British interests.[103] Moreover, according to the School of Oriental and African Studies' Annabelle Sreberny and Massoumeh Torfeh, the contents of the BBC's Persian service were also 'partially dictated' by the Foreign Office, and this left many Iranians 'with the impression that the BBC was an arm of the British government'.[104]

With spiralling discord in Tehran and fingers pointing in the wrong directions, the Shah was asked by the CIA to prepare decrees calling for the replacement of Mosaddegh with Zahedi, who by then had had to be moved to US safe houses as Britain's embassy had been closed on the correct grounds that it was plotting against the government.[105] But Mosaddegh refused to abdicate and went on national radio to reiterate that he was Iran's elected prime minister and to state that the Shah was being 'encouraged by foreign elements to attempt a coup d'état'. Although the Shah fled, the same agitators that had posed as *Tudeh* militants poured back onto the streets, but this time with pro-Shah banners, calling for his return.[106]

Finally installed with the pretence of popular support, Zahedi's position was still far from secure, with a nine-hour battle raging through Tehran as many army officers remained loyal to Mosaddegh. Tipping the balance, the US military mission in Iran began to support actively the pro-Zahedi camp, as the operation seemingly needed more resources than the CIA had originally envisaged. As a former major general testified to Congress, 'We violated our normal criteria ... we provided [them] immediately with blankets, boots, medical supplies that permitted and created the atmosphere in which they could support the Shah. The weapons, armoured cars, radio equipment ... were all furnished through the military defence assistance programme.'[107] Still serving the CIA's narrative, however, the *New York Times* claimed that the eventual military defeat of Mosaddegh's forces was 'nothing more than a mutiny by the lower ranks who revered the Shah'.[108]

From the British side, but with clear US cooperation, a less well-documented MI6 plan to undermine Mosaddegh's position also seemed to have been underway. Not dissimilar to its concurrent support for the

Muslim Brotherhood's agitation against the new Egyptian republic, and in many ways its earlier alliance with the *Basmachi* militants against the Bolsheviks, Britain had again identified conservative Islamic forces as natural allies against a largely secular and progressive new state that threatened Western interests. Reaching out to some of the more militant members of Iran's clergy, many of whom felt threatened by Mosaddegh's intended reforms, Britain effectively added another and arguably more dangerous element to the street protests as it sought to destabilize further the already precarious situation. Although, as former Iranian officials have claimed, a young Ruhollah Khomeini took part in the demonstrations, Britain's point man at the time was Ayatollah Abol-Ghasem Kashani. Having served as speaker of the Iranian parliament before being dismissed, Kashani had earlier worked with Nazi agents during the Second World War and had helped found the *Fadayan-e-Islam*, or 'Devotees of Islam'. A militant organization, it had been held responsible for the 1951 assassination of Mosaddegh's predecessor, Ali Razmara, who had been the first to entertain seriously the notion of renegotiating the APOC concession.[109] While some have sought to place Kashani in the nationalist camp, at least during the crisis,[110] this claim has been undermined by the contents of a 1952 CIA report, which identified him as having followers that could give Mosaddegh a 'contest in the streets … [that] would be bitter and destructive'.[111]

Channelling funding to Kashani and his supporters was obviously politically explosive if uncovered. Ann Lambton, a historian who advised the British government on the overthrow of Mosaddegh and was described in her *Telegraph* obituary as 'providing a valuable aid to Britain's eventual success', had urged the deployment of a British academic specializing in eastern religions and working as an MI6 agent to serve as an interlocutor.[112] Nonetheless, Lambton admitted that 'Kashani has [already] received large sums of money from somewhere.'[113] But the 'somewhere' was not so mysterious, with a former Iranian ambassador to the UN having since described how a funding stream to Kashani's men was by then well established, as 'the British would bring suitcases full of cash and give it to these people. For example, people in the bazaar, the wealthy merchants, would each have their own ayatollah that they would finance. And that's what the British were [also] doing.'[114] CIA funding to Kashani also now seems confirmed, with a former CIA station chief admitting that 'it was money both to Kashani and his chosen instruments, money to finance his communication channels.'[115] Moreover, Lambton also seemed unaware of the extent of Britain's 'Oudh Bequest', which was a long-standing and indirect means of paying retainers to Shia clerics in Iraq and Iran so as to maintain influence in the holy Shia cities of Karbala and Najaf. This mechanism was favoured by London as it allowed British embassy officials some leeway in being able simultaneously to give public support to the urban Sunni elites in Baghdad, even when they were putting down Shia uprisings. In 1903, for example, Britain's representative in Iran had noted that the bequest was a strong means of 'cultivating friendly personal relations with the chief priests as [it] would enable us to use them if necessary as a lever should Persia follow an unfriendly policy'.[116]

Noting in his memoirs that 'the British had their fingers in strange pies ... [they] had ties to the most reactionary clergy in the country,' the Shah also admitted that during this period '[he had] a longstanding suspicion of British intent and British policy'.[117] Writing from exile, his sister even argued that if you turned a cleric's beard upside down you would have seen 'Made in England' stamped underneath it.[118] Vaguely aware that Britain had been pursuing an Islamist back-up plan on the sidelines of the mainstream CIA coup strategy, the Shah's family was nonetheless probably unaware that Britain had been contemplating the ayatollahs actually seizing power outright if the Shah or his new prime minister ever proved uncooperative in the post-Mosaddegh era. Britain's foreign secretary, for example, had already discussed with the US the possibility of Kashani being a 'client political leader' if some sort of *modus vivendi* could be established.[119] Such an eventuality was not so unlikely, as declassified CIA documents have since revealed the rampant corruption and nepotism in the post-coup Zahedi government along with its divisive efforts to get Mosaddegh executed.[120] Sensing their vulnerability and, so it seems, their reliance on support from the Islamist camp, both Zahedi and the Shah paid personal visits to Kashani. According to the Iraqi ambassador to Tehran, they kissed his hand and thanked him for all of his help.[121]

Either way, with Mosaddegh removed the Iranian government quickly issued a new tender for foreign oil companies, but this time granting US firms forty percent of the concessions while Britain's share was reduced to the same level.[122] In this sense, the new Iranian dictatorship proved a good microcosm of the broader shift in influence in the Middle East from Britain to the US, with the CIA's heavy lifting seeming to warrant the Eisenhower administration's abandonment of the earlier promises to Britain that 'Persian oil is yours'.[123] Handsomely rewarded for his role in the US's first significant Middle Eastern counter-revolution, Kermit Roosevelt left the CIA in 1958 and joined one of the largest US oil firms that had won an Iran concession.[124] He also founded a consultancy company which received $116,000 a year from the Iranian government and helped facilitate further deals between US companies and Iran. Meanwhile, another US concession-winning company became a client of the same law firm of which both Dulles brothers were members.[125]

Most grimly, as a sort of counter-insurgency 'after service', the Shah's dreaded internal security services – the Organization of National Security and Information, or *Savak* – had by the early 1960s already received $500 million of US aid for the purchase of riot-control equipment. It was also receiving CIA and MI6 training, which, according to a former CIA analyst, was intended to 'deal with any likely and foreseeable civil disturbance in Tehran' and was 'based on German torture techniques from the Second World War'.[126] By the 1970s the increasingly repressive regime was one of Britain's biggest trade partners, with most of the Western oil majors successfully renegotiating their concessions.[127] During a visit by opposition leader Margaret Thatcher in 1978, shortly before her election victory and the collapse of the Shah's regime, the future British prime minister gushingly declared that 'his imperial majesty [is] … one of the world's most far-sighted statesmen whose experience is unrivalled … no other leader has given his country more dynamic leadership. He is leading Iran through a twentieth century renaissance.' She also claimed that 'it is a source of pride that British contractors are going to build the new military industrial complex at Isfahan; and have helped to construct the dockyard at Bandar Abbas.' Putting it bluntly, she concluded that 'defence sales generate employment in Britain, which we badly need … Iran's purchases of British fighting vehicles provide many thousands of jobs throughout our engineering industries … Iran has become by far our largest market in the Middle East … our sales to Iran now amount to more than £1 billion a year. We should like to do even better.'[128]

In 2013, to mark officially the sixtieth anniversary of the coup and, perhaps just as importantly, following a series of earlier lawsuits against the CIA, the US's National Security Archive published a series of recently declassified CIA documents on Iran. These included the first formal acknowledgement from the CIA that it had planned and helped to execute the coup. Summarizing the files, the National Security Archive described them as 'reinforcing the conclusion that the US, and the CIA in particular, devoted extensive resources and high-level policy attention toward bringing about Mosaddegh's overthrow, and smoothing over the aftermath'.[129] The documents' existence and contents contrast sharply with a report in the *New York Times* in 1997 that quoted CIA officials stating falsely that most of the documents relating to Iran in 1953 were either lost or destroyed in the early 1960s, allegedly because the record-holders' safes 'were too full'.[130] In much the same way, there was also a British cover-up, with Foreign Office documents written at the time the Shah's rule was disintegrating in 1978, but since declassified, indicating that its Iran desk officer had warned that if any records relating to the coup were ever released they risked 'possibly damaging consequences not only for London but for the Shah of Iran, who was fighting for survival', and that they contained 'very embarrassing things about the British'.[131] A year later other British officials warned that 'as the revolution [in Iran] is upon us, the problem is no longer Anglo-American: the first revelations will be from the Iranian side.'[132] Even today the British government does not acknowledge its involvement in the Mosaddegh crisis, although in 2009 Foreign Secretary David Miliband equivocally referred to Britain's role as part of a series of 'many outside interferences into Iran's affairs'.[133]

REMOVING THE RIVALS – TAKING ON THE ARABS

Emboldened by their successes in Iran, the US and its intelligence organizations soon woke up to the importance of Egypt and began to assume prime responsibility for countering most of the other Arab nationalist movements in the Middle East and North Africa. Worryingly for Washington, its enemies had even reached Israel's gates as a series of ineffective military dictatorships in Syria came to an end in 1954 when Syrian 'free officers' restored free and fair elections.[134] With the nationalist People's Party and the Arab Socialist Renaissance Party – the *Ba'ath* – winning a combined 55 out of 140 seats and thus representing the biggest bloc in parliament, the former French protectorate seemed finally poised to pursue an independent foreign policy.[135]

Refusing all US aid and staking out its Cold War neutrality, the new Syrian government confirmed the Department of State's fears, with embassy cables from Damascus warning that 'if the popular leftward trend in Syria continues … there is a real danger that Syria will fall completely under left-wing control.' Unsurprisingly, given the still gestating Eisenhower doctrine, the embassy also made multiple claims that the Syrian Communist Party was actively penetrating the government and the army, even though the party had won only one seat in the general election.[136] Without evidence, one cable stated: 'If the present trend continues there is a strong possibility that a communist-dominated Syria will result, threatening the peace and stability of the area and endangering the achievement of our objectives in the Near East.' On this basis it recommended that 'we should give priority consideration to developing courses of action in the Near East designed to affect the situation in Syria.' But even within the embassy there was confusion, as another cable stated: 'In fact the [Syrian] Communist Party does not appear to have as its immediate objective seizure of power. Rather it seeks to destroy national unity ... and to exacerbate tension in the Arab World.'[137] British government reports were much the same, warning that '[Syria's] army is deeply engaged in politics and increasingly under the influence of the extreme left; and there's much communist penetration.' Foreign Office records also reveal that the British cabinet agreed an attempt should be made to 'swing Syria on the right path'.[138]

Keeping it in the family, Kermit Roosevelt's cousin Archibald took the lead after a meeting with the leader of Syria's conservative Populist Party.[139] The memoirs of a former National Security Council official indicate that, after a discussion of what aid the US could supply to bring them to power, money was given to the party so that it could buy off military officers, radio stations, and newspapers.[140] Reprising its CIA-supporting role, MI6 meanwhile arranged for a Turkish border incident to take place. Serving as a distraction for the Syrian military, it was to allow British-funded Iraqi tribes to rise up and cross Syria's eastern border while Lebanese elements would come in from the west. Moreover, in the same vein as its outreach to Egypt's Brotherhood and Iran's ayatollahs, Britain also began to put into effect its usual Islamist 'Plan B' by contacting the Syrian branch of the Brotherhood and encouraging it to stage simultaneous demonstrations in Syria's cities. The aim, it seems, was for the ensuing confusion to create a state of anarchy requiring intervention from the still pro-British Iraqi armed forces.[141] Worryingly, British foreign secretary Selwyn Lloyd also wrote to the new prime minister, Anthony Eden, with details of a longer-term plan. According to their correspondence, after the CIA- and MI6-sponsored coup had taken place an effort would then be made to 'attach Syria to the Iraqi state ... in connection with the development of the fertile crescent'.[142] A date for the coup, known as 'Operation Straggle', was set for late October 1956, while an aftercare plan was drawn up involving the sealing off of all Syrian border posts and with the US immediately granting recognition to the new government.[143]

Although the Suez Canal crisis derailed Straggle, with Eden asking for it to be aborted on the grounds that anti-Western sentiments were running too high in the region, within three months Damascus was back in the spotlight after it signed a technical aid agreement with the Soviet Union. According to Department of State reports, 'the British [were] believed to favour active stimulation of a change in the present regime in Syria, in an effort to assure a pro-Western orientation.' By summer 1957 a new coup was thus prepared, this time with Kermit Roosevelt back at the helm. Known as the 'Preferred Plan', it was again to rely on Brotherhood demonstrations along with the arming of 'political factions with paramilitary capabilities'. As before, violent border incidents were to be staged, but this time they were to be false flag operations so as to place the blame on the Syrian government. More drastically, Eden also authorized the assassination of a number of Syrian officials including the head of military intelligence and the chief of the general staff. Rather than relying on the Populist Party to take power, the US and British fell back on the more tried and tested strategy of installing a strongman after the expected collapse of the government.[144] Opting for Adib Shishakli as their Syrian version of Iran's Fazlollah Zahedi, London and Washington consciously backed the country's former military dictator who had staged an election in 1953 to install himself as president and had then banned all newspapers critical of him.[145]

One of the CIA officers who had been involved in the Tehran coup was sent to Damascus, and Shishakli's former chief of security was brought to Lebanon so that he could then be smuggled across the border in a US diplomatic vehicle. The stage was set for the Preferred Plan.[146] Or so it seemed. In fact a number of the US's paid informants in the Syrian military had handed over their cash payments to Syrian intelligence along with the names of the CIA agents involved. They also revealed that the US had promised the Shishakli faction between $300 and $400 million in aid if it made peace with Israel once it had seized power. The idea of a continuing US presence had quickly become untenable. Especially bitter, the expelled US Army attaché ran his Syrian motorbike escort off the road as he reached the Lebanese border, shouting to him that the Syrian chief of intelligence 'and his commie friends' would have 'the shit beaten out of them by him with one hand tied behind his back if they ever crossed his path again.'[147]

Smarting from two failed coups and forced to gaze in from the outside, the US's focus on Syria nonetheless remained strong, with the Syrian government repeatedly complaining of 'unidentified aircraft flying over Latakia' – the Mediterranean port where most foreign ships docked. As a NATO member since 1952, Turkey also seemed willing to be drawn into the stand-off, likely in an attempt to underscore its role as an Eisenhower Doctrine enforcing state. Indeed, at one point Eisenhower himself stated that the Turks were massing on Syria's border with a 'readiness to act' due to 'anticipated aggression' from Syria, and that 'the US would undertake to expedite shipments of arms already committed to the Middle Eastern countries, and further, would replace losses as quickly as possible.'[148]

On top of these pressure-building tactics the US media continued its campaign to brand Syria a 'Soviet satellite', even though there was little evidence to support such assertions. Certainly by 1958 this seemed wholly implausible as under the terms of Syria's merger with Egypt to form the United Arab Republic both states had declared their respective communist parties to be illegal.[149] As a *New York Times* correspondent later described, a number of reports were nevertheless still filed, mostly describing Soviet arms and aircraft arriving in Syria, but these later proved to be false.[150] Even the Department of Defense was reluctant to buy into the ongoing CIA and Department of State Soviet–Syria narrative, with one of its reports stating that 'the Soviet Union has shown no intention of direct intervention in any of the previous Middle Eastern crises, and we believe it is unlikely that they would intervene, directly, to assure the success of a leftist coup in Syria.'[151] Furthermore, on the subject of the anti-communist Turkish antagonism, one of Eisenhower's own advisers later wrote of how the undersecretary of state 'reviewed in rueful detail ... some recent clumsy clandestine US attempts to spur Turkish forces to do some vague kind of battle against Syria.'[152]

Although a glimmer of hope came for the White House in 1961 following an army-led coup d'état that took Syria out of the short-lived United Arab Republic and restored Syrian independence, in many ways its only real function was to reverse Egyptian encroachment and end Damascus's status of subordination to Cairo.[153] Weak and lacking popular support, the post-coup regime was soon vulnerable to an increasingly militant wing of the *Ba'ath* and its numerous sympathizers within the armed forces. After seizing power in 1963, the *Ba'ath* renamed Syria the 'Syrian Arab Republic'[154] and sought to reaffirm its nationalist credentials, albeit outside Nasser's sphere of influence. Pro-*Ba'ath* military officers were promoted, including a prominent lieutenant colonel, Hafez al-Assad, who was made commander of the air force, while his brother Rifaat assumed control over the party's militia.[155] As this worst-case scenario unfolded, the US and British leaders met but were only able to agree upon a vague path forward that sought the 'penetration and cultivation of disruptive elements in the Syrian armed forces ... so that Syria can be guided by the West'.[156]

Next door in Jordan, however, things had been going a lot more smoothly. The young and British-installed King Hussein bin Talal, whose Hashemite family claimed descent from the Prophet Muhammad, was proving much better at keeping his opponents at bay. Five years into his reign, in 1957, the first significant challenge emerged as the increasingly popular prime minister Sulayman al-Nabulsi sought to affirm Jordan's neutrality and bring it closer to Syria and Egypt. Having won elections a year earlier, described by British officials as the 'first approximately free ones in the history of Jordan', he had also begun to use his mandate to reject offers of US aid on the grounds that it came with strings attached, notably the normalization of relations with Israel and the severing of ties to Nasser. As a final straw he also declared that 'communism is not dangerous to Arabs' and began to establish diplomatic relations with the Soviet Union.[157]

With all the alarm bells ringing, the usual suspects soon swung into action as CIA agents encouraged Hussein to dismiss al-Nabulsi on the grounds his supporters were plotting a coup. With no apparent evidence, Hussein duly claimed 'international communism and its followers' were responsible for 'efforts to destroy my country' and declared that 'we want this country to be inaccessible to communist propaganda and Bolshevik theories.'[158] Having purposefully used the buzzwords of the Eisenhower Doctrine, the king's plea prompted the US to move naval units to the eastern Mediterranean while Saudi troops moved into the southern port of Aqaba, effectively landlocking Jordan. In case a more full-blown intervention was needed, the US even began to deploy marines in Lebanon. Back in Amman, Hussein declared martial law and set about banning all political parties.[159]

Boxed in on all sides, al-Nabulsi's movement had lost its momentum as the monarchy's autocratic powers were entrenched and the US's show of force seemed to have had the desired effect. As a *Washington Post* investigation in the 1970s later revealed, this didn't come cheap, as the CIA had begun a series of post-al-Nabulsi annual payments to Hussein; these were to continue for the next twenty years and were in exchange for the agency having unfettered access to all of Jordan.[160] In his report to the foreign secretary, one British diplomat acknowledged that the new CIA-backed Jordanian regime was 'frankly repressive', but rather chillingly explained that '[Britain's] interest is better suited by an authoritarian regime which maintains stability and the Western connection than by an untrammelled democracy which rushes downhill towards communism and chaos.'[161]

Staying in the shadows, other British officials advised Hussein to strengthen himself further by cultivating a stronger relationship with the Jordanian branch of the Brotherhood. Although one such diplomat noted that the Brotherhood's official publication in Jordan had been identifying Arab Christians and the British as the organization's two main targets, and admitted that it was led by 'parochially minded local fanatics', he nonetheless recognized that it was also 'opposed to powerful left-wing parties.'[162] Thus, with Islamism again identified as a useful counterweight to unwanted ideologies, the heavily British-influenced Jordanian military began to provide military training to Brotherhood paramilitary forces.[163] In particularly restive Jericho the Brotherhood was even provided with arms so as to serve as 'strong arm opposition' to unsubdued leftist elements in the area.[164] As a further appeasement Hussein allowed the Brotherhood to field candidates in the next parliamentary election, while of course all nationalist and communist parties continued to be suppressed.[165] In 1970 the volatile alliance seemed to have paid off, with Brotherhood militias helping the Jordanian monarchy put down the extensive 'Black September' uprising led by a combination of Nasserists, Marxists, Palestinian Liberation Organization members, and even a faction of the Syrian armed forces.[166] As a reward for its loyalty, the Brotherhood had some members promoted to positions within the Jordanian government, while others were permitted to run militia training camps for Syrian Brotherhood recruits.[167]

The other Hashemite kingdom, Iraq, had not fared so well, with the British-backed King Faisal II succumbing to a nationalist coup d'état in 1958 and paving the way for Abd al-Karim Qasim's revolutionary government. As with the Syrian nationalists, Qasim's administration did not align itself with Egypt and actually put down a Nasserist uprising in Mosul in 1959, but very soon it started to trigger all the usual warnings for the Western powers. With more political freedoms the Iraqi Communist Party had been able to gain 'unprecedented influence over government and government-sponsored associations', and by 1962 more than a thousand Soviet engineers were in the country as Qasim confiscated the unused concession areas previously held by the Anglo-American Iraq Petroleum Company.[168]

While Qasim's stated claims on Kuwait may, as described, have actually played into Britain's hands in 1961, the overall tenor of his foreign policy was deeply unsettling. His strong support for the Organization of the Petroleum Exporting Countries was a cause for concern, as was his termination of a US-funded Iraqi police training programme.[169] Furthermore, his control over the city of Baghdad symbolically undermined the earlier 'Baghdad Pact', signed in 1955, that had grouped together Iraq, Iran, Turkey, and Pakistan in an anti-Soviet and pro-NATO alliance nominally headed by Britain. Embarrassingly the pact had to be renamed the Central Treaty Organization and have its headquarters shifted to Ankara before being nicknamed the 'forgotten alliance' and then eventually dissolved in 1979.[170]

In February 1963, following student demonstrations and an armed putsch by the Iraqi version of the *Ba'ath* Party, the US found itself confronted with an unusual dilemma. Briefly deviating from the stand-ard Anglo-American pattern of backing monarchs, Islamists, or other reactionary forces, the Kennedy administration appeared to consider any enemy of Qasim as a potential friend and, so it seems, had already been covertly assisting the Iraqi *Ba'ath*. With no formal connections to the more progressive Syrian *Ba'ath*, the new Iraqi regime had a much smaller political base, with the party perhaps having less than a thousand members and being reliant on the support of key army officers including Abdul Salam Arif, who became president, and Ahmed Hassan al-Bakr, who became prime minister. Brutally suppressing the country's Kurdish minority, but at the same time also trying to destroy the Iraqi Communist Party, Arif and al-Bakr were useful but dangerous US allies. As such, the history of the US's involvement with the first Iraqi *Ba'ath* regime remains highly sensitive, with most CIA and Department of Defense records of the episode either remaining classified or still not having been catalogued. Nevertheless, Weldon Matthews has been able to piece together much of the story using available archival sources, the Iraqi press, and various memoirs, while a recent London School of Economics doctoral disserta-tion written by Bryan Gibson has added a further layer of understand-ing by supplementing existing sources with interviews and other newly available material.[171]

As Matthews describes, the US officials had tried to paint a picture of the Iraqi *Ba'ath* regime as being a 'modernizing, even democratizing, anti-communist movement ... that was generally favourable to US strategic interests and Iraq's development'. In some cases it was even described as a 'liberal government'. Most incredibly, it seems that the US had already established a relationship with the *Ba'ath* before the putsch, with train-ing having been provided for pro-*Ba'ath* police commanders. Moreover, there is evidence that US officials had prior knowledge of the putsch's date, and had been informed of the likely membership of the new *Ba'ath* government.[172] Intriguingly a Department of State document refers to how '[US] officers assiduously cultivated' the university strikes that helped to undermine Qasim.[173] It was also clearly intended that CIA staff would come to Baghdad to brief US embassy staff on the plan of action. Among them was to be George Carroll, one of Kermit Roosevelt's CIA colleagues who had helped plan the overthrow of Mosaddegh and had then helped the Shah with 'counter-insurgency improvements' using his diplomatic cover in Tehran.[174]

Although Qasim's supporters and Iraqi Communist Party members continued to fight after the putsch was launched, the well-trained *Ba'ath* militias were able to mop them up within a few months. Department of State officials at the time lamented, rather accurately, that 'the conclusion that the US is somehow behind this coup has wide currency and communists are already trying to use this to charge the new government as a US stooge.'[175] Similarly it was also noted that there was a strong belief the US was 'certainly sponsoring operations in Iraq that were conducted by non-US personnel.'[176]

Based on his study of interactions between US officials and the Iraqi national guard, Matthews also demonstrates that the US was well aware of how the *Ba'ath* regime was detaining without trial several thousand Iraqis, most of whom were Iraqi Communist Party members. Matthews contends that US officials had good reason to believe that detainees were regularly executed or tortured and argues that 'in the application of counter-insurgency policy, the Americans were uninterested in reports of the regime's human rights violations and were even protective of it.'[177] When the *Ba'ath* fell in November 1963 to another military coup, having lasted less than a year, the new Iraqi government published an exposé containing gruesome photos and government documents revealing the extent of the torture and suffering of the prisoners.[178] Post-1963, US diplomats in Iraq began to corroborate much of this, reporting that embassy officials had been interviewing torture victims, with one diplomat predicting that 'the popular revulsion against the *Ba'ath* is largely justified, and will have a more or less permanent effect on the political development of Iraq.'[179]

Over in Lebanon, a different US strategy had been, in effect, intended to prevent the sort of uncomfortable election victories that had occurred in Syria and Jordan, or the type of nationalist government that Qasim had formed in Iraq. In receipt of considerable US aid, President Camille Chamoun was considered one of Washington's most steadfast and valuable allies in the region. Taking no chances, CIA election propaganda specialists were deployed to Beirut to ensure that pro-status quo candidates were out in front for the summer 1957 general election.[180] Although these 'independents' duly won a landslide fifty-one seats, with the various socialist and nationalist parties only winning fifteen seats between them, the CIA campaign had not quite been enough, with nearly half of voters staying away from the polls and with anti-government demonstrations rippling through the country for most of the next year.[181]

With the public fearing Chamoun would use the election result to extend unconstitutionally his presidential term by another six years, Lebanon seemed to be drifting out of the US's orbit. To make matters worse, the assassination of an anti-government newspaper editor in May 1958 gave fresh impetus to the protests, even sparking a full-blown rebellion in many parts of the country. With Chamoun's legitimacy in tatters and its hard work seemingly undone, the CIA quickly upgraded Lebanon to Eisenhower Doctrine status, with John Foster Dulles stating 'international communism' was the source of the conflict. Even Eisenhower waded in, explaining that 'behind everything was our deep-seated conviction that the communists were principally responsible for the trouble and that by seeking an additional term President Chamoun was motivated only by a strong feeling of patriotism.'[182]

With spurious grounds for intervention established, US Navy warships were dispatched to Lebanon's coast while US supplies were provided to the Lebanese police force along with tanks and weapons for the armed forces. Anti-communist US propaganda detailing purported Soviet interference was pushed by new local radio stations, such as the *Voice of Justice* and the *Voice of Iraq*, which went on air at this time. These were described as 'mysterious Arab radio stations' as nobody knew their origin. But a UN Observation Group answering to Dag Hammarskjöld reported no significant interference from the Egyptian–Syrian United Arab Republic, nor any at all from the Soviet Union.[183] Even more awkwardly, Lebanese fingers were also publicly pointing in other directions, with the beleaguered Chamoun complaining to Britain's foreign secretary of the 'evil influence of the Saudi money all over the Middle East.'[184] Writing a few years later, the co-founder of the Institute of Policy Studies, Richard Barnet, admitted that Nasser certainly may have tried to exploit the situation in Lebanon, but was adamant that 'he did not create it.' Barnet also claims that there were more than enough arms already in Lebanon to fuel the rebellion without the need for outside supplies, and that 'once again a government that had lost the power to rule effectively was blaming its failure on foreign agents.'[185]

With Lebanon still spiralling out of Chamoun's control, the US seized on the July 1958 revolution in Iraq as a pretext for an even heavier intervention on the grounds of protecting the small democratic country. By the end of the summer more than fourteen thousand US troops had arrived – more than the Lebanese police and armed forces combined.[186] In an apparent case of overkill, the large US presence seemed to backfire when even the Lebanese army's commander-in-chief told Eisenhower's envoy that his men were becoming restless, that the Lebanese people wished to see Chamoun resign, and that US troops should leave.[187] Although this provided an obvious opportunity for negotiation and the assuaging of the commander's fears of US motives, the envoy reportedly instead pointed to an offshore US warship and replied that 'just one of its aircraft, armed with nuclear weapons, could obliterate Beirut from the face of the earth.' To press his point home, he then added that 'he had been sent to make sure that it wouldn't be necessary for US troops to fire a shot' and stressed to the commander that he should make sure there were 'no provocations on the Lebanese side.'[188]

With less CIA operational experience and fewer British contacts to draw upon, the US's ability to head off threats in French-speaking North African Arab states was much more limited. Nevertheless, if either nationalist movements or Soviet penetration seemed likely, significant efforts were still made to apply some of the same counter-revolutionary strategies. In Algeria, for example, four French generals had launched a coup in 1961 in the midst of a post-independence civil war, in an effort to maintain Algeria's union with France and stand up to President Charles de Gaulle, who had pushed for an independent 'Algeria for Algerians'. In this scenario, it seemed, an independent and free Algeria would have immediately smoothed the path for the National Liberation Front – the most prominent socialist and pro-independence movement – to stage some sort of communist takeover.[189]

Several major newspapers, including prominent European dailies, soon began to suggest that the CIA had been involved. The French ministry of foreign affairs refused to dispute the allegations, but the leading newspaper *Le Monde* concluded that 'it seems established that US agents more or less encouraged Challe [the leader of the coup].'[190] The US media reaction was more mixed, with most outlets rejecting Le Monde's allegations, and some claiming that France sought a 'scapegoat', while others hinted at a Moscow-hatched plot to sour US-French relations.[191] Nonetheless a New York Times report stated that 'the CIA was involved in an embarrassing liaison with the anti-Gaullist officers who staged last week's insurrection in Algiers ... [this has led to an] increased feeling in the White House that the CIA has gone beyond the bounds of an objective intelligence-gathering agency.'[192] As well as Maurice Challe, who as a former commander-in-chief of NATO's European forces was an ideal point man for the US, it also transpired that in 1960 CIA agents had begun to acquaint themselves with a former French governor general of Algeria who had reportedly warned them that De Gaulle was about to allow Algeria to become a 'Soviet base'.[193] Other meetings between US officials and Algerian provocateurs reportedly took place in Spain, which – according to an investigation published by The Nation – prompted a CIA promise that if the generals succeeded, then the US would recognize the new military-led Algerian state within forty-eight hours.[194]

More broadly the coup's objectives may have reflected the CIA's ambitions to weaken De Gaulle's position in France. Increasingly distrusted in Washington, he had already refused to incorporate French forces into NATO's integrated command structure, and – perhaps most problematically – had objected to exclusive US control over NATO's combined nuclear arsenal. He had also called for the removal of all US military bases from French territory and for the US to remove itself from Indochina.[195] Although the Algeria coup failed, De Gaulle remained dogged by its remnants, who formed the remarkably well-organized paramilitary Organisation de l'Armée Secrète. Operating branches in both Algeria and metropolitan France, its covert anti-government operations were fictionalized a few years later in the best-selling thriller The Day of the Jackal.[196] Interviewed much later, former head of French intelligence Pierre Lacoste revealed that the CIA had indeed provided support to the OAS in its efforts to attack De Gaulle during the 1960s.[197]

Further west, in Morocco, the challenge was somewhat more straightforward, with Le Mouvement des Officiers Libres becoming increasingly active in the 1970s in its attempts to remove the Moroccan Alaouite monarchy, improve human rights, fight corruption, and set up a 'Democratic

Arab Islamic Republic of Morocco'. In this sense its members were similar to the first wave of Arab nationalists, albeit without the emphasis on secularism. Having tried to shoot down King Hassan II's aircraft in 1972, the movement began to grow in strength and by the early 1980s seemed to have infiltrated many of the country's key institutions. As far as the US was concerned, the fall of Hassan II was unthinkable, as his armed forces had been helping both the UNITA militias in Angola and aiding US strategy in Zaire. With more than a hundred US nationals reportedly embedded within the Moroccan military, and with the US assistant secretary of defense for international security having visited the king with a team of twenty-three experts, the Moroccan capital by this stage was considered one of the CIA's most important outposts in Africa.[198]

In 1983 local newspapers reported that the head of Moroccan security, General Ahmed Dlimi, had been killed in a car accident. As William Blum notes, he was likely a secret member of the revolutionary movement. *Le Monde*'s correspondent on the ground was certainly suspicious of the accident's circumstances and suggested that Dlimi's death required further investigation. Unsurprisingly, the correspondent was promptly expelled from the country.[199] Since then *Le Monde*'s view has been backed up by exiled dissident Ahmad Rami's autobiography, which claims that Dlimi was in fact arrested, interrogated, shot, and then later placed in the car he was discovered in. According to Rami, Dlimi had been advocating a closer relationship between Morocco and France so as to reduce Rabat's dependency on the US, and in December 1982 the two men had met in Sweden to discuss this. Rami claims that the CIA managed to record a microfilm of their meeting and handed this to Hassan II shortly afterwards, claiming this was 'enough for [Dlimi] to be eliminated'. In 2001 these allegations were further corroborated by a former Moroccan army officer.[200]

STRENGTHENING THE STATUS QUO – THE ARMS TRADE

With its counter-insurgency strategies able to head off most but not all threats to the Middle Eastern status quo, the US's need to buttress directly its oil-producing clients from both external and internal threats continued to grow. Soon generating an important and highly lucrative side trade, advanced and very expensive weaponry, sometimes even superior to that being fielded by the US and other Western armed forces, began to be exported to states that were 'on the same side' as the NATO powers. On paper at least, these expensive arsenals provided some sort of deterrent ability in an ever more volatile neighbourhood along with giving ruling families a feeling they had made a down payment for future Western protection. Meanwhile, the vast chunks of gross domestic product being assigned by these autocratic states to Western arms procurement – sometimes in excess of ten percent – effectively meant significant portions of their oil revenues were being recycled back to the economies of their biggest energy customers, and of course converted into dollars or sterling.

Throughout the 1970s the ever more repressive Shah of Iran was one of the biggest cogs in the wheel, purchasing large quantities of US and British equipment, including the latter's Chieftain tanks. With an order placed for a massive fifteen hundred of the vehicles, and payment made entirely up front, only 185 were delivered to the Shah's armed forces by the time of the 1979 revolution, thus allowing the manufacturer and Britain's Ministry of Defence to pocket an estimated £400 million and cease all further deliveries.[201] Already beginning to eclipse Iran, however, the six Arab Gulf monarchies soon emerged as an even greater prize for the West's increasingly export-focused arms industries.

Formed in 1981 and headquartered in Riyadh, the new Gulf Cooperation Council – ostensibly a political and economic union – was also envisaged as a new Western-equipped military bloc to counter supposed threats to the regional order from revolutionary Iran and elsewhere.[202] In this sense, the GCC was the latest attempt at building a NATO-armed Middle Eastern fortress, replacing the ill-fated Baghdad Pact, the Central Treaty Organization, and the even shorter-lived 'Middle East Command' that had briefly tried to link the Western powers with Turkey, Israel, and Jordan.[203] Within a few years Saudi Arabia alone had bought more than $2 billion of US arms, most of it never to be used, while Britain's arms exports to other GCC members – most of which were heavily promoted by the Ministry of Defence's newly formed Defence Export Sales Organization – soon rose to nearly £800 million per annum.[204]

As important as the protection it was supposed to offer, and the petrodollar generation it clearly facilitated, the fast-growing Middle East arms trade also enriched numerous powerful individuals on both sides of the fence. As Fred Halliday observed, even by the mid-1970s the flow of weapons from the West to the Gulf had already led to 'corruption on a hitherto undreamt of scale'. In one remarkable case, a British 'fixer' who had previously been a military officer had even tried to take legal action against a British Aircraft Corporation salesman whom he alleged had agreed to pay him commissions of between five and ten percent on all arms sales to Arab countries. The disgruntled intermediary confidently claimed to the court that he had only received £40,000 of the funds he was 'owed'.[205] In numerous other cases prominent Saudi and American interlocutors, some of whom are still alive today, were able to broker commissions of hundreds of millions of dollars per deal, creating a new subset of the world's richest men by the end of the twentieth century.

By far the biggest deal and, so it would seem, one of the most corrupt, was the one agreed between the British government and Saudi Arabia in the late 1980s. Worth around £50 billion and thus the biggest arms contract in history or, as one wit claimed, 'the biggest British sale ever of anything to anyone', Saudi Arabia had effectively paid the Ministry of Defence to modernize and re-equip its entire army and air force. Known ironically as *Yamamah*, which translates as 'dove', the circumstances in which the contract was signed continue to provide one of the best insights into the Western governments' secretive relations with their Middle Eastern clients at the height of the oil era. As a former MI6 officer told the BBC, Britain reached pole position on *Yamamah* only because MI6 had been supplying British businessmen with information on their rivals, notably the French, and – more disturbingly – had provided intelligence on which Saudi officials their competitors were intending to bribe.[206] Others, meanwhile, have claimed that Britain's no-questions-asked approach made it the most attractive weapons supplier at that time, with London quick to confirm that arms sold under *Yamamah* would be exempt from export licensing, which in effect meant that Saudi Arabia would be free to do whatever it wanted with them.[207]

The deal was viewed by many as a step too far, and recently declassified documents have revealed that at the time of negotiations more than fifty US congressmen co-signed a letter of protest delivered to Prime Minister Margaret Thatcher. Expressing grave concerns with regard to the supplying of such equipment to Saudi Arabia, on the basis it would 'undermine peace in a turbulent region', they further claimed that 'your government's arms sale will simply increase the level of violence.' But with the White House almost certainly preferring that Britain, rather than any other European state, supplied Saudi Arabia, the declassified papers reveal that Thatcher herself had begun to micromanage *Yamamah* and had taken a personal interest in its progress. Notably, she wrote to the Saudi minister for defence to tell him he had made a 'wise decision' and to guarantee him that the contract would be entirely handled by the British government. She also stressed to him that it was 'vital' that there be no publicity and that '[he] may be confident of our complete discretion'.[208]

In many ways Thatcher's *Yamamah* letters fit a broader and illustrative pattern of personal correspondence that had developed between her and the Saudi royal family during this period, with other declassified papers revealing how she had apologized to King Fahd bin Abdul-Aziz al-Saud for an 'inaccurate news item' on the BBC. She explained to Fahd that 'I and all my colleagues attach the highest importance to friendship and co-operation with the kingdom of Saudi Arabia and share your majesty's wish that nothing shall disturb this relationship.' The offending BBC report was in fact based on a very real incident that had taken place during the *hajj* pilgrimage and involved the mistreatment of foreign pilgrims. The British ambassador to Saudi Arabia himself had referred to it using diplomatic channels, and even the Saudi ministry of the interior had confirmed some of the incident's details. Thatcher's obsequious response prompted a Foreign Office official later to write in the archived letter's margins that there was 'an object lesson somewhere here. [The] prime minister is very oily to kings but matter of fact to lesser mortals. We can agree with this text.'[209]

With criticism in the British media continuing to mount, Thatcher was obliged to keep publicly justifying *Yamamah* even after she left parliament. In 1993, for example, she stated in a Chatham House speech that 'I am proud to have played a part as prime minister in helping Saudi Arabia to make provision for its own self-defence through the historic government-to-government agreement.' She reasoned it had 'since brought such great benefit to both our countries' and, with reference to protestors standing outside in St. James's Square, claimed that 'those who argue that arms sales to Middle Eastern countries are in themselves dangerous because they increase the likelihood of future conflicts are totally misguided.'[210] With Thatcher's powerful allies capable of delaying an inquiry into possible wrongdoings, it was only in 2004, more than a decade later, that Britain's National Audit Office finally launched an investigation into *Yamamah*. But even then the forces aligned against it were considerable and the office's work was abruptly brought to a halt two years later.

As the *Guardian* later revealed, the National Audit Office was forced to drop the case on the basis that 'the Saudis began issuing their own threats. They claimed they would stop supplying vital intelligence about terrorists to Britain if the investigation was allowed to continue.' Meanwhile, Serious Fraud Office investigators who had also been looking into *Yamamah* were dramatically told by British government officials that, if they carried on, they would be facing the loss of 'British lives on British streets'. Having reportedly written a secret letter to the attorney general, Prime Minister Tony Blair was also understood to have been urging the end of the *Yamamah* inquiry, on the grounds that there was a 'real and immediate risk of a collapse ... in British-Saudi security, intelligence and diplomatic cooperation'. Despite all of this, it was reported that the National Audit Office did get as far as ascertaining that about fifteen percent of the deal's costs had gone directly to Saudi ruling family members – the only NAO report ever to have been withheld from publication. Following up on this, a BBC probe in 2007 made the allegation that the payments were 'made with the full knowledge of the Ministry of Defence' and that two transfers of £120 million were sent to accounts operated by the Saudi embassy in Washington that were personally used by senior princes. In 2010, BAE Systems, one of the main *Yamamah* beneficiaries, finally admitted wrongdoing, but only after a separate US Department of Justice investigation had begun to look in their direction. Agreeing to pay £300 million in penalties to settle the matter, BAE Systems accepted the Department of Justice's claim that 'BAE agreed to transfer sums totalling more than £10 million to a bank account in Switzerland controlled by an intermediary. BAE was aware that there was a high probability that the intermediary would transfer part of these payments to the [Saudi] official.'[211]

With the *Yamamah* controversy far from an isolated case, the specifics of several other long-running deals have also slowly started to emerge. In 2010, for example, it was finally confirmed that the US Department of

Defense had earlier agreed to supply $60 billion of arms to Saudi Arabia. With a significant emphasis on improving the 'inter-operability' of the Saudi armed forces, the contract strongly suggested possible joint US–Saudi operations should the need arise.[212] Several years in the making, it had originally been justified to Congress on the basis that seventy-five thousand jobs in the US arms industry would be protected.[213] Meanwhile, back in Britain, a former army officer who had worked for GPT Special Projects Management, a subsidiary of Airbus, came forward as a whistle-blower on a £2 billion contract to supply communications equipment to the Saudi Arabian national guard. Backed by two other former GPT employees, he revealed details of questionable transactions involving Ministry of Defence officials, gifts including luxury cars given to Saudi officials, and illicit payments being routed through the Cayman Islands. In 2012 the Serious Fraud Office launched an investigation and arrested several people connected to the deal. In April 2015, with the story refusing to go away, a freedom of information request filed by *Private Eye* magazine led to a tribunal in which two government officials were required to answer questions. With much of the case held in private, the public section of the tribunal saw one of the officials justifying the lack of any earlier inquiry on the grounds that the *Yamamah* investigation had also been closed, and that 'releasing the documents would cause harm to our relations with the Kingdom of Saudi Arabia.' He also stated that Britain's maintaining of relations with 'a few [senior] Saudi princes ... is vital to the achievement of our national security interests, particularly counter-terrorism'. In support of this he cited 'tip-offs' received from Saudi Arabia that had purportedly allowed British security services to discover bombs placed on aircraft.[214] Unnervingly, a few months later, the tribunal ruled that the details of the case could remain a secret on the grounds that 'public disclosure of the withheld information would prejudice relations between the UK and Saudi Arabia' which in turn might lead to 'real and significant harm' for Britain.[215]

STRENGTHENING THE STATUS QUO – MILITARY BASES

Closely tied to the arms trade and helping reinforce further the terms of protection offered by the US to its oil-producing allies, the number of

Western military bases on and around the Arabian Peninsula began to mushroom in the latter part of the twentieth century. With roots dating back to the old network of British installations in Kuwait, Oman, and the Trucial States, along with the US's original airbase in Saudi Arabia's Dhahran, in many cases these newly expanded facilities soon began to host sizeable NATO member deployments.[216] A $400 million Anglo-American air defence programme was also launched, and the US Navy eventually re-established its old Second World War-era Fifth Fleet at a naval support facility in Bahrain.[217] More recently the US Air Force set itself up in Qatar after the US government was told by its ruler, Hamad bin Khalifa al-Thani, that he would like to see 'up to 10,000 US servicemen permanently based in the emirate'. Duly shifting personnel from a more discreet camp at Saudi Arabia's Prince Sultan airbase, the US formally turned Qatar into CENTCOM's forward headquarters and soon added accommodation for an array of special forces, and a CIA outpost.[218] By 2010 at least four of the Gulf monarchies that had purchased the latest US anti-missile system had been promised by CENTCOM that Aegis destroyers equipped with early warning radars would be on patrol in the Persian Gulf at all times.[219]

Although no US bases were built in the UAE, the country's ports were heavily used by the US, with Dubai's Jebel Ali quickly becoming the US Navy's most highly visited 'liberty port'.[220] Shrouded in secrecy for many years, Abu Dhabi had also leased sections of its Al-Dhafrah airbase to the US Air Force and to the CIA, with unmanned reconnaissance aircraft and tanker aircraft using its facilities to support US operations elsewhere in the region. Somewhat embarrassingly, it was revealed in summer 2005 that US drones and U2 aircraft were also being serviced there following the crash landing of a spy plane on its return to Abu Dhabi from a mission in Afghanistan.[221] Meanwhile, the UAE had also been secretly making available an airbase in Pakistan to the US military. Following a leaked US diplomatic cable and a Reuters report describing it as a 'mystery wrapped in a riddle', it emerged that the Al-Shamsi base in Baluchistan had been leased by the Pakistani government to the UAE since 1992, but had then been subleased by the UAE to the US.[222]

Despite pleas and offers of financial aid from some Gulf monarchies to keep British servicemen based in the region after independence, Britain's military role in the region was greatly reduced after 1971, as the US effectively stepped in to plug most of the gaps. Nonetheless the Royal Air Force continued to station an expeditionary air wing in Qatar and established its own desert airbase at Thumrait in southern Oman.[223] In a statement to the House of Commons Select Committee on Defence in 2000, a Ministry of Defence spokesperson helped confirm what many assumed to be an unwritten defence pact between Britain and these states. After explaining that 'all of the Gulf countries have an expectation that [Britain] would assist them in times of crisis,' he noted that 'many of the [Gulf] countries do not feel the need for an agreement because we have continually assured them of our commitment to the stability of the region.'[224] The committee's report also revealed that nearly three hundred British military personnel were stationed in Gulf states at that time, and that Britain had trained more than eight hundred personnel from these countries over the previous year.[225] When questioned on this, the minister of state for foreign affairs argued that this was an 'obvious manifestation of our commitment to enhancing the military capability of the region. These contacts help to build bridges. But they also enhance and make more credible the ability of the Gulf States to deter would-be aggressors.'[226] Among the report's other findings was that the Ministry of Defence had by then set up a specific Saudi Arabian Projects Unit within the Defence Exports Sales Organization. Described as acting on behalf of the Saudi government to ensure that the ministry's prime contractor, BAE Systems, met its contractual obligations, it was understood to be staffed by a mixture of RAF, Royal Navy, and civilian personnel. The committee stated that the precise arrangements surrounding the unit were 'sensitive' but did not elaborate further.[227] In fact, it recommended even deeper ties with Saudi Arabia and for the Ministry of Defence to be even more forthright in connecting further arms sales to formal military arrangements between the two countries. It concluded that 'the [Ministry of Defence] should be prepared, on occasions, to be more direct in linking the promotion of British equipment to military assistance. Otherwise it risks the British defence industry being disadvantaged to the benefit of our less coy allies and competitors.'[228]

Beyond the US and Britain, numerous bases in the region were soon established by other Western powers. Canada, for example, built the secret 'Camp Mirage' outside Dubai and used it as a rest and supply station for Canadian and Australian troops working elsewhere in the Middle East.[229]

In 2009, France also opened a base in the UAE after a new and more hawk-ish leadership in Abu Dhabi succeeded the more cautious former ruler Zayed bin Sultan al-Nahyan, who had long resisted the overt presence of Western servicemen.[230] Certainly France's *Camp de la Paix* was inaugurated with considerable fanfare, with even President Nicolas Sarkozy appearing in person.[231] It was followed up by announcements that the French Navy would begin using facilities at Port Zayed, and that UAE diplomats could begin using French embassies in countries where there was no UAE pres-ence. Writing an article for one of the UAE's state-backed newspapers, Sarkozy made the relationship even clearer by explaining that 'we have been strategic partners for fifteen years, linked by the defence accord we signed in 1995. With this permanent base, our commitment alongside you becomes even stronger.' He also claimed that the base 'proves that France is prepared to take every risk for its friends, the message is clear, we will stand by you under all circumstances, even the most difficult' and that 'you should know that you can always count on us if the security of the region were ever to be threatened.'[232]

STRENGTHENING THE STATUS QUO – MERCENARIES

Providing a further line of defence for the Western-backed oil monarchies have been large numbers of foreign mercenaries. At all ranks and files, from foot soldiers up to senior military advisers, the dependence of Gulf rulers on their presence has historically provided the US, Britain, and other Western governments with some considerable comfort, especially if their own expatriates are there on the ground. Observing in the mid-1970s that 'the Middle East oil producers of the more conservative kind are probably the most obvious example of countries which are permitted to recruit British military personnel,' Fred Halliday usefully outlined the several types of mercenaries he had already noticed in the region. Among these were what he called the 'stereotype soldiers for hire' who had simply been brought in to provide training in communications and sometimes specialized offensive operations. As he put it, in the 'oil rich states of the Arabian Peninsula … their continued use [is] essential to maintaining the anti-democratic system that prevails'.[233]

Legally of course there were no impediments to the export of such mercenaries to allied states, especially in Britain's case, as the Diplock Committee's report in 1976 confirmed that the British government retained the right to decide which countries British mercenaries could go to.[234] In other words, Britain made it clear that it was not opposed to its citizens working overseas as self-employed soldiers as long as the conflict or situation tied with British foreign-policy goals. Indeed, there is evidence that retired servicemen were being actively hired by the British government for the purpose of their export to the Middle East. Notably, in the 1960s, with the described conflicts in Yemen and Oman still raging, a front company for the Ministry of Defence had begun to recruit and supply former RAF pilots to go and train the Saudi air force.[235]

On a more senior level were those who ended up running entire armies behind the scenes along with numerous former intelligence officials and policemen employed to maintain the Gulf monarchies' internal security services.[236] As the right-hand man of the Bahraini ruler between 1924 and 1956, Charles Belgrave provides a good early example, as does the Cambridge-educated St. John Philby, who served as adviser to King Abdul-Aziz bin Saud or 'Ibn Saud', and even negotiated oil concessions and international alliances on his behalf during the 1920s and 1930s.[237] Visitors to Oman in the 1970s similarly claimed real power was held by a 'shadowy duo of British advisers', including a senior British intelligence official with a background in psychological warfare who had initially been part of an official Foreign Office delegation sent to Oman's ministry for information.[238] In Qatar 'enormous power' was also thought to be held by two British expatriates, one who controlled the army while the other ran the police force.[239]

Continuing to tap Western intelligence communities for its senior staff long after Philby's death, Saudi Arabia ended up hiring numerous former CIA, MI5, and MI6 officers throughout the twentieth century.[240] But providing an even better recent example of this has been Bahrain, where a steady stream of Westerners has been responsible for the evolution of the island's ill-reputed security services. Referred to by visitors as a 'mysterious officer', the same Ian Henderson involved in putting down the *Mau Mau* rebellion in Kenya had soon been hired by the al-Khalifa ruling family to protect their regime from steadily growing public dissent.[241] Bumping into Henderson at a party in 1973, when studying on a Fulbright scholarship, former CIA official Emile Nakhleh recalls being told that he and everyone else was already under surveillance.[242] Earning the nickname 'Butcher of Bahrain', Henderson was in many ways just the tip of the iceberg, as dozens of other British and Western expatriates later arrived.[243]

Despite numerous accusations of Henderson's personal involvement in torture in Bahrain, many of which continue to be made after his death, he was never questioned on his numerous return trips to Britain and in 1984 he was decorated with a CBE by the Queen.[244] In 2015 a secret Foreign Office report dating from 1977 and entitled *Internal security in Bahrain* was considered for declassification following a freedom of information request by a Bahraini rights organization.[245] Some parts of the document were declassified and revealed that Henderson had been in close contact with British officials and that nine officers were on loan to Bahrain from Britain's Special Branch.[246] The other parts of the document were however kept classified on the grounds that 'international relations could be damaged were they to be released.' Although the British government's spokesman insisted on making most of his comments during a secret portion of the hearing, he did note in the public part that any further disclosure of the paper could also harm current British efforts to 'reform' Bahrain's security forces.[247]

Another category of mercenaries present in the region have been active military personnel seconded to Gulf governments in order to smooth the flow of weapons sales and for the Western governments to 'make a profit' from their deployment. The test case for this strategy was Oman in the 1970s where the newly installed sultan had begun to pay the British and other Western governments directly out of Omani oil revenues in exchange for the large numbers of staff they had transferred to his fledgling armed forces. Other examples are plentiful, especially during this period, with a 140-strong 'Kuwait liaison team' being sent by Britain in 1977 to train the Kuwaiti army in the use of tanks, presumably in an effort to persuade Kuwait to buy British tanks in the future.[248]

In Saudi Arabia, the staffing of the national guard has been particularly important given its de facto role as the last line of defence for the monarchy. Since the 1970s it has received training from SAS soldiers seconded on 'special duties in connection with the personal safety of His Majesty the King', with a unit of SAS veterans later being assigned to protect the Saudi minister for oil and mineral resources, Ahmad Zaki Yamani.[249]

The Ministry for Defence has since admitted that short-term training teams have continued to conduct 'low level internal security training' for the national guard, while on a bigger scale a good few hundred US military personnel along with more than a thousand employees of Vinnell Corporation have also been seconded to its headquarters, the latter being a private security company that is a major US government contractor and is owned by Northrop Grumman, one of the US's largest arms manufacturers.[250]

A harder type of mercenaries to identify and measure have been the 'mercenary migrants' recruited from poorer countries in the broader region and often organized by Western middlemen or other such intermediaries. As Halliday put it, these were mostly men driven to the Gulf monarchies 'by hunger' who would end up 'fighting and suppressing their class counterparts in other states'.[251] In the early 1960s, Pakistan allowed many of its citizens to go to Saudi Arabia to bolster defences as the Yemen war raged along the kingdom's southern flanks. Among their number was the young Muhammad Zia-ul-Haq, the future military dictator of Pakistan, who was himself British- and US-trained and who later took part in mercenary activity in Jordan to help the monarchy survive the Black September uprising. After taking power in 1978, Zia-ul-Haq deepened his relationship with Riyadh further by 'assuming responsibility for some of Saudi Arabia's internal security needs'.[252]

Similarly in Oman, huge numbers of South Asian fighters became integrated into the official armed forces with an estimated forty percent of all Oman's soldiers at one point being Baluchi. In this sense the Omani army was increasingly taking the form of earlier British-led forces in Africa and India in which militias were not only made up of natives, but also the natives of poorer nearby colonies.[253] The armed forces of other Gulf monarchies quickly adopted much the same format, notably Bahrain where perhaps an equally high percentage of its troops hailed from Baluchistan and other parts of Pakistan. Controversially, by the time of the US-led military build-up to liberate Kuwait in 1991, there is evidence that members of the Gulf monarchies even considered US troops to be 'brought-in mercenaries'. Interviewed by the *Wall Street Journal*, one Saudi official replied 'you think I want to send my teenage son to die for Kuwait? We have our white slaves from the US to do that.' Describing it best, a Saudi academic stated that 'the US soldiers are a new kind of foreign worker here. We have Pakistanis driving taxis and now we have Americans defending us.'[254]

3

THE ROAD TO AL-QAEDA –
THE CIA'S BABY

SEARCHING FOR AN ISLAMIC STATE – BRITAIN'S CALIPHATE

Having repeatedly identified conservative and reactionary Islamist movements as strategic allies in numerous conflicts and stand-offs, whether against the Bolsheviks in the early 1920s or against revolutionary Egypt and the democratically elected prime ministers in Iran and Jordan in the 1950s, British officials had also been dabbling with those who propagated a much grander and transnational 'Islamic state' project. In this sense, Britain had long recognized not only the 'one-off' usefulness of those committed to building traditionalist sharia law states in specific countries, but also the broader value of being able to liaise with some sort of truly pan-Islamic organization that could serve as a powerful counterweight to Britain's primary and largely secular enemies in the region, including the various national liberation movements, communists, and all who sought an end to British monopolies over their nations' valuable resources and markets.

For much of the nineteenth century Britain had supported the Ottoman Empire and its constituent caliphate as an effective buffer against Russian encroachment into the Middle East and South-Eastern Europe. The two powers had of course even fought alongside each other in the Crimean War from 1853 to 1856, immortalized for most Britons today by tales of the heroic 'Charge of the Light Brigade'. But with the Ottoman Empire known as the 'sick man of Europe' and in steady decline by the end of the century, its ability to protect and project the power of the caliphate was increasingly questionable.[1]

Hedging their bets, in 1885 British intelligence officials held a meeting with regional activists to discuss the prospect of a new and more conservative 'pan-Islamic alliance' that could be used to confront both Russia and, so it seemed, the *Nahda* or 'awakening' that had been sweeping from Egypt into the Levant and other Ottoman territories, and had catalysed a period of intellectual modernization and reform.[2] As Robert Dreyfuss describes, referring to the meeting, 'there was a pattern here that would endear right-wing Islamism to Western imperial strategists for generations to come ... the opposition to nationalism, and their support for vague notions of an Islamic state.'[3] Notably, the fact that the same activists the British officials met had also been publicly calling for the restoration of Islamic rule 'over all lands that have once been Muslim', which presumably included parts of Europe, did not seem to ring alarm bells. Or if it did, it was likely deemed manageable blowback, as many of these Islamic state proponents went on to assume prominent positions, including that of grand mufti, in British-ruled Egypt.[4]

As a final straw, the Ottoman Empire's alignment with Germany during the First World War prompted even stronger efforts in London to make sure that Istanbul would no longer have any claims to Islamic leadership. Having supported the 1916 Arab Revolt against the Ottomans, Britain had entered into agreement with the Sharif of Mecca, Hussein bin Ali of the Hashemite dynasty, and had promised not only future British-backed Hashemite kingdoms in Jordan and Iraq for his sons, but also one for Hussein himself on the Arabian Peninsula. Under this arrangement the post-First World War Middle East would have a new caliphate in Mecca, and one which this time was entirely under the control of the British Empire. As Secretary of State for War Herbert Kitchener explained, 'If the caliphate were transferred to Arabia, it would remain to a great extent under our influence.'[5] Meanwhile, other British officials confirmed that 'one of [Britain's] fundamental traditions is to be a friend of Islam ... and to defend the Islamic caliphate even if it was a caliphate of conquest and necessity as the Turkish caliphate, which England had defended with money and men and influence several times.' Moreover, they stated that 'there is no nation among the Muslims which is now capable of upholding the Islamic caliphate except the Arab nation,' and they promised to protect Mecca and 'guarantee the holy places against all external aggression'.[6]

Unfortunately for Hussein, he himself was part of a bigger double-bet on the future of Arabia, with London having long since established relations with the powerful al-Saud dynasty from the central province of Najd. As volatile and ruthless as their rule may have been, the Saudis nonetheless ticked many of Britain's boxes as they offered another alternative, albeit still localized, to the collapsing Ottoman caliphate. Underpinned by ultra-conservative 'Wahhabism', which was based on the teachings of the eighteenth-century Islamic revivalist Muhammad Abd al-Wahhab, who had called for the purging of non-Islamic 'impurities', the proto-Saudi kingdom was understood to be a highly reactionary Sunni Islamic state expanding out of the Arabian Peninsula's hinterland.[7]

Forged through conquest, the Saudi-Wahhabi entity was also brutally sectarian, repeatedly attacking Shia communities along the coastline of the Persian Gulf in the 1790s, and pillaging Shia shrines in Iraq in 1801 and 1802.[8] In Karbala, scene of an ancient battle between the Sunni caliph and the Shia, represented by the Prophet Muhammad's grandson Hussein, the Saudis slaughtered most of the town's population, destroyed the dome over the grave of one of Shiism's founders, and 'looted property, weapons, clothing, carpets, gold, silver and precious copies of the Qur'an'.[9] The smashing of the Karbala dome along with others in Mecca has been described as the 'signature activity' of Wahhabism at the time.[10]

Despite such barbarity, by 1899 the Saudis were being encouraged by Britain to use its protectorate of Kuwait as a launch pad to further their campaign against rival tribes and the Ottomans. Capturing Riyadh in 1902, Ibn Saud and his Wahhabi militia, the *Ikhwan*, quickly went on to conquer most of the other central and eastern parts of Arabia. Signing a treaty with Ibn Saud in 1915, Britain 'formally recognized [him] as the independent ruler ... under British protection. In return he undertook to follow British advice.'[11] Remarkably, in 1917, a year after the Sykes–Picot agreement had already promised Arabia to the Hashemites, and at exactly the same time that both Mark Sykes and François Georges-Picot visited Mecca to discuss their plans with Hussein, Britain had also decided to put Ibn Saud on a handsome monthly retainer of £5,000. Described as a 'Bedouin chief for hire', his son Faisal was even invited to take a tour around London.[12]

With the First World War drawing to a close it still seemed Hussein was in pole position, as his monthly retainer was £12,000, and an estimated £11 million – an enormous sum for that time – had been transferred to the Hashemite coffers.[13] Having coordinated much of the Arab Revolt via their man on the ground, Colonel Thomas Lawrence, or 'Lawrence of Arabia', Britain's Cairo-based Arab Bureau continued to back the Mecca plan on the basis they would be best placed to oversee the process of switching the caliphate from Turkish to Arab control. The bureau chief, David Hogarth, was unequivocal in his views, having described the Saudi pretenders as having a 'fanatical creed unsuited to most of the Islamic world'. With the Ottoman Empire all but finished by 1919, Hussein duly pleaded with Hogarth and others to ensure that Ibn Saud's power was held in check and that the Ikhwan was destroyed, because it was a 'political society in the cloak of religion'.[14] By the end of the year it seemed London was heeding such calls and was prepared to fulfil the Sykes–Picot promises, as at one point even the Royal Air Force was used to support Hussein's attempts to roll back the Saudis.[15]

In many ways, however, Britain's actions against the Ikhwan were just part of a 'friendly rivalry', as London secretly continued to back both sides at the same time. The India Office in particular seemed to favour Ibn Saud over Hussein on the basis that the Ikhwan's ferocity would help ward off other rival powers from entering the Persian Gulf.[16] Although posthumously transformed into the blond-haired, blue-eyed Hollywood hero of the Arab people, even Lawrence was wholly at ease with the duplicitous double game. Commenting in a secret intelligence report on the British plan, he described Hussein as 'beneficial to us, because [he] marches with our immediate aims, the break-up of the Islamic "bloc" and the defeat and disruption of the Ottoman Empire, and because the states he would set up would be as harmless to ourselves as Turkey was'. The ideal scenario for Lawrence, it seemed, was 'if properly handled [the Arab states] would remain in a state of political mosaic, a tissue of jealous principalities incapable of cohesion, and yet always ready to combine against an outside force'.[17] He also later explained that 'Hussein was ultimately chosen because of the rift he would create in Islam. In other words, divide and rule.'[18] The

India Office similarly noted the advantages of such a strategy, with one report stating: 'What we want … is not a united Arabia, but a weak and disunited Arabia, split up into little principalities so far as possible under our suzerainty.'[19] On the subject of manipulating dangerous elements such as the Ikhwan, Lawrence was also quite comfortable, pointing out that when a 'Wahhabi-like Muslim form of Bolshevism' had welled up in southern Iraq, it was easily put down by British aircraft and on-the-ground spotters.[20]

The Saudi-Wahhabi killing spree that ensued as Lawrence's 'tissue of jealous principalities' continued to pull each other apart led to an estimated 400,000 dead with 40,000 public executions, 350,000 amputations, 'scorched-earth' battlefields, and the displacement of an estimated one million persons, most of whom fled to neighbouring countries. With the Ikhwan responsible for much of the carnage, Ibn Saud claimed to his British employers that they were operating independently of his control. Perceptive British officials however stated that '[Ibn Saud] does not want it to be known that he himself is at the bottom of the whole thing, and is fostering and guiding the movement for his own ends.'[21] As colonial secretary, Winston Churchill was similarly well aware of the reality, having informed parliament at the time that the Ikhwan was 'austere, intolerant, well-armed, and bloodthirsty … they hold it as an article of duty as well as of faith, to kill all who do not share their opinions and to make slaves of their wives and children … men have been killed for smoking a cigarette.'[22] Moreover, Churchill had earlier warned of the dangers of using such extremist Islamist militias in Britain's wars in Sudan, having written that 'no stronger retrograde force exists in the world. Far from being moribund, Muhammadism is a militant and proselytizing faith.' He also claimed it led to a 'fanatical frenzy, which is as dangerous in a man as hydrophobia in a dog.'[23]

Hussein and his supporters soon proved no match for this bloodthirsty force, even after his 1924 declaration that the caliphate was restored. The facts on the ground meant that the Hashemite dream of control of Mecca was already over, as the British-financed proto-Saudi state had effectively been given both the resources it needed and a green light to expand during its crucial infancy. Despite his reservations, Churchill himself had increased Ibn Saud's retainer to a much larger £100,000 per year and had thus made the al-Saud one of the richest ruling families in the region. Closely tallying with philosopher Ibn Khaldun's fifteenth-century examples of how new-born kingdoms could emerge on the periphery of great empires, Ibn Saud had thus been able to conquer most of his neighbours within careful limits set out by Britain. With no objections to the strengthening of his religious legitimacy, Britain naturally did nothing to prevent his eventual takeover of the western Hijaz province and the holy cities of Mecca and Medina.[24] In this sense the quickly consolidated Saudi kingdom and its supremacy within Islam was, according to historian Madawi al-Rasheed, very much a 'British invention'.[25]

Although firmly in control of his territories, Ibn Saud still showed no signs of bringing the bloodletting to an end. At the same time that Britain signed a fresh treaty in 1927 recognizing Saudi Arabia's full independence in exchange for Ibn Saud conceding control over foreign affairs, Wahhabi scholars were continuing to 'forcibly convert' Shia in the Eastern Province.[26] Even the camel-borne *Ikhwan* remained at large for another two years until they rose in rebellion against the British in Iraq and were slaughtered by troops armed with machine guns at the Battle of Sabilla.[27] The *Ikhwan*'s remnants were then incorporated into the new Saudi armed forces and religious morality police, but Britain still had to contend with blowback as Saudi military encroachments continued for many more years, especially into Yemen, with Britain having to broker the Treaty of Taif in 1934 between Ibn Saud and its client rulers in northern Yemen.[28]

SEARCHING FOR AN ISLAMIC STATE – WAHHABISM AND THE
MUSLIM BROTHERHOOD

By the late 1940s, with the Cold War in full swing and with the need to safeguard the resource-rich Persian Gulf in the wake of British decline, the usefulness of Saudi Arabia's religious conservatism was also becoming apparent to Washington. According to Dwight Eisenhower's memoirs and the reports of a number of British diplomats, even the White House had identified the need to build up Ibn Saud into a 'spiritual leader' for the entire region so that he could serve as a 'counterweight to Nasser' and ultimately as 'the great gookety gook of the Muslim world'.[29] In other words he was to perform the role originally auditioned for by the Sharif of Mecca; one which, as Arabist Jean-Pierre Filiu argues, was part of an unwitting US effort to recreate the manipulable thirteenth-century Abbasid caliphs who had provided legitimacy for the non-Arab Mamluk rulers in Cairo and Damascus.[30]

As an old man, however, the failing health of Washington's new proto-caliph was a great cause of concern. In fact, it even became a matter of US national security, with a US Air Force doctor sent to attend to Ibn Saud's deteriorating eye condition and then, in 1950, a secret mission launched to insert Eisenhower's personal physician covertly into Riyadh to treat the king's chronic osteoarthritis. Given the sensitivity of the trip, due to 'many Saudis, including the more conservative religious authorities, being increasingly against any US military presence', the Saudi government reportedly sent an emergency telegram to its ambassador in Washington to ask the White House 'not to permit any news either press or radio concerning the medical team coming here'. According to Secretary of State Dean Acheson, who referred to a subsequent US–Saudi defence pact, the secret medical trip was 'a diplomatic stroke which paved the way for the signature of an extremely favorable US–Saudi Arabia agreement'.[31]

Succeeding his father in 1953, Saud bin Abdul-Aziz al-Saud was quick to assure the US that things would be business as usual and conveniently requested the Wahhabi religious establishment to issue a *fatwa* or religious ruling that forbade Muslims from accepting aid from the Soviet Union. Still mostly staffed by US nationals, even Aramco got in on the act by funding a 'print shop and broadcasting station in Riyadh for the propagation of religious tracts'.[32] After all, the more conservative the Saudi population was, the better the *fatwa* would stick. The US consul general in Dhahran gleefully reported back to base that the new Saudi king believed that both Christians and Muslims were threatened by communism, and concluded that because Saud was 'the head of the Wahhabi movement to restore the pure faith of Islam, [he] is without any doubt the most representative and influential Muslim in the world today'. The same diplomat also noted that the king wished to 'spark plug a pan-Islamic movement' and concluded that '[the US] would welcome such a movement under his leadership because we are sure that it would be friendly'.[33]

To make the White House's new 'pan-Islamic movement' work, the Wahhabi establishment's various edicts of course needed to be heard and heeded by a much greater Islamic population than that of Saudi Arabia. The plan, it seems, was to somehow facilitate a pragmatic link-up between Riyadh and the various chapters of the Muslim Brotherhood so as to form an even stronger and transnational conservative Islamic front. On the one hand Saud could bring considerable resources to the table and channel his increasing oil wealth into a worthy cause that would suit US interests, while on the other hand the Brotherhood continued to claim a vast membership in Egypt, Jordan, Syria, and elsewhere, and had already proved to be an on-the-ground asset against nationalist and socialist movements in these countries. Most importantly, all parties were willing to speak loudly the language of the Cold War, with the Brotherhood's leadership publicly distancing itself from earlier episodes of anti-British violence, while its official newspaper began to carry a daily column entitled *The Fight Against Communism*.[34]

According to Georgetown University's John Voll, the rebranded Brotherhood by this stage was a 'smart intelligence vehicle' for the CIA, and, as he argues, the US would have been 'stupid not to have had a relationship with them'.[35] The point man, it seems, was Hassan al-Banna's son-in-law, Said Ramadan. As a young ideologue who had become the Brotherhood's chief international organizer, he had been secretly evaluated by US embassies in the region and deemed a potential US asset. Not so secretly, the US government then began to fund his trips to the US and facilitate his participation in academic symposia on Islamic culture.[36] Prior to one such event, held at Princeton University in 1953, the US ambassador to Egypt had rather aggressively recommended Ramadan's attendance to the university organizers on the basis that 'his scholarly attainments are sufficient ... [and that] his position within the Brotherhood makes it important that his desire for an invitation be considered carefully in light of the possible effects of offending this important body'.[37] When hosting Ramadan in Switzerland in the 1960s, the somewhat suspicious Swiss authorities built a dossier on him which was later leaked and published by Geneva's *Le Temps* in 2004. It contained several references to his connections to 'certain Western secret services'.[38] Similarly, according to a *Wall Street Journal* investigation, German intelligence had recorded that Ramadan's expenses were being financed by the 'American side', that he met with CIA agents in Germany, and that a

European Muslim congress he organized had been co-funded by a CIA front company.[39]

As Robert Dreyfuss puts it, the Brotherhood's 'ace-in-the-hole' was of course not just CIA funding, but rather the US-sanctioned transfer of financial support from Saudi Arabia to the organization's coffers. Although former CIA station chief Ray Close has revealed that Riyadh was 'adamantly opposed to its activities inside Saudi Arabia', and had blocked its efforts to set up a formal branch in Mecca in 1946, he explained that the al-Saud were 'very tolerant [of the Brotherhood] and encouraged it in Egypt, Sudan, and elsewhere'.[40] As with most elements of the Saudi–Brotherhood relationship, such support was nothing new, with a US diplomat based in Jeddah during the 1940s having described al-Banna as a 'frequent visitor, because Saudi Arabia was his principal source of financing' and that he had 'no hesitation in meeting Westerners'. Al-Banna was also described by the same diplomat as having held follow-up meetings at the US embassy in Cairo and being 'perfectly empathetic'.[41] Under King Saud and Ramadan, such arrangements of course became even tighter, but it was to be under one of Ibn Saud's other sons, Faisal bin Abdul-Aziz al-Saud, that the relationship really took off.

As crown prince and then also prime minister of Saudi Arabia, and with his mother a direct descendant of Muhammad Abd al-Wahhab, Faisal was a man after the CIA's heart. He had toured around Muslim countries describing Marxism as 'a subversive creed originated by a vile Jew', and had declared that 'the communists fear the expansion of our [Islamist] movement because it will reach the Islamic territories that have fallen under their oppressive domination.'[42] In 1961 he had established the Islamic University of Medina before even setting up the kingdom's first television station.[43] As an intended counterweight to the Gamal Abdel Nasser-controlled Al-Azhar University in Cairo, Faisal's brainchild received lavish ruling family funding and was heavily staffed by exiled Brotherhood members and sympathizers, including Sayyid Qutb's brother Muhammad.[44]

More importantly, Faisal had also begun to establish a system of international institutions that would serve for the next half century as the primary international conduits of Saudi oil wealth to the Brotherhood, and eventually far more extremist organizations. Most notably, in 1962, he had set up the Mecca-based Muslim World League with Ramadan as his co-founder.[45] Described as a 'who's who' of right-wing Islam at the time, the new organization was considered by a former British ambassador to have been an 'instrument for whipping up interest in and support for Saudi policies' and a vehicle to place Faisal in a 'friendlier Islamic environment than being surrounded by Arab nationalist states'.[46]

With all of this underway there was understandably great impatience for Faisal to become king, especially given lingering concerns that his brother might ultimately prove unable to counter the advances of national-ist movements on his doorstep. Indeed, a secret Foreign Office report in 1963 warned that Saud was 'struggling to speed evolution in order to avert revolution'.[47] Having already begun to plan for Faisal's formal succession, the US and British governments soon had their way, as within a year of the Foreign Office's warning another well-timed Wahhabi establishment *fatwa* had justified Faisal's supplanting of his brother.[48]

Doing his backers proud as the new king, Faisal soon not only founded and funded Ramadan's Islamic Centre in Geneva but also went on to estab-lish the Organization of the Islamic Conference.[49] The usefulness of the latter, just like the Muslim World League, was also confirmed by Western officials, including a British Foreign Office minister who in 1966 described it as a 'congress [that would help] oppose communism and defend the faith'.[50] A US Department of State report filed a few years later similarly praised Faisal's new state-backed entities and revealed that a discussion had already been held with him on the best way for oil revenues to be spent in order for the kingdom to build up influence in the 'Third World' and among 'less favoured nations'. Notably, Riyadh's 'formidable financial and petroleum reserve' was recognized as a key plank in its 'diplomatic talents in the international community for and on behalf of [US] strategy'.[51]

To back all of this up, a new network of 'Islamic banks' and other such financial institutions was obviously necessary. Wholly encouraged by the Western governments, they were often set up with the assistance of Western companies and consultants, while teams of academics drawn from both the Islamic world and the West were tasked with finding 'sharia compliant' solutions to ease the sector's integration into global finance.[52] By the time of Anwar Sadat's succession, the entry of these banks into the Egyptian market was considerably smoothed following his new *infitah* or 'openness' policy, which was seen as a huge opportunity for both 'right-wing Islamists and conservative business owners' to get a bigger stake in the country's economy. After claiming that 'most of the commanding levers of the policy of economic opening are now in the hands of former Muslim brethren who were in exile and have now returned to Egypt,' the Brotherhood's leaders even issued a formal declaration requiring their members to support the *infitah*. Indeed, some actively took part in strike-breaking against workers who tried to resist the new capitalist structures.[53]

As arguably Egypt's first Islamic bank, Mit Ghamr was set up by German experts and had a founder who stated that he had established it to prevent 'the Islamic identity fading away ... in preparation to shift to Marxism'.[54] With a system that did not charge interest but yet was still able to cooperate fully with overseas banks and investors, it had become a useful vanguard for Saudi capital in what was once an inhospitable environment. Soon after, a number of Gulf-based Islamic banks were directly able to establish branches in Egypt. Among these was the Faisal Islamic Bank of Egypt, which was owned by Faisal's son Muhammad and approved by Egypt's grand mufti. With Sadat eventually sponsoring a special new law to charter the institution, it was to be protected from nationalization and granted immunity from various Nasser-era taxes. Unsurprisingly its board of directors included the Brotherhood-linked theologian Yusuf al-Qaradawi, along with other reactionaries such as Abdel-Latif al-Sharif and Omar Abdul Rahman, the latter being a 'spiritual adviser' to Egypt's Islamic Jihad organization and later convicted for his role in the 1993 New York World Trade Center attack.[55]

As Tufts University's Ibrahim Warde explains, by the time these Islamic banks were establishing themselves, 'ideologically both liberalism and economic Islam were being driven by their common opposition to socialism and economic dirigisme.'[56] Moreover, as Dreyfuss describes, by this stage it was very normal to see major figures in the new Islamic banking sector being non-Muslim Westerners, 'many of whom were readily able to quote narrowly Qur'anic interpretations supporting the view that Islam was essentially a free market-supporting religion'. As he also contends, the bulk of Islamic banking activity probably wasn't even taking place in Muslim-majority countries, with most taking place in Western capitals or Britain's various offshore banking havens. Indeed, one of Muhammad bin Faisal's other sharia-friendly businesses, the House of Islamic Funds, was incorporated in the Bahamas and then subsequently operated from Geneva.[57]

Not all US officials agreed with Faisal's new pan-Islamist empire, with some in the 1960s having cautioned that such close relations between the US, Saudi Arabia, and the Muslim Brotherhood could easily backfire and ostracize the US from the rest of the Arab world. As the National Security Council's Robert Komer argued, 'It's one thing to defend the Saudis against aggression [but] it's another to declare we choose the kings over the bulk of the Arab World; that would be the real way to lose our oil.'[58] Others simply described Saudi Arabia and the other Western-backed Arab monarchies as 'representing historical anomalies, and their survival over the long range is in doubt',[59] while many officials were particularly alarmed by Faisal's speech in Washington in 1966 in which he had stated 'the Jews around the world support Israel ... we consider those who provide assistance to our enemy as our own enemy.'[60]

A Council on Foreign Relations task force on the Middle East meanwhile concluded that the sort of political Islam espoused by Saudi Arabia and the Brotherhood was an unsuitable ally against communism due to its fundamental 'revulsion against the West'.[61] Similarly a British official and eventual ambassador to Saudi Arabia remarked in 1973 that Nasser's 'anti-imperialism' had 'forced us ... to support regimes which were obscurantist, reactionary, and discreditable to their supporters', while another British ambassador had warned with reference to the pro-Faisal *fatwa* that 'what may also be serious in the long-term ... is the bringing of the [religious establishment] into the picture and they may exact a price for their support.'[62] Others had more specific concerns about the US and Britain being too openly identified with Faisal's new international organizations, with a Foreign Office minister making it clear to the Saudis that although he wished them every success, since they 'made for stability', any 'suggestion that Britain [officially] supported these developments was bound to damage their prospects'.[63]

Confirming such fears, but ultimately doing little to dampen the West's enthusiasm for Faisal's role or reduce the flow of Western armaments to the kingdom, was a rare 'general principles' statement issued by Riyadh in 1975. Setting out to explain the kingdom's new defence policy, and drawing heavily on both Wahhabism and the rhetoric of leading Brotherhood scholars, it stated that 'the doctrine of jihad is something that will remain in existence until the Day of Judgement ... the kingdom's defence system is guided by the sharia rules of conduct for war that are contained in the Holy Book, the Sunnah of the Prophet, and the guidelines of the Four Great Caliphs.'[64]

MOBILIZING JIHAD – THE CASE OF AFGHANISTAN

In less than two years the holy war doctrine espoused by the government of Saudi Arabia and backed by the expanding Brotherhood network was fully mobilized. The well-resourced and now well-organized Islamic front was to get its first big opportunity in Central Asia, where circumstances arising in Afghanistan had not only opened the door for a US-planned, Saudi-endorsed, and oil-financed jihad against a problematic government that might align itself with the Soviet Union, but had also created conditions in which a powerful and conservative Islamic fighting force could be placed right on the border of the Soviet Union's own Muslim-majority republics.

In the 1970s the Afghan government had initially been pro-Soviet and backed by nationalist officers of the Afghan armed forces, but had then begun to tilt to a more pro-Iran, and thus pro-US, stance. It had been planning to ban all parties other than the ruling clique under a new constitution, and its security forces had begun to assassinate leftist and communist sympathizers. Power behind the scenes, according to research based on the Soviet archives, was effectively being wielded by the Shah's dreaded *Savak*, and with Iranian assistance the Kabul regime managed to stave off several Islamist extremist insurgencies in the mid-1970s backed by a Pakistani administration that was increasingly concerned about the prospect of a viable Afghan state or even a 'greater Afghanistan' on its doorstep.[65]

A coup by the People's Democratic Party in 1978 ousted the decaying regime and tried to pull Kabul from the grasp of Tehran and Islamabad. Making no claims to be communist, and stressing its non-aligned status,[66] but recognizing the dangers its neighbours posed, the PDP signed not only a friendship treaty with the Soviet Union but also sought backing from Moscow to support a radical programme of reform, including the introduction of basic social services and public infrastructure. On visiting Afghanistan in 1979 Fred Halliday remarked that more development had taken place under one year of the PDP than over the previous two centuries. Writing for the *New York Times*, he described how feudal practices were being abolished, peasant debts were being forgiven, and hundreds of schools and medical clinics were being built in the countryside. He also noted the introduction of reforms to limit child marriage and to teach women to read.[67]

With the initial resistance to the PDP being led by the old landowning classes and conservative religious forces, accusations were made that the new government was curtailing Islamic traditions and endangering a centuries-old way of life. But as the *Economist* reported, these were largely false claims, with little evidence that the PDP sought to limit anyone's religious rights. As the *New York Times* concluded, Islamic issues were being used primarily by fundamentalists and those who opposed the government's land reform policies or its efforts to dismantle feudal structures.[68] This view was repeated by the newspaper on a least one other occasion over the course of the year, with its correspondent reporting that it was the 'revolutionary government's granting of new rights to women that pushed orthodox Muslim men ... in the eastern villages of Afghanistan into picking up their guns'. Moreover, he stated that the 'land reform attempts undermined their village chiefs' while 'portraits of Lenin threatened their religious leaders'. As one of the Islamist fighters he interviewed claimed, 'the government said our women had to attend meetings and our children had to go to schools ... this threatens our religion. We had to fight.' Meanwhile, another fighter who used to be a school headmaster described how the PDP had been trying to 'break down Islamic ethnic rule in the villages' and complained how its representatives had been 'preaching socialism, and had invited women to attend their meetings'. He also lamented that the new government was trying to 'impose various ordinances allowing women freedom to marry anyone they chose without their parents' consent'.[69]

Although not all villagers seemed keen to join a jihad against the government, with some of the *New York Times*' interviewees stating that 'sometimes we have to catch [other villagers] and bring them with us forcefully until they see that our cause is right,' violence nonetheless spread across the country, with hundreds of teachers, civil servants, and other public sector workers being killed.[70] In Robert Dreyfuss' words, this soon became a 'Pol Pot-style attack against secular and educated Afghanis'.[71] Headed by the Tajiki scholar Burhanuddin Rabbani, an Al-Azhar graduate who drew inspiration from the Brotherhood's leading thinkers, and with the Pashtun graduate Gulbuddin Hekmatyar serving as its deputy, the Afghan branch of the *Jamaat-e-Islami* organization quickly came to the fore. Importantly, Rabbani and Hekmatyar were able to count on immediate cross-border support from the much bigger Pakistani branch of the *Jamaat-e-Islami*. Led by the elderly Abul A'la Maududi, the Pakistani group had already been calling for people to be educated in preparation for an Islamic revolution and the building of an 'Islamic state' in the wake of modern civilization's inevitable collapse and the ending of the *jahiliyyah* or 'period of ignorance' the world was living in.[72] As a key intellectual proponent of the Islamic state project, Maududi had already been evaluated by British agents as being 'ambitious and unscrupulous' with a wish to establish a state 'which will be run as nearly as possible in accordance with the tenets of the Qur'an and Sunnah ... virtually a dictatorship ruled by an emir following the precedents of the earlier caliphs'.[73]

Galvanized and equipped by its Pakistani allies, the emerging Afghan Islamic state became increasingly militant, bombing cinemas and cultural centres, and even managing to detonate explosives in the dining room of Kabul University.[74] Some of its fighters, who were interviewed by the US media, freely told stories of how they had put to death dozens of government officials after capturing them alive.[75] Despite the ferocity of the Islamist insurgency, the PDP tried to maintain its programme of reforms, although it understandably became more cautious over 'confronting traditional structures head-on'. By way of appeasement, or perhaps basic survival, the government made sure to release jihadist prisoners, rebuild mosques, and exempt properties owned by religious leaders from its new land laws. With its commitments to modernization balanced against its efforts to remain inclusive to more traditional elements, the PDP was understood to have 'won grudging tolerance from many members of the modern-minded middle class'.[76]

Fearing the worst, and undoubtedly mindful of the numerous US-sponsored counter-revolutions taking place elsewhere in the world, the mayor of Kabul tried to appeal to the US for clemency by pleading to the *Los Angeles Times* that 'we only hope that the people of the US take a good look at us. They think we are very fanatic communists, that we are not human beings. We are not fanatics. We are not even communists.'[77] But others in the Kabul government were much more realistic and seemed to know what was coming, with one US embassy officer reporting that the PDP had begun referring openly to the Islamist insurgent leaders as the 'made-in-London mullahs'.[78]

The eventual US role in the conflict, as feared by the poor mayor, is usually narrated as some sort of reaction to Soviet invasion. But this is far from the truth, as in summer 1979, some four months before Soviet forces entered Afghanistan, the White House had already begun covertly to support the Islamist insurgents with the clear objective of destabilizing the PDP and baiting Moscow into a military response. As a Department of State report argued at the time, 'the US's larger interests ... would be served by the demise of the [PDP], despite whatever setbacks this might mean for future social and economic reforms in Afghanistan ... the overthrow would show the rest of the world that the Soviets' view of the socialist course of history being inevitable is not accurate.'[79]

In a remarkably candid interview given nearly twenty years later that should now be essential reading for all students of US foreign policy, President Jimmy Carter's national security adviser at the time, Zbigniew Brzezinski, explained that 'according to the official version of history CIA aid to the mujahideen began during 1980, that's to say, after the Soviet army invaded Afghanistan. But the reality, kept secret until now, is completely different: on 3 July 1979 President Carter signed the first directive for secret aid to the opponents of the pro-Soviet regime in Kabul.' Pressed by his interviewer on this point, Brzezinski also claimed: 'We didn't push the Russians to intervene, but we knowingly increased the probability that they would ... the secret operation was an excellent idea. It had the effect of drawing the Russians into the Afghan trap.'[80]

Tellingly, even when the Soviet Union began its intervention, on the grounds that it shared the PDP's fears of a rising extremist Islamic state, the Department of State made no charge that Moscow had invaded and privately acknowledged that Kabul had invited Soviet troops to assist.[81] Nevertheless, the new Soviet front line was publicly described by US officials as both an offensive operation and part of a pre-planned Soviet expansion that intended to use the PDP as a Central Asian conduit to the Middle East. The exiled Shah of Iran claimed the Soviets even intended to threaten Persian Gulf oil supplies, while Carter stated that 'the Soviet invasion of Afghanistan is the greatest threat to peace since the Second World War.'[82] Running with the story, the Department of Defense began to set up the regional rapid deployment task force that eventually turned into CENTCOM, while also drawing up plans to fire 'small nuclear missiles' at Afghanistan's border with Iran so as to block mountain passes from any further Soviet advance.[83] CIA officials meanwhile demanded new locations for listening posts close to the southern flanks of the Soviet Union, and with the crisis soon hitting mainstream debates the US media called for even more military bases in the Middle East and for the CIA to be given greater powers to provide covert aid to the Afghan 'freedom fighters'.[84]

On a political level, Carter also used the Soviet intervention to follow in Truman and Eisenhower's footsteps by announcing his own 'Carter Doctrine' that stated: 'An attempt by any outside force to gain control of the Persian Gulf region will be regarded as an assault on the vital interests of the US.'[85] In turn, as US ambassador to Saudi Arabia James Akins later pointed out, the Afghan-justified doctrine also helped appease a lingering fear within the Department of State that if major oil exporters ever proved uncooperative then the US would need to have a much stronger military presence in the Gulf. Henry Kissinger, who is understood to have raised the issue repeatedly while serving as secretary of state in the 1970s, reportedly stated that, if need be, there would be 'massive political warfare [against such countries] to make them risk their political stability if they did not cooperate'. As a former CIA official describes, Kissinger even had a specific plan to 'teach Saudi Arabia a lesson' by choosing a smaller monarchy and then having its ruler overthrown. According to the official 'the idea was to do it in Abu Dhabi or Dubai.'[86]

In this light, with significant military and political benefits for the US's position in the Middle East, and with the prospect of creating a slow-bleeding conflict for Moscow, or a 'Soviet Vietnam' as both Brzezinski and the veteran Texan congressman Charlie Wilson put it, there were strong incentives for the Afghan insurgency to be intensive but not necessarily fast in achieving its objectives. As the Pakistani newspaper

The Muslim observed, 'Washington does not seem to be in any mood to seek an early settlement of a war whose benefits it is reaping at no cost to US manpower.'[87] Indeed, on arriving in Pakistan, CIA director William Casey explained in frank terms to assembled Pakistani generals that 'we can do a lot of damage to the Soviet Union.'[88]

More grandly, there is evidence that the Afghan campaign was seen by some as the first in a whole series of Islamist rebellions that would eventually bring the Soviet Union to its knees. Although seemingly having had their fingers badly burned by Islamic fundamentalism in Iran, with the Shah's compliant regime having finally collapsed by the beginning of 1979, a powerful faction in the US continued to argue that conservative Islam remained the West's best bet in the region. Publishing a policy paper entitled *The Return of the Great Game*, the future US ambassador to Kabul argued that the Soviet Union's influence in Central Asia was at even greater risk after the emergence of the Islamic Republic in Iran. By his logic, if much the same sort of state could emerge in Afghanistan then things would be even worse for Moscow.[89]

When asked by his interviewer if he regretted supporting Islamic fundamentalism, Brzezinski seemed to confirm such an ambitious project. Choosing to reply with questions of his own he asked, 'What is more important in world history? The Taliban or the collapse of the Soviet empire? Some agitated Muslims or the liberation of Central Europe and the end of the Cold War?'[90] As Dreyfuss argues, the US support for the Afghan insurgency was therefore likely viewed as merely the first step in forming an Islamist 'Maginot Line' or 'green belt' along the Soviet Union's southern flanks, given that all the nations between Greece and China were predominantly Muslim. In his words, 'Adventurous [US] policymakers imagined that restive Muslims inside the Soviet Union's own Central Asian republics might be the undoing of the Soviet Union itself, and they took steps to encourage them.'[91]

Although undoubtedly spurred by a census in the Soviet Union that revealed Muslim populations were increasing at a much faster rate than all other constituents, the US's identification of Islam in Central Asia as its enemy's Achilles heel in fact had a long legacy.[92] Back in the 1950s the CIA's chief specialist on Islam had been conducting research into the extent to which Soviet Muslim communities in outlying republics could be mobilized against Moscow.[93] Harvard University's Richard Pipes, who later worked closely with the White House's Foreign Intelligence Advisory Board, argued in 1955 that a new Muslim state might one day form in Central Asia and would likely orient itself to the Middle East rather than Russia.[94] Making much the same point, many of Russian exile Alexandre Bennigsen's publications in the 1960s, notably *Islam in the Soviet Union*, claimed that the only significant resistance to the Bolsheviks came from the underground Sufi movement, because only they were capable of launching a holy war against the Soviet Union.[95] Then teaching at London's School of Oriental and African Studies, Princeton University's Bernard Lewis was soon on the same page, describing how Muslims in Central Asia could potentially serve as a powerful fifth column.[96]

Britain was naturally fully on board with all aspects of Brzezinski's plan, including both the immediate objectives of the insurgency and its grander, longer-term designs. The newly elected Margaret Thatcher soon announced to an audience at the Foreign Policy Association in the US that she was going to call the next decade 'the dangerous decade'. Worryingly she revealed that Britain intended to double down on its support for the pan-Islamic 'resurgence' by stating: 'It is in our interests as well as in the interest of the people of that region that they build on their own deep religious traditions. We do not wish to see them succumb to the fraudulent appeal of imported Marxism.'[97] Over the next two years Thatcher reinforced her position on conservative Islam and the emerging Afghan Islamic state, even telling Afghan refugees in a Pakistani camp that 'you refused to live under a godless communist system which is trying to destroy your religion.' Promising them that 'we in Britain will continue to help you in every way we can,' she claimed that 'the hearts of the free world are with you and with those of your countrymen who have stayed behind in Afghanistan.'[98] Soon after, she also informed parliament that Afghanistan was an 'Islamic country ... the Soviet Union has driven a wedge into the heart of the Muslim world ... these are the facts. They are a cause for alarm both to the countries of the region and to ourselves.'[99]

Like Brzezinski, the secretary of defense at the time, Caspar Weinberger, has also since commented on the strategy. Seeking the moral high ground, he argued that 'we knew we were involved with Islamic fundamentalists ... we knew they were not very nice people, and they were not all people attached to democracy. But we had this terrible problem of making choices.' Importantly his answers also help confirm that, when faced with a choice, the US deliberately chose to back the most dangerous elements of the insurgency. In particular, when asked if the US had attempted to reach out to non-fundamentalist oppositionists in Afghanistan, Weinberger replied that 'there was some attempt to do that, but the real point is that we had to make choices.'[100] Casting a bit more light on the policy, a former Department of State official has since clarified that 'the people we did support were the nastier, more fanatic types of mujahideen ... if you want to win the Cold War and defeat the Soviets in Afghanistan, you can't use the Salvation Army.'[101]

As some have claimed, somewhat moderate options on the ground were available to the US, including the militias fighting under Ahmad Shah Massoud, a prominent resistance commander who had initially been supported by Britain and who rejected both the Soviet Union and the founding of an Islamic state.[102] But as CNN investigative journalist Peter Bergen has demonstrated, the US deliberately gravitated to the likes of Rabbani, Hekmatyar, and the various allies of *Jamaat-e-Islami*. Promising the largest numbers, the greatest zealotry, and apparently better linked to Pakistani intelligence and wealthy Saudi donors, they were Washington's ideal Cold War allies. Even their kidnapping of the US ambassador earlier in 1979 did not seem to matter; nor did their frequent chants of 'Death to America' and the CIA's evaluations of Hekmatyar as being 'vicious', a 'fascist', and 'definite dictatorship material'.[103] A Congressional task force that had identified Hekmatyar's supporters as the most corrupt of the many Afghan fighting groups also seemed to be ignored, as did accusations that he had personally skinned prisoners alive and thrown acid into the faces of women.[104] As a former CIA official described, 'We didn't think that we would defeat the Soviets ... but we did want to kill as many Russians as we could, and Hekmatyar seemed like the guy who could do that.'[105]

Even after US support for the insurgency began, several Westerners were killed by groups connected to Hekmatyar, while a US military attaché was pulled from his car and attacked.[106] In something of a diplomatic absurdity Reagan nonetheless dedicated a US space shuttle flight to the 'anti-Soviet insurgents', and in 1985 hosted several of the Afghan jihadist leaders in the White House, referring to them as 'the moral equivalent of

America's founding fathers'.[107] With the British government in lockstep, Thatcher invited another prominent commander, Hadji Abdul Haq, to London a year later. Despite having already admitted to a 1984 terror attack at Kabul airport that had killed twenty-eight people, most of them students en route to the Soviet Union, Haq was hosted as a government guest. Similarly, Thatcher invited Hekmatyar in both 1986 and 1988, with the extremist known to have visited Downing Street and met various Foreign Office officials.[108]

OPERATION CYCLONE – ANGLO-AMERICAN JIHAD

With close parallels to the third-party led training and arming of the Guatemalan, Cuban, and eventual Nicaraguan contras, the CIA's covert support for its new Afghan allies, known as 'Operation Cyclone', was greatly facilitated by an increasingly cooperative Pakistan. Having itself moved much further to the Islamic right, Islamabad in many ways became the US's perfect partner, especially after an Islamist military coup had brought to an end Zulfiqar Ali Bhutto's 'parliamentary experiment' in 1977.[109] Led by the former mercenary Muhammad Zia-ul-Haq who, as described, had earlier fought on behalf of several Arab monarchies, the junta executed Bhutto in 1979 and had implemented sharia law in Pakistan. Receiving the backing of Abul A'la Maududi and *Jamaat-e-Islami*, Zia-ul-Haq was at the helm of a burgeoning Islamic state with a powerful military and an elaborate intelligence apparatus that stretched well into Afghanistan. Naturally, this newly useful Pakistani government received public backing from the West, with the British government stating that 'Zia-ul-Haq had announced holding elections … and there is no reason to think that he does not genuinely wish to carry out this intention,' and the US being quick to 'whitewash the legacy of the coup and decide that bygones were bygones'.[110] Building a particularly strong rapport with Zia-ul-Haq, Charlie Wilson sought to sweeten the deal further, with Pakistan soon receiving billions of dollars in economic and military aid from the US, while Congress eventually approved sales of the coveted F-16 jet fighters to Islamabad.[111]

With its willing partner firmly in place, Cyclone's annual budget soon grew to between $20 and $30 million.[112] For obvious reasons a circuitous

105

route was needed to get US weapons to Pakistan, so with Anwar Sadat's approval US cargo flights began to ferry weapons from Egypt. Moreover, given the CIA's desire to mask its role thoroughly from Soviet forces in the field, the guns needed to be older Nasser-era Soviet-made arms rather than anything produced in the West. In fact, when it became difficult to find such weapons, a 1950s-era arms factory in Cairo was resuscitated and brought back into operation.[113]

Keeping a low profile in Afghanistan, and clearly mindful of its embarrassments in Central America, the CIA never had more than ten operatives in the field during the early years of the campaign. According to Peter Bergen, even then they shied away from dealing directly with the jihadists, preferring to communicate through trusted intermediaries in Pakistani intelligence.[114] As the war correspondent Steve Coll describes, by this stage a 'ceaseless stream' of CIA and Department of Defense officials was visiting command centres in Pakistan, while 'CIA operations officers helped Pakistani trainers establish schools for the mujahideen in secure communications, guerrilla warfare, urban sabotage, and heavy weapons.'[115]

After 1985, US funding for Cyclone dramatically accelerated following the secret National Security Decision Directive 166. With spending rising to over $600 million per annum, it was later described by the *Washington Post* as 'sharply escalating US covert action in Afghanistan' and was interpreted as the 'abandoning of a policy of simple harassment of Soviet occupiers' and instead 'letting loose on the Afghan battlefield an array of US high technology and military expertise in an effort to hit and demoralize Soviet commanders and soldiers'.[116] The new directive made sure that the insurgents received 'plans for military operations based on US satellite intelligence, intercepts of Soviet communications, and secret communications networks for [them to use]'. It also provided them with a staggering array of new equipment including 'delayed timing devices for tons of C-4 plastic explosives for urban sabotage and sophisticated guerrilla attacks, long-range sniper rifles, a targeting device for mortars that was linked to a US Navy satellite, and wire-guided anti-tank missiles'.[117] As Dreyfuss claims, some Afghan fighters may even have been brought to the US to receive training from special forces in how to use explosives and detonators.[118] Most infamously, as the *Washington Post* later reported, the

US also set up 'a secret mujahideen Stinger [anti-aircraft missile] training facility in Rawalpindi, complete with an electronic simulator made in the US'. This simulator apparently allowed 'mujahideen trainees to aim and fire at a large screen without actually shooting off expensive missiles … the screen marked the missile's track and calculated whether the trainee would have hit his airborne target.'[119]

Almost all of this new US assistance to its jihadist allies, including the transfer of Stingers, was brought to the Western world's cinema screens with the 1988 action movie *Rambo III*. At the time it was the most expensive Hollywood production in history, costing $58 million.[120] The credits of the original release included the line 'Dedicated to the brave mujahideen fighters', but after 9/11 this was quietly changed to 'Dedicated to the gallant people of Afghanistan'.[121] According to a Pakistani general, by this stage approximately sixty-five thousand tons of weapons were being shipped annually to help the cause, but others have estimated that as much as a third of the shipments never made it to their intended recipients. In aggregate, or at least over the course of the 1980s, Cyclone is thought to have cost over $2 billion, making it the biggest US covert operation since the Second World War.[122] The true total may be even higher, as some of the funds laundered through drug traffickers under the aegis of the CIA, as with the contemporaneous Nicaraguan operation, also seem to have been redirected back to mujahideen recruiters in Pakistan. As Mark Curtis explains, at least ninety percent of the world's heroin was being produced from Afghan opium exports at this time as the country's plentiful poppy fields increasingly fell under the insurgency's control. As a former SAS officer in Afghanistan has since claimed, when he reported to US intelligence officers what he saw he was told: 'If you see anything connected with opium again, just ignore it completely.' This led him to surmise that the opium trade had the tacit approval of the CIA, and that it was inconceivable that MI6 was not also aware of the arrangement.[123] By 1993 Afghanistan was described by the US Drug Enforcement Agency as the 'new Colombia of the drug world', while US officials admitted 'they had failed to investigate or take action against the drug operations because of a desire not to offend their Pakistani and Afghan allies.'[124]

With its role underestimated and often assumed to have been limited to providing political support to the US and Pakistan, Britain was in fact also heavily involved in the conflict. Likely seen by the Thatcher government as both a means to accelerate the demise of the Soviet Union and another golden opportunity for Britain to cement its role as the US's chief ally, by the late 1980s MI6 was effectively running its own mini version of Cyclone. Although Thatcher formally denied any British engagement in Afghanistan and stated that London only sought diplomatic solutions, she nonetheless also told parliament that the jihadists were 'genuine freedom fighters, fighting to free their country from an alien oppressor', and there is now considerable evidence that Britain had begun to supply the insurgents with an array of sophisticated weapons.[125] Among these were Blowpipe shoulder-mounted surface-to-air missiles, with the Ministry of Defence apparently keen to rid itself of unwanted stocks of the missiles after they received bad press following poor performance during the Falklands conflict. Ironically Britain had first tried to sell them on to Saudi Arabia, but the US had warned against this on the basis that they may end up in the hands of terrorists, and claimed it had not sold Stingers to Riyadh for the same reason.[126]

By far Britain's biggest contribution, however, was its role in training jihadist 'special forces'. A British private security firm known as KMS or Keenie Meenie Services, apparently named after the pro-British mercenaries who had fought against the *Mau Mau* in Kenya, became the effective front organization. Staffed by SAS veterans who had been training Omani officers and had served as advisers to the Nicaraguan contras, it had also begun to train small teams of Islamist fighters at a base in Afghanistan and at an MI6 base in Oman. As both Curtis and investigative journalist Anthony Kemp note, some KMS men even ended up performing scouting and backup roles for the front-line insurgents.[127]

In 1987, Britain's *Observer* newspaper published a leaked KMS proposal to the CIA in which the company offered to train Afghans in a range of activities including demolition and sabotage.[128] But there is no doubt that its strongest connection was with the British government, with KMS found to have been advertising in publications produced by a wholly owned commercial subsidiary of the Ministry of Defence.[129] When Thatcher was questioned in parliament about KMS's activities, she not only implied that she had knowledge of the company but hinted that it may have been operating as a subcontractor for the US, stating that 'it has been the practice

108

of successive governments not to answer questions about the details of discussions which may have taken place with foreign governments.'[130]

Unfortunately for Whitehall, a former SAS officer who claimed to have been involved in the operation later came forward and revealed more details to the BBC. He described how in 1983 he had helped train 'mujahideen commanders' in Scotland and northern England after they had been smuggled into the country posing as tourists. He explained that they were 'already excellent soldiers committed to their cause' and that Britain saw the relationship as a 'marriage of convenience between two organizations that had nothing else in common.'[131] A former CIA agent based in Afghanistan has since helped put these training missions into perspective claiming that '[the British] had a willingness to do jobs I couldn't touch. They basically took care of the how to kill people department.'[132] Further corroboration has been provided by a former Libyan jihadist who, in an interview with the Jamestown Foundation, has described his experiences after arriving in Afghanistan in 1989 towards the end of the conflict. He described having received 'training in all types of guerilla warfare' along with celestial navigation and claimed that 'all weapons training was with live ammunition', with ammunition being plentiful. More significantly he told the interviewer that 'we were trained by the elite units of the mujahideen who had themselves been trained by the Pakistani special forces, the CIA, and the SAS ... we also made extensive use of manuals from the US and British military.'[133]

On top of their military assistance for the insurgents, the US and British intelligence agencies were also engaging in 'propaganda and other psychological operations in Afghanistan on their behalf', with the CIA having taken a lead role but with MI6 also known to have launched an information-based 'disruptive action' campaign at the beginning of the war.[134] Providing another layer of support for the operation was the financial co-option of key opinion makers and civil society organizations in Afghanistan, including the creation of fake non-governmental organizations. An estimated $500,000 of initial US funding was provided to pro-insurgency Afghan journalists to use 'television, radio and newspapers to advance their cause', while a number of CIA-backed NGOs were set up under the cover of religious or charitable organizations.[135] Despite their supposedly humanitarian missions, they were not apolitical, with one having circulated the claim that Soviet soldiers were burning babies alive.[136]

Outlined in Craig Davis's seminal *World Policy Journal* article, entitled 'A is for Allah, J is for Jihad', which was based on extensive fieldwork in Afghanistan, the US Agency for International Development was also involved. It had paid $50 million for the University of Nebraska to produce specially commissioned school textbooks which were then supplied to Pakistan and Afghanistan. The books contained examples justifying jihad including 'drawings of guns, bullets, soldiers and mines'. Disturbingly, the books also promised children rewards in the afterlife if they were to 'pluck out the eyes of the Soviet enemy and cut off his legs'. The same books were later approved by the eventual hard-line Islamist government in Afghanistan under the Taliban, and then became 'part of the Afghan school system's core curriculum' and frequently appeared in militant *madrasa* schools in Pakistan.[137]

In many ways these propaganda strategies had a long pedigree in the country, as ever since the 1950s the US-backed Asia Foundation had been providing funding to members of staff at Kabul University, with a focus on mobilizing the country's Muslim communities and establishing links between leading Afghan Islamists and US policymakers.[138] With the help of such NGO work, by the 1970s the US embassy had identified a particularly conservative clerical family as having leadership potential and the ability to 'set back the leftist cause, at least in the countryside'. Another possible leader was a professor whose theology department had been one of the biggest recipients of Asia Foundation funding. Members of his secret Organization of Muslim Youth, along with many of his students, ended up meeting US officials on several occasions.[139] According to political scientist Robert Wirsing, and confirmed by a former Pakistani official, CIA funding to such individuals, including the leaders of the *Jamaat-e-Islami*, seems to have begun shortly after.[140]

FOREIGN FIGHTERS, FOREIGN CASH

No major Anglo-American Cold War counter-revolution would have been complete without the deployment of large numbers of foreign fighters. This time, however, given the nature of the conflict, they were no longer mere mercenaries or even regular troops sent by friendly regimes, as they had been in Oman, Vietnam, and elsewhere. Instead the ideologies underpinning the insurgency allowed for the mass recruitment of jihadists from all over the Islamic world, most of whom flocked to Pakistan and then entered Afghanistan to fight for what they believed was the best chance yet of establishing an ultra-conservative Islamic state. Over the course of the 1980s an estimated one hundred thousand such fighters arrived, with most gaining important war zone experience and invaluable training in how to operate advanced weaponry and other sophisticated military equipment.[141] As an endowed professor at Columbia University, Mahmood Mamdani, has since described, 'This [was] the context in which an American-Saudi-Pakistani alliance was forged, and religious *madrasas* turned into political schools for training cadres. The Islamic world had not seen an armed jihad for centuries. But now the CIA was determined to create one.' Adding to this, Mamdani also explained that the prospect of uniting Muslims from across the world behind a new 'holy war against the Soviet Union' had become an 'important prong of the Reagan administration's Cold War stance.'[142]

Naturally the global 'rat lines' to get the jihadists to Central Asia were approved by the Western powers and, for those coming from the conservative Gulf monarchies, facilitated by their own governments. According to former CIA director Robert Gates, the agency was well aware of the system but did nothing to discourage the recruitment of these 'Arab Afghans.'[143] Delegations of fighters even began to arrive in Pakistan from London in 1981 and, according to the *Daily Telegraph*, 'Black Muslims' from the US were also soon turning up.[144] Indeed, a former Department of State official, interviewed by the author, estimates that more than fifty recruiters were operating in different US cities at this time, either soliciting donations or facilitating the flow of fighters out of the country.[145] Meanwhile, in the case of Egyptian volunteers, many of whom were prisoners released by Anwar Sadat, US instructors were sent to train them up before they were then transferred to Afghanistan. As a former CIA official who had been based in Pakistan during this period remarked, 'Muslim governments emptied their prisons and sent these bad boys over there.'[146]

Perhaps unsurprisingly, given their motives and backgrounds, the foreign fighters were widely considered to be the most brutal of the conflict's belligerents. According to US media reports, an apparent tactic of these jihadists was the mutilation of victims, including cutting off noses, ears, and slices of skin.[147] In 1985 the *Washington Post* noted how their prisoners were living 'lives of indescribable horror' and were often held in animal cages.[148] By the end of the war they were described by the *Los Angeles Times* as having turned on each other many times, with mass political killings in refugee camps, drug wars, and 'gangland style in-fighting'.[149] As a former jihadist recalled, the foreigners also injected a sectarian element to the war, many having come not only to fight the Soviet Union but also to cleanse Afghanistan of its Shia minority.[150] Moreover, they were also blamed for introducing suicide missions to the insurgency, with Steve Coll observing that it was 'only the Arab volunteers from Saudi Arabia, Jordan, Algeria, and other countries ... who later advocated suicide attacks'. In contrast, as he explains, most of the indigenous combatants were still 'tightly woven into family, clan, and regional social networks' and thus 'never embraced suicide tactics in significant numbers'.[151]

Despite the vast funding already assigned to Cyclone, the US made sure it also helped the growth of the jihadists' nascent global financial networks. Under its new intelligence chief, Turki bin Faisal al-Saud, Saudi Arabia had agreed to match all US funding for Afghanistan, dollar for dollar, with grand mufti Abdul-Aziz bin Baz – the founding vice president of King Faisal's Islamic University of Medina – having usefully issued a *fatwa* calling for a wealth tax to support the fighters in Afghanistan.[152] Moreover, as numerous sources have claimed, whenever Saudi payments were late, Cyclone's frontman, Charlie Wilson, would fly to Riyadh to place pressure on the government.[153]

By this stage Saudi Arabia's eagerness to help was likely not only a function of its interdependent oil-for-protection relationship with the US and its proximity to the Muslim Brotherhood, but also due to its fear of an internal Islamist uprising against its increasingly decadent and overtly pro-Western monarchy. Having witnessed the rapid replacement of the US-backed Shah of Iran by a revolutionary Islamic republic, it had also been jolted by the attack and seizure of the Grand Mosque in Mecca in November 1979. Taking hostages and holding them for two weeks, the armed protestors represented a conservative Wahhabi sect that intended to consecrate one of its members as the *Mahdi* or 'messianic redeemer' of Islam. Led by Juhayman al-Utaybi, a descendant of one of the same tribes that had fought with the *Ikhwan* in the 1920s and taken part in its battle with the British, the revolt served as an urgent reminder for Riyadh that it needed to reaffirm its ultra-conservative credentials.[154] As the veteran journalist Abdel Bari Atwan, historian Stéphane Lacroix, and others have argued, the Saudi state's response largely became one of supporting home-grown Saudi jihadists but making sure they exported their jihad elsewhere.[155]

Given the scale of Operation Cyclone and the US's requirement that funding channels remained as discreet as possible, most of the Saudi financial support ended up being routed through a circuitous network of overseas banks, front companies, and ostensibly non-governmental organizations. The UAE-based Bank of Credit and Commerce International, which was part owned by the Abu Dhabi ruling family and run by expatriate Pakistani bankers, was one such conduit, with both CIA and Saudi funds destined for Afghanistan being placed there along with an estimated $245 million of 'unrecorded deposits' from the Faisal Islamic Bank of Egypt.[156]

Eventually collapsing in 1991, the bank was subsequently the subject of an investigation and report, prepared for the US Senate's Committee on Foreign Relations by senators John Kerry and Hank Brown, and providing one of the best insights into its murky role. Describing its 'unique criminal structure' that involved an 'elaborate corporate spider web', the report details billions of dollars in laundered funds along with transactions connected to arms trafficking and international terrorism. Most damningly, Kerry and Brown concluded that 'by early 1985, the CIA knew more about BCCI's goals and intentions ... than anyone else in government', and that even 'after the CIA knew that BCCI was as an institution a fundamentally corrupt criminal enterprise, it continued to use both BCCI and First American, BCCI's secretly held US subsidiary, for CIA operations'. The investigators also complained that 'initial information that was provided [to them] by the CIA was untrue; later information that was provided was incomplete; and the agency resisted providing a full account about its knowledge of BCCI until almost a year after the initial requests for the information.' It also suggested that 'the relationships among former CIA personnel and BCCI front men and nominees ... requires further investigation.'[157]

Adding to the picture, in 2003, David Kaplan and his colleagues at *US News* published their findings after conducting a five-month investigation. Their unequivocal conclusion was that the primary sources of funds for the 1980s jihadists were Saudi Arabia's 'quasi-official charities', including many of the same US-approved but poorly scrutinized institutions that had been set up in the 1960s by King Faisal. Citing US officials, they claimed that 'key charities became the pipelines of cash that helped transform ragtag bands of insurgents and mujahideen into a sophisticated, interlocking movement with global ambitions' and that the funds were being used in some twenty countries to run paramilitary training camps, buy weapons, and recruit new members.[158]

Among these was the Jeddah-based International Islamic Relief Organization, which was understood to have been supplying foreign fighters and, according to a 1996 CIA report, had been funding six 'militant training camps' in Afghanistan.[159] Similarly the Riyadh-based Al-Haramain Foundation was believed to have been another major source of funds, especially for those intermediaries in Pakistan responsible for transferring the 'Arab Afghans' across the border.[160] Though its chairman was stripped of his position when the foundation was eventually closed down in 2004 following post-9/11 pressure from the US, he was quietly acquitted of all charges by the Riyadh court of appeals in 2014.[161]

Beyond support for fighters, the well-established Organization of the Islamic Conference was understood to have been providing aid to the populations in Afghanistan that fell under the control of the Islamist insurgents, or to those who had fled and were languishing in Pakistani refugee camps. In this sense, it represented Saudi Arabia's bankrolling of the softer 'hearts and minds' side of the campaign. Naturally its work received high praise from Western officials visiting the region whose primary aim was to lay blame for the unfolding humanitarian crisis on the Soviet Union and, so it seemed, to divert attention away from the conflict's root causes. In 1981 even Thatcher referenced the organization, telling refugees that 'helping you live here is no substitute for trying to help you to return to your own homes to live in peace and freedom ... we shall continue, together with Pakistan, the Islamic Conference ... to work for a solution to the problems brought about by the invasion of your country.'[162]

Most important, however, was the role played by the Mecca-based Muslim World League, which by then was serving as a sort of umbrella for a number of these charities, including the IIRO. Closely tied to key Saudi government officials and ruling family members, it was repeatedly presented to the international media as a non-governmental organization, but a growing body of evidence suggests it was a de facto arm of the Saudi state as of course both King Faisal and the US Department of State had clearly intended it to be some twenty years earlier. In 1999, for example, the proceedings of a Canadian court case confirmed it to be a fully Saudi government-funded organization, while in 2013 an extensive report prepared for the European parliament made the allegation that both the Muslim World League and its IIRO subsidiary were extensively used by Saudi intelligence during this period as vehicles to transfer money to the jihadists.[163]

By the early 1980s, the Muslim World League's secretary general was a former Saudi minister for Islamic affairs and it had expanded its reach across the world with branches in almost all Muslim countries.[164] While employing local staff in its outposts, Saudi embassy staff usually also helped to run the show. In the Philippines, for example, the Saudi ambassador was one of its board members, while others were described as having been 'politically well connected, including with the Saudi royal family and the top echelons of [Saudi] society'. But despite the wealth it showered on poorer countries, the Muslim World League was not always welcome, with some Asian governments claiming that it wielded huge leverage over them by controlling employment visas for their thousands of citizens who relied on employment in Saudi Arabia.[165] Meanwhile, in Morocco, which prior to this time did not have much history of Islamic extremism and certainly none of exporting jihadists to other conflicts, increased financial aid from the Muslim World League to help Morocco fight its war in the Western Sahara has been blamed for promoting the 'Wahhabization' of Moroccan society. As historian Muhammad Darif explains, 'When Saudi Arabia gave the money, [Morocco] had to welcome its preachers. There was a political price to pay.'[166]

Operating underneath and sometimes intersecting with these various front organizations was also a substantial network of wealthy individual donors, most of whom were ideologically sympathetic to the cause and, as part of a longer-term project, committed to building up an international Islamist fighting force. It is difficult to gauge exact numbers, but some have suggested that the total donations from those based in Saudi Arabia and other oil-rich Gulf monarchies such as Kuwait and the UAE easily exceeded the CIA's funding for Cyclone and may well have eclipsed the

Saudi government's support. As a former Pakistani intelligence officer has since complained, it was neither Washington nor Riyadh that really propped up the jihad, but rather 'cash from rich individuals or private organizations in the Arab world ... without these extreme millions the flow of arms actually getting to the mujahideen would have been cut to a trickle.'[167]

Describing much of this phenomenon in her well-researched 2006 book, *Thicker Than Oil: America's Uneasy Partnership with Saudi Arabia*, Rachel Bronson, former director of Middle East Studies at the Council on Foreign Relations, made the allegation that the governor of Riyadh at the time, Salman bin Abdul-Aziz al-Saud, was 'organizing funds flowing to Afghanistan' and that he 'helped to recruit fighters destined [for Afghanistan]'. She also explained how the grand mufti himself had supplied $25 million to a key Afghan commander so that a new 'party' could be founded.[168] Later described by the Washington Institute as 'the most senior Islamic authority to open the door to the religious legitimization of Palestinian terrorism', the grand mufti's role in Afghanistan was also understood to fit with his 'persistent attempts to move Saudi Arabia in the direction of strict and severe fundamentalism'.[169] Named after him, the Abdul-Aziz bin Baz Foundation still survives and describes itself as continuing to be 'blessed with direct and continuous support' from Salman, who is of course the current king.[170]

A former CIA officer has since estimated that over the course of the 1980s such private Saudi donations to the Afghan jihad reached over $20 million per month.[171] According to Kaplan's study, by the end of the decade there was so much private Saudi money in the region that even 'mid-level jihadists' were making seven times Pakistan's average wage.[172] A former CIA station chief based in Saudi Arabia has corroborated much of this by explaining that this led to a situation in Afghanistan where 'there was always somebody ready to give money to someone. There was a lot of free enterprise going on.'[173] Indeed, as a former jihadist and veteran of the conflict recalls, for those private financiers who preferred to avoid direct money transfers, expensive cars were simply imported into the Gulf monarchies and then driven via Iran and Afghanistan to Pakistan, where they would be sold for a high price with no taxes paid, before the proceeds were passed on to trusted recruiting sergeants.[174]

Among the most able and best connected of these local fixers was Abdul Rasul Sayyaf, an Afghan commander who was the main recipient of the Saudi grand mufti's donations and served as a mentor to the eventual alleged 9/11 mastermind Khalid Sheikh Muhammad, along with others operating out of the Muslim World League's office in Peshawar. Among the latter was the Palestinian professor Abdullah Azzam, who had previously taught at the ultra-conservative King Abdul-Aziz University in Jeddah before being moved by the Muslim World League in 1980 to a teaching position at an Islamic university in Pakistan.[175] Even while working in Saudi Arabia he had been publishing a magazine entitled *Al-Jihad* which repeatedly called for the establishment of an Islamic state stretching from Spain to the Philippines, thus earning him the nickname 'the father of global jihad'.[176] In particular, he had stated in suitably Cold War-friendly terms that 'a viable Islamic state could be constructed [beginning in Afghanistan] on the ashes of communist hegemony,' and that true Muslims were obliged to perform *hijra*, the act of migrating to an Islamic state.[177] He also became known as one of the main proponents of promoting a sectarian edge to the Afghan conflict, a call which was thought to have intensified as Saudi and other Gulf donations increased, and as an advocate of suicide bombing given his emphasis on the rewards that martyrs could expect to receive in their afterlife.[178]

But it was the arrival in Pakistan of the young Saudi protégé Osama bin Laden that really transformed the jihadi landscape. Having read economics and business administration at King Abdul-Aziz University, his real interest had quickly turned to religion and he duly fell under the sway of Azzam. With private wealth, and hailing from the powerful and well-connected bin Laden business dynasty, he was quickly able to cultivate supporters of his own and sponsor causes of his choice. After being approached by key Saudi princes and Saudi intelligence officials in 1978 or 1979, his help had first been sought in inserting jihadist fighters into Yemen to combat the People's Democratic Republic, before he was later asked to help recruit fighters for the Afghan campaign.[179] Reconnecting with his old teacher in Pakistan, and forming a relationship with Sayyaf, bin Laden had set up a new organization in a house he had bought in Peshawar with their help.[180] Known as the Afghan Services Bureau, or *Maktab al-Khidamat*, it was designed to serve as a conveyor belt for foreign recruits and was backed for several years to the tune of $600 million by a shadowy network of Gulf-based patrons known as the 'Golden Chain'.[181] Significantly, it also became proactive in identifying new donors, with bin Laden and Azzam dispatching 'road shows' around the Gulf to solicit further aid. One such trip was undertaken by an organization calling itself the Islamic Union for the Liberation of Afghanistan, which was invited to Abu Dhabi by a group of sympathetic journalists and a former Afghan judge working as a preacher in the UAE.[182]

By the mid-1980s *Maktab al-Khidamat* was understood to have become the pre-eminent recruitment agency, with former jihadists claiming it offered fighters the 'best opportunity to see action'.[183] According to former CIA director Robert Gates, its Arab recruits were often signed up after being told they would be paid $300 a month by bin Laden.[184] With business booming, the organization became bigger and more complex, eventually morphing at some point in 1988 or 1989 into al-Qaeda or 'The Base', in reference to one of bin Laden's most prominent training bases in eastern Afghanistan.[185] Despite Azzam's long history with the Muslim World League, and the fact that another of al-Qaeda's founders, the Saudi citizen Wa'el Hamza Julaidan, was also one of its former employees and had previously been working in Arizona, *Maktab al-Khidamat* did not seem as directly connected to the Saudi state or the CIA's Operation Cyclone as some of the other Pakistan-based fronts.[186]

Nonetheless, there are strong indications that at the very minimum they were indirectly supported and encouraged throughout the conflict. Writing in the *Guardian* three weeks before his death in 2005, former British foreign secretary Robin Cook claimed 'Bin Laden was … a product of a monumental miscalculation by Western security agencies.'[187] As investigative reporter John Cooley has described, in the early 1980s the CIA had immediately recognized bin Laden's 'impeccable Saudi credentials' and had thus given him 'free rein in Afghanistan to organize Islamist fighters'.[188] He was also thought to have disbursed aid received from US and British sources and, in 1986, as is now clear, the CIA, in cooperation with bin Laden, had even helped to build a large underground camp in Khost, which was to serve as field hospital and weapons store for *Maktab al-Khidamat* and later al-Qaeda.[189] Most damningly, as revealed by US Department of Treasury reports and witness interview transcripts collected by lawyers in a recent US court case, US raids that had later taken place on the offices of a Saudi-linked charity in Bosnia discovered hand-written notes between bin Laden, Azzam, and Julaidan that were written on Muslim World League and Saudi Red Crescent Society letterheaded paper. Among the messages were requests for 'weapons to be inventoried' and for 'an extreme need for new weapons'.[190]

THE ISLAMIC REPUBLIC OF IRAN – A SECRET RELATIONSHIP

In contrast to the heavily stage-managed Afghan jihad and the US-sponsored efforts to establish a fundamentalist Sunni Islamic state in its wake, the conservative Iranian religious establishment's ability to hijack the long-running Tehran protests of 1978 and 1979, oust the US-compliant Shah, and then found a hard-line Islamic republic of its own had initially shocked the Western powers but not necessarily worried them. Even though the US had, as Robert Dreyfuss argues, 'catastrophically underestimated' the new-found power of political Islam in Iran,[191] this was not necessarily a complete surprise given the US and Britain's earlier described support for Ayatollah Abol-Ghasem Kashani. Far worse, in both Cold War and commercial terms, would have been a secular, nationalist, or pro-democracy movement capable of gaining control over a key Western ally and then developing its own economic and foreign policies.

In academic circles, such a nightmare scenario was considered more likely than an Islamic revolution, with Fred Halliday's partly prophetic *Iran: Dictatorship and Development*, published in 1978, having downplayed the influence of the Islamic right, as did political scientist James Bill in his article for *Foreign Affairs* published at the end of the year. Arguing that the most probable alternative to the Shah was a 'left-wing, progressive group of middle-ranking army officers', Bill reasoned that 'other future possibilities included a right-wing military junta, a liberal democratic system based on Western models, and a communist government.' Of the leading ayatollahs, whom he likely still regarded as potential US allies, Bill described them as 'generally men of great learning, integrity and popularity. They are renowned for the simplicity of their standard of living and are among the most democratically chosen grassroots leaders in the contemporary Middle East.'[192]

The story was much the same in US policy circles, with intelligence reports right up until the Shah's final days not only assessing his crumbling regime as still secure, but also claiming that any successful anti-Shah movement would most likely be led by left-wing or nationalist 'Mosaddegh disciples' rather than the ayatollahs. Most analysts seemed to base their assumptions on a 1977 National Intelligence Estimate entitled *Iran in the 1980s*, which concluded there would be 'no radical change in Iranian political behaviour in the near future', and a CIA assessment from 1978 that stated: 'Iran is not in a revolutionary or even pre-revolutionary situation.' All told, the view of Jimmy Carter's national security team was thought to be 'coloured by the insistent, though absurd, belief that the Soviet Union was behind the trouble in Iran'. As Dreyfuss argues, such advisers likely questioned 'how could so powerful an American ally as the Shah of Iran be toppled if it weren't Moscow's doing?'[193]

With the KGB later confirming that there were only ever a handful of Soviet agents in Iran at the time, much of the US analysis was indeed spectacularly far off the mark.[194] With the revolutionary mantle only briefly being worn by disorganized secular demonstrators, it was increasingly vulnerable to an Islamist takeover and, as Columbia University's Hamid Dabashi explains, what began as a 'multifaceted cosmopolitan revolution was violently Islamicized by a succession of cultural revolutions, university purges, mass executions, forced exiles, and the conniving abuse of a regional crisis'.[195] Similarly, as Iranian-born journalist Jasmin Ramsey has since claimed, many of the Iranians who welcomed the revolution didn't necessarily support the new religious state; instead '[they] wanted an anti-imperialist, democratic revolution'.[196]

The US embassy staff in Tehran were naturally more aware of the situation on the ground than their counterparts in Washington, but even they were caught unawares by the fall of the Shah. Nonetheless, they remained positive about the prospect of a theocratic state forming, and they continued to frame its likely leaders as potential Cold War allies. If anything, they reasoned that an Islamist regime was going to be better for US interests than the outgoing monarchy as the ayatollahs would enjoy greater popular support and at least some sort of in-built legitimacy. Filing a report just hours after Ayatollah Ruhollah Khomeini's triumphal return to Iran, one diplomat claimed that 'the Shia Islamic movement is far better organized, enlightened, and able to resist communism than its detractors would lead us to believe ... In many ways it supports a reformist-traditionalist view of Iran which is far more attractive to most Iranians at this time than the models of communism.'[197] Even the ambassador-designate to Iran, Walter Cutler, tried to put Khomeini's supporters in a Cold War context by later stating that 'the fact that the Iranian revolution was based on Islam, not left-wing nationalism, was something that encouraged many US policy makers ... I thought that we could handle the possibility that the Soviet Union might try to increase its influence, because of the strength of Islam ... if you're looking for common interests.' Meanwhile, in the absence of an ambassador, the senior US official in Tehran, Bruce Laingen, explained that 'we saw our mission as to reiterate our acceptance of the Islamic revolution, and to communicate that we were [also] a spiritual-minded country. That it was feasible for the US to come to an understanding with political Islam, and that the Shah had no future.'[198]

Unsurprisingly perhaps, Zbigniew Brzezinski was similarly pragmatic. As former CIA official Richard Cottam has described, and as very recently declassified US cables have confirmed, Brzezinski immediately sought 'de facto alliance with the force of Islamic resurgence and with the regime of the Islamic Republic of Iran'.[199] Putting this into context, the CIA's former vice chairman of the National Intelligence Council, Graham Fuller, has since explained that at the time US interests were not necessarily incompatible with Shia fundamentalism as, after all, it was seemingly just another expression of the same Islamic right that suited the US's Cold War interests elsewhere. Moreover, he pointed out that if the Khomeini regime were to falter then the US, which 'had almost no cards to play', would likely lose out to a 'Soviet-backed leftist government'.[200]

With arguably just as much at stake in Iran, Britain seemed to adopt much the same stance and, as evidence seems to support, may have been even more proactive in forging relations with the ayatollahs. According to reports filed by the British ambassador in Tehran, even as the Shah was still clinging to his throne, secret discussions had begun on how best to reach out to Khomeini. A dispute between Prime Minister James Callaghan and Foreign Secretary David Owen reveals that Callaghan and other British officials thought it necessary to 'reinsure' on Iran, while Owen felt it best to stick with the old regime and not establish contact with Khomeini's entourage. By the end of 1978 it seemed the British ambassador had even informed the Shah that Britain was establishing contacts with unnamed elements of the opposition, perhaps to cover tracks in case of *Savak* surveillance.[201]

British officials had also been making it clear that they were willing to do business with whatever new government formed, with Cabinet Secretary John Hunt referring to several pending arms sales and arguing that 'we should lose no opportunity to foster our relationship with the new government.' Soon even Owen grudgingly made clear that the Shah would be denied political asylum in Britain based on 'the cold calculation of national interest'. He did, however, record that this was 'despicable' and that there was 'no honour in my decision.'[202] Remarkably by this stage the BBC's Persian service, which had so firmly backed the Shah's position against Mosaddegh in the 1950s, was now commonly being referred to as 'Ayatollah BBC', given its heavy criticism of the Shah and widespread Iranian speculation that Britain had already begun covertly to back Khomeini. As the Israeli investigative reporter Ronen Bergman has described, '[BBC Persian] gave Khomeini a platform. His regular broadcasts made him the unchallenged leader of the Iranian revolutionary movement.'[203]

But far more than Brzezinski or the British, it was to be US presidential candidate Ronald Reagan and his campaign team that made the greatest inroads into building up a secret connection with Khomeini. Despite a mix of fifty-two US embassy staff and citizens being taken hostage in Tehran in November 1979, a working relationship quickly developed between the two camps. According to the memoirs of the short-lived first post-revolution Iranian president, Abolhassan Banisadr, his staff had 'proof of contacts between Khomeini and the supporters of Ronald Reagan as early as the spring of 1980'. Banisadr also stated that other members of the religious establishment including 'Rafsanjani, Beheshti, and Ahmad Khomeini [Ruhollah's son] played key roles.'[204] Writing again in 2013, in the form of a complaint about factual inaccuracies in the Hollywood movie *Argo*, Banisadr repeated his claims but provided even more detail, stating that 'Ayatollah Khomeini and Ronald Reagan had organized a clandestine negotiation, later known as the October Surprise, which prevented the attempts by myself and then-US president Jimmy Carter to free the hostages before the 1980 US presidential election took place.' The purpose of this, he argued, was to 'tip the results of the election in favour of Reagan'. Moreover, Banisadr revealed that 'two of my advisers, Hussein Navab Safavi and Sadr al-Hefazi, were executed by Khomeini because they had become aware of this secret relationship between Khomeini, his son Ahmad, the Islamic Republican Party, and the Reagan administration.'[205]

In fact, after the majority of the hostages were finally released on 20 January 1981, the very day that Reagan was sworn in and 444 days after their capture, a former Reagan campaign team member had gone on to leak that Banisadr knew that the Khomeini faction had 'made a deal with Reagan that the US hostages should not be released until after Reagan became president'. The other end of the deal, according to this whistle-blower, was that 'in return, Reagan would give [Khomeini] arms'. To support his accusations, he also stated that 'we have published documents which show that US arms were shipped, via Israel, in March 1981, about two months after Reagan became president.'[206]

Backing up these and Banisadr's own claims, former Carter administration National Security Council member Gary Sick has published more details about the so-called October Surprise. Writing in the *New York Times*, he outlined how the Reagan–Khomeini military relationship had actually begun in 1980, with Israel as the middleman secretly shipping spare parts for tanks, armoured personnel carriers, and F-4 fighter aircraft to Iran, and with all of this taking place without the Carter administration's knowledge. Sick also points out that the US hostages were released 'exactly five minutes after Reagan took the oath of office' and, with the Iran–Iraq War already in full swing, that Israel's bombing of Iraq's nascent nuclear facility in summer 1981 was effectively an extension of the deal. In this sense US approval was given to the strikes on the basis that Iran's air force wasn't up to the task and that the US could not intervene directly as it was officially supposed to be providing intelligence to Baghdad on Iran's troop movements.[207]

As other reports demonstrate, the US's supply of arms to Iran continued right up until 1988, most famously via the described Iran–Contra arrangement.[208] Among the weapons were US-made machine guns and cannon shells, along with various Soviet-made items, some of which were sold to Iran in exchange for its help in releasing Western hostages held by an Iran-allied militia in Lebanon.²⁰⁹ With the intermediary being none other than a son of the West's old ally Kashani, Sick has argued that in many ways the Iran–Contra affair was 'less of an aberration in US policy but rather the re-emergence of a strategy that had begun long before the Reagan administration ever took office'.²¹⁰

Playing its usual supportive role, the British government was following closely on Reagan's heels. Although it may have ceased arms shipments to Iran during the US hostage crisis, statements made by Thatcher indicate that Britain had nonetheless continued to train Iranian military officers throughout the period.²¹¹ After Reagan took office and the hostages were released, the green light seems to have been given for much more intensive collaboration, although, as with the US, Britain was officially supporting Iraq in the Iran–Iraq War, so it had to take suitable precautions. Using the Iranian-born fixer Jamshid Hashemi as its go-between, Britain began to supply foreign-manufactured arms to Iran, including Chinese silkworm missiles. In 1985, for example, MI6 sent an undercover female agent to China, ostensibly acting as the middleman's secretary, to help arrange the deal, which was ironically codenamed the 'October Contract'.²¹² Other British deliveries included 'non-lethal' parts including tank engines, sent so that Iran could keep its British-built fleet of Chieftain tanks running, along with hundreds of Land Rovers and British-manufactured air defence radars.²¹³ British naval guns were meanwhile being shipped via Singapore, while Greece was also used as a transit point for the same British-made gunboats that were eventually used by Iran against civilian shipping in the 'tanker war' phase of its conflict with Iraq.²¹⁴ Most remarkably, by the late 1980s, a British government-owned company, Royal Ordnance, shipped explosive powder and other chemicals to Iran.²¹⁵

On an intelligence level, US and British cooperation also deepened, with arguably an even better relationship developing with the Islamic Republic than they had enjoyed with Iran in the latter years of the Shah's reign. In 1983, following the debriefing of a formerly Iran-based KGB agent who had defected to Britain, the CIA and MI6 jointly began to pass on information to the Tehran regime about Iranian communists and other leftists. Going far further than the Shah ever had, Khomeini made over a thousand arrests and executed several leaders of the *Tudeh* Party. As James Bill describes, this was regarded in the West as successfully 'completing the dismantling of the Iranian left', even though the CIA and MI6 had long been aware of the Islamic Republic's propensity for executing political prisoners without trial.[216]

Battlefield data also flowed to Iran, with CIA director William Casey having helped set up a system to provide information on the Iraqi armed forces. Secret meetings were held between Casey, National Security Council members, Israeli intelligence agents, and their Iranian counterparts including Akbar Hashemi Rafsanjani.[217] In return, notwithstanding the anti-Shia sectarian element that had been introduced by Abdul-Aziz Azzam and others to the concurrent Afghan jihad, Iran also seems to have done its bit for Operation Cyclone. As Abdel Bari Atwan notes, it is often forgotten that eight of the insurgency's main brigades, including the Afghan Hezbollah and *Harakat-i-Islami*, were made up of Shia fighters.[218] Often carrying pictures of Khomeini in their pockets, they were frequently reported to be receiving supplies from across the border and, as claimed by the US media, their commanders were sometimes even seen transferring heavy weapons, including Stingers and rocket-propelled grenade launchers, to the Iranian army.[219]

4

ALLIED TO JIHAD – USEFUL IDIOTS

THE TALIBAN – AMERICA'S NEW ALLY

F acing mounting internal pressures including low oil revenues, severe government retrenchment, and secessionist calls from its outlying republics, by the late 1980s the Soviet Union was sending out strong signals that it sought disengagement from its bloody misadventure in Afghanistan.[1] Agreeing to pull out in early 1988 on the condition that the Western powers and Pakistan ceased arming *basmachi* extremists, thus using the same term applied to the British-backed Turkmen Islamists earlier in the century, Moscow's white flag was nonetheless rejected by the outgoing Ronald Reagan administration. In what some have deemed an 'illegal decision', the White House's renewed commitment to the insurgency nonetheless helped confirm that the true purpose of Operation Cyclone was never just to achieve control over Afghanistan, but was also to help engineer the total collapse of the Soviet Union, by founding Islamic states in Central Asia. Certainly, despite the conventional wisdom that the US withdrew its funding and support for the insurgents when Moscow finally made its withdrawal a year later in 1989, nothing could be further from the truth.[2]

Warning the US of the rise of a hard-line state in the wake of its retreat, the Soviet foreign minister Eduard Shevardnadze also reportedly asked for 'US cooperation in limiting the spread of Islamic fundamentalism'. Similarly, when meeting with his CIA counterparts, KGB director Vladimir Kryuchkov lamented the 'rise to power in Afghanistan of another fundamentalist government, a Sunni complement to Shia Iran', while even Pakistani prime minister Benazir Bhutto told the newly installed President George H. Bush that he was 'creating a Frankenstein' in the region.[3]

But with the prize of full Cold War victory within sight, all such warnings fell on deaf ears as funding and weapons continued to flow to the jihadists, some of whom were even mounting cross-border incursions into Soviet territory. According to former Pakistani intelligence officials, hundreds of fighters were pushing up to twenty-five kilometres across the border, while thousands of CIA- and Saudi-printed copies of the Qur'an translated into Central Asian languages were being smuggled into Soviet border towns and cities.[4] With the US keeping the pressure on Moscow even after the Soviet Union formally came to end and the new Commonwealth of Independent States had been declared, Russian officials complained that over five thousand jihadists who had been training in Afghanistan had turned up in Tajikistan to fight its government, while in 1991 Charlie Wilson managed to secure a final $200 million tranche of funding for the insurgency.[5]

According to available photographic evidence and the accounts of campaign veterans, even those fighters who briefly returned to Saudi Arabia that year to help shore up the kingdom against a possible Iraqi invasion were rewarded by the US, which turned a blind eye to their pillaging of heavy weaponry from Saddam Hussein's fleeing forces in Kuwait. With cooperation from Pakistani intelligence, much of this new jihadist firepower was then sent back in convoys to Afghanistan before being passed on to the so-called 'Haqqani network'. Led by Jalaluddin Haqqani, it was by then running one of the biggest militias and was understood to be closely intertwined with al-Qaeda.[6]

With such powerful paramilitaries easily able to subdue most remaining post-Soviet resistance, and with no functioning Afghan government left for the United Nations to transfer any transitional authority to, the US vision of an Afghan Islamic state was getting close to reality. Able to enter the shattered city of Kabul, the jihadists quickly rolled back all of the People's Democratic Party's earlier reforms, stripped women of their rights, banned alcohol, restarted public executions, and implemented sharia law.[7] With the Taliban – or 'students' – organization emerging as the dominant politico-religious force by the mid-1990s, it was soon the de facto government and even began to appoint ministers. Having forged working relationships with the likes of Haqqani and Gulbuddin Hekmatyar, it also reached out to Osama bin Laden and the many remaining 'Arab Afghans', and effectively offered them permanent sanctuary. With Afghanistan now one of the most repressive and backward regimes on the planet, the US could of course not afford to establish a formal relationship with the Taliban, but regional allies such as Saudi Arabia, the UAE, and Pakistan were free to do so. As al-Qaeda defector transcripts recently released by a US court have revealed, the Saudi government was in fact the first to grant official recognition to the Taliban in a move almost certainly approved by the US Department of State.[8]

In addition to such intermediaries there is evidence the US also began to develop some low-key links of its own. In 1997 an Amnesty International report described how 'many Afghan analysts believe that the US has close political links with the Taliban militia. They refer to visits by Taliban representatives to the US in recent months and several visits by senior Department of State officials to Kandahar including one before the Taliban took over Jalalabad.'[9] In part it seems these meetings were propelled by increasing US interest in building trans-Asian energy infrastructure through Afghan territory. Brought all the way to the Unocal oil company's offices in Sugarland, Texas, in December 1997, a 'senior delegation' of Taliban officials had been asked to support a pipeline project that aimed to supply Central Asian gas to South Asia and ultimately Pakistani ports on the Arabian Sea, thus allowing Unocal to bypass Russia, Iran, and China. As the BBC reported, Unocal already had a deal in place to buy gas from Turkmenistan and sell it to Pakistan, but was worried that a rival Argentinian firm was also interested. Trying to gain the upper hand, Unocal offered the Taliban a fifteen percent cut for every thousand cubic feet pumped through Afghanistan and promised to train 140 Afghans in the necessary pipeline-construction skills. In another link to the University of Nebraska, Unocal had already commissioned the institution to train the men in Kandahar.[10]

With so much at stake, many US officials unsurprisingly soon came to terms with doing business with the extremist regime. In 1997 one diplomat explained that 'the *Taliban* will probably develop like the Saudis ... there will be [an equivalent to] Aramco, pipelines, an emir, no parliament and lots of sharia law. We can live with that.' Similarly, a Department of State spokesperson claimed that the US found 'nothing objectionable' in the Taliban's takeover of Kabul.[11] A future US ambassador to Afghanistan, who at the time was one of several US officials employed by Unocal to promote its scheme, even reasoned that 'the *Taliban* does not practise the anti-US style of fundamentalism practised by Iran – it is closer to the Saudi model. The group upholds a mix of traditional Pashtun values and an orthodox interpretation of Islam.'[12] Britain, meanwhile, was already running its own version of a Taliban embassy in London after having granted sanctuary to a former commander of one of the militias it had helped train in the 1980s and who had then gone on to become the Taliban's 'European representative'.[13] As Mark Curtis notes, by then the British-manufactured Blowpipe missiles earlier supplied to the mujahideen had even started to reappear as part of the Taliban's official arsenal.[14]

Although there was no Cold War left to win, there are suggestions that on top of the pipeline prospects the US was equally keen to keep manipulating the Taliban's rise and survival as its continued existence helped to keep on edge many of the newly independent Muslim-majority Central Asian republics. Worried over the spread of Taliban-like extremist Islam in their own backyard, their governments became much more amenable to US overtures to establish and lease military bases in their territory.[15] With many such US missions successfully set up by the end of the 1990s, US congressman Dana Rohrabacher's statement to a Senate Foreign Relations subcommittee in 1999 that the US government was continuing to conduct a covert policy of supporting the Taliban 'on the assumption that the Taliban would bring stability to Afghanistan' seems to have represented only half the story. He did, however, make quite clear that the Taliban was the 'most anti-Western, anti-female, anti-human rights regime in the world'.[16]

KEEPING BIN LADEN ON BOARD

Remaining a key figure in Afghanistan and Pakistan, but also increasingly active across the broader Islamic world, Osama bin Laden had continued to rise in prominence even after the end of the anti-Soviet war. According to Flagg Miller, a linguistic anthropologist who spent ten years studying a batch of audio tapes discovered in bin Laden's Kandahar residence, it was only in the early 1990s that he assumed supreme leadership over al-Qaeda, as prior to that other militants fighting in Afghanistan had regarded him cautiously due to his wealth and Saudi nationality. Moreover, as Miller notes, an overlooked clause in al-Qaeda's founding charter had stated that the 'commander of the guards' was not supposed to come from the Gulf monarchies or Yemen.[17]

Running into trouble when trying to return to Saudi Arabia in 1991, given Riyadh's wariness of welcoming back hardened jihadists from their Afghan campaign, bin Laden had briefly been put under house arrest, with local state-owned media later attributing this to his 'irresponsible behaviour that contradicts the interests of Saudi Arabia and harms sisterly countries, and his refusal to obey instructions issued to him'.[18] But according to a classified US intelligence report obtained by investigative journalist Gerald Posner, the US was aware of an 'unwritten truce' that had already been reached between bin Laden and Riyadh. Having promised that al-Qaeda-linked fighters would refrain from targeting the kingdom, bin Laden had been allowed to leave Saudi Arabia and was guaranteed continuing access to his assets even after being stripped of citizenship. As with the Haqqani fighters who had earlier helped defend Saudi Arabia's northern border, bin Laden seems to have also offered such assistance. Although Riyadh appears to have declined, a number of al-Qaeda veterans were nonetheless understood to have then joined the Saudi Arabian national guard after bin Laden finally left and moved to Sudan.[19] Meeting him there, prominent British journalist Robert Fisk eulogized him as a retired jihadist who by then was more interested in using his men to build roads and infrastructure. Bin Laden in Fisk's words was simply 'an anti-Soviet warrior putting his army on the road to peace'.[20]

Behind the scenes of course, the Saudi quasi-government funding and private donations to al-Qaeda and other such groups continued to grow, with a report prepared for the European Parliament claiming that the same big charities that had earlier channelled funds to the Afghan jihad were by the early 1990s still diverting between fifteen and twenty percent of their resources to such extremists.[21] Doubtless aware of this and certainly of the 1980s arrangements, given her access to extensive intelligence, former British prime minister Margaret Thatcher nevertheless stated, in a keynote address at a 1993 Chatham House conference entitled *Inside Saudi Arabia*, that 'the kingdom of Saudi Arabia … [is] a leader of the wider Islamic family of nations, and is a strong force for moderation and stability on the world stage.'[22]

If anything, by the mid-1990s, an even more formal funding flow had been established, with later US court proceedings indicating that a meeting took place in 1996 in a Paris hotel, close to the Saudi embassy, between a group of Saudi princes and businessmen who came to an agreement to resume their financing of bin Laden's operations.[23] Apparently another example of the old 'Golden Chain' in action, the eventual 9/11 Commission's report corroborated this by stating that evidence was available indicating that the shadowy network had resumed its support for al-Qaeda during this period so as to help maintain its influence in Central Asia after bin Laden's return from Saudi Arabia and Sudan.[24] According to Posner in the *New York Times*, the 9/11 report could have gone further, as the evidence on the Golden Chain was understood to implicate 'a former government minister in Saudi Arabia, three billionaire banking tycoons and several top industrialists'.[25]

Having visited bin Laden in person in 1996, Abdel Bari Atwan explains that the Saudi funders also requested that bin Laden issue a statement declaring that the king of Saudi Arabia was a 'true Muslim'.[26] In this sense it seemed powerful Saudis were still keen to keep al-Qaeda onside and have at least some degree of control over it. Particularly alarming for them had been a widely circulating bin Laden *fatwa* published earlier in the year by a London-based Arabic language newspaper. This called for a 'declaration of war against the Americans occupying the land of the two holy places', in reference to Mecca and Medina.[27] Indeed, French intelligence reasoned that the secret Paris meeting was primarily held in response to two attacks that had recently taken place on US personnel in Saudi Arabia and the subsequent fears expressed by ruling family members that al-Qaeda was beginning to turn on the kingdom. As per sworn statements later made by the Taliban's former intelligence chief Muhammad Khaksar, it was alleged that within two years of the meeting Saudi Arabia's intelligence chief had managed to reach a more solid agreement with bin Laden that guaranteed him further Saudi funds and no extradition requests, in return for no further al-Qaeda attacks on targets within Saudi Arabia. According to Simon Henderson, a research fellow at the Washington Institute for Near East Policy, US and British official sources were aware of how these funds were being transferred to bin Laden by two Saudi princes and that it was 'official money ... not their own', and amounted to hundreds of millions of dollars.[28]

The fresh Saudi financing was partly spent on supporting extremist *madrasas* in Pakistan's north-western frontier province. Among these was the Haqqania Madrasa, which had earlier been home to Haqqani himself and various Taliban members and was by then known as the 'University of Jihad'. The Combating Terrorism Center at West Point has since detailed how Haqqani and his close relatives were able to travel freely to Saudi Arabia during this period to perform pilgrimage and raise additional funds for their expanding network.[29] Spread more widely, some of the new resources were evidently disbursed elsewhere across Central Asia and the Middle East, with an MI6 report prepared for the Foreign Office entitled *Islamic Fundamentalism in the Middle East* explaining that 'private Saudi and Gulf money donated for Islamic causes is a common factor in much of the region.' The report also put forward the rather convoluted reasoning that while the British government may have reservations over the 'the strong anti-Western streak' exhibited by the main groups involved, and that the 'wider objectives [of the groups] are more or less incompatible with Western liberal principles', their 'fundamentalism is not necessarily synonymous with political radicalism or anti-Western policies'. Seemingly still framing the problem in Zbigniew Brzezinski-style Cold War logic, MI6 also claimed that any threat of blowback to the West was unlikely to be serious as '[Islamic] fundamentalism does not pose a coherent and monolithic threat to Western interests in the way that communism once did ... dealings with extreme fundamentalist regimes would be highly unpredictable but not necessarily unmanageable.'[30]

Certainly there is ample evidence that British intelligence actively tolerated al-Qaeda's presence in London for much of the 1990s. Having set up a Wembley-based front company in 1994 called the Advice and Reformation Committee, bin Laden is understood to have visited in person, as noted in a later report prepared for the US Congress in 2001.[31] With bin Laden finally indicted by a US federal grand jury in New York for his role in al-Qaeda's bombings of US embassies in Tanzania and Kenya in 1998, the court proceedings provided much more information about his London connections. Embarrassingly for Britain, it was revealed that 'on or about 11 July 1994, the defendant Osama bin Laden created the London office of al-Qaeda, naming it the Advice and Reformation Committee and placing the defendant Khalid al-Fawwaz in charge.' The proceedings also stated that the office 'was designed both to publicize the statements of Osama bin Laden and to provide a cover for activity in support of al-Qaeda's "military activities", including the recruitment of military trainees, the disbursement of funds and the procurement of necessary equipment including satellite telephones and necessary services'. Furthermore, 'the London office served as a conduit for messages, including reports on military and security matters from various al-Qaeda cells, including the Kenyan cell, to al-Qaeda's headquarters.'[32]

Most remarkably, shortly before its shutdown, al-Qaeda's London office had not only been responsible for publishing bin Laden's anti-American *fatwa*, but had also issued another declaration calling for an 'international front for jihad against the crusaders and the Jews.'[33] Meanwhile, bin Laden's co-defendant and 'de facto ambassador in Britain', as British intelligence described his Saudi associate al-Fawwaz, was understood to have been making enquiries to the Home Office about possible political asylum for bin Laden in Britain.[34] As Atwan recalls, a leading figure of this 1990s 'Londonistan' jihadist community, Abu Musab al-Suri, had later confirmed to him that 'a tacit covenant was in place between MI6 and the extremists.'[35]

THE WAR AGAINST SERBIA – BOSNIAN JIHAD

With Operation Cyclone long since finished and the Commonwealth of Independent States hardly a threat to Western interests, it is important to understand what these 1990s al-Qaeda 'military activities' actually were, and why the Western intelligence agencies seemed so keen to tolerate them. This time it seemed at least part of the answer lay within Europe itself, and more specifically the Balkans. Following Croatia's and Slovenia's declarations of independence from the former Soviet-sponsored federation of Yugoslavia in 1990, and in the wake of a referendum in February 1992, the Muslim-majority Bosnia-Herzegovina also declared independence. With the rump Yugoslavia dominated by non-Muslim Serbia, still officially known as the Socialist Republic of Serbia and regarded by Washington as 'the last communist government in Europe', a golden opportunity had emerged to remove one of the biggest stumbling blocks for NATO's eastwards expansion, European Union enlargement, and Western access to markets in Eastern Europe. As Mark Curtis explains, Serbia's 'independent domestic policies posed the last real barrier to openly expressed British, EU, and US aims in Eastern Europe'.[36]

Militarily backing the substantial minority of Bosnian Serbs, most of whom were opposed to the new breakaway state and had boycotted the referendum, Serbian president Slobodan Milošević was soon accused by the Western powers of engaging in 'ethnic cleansing' against the pro-referendum Bosniaks and Bosnian Croats.[37] With no apparent diplomatic options on the table to remove him peacefully from power, a 1992 MI6 paper had quickly demonstrated 'the need to assassinate President Milošević of Serbia'. Thus, when NATO's extensive 'Operation Deny Flight' operation began a few months later in 1993, ostensibly to provide no-fly-zone cover for the Bosnian separatists, Milošević's personal residence in Belgrade was specifically targeted by NATO aircraft.[38]

With Milošević managing to survive such attacks and with little movement on the battlefield, the campaign soon developed into a full-scale air-strike campaign against Serbia. Known this time as 'Operation Deliberate Force', by the end of 1995 it was even accompanied by an unprecedented sixty-thousand-strong NATO 'implementation' ground force.[39] To provide the *casus belli*, Western intelligence agencies had earlier reported that Bosnian Serb paramilitaries had committed genocide and were responsible for the 'Srebrenica Massacre' of about eight thousand Bosnian Muslims that summer.[40] The International Court of Justice has since confirmed that the Serbian and Croatian governments 'deliberately forced minority ethnic groups out of areas they controlled', but has problematically cleared both governments of genocide, with Judge Peter Tomka stating in February 2015 that 'forces on both sides had carried out violent acts during the war ... However, neither side had provided sufficient evidence to demonstrate the specific intent required for acts of genocide'.[41] In summer 2015 newly declassified documents shed more light on the massacre and its apparent manipulation by NATO, with research findings collated by a former *Le Monde* journalist revealing that the British, French, and US intelligence services had all anticipated it. Indeed, Western officials were understood to have already been aware that the UN-protected safe area in Bosnia was 'untenable' and that 'as the killing hit full throttle, top Western negotiators did not raise the issue of mass murder [with Serbia], even though unclassified US cables showed that the CIA was watching the killing fields almost "live" from satellite planes.'[42]

Meanwhile, in the year leading up to Operation Deliberate Force, there is evidence that the US had begun to supply the Bosnian separatists with weapons and had thus been contravening both the UN arms embargo on the conflict and the terms of the no-fly zone. UN peacekeepers of the Nordic Battalion had reported spotting C-130 transporter 'black flights' landing at airstrips in eastern Bosnia. Although NATO and the US denied knowledge of these flights at the time, a later BBC investigation confirmed that these secret missions were supplying 'vital, high value supplies: anti-tank guided weapons to counter Bosnian Serb armour, Stinger surface-to-air missiles to ward off helicopters, night vision goggles'. The BBC also contended that on the designated nights of the 'black flights', the NATO no-fly zone was being monitored by 'US Navy Awac surveillance planes rather than NATO aircraft with their multi-national crews.'[43] It remains unclear, however, whether the aircraft and weapons involved actually originated from the US or were merely from US partners. A plausible claim has been made that it was in fact Iran, with full knowledge of the Western powers, that had, for about a year from the beginning of the conflict and then again from 1994 to 1995, been making three covert flights a week to Bosnia.[44]

Equally worryingly, a UN negotiator at the time and a former Norwegian foreign minister, Thorvald Stoltenberg, has since stated that 'over 100 operators from across the spectrum of US intelligence agencies were on the ground in Bosnia' and that 'this intelligence-gathering was aimed as much at the UN as the Serbs, and intelligence was passed directly on to the Bosnian Government.' He also explained that 'this information was often used to ratchet up the pressure on UN commanders to [call for] punitive air strikes on the Serbs.'[45] A former Bosnian fighter has similarly described how US special forces were active in Bosnia at the time, providing training to a number of fighters, some of whom were Islamist militants.[46] Rather than being official US troops, these 'special forces' trainers seem more likely to have been part of a contract awarded to a private US company.[47] In 2010 a group of Serbs launched a lawsuit in the Federal Court of Chicago against such a company, on the basis that it had 'participated in genocide' and had supplied weapons and training to combatants in violation of the embargo. Crucially, they claimed that activities relevant to the company's contract in Bosnia had also taken place in Virginia.[48]

Britain's involvement in Bosnia has rarely been discussed, but the reports that are available strongly suggest it had reprised its tried-and-tested Cold War strategy of either nurturing or tolerating the Islamicization of a conflict. With little history of indigenous Islamic extremism, Bosnia certainly seems to have become home to a sizeable number of foreign jihadists and preachers during this period. With British MPs concerned that the Balkans were becoming the new focal point for the international jihad, and that Britain was doing nothing to stop it from happening in 'Europe's own backyard', a Foreign Office minister tried to downplay the number of foreign fighters involved.[49] Nonetheless, successive claims have been made that British intelligence had been allowing poorly regulated Islamic 'convoys of mercy' to set off from Britain to Bosnia. Organized by British Muslim charities, the trucks were ostensibly supplying aid but, as revealed by an extensive *Sunday Times* report based on the court testimonies of a British jihadist held in Karachi, they were in fact 'organizing clandestine support for the Muslim fighters' and ferrying jihadists into Bosnia.[50] Similarly, as Mark Curtis has described, the Finsbury Park-based extremist preacher Abu Hamza al-Masri, who had already set up his 'Supporters of Sharia' organization to 'support the mujahideen around the world', was also helping to prepare the convoys. This was done by supplying food and medical supplies, but also by assisting the flow of fighters out of Britain and then back into Britain without being questioned by the authorities.[51] In this light British citizens can perhaps better understand not only why bin Laden's office was freely functioning in London at this time, but also why characters such as al-Masri, who had repeatedly expressed support for bin Laden and the need to create an Islamic caliphate, were still very much at large. Reportedly even the Queen had expressed bewilderment as to why al-Masri had not been arrested. In fact, it was only in 2004, and only then following a US extradition request, that the British police finally arrested him.[52]

To some extent it seems the US had also chosen to go a bit further than just supporting the native separatists, as the Department of Defense and the CIA were both understood to have brokered further Operation Cyclone-like alliances with the international jihadists. According to Richard Holbrooke, former US chief negotiator in the Balkans, this led to yet another 'pact with the devil' as 'the [Bosnian] Muslims wouldn't have survived without this help.'[53] From the US itself, in a sort of parallel to the British 'convoys of mercy', American Muslim veterans of the Afghan jihad were being recruited by al-Qaeda-sponsored Egyptian networks and then brought over to Bosnia to fight as soldiers or serve as trainers.[54] The majority of the foreign jihadists, however, appear to have been the old 'Arab Afghans' whose fight in Central Asia had come to an end and who sought redeployment to the next battlefield. Estimates for the total jihadist migration vary greatly, with anywhere between 850 and 4,000 such fighters arriving to help against the Serbs, and in some cases they may have even been airlifted from Afghanistan to Europe by the US.[55]

The emir of the resettled Arab Afghans in Bosnia was thought to have been a Saudi citizen of Indian descent who had fought in Afghanistan and had then set up his new headquarters in Travnik – a small town in the mountainous central canton of Bosnia.[56] Overseeing several training camps in the region, the emir was understood to have relied upon a small core force from the Gulf monarchies which included two of the eventual Saudi 9/11 hijackers and Khalid Sheikh Muhammad. But there were also contingents from elsewhere in the Middle East and North Africa, most of whom were disaffected, often unemployed youths.[57] According to a Bahraini al-Qaeda defector who later testified to a UN panel, he had previously trained in Afghanistan camps before joining a unit in Bosnia comprising 'seventy Arabs, twenty-five Turks, and only about twelve Bosnians'.[58]

Officially the jihadist 'foreign legion' was affiliated with regular Bosnian military units, but in practice they were operating as separate 'shock troops ... independently of formal military control'. By 1995 their infrastructure in Bosnia was thought to have been so strong that they were able to send many of their new local comrades to training camps in Afghanistan and Pakistan. Returning to Europe suitably radicalized, these new Bosnian

jihadists are thought to have been responsible for the first organized suicide bombings in modern Europe.[59] Among their notable targets was the
Rijeka police station, attacked in an apparent effort to force the authorities
to release one of their spokesmen.[60]

Marking the twentieth anniversary of the Srebrenica Massacre, in
2015, a BBC *Our World* documentary attempted something of a revi-
sionist history of the conflict. Admitting that Bosnia in the 1990s was
the 'cradle of modern jihad', the first few minutes showed how black
jihadist flags were still flying in 2015 and quoted a former Arab fighter in
Bosnia who had later become an MI6 agent.[61] As he put it, the Bosnian
campaign was the first real occasion when the jihadists' anti-Western
narrative became explicit. The narrator acknowledged that of the hundreds of Arab fighters who arrived, some went on to be the world's most
notorious terrorists and 'cadres of al-Qaeda', including the organization's
future leader in Saudi Arabia.[62] The BBC also depicted the brutality of the
foreign legion's methods including public beheadings, the desecration
of churches and monasteries, the kidnapping and murdering of foreign
aid workers, the setting up of ad hoc sharia courts, and the patrolling
of streets 'hunting for non-believers'. Making the important point that
Bosnia's Muslims were 'not devout' before the foreigners came and the
'wave of radicalization' began, the BBC further claimed that by the end
of the war Bosnia's increasingly concerned generals had asked the jihadists to leave the country.[63]

Going only halfway, however, the documentary offered no explanation of how so many jihadists had been able to move to Bosnia, and nor
did it include any discussion of the role played by the Western powers
and their Arab allies in the previous Afghan jihad. Showing footage of
UN peacekeeping armoured personnel carriers returning fire in 1993,
the BBC claimed these were the 'first salvos in the British Army's fight
against jihadism' before explaining that this was part of a UN mission,
to which Britain was contributing, aimed at protecting and evacuating
Bosnian villagers trapped inside a monastery under ongoing attack by the
'mujahideen battalion'.[64] It further explained how BBC correspondents at
the time had 'seen many times how peacekeeping forces helped Bosnia's
Muslims'. Importantly, though unwittingly, the documentary also depicted
the buildings that used to serve as the jihadists' forward headquarters in

the town of Zenica. Largely untouched, these were big structures including a substantial factory complex that should have been easily identified and targeted by the NATO air strikes.[65]

THE WAR AGAINST SERBIA – KOSOVAN JIHAD

Although the Bosnian war ended inconclusively in late 1995 with Slobodan Milošević remaining in power, a fresh opportunity nonetheless soon arose to undermine further the Serbian government and perpetuate the jihadist movement in the Balkans.[66] On Serbia's southern flanks, the landlocked Muslim-majority province of Kosovo, mostly made up of ethnic Albanians, was becoming increasingly restive. Having attacked several Serbian refugee camps, Serbian officials, and police stations, the paramilitary Kosovo Liberation Army had already been designated a terrorist organization by the US and, as late as 1998, the British government was continuing to describe it as 'without any question a terrorist group', with Foreign Secretary Robin Cook condemning the 'terrorism of the self-styled KLA'. Moreover, according to US special envoy to Kosovo, Robert Gelbard, it was also being investigated for apparent links to organized crime in Britain and its involvement in the international drug trade.[67] Within a few more months the trans-European police authority, Europol, began to prepare a detailed report on the KLA's narcotics operations after collating a range of intelligence reports produced by Sweden, Switzerland, and Germany.[68] Most grotesquely the UN later launched an investigation into what were described as credible claims that at this time the KLA had also been trafficking human organs harvested from kidnapped Serbians.[69]

Thought to have grown to about thirty thousand men, the KLA was still far from being an Islamist force or avowedly sectarian. But by this stage numerous reports had begun to circulate of its increasing contacts with al-Qaeda in Bosnia, and of such fighters beginning to join its ranks.[70] One such Kosovo-based al-Qaeda unit was thought to be headed by Muhammad al-Zawahiri, the brother of bin Laden's deputy, Ayman, who over the course of 1998 had helped to plan and execute the US embassy bombings in Kenya and Tanzania.[71] Although the 1995 Bosnian peace agreements had required all of the foreign combatants to leave the Balkans, several hundred were thought to have remained after the Bosnian government handed out passports en masse. Indeed, in an article published several years after the conflict, the *New York Times* matter-of-factly stated that those Arabs who had come to fight were given citizenship in return.[72] Commenting on this development to another US newspaper, a Department of Defense official had claimed 'these are the bad guys – the ones you have to worry about', while a counter-terrorism official agreed that hundreds remained in the Balkans but concluded: 'Are they a threat? Absolutely. Are we all over them? Absolutely.'[73] Less optimistically, but rather prophetically, the director of a congressional task force on terrorism and unconventional warfare warned that such 'Bosnian operatives would be able to carry out a series of terrorist operations which could be attributed to a Kosovo Albanian organization'. He reasoned that this could provoke a strong Serbian response which in turn could 'be used to induce Western military intervention against Yugoslavia itself'.[74]

As well as the newly naturalized 'Arab Bosnians' streaming into Kosovo, other extremists came across the border from Albania. According to the proceedings of a 1998 French court case involving a former French jihadist in Kosovo, al-Qaeda had earlier established a transit hub in Albania following a personal visit from bin Laden.[75] As with the earlier British 'convoys of mercy' to Bosnia, there is also evidence that a London-based organization was helping to send British jihadists to Kosovo, with former US Department of Justice prosecutor John Loftus accusing British intelligence of collaborating with an entity known as *Al-Muhajiroun* or 'The Emigrants' despite it having been repeatedly blacklisted as a terror cell.[76] Soon the CIA and Albanian intelligence estimated that fighters hailing from at least six Middle Eastern countries were active alongside the KLA.[77]

With the prospect of a new jihadist alliance, by the beginning of 1999 both the US and British governments were understood to be circumventing their official terror designations by discreetly initiating contact with the KLA's increasingly al-Qaeda-influenced leaders. Following secret meetings held by the US special envoy to Kosovo and British embassy staff in Belgrade, Cook confirmed that he was holding telephone conversations with the KLA, and soon after it was reported that 'contacts are taking place on a regular and amicable basis between the KLA and American and NATO officials' and that the 'rebel army' had begun to serve as 'NATO's eyes and ears in Kosovo ... providing crucial aid to the alliance, acting as spotters on the ground'.[78]

By spring 1999 the BBC was not only reporting that NATO was openly cooperating with the KLA, but that Britain's SAS was already 'on the ground'.[79] Unreported in the British media, however, was that this was a clear contravention of UN Security Resolution 1160, which in 1998 had forbidden the 'sale or supply to the Federal Republic of Yugoslavia including Kosovo ... of arms and related materiel of all types ... and shall prevent arming and training for terrorist activities there'.[80] In 'Operation Picnic', as it was known, the SAS's role was to help the KLA set up 'picnic teams' to root out Serbian forces based in Kosovo, with each British-assembled team comprising twenty to thirty 'allied soldiers'.[81] Although London's official position remained that there was no evidence of 'systematic involvement' of jihadist fighters among these allies, photographs nevertheless emerged showing them to be embedded within the KLA.[82] Interviewed by the *Independent*, a senior KLA commander explained that 'the missions were supposed to be what the US Army calls "sterile", which meant the soldiers either wore uniforms that could not be traced to any allied unit or were disguised in the combat fatigues of the Black Hand Serb paramilitaries'.[83] Revealing a little more about Picnic's chain of command, an account in the *Scotsman* quoted a senior British military source who claimed that the Ministry of Defence had first been approached by the US Defense Intelligence Agency before then subcontracting the work to two private companies that hired former SAS soldiers.[84]

Effectively resuming their earlier Bosnia-supporting air strikes, by the summer of 1999 NATO had bombed Serbia for eleven straight weeks, albeit this time in defence of Kosovo. One academic study, later supplied to the International Criminal Tribunal for the former Yugoslavia, estimated that $100 billion of damage had been done, including the destruction of bridges, railways, schools, hospitals, civilian airports, and even medieval monasteries and shrines.[85] A former US attorney general who was appalled by the Western powers' role in the conflict even filed a complaint of war crimes against Britain at the International Criminal Court.[86] Nonetheless, the mass destruction of Yugoslavia's infrastructure was justified by the Western governments on the basis of 'preventing an impending humanitarian disaster'. The *Independent* largely bought the story, seemingly on the basis that because Kosovo was not oil rich it could not possibly be targeted for any other reason, while the *Guardian*'s Polly Toynbee argued that the bombings were 'a brave and probably only chance for the West collectively to create a more ethical foreign policy ... [and showed] purity of motive, freedom from self-interest'. Even the *New Statesman* claimed of the campaign that 'the most powerful states are willing to fight for human rights.'[87]

With Western assistance from the air and on the ground, and with al-Qaeda's veterans again clearly involved, the KLA was, as Human Rights Watch described, soon able to evolve from being a 'scattered guerrilla group' to becoming 'ultimately a more formidable armed force engaged in military tactics that put civilians at risk'. In an extensive report published in 2001, Human Rights Watch noted that 'KLA units sometimes staged an ambush or attacked police or army outposts from a village and then retreated, exposing villagers to revenge attacks. Large massacres sometimes ensued [which] helped publicize the KLA's cause and internationalize the conflict.' The report also detailed how the conflict soon gained a sectarian edge, as 'immediately following NATO's arrival, there was widespread and systematic burning and looting of homes belonging to Serbs, Roma, and other minorities and the destruction of Orthodox churches and monasteries. This destruction was combined with harassment and intimidation designed to force people from their homes and communities.'[88]

Estimates for the total death toll vary greatly, but according to the director of the Transnational Foundation for Peace and Future Research the KLA was understood to have killed about a thousand Serbs by the end of the war, while approximately 210,000 ethnic Serbs had had to flee Kosovo.[89] Including both Serbs and Kosovans, the British government initially claimed that ten thousand died in Kosovo in 1999, but later clarified that only two thousand had died prior to the NATO air strikes. Documents since released by the German ministry of foreign affairs indicate that the air campaign in fact did not even have any strategic justification. In February 1999, a month before the strikes began, German intelligence reported that 'the often feared humanitarian catastrophe ... has been averted' and that 'public life has since returned to relative normality.' The documents also state quite clearly that 'the measures taken by the [Serbian] armed forces are in the first instance directed towards combatting the KLA' and that 'events since 1998 do not evidence a persecution programme based on Albanian ethnicity.' Similarly, subsequent studies published by the Organization for Security and Cooperation in Europe have argued that the Serbian army's increased use of public violence in Kosovo occurred only after the NATO campaign began. Even the chairman of NATO's military committee admitted on British television that 'definitely some of the atrocities which happened were caused by NATO bombs, since [these provoked] this vendetta feeling.'[90] Britain's House of Commons Foreign Affairs Committee's inquiry concluded that 'it is likely that the NATO bombing did cause a change in the character of the assault upon the Kosovan Albanians. What had been an anti-insurgency campaign [against the KLA] ... became a mass, organized campaign to kill Kosovo Albanians.'[91]

Amid the bombing and fighting, Robin Cook was questioned in parliament over the length and severity of the operation, to which he replied, 'No one would be happier than President Milošević if we were now to suspend the military campaign ... [it] would not assist a solution, but would ensure that it would be longer before we could secure the only solution that will bring justice to Kosovo – the return of the refugees under international protection ... until we can secure that objective, it would be foolish of the House to suggest that we should cease the bombing campaign.'[92] Significantly he even went as far as blaming Milošević personally for the rise of the KLA. Avoiding all references to Britain's role in the conflict, and using language now eerily familiar to those following British policy on Syria, he stated that 'we have to face the fact – as must Milošević – that his behaviour and his brutality are the best recruiting sergeant for the KLA. That army has grown in strength during the period in which he has claimed to be wiping it out.'[93]

When interviewed by the *New Statesman* just days after the end of the bombing campaign in July 1999, Cook went into more depth about Britain's priorities in the Balkans and its necessarily hard-line stance on Serbia. Stating that 'our key tasks are first of all to increase trade, open up [Yugoslavian] markets and help them with economic progress, to intensify the integration with European structures,' he then moved on to explain that 'we must increase their ties with NATO in order to make sure that they do have a greater sense of security and we must take a stronger part in their security.'[94] Two years later a Foreign Office minister even linked these objectives directly to the scale of destruction wrought by the air strikes, remarking in a speech to the Confederation of British Industry in the presence of the new and more compliant post-Milošević Yugoslavian president that 'Britain can continue to benefit from the reconstruction of Yugoslavia including bilateral investment promotions.'[95] As for Kosovo, the supposed focus of the conflict, after a few more years Britain and the US unsurprisingly became the first states to recognize its independence.[96] But this met with tepid international reaction, with Russia, China, India, and many other states continuing to refuse to acknowledge its secession from Serbia.[97]

Funding patterns for the new European jihadist campaigns, first in Bosnia and then in Kosovo, appear to have mirrored closely the Afghanistan campaign. Nonetheless, it appears that this time far less financing came directly from the Western governments and intelligence agencies; instead a much greater proportion came from the West's Middle Eastern allies. Again serving as de facto al-Qaeda sponsors, many of the same state-backed Saudi charities and NGOs resumed their leading role, as of course did the existing network of private financiers. The seven-member Bosnian presidency was quick to recognize the advantages of playing host to the Arab–Afghan foreign legion in Travnik, and thus became cognizant not only of al-Qaeda's battlefield abilities, but also of its mascot-like role in generating substantial funding from across the conservative Islamic world.[98] Indeed, as extra-early recipients of Bosnian passports in 1993, both bin Laden and Khalid Sheikh Muhammad were reportedly welcomed in Bosnia several times during the conflict.[99]

With such trusted intermediaries in place or at least making visits, by 1994 Saudi donors were understood by the US embassy in Riyadh to have already dispatched $150 million to Bosnia, most of which had been collected in mosques across the kingdom.[100] On a more formal level, a UN-sponsored investigation concluded that another $120 million had been sent to Bosnia by the Saudi High Commission for Relief via the Third World Relief Agency.[101] As security analyst Evan Kohlmann notes, the latter was being managed by a member of the Sudanese National Islamic Front and about half of its eventual total of $350 million in aid was used to supply weapons for the conflict.[102] Recent US court proceedings have largely corroborated this, revealing Western intelligence agencies' estimates that most of the funds channelled by these entities had been spent on arming fighters rather than humanitarian aid. A Bahraini former jihadist's testimony to the UN has also made the allegation that these organizations 'participated extensively in supporting al-Qaeda in Bosnia.'[103]

Other Saudi charities were also involved but on a smaller scale, with the Al-Haramain Foundation having funded a jihadist battalion in Bosnia, and with a member of the Egyptian Islamic Jihad fronting an office for it in Albania that was used to help recruit fighters for the Kosovan campaign.[104] Many years later, in 2014, Kosovans understood to have been connected to the foundation during this period were arrested for terrorism offences along with the laundering of hundreds of thousands of Euros.[105] As Georgetown University's John Esposito notes, even some of the non-lethal Saudi aid to the Balkans was also highly questionable, with there being something of a policy of 'destruction or reconstruction of many historic mosques, libraries ... because they did not conform to Wahhabi aesthetics'.[106]

A CIA investigation in 1996 determined that a third of such Islamic charities operating in the Balkans were 'facilitating the activities of Islamic groups that engage in terrorism, including plots to kidnap or kill US personnel'. It also made the allegation that 'even high-ranking members of the collecting or monitoring agencies in Saudi Arabia, Kuwait, and Pakistan – such as the Saudi High Commission – are involved in illicit activities, including support for terrorists.'[107] Moreover, as David Kaplan's team discovered, by this stage US intelligence agencies were also 'picking up disturbing chatter out of Saudi Arabia', with several intercepts reportedly implicating some of its wealthiest businessmen. According to one senior US official, 'It was not definitive but still very disturbing ... That was the year we had to admit the Saudis were a problem.'[108] Nonetheless, despite the ample warnings and of course the illegality of contravening the UN arms embargo on supplying weapons to participants in Yugoslavia, it appears that the Western governments continued to give a green light to the campaign. According to Kohlmann, one senior Western diplomat who went as far as questioning the legality of the Third World Relief Agency's activities was effectively told to 'back off' on the grounds that this was at least one way that the US could help the Bosnians.[109]

THE LIBYAN ISLAMIC FIGHTING GROUP - BRITAIN'S NEW ALLY

Having joined the Libyan military in the early 1960s with the express purpose of launching a coup against the Western-backed monarchy, Muammar Gaddafi had seized his opportunity in 1969 when the unpopular and politically distant King Idris al-Senussi was out of the country receiving medical treatment. Arresting Idris's nephew and heir, the crown prince, the 'free officers' of Libya duly installed their transitional government and Gaddafi, still only a colonel, read out the 'communiqué number one' that confirmed the birth of the Libyan Arab Republic.[110] Immediately costing Britain an estimated £100 million in lost oil infrastructure investments and access to military bases, Gaddafi was nonetheless grudgingly regarded by British officials as being a very popular leader.[111]

The US had been less badly damaged by Gaddafi, despite the rhetoric of President Richard Nixon's administration. Staff at its Wheelus airbase in Libya had already been preparing for a full withdrawal, as an agreement signed under Idris was due to come into effect in 1970.[112] Nonetheless, like Britain, the US soon began to formulate scenarios to bring Gaddafi's regime to an end, as it was not only accused of trying to build the world's largest poison gas plant, but was also known to be funding countless governments and movements around the world that were antagonistic to Western interests, in some cases as far afield as Thailand, Indonesia, and the Philippines.[113] Searching for a *casus belli*, in 1981 the US announced that a Libyan hit team had been intercepted while trying to assassinate Ronald Reagan, who himself stated to the media that 'we have the evidence, and [Gaddafi] knows it.' Problematically, however, a task force to investigate the plot had been set up by Deputy Secretary of State William Clark and years later officials involved in it admitted that 'we came out with this big terrorist threat to the US government. The whole thing was a complete fabrication.'[114] In fact, as later reported by the *New Statesman*, the 'hit team' turned out to be made up of Lebanese citizens who had been in the US to assist with negotiations to release US hostages in Beirut. They were understood to have had no connection whatsoever to Gaddafi.[115]

By 1986 Reagan's administration was nonetheless ready to try again, especially after Libya was condemned for firing missiles at US aircraft and its intelligence services were publicly blamed for the bombing of a West Berlin discotheque frequented by US military personnel. Both charges seemed to stick, and within ten days of the Berlin tragedy the US began to launch supposedly retaliatory strikes on both Tripoli and Benghazi.[116] It soon transpired, however, that 'Operation El-Dorado Canyon' was far more than just an effort to punish Gaddafi and, as is now becoming clearer, also had nothing to do with either the missile attacks or the disco bombing. As a former US pilot and squadron leader who served in the operation has since described, El-Dorado Canyon had in fact been in the planning stage 'for about four months from the beginning of 1986'. He understood it to have primarily been an assassination attempt on Gaddafi using the pretext of broader air strikes.[117] Certainly Gaddafi's personal compound at Bab al-Aziziya in Tripoli was directly and heavily targeted, with nine of the forty-five aircraft involved in the operation having been assigned to it.[118] Four bombs were dropped on the building thought to be Gaddafi's house within the compound, but due to warnings from either a Maltese or an Italian politician, Gaddafi had managed to escape beforehand.[119]

Although a later US trial took the view that the Berlin bombing had been 'planned by the Libyan secret service and the Libyan Embassy', a trial held in Germany after its reunification had concluded that while 'Libya [bore] at the very least a considerable part of the responsibility for the attack' there was nonetheless no proof that Gaddafi was personally responsible.[120] As for the missile attacks, the original account seems equally spurious, as a group of British electronic engineers who had been based in Libya at the time later described to the *Sunday Times* how they had watched on their radar as the US aircraft flew deep into Libyan territory. As one of the men stated, 'I don't think the Libyans had any choice but to hit back. In my opinion they were reluctant to do so.'[121] Meanwhile, in other reports, anonymous British officials were quoted as saying that the US's intelligence on Libya was 'wildly inaccurate' and had been passed on to Britain in an effort to 'deliberately deceive'.[122]

Still surviving, by the 1990s, Gaddafi's government was proving particularly problematic as it had convinced itself, with some considerable accuracy, that Saudi Arabia was at the root of the dramatic resurgence in Islamic fundamentalism across the region. Awkwardly for the US and Britain, both heavily implicated in all of the Saudi-funded jihads thus far, the Libyan government became the first in the world to collect evidence on Osama bin Laden's activities and to begin supplying it to Interpol.[123] In early 1998, some five months before al-Qaeda's US embassy bombings, Gaddafi had formally requested an Interpol arrest warrant for bin Laden.[124] According to a former adviser to the French president Jacques Chirac and a French investigative journalist, both the CIA and MI6 had then actively tried to stop the Interpol warrant from being issued and had sought to 'downplay the threat' posed by bin Laden.[125]

From the Libyan regime's perspective, not only was the Arab world under threat from the scourge of religious radicalization, but so also was its own domestic survival as a large number of the 'Arab Afghans' earlier recruited by bin Laden and his associates were actually Libyan citizens. Established in the dying days of the Afghan campaign, the Libyan Islamic Fighting Group (LIFG) was the most prominent cluster, but there were others too, including a number of smaller Libyan units that 'mostly consisted of a leader and a handful of followers'.[126] Those who had not moved on from Afghanistan to the Balkans had returned to North Africa and most had brought with them both military experience and strong convictions about the secular nature of Gaddafi's republic. According to one former Libyan jihadist, the reason they had gone to Afghanistan in the first place was that 'a lot of young [Libyans] felt desperate because the regime made it very hard for people of Islamic persuasion to express their opinion.'[127]

Disturbingly, however, a number of key LIFG members had also moved to Britain. With most living in London and Manchester they appeared to have been offered sanctuary, and they soon began to make repeated public calls for the overthrow of the Gaddafi regime.[128] Naturally Britain had not designated the LIFG a terrorist organization despite its obvious connections to al-Qaeda and other extremist groups in Central Asia, as it was clearly a useful if potentially volatile ally against Tripoli. Among its members was Nazih al-Ruqail, also known as Abu Anas al-Libi, who arrived in Britain in 1995 and was granted political asylum. He was known to have participated in an earlier failed al-Qaeda plot to assassinate Egyptian president Hosni Mubarak and was later implicated in the 1998 US embassy bombings after having flown to Nairobi to train al-Qaeda members in surveillance techniques.[129] Described by a former jihadist as having been a key player in al-Qaeda in Afghanistan since the early days, al-Libi eventually fled Britain in 2000, with a subsequent raid on his Manchester flat leading to the discovery of a 180-page 'terrorist training manual'.[130] Meanwhile, other key LIFG members had been living freely in Ireland, with one remaining in Dublin until 2004 when he left to join the growing Islamist insurgency against the Iraqi and US coalition forces.[131]

Going a long way towards explaining their tolerated presence in Britain, in 1995 and 1996, al-Libi and his LIFG associates had been working closely with British intelligence. Having correctly identified Gaddafi's vulnerability to jihadist organizations, MI6 had developed a plan that would involve Libya-based LIFG veterans leading an assassination attempt and 'producing unrest' across the country, while a simultaneous coup by army officers would take control of the capital.[132] Although six innocent bystanders were killed, the LIFG attack failed and the regime remained in place. With fingers soon pointing at Britain, Foreign Secretary Malcolm Rifkind unequivocally denied any British involvement in the plot.[133] Unfortunately for Rifkind, however, two years later former MI5 officer David Shayler came forward and gave an interview to the BBC in which he claimed that MI6 had indeed reached out to the LIFG and had paid it £100,000 and provided it with 250 weapons on the basis that it would carry out an assassination of Gaddafi.[134] Shayler's allegations were substantially reinforced in 2000 when a leaked MI6 document corroborating most of these details appeared on a US-based server. Marked 'UK Alpha Eyes Only', the document was reported on by the BBC and its authenticity was confirmed to the British press by Whitehall sources, while the secretary of Britain's 'D Notice' censorship committee requested that the document's contents not be published.[135]

Rather belatedly, in February 2004, former CIA director George Tenet told the US Senate's Select Committee on Intelligence that 'one of the most immediate threats [to US national security] is from smaller Sunni extremist groups that have benefited from al-Qaeda links. They include ... the Libyan Islamic Fighting Group.' Tenet repeated his assessment to the 9/11 Commission the following month, with the US finally designating the LIFG a terrorist organization shortly after and issuing a $5 million bounty for the capture of al-Libi.[136] After another year Britain belatedly followed suit after the Home Office Special Immigration Appeals Commission stated that the LIFG's primary aim had been to 'overthrow the Gaddafi regime and replace it with an Islamic state'.[137] Only in 2007 was it officially considered by Western intelligence agencies to be a part of al-Qaeda.[138]

THE ROAD TO 9/11 - MANAGING BLOWBACK

Despite some internal discussion having taken place within the Western intelligence community on possible future blowback from its various relationships with al-Qaeda and other extremist groups, by the end of the 1990s it seemed the majority of senior US and British planners still held the view that such an eventuality was ultimately manageable or containable. In other words, the strategic benefits of retaining links to international jihadist organizations and their primary funders still outweighed potential national security complications, even in the post-Cold War era. After all, as was being seen in Yugoslavia, Libya, and doubtless elsewhere, alliances with ultra-conservative Islamist militants were continuing to pay dividends for the Western powers and were likely to do so again in the future.

In this light, major but nonetheless isolated terrorist attacks, such as the 1993 bombing of the US World Trade Center by veterans of the Afghan jihad, and even al-Qaeda's 1998 embassy bombings which killed 224 people including twelve Americans, were all ascribed to rogue elements having stepped out of line.[139] With President Bill Clinton's administration retaliating to the latter by launching limited cruise missile strikes against purported terrorist installations in Afghanistan and the Sudan, and with the CIA finally beginning to refer to al-Qaeda by its name later that year following the indictment of Osama bin Laden in US courts, red lines at last seemed to have been drawn for the most prominent jihadist organization. But at the same time it was clear that the US had no intention of seeking its destruction or even dismantling. Indeed, while CNN gushingly reported that the US had 'pounded targets' in Afghanistan and the Sudan on the basis that, according to Clinton, 'our target was terror,' the operation's reality was somewhat different.[140]

The Sudanese target, for example, was a pharmaceutical factory that the CIA claimed was producing nerve gas, but a year later the US Bureau of Intelligence and Research published a report claiming the CIA's evidence was weak and requested that the assistant secretary of state press the CIA for clarification. Although no details were forthcoming as the CIA claimed there was no additional evidence, several years later the *New York Times* reported that US officials were conceding that 'the evidence that prompted President Clinton to order the missile strike on [the factory] was not as solid as first portrayed ... there was no proof that the plant had been manufacturing or storing nerve gas, as initially suspected by the Americans, or had been linked to Osama bin Laden.' It was also claimed by the paper that the Sudanese authorities had actually invited US investigators to visit the target site to test for chemical deposits but that their invitation had not been accepted.[141] More intriguingly, the targets in Afghanistan, which included some of the old 1980s training camps first used by al-Qaeda, were reportedly almost empty at the time of the strikes. Although Clinton had described them as being 'the most active terrorist bases in the world', and the US made it clear that they had been seeking to kill bin Laden, it appears that only a handful of militants were killed, and perhaps as few as six.[142] Reportedly alerted to the possibility of strikes by the arrest of one of his aides two weeks earlier, bin Laden had ordered the camps to be cleared, later joking that only a few camels and chickens had died.[143] Remarkably the director of Pakistani intelligence has since claimed that 'more than half the missiles fell in Pakistani territory' and that he had tipped off the Taliban himself.[144]

Published in 1999 just months after the embassy bombings, the US National Intelligence Council's forward-looking *Global Trends 2015* report made no mention at all of Islamic fundamentalism in its 'key future threats' section. As the Council's vice chairman later admitted, they had 'shied away' from the issue because 'it might be considered insensitive and unintentionally generate ill will.'[145] But soon after its release the prospects of more serious blowback from al-Qaeda seemed higher than ever. Known as the 'Millennium Plot', four bombings planned by the group to take place in Jordan on 1 January 2000 were thwarted, as was an attempt to blow up the USS *The Sullivans* off the coast of Yemen.[146] Also planned for January was an audacious plot to bomb Los Angeles airport using a cache of explosives which, according to later US court proceedings, were thought to be forty times more powerful than a regular car bomb.[147] Despite being an almost copycat mission, al-Qaeda effectively repeated its USS *The Sullivans* attack later that year when it managed to hit the USS *Cole* with suicide bombers. With seventeen killed and thirty-nine injured the US response was not, as might be thought, to target the international infrastructure of al-Qaeda or the ultimate backers of the attack's Saudi-born alleged mastermind, Abd al-Rahim al-Nashiri, but rather to place most of the blame on the government of the Sudan. Indeed, a US federal court judge later ruled that al-Qaeda could not have carried out the attack without the support of Sudanese officials and that 'the government of Sudan induced the particular bombing of the USS *Cole* by virtue of prior actions of the government of Sudan.' The court even ruled that millions of dollars in frozen Sudanese state assets were to be paid out to the victims' families as compensation.[148]

9/11 - SAVING SAUDI ARABIA

Less than a year after the USS *Cole* was hit, the 11 September 2001 terror attacks on US soil were of such magnitude that they not only served as an alarming reminder that al-Qaeda and its funding networks were intact and fully functioning, but that the group's central command was by this stage completely committed and capable of serving up increasingly deadly blowback against its former patron. With as of yet unknown motivations, but likely intended either as a grand status symbol to cement its pre-eminence within the international jihadist community, or to serve as a warning to the US and Saudi Arabia over their too-close relations, al-Qaeda's quadruple suicide plane hijacking captured the world's attention for weeks, with globally broadcast images of its deadly aftermath being seared into the minds of an entire generation of human beings. Hitting three out of their four targets, two civilian airliners crashed into the twin towers of the World Trade Center killing more than 2,800, including eleven unborn babies, while a third managed to strike the side of the Department of Defense's iconic Pentagon headquarters, killing a further 125.[149] The fourth aircraft, United Airlines Flight 93, fell into a field after an apparent struggle on board, but most have assumed it was intending to hit either the White House or the Capitol.[150]

With fifteen of the nineteen hijackers understood to have been Saudi citizens, and with veteran journalists claiming at the time that more than eighty percent of the Saudi security services sympathized with bin Laden, rumours naturally began to swirl.[151] Forced into picking the least bad option, the US government quickly publicly denounced al-Qaeda and promised severe punitive action against its former ally. Meanwhile, parallel and very extensive efforts were made to isolate Saudi Arabia from the situation and nudge both debate and policy away from the US's still strategically vital relationship with the kingdom and its other Middle Eastern allies. In many ways this was easier than it sounds, as a later investigation into Saudi–US ties revealed that by this stage 'billions of dollars in [Saudi] contracts, grants, and salaries had gone to a broad range of former US officials who had dealt with the Saudis ... [including] ambassadors, CIA station chiefs, and even cabinet secretaries.'[152]

Overall, the President George W. Bush administration's efforts paid off, with most mainstream media coverage focusing on the apparently dramatic emergence of al-Qaeda and its mysterious cave-dwelling figurehead. Almost no attention was given to the US's historic relationship with al-Qaeda, the jihads both had supported in Afghanistan and the Balkans, or the US's ongoing and active relations with states such as Saudi Arabia whose government-backed organizations and wealthy citizens had been long-standing supporters of the jihadist movement.

Helping further to deflect attention from the key issues were a range of seemingly well-resourced 'truther' organizations, some of which were even able to set up their own television and radio shows. Concentrating suspicious American minds on largely implausible 9/11 conspiracy theories, they mostly dwelled on 'inside jobs', the FBI's purported ignoring of early warnings, evidence planted at 'Ground Zero', or the possible role of Israeli intelligence. In fact, the latter was even adopted by Riyadh as its official position, with the US ambassador at the time having since described how the governor of Riyadh and present-day king, Salman bin Abdul-Aziz al-Saud, had told him categorically that 9/11 'was not the work of Saudis, we couldn't possibly have done this, this must have been an Israeli plot, the Mossad must have done this'. The ambassador also claims to have received the same response from Minister of Interior Nayef bin Abdul-Aziz al-Saud, and recalls how he even tried to enlist CIA briefers to show Salman and Nayef hard evidence that Saudi hijackers were indeed responsible.[153] As others have reported, as late as December 2001 Nayef was still stating that there were no Saudis involved in the hijacking, and even when he admitted there were in February 2002 he then went on to say there were 'big question marks' and we must 'ask who committed the events of 11 September and who benefited from them ... I think the Zionists are behind these events.'[154]

With its priorities clear, the White House had moved fast to save Saudi Arabia as much embarrassment as possible and had even allowed a secret Saudi-bound flight to take off on 13 September despite the Federal Aviation Administration having placed a block on all private flights until the following day. Believed to have had top Saudi businessmen and ruling family members on board, and to have originated in Tampa Florida before flying on to Lexington Kentucky to pick up more passengers, the flight was initially denied to have taken place by the US government and the FBI, but the 9/11 Commission report later confirmed that it had indeed taken place on that day. On boarding the flight, one passenger reportedly told the security guards that he had managed it because 'his father or his uncle was good friends with George Bush Senior.'[155] Asked in a CNN interview two years later if he could unequivocally state that nobody on board the evacuation aircraft had any knowledge of the 9/11 attacks, the Saudi embassy's information officer replied by saying he was sure of only two things: 'there is the existence of God, and then we will die at the end of the world. Everything else, we don't know.'[156]

Since then, the US government has mostly succeeded in shielding Saudi Arabia from further scrutiny, with neither the White House and Congress-organized 9/11 Commission nor a joint congressional inquiry seeming to have provided enough of a 'smoking gun' to warrant further investigation. Publishing its report in 2004 the former had concluded that the CIA and the FBI were primarily responsible because they had failed to prevent the attacks occurring, while little attention was given to US foreign policy or the role of other states.[157] Seemingly providing further evidence of US incompetence are the claims made in the recent memoirs of Michael Springmann, a former US diplomat who once served as head of the visa section at the US consulate in Jeddah and later worked for the Department of State's Bureau of Intelligence and Research. Describing how the CIA had heavily infiltrated the visa section in the kingdom while he was there, he stated that highly questionable decisions were being made to hand out US visas to numerous Saudi travellers.[158] When interviewed by the author he agreed that this practice likely continued long after he left and right up until 9/11.[159]

Certainly Springmann's revelations help confirm the findings of a 2002 report published by the *National Review* which had managed to track down the visas for the fifteen Saudi 9/11 hijackers and had found very obvious evidence that every one of them should have been denied entry to the US. Not one application was filled out properly, with some having put down unrecognizable town names as their supposed US destinations, while others made up the names of schools they were claiming to be employed by. The Saudi who was to become the pilot of the plane that hit the Pentagon had simply put 'hotel' as his US address, while others did not even list their nationality or gender. As the *National Review*'s contributing editor put it, 'I really was expecting al-Qaeda to have trained their operatives well, to beat the system ... [but] they didn't have to beat the system, the system was rigged in their favour from the get-go.'[160]

Two key figures in the Saudi regime also tried to contribute to the 'US incompetence' explanation, with the Saudi ambassador to the US at the time, Bandar bin Sultan al-Saud, having stated in 2007 that 'Saudi security had been actively following the movements of most of the terrorists with precision [prior to 9/11] ... If US security authorities had engaged their Saudi counterparts in a serious and credible manner, in my opinion, we would have avoided what happened.' Similarly, Turki bin Faisal al-Saud has since claimed that when he was the Saudi intelligence chief back in 1999 and 2000, his officers had provided the CIA with background on some of the eventual 9/11 hijackers. CIA spokesmen have stated there is no evidence to support Turki's assertions and no such Saudi information was ever passed on to the US authorities.[161]

Nonetheless, a serious challenge to the official narrative has now emerged, with dozens of senior US politicians, both Republican and Democrat, having begun to press more firmly for the release of a redacted section of the joint congressional inquiry's report that is understood to point to a working relationship between al-Qaeda and at least some elements of the Saudi state. Seeking compensation from Saudi Arabia, a long-running class action lawsuit representing the families of the victims of 9/11 got its big break in 2014 when a New York federal court judge ruled that the Saudi Arabian government was not allowed to claim sovereign immunity, and was thus liable to be sued for damages if the link could be proven.[162] In other words, for more than a decade Saudi Arabia had been shielded from exactly the same type of legal action that had been used against the Sudanese government in the wake of the USS *Cole* attack in 2000. Former US officials submitted affidavits claiming that agents of the Saudi government were at the 'centre of a US-based support network that received several of the hijackers upon their arrival in the US, and provided assistance to those hijackers critical to the success of the 9/11 plot'.[163] Moreover, making two sworn statements to the court that he had seen twenty-eight of the redacted pages from the joint congressional inquiry's report in his earlier role as co-chairman of the congressional inquiry, Senator Bob Graham stated unequivocally that elements of the Saudi state were implicated in 9/11. Other senators such as Thomas Massie have similarly come forward to claim that 'the information in these 28 pages establishes a chain of liability [for 9/11].' At a March 2014 press conference he even stated that the pages were so shocking that 'I had to stop every couple pages and ... try to rearrange my understanding of history. It challenges you to rethink everything.' Senator Stephen Lynch, meanwhile, has called for the pages to be released so as 'to hold accountable those who aided and abetted these savage attacks on our homeland'.[164]

The new openings in the case also prompted the publication of an extensive essay in the *New Yorker* in September 2014 that deemed the twenty-eight redacted pages to be a 'void in the history of 9/11'.[165] Many other such articles have subsequently appeared in leading US and British broadsheet newspapers and in early 2015 a bipartisan congressional bill, House Resolution 14, was finally launched. Sponsored by Senator Walter Jones it quickly attracted more than twenty co-sponsors, and without any signs of the movement losing momentum, and with fresh details from other sources continuing to emerge, it will likely prove much harder for future US administrations to prevent publication of the controversial pages.[166]

In March 2015, for example, a report published by a Congress-organized independent review of US homeland security cited an earlier FBI document that claimed an accredited diplomat at the Saudi consulate in Los Angeles, who also served as a preacher in the city, had 'immediately assigned an individual to take care of [two of the 9/11 hijackers who had just arrived] during their time in the Los Angeles area'. Allowed to return to Saudi Arabia, a separate 9/11 Commission record of interrogation document reveals that the diplomat was then interviewed twice in Riyadh by US investigators in 2004. After the second interview it was noted that the man continued to deny knowing another key suspect despite evidence of 'numerous phone calls' between the two and despite witnesses' claims that the men had met each other on several occasions. More significantly, in July 2015 the lawyers representing the families of the victims successfully appealed for the declassification of a previously secret 2003 memorandum that had been prepared for the 9/11 Commission by some of its staffers. Listing dozens of Saudi citizens living in the US, it revealed that the FBI was aware of two Saudi naval officers based in San Diego who had made 'telephonic contact' with some of the hijackers, and a third naval officer based in Pensacola, Florida, who was 'in contact with at least one of the hijackers' possible associates'. The memorandum also detailed a Saudi suspect in San Diego – a former employee of the Saudi government's educational mission in Washington, who had been earlier described by the FBI as a 'vocal supporter of Osama bin Laden', and who was understood to have received 'considerable funding' from two Saudi royals 'supposedly for his wife's medical treatments'. Crucially the man was understood to have already admitted to an FBI asset that he had had contact with the hijackers, although he reportedly 'denied this in later conversation'.[167]

Soon after, the lawyers were able to add even more weight to Graham's and Massie's assertions after forcing the FBI to reveal new information that was originally withheld from both the 9/11 Commission and the joint congressional inquiry. Through a series of freedom of information requests they determined that at some point in 2001 the FBI had begun to investigate a 'well-connected' Saudi family renting a house in Sarasota, Florida, after receiving reports from suspicious neighbours. FBI agents had found multiple contacts between the family and some of the hijackers who were training nearby, before the family fled the US very shortly prior to the attacks taking place. Indeed, this was the same 'luxury house' which, according to a later report in the local Florida media, had been vacated just two weeks before 9/11, with the residents having left 'a brand new car in the driveway, a refrigerator full of food, fruit on the counter – and an open safe in the master bedroom'. In a remarkable twist, the newly released FBI information also showed that it knew the house was owned by an adviser to Ahmad bin Salman al-Saud, a son of Salman and thus a nephew of the king at the time, Fahd bin Abdul-Aziz al-Saud.[168]

Crucially, according to Gerald Posner's earlier investigation for the *New York Times*, Ahmad was understood to have been on board the secret 13 September flight that left from Tampa, which is about an hour's drive away from Sarasota. Although the prince's well-known racehorse *War Emblem* went on to win the Kentucky Derby in May 2002, his name along with two other Saudi princes was mentioned soon after by a senior al-Qaeda captive during a US interrogation that involved eighty-three waterboarding sessions.[169] Within six weeks of the derby, Ahmad was reported to have died suddenly in Riyadh, aged 43; the cause of death was recorded as being a heart attack.[170] Worryingly, the two other Saudi princes named by the al-Qaeda captive had their deaths announced the very same week, with one having died in a car accident and the other of 'thirst'.[171] An exhaustive review of available police reports, photographs, and media coverage in Saudi Arabia at the time has shown there is no firm evidence that a car accident involving a member of the ruling family took place on the date and at the location claimed, while the 'thirst' incident appears to have been a desert hiking trip that had gone unusually wrong and had involved no witnesses.[172]

In a *Washington Post* article published only a few months after the three princely deaths in Saudi Arabia, and which is no longer available on its website, it was described how a US National Security Council task force had been preparing to 'present the Saudis with intelligence and evidence against people and businesses suspected of backing al-Qaeda and other terrorist organizations, coupled with a demand they be put out of business'. Quoting an official with knowledge of the task force, the deleted article explained that the US's stance on Saudi Arabia was that 'we don't care how you deal with the problem; just do it or we will after ninety days' and that '[we] would press the Saudis to act even if there was not enough information to secure a conviction.'[173]

9/11 – PROTECTING THE FUNDING NETWORKS

As with the mostly successful protection of the vital US–Saudi alliance, the deflection of attention from international funding networks historically sponsored by Saudi Arabia and other wealthy US-backed Gulf monarchies was also largely accomplished, at least for a decade or so. Despite occasional glitches, and some internal dissent within the US policy community, the various organs of the US government allowed the majority of the numerous state-backed charities, aid organizations, and wealthy individuals that had served US foreign-policy goals so well since the early 1980s to escape the aftermath of 9/11 almost completely unscathed. As a critical 2002 report published by the Council on Foreign Relations put it, 'Any [US] crackdown on Islamic banks, charities and wealthy sponsors of al-Qaeda would create a backlash that would jeopardize the survival of the Saudi government.'[174]

The biggest headache, it seemed, was the Saudi High Commission, which, as described, was understood to have been a major funder of the 1990s Balkans campaign, and was inextricably linked to powerful ruling family members. As former CIA official Bruce Riedel has alleged, Salman bin Abdul-Aziz al-Saud had effectively been Saudi Arabia's leading fundraiser for jihadists in Bosnia and earlier in Afghanistan, when his half-brother King Khalid bin Abdul-Aziz al-Saud had chosen him for the role. David Weinberg, a senior fellow at the Foundation for the Defense of Democracies, has similarly made the allegation that Salman was 'in essence, Saudi Arabia's financial point man for bolstering fundamentalist proxies in war zones abroad'. With the SHC having collected $600 million for Bosnia and Kosovo by 2001, a NATO force raided its office in Sarajevo in the wake of 9/11 and discovered what has been described as a 'treasure trove of terrorist materials' including al-Qaeda materials, instructions on how to fake US identification badges, and maps highlighting government buildings in Washington DC.[175] The raid also found a stash of 'before and after' photos of the destroyed World Trade Center in New York.[176] Although the US Joint Task Force Guantanamo responded by adding the SHC to its list of suspected terror entities, this designation was later quietly dropped.[177]

More recently further revelations from the US court case involving the families of the victims of 9/11 have created fresh trouble for the SHC. In the court's proceedings the SHC at the time of 9/11 is described as 'itself one of al-Qaeda's most important charity collaborators, and the theories of jurisdiction and liability as to the SHC rest on its own tortious [wrongful] conduct in directly providing funding, logistical support, and other resources *to* al-Qaeda. The proceedings also pointed to a possible SHC role in funding the 9/11 attacks themselves, explaining that 'since 2005 ... the FBI has declassified hundreds of documents relating to the investigation of Omar al-Bayoumi, a Saudi intelligence agent who provided direct assistance to several of the 9/11 hijackers in support of the 9/11 attacks ... This information bears directly on the theories advanced against the Kingdom and SHC.'[178] Incredibly, in a separate US court hearing that took place in September 2015, and which made no reference to the afore-mentioned US court ruling on the government of Sudan, it was decided that the SHC was to enjoy sovereign immunity from such investigations on the basis that it was part of the Saudi state.[179]

Beyond the SHC, claims were made in a UN report published in 2002 that $16 million from other Saudi sources had still managed to reach al-Qaeda after 9/11. Meanwhile, a little later in the year, even the CIA admitted that there was 'incontrovertible evidence that there is support for [al-Qaeda] within the Saudi government'.[180] A former CIA consultant on religious conflict described this spending as part of the 'largest worldwide propaganda campaign ever mounted', while an independent task force sponsored by the Council on Foreign Relations reached much the same conclusions, stating that 'for years, individuals and charities based in Saudi Arabia have been the most important source of funds for al-Qaeda. And for years, Saudi officials have turned a blind eye to this problem.' Despite the eminence of its contributors, the task force's findings were dismissed as being 'ill-informed and politically motivated' by one of the Saudi king's foreign policy advisers, who is now the Saudi minister for foreign affairs.[181] Citing US officials, David Kaplan's investigation estimated that $70 billion had been spent by Saudi Arabia up to that point on promoting 'fundamentalist Wahhabi' organizations, including international charities. This enormous figure was challenged by the same Saudi adviser on the basis that 'these people may have taken advantage of our charities ... We're looking into it, and we've taken steps to ensure it never happens again.'[182]

By this stage, however, Saudi funding seemed not only to be still going to bin Laden's 'al-Qaeda central' in Pakistan and Afghanistan, but also to a new and much more sectarian jihadist campaign committed to forging an Islamic state in Iraq and which was in effect leading the Sunni upris-ing against both US occupying forces and the new Shia-dominated Iraqi government. Published in 2006, a report by the US Iraq Study Group outlined how 'private Saudi citizens are giving millions of dollars to Sunni insurgents in Iraq and much of the money is used to buy weapons, including shoulder fired anti-aircraft missiles.' Backing up the group's claims, the Associated Press's correspondents cited one-to-one interviews they had held with truck drivers in Iraq who 'described carrying boxes of cash from Saudi Arabia into Iraq, money they said was headed for insurgents'. Iraqi officials were also quoted as saying that '$25 million in Saudi money went to a top Iraqi Sunni cleric and was used to buy weapons, including Strela, a Russian shoulder-fired anti-aircraft missile. The missiles were purchased from someone in Romania, apparently through the black market.'[183]

According to US officials cited by investigative reporter Seymour Hersh in 2007, senior Saudi princes had assured the White House they would 'keep a very close eye on the religious fundamentalists [in Iraq]'. Incredibly they had also told the US that 'we've created this movement, and we can control it ... It's not that we don't want the [jihadists] to throw bombs; it's who they throw them at.' Hersh nonetheless managed to find one outspoken Saudi diplomat who conceded that he was worried about such sponsorship of Sunni extremists in Iraq, arguing that '[they] are sick and hateful, and I'm very much against the idea of flirting with them.' Rather prophetically he also explained that 'they hate the Shia, but they hate Americans more. If you try to outsmart them, they will outsmart us. It will be ugly.'[184]

In 2007 the Congressional Research Service reported that the undersecretary of the treasury for terrorism and financial intelligence, Stuart Levey, had said, 'If I could somehow snap my fingers and cut off the funding from one country, it would be Saudi Arabia.'[185] A year later Levey doubled down on his conclusions by telling a Senate committee that Saudi Arabia was still the leading source of funding for al-Qaeda along with 'other extremist networks'. Hinting that the US had not really been putting the kind of post-9/11 pressure on Saudi Arabia that it was supposed to have done, he also admitted that 'the Saudi government has not moved to publicly hold accountable those within the kingdom who have been the subject of enforcement actions by the US and other authorities.'[186]

More damningly, despite the US embassy in Riyadh having reported to the secretary of defense in mid-2009 that the kingdom was 'part of the solution, not part of the problem [of terrorism]', on the basis that Saudi Arabia had finally started to share aircraft passenger lists with US authorities and had claimed to have tightened up the cash flows of various charities,[187] only months later a secret cable written by Secretary of State Hillary Clinton to other Department of State officials explained that 'donors in Saudi Arabia constitute the most significant source of funding to Sunni terrorist groups worldwide.' Clinton's cable also complained that despite the opening of a Department of the Treasury attaché office in Riyadh the year before, 'more needs to be done since Saudi Arabia remains a critical financial support base for al-Qaeda, the Taliban, *Laskhar-e-Taiba* [another group in Pakistan co-founded by Abdullah Azzam], and other terrorist groups.' She also observed that 'Riyadh has taken only limited action to disrupt fundraising for the UN 1267-listed Taliban and *Lashkar-e-Taiba* groups that are also aligned with al-Qaeda and focused on undermining stability in Afghanistan and Pakistan.' The cable pointedly referred to the role of Saudi charities, along with a 'multilateral organization' the name of which was redacted in the cable but which almost certainly refers to the Golden Chain.[188]

Other extremist entities still backed by Saudi Arabia but not mentioned in the Clinton cable included various groups committed to founding an 'Islamic mini state' in northern Lebanon. Understood to have received training in al-Qaeda's Afghan camps before returning home, Lebanese jihadists appear to have been supported by prominent Lebanese Sunnis who in turn were in receipt of Saudi and perhaps even US funding. Described by a former National Security Council aide in 2007 as having been 'amateur hour', another former US intelligence official claimed that 'we are in a programme to enhance the Sunni capability to resist Shia influence, and we're spreading the money around as much as we can.' Acknowledging that 'the money always gets in more pockets than you think it will' he agreed that the US's role meant that 'we're financing a lot of bad guys with some serious potential unintended consequences. We don't have the ability to determine and get pay vouchers signed by the people we like and avoid the people we don't like. It's a very high-risk venture.' Featured in the same report, published by the *New Yorker*, were accounts of how arrested jihadists were bailed out of jail by such externally backed Sunni politicians, while a senior Lebanese government official admitted that extremists were operating freely across the country because 'we have a liberal attitude that allows al-Qaeda types to have a presence here.'[189]

Casting more light on the situation is another secret cable from 2009, which was filed following a briefing given by Saudi ministry of interior officials to Richard Holbrooke, the US envoy to Afghanistan and Pakistan. In it, the author warns that 'the *hajj* is still a major security loophole for the Saudis, since pilgrims often travel with large amounts of cash and the Saudis cannot refuse them entry into Saudi Arabia.' It also cites US officials as admitting that the *hajj* is 'a vacuum in our security as it offers a prime opportunity for militants and their donors to enter [Saudi Arabia] and either launder funds or receive funds from government-backed charities'.[190] This situational assessment tallies well with numerous reports of front companies having been established in Saudi Arabia to solicit donations for most of the organizations mentioned by Clinton, including *Laskhar-e-Taiba* which had set one up in Riyadh via its charity wing just three years before it carried out the 2008 Mumbai massacre.[191] As recently as 2013, much the same conclusions were being drawn by the Directorate-General of External Policies for the European Parliament. In its report, entitled *Salafism/Wahhabism in the support and supply of arms to rebel groups around the world*, assertions are made that 'Saudi Arabia has been a major source of financing to rebel and terrorist organizations since the 1970s' and that the number of 'indoctrinated jihadist fighters' will continue to increase.[192]

Alongside Saudi Arabia, the extensive extremist funding networks running through neighbouring wealthy states such as Kuwait were also understood to have survived 9/11 more or less untouched. With state-backed charities and numerous powerful individuals in the emirate having been heavily involved in the earlier Afghan and Balkans campaigns, in many ways the 2000s just represented 'business as usual'. In 2005, for example, the US repatriated a prominent Kuwaiti Guantanamo inmate who had been captured in Afghanistan, but then learned he had been released by the Kuwaiti authorities just four months later. He was known to have left Kuwait and then committed a suicide attack on behalf of al-Qaeda in Iraq.[193] The 2009 Clinton cable certainly complained that 'al-Qaeda and other groups continue to exploit Kuwait both as a source of funds and as a key transit point', and claimed that Kuwait had proven 'less inclined to take action against Kuwait-based financiers and facilitators plotting attacks outside of Kuwait'. More speciously, given the evidently massive cash flows moving through organizations in Saudi Arabia, the cable also asserted that 'Kuwait remains the sole Gulf Cooperation Council country that has not criminalized terrorist financing.' To back this point up, an especially problematic Kuwaiti NGO was singled out, with the cable noting that 'a particular point of difference between the US and Kuwait concerns the Revival of Islamic Heritage Society.' In June 2008 the Department of the Treasury had apparently designated all of the society's offices as terror sponsors on the basis they were 'providing financial and material support to al-Qaeda and UN 1267-listed al-Qaeda affiliates, including *Laskhar-e-Taiba, Jamaat-e-Islami,* and [Somalia's] *Al-Itihaad al-Islamiya'*. Meanwhile, with reference to private Kuwaiti individuals, the cable stated that 'our information indicates that Kuwaiti donors serve as an important source of funds and other support for al-Qaeda and other terrorist groups.'[194]

On the UAE, Clinton's secret analysis was not much rosier, with the cable revealing that 'UAE-based donors have provided financial support to a variety of terrorist groups, including al-Qaeda, the Taliban, *Laskhar-e-Taiba*, and other terrorist groups' and lamenting that 'the UAE's role as a growing global financial centre, coupled with weak regulatory oversight, makes it vulnerable to abuse by terrorist financiers and facilitation networks.'[195] This gloomy assessment matched another leaked US diplomatic cable from a year earlier that described how in 2005 organizations in the UAE and Saudi Arabia that 'ostensibly had the support of those governments' had begun to finance jihadist recruitment centres in the Punjab in northern India. At these centres, youths were reportedly being 'indoctrinated in jihad', while their parents had been promised that their children would receive employment afterwards, either as clerics or being sent to jihadist training camps in federally administered tribal areas. The cable's author estimated that about $100 million a year was being sent from the UAE and Saudi Arabia to fund the programme.[196]

Although a relative backwater during the 1980s and most of the 1990s, given its more modest oil revenues and thus more limited capacity to engage in Western-backed jihadist-sponsoring foreign policies, by the 2000s the emirate of Qatar had nonetheless begun to emerge as another key donor hub for extremist organizations. With its natural gas exports having commenced in 1995 and then risen rapidly to overtake Indonesia by 2007 to become the greatest in the world, within the space of a decade Qatar had become one of the wealthiest per capita states in the region.[197]

Moreover, unlike the other small Gulf monarchies, Qatar was the only other state beyond Saudi Arabia in which Wahhabi thought remained predominant, with key members of its religious establishment, behind closed doors at least, understood to be no less conservative than their counterparts in Riyadh.[198]

Perhaps unsurprising, given that all the right ingredients seemed to be in place, there was evidence presented to the US Congress as early as 2003 that Qatar-based charities were helping to launder al-Qaeda-linked money along with 'providing employment and documentation for key figures in the operation.'[199] In particular, a former business aide of bin Laden testified that the Qatar Charitable Society had long been a source of al-Qaeda funding, with its director having helped provide travel documents and other forms of assistance.[200] Later that year the *National Geographic* published an extensively researched essay which not only portrayed Qatar as the second most-conservative Gulf monarchy after Saudi Arabia, but cited a professor of politics at Qatar University as saying that after 9/11 the presence of the US military in his country was 'a very provocative element'. As the academic pointed out, 'It is not just my students who are saying this ... Go to the [market], go downtown, go to any café. The attitude is decidedly anti-American.' Although the *National Geographic* noted 'there are no militant groups here, no radical clerics calling for jihad,' it nonetheless admitted that some Qataris were admirers of bin Laden and described how there was now considerable religious activism in the country with 'Qataris having joined scattered missionary groups known as *dawah* that are proselytizing and actively recruiting, especially among the young, in their advocacy of a more rigid form of Islam'. These Qatari dawahists were to be recognized by their 'long, broad beards and white calf-length robes that are emblems of devout Wahhabi faith in Saudi Arabia.'[201]

By the end of the 2000s, the situation seemed even worse than the initial concerns brought to Congress, with George W. Bush pointedly leaving Qatar out on his final tour of the Gulf in 2008 despite its hosting of US CENTCOM. As some suggest, this likely reflected that some elements in the US government had lingering suspicions that Qatar was not doing enough to stop its dirty laundry from being aired in public. Indeed, just before Bush's trip an inter-agency US task force had made the allegation that an organization called Qatar Charity was a 'terrorism support entity.'[202] Furthermore, as the Baker Institute's Kristian Ulrichsen describes, 'Some in the CIA were convinced that Al-Jazeera [the Qatar-based news network] was the publicity arm of international terrorism.'[203] The 2009 Clinton cable certainly pulled no punches on Qatar, complaining that its counter-terrorism cooperation with the US was the 'worst in the region' and that Qatar had been 'hesitant to act against known terrorists out of concern for appearing to be aligned with the US and provoking reprisals.'[204] But as with Saudi Arabia, Kuwait, and the UAE, no practical US steps to remedy the situation appeared to have been taken. Symbolically, perhaps, a man alleged to have helped Khalid Sheikh Muhammad escape Qatar in the 1990s with assistance from a senior Qatari minister apparently then went on to serve as a notional minister himself and was allowed to remain in his post right up until 2013 when a cabinet reshuffle took place.[205]

THE FAKE 'WAR ON TERROR' – AFGHANISTAN

As destabilizing as 9/11 was, especially for the US's historic relations with Saudi Arabia and more broadly with ultra-conservative Islamic forces, most of the immediate blowback for senior US policymakers was successfully contained. As intended, almost all public blame was effectively and narrowly focused on al-Qaeda itself, which was framed by US officials and in turn by the mainstream media as a largely independent and sovereign-like organization. Rarely were mentions made of al-Qaeda's long-standing financial and material connections to vital US allies or the US itself. Meanwhile, Osama bin Laden was now colourfully portrayed by the US tabloids as an enigmatic global terrorist mastermind busily plotting further barbaric attacks on the US and its friends.

With a clear 'enemy state' identified and a suitably distinctive leader to eliminate, the White House was empowered to respond to 9/11 with what was really a conventional military campaign with definable objectives. This 'War on Terror' was, in many ways, the masterstroke of the George W. Bush administration as it not only helped shift all remaining attention away from the root causes of 9/11 and allowed potentially still useful albeit volatile structures to remain in place, but effectively it also gave the US carte blanche to intervene forcefully in any part of the world where it could claim that al-Qaeda had established a presence. In this sense the White House created a neo-imperial mandate for itself to enter into countries in a manner not seen since the old British and French empires. This would apply to countries in which problematic governments or rulers needed to be toppled in order to safeguard access to valuable natural resources, lucrative markets, or other economic assets. The timing in many ways could not have been better, as exactly ten years earlier, Undersecretary for Defense Paul Wolfowitz had informed eventual NATO supreme commander Wesley Clark that 'we [have] learned we can intervene militarily in the Middle East with impunity ... We've got about five to ten years to take out these old Soviet "surrogate" regimes before the next superpower comes along to challenge us in the region.'[206]

Ticking all boxes by the time of 9/11 was Afghanistan. Not only easy to frame as an al-Qaeda haven, it was also tantalizingly close to the emerging energy-rich Central Asian region. With the previously described Unocal project having floundered as the Taliban proved increasingly unable to quell opposition, US officials were becoming markedly less tolerant of the Kabul regime. As a number of analysts have described, a meeting had taken place in July 2001 to try to improve the situation, with the US bringing the Taliban to the same table as their rivals to try to forge a new national government. The deal, it seemed, was that if the Taliban could come to some sort of compromise, they would immediately receive economic aid. But when they remained unforthcoming, they were reportedly informed by a US official: 'Either you accept our offer of a carpet of gold, or we bury you under a carpet of bombs.' According to former Pakistani foreign minister Niaz Naik, who was also present at the July meeting, US officials had privately informed him that military action would be taken against the Taliban by October 2001. In fact, Naik revealed this in a BBC interview a few days before 9/11.[207] The intention, it seemed, was that if the Taliban needed to be removed, then the rival 'Northern Alliance' would serve as the de facto ground forces under substantive US air cover.

In many ways the die was cast much earlier than just three months before 9/11, and probably before the Bush team had even taken office. Speaking on the imminent centrality of Afghanistan to US interests in 2000, before being installed as Bush's vice president, Dick Cheney had already stated that 'I cannot think of a time when we have had a region emerge as suddenly to become as strategically significant as the Caspian.' Similarly, a report published by the US Army War College's Strategic Studies Institute the same year had made clear the future necessity of US influence over the potentially vast energy reserves in Transcaucasia and Central Asia. The report contended that the region's resources were going to be needed as an important backup to the 'unstable Persian Gulf', but warned that Russian political influence in the region would be able to 'sabotage many if not all forthcoming energy projects'. To avoid such a problem, the report recommended creating a 'win-win situation' in which 'some external factor must be permanently engaged and willing to commit even [US] military forces if need be, to ensure stability and peace.' It concluded that 'without such a permanent [US] presence ... Russia will be able to exclude all other rivals and regain hegemony over the area.'[208] The British press had also made the link between future Russian rivalry and US energy interests in the region, with pre 9/11 reports having identified a proposal for a new pipeline to run through Afghanistan that would massively undercut an existing plan for a $3 billion pipeline from Georgia and Turkey to the Mediterranean. As one correspondent put it, 'Russia [was] fearing that is exactly what the Americans want'.[209]

Speaking in November 2001, just weeks after the US-led invasion of Afghanistan had begun, Assistant Secretary of State Elizabeth Jones effectively confirmed that the real reason for the intervention had little to do with al-Qaeda: 'When the Afghan conflict is over we will not leave Central Asia. We have long-term plans and interests in this region.' Moreover, as Mark Curtis notes of the eventual military campaign, it soon became less about mopping up Taliban remnants and much more about establishing a new chain of Central Asian US military bases that were to form a Russia-bordering arc from Georgia up to Uzbekistan.[210] Although eventually serving as the US-approved president of Afghanistan for ten years after taking office in 2004, in one of Hamid Karzai's first post-retirement interviews in 2015 he told Al-Jazeera in no uncertain terms that al-Qaeda's purported presence in his country in 2001 was practically non-existent and a 'myth'. He also stated his certainty that the 9/11 attacks were neither executed nor planned from Afghanistan.[211]

As a former US client, Karzai's frustration is perhaps best explained by the US's eventual hedging on the Taliban, especially after it began to regain momentum and as the US and its allies encountered much greater resistance than they had envisaged in stabilizing the country themselves. As early as 2004 the Pakistani press had begun to claim that Britain had entered into talks with the Taliban on behalf of the US, with the respected *Dawn* magazine reporting that the US was seeking an 'honourable American exit' from the conflict ahead of presidential elections.[212] By 2008 negotiations seemed to have intensified, with Britain having brokered a meeting in Saudi Arabia bringing together representatives of the various Afghan factions, including the Taliban and Gulbuddin Hekmatyar's militias.[213] In 2012, with the US having stated its intent to withdraw from Afghanistan in 2014, the Barack Obama administration's Taliban policy had effectively reverted back to a 1990s level of cooperation. With an official flag-flying Taliban office opening in Qatar, barely a few kilometres from CENTCOM and various other US facilities, the group's leaders had essentially been brought to neutral ground to facilitate more urgent negotiations with US and British officials.[214]

A Taliban spokesman explained shortly before the Qatar operation opened for business, 'We are at the moment, besides our powerful presence inside [Afghanistan], ready to establish a political office outside the country to come to an understanding with other nations.' US diplomats similarly told the *New York Times* that 'the opening of a Taliban mission would be the single biggest step forward for peace efforts that have been plagued by false starts.'[215] Certainly by then all of the US's contacts with the Taliban were being channelled through Qatar, apart from some bizarre public sparring on Twitter between the NATO International Security Assistance Force and the Taliban's official account, which had been running uninterrupted for years.[216] Since the US's withdrawal from Afghanistan, Qatar has clearly retained this 'Taliban portfolio', although a Taliban spokesperson stated to the Pakistani media in early 2015 that they had also been using the UAE as a 'frequent meeting point with foreign delegates'.[217]

THE FAKE 'WAR ON TERROR' – IRAQ

Moving beyond Afghanistan, by early 2002 the George W. Bush administration had begun to mark up additional regimes that, like the Taliban, were similarly uncooperative and in command of resource-rich and strategically significant territories. Unable to establish the same sort of links between these states and al-Qaeda, the US moved to an effective second stage of the 'War on Terror', with Bush's January 2002 State of the Union address declaring that Iraq, Iran, and North Korea were all part of an 'Axis of Evil' that more broadly supported terrorism and sought to produce weapons of mass destruction.[218] Borrowing from Yossef Bodansky's 'New Axis Pact' – as described in a 1992 paper prepared for the House Republican Research Committee – Bush's target list was soon supplemented by his equally neo-conservative colleagues. In May 2002 Undersecretary of State John Bolton announced his 'Beyond the Axis of Evil', adding Syria, Libya, and Cuba as fellow travellers, while a few years later Secretary of State Condoleezza Rice added a few more to her 'Outposts of Tyranny'.[219] Naturally none of the lists included any of the US's well-documented terror-enabling allies such as Saudi Arabia, Kuwait, and Qatar.

First up was Iraq in 2003, and if all had gone to plan with a new US-compliant government in Baghdad, and Afghanistan managing to stabilize, then it seems likely that the other 'axis' states would have quickly been lined up as sequels. The decision to choose Iraq for this important role was likely multidimensional and driven by the US public's existing anti-Iraq sentiments combined with long swirling rumours of an Iraqi WMD programme and an annoyance that Baghdad had begun to sell oil in euros rather than dollars under the UN-sponsored 'oil for food' scheme.[220] As with Afghanistan's pipeline potential, others have also pointed to Iraq's great but frustratingly inaccessible unexploited oil reserves. Just weeks before the US-led invasion in March 2003, which eventually led to a Western-organized interim government enshrining the privatization of Iraqi oil companies into Iraqi law, a widely circulated British Department of Trade and Industry White Paper, complete with a foreword by Tony Blair, had warned that Britain would become a net importer of oil by 2010 and 'by 2020 we could be dependent on imported energy for three quarters of our total primary energy needs.' Implying strongly that most of this energy would need to come from the Middle East, the paper stated that the Western powers should not only protect existing oil producing states, but they should also focus on 'promoting regional stability and economic reform in [other] key producing areas.'[221]

As with the need to secure Afghanistan's resources, the attempted re-entry of Western companies into Iraq's oil markets and the decision to remove Saddam Hussein's regime can also be traced back much further, and certainly well before 9/11. In 1996, for example, the CIA Iraq Operations Group had even launched a coup attempt. Known as 'Operation Silver Bullet', it was part of an effort to ease pressure on the White House in the run-up to presidential elections, with the Bill Clinton administration needing to be seen to have done something about Iraq. Soon becoming incredibly complex with far too many moving parts, it had failed spectacularly and is understandably rarely discussed today. According to Scott Ritter, the former US captain in charge of liaison with the UN Special Commission or 'Unscom', which ran the UN's weapons inspections programme in Iraq, the CIA's plan involved not only the complicity of Unscom's senior executives but also help from both MI6 and Israeli intelligence. Having seen how Unscom's inspectors were increasingly gaining access to some of the most sensitive sites in Iraq, including bases belonging to the Special Republican Guard, Ritter has explained how CIA-trained Iraqi defectors were being prepared to move in on these positions thus removing Saddam's most loyal units and paving the way for a new political authority, the Iraqi National Accord, which was already being funded by the US and Saudi Arabia.[222]

But with some of the defectors serving as double agents for Saddam's security services, the 'Mukhabarat [internal security] learned every detail of the plan – including the fact that the CIA was linking the timing of the coup with the [next] Unscom inspection in early June'. As Ritter describes, the Mukhabarat even used a seized CIA-provided satellite phone in Baghdad to call up the CIA station in Jordan and inform them that the coup was over, while the Iraqi government announced that one of its Special Republican Guard units had had to be 'liquidated' with all of its staff placed on 'administrative leave'. Given that this was the same unit that the CIA had requested to be off-limits for the impending Unscom inspections, Ritter speculated it had earlier signalled its willingness to defect and that the CIA intended for it to join the coup.[223]

By 1998 the strategy seemed to have shifted to one of building an international consensus for much greater military intervention against Saddam, with limited US air strikes on Iraq being overshadowed by widespread reports in the Western media warning of an Iraqi plot to spread anthrax in Britain, and with numerous articles claiming that it was the Baghdad regime, rather than any sanctions, that was most responsible for an apparent upsurge in child deaths in Iraq.[224] The latter reporting, as Abdel Bari Atwan recalls, was largely oblivious to descriptions of the ongoing UN embargo on goods entering or leaving Iraq as being 'even more punitive than the Treaty of Versailles, as it even included foodstuffs and basic medication'.[225] Within another year the *Guardian* had learned that the unusually intensive media coverage of Iraq was part of a '[British] government propaganda campaign unprecedented since the end of the Cold War' and was being directed, in Britain at least, by an 'Iraq media group' which had the goal of 'blackening Baghdad and preparing [Western] public opinion'.[226]

In parallel to the media campaign, senior Western politicians had of course also begun to paint a picture of Iraq as a determined producer of WMD, regardless of the opinions of international organizations or experts. Having stated in 1997 that 'we do not agree with the nations who argue that if Iraq complies with its obligations concerning WMD, sanctions should be lifted,' Secretary of State Madeleine Albright had already made the US's position quite clear. Similarly, in a speech to parliament in 1998 Tony Blair had explained that 'a broad objective of our policy is to remove Saddam Hussein and to do all that we can to achieve that ... If we can possibly find the means of removing him, we will.' By 2002, with the 'War on Terror' already raging and the Western public still spooked by the al-Qaeda spectre, the opportunity to push even harder on Iraq finally seemed to have come. As *The Times* reported, 'Key figures in the White House believe that demands on Saddam to readmit UN weapons inspectors should be set so high that he would fail to meet them,' while a US intelligence official was quoted as saying the White House would 'not take yes for an answer'.[227]

Problematically, the evidence to support such a belligerent stance was sorely lacking, with Unscom's chief having stated in 2002 that 'ninety to ninety-five percent of Iraq's WMD have been verifiably eliminated' and with the International Atomic Energy Agency director general Muhammad el-Baradei claiming that the IAEA had 'destroyed, removed, or rendered harmless all [of Iraq's] facilities and equipment relevant to nuclear weapons production'.[228] Furthermore, the US intelligence based on information obtained from an Iraqi defector known as 'Curveball', who had provided hundreds of supposed first-hand accounts of Iraqi WMD installations that were then relied upon by Secretary of State Colin Powell in a UN presentation to gather further support for a military intervention, was soon debunked by German intelligence, while the CIA also eventually admitted that Curveball was a fraud.[229] Meanwhile, despite the Blair administration's public message, British officials were privately admitting there was no 'killer evidence' about Iraqi WMD. To make matters worse, a Whitehall source was quoted as saying that the information in a forth-coming British government dossier on Iraqi WMD was based entirely on the period prior to 1998.[230]

A more public obstacle, for Britain especially, was the expert opinion of David Kelly, a former Unscom inspector and noted authority on bio-logical warfare employed by the Ministry of Defence. Having told a BBC journalist that the dossier's claim that Iraq could deploy WMD within forty-five minutes was bogus, he was called before the Foreign Affairs Select Committee and questioned about his comments before being found dead two days later.[231] Although officially a suicide, with the results of the post-mortem originally being sealed for seventy years to protect Kelly's family, repeated demands have been made for a fresh investigation into his death, with a group of doctors voicing their suspicions in 2009, and a British MP who spent a year researching Kelly's death also having claimed foul play.[232] Sticking to their guns, in 2013 the group of doctors published an open letter in the *Guardian* in which they stated: 'We have multiple serious concerns about the medical, forensic and other evidence supporting the official story that Dr Kelly committed suicide.' They also asserted that the Thames Valley Police's investigation into his death was 'deficient and dishonest'.[233] Likely contributing to this conclusion, a few weeks earlier one of the doctors had received a rejection of his freedom of information request to the Cabinet Office to determine whether Kelly had received any correspondence or telephone calls from the prime min-ister or the chairman of the Joint Intelligence Committee in the period before his death. According to the Cabinet Office, the rejection was made because 'the cost of dealing with it would exceed the appropriate limit. The appropriate limit has been specified in regulations and for central government this is set at £600.'[234]

In some ways the attempts to frame Iraq as a terror-supporting al-Qaeda enabler were more successful, even though Western intelligence sources at the time were indicating that the Iraqi regime was actually an obstacle to al-Qaeda expansion and, according to an eventual Senate Select Committee on Intelligence report, none of the pre-war intelligence reports managed to link Iraq to al-Qaeda.[235] Years later even former CIA director George Tenet told CBS's *60 Minutes* that 'We could never verify that there was any Iraqi authority, direction and control, complicity with al-Qaeda for 9/11 or any operational act against America. Period.'[236] Nonetheless a recently leaked White House memorandum from 2002 reveals how Blair had already pledged full British support for a US intervention in Iraq on the basis that he would help to outline 'the strategic, tactical, and public affairs lines that he believes will strengthen global support for our common cause'. The memorandum also claimed that Blair would 'suggest ideas on how to make a credible public case on current Iraqi threats to international peace'.[237]

Simultaneous with the political manoeuvrings, but still rarely discussed, were the US- and British-led efforts to transform illegally the existing no-fly zones over northern and southern Iraq into concerted attacks on Iraqi infrastructure, even before 9/11. At least 28,000 sorties had dropped 18,000 bombs on 450 targets in these zones over the course of the 1990s, with the British government admitting in 1999 that the 'self defence policy' in no-fly zones had already morphed into an 'active campaign aimed at fatally weakening the Iraqi regime'.[238] As the intelligence company Stratfor reported, these air strikes seemed to be 'at least paving the way for opposition activities on the ground'.[239] By 2002, with preparations for the full 'War on Terror' military intervention entering their final phase, a significant surge in such attacks took place, with an Anglo-American bombing mission involving a hundred aircraft striking an Iraqi air defence centre close to Baghdad and thus hundreds of miles beyond the no-fly zone limits.[240] As the *Guardian* explained, 'British defence sources have now given up the pretence that the southern no-fly zone is a humanitarian exercise designed to protect Iraqi Shia and Marsh Arabs.'[241] Also using the umbrella of the no-fly zones, fellow NATO member Turkey had been making its own frequent incursions into Iraqi airspace, mostly to hit Kurdish targets. As Curtis notes, these were known to the US and British air forces as 'Turkish

Special Missions', with US and British pilots often protesting at being recalled to their airbases while these flights took place, and then reporting seeing 'burning villages, lots of smoke and fire' when eventually returning to the skies. Meanwhile, the Turkish army had also been entering Iraqi territory, sometimes with several thousand troops, and by the time of the 2003 invasion there were thought to be even larger numbers already within Iraq's borders, ready to assist the US with its final push.[242]

5

THE ARAB SPRING – A SYSTEM THREATENED

A NEW CHALLENGE, A NEW HOPE

S oon known as the 'Arab Spring', the wave of uprisings and revolutions in 2011 that spread like wildfire from North Africa across to the Arabian Peninsula sparked much hope, both in the Arab world, where anything suddenly seemed possible, and in the international community, which for the first time in generations had a glimpse of a more progressive and even democratic future for the Middle East. But above the level of jubilant street protests and the toppling of corrupt dictatorships, the Arab Spring also represented a significant threat to almost half a century of protected status quo. The largest and most powerful revolts, and seemingly the only ones capable of removing regimes without needing external intervention, had all taken place in states firmly allied to the Western powers.

In this sense, in much the same way that 9/11 a decade earlier had severely troubled the West's relations with extremist Islamist forces and the conservative monarchies that helped to finance them, the Arab Spring seemed poised to deliver a similarly disruptive and maybe fatal blow to its other authoritarian clients in the region. After all, for all their faults these post-Cold War Arab regimes had mostly met the political and economic needs of the Western governments. They had proven worthy diplomatic and security partners for the 'War on Terror' while at the same time consistently supplicating themselves to the multinational companies who sought easy access to their countries' markets and resources.

Difficult to categorize and, unlike most previous Middle Eastern revolutions, with few common ideological underpinnings, the 2011 uprisings were also clearly far from being isolated or quickly containable chaotic events. If anything, most evidence soon started to point to a fulmination of years of steadily building and hard-to-fix socio-economic pressures in states that were increasingly unable to meet the basic needs of their citizens. Moreover, with clear parallels between the Arab Spring and concurrent protests elsewhere in the world, the outward-looking and forward-thinking revolutionaries also seemed to represent something bigger than mere political transformation. As some suggested, they were on the cusp of rediscovering long-suppressed notions of Arab cosmopolitanism, dignity, and modernity that would help place the revolutions more firmly on the 'right side of history', both in the eyes of the region's people and of those across the globe watching events unfold in front of their television screens.

THE ROAD TO 2011 – REGIMES IN DECAY

By the turn of the twenty-first century the entire region appeared socially and politically moribund, with no real alternative to dictatorship and tyranny. With pan-Arabism and Arab nationalism long dead, with Arab socialism and communism a fading memory, with almost no functioning democratic institutions, and with some of the lowest political rights and civil liberty scores in the world, the people of the Middle East seemed destined to remain under the yoke of corrupt and violent states that clearly served the interests of outside powers and businesses ahead of their own citizens.[1] In 2002 the UN's first report on Arab human development had declared the need for an urgent 'Arab awakening', but apart from stressing the need for some serious critical thinking its authors offered few substantive suggestions on how best to tackle or even identify the underlying forces holding back the development of such a resource-rich region.[2]

In many ways, however, people were already on the move. Having witnessed the 'Autumn of Nations' demonstrations and wave of democratic transitions through much of Eastern Europe in the wake of the Soviet

Union's collapse and, closer to home, a contemporaneous surge of popular protests in no less than twenty-eight sub-Saharan African states between 1988 and 1992, which had led to eleven democratic elections a few years later, the Arab world and especially Egypt, its most populous state, had soon started to mobilize.[3] Spilling out onto Cairo's streets in support of the second Palestinian *intifada* uprising in 2000, and once again in 2003 to demonstrate against the US-led invasion of Iraq, the increasingly emboldened protest movement was soon even publicly chanting against President Hosni Mubarak.[4]

Organized into the *Kifaya* or 'Enough' movement, within a few more years secular youth activists had assumed leading roles and, as scholars have since argued, this period 'sowed the seeds of a broader protest culture and helped create a cross-ideological pro-democracy network'.[5] By 2008 such youth networks were firmly at the fore, having mobilized many different sections of society to support mass strikes in the textile industry that had been sparked by low wages and rising food costs.[6] With three killed and hundreds more arrested many saw the episode as 'a dress rehearsal for revolution'.[7] As the School of Oriental and African Studies' Reem Abou el-Fadl has explained of these groups, many of which were to be at the forefront of the Arab Spring, they had 'a rich tradition of protest ... articulated with pan-Arab and anticolonial concerns', while as Durham University's Jeroen Gunning and Ilan Baron put it, the Egyptian events of 2011 'did not come out of nowhere'.[8]

Elsewhere in the Arab world, people had meanwhile watched transfixed as the Lebanese took to their streets in 2005 to declare the 'Cedar Revolution', named after the lush Mediterranean state's endangered national tree. They demanded a new government, one that would be independent and free of external interference. Enraged by a series of political assassinations including that of former prime minister Rafic Hariri, the well-organized crowds represented all religions and sects, both genders, and many different backgrounds. In what would have been unimaginable to many at the start of the year, within just three months the protestors ostensibly succeeded in prompting the withdrawal of over fourteen thousand Syrian troops and forced the disbanding of Lebanon's historically pro-Syrian government.[9] Less than three years later the Arab world was again galvanized, but this time by events in Iraq. Having hurled his shoe at George W. Bush at a press conference in Baghdad and then shouting, 'This is a farewell kiss from the Iraqi people, you dog!', the infamous 'shoe thrower' journalist was merely met with nervous laughter by an evidently frightened and shocked US president.[10]

In many ways, however, it was in Iran that the Arab Spring may have had its strongest antecedents, with Tehran's 'Green Revolution' soon synonymous with the non-ideological demand *ra'i-ye-man kojast*, or 'where is my vote', following the disputed summer 2009 re-election of President Mahmoud Ahmadinejad. Although the extent of the electoral fraud was likely exaggerated, with the international media mostly ignoring the rural and conservative constituencies likely to favour Ahmadinejad, and with a telephone poll in Iran conducted by a consortium of US-based organizations including the Center for Public Opinion and the New America Foundation having found that a considerable majority were fully intending to vote for Ahmadinejad, there was nonetheless something happening on the streets of the capital.[11] As the University of Michigan's Juan Cole has claimed, there was little that could properly explain such a 'vast swing' to the incumbent in the final polls, and a mass pro-democracy movement had quickly emerged that seemingly had little to do with class, gender, or even religion.[12] Indeed, as Hamid Dabashi euphorically claimed, Tehran was destined to become the 'ground zero of a civil rights movement that will leave no Arab or Muslim country, or even Israel untouched'.[13] Although ultimately unsuccessful in the face of stiff repression from the Islamic Republic's security services and its various paramilitary loyalists, Dabashi was at least half-right as Iran's urban youth certainly sent shockwaves across the Arab world. With the largest protests numbering between one and three million, the media beamed back images into Arab capitals of 'young, hip Iranians decked out in green' who were challenging their hitherto unassailable politicians and religious leaders.[14]

TUNISIA – THE JASMINE REVOLUTION

Having sought to separate religion from political power as early as the 1860s, and with a modern constitution in place long before France's arrival in 1881, it was perhaps fitting that the Arab Spring should begin in the historically progressive state of Tunisia.[15] When a municipality inspector closed down the stall of poor vegetable vendor Muhammad Bouazizi and then, by most accounts, slapped him in the face, what was likely a daily episode of public humiliation in the town of Sidi Bouzid dramatically escalated following Bouazizi's self-immolation on 17 December 2010.[16] With unnerving similarities to Jan Palach, the man who set himself on fire in 1969 to protest against the Soviet Union's occupation of Czechoslovakia and whose subsequent sympathizers had eventually paved the way for the 'Velvet Revolution' some twenty years later, Bouazizi's actions unleashed a wave of public dissent, including over a hundred further attempts at self-immolation in Tunisia and several elsewhere across the Arab world.[17]

Having been in power for twenty-three years, but quickly pledging not to seek re-election in 2014, a distant and unsatisfactory three years into the future, President Zine el-Abidine Ben Ali soon found himself running out of options and having to resort to ever more repressive measures in order to hold on to the capital. With two protestors shot dead by his widely unpopular police force on 24 December, the revolution soon spread to all parts of the country.[18] With more than two hundred others killed over the next week, the eventual death of the heavily burned Bouazizi on 4 January 2011 led to a further and seemingly unstoppable surge in the protests, despite Ben Ali having personally visited the dying man in hospital. Renaming a central square in Tunis after their martyr, thousands of students gathered in front of the prime minister's office while teachers, lawyers, and a host of civil society organizations all joined in. Although having largely cooperated with the regime for many years, the General Tunisian Labour Union also broke ranks, especially at the lower levels, with many of its democratically elected local committees rising up and joining the protests.[19] With hundreds of thousands on the streets – far beyond anything the police could deal with – the armed forces had begun to deploy. But having refused to carry out the president's shoot-to-kill order against protestors in Kesserine on 12 January, they had ultimately chosen to side with their compatriots against the remnants of the presidential guard.[20] As political scientist Robert Springborg describes, by doing so the military commanders had effectively become the 'midwives of the revolution' and, arguably, the rest of the Arab Spring.[21]

Likely encouraged by a French minister's offer on the same day as the events in Kesserine to send French police to 'help restore calm' in Tunisia, Ben Ali took to the skies two days later and fled in the direction of France, presumably intending to regroup and return.[22] But with the Nicolas Sarkozy administration ultimately denying him permission to land, having undoubtedly recognized the public relations scandal his arrival would have caused, Ben Ali was humiliatingly rerouted to exile in Saudi Arabia, the only state that still seemed willing to touch him.[23] At the end of January, and throughout February, the protest leaders repeatedly reconvened and, under the banner of the National Council to Protect the Revolution, they successfully pressured the remaining government officials to reshuffle the cabinet of ministers and then force the resignation of the Ben Ali-appointed prime minister. Demanding the election of a constituent assembly and the writing of a new constitution, the revolution was then symbolically completed with the dismantling of the much-hated State Security Administration, along with the dissolution of the old ruling party and the confiscation of its assets on the grounds of corruption.[24]

EGYPT – THE REPUBLIC OF TAHRIR

With already extensive protest networks lying in wait, and with a series of equally evocative Bouazizi-like catalysts of its own, it seemed almost inevitable that *umm al-dunya* or 'mother of the world', as Egypt is known, would rise in the wake of Tunisia. Having uploaded videos to YouTube of police officers doing drug deals, a young businessman from Alexandria called Khalid Said had been dragged from a cybercafé on 7 June 2010 and beaten to death on the pavement.[25] Although he became the nation's iconic martyr, with his online memorial page *We are all Khalid Said* soon a focal point for resistance, there were soon many more, including self-immolations outside the Egyptian parliament by protestors who, as with Bouazizi, felt they had nothing left to lose given the hopelessness of their daily lives.[26]

With highly restricted parliamentary elections in November and December 2010 that effectively removed the last remaining opportunities for MPs to debate properly with the government, the mood became even more febrile. Opposition parties chose to boycott the elections on the grounds that Hosni Mubarak sought the most pacified and rigged parliament possible, while others contended that the whole episode was designed to smooth the path for his much-despised son Gamal to stand in presidential elections the following year.[27] As Stanford University's Fouad Ajami explained, by this stage Gamal embodied the dynastic ambitions of his father,[28] while as Jean-Pierre Filiu claims he had also become the 'living symbol of crony capitalism' in an increasingly unequal Egypt.[29] Having earlier had to rebuff the prospect of his succession and, as a leaked US Department of State cable from 2008 indicates, not considered to have the full backing of Egypt's state security apparatus or the powerful military, it would seem Gamal's plan was for a wholly acquiescent new parliament to provide him with the illusion of support he needed.[30]

Having already witnessed Ben Ali's undignified exit from Tunisia, the tipping point for Egypt came just a few weeks later on 25 January 2011. In a sort of reverse celebration of the National Police Day huge crowds had begun to gather for a 'day of rage'. Chanting 'Tunisia is the solution' along with 'bread, freedom, social justice, and human dignity', demands were made for the resignation of the minister of interior, the repeal of the never-ending 'emergency laws' that had been running continuously since 1981, a minimum wage, and fresh limits on future presidential terms. With these demands unmet, and with the government cutting off the Internet, a second and even bigger day of rage was unleashed on 28 January. Although there is some dispute over how big the crowds became, credible estimates seem to indicate they were within the range of eighteen to twenty-eight percent of Egypt's entire population.[31] Despite sacking the prime minister and quickly filling the long-vacant position of vice president with someone other than his son, Mubarak's measures were deemed too little and far too late. After all, the new prime minister was considered little different to his predecessor while the new vice president, Omar Suleiman, was none other than the former intelligence chief.[32] Within three more days, the 'marches of the millions' saw the protestors escalate their demands to immediate political change, including the removal of Mubarak himself.

Importantly the streets were filled with Muslims and Christians marching alongside each other, with twenty-six mosques and seven churches having been chosen by the organizers as the main rallying points.

As eyewitnesses describe, Christians watched out for Muslims while they paused to pray, while masses were held in public squares and even a secular wedding took place.[33] Christian songs were played through improvised loudspeakers and were interspersed with the old songs of the 1919 rebellion, while placards appeared depicting Islamic crescents embracing Christian crosses. Arriving in Cairo to lead public prayers was none other than Yusuf al-Qaradawi, who made sure to refer to the efforts of both Muslims and Christians alike as crowds chanted 'one fist' in reference to their shared goals and objectives.[34] Most symbolically, perhaps, at least for the teenagers, the singer of the well-known Arabian Nights band had by then 'discarded his usual homeboy outfit and had put on a blue T-shirt claiming he was at the same time Sunni, Shia, and Sufi'.[35]

As for the Brotherhood's regular members, many of the younger ones were spotted 'working seamlessly with everybody else and remaining invisible' as they 'defended, organized, and managed ... from manning the barricades to clearing the garbage'.[36] When even more religiously conservative 'Salafists' also appeared on the streets and began to put up banners proclaiming the *shahada* – 'there is no God but God' – and even the occasional Osama bin Laden poster, there was initially some worry, but when the time came for Friday prayers the combined crowd's chant had morphed into a more pluralistic mixture of 'God is Great' and calls for 'change, freedom, and social justice'.[37] Such an atmosphere had finally enabled even the staunchest of 'secularists' to feel connected with their more religious compatriots,[38] and in this sense the regime's long cultivated binaries of Muslim/Christian or secularist/Islamist seemed to have been greatly undermined. Certainly in their freshly created new public spaces Egyptians holding widely different views on how religious their new state should be seemed willing to tolerate often wildly competing opinions on the grounds of freedom of speech.[39]

Equally significantly all classes seemed to be represented, too, with 'affluent neighbourhoods [of Cairo] like Giza having their share of disturbances [as with] working class districts affected by the growing number of strikes'.[40] Indeed, almost all types of Egyptian workers seemed to be coming together, with everyone from airport staff to agricultural workers all eventually joining in as mass trade-union-led demonstrations swept through the streets from 8 February onwards, denouncing corrupt officials and reaffirming the protestors' demands. Some announced the existence of the Popular Socialist Alliance Party, and leaflets were distributed calling for proper and more powerful post-revolutionary trade unions, while soon after the new Federation of Independent Labour Unions began to meet under their red banner.[41] On realizing that the masses were not focused on looting and pillaging, the middle classes most definitely played a role too, and perhaps a pivotal one, with neighbourhood committees forming to manage, protect, and clean areas. As the journalist Robin Yassin-Kassab claimed, the 'previously snooty were now treating their inferiors with exaggerated respect', while in the words of the *Economist*'s correspondent Max Rodenbeck, 'the urban middle class expected the rabble to destroy everything. When that didn't happen, the bourgeoisie joined the revolution. It was their participation that tipped the balance.'[42]

The protests were also very much about female emancipation, too, with uncovered, liberally dressed women described as 'moving more proudly than usual' even in front of obviously conservative men.[43] Newly organized anti-harassment groups staffed by both women and men were even set up to try to curb the harassment of women amid the protests. As academic Vickie Langohr has argued, on a deeper level these groups also helped push back against the 'insidious discourse' of the Mubarak regime that had 'caricatured women's rights activists as inauthentic Egyptians, more attuned to the concerns of Western funders and international organizations than to those of the Egyptian street'.[44]

In a crude and hastily improvised attempt at counter-revolution the embattled dictatorship focused heavily on trying to drive wedges between what seemed an increasingly united population. Indeed, Mubarak's *après moi le déluge* moment had come: having ordered the withdrawal of the police force at the same time that prisons containing hardened criminals were opened up, the regime had also been inserting hired arsonists and *baltagiyya* thugs into the crowds. Tragi-comically, groups of camel-borne raiders equipped with clubs and sticks had even been cobbled together to charge the crowds in the 2 February 'Battle of the Camel', while more sinisterly protestors reported seeing snipers appear on rooftops.[45] Foreigners were understood to be especially vulnerable, along with anyone who 'looked different', as the regime seemingly sought to blame the revolution on foreign agents.[46]

With several seemingly unstoppable attacks on Christian churches and shrines in the wake of deadly arson on a Coptic church in Alexandria on New Year's Day, it seemed Mubarak was also engaging in a 'clumsy ploy to scare the Christians into loyalty' and thus attempting to divide what was threatening to become an inter-faith or even secular protest movement. Although the regime's security services were still publicly portraying themselves as the protectors of religious minorities, claims were made that they rarely intervened or were slow to do so when such bouts of sectarian violence were taking place.[47] In mosques, meanwhile, state-sponsored preachers were heard giving sermons telling protestors to go home, while the head of Al-Azhar's *fatwa* committee predictably condemned the uprisings as *haram* or 'forbidden' and cast doubt on the 'very legitimacy of peaceful demonstrators'.[48] Also in Mubarak's camp, it seemed, even the Coptic pope publicly called for his congregation to support the government.[49]

Largely undeterred, by the second week of February, the protests had spread to almost all cities and regions, with particularly violent clashes erupting in Suez and the Sinai. But with the focus firmly remaining on Cairo, a de facto 'protest capital' had already been established in the giant Tahrir Square. Named after Egypt's formal 'liberation' from Britain in 1949, Tahrir had both logistically and symbolically become the nerve centre for the final phase of the 2011 revolution. As the prominent British Muslim journalist Ziauddin Sardar observed, the square was now the home for Egypt's 'traditionalists, liberals, secularists, mystics, modernists, postmodernists, believers as well as agnostics and atheists' as it had allowed them 'all [to] come together to demand freedom from tyranny'. And, as he and others have also pointed out, this was not just about lofty ideals, as the revolutionaries also made sure to clean up Tahrir from the debris of the protests, with some even scrubbing pavements clean with their toothbrushes.[50]

Rather than marching on Mubarak's presidential palace, as foreign reporters had expected, the protestors remained defiant in Tahrir. With most of the world's television cameras relaying images of their giant and continuous gathering, the organizers declared it to be a space liberated from the Mubarak regime and thus a 'free republic'.[51] Crucially the new 'Republic of Tahrir' created a physical territorial space for the revolution's ideals and values, which is often thought to be an important precondition for real political transformations to actually take place.[52] Building on this, Gunning and Baron describe how Tahrir had become an 'autonomous commune where the normal rules of politics were suspended' which in turn allowed the square to meet Karl Marx's definition of a transitory organ of revolutionary action.[53]

Ultimately unsuccessful in countering the powerful forces aligned against them, both Mubarak and Suleiman resorted to a final flurry of paternalistic messages, pleading with parents to take their children off the streets, warning that their departure would lead to chaos, and blaming a foreign conspiracy that only they could protect against.[54] Likely fearing a revolution within their own ranks and a subsequent loss of their long-standing economic and social privileges, the Egyptian military's chiefs seemed to follow the lead of their Tunisian counterparts by refusing to open fire on the revolution and ultimately separating themselves from the crumbling dictatorship.

Evoking the spirit of 1952, the Supreme Council of the Armed Forces (SCAF) issued two communiqués to the Egyptian people on the 10th and 11th of February. Assuring all citizens that the military was safeguarding their interests and intended to oversee a peaceful transfer of power, free elections, and an eventual end to the state of emergency, the second communiqué was pointedly issued on the same day that Suleiman had to appear in front of a television camera and announce Mubarak's resignation.[55] Just two days later, on 13 February, the SCAF dissolved the controversial new parliament and suspended the constitution, while the minister of interior was charged with embezzlement.[56] After a few more weeks the ruling National Democratic Party was dissolved, with its organizational secretary being arrested on corruption charges.[57] Having already fled to an internal exile in the Red Sea resort of Sharm el-Sheikh, Mubarak himself was then placed under house arrest.[58]

YEMEN – REVOLUTION IN ARABIA

Although a lot more complex, and with much less clear-cut results than the movements in Tunisia and Egypt, the concurrent uprising in Yemen effectively turned into the third successful revolution. With protests having begun on 15 January 2011, the day after Zine el-Abidine Ben Ali's demeaning departure, they soon grew in size as Yemenis witnessed the apparent early successes of their comrades in North Africa. Egyptian slogans and songs swept through the crowds, especially as Hosni Mubarak seemed to be teetering. Shrewder, savvier, and certainly more experienced than his fellow dictators as he entered his thirty-third year as president of Yemen in one form or another, Ali Abdullah Saleh had ordered a pre-emptive takeover of Sana'a's own Tahrir Square. But by 23 January the protestors had still managed to get there, as well as to other key sites in the capital.[59] Closely mirroring the Egyptians, the Yemenis launched their own 'day of rage' on 3 February after Saleh refused to resign and had instead merely promised a new constitution and to stand down in 2013.[60]

Much like the Tunisian and Egyptian protests, Yemen's *Thawrat al-Taghir*, or 'Change Revolution', was characterized by its largely non-violent nature and the formation of its own transitory organs including 'tent cities' and volunteer 'people protector' brigades that began to encircle the revolution's public spaces. To articulate better the crowd's demands, a media collective called #SupportYemen was also established along with a number of non-partisan grassroots organizations such as Resonate Yemen. Uniting youth, farmers, and workers from all over the country, the protests in Sana'a have since been described by political ethnographer Stacey Philbrick Yadav as having 'represented diverse backgrounds and political affiliations, bringing about an opportunity for interaction that never existed before' and with those involved 'recognising – some for the first time – that they had a stake in defending each other's right to difference'.[61] The *New York Times* also highlighted the role of women in the movement, arguing that it gave Yemen 'a brief moment before women were pushed aside again'.[62] Moreover, as a team of US-based academics have pointed out, the protestors were mostly focused on making national and secular demands rather than the more divisive long-standing demands of groups such as the Southern Movement separatists in Aden or the paramilitary Zaydi-Shia Houthi movement in the north.[63]

Unable to contain the situation and with protests continuing to swell as the weeks went by, Saleh's police force fatefully began to open fire on the crowds. With fifty-two dying on 18 March alone, soon known as 'Bloody

Friday', and with further killings over the next few months including unidentified snipers shooting dozens dead in Taiz, the Yemeni revolution seemed sadly set to take a more violent path than those in North Africa.[64] But with unabated demonstrations and, as Fouad Ajami described, an even greater determination to see the back of Saleh, the spirit of the Arab Spring still seemed to live on. As he put it, 'The men and women who went out into the streets ... sought the rehabilitation of their country ... a more dignified politics than they have been getting from the cynical acrobat at the helm for more than three decades.'[65] Crucially they were not alone, as a string of key defectors soon joined their ranks. Among them were powerful generals and tribal chiefs,[66] while even an armoured brigade commander from Saleh's own tribe made his move when Saleh attempted to promote his son Ahmad within the armed forces.[67] Agreeing on 23 April 2011 to step down in return for immunity from criminal prosecution and then a few weeks later signing a deal with opposition groups in which he guaranteed to resign within a month, Saleh finally appeared to be on the way out and, so it seemed, was the Arab Spring's third scalp.[68]

BREAKING THE FEAR BARRIER – A CHANCE FOR COSMOPOLITANISM

As with the Iraqi shoe thrower and the earlier Cedar and Green revolutions in Lebanon and Iran, it seemed that the people of Tunisia, Egypt, and Yemen, plus those in many other restive Arab states, were effectively breaking through the 'fear barrier' of authoritarian rule. On top of whatever shift in political order was taking place across the region, there was a feeling that perhaps at last the 'social death' of the Arab people was coming to an end.[69] As political scientist Francesco Cavatorta contends, once there has been 'the tearing down of the wall of fear surrounding citizens vis-à-vis their regimes it renders authoritarian governance much more difficult'.[70] Applying this revolutionary moment to the Arab Spring, Jean-Pierre Filiu described how a 'social body paralyzed by autocracies' had been reawakened in 2011 and a reaction was taking place against 'the sterilization of ambitions, the privatization of the nation state, the obliteration of its future'.[71]

189

Although the events in Tunisia, Egypt, and Yemen may not quite have met the conventional definitions of revolutions given that there were no particularly rapid or clear changes in deeper state structures, some have argued that genuine 'revolutionary situations' certainly did emerge.[72] Jeroen Gunning and Ilan Baron have, for example, convincingly shown how Egyptian society had begun to organize itself freely through 'informal networks based on shared beliefs and solidarity which in turn were able to mobilize against conflictual issues'.[73] Most of the Arab Spring protests also seemed to fit firmly within the expectations of the University of Connecticut's Cyrus Zirakzadeh for 'social movements': typically, diverse groups of people from a range of socio-economic and religious backgrounds had begun to come together, including those who previously had no means of articulating themselves through formal political institutions.[74]

As well as seeing societies emboldened against dictatorships, Ziauddin Sardar argues that the Arab Spring was also most definitely a pushback against religious politics, as none of the major uprisings in 2011 could be considered 'Islamic revolutions' and in almost all cases the leading protest movements made concerted efforts to stick to wholly secular objectives. Writing prophetically in 2012, he contended that 'Islam or the creation of the legitimately feared "Islamic state" is not the goal of these revolutions ... Rather they are motivated by something altogether different: the aspirations of all segments of society ... for freedom, social justice, and accountable governance.'[75] Indeed, the people who congregated in Tahrir Square have been described as a 'thriving cosmos of a different vision of society', not only because they held markedly different beliefs, including differing religions, but also because they were able to reach agreement over common causes, even if sometimes it was just 'the fall of the regime'.[76] As Columbia University's Rashid Khalidi claims, this meant that the revolutionary emphasis was first and foremost on the strengthening of society itself and on dealing with the internal problems of 'democracy, constitutions, and equality'. In this sense the 2011 uprisings were quite different to the Arab revolutions of the twentieth century, most of which were focused on national liberation from external rule.[77]

The London School of Economics' Mary Kaldor was equally optimistic when she argued in February 2011, just days before Hosni Mubarak's ouster, that what was happening was the re-emergence of a new and more active Arab civil society that would in turn herald a movement for democracy across the whole region. She explained that 'the people in Tahrir Square and elsewhere are giving us back the meaning of civil society – a place where people can talk, discuss, and act freely,' and she even evoked the spirt of the Eastern European revolutions by contending that what was happening in North Africa was 'the completion of 1989'.[78] Less than a week later, journalist Jacqueline Head joined the same bandwagon by suggesting we were witnessing 'the Arab world's 1989 revolution' and predicting a 'ripple effect' from a 'wave of democracy finally crashing on the North African shore'.[79] In this sense both Kaldor and Head had understood the Arab Spring, or as much of it as they could see at the time, as a continuation of the 'Third Wave' of democratization that, according to Samuel Huntington, had begun with the earlier described 'Carnation Movement' in Portugal in 1974 and had then swept through Latin America and Pacific Asia before reaching the satellites of the old Soviet Union.[80]

A little harder to define than re-emerging civil society, there was also a sense that the new 'Arab voice' of 2011 was also calling for a greater sense of dignity, with *karama* soon emerging as one of the protestors' key demands. As a Lebanese businessman observed, 'Whatever tribe, clan, religion, sect or ethnic group [they] belonged to, citizens asked for dignity before anything else.'[81] Making much the same claim, the University of Maryland's Shibley Telhami argued that the uprisings were primarily about restoring dignity, as until 2011 the Arabs could never 'fully divorce the authoritarianism of their rulers from the Western-dominated international order'.[82] Going further, Khalidi asserted that in Tunisia and Egypt at least, the need for dignity had in effect morphed from being a quest for moral virtues to becoming a political force in its own right.[83] Indeed, the initial calls for *karama* were soon buttressed by a host of other pleas, all for things completely unheard of under the old regimes. Among these were demands for *huriyya* meaning 'freedom'; *silmiyya silmiyya* meaning 'peaceful peaceful'; *adalah al-ijtima'iyah* meaning 'social justice'; and perhaps most memorably *al-sha'b yurid isqat al-nizam* meaning 'the people want the overthrow of the regime'.

Above and beyond the calls for dignity and the surging use of emancipatory language, cosmopolitan ideals were also clearly being expressed by this powerful new collective voice, as the people in these giant public spaces were effectively trying to form single communities as a function of their shared humanity and morality.[84] In this sense the Arab Spring had far more than just a political agenda, as it was also 'a retrieval of organic cosmopolitan cultures' for an Arab civilization that had been suppressed for centuries 'under a dialectic sustained between domestic tyranny and globalized imperialism'. More specific to the Western powers, the people of 2011 had begun to 'retrieve the worlds that are buried under two hundred years of colonial and imperial domination'.[85] Importantly, this was not just about Arab cosmopolitanism, as the protestors were soon aware that their movements were connected to the rumblings of a much bigger and perhaps even worldwide protest movement that was continuing to gather pace. Already wearing '1848' T-shirts and carrying banners referencing the Russian Revolution, the Spanish Civil War, and other pivotal historical episodes, the Arabs were also donning the Guy Fawkes masks first popularized by the movie *V for Vendetta* and then commonly associated with the global anti-capitalist movement.[86]

Symbolically perhaps, during the same week Mubarak fell, crowds outside Wisconsin's capitol building protesting against lack of government accountability and the break-up of public employee unions had begun to chant Egyptian slogans. Vice versa, the Cairenes had begun to copy Wisconsin's slogans. Although rarely mentioned, the Arab street was also adopting many of the same images and mottos used in Iran's Green Revolution, while crowds in Tehran simultaneously gathered to voice their support for the Arabs.[87] Worried at the prospect of such a progressive and secular movement spreading to their borders and sparking a repeat of 2009, the ayatollahs were visibly shaken and Iran's state-controlled media tried all it could to frame the Arab Spring as another 'Islamic revolution'.[88] By the summer of 2011 even the Israelis had heard the 'Arab voice', with hundreds of thousands joining the 'Tent Movement' which was protesting against the rising cost of living and the declining quality of public services. Not only sharing the language of the Arab Spring they also began to copy the Tahrir Square tactics of claiming physical space and then defending their liberated territory.[89] Similarly, the anti-austerity protests of the '15-M Movement' in Spain and then the 'Occupy Wall Street' campaign for social and economic equality owed considerable debts to their Arab antecedents. As *Der Spiegel* put it, there was a 'Tahrir Square in Madrid ... Spain's lost generation had found its voice.'[90] Meanwhile, as the New America Foundation's Anne-Marie Slaughter explained, despite their differences, Occupy Wall Street and the Arab Spring were inextricably linked as 'they shared the same fundamental drivers: a deep sense of injustice and invisibility.'[91]

THE ECONOMIC STORM – ENTER NEO-LIBERALISM

Explanations abound as to why 2011, or strictly speaking late 2010, became such a tipping point for the Arab World. Going beyond the demonstration effect of the protest movements in Eastern Europe, Africa, Iran and elsewhere, some have focused on the specific catalysts, such as the deaths of Muhammad Bouazizi and Khalid Said, while others have pointed to particularly incendiary speeches or incidents involving incumbent rulers and their designated heirs. While all such things undoubtedly played a role, the most plausible scenario – and one that seems to be emerging as a consensus within academia – is that a number of steadily building pressures resulting from deep-seated structural problems had begun to boil over at more or less the same time. In other words, a 'perfect storm' of region-wide socio-economic and political concerns, some of which had been fermenting for decades, had finally all caught up with each other.

Most obviously, it would seem, the Arab people collectively had a sense that their supposed stake in their countries' economies was being rapidly eroded. Suitable and sufficient employment seemed to be drying up, for both the working and middle classes, while inequalities within society were deepening. Egypt's earlier *Kifaya* movement had, after all, clearly linked economic discontent to an anti-regime stance, while Iran's Green Revolution was not just about elections and human rights but also very much focused on soaring unemployment and rising inflation. Indeed, a good chunk of the protestors in Tehran 'seemed apolitical', while many could not be considered part of an urban middle class as often they 'didn't have jobs, couldn't leave, and couldn't marry'.[92]

While most of the headlines about the 2011 revolutions understandably centred on the grand demands made in public squares, the protests were also very much characterized by 'factory occupations, demands for renationalization of industries, and demands for minimum wage levels'.[93] In this sense, at least some of the Arab Spring protestors seemed to have been taking part in the type of socio-economic revolution that Marxist scholars would have anticipated. Using Karl Korsch's terms, by 2011 the Arab World had apparently reached the point in its development in which 'the material productive forces of society [had begun to] come into contradiction with the existing production-relations within which they hitherto moved.' From this perspective old, regressive, or unfair economic policies being pursued by the region's dictators would not only become 'fetters upon the forces of production' but also grounds for discontent, renegotiation, and even revolution.[94] Certainly the particular policy paths chosen by Hosni Mubarak's regime had clearly made it highly vulnerable by 2011 as it had become the 'focus of not just political but also economic discontent, while becoming associated with excess privilege'.[95]

Putting this another way, most of the region's states, and certainly those in which mass uprisings occurred, had long been pursuing divisive and ultimately destabilizing economic strategies which, by 2011, were broadly perceived as serving the interests of foreign investors and global capital ahead of the population's basic needs. At first glance this seems perplexing given the previously described mid-twentieth-century revolutions that brought many of these regimes to power on tickets of anti-imperialist economic nationalism or even Arab socialism. After the collapse of the Western-backed client rulers, the successive presidents of the new regimes were supposed to be building fairer and more equal societies, as well as protecting their citizens from predatory postcolonial exploitation.

With fast-growing youthful populations, and having to satisfy their citizens' lofty expectations, many of these nascent states had quickly introduced 'redistributive social policies' which allowed the new governments to 'consolidate patterns of state-society relations anchored in authoritarian bargains'. In turn, these socio-economic contracts forged in the 1950s and 1960s between the Arab nationalist presidents and their people 'guaranteed economic security in exchange for political quiescence'.[96] Moreover, the 'statist' or state-led economies that emerged suited the political rhetoric of Gamal Abdel Nasser and his contemporaries as they allowed such politicians to preside over popular land reform measures and the nationalization of industries and assets once owned by the old colonial oligopolies.[97] As an added bonus, even though the Western powers were actively trying to overthrow or destabilize many of their governments, the new republics' economic policies more or less tallied with the recommendations being made by most of the international financial institutions (IFIs) of the day. Inspired by the concept of 'embedded liberalism' and the work of British economist John Maynard Keynes, the IFIs' aim was to build on the post-Second World War conferences that had called for countries to balance their openness to global trade with meeting the requirements of their populations.[98] In particular, states were to be left with active responsibility for redistributing wealth, providing social justice, and 'fine-tuning economic expansion and ensuring that incomes and demand grew in a regular manner'.[99] The International Bank for Reconstruction and Development, for example, had been encouraging the Arab world to have large public sectors to make up for their weak private sectors and had been promoting the need for import-substitution industrialization so as to improve self-sufficiency and generate employment.[100]

By the 1970s, however, the Arab republics were not only struggling with the impact of a global downturn and consequent labour strikes and bread riots, but were also beginning to be overrun by a growing state bourgeoisie.[101] Able to enrich itself after gaining commanding roles in the public sector, the new group was fast turning into the same sort of uncontrollable bureaucratic class Trotsky had earlier warned would subvert the Soviet Union.[102] Struggling to fund giant welfare states and maintain subsidies, the new elites gradually started to push the old socialist policies to the wayside as they began the 'mimicking of neo-liberalism' and applying 'elements drawn from a global repertoire of models of governance and social policy'.[103] Certainly, with the IFIs increasingly dominated by Western governments, most of the models being suggested to these states had clearly evolved into recommendations for rapid economic liberalization. On the one hand such struggling states that began to denationalize assets and remove barriers to foreign investment would get some immediate relief from their fiscal pressures, but on the other hand Western and multinational companies could once again enter markets with the complicity of local bureaucrats still pretending to represent socialist republics. By the end of the 1980s such IFI policy prescriptions for the developing world were all part of the new 'Washington Consensus', in reference to the common location of the headquarters of the IMF and World Bank, and their close proximity to the US Department of the Treasury.[104]

With states in the Arab world building up debts and facing successive currency crises in the 1990s, the situation had deteriorated much further, making most of these states even more vulnerable to IFI-provided solutions such as the 'structural adjustment packages' agreed by the governments of Tunisia, Egypt, Morocco, and others.[105] Described in a subsequent World Bank report entitled *From privilege to competition: unlocking private-led growth in the Middle-East and North Africa*, these were intended to transform the private sector into the main engine of growth.[106] Similarly, another World Bank report, entitled *Trade, investment, and development in the Middle East and North Africa: engaging with the world*, had argued that this was an essential step for the Arab world so that it could join the 'new global economy'.[107] In most cases the packages and their follow-up agreements involved removing local labour rights, weakening the power of trade unions, introducing tax advantages for foreign companies, and outsourcing welfare provision to either private networks with regime links or to 'religious organizations' such as the Muslim Brotherhood.[108]

In Tunisia, for example, problematic trade union officials were purged and replaced by Zine el-Abidine Ben Ali loyalists, while insiders were given access to unsecured state bank loans to help them quickly buy up former national assets.[109] In Egypt's case there was a little more resistance to the new order as, after all, Mubarak had often referred to the IMF as a 'quack doctor'. But in any case Egypt was already exporting about a third of its labour overseas and since 1991 had begun to receive considerable external debt relief, in return for promising to 'deepen economic reform' and agreeing to the participation of its armed forces in the US-led coalition to liberate Kuwait. By the end of the 1990s most of the Nasser-era land reforms had been effectively reversed as peasants were evicted from their holdings and seven percent of the population ended up owning more than sixty percent of the land. Meanwhile, further Mubarak 'reforms' had led to new labour laws giving employers the right to dismiss workers, substantial tax cuts for the emerging entrepreneurial and landowning class, and lucrative foreign partnership franchises created and then distributed to ruling party members and other 'crony capitalists'.[110] Such liberalization also helped Mubarak keep the military on board, as not only did most of the US aid flow to its generals, but as a sort of conglomerate in its own right it was well placed to buy up and manage former state assets through entities such as the Arab Organization for Industrialization and the Egyptian National Service Projects Organization. In many cases, individual officers were able to enrich themselves with new business opportunities, as were those retirees who were well placed to invest their substantial 'loyalty allowances' in the new private sector. The new relationship that formed between the civilian regime and the business-focused military also seems to have boosted Mubarak's ability to marginalize remaining opponents, including Egypt's former defence minister Abd al-Halim Abu Ghazala. Tellingly perhaps, whenever the US Congress debated steering more of its Egyptian aid to actual development projects, both Mubarak and the military pushed back hard against such changes.[111]

In this sense, what seemed to be happening to large parts of the Arab world in the late twentieth century was more or less what Korsch had warned against in the European context back in the 1930s, when he cautioned that 'state-monopoly capitalism [will lead to] the monstrous oppression of the labouring classes by a state which becomes increasingly intertwined with the all-powerful capitalism'.[112] Moreover, in terms of the Arab states' international relations and the apparent reinforcing of their postcolonial subordination as a result of these new packages and agreements, the fears of other Marxist scholars also seemed to be playing out. Writing in 1914, philosopher Karl Kautsky had predicted that eventually the Western capitalist states would suppress their rivalries and nationalist tendencies and reach a sort of 'unified imperialism' to allow their collective exploitation of the developing world and especially those regions such as the Middle East and North Africa, where they continued to enjoy influence and benefit from imperial legacies.[113]

Putting this in Vladimir Lenin's language, the new system would mean that any nominally postcolonial Middle East would still remain colonial because capitalism had reached a more advanced stage in which the exporting of finance-capital via local clients would take over from earlier patterns of straightforward trade with colonial administrations. As the rulers of 'semi-colonies', to use the Communist International's definition or, as others have called them 'semi-industrialized dependent countries', such clients would get to stay in power by channelling their 'super profits' into a patronage network to buy off military and labour leaders.[114] They would therefore become an integral link in the sort of 'core-periphery' chain of relations envisaged in sociologist Immanuel Wallerstein's world systems theory,[115] but with the more negative features of vast wealth flows out of the region and with the bulk of the population left unprotected from the impact of unbridled international capitalism.

By the beginning of the twenty-first century, and certainly by the time of the *Kifaya* movement, the situation seemed well established. For Egypt, Tunisia, and most of the other states that had committed themselves to the 'restructuring' of their economies, their elites were not necessarily orbiting just one centre of imperial gravity as they might have done prior to the nationalist revolutions, but they were nevertheless ever more responsive to the kind of postmodern empire convincingly described by the post-Marxist philosophers Michael Hardt and Antonio Negri[116] – one that represented the interests of powerful governments and multinational corporations and which had clearly managed to gain huge stakes in Arab economies and access to their most valuable resources. Based on Robin Yassin-Kassab's description of the new Egyptian elites, they had perhaps become the best example of this, as in his words they treated 'regular Egyptians' as second-class citizens while their own families 'lived like colonialists, residing in gated communities, educating their children in foreign languages and foreign universities, viewing the people as a threatening rabble.'[117]

As for the Western powers, as well as clearly having evolved into Kautsky's 'unified imperial' front, by this stage important changes within their own countries also seemed to be feeding into their increasingly collective Middle East policy. From a neo-Marxist perspective, or in the terms of sociologist Jürgen Habermas, many of these former empires seemed to have been entering a 'late capitalist' or 'advanced-capitalist' stage in their own development.[118] Although still democratically elected, governments needing to ensure continuous growth for capitalist economies in order to maintain and improve standards of living seemingly had little choice but to commit to serving the interests of big businesses and their need for continuous global expansion, while at the same time finding ways to legitimize necessarily predatory foreign policies and dissipate any domestic opposition to the system.

Britain perhaps represents the strongest case of this, with the Labour government that took power in 1997 having made it even clearer than earlier Conservative administrations that its foreign policy, most of which was focused on the Middle East and North Africa, would be conducted on a 'trade first' basis and would encourage capital accumulation in the developing world so that populations would eventually benefit from a 'trickle down' effect. In 2001 this vision of how developed and underdeveloped countries could help each other within a neo-liberal framework was formalized by its proposed 'Global New Deal'. As Chancellor of the Exchequer Gordon Brown stated, it had become an obligation for richer countries to 'open markets and to transfer resources' while in return for this poorer countries were obliged to 'pursue stability and create the conditions for new investment'. With no reference to the promotion of democracy or rights in such countries, and making a mockery of Franklin D. Roosevelt's social welfare-focused 'New Deal', Brown's emphasis on 'stability' was of course another facet of the neo-liberal model, as Western governments and business leaders hoped that politics could be separated from economics in the developing world and that anything resembling debate could be restricted to members of the client elites. Britain's secretary for trade was even more candid, not only confirming that 'we want to open up protected markets in developing countries' but claiming a few weeks after 9/11 that it was above all 'an attack on global trade ... so we must respond by launching a new trade round [and] fight terror with trade'.[119] Unsurprisingly Britain's secretary of state for international development did not have much time for trade unions or meaningful labour legislation in the target countries, arguing that 'by far the best approach is for enterprises themselves to ensure they respect the rights of workers ... voluntary codes ... are often more effective than regulation.'[120]

By 2003 London had doubled down on its strategy, especially in relation to getting access to energy markets in the developing world and thus implicitly the Middle East. In the earlier described White Paper, which had warned Britain was about to become a net importer of oil, calls had been made for the government to 'promote conditions for foreign direct investment through stable financial regimes, transparent legal frameworks, predictable domestic energy policies and predictable foreign investment terms'. Seeking to co-opt international organizations for the mission, it also recommended 'promoting the liberalization of energy markets including through the World Trade Organization.'[121] Indeed the latter had long been 'locking in' developing states, regardless of how poor they were, with various agreements that required their governments and regimes to promote economic liberalization above all else. In the words of a former WTO director-general, the organization used trade negotiations with such countries to ensure that liberalization was extended to 'most aspects of policymaking' related to the economy.[122] As others have put it, the WTO's rules soon had the effect of 'massively restricting the ability of [these] governments to promote policies in their own national interests', and the organization seemed to be actively 'deepening globalization to an extreme form of worldwide economic liberalization that would turn the global economy into a playground for corporations.'[123]

To a great extent the UN Sub-Commission on the Promotion and Protection of Human Rights agreed with this assessment, having noted that 'the assumptions on which the rules of WTO are based are grossly unfair ... those rules reflect an agenda that serves only to promote domi-nant corporate interests that already monopolize the arena of international trade.' It also warned this would lead to a 'veritable nightmare' for develop-ing states.[124] Moreover, from the perspective of development economists, many of the WTO's ensuing agreements with Middle Eastern states seemed to preclude the exact policies that had been pursued by some of the late twentieth century's biggest development success stories, notably the 'Asian Tigers' whose governments frequently imposed strong import controls, taxes on foreign companies, and made considerable interventions into the private sector.

THE ECONOMIC STORM – THE RISE OF CRONY CAPITALISM

By the 2000s, with a raft of international trade agreements in place, with the denationalization process well underway, and with readily identifiable client elites pulling most of the strings, the type of authoritarian capital-ism practised across most of the Arab world was being widely criticized across a vast spectrum of political scientists, economists, and sociologists. With the best retrospective analysis, the Belgian academic Koenraad

Bogaert explains how 'the neo-liberal reforms reflected a profound shift from state-developmentalism toward intrinsically authoritarian modalities of neo-liberal government.' As a consequence of this he argued that 'authoritarianism in the region has been transformed by the ways in which the interests of ruling domestic elites and global economic elites became increasingly intertwined.' Moreover, he identified this phenomenon as a key driver of the Arab Spring, contending that 'what many observers failed to recognize, especially in the beginning, was that the popular uprisings ... were rooted not just in demographic trends and the problems of youth unemployment ... the uprisings are not just a revolt against authoritarian regimes but also expressions of a systemic crisis, a structural crisis of the social order of neo-liberal globalization.' In turn this had led to 'material decline for the middle and working classes mainly due to the loss of income redistribution mechanisms'. Putting it more simply, the Arab Spring was really about 'people being drawn to the streets by the pressing economic grievances and uneven development that are a result of more than thirty years of neo-liberal policies'. Indeed, barely months and weeks before the uprisings began, the World Bank and the IMF were continuing to praise countries such as Egypt and Tunisia for their 'sound economic policies and market reforms'.[125]

Making much the same argument, political scientist Steven Heydemann has described how a sort of dystopia of 'poor capitalism' had developed, while Hamid Dabashi observed how the extreme unevenness that had become apparent, especially following the 2008 credit crunch, had led to the 'globalized disempowerment' of the Middle East and North Africa.[126] Focusing on the deteriorating relationship between governments and the people, journalist Simon Assaf makes the case that 'regimes had [earlier] made a social contract with their populations that promised development and provided a certain level of economic security. This social contract was undermined and weakened by neo-liberal reforms.'[127] This broken deal, as far as development economist Adam Hanieh was concerned, was evident not only in the region's cities but also its hinterlands, as the commodification of rural land had 'increased the precariousness of farmers' lives and their ability to remain on the land [as a result of] liberalizing land ownership laws and rent controls, and integrating rural agricultural production into regional and global agribusiness chains'. He has also shown

201

how this was leading to a massive growth in urban slums as the changes to land ownership and tenancy rights 'precipitated extensive rural-to-urban migration'.[128]

Meanwhile, as the suffering of the people was increasing, the ruling elites seemed to be growing even richer, with the University of St Andrews' Raymond Hinnebusch contending that by the time of the Arab Spring the neo-liberal 'solutions' adopted by many of the region's states had simply reinforced 'new state-crony capitalist coalitions to exclude labour as well as deepen dependencies on global finance capital'.[129] In Hanieh's words this ruling coalition was now an 'upper bourgeoisie ... fully incorporated into international circuits of capital accumulation', while Heydemann saw it as an ever-tightening 'inner circle' of regime loyalists who were able to engage in 'predatory rent-seeking as neo-liberal reforms gathered pace'.[130]

On top of the growing sense of unfairness, others have tried to show how the new elites were increasingly regarded as corrupt and nepotistic by the bulk of the population. The new neo-liberal structures were often more opaque than those of the old statist system and this was encouraging rather than diminishing corruption among the ruling class, which was becoming a 'large scale mafia'.[131] Similarly, it was often the most powerful families with connections to key government institutions, including authoritarian agencies, that were effectively 'taking the helm in pseudo-private activities' and thus evolving into a 'gangster-capitalist' class.[132] In this context, by 2011, any feelings of paternal respect for presidents from the region's youth seemed to be long gone, as old patterns of social paternalism in these states were now 'limited by the predatory tendencies of the ruling clique, a close-knit network of families and clients, which [has ended up] controlling a substantial part of the national resources and the related job allocations'. As Filiu saw the build-up to the Arab Spring, 'the two demons of corruption and nepotism [had begun] to haunt some of the young Arabs, because they feel like outsiders in their own country.'[133]

In Egypt's case, the country's neo-liberal elite was personified by both Hosni Mubarak's disliked son Gamal, along with what has been described as an 'exclusive business clique' that had surrounded him.[134] Many members of this set had been buying into 'Porto' resorts constructed by the Amer

Group, a private developer that had been established by a former public prosecutor. Dotted along Egypt's coastline, these gated communities were seen to epitomize the separation of the nouveau riche from the desperate Egyptian masses.[135] For the poor, meanwhile, the mass housing projects that were supposed to provide them with some sort of basic dignity had also been placed in the hands of the private sector, with Gamal's partners having 'aggressively courted private sector alliances with significant tax subventions and opaque property rights transformations' to get them built. As the population continued to shift to these miserable out-of-town developments the prospect of an urban revolt was not seen as immediate but, as political scientist Pete Moore claims, 'The importance of these [new] political geographies to social movements and perceptions of inequality mounted.'[136] Perhaps most symbolic of the growing divides at this time was the rising discontent over a controversial Egypt–Israel gas deal. Deemed by many to have been larceny, when the crowds eventually took over Tahrir Square they demanded to know: 'Who sells his resources cheap to his enemy?'[137] Put together by retired members of Egyptian intelligence in cooperation with a senior minister and other such cronies, the deal had seen an Egyptian–Israeli joint venture buying up Egyptian gas for only $1.50 MMBtu and then selling it on to the Israeli Electric Company for $4 MMBtu. By the time the regime fell it was estimated that Egypt had lost over $400 million.[138]

In Tunisia the relatives of Zine el-Abidine Ben Ali, and especially those of his wife, Leïla Trabelssi, were seen as performing much the same role as Gamal, with many well placed to become the country's biggest business owners as state assets were gradually privatized by governmental 'secret committees'. Described as 'unelected, unaccountable, and pushing policy through before any debate or discussion', the committees were nevertheless understood to be 'consciously supported' by the IFIs given their commitment to rapid economic liberalization.[139] For those on the outside who intended to survive in business and avoid a 'shakedown' by the increasingly corrupt government, there were little option but to join the ruling party. By 2010 the Democratic Constitutional Rally's ranks had duly swelled to over two million but with 'very few due to genuine conviction' and with 'most of them [doing so] to be left alone'. Moreover, with 'racketeering by the presidential clan in the major branches of the economy so intense' the genuine private sector effectively had to self-limit its activities and stay out of trouble.[140]

Far from exempt, the poorer Arab monarchies also seemed to be finding it harder to bridge the divide between their new crony-capitalist classes and the broader masses. In Jordan, for example, similar cliques formed around the ruling family and key government officials while, in reference to the locations of foreign companies, the neighbourhoods closest to the 'centres of foreign capital' were those that began receiving disproportionately the best public services and public infrastructure. In turn this was leading to highly visible 'sites of inclusion and exclusion ... [that] effectively created different sets of rights and opportunities for different segments of the population'.[141]

As for Morocco, King Mohammad VI had quickly become the country's top businessman courtesy of his 'unholy marriage between power and the world of business and finance'. Controlling the country's biggest holding company, the National Company for Investments, he effectively had major stakes in Morocco's banking, insurance, communications, and agricultural sectors. As economist Naguib Aqsabi argues, this meant 'Moroccans were no longer simply sponsors denied the right to discuss the king's portion of the general budget and to question the source of his riches. Instead, they have also become customers who help to multiply his wealth.'[142]

Though a little less obvious, similar patterns had soon begun to appear in the more indigent of the Gulf monarchies. In Bahrain, for example, an extensive *Financial Times* report has since revealed how more than $40 billion of public land had been sold off to private companies. Unsurprisingly most of the buyers appeared to enjoy close links to the ruling family, as in 2002 the king had already given himself the sole rights to sell off state land. Rather innovatively some of the companies were being sold underwater plots for land that the government was promising would eventually be reclaimed from the sea using state resources.[143] Casting even more light on such murky practices is a secret 2009 US diplomatic cable on Oman. Candidly discussing the extent of high-level corruption within the sultanate as its government sought to diversify the economy away from oil and gas, it details how a handful of well-connected local families 'parlayed their privileged positions and government ties into developing new business opportunities'. It also observed that the government's promises of support for small and medium-sized new businesses had floundered as Oman's private sector instead became an oligopoly with almost all of the big businesses 'owing their fortunes in part to ties to the sultan or members of his government'. Adding that 'as a result, they control conglomerates that operate in a wide array of sectors, from construction to cars, and from manufacturing to hotels,' it also explained that Qaboos bin Said al-Said had a 'kitchen cabinet' of key individuals who were not government members but gave him advice, and how several of these were also the heads of the same business empires that had been benefiting from the privatization of Oman's economy.[144]

THE ECONOMIC STORM - THE RISE OF GULF CAPITALISM

For the wealthier Gulf monarchies with still considerable oil and gas revenues the 2000s not only saw an intensifying of local crony-capitalist networks, as with Bahrain and Oman, but also the increasing clout of their biggest companies across the whole region. In this sense Gulf-based conglomerates that were often subsidized from state coffers and led by mixtures of ruling family members and well-connected merchants were effectively able to operate alongside Western multinationals as conduits for international capital into the Arab and broader Islamic world. Mostly managed and advised behind the scenes by expatriates headhunted from the best-performing London and New York firms, their indigenous chief executive officers were able to emerge as the successful Arab faces of the Washington Consensus and Britain's Global New Deal.

Although most commonly associated with their giant sovereign wealth funds, most of which spent the twentieth century investing hydrocarbon surpluses into Western treasuries and blue-chip stocks, some of the Gulf states had also long been identified as potential investment allies in the Middle East itself, especially in tricky-to-access areas for the multinationals.[145] US planners, for example, had already envisaged such a role for Saudi companies, with earlier secret embassy cables having discussed proposals for Saudi Arabia to participate more fully in the work of the IFIs and to help get its officials some voting rights. Among the recommendations was the provision of 'creative suggestions for channelling Saudi resources into intermediate level developing states in combination with US technology and know-how and [the assigning of] additional embassy personnel, including an officer who could devote full time to financial matters'. Joint ventures between US and Saudi companies were also encouraged, especially in the petrochemicals sector and, as a sort of side benefit for the US government, any surplus Saudi revenues were expected to be used to 'help meet the capital shortage in the US'. In something of a parallel to the earlier described arms trade, in which Saudi oil profits were already being recycled back to the West in the form of substantial weapons purchases, the cable called for the new capitalist kingdom to purchase treasury bonds and long-term assets in the US rather than just paper money.[146]

While Saudi petrochemical companies, along with finance houses and telecommunications providers, soon became household names across the region, in more recent years it was perhaps the UAE's wealthiest emirate of Abu Dhabi that became the most creative example of such state-led 'Gulf capitalism'.[147] With a range of government-backed or ruling-family-owned corporations having used injections of oil-derived sovereign wealth to establish relationships with dozens of leading international companies, the resulting joint ventures went on to penetrate dozens of other markets and resource-rich states including 'frontier economies' stretching from West Africa to South-East Asia that had previously been off limits to Western investors.[148]

In terms of the IFI-endorsed neo-liberal charge, however, it was undoubtedly the model adopted by the UAE's second emirate of Dubai that was to become the real poster boy for the Arab world. With a long history as one of the region's premier 'free ports' courtesy of its laissez-faire attitudes and business-friendly reputation, its major conglomerates were soon investing wherever they could in the Middle East and then far beyond. Leveraging Dubai's experience and expertise in ports and communications, they took control of dozens of foreign shipping and trade facilities and, following a bout of property ownership relaxations at home and a subsequent real estate boom, they quickly took their newfound skills on the road too. By the time of the 2008 credit crunch Dubai's biggest developers such as Emaar and Nakheel were synonymous with high-end, foreign-investment-focused real estate projects in almost every Arab state. Moreover, with teams of British advisers having long since helped Dubai's ruling al-Maktoum family pioneer the concept of Middle Eastern export processing zones, by the 2000s the emirate was turning into a base for dozens of low tax, sector-specific 'free zones' that allowed companies from all over the world to gain an easy foothold in the region's markets. Ranging from basic manufacturing and foodstuffs to Internet services and media, they soon branched out into healthcare tourism and even a 'Knowledge Village' for foreign universities to come and set up campuses.[149] As expected, other states attempted to follow the same path, with Jordan's Aqaba Special Economic Zone adopting most of the Dubai model, and several others being launched in Egypt, Morocco, and Oman.[150]

Barely affecting the lives of regular citizens in most of these states, many of the gated and out-of-bounds special zones and property developments were regarded as little more than enclaves of Gulf and international capital. By the time of the Arab Spring any promises of technology transfer to domestic economies or at least some improvement in overall standards of living did not seem to have materialized. If anything, those dwelling in the old Arab cities beyond the fences of the shiny new constructions seemed much worse off than before. The effect of Gulf capital had become one of 'accentuating the uneven development of the region as a whole – one in which Gulf capital is both a prime mover as well as a prime beneficiary' while, with regard to the new rules and authorities that were often created for the special zones, the Gulf's neo-liberal strategies had led to national territories becoming ever more uneven political spaces.[151]

In many ways this increasing imbalance in the Arab world was best symbolized by a catchy and controversial article penned two years after the Arab Spring by UAE journalist Sultan al-Qassemi. Entitled *Thriving gulf cities emerge as new centres of the Arab world*, it provoked a maelstrom of reaction across the region and especially from those dwelling in ancient but impoverished cities such as Cairo and Baghdad. With the article's main points being clear and largely uncontestable, focusing on the Gulf's massive GDP vis-à-vis the rest of the Arab world and its new-found ability to engage in a 'cultural renaissance' by buying in expensive foreign museums and universities, al-Qassemi described colourfully how 'decades of underinvestment and full-blown civil wars have resulted in the historic Arab cities of North Africa and the Levant having poor and inadequate infrastructure, from archaic roads to outdated academic curricula and teaching methods.'[152]

FROM MODERNIZING ARABS TO REVOLUTIONARY ARABS

In parallel to the build-up of socio-economic pressures, the increasing unevenness accentuated by decades of untamed economic liberalization, and the arrival of Gulf capitalism, compelling arguments have been made that by 2011 the Arab world was also beginning to experience the impact of particularly powerful new 'modernizing forces' that had begun to combine with more slow-burning, pre-existing ones such as urbanization and education. As historian Alexis de Tocqueville had already observed during his tour of the United States in the 1830s in search of 'the secret of democracy', real political maturity only seemed possible if a new 'mass society' could form on top of an increasingly urban, educated class that had the tools and opportunity to build civil society organizations.[153]

In some ways, Tocqueville's theory was soon to tally with Karl Marx's thoughts, as the latter agreed that the masses would never be able to rise up in proletarian revolution if their country was too backward.[154] Pushing this further, and as a strong portent of twentieth-century scholarship, Friedrich Engels had also argued that 'wherever the power structure of a country contradicts its economic development even politicians with the capacity to repress would eventually fail.'[155] Still more or less in line with Marx, by 1959 sociologist Seymour Martin Lipset had asserted that the wealthier a nation became, and the more its population was exposed to modernizing forces, then the better would be its chances of sustaining democratic institutions.[156] Similarly, the following year, political scientist Karl Deutsch packaged these forces and processes under his 'theory of social mobilization', stressing both their cumulative impact and their inevitable or extremely likely capacity to transform political behaviour.[157] Published in 1968, Samuel Huntington's landmark *Political Order in Changing Societies* contended there would even be a 'law of rising politicization' and that a 'king's dilemma' would inevitably be faced by traditional rulers and governments, most of which would find it difficult to maintain power in the face of economic development and a modernizing society.[158] Meanwhile, on the Middle East itself, economist Daniel Lerner had already predicted in his *The Passing of Traditional Society: Modernizing of the Middle East* that most of the region's societies would pass through a series of distinct phases beginning with urbanization and then proceeding through literacy and mass communication before eventually reaching political participation.[159]

By this time, however, the realities of the Cold War and the increasing interest of the Western powers in managing the economic and political affairs of large tracts of the developing world were already leading to the subversion of so-called 'modernization theory'. Having latched on to its usefulness, special adviser Walt Rostow made it quite clear to the John F. Kennedy administration that if former imperial colonies and other poorer countries could experience Western-style socio-economic development under US tutelage then their modernizing populations would be more likely to resist communist revolutions or the crude type of 'national libera-tion wars' understood to be sought by Nikita Khrushchev.[160] In this sense a more academic and long-term US strategy was forming that could perhaps eventually reduce the need for the US's heavy-handed counter-insurgency operations. As Weldon Matthews notes, the US was particularly keen on building up foreign militaries as their partners in modernization, as these would allow the US to 'work with authoritarian regimes as their societies passed through a fragile transition, after which democracy could emerge' or, in Rostow's words, after which people could enjoy 'increasing degrees of freedom'.[161]

Still primarily focused on imperialist tactics for ensuring order in its former possessions, the British government nonetheless also soon began to make Rostow-style references to modernizing 'guardian regimes'. In Foreign Office statements during the Oman war, for example, officials not only defended the government's role on the basis that it was 'provid-ing assistance to the Sultan of Oman, a sovereign state with which we enjoy friendly relations, against a professionally-organized and externally supported armed subversive movement which threatens the stability of the area', but also on the grounds that 'under the present sultan, Oman is making great social and economic advances for the benefit of the people and [the British government] believe it is right to give this development every encouragement'.[162]

Since then numerous US and British government documents have continued to stress the need for such modernization, but in almost all cases linking it to Western norms of development and the prescriptions of the Washington Consensus and the Global New Deal. Recent academic scholarship has for the most part joined suit, with, for example, Dietrich Rueschmeyer et al's influential *Capitalist Development and Democracy* having even tried to demonstrate an explicit link between international capital and political modernization on the basis that capitalism's factories increase urbanization, thus bringing people together and creating better conditions for civil society to form.[163] Others, however, have still tried to approach modernization from a class-based perspective, contending that the increasingly conscious populations of Arab states seemed to be approaching a situation where some form of struggle or contest with elites was necessary, otherwise more simplistic revolutions or coups d'état would just see political entrepreneurs manipulating mass mobilization while class structures remained unaltered.[164]

Cautioning against placing too much weight on modernization theory, or at least the role of economic development, Brandeis University's Eva Bellin has noted that four decades of research on democratization reveals there is still little economic determinism governing democratic transitions, with plenty of examples of 'materially inhospitable' poverty-stricken countries transitioning to democracy courtesy of good leadership, while plenty of relatively well-developed states have sustained authoritarian regimes long after what may seem their sell-by dates.[165] Moreover, as others have warned, there is a danger of both scholars and governments framing modernization in an orientalist context that requires traditional societies to somehow 'catch up' with Western standards.[166] In this sense, proponents of economic-focused modernization theory may be accused of keeping the Arab world in a postcolonial state, with both its regimes and very often its oppositions having been urged to focus on pedestalized Western models and objectives.

COSMOPOLITAN COMMUNICATIONS – FROM SATELLITES TO SOCIAL MEDIA

The wildly differing levels of socio-economic development of the states experiencing Arab Spring revolutions in 2011 at first seem to confirm the suspicions of a divided academia and a sceptical commentariat. Although most of the commonly used indicators only ever tell us part of the story about countries' development, they at least tell us something. With a GDP per capita of around $10,000 and an adult male literacy rate of nearly ninety percent in 2010, the middle-income and well-educated Tunisian people who were the first to revolt seemed to tick at least some of the boxes that Daniel Lerner and Samuel Huntington would have expected to see ticked, while the preceding decade of rampant neo-liberal reforms under Zine el-Abidine Ben Ali also seemed to validate the capitalist expectations of Dietrich Rueschmeyer *et al*. Egypt on the other hand seemed to have some of the characteristics of a more modern population capable of demanding political reform, but yet still had vast chunks of its population living in impoverished and rural circumstances. Although estimated to have a GDP per capita of about $6,600 and a literacy rate of eighty percent on the eve of the revolution, the yawning disparities between the ultra-modern and the very traditional among its eighty million people will likely never be known. As for Yemen, apart from a small minority living in the biggest cities, most of its citizens sadly seemed as distant as ever from the sort of standards expected by modernization theorists, with a GDP per capita of only $1,300 and a literacy rate of just sixty-six percent in 2010.[167]

Nonetheless, what does seem to have been a common modernizing thread linking most of the Middle East and North Africa over the past few years is the rise of increasingly powerful communications technologies. Earlier modernizing forces such as access to newspapers, radios, televisions, and mobile phones have of course all been considered important drivers behind the growth of a more informed civil society and ultimately demands for political reform. But under most of the authoritarian regimes in the Arab world many of these forms of communication were also seen as double-edged swords as states soon proved able to censor problematic media and to control and sponsor their own, more compliant media. Even in the early days of the Internet an argument can be made that most of the Arab governments were actually able to increase their control over the population, as critical web pages could be blocked while emails and other personal communications could be intercepted and read. As the University of California's Babak Rahimi puts it, the Internet at this time was not necessarily liberating but rather 'obfuscating and depoliticizing of activism in the true sense ... it is not characterized by revolutionary empowerment, but by loss of power and, at worst, state control over citizens.'[168] Indeed, as Jean-Pierre Filiu observed of the Arab world, 'All the regimes had understood over the years that close monitoring of the Internet was far more efficient than its brutal prohibition.'[169] Certainly few rulers ever shut off the Internet for long, with Syria's Bashar al-Assad only ever doing so on a temporary basis, and Hosni Mubarak only attempting it after more than a fortnight of escalating protests.[170]

More sophisticated strategies have included the setting up of 'honeypot' websites to lure citizens into handing over passwords, while cyber cafés have been routinely installed with keyboard loggers. Smartphones, too, have been targeted, ranging from the crude sending out of pro-government messages to protestors in Egypt, Oman, and Libya during 2011, to the installing of spyware on users' devices, most famously on BlackBerry handsets so as to crack its encrypted messaging service.[171] For the Gulf monarchies and other states with plenty of resources, their intelligence agencies have also been able to spend heavily on military-grade software to allow 'deep packet inspection' of web traffic. In Bahrain, for example, a research team from the University of Toronto made the allegation that it had found traces of British-made spyware on activists' computers, while after Mubarak's ouster it was discovered that the same company had also been making sales pitches to Egyptian intelligence.[172] More recently, following a hack on an Italian cyber security firm, the company's records revealed that its 'lawful interception' and 'offensive technology' products were being marketed to many of the most repressive regimes in the world. The leaked documents indicated that the company had contracts with Saudi Arabia, Bahrain, the UAE, and a number of other states in the region, while the University of Toronto team made the allegation that it had found evidence of its spyware on the computers of targeted Moroccan media organizations and UAE human rights activists.[173] Incredibly the leaks also detailed how at one point the Saudi intelligence chief had even considered buying the company outright for $42 million.[174]

On the eve of the Arab Spring, however, there seemed to be at least two forms of communication that were both in very widespread use and were proving almost impossible for regimes to co-opt or censor. One of these, satellite television, was of course not a new technology, with the Arab world's most watched Al-Jazeera channel having been established some fifteen years earlier. As US political scientist Marc Lynch claimed

212

of the Qatar-based network in his *Voices of the New Arab Public*, it was the region's first major media platform that had seriously discussed the notions of political reform, democracy, and social justice, while as Chatham House's Nadim Shehadi noted, it had already been successfully challenging the narratives of both terrestrial state-controlled television networks and the Western media.[175] But it was in the years immediately prior to the Arab Spring that Al-Jazeera had really begun to take off, with its reach and resources truly mushrooming after being assigned a colossal annual budget of $650 million, and with an English-language offshoot helping to universalize its message even further.[176] Its finest hour, it seemed, had come during the Egyptian protests when brave correspondents in almost cut-off cities such as Suez continued to file their reports. Talking directly to protestors on the ground and relaying their reports back to a rapidly growing regional and global audience, their coverage provided what some have called 'electrifying proof of the scale of the uprising'.[177] Even the English-language version was booming, with its twenty-four-hour dedication to live-streaming the events in Cairo increasing its viewing figures by over 2,500 percent.[178] Beyond Egypt, the *New York Times* soon insisted that 'the protests rocking the Arab world this week have one thread uniting them: Al-Jazeera ... whose aggressive coverage has helped propel insurgent emotions from one capital to the next', while Lynch reasoned that 'it's almost impossible to imagine all this happening without Al-Jazeera.'[179]

The other form of communication that really seems to have made a difference is social media, but as yet its true impact has proven difficult to measure. As part of a second wave of Internet technologies allowing people to move away from the old easy-to-censor platforms to much broader-based peer-to-peer networking that can more easily connect larger sections of the population and spread 'viral' messages, social media websites and applications such as Facebook and Twitter have certainly taken their fair share of the credit for igniting and sustaining the 2011 revolutions. With apparently millions in countries such as Tunisia and Egypt able to access each other's thoughts and instructions at the click of a button and, perhaps equally importantly, able to liaise virtually with millions more across the region and indeed the world, the technology's power and potential seemed to fit well with the notion of 'cosmopolitan communications' put forward just two years earlier by the University of Michigan's Ronald Inglehart and

213

Harvard University's Pippa Norris. Although their emphasis was really on the impact of such global communications on cultural diversity, the study nonetheless clearly demonstrated the potential for such technologies to take their users far beyond their local communities and even the 'firewalls' of nation states.[180]

With some describing it as 'digitally enabled democratization' while others have pointed to how it 'irreversibly narrowed the bounds of acceptable state behaviour in the Arab world, even in the most authoritarian states', the technology's revolutionary role arguably attracted more attention than satellite television and of course much more than the region's less glitzy but steadily building socio-economic pressures.[181] In some ways social media as a protest tool was not quite new to the region, with even the Egyptian strikes of 2008 and the associated '6 April Movement' having spawned a popular Facebook page. In Iran, too, the Green Revolution had also taken to cyberspace with Twitter thought by many to have served as a particularly powerful organizing platform. Although officially blocked by the government, young Iranians were still able to access it using 'virtual private networks' and, as some have claimed, it quickly became a 'citizen-fuelled news bureau of video reports filed straight from the streets of Tehran, unfiltered'.[182] Most notably after the street murder of the young female student Neda Agha-Soltan – which the Western media reported to have been committed by regime thugs – her pictures and videos were all over the Internet within minutes, appearing to galvanize the movement even further. Remarkably, at the height of the protests it was reported that the US Department of State had contacted Twitter to ask it to delay a scheduled upgrade so that Iranians using the service would face no interruption.[183]

Fairly or not, the 2011 Egyptian revolution soon became synonymous with Facebook, with a reinvigorated 6 April Movement page having been joined by the popular 'We are all Khalid Said' commemoration page. Set up by Google marketing executive Wael Ghonim, the latter served as an important case study in his eventual bestseller *Revolution 2.0*, which in many ways heralded the arrival of social media in politics. Reviewed by the *Daily Telegraph*, it was described as delivering 'lessons in thoroughly modern revolution'.[184] As in Iran, Twitter also proved powerful, but in an even more innovative way, with the 'hashtag' #Jan25 allowing users all over the world to follow live-streaming events on the ground in Tahrir

Square. With tweets in both Arabic and English it arguably gave birth to the phenomenon of 'hashtag graffiti', as activists involved in almost all significant political events around the world since then have crafted their own similar tags. Bringing everything together, and in something of another Egyptian innovation, was a 'media camp' set up in the heart of Tahrir. Described by one activist as being 'two tents with laptops, memory readers, and hard disks', he explained that 'we had all the physical means with us and we hung a sign in Arabic and English on the tent itself saying [it was a] focal point to gather videos and pictures from people in the street.' He claimed they 'received a huge amount of videos and pictures and then we [went] back online and kept posting them.' As the coordinator of Cambridge University's digital humanities project recalled of her visit to Tahrir at the time, it was 'one of the most self-consciously mediated spaces' she had ever entered.[185]

In Tunisia there were many close parallels, with the seemingly pivotal role played by social media later symbolized by the appointment of a thirty-something former blogger as the country's minister for youth and sports.[186] Allowing for links to longer-form protest essays to circulate, the new platforms also effectively brought to an end the era of Tunisian 'heroic solo blogger-activists' and replaced them with more collaborative and much more widely read projects put together by teams of activists and citizen journalists who were collectively less vulnerable to regime intimidation. As US political scientist David Faris notes of Tunisia and the rest of the Arab world at this time, 'the flames of dissent were being carried by outfits that look much more like digital magazines than blogs.'[187] Among the new social media-driven publications in Egypt was *Mada Masr*, which soon covered its costs with commercial advertising and, in an effort to expand readership further, often included sections on lifestyle and culture as well as politics. Others, such as *Rassad News Network*, even experimented with paid subscriptions.[188]

Crucially even simple tweets and basic Facebook posts were often being posted in both Arabic and English, with either translators doubling up as activists or with some using early versions of online translation tools. Bilingual Tweeters overseas also played a role, with some such as the UAE-based Sultan al-Qassemi making a name for himself while virtually live-tweeting English versions of Mubarak's final speeches. In many cases they even served as bridges to mainstream Western media, especially for news outlets unable to get their correspondents into the revolutionary states. One thing was for sure: any notion that social media was going to be an overwhelmingly Westernizing force that would eventually shift large chunks of the world's population towards English seemed thoroughly debunked by the Arab Spring, as there was an undoubted surge in the use of online Arabic.[189] In fact, if one was trying to follow events on the ground relying only on English sources then there were often delays of several hours or even more than a day before being able to learn about key events. More broadly, perhaps, this also pointed to a resurgent modern standard Arabic, as well as the survival of more vernacular versions, as social media users from Morocco to Saudi Arabia were not only learning how to link up with each other, but were sometimes even teaching each other how best to use the more cosmopolitan version of their language. As Filiu puts it, the Arab Spring youth had become the 'first generation to experience and speak a truly popular Arabic after centuries of elitist and religion-oriented teaching'.[190]

Further to social media's new-found translatory functions, many have also pointed to its role in the mass distribution of Arabic versions of the 'Wikileak' cables based on secret US diplomatic correspondences. First posted online only weeks before the revolutions began, a large number of the documents emanated from US embassies in Arab capitals and often featured detailed and unflattering assessments of Arab leaders and their governments. The quickly produced and far more accessible Arabic translations of the leaks thus became political dynamite in the hands of well-connected activists, with Stirling University's Muhammad Idrees Ahmad pointing out that it was the evident 'blurring of diplomatic and clandestine functions [of the Arab governments] ... some of which verged on criminality' that caught most of the public's attention.[191]

Arguably a direct catalyst for the entire Arab Spring, one such leak that had appeared in the Arabic daily *Al-Akhbar* on 7 December 2010 caused the Tunisian authorities to block access to it online, thus prompting almost every Tunisian with Internet access to find it and share it using Facebook and Twitter. Dating from the year before, the cable in question included the US ambassador's description of the Zine el-Abidine Ben Ali regime as having 'lost touch with the Tunisian people' and 'increasingly relying on the police for control and focus on preserving power'. To make matters worse, the ambassador had also alleged there was corruption within the first lady's Trabelssi family, and had remarked that the 'risks to the regime's long-term stability are increasing'. Most colourfully, the cable even revealed how Ben Ali's son-in-law was serving dinners 'with ice cream and frozen yoghurt brought in by private plane from St. Tropez', and that he owned a pet tiger that was fed four chickens a day. When Ben Ali finally fled, many Tunisians suggested it was the combination of Wikileaks, *Al-Akhbar*, and social media that had 'drawn first blood'. In Egypt, media activists were similarly poring over leaks that outlined extensive corruption within the ruling party and the Mubarak family, while in Yemen the protestors found out that Ali Abdullah Saleh had been actively assisting the US in executing Yemeni citizens by 'providing corridors for drone and cruise missile attacks, and then assuming responsibility for the attacks as the Yemeni government's own'.[192]

Others, however, have been a little more sceptical over the extent to which social media drove the uprisings, and have argued that there has been too much technological determinism in analyses of 2011. In some ways expectations were probably running far too high, with the BBC having already tried to describe the spring 2009 pro-Western Moldova street protests against the democratically elected Communist Party as being a 'Twitter Revolution', and with most of the Western media then quickly reapplying the same name to Iran's Green Revolution a few months later. As the *Guardian*'s Matthew Weaver explains, this was really 'fuelled [more] by Western fantasies for new media than the reality in Iran'.[193] Indeed there are claims that there were probably less than a thousand properly active Twitter users in Iran at the time of the protests, with most of the revolutionary accounts really being outside of the country, and tweeting in English rather than Farsi.[194] Moreover, as journalist Jasmin Ramsey reflected two years later, 'the use of social networking ... was certainly important, but even in 2011 I noticed that word of mouth [was] still the dominant mode of communication.' She also described how landline phones and information passed via taxi drivers was really the paramount source of news in Tehran.[195] In his book *The Net Delusion*, Evgeny Morozov was similarly cautious, arguing that the Internet in Iran was primarily a device for surveillance and state control rather than something emancipatory.[196]

Admitting a role for social media, but drawing much the same conclusions as Ramsey and Morozov on Iran, a number of scholars who have focused deeply on the Egyptian revolution have sought to portray it as more of an enabler than a driving force. While visiting Tahrir Square one British academic observed how 'the surge in Facebook sign-ups, the flowering of new online networks, the surge in YouTube videos are reflections of, rather than substitutes for a ferment of new offline political organizations.'[197] Similarly, although Jereon Gunning and Ilan Baron argue that such technologies played a key part in helping to expose regime abuses, they admit that '[social media's] role in the 25 January revolution was more limited ... Much of the mobilization was carried out offline in order to evade police attention, and many ... would not have had regular Internet access.' As such, 'What persuaded online adherents to become offline activists was thus something other than the Internet.'[198] Filiu's view is much the same, claiming that the 'day of rage' was primarily the result of extensive, underground militant networking involving the preparing of several rally points for protestors. Some of these were never announced online, including the one for the key group that managed to converge in front of El-Mugamma, the central government building.[199] Even a study of the prominent #Tahrir Twitter hashtag at the time seems to show that the revolutionary turmoil in Egypt did not come 'out of the blue' or mainly through social media activism. As its author noted, it was instead 'precipitated through many years of internal pressures and growing social movements.'[200]

Meanwhile, some have tried to show how more traditional forms of communication still played a significant and perhaps even leading role. With many expecting mobile phone signals to be cut, landline numbers were being passed around, while groups such as the Front to Defend Egyptian Protestors were known to have relied primarily on text messages rather than social media postings. These were received on a hotline which was used to gather testimonies about police brutality and put people in touch with lawyers.[201] As Rahimi has also pointed out, when the regime cut off the Internet the sudden absence of social media did not seem to have slowed the revolutionary momentum and may have actually accelerated mobilization and expanded decentralized dissent.[202] The perception in other Arab Spring states seems to have been much the same, despite the relentless framing of the uprisings in the Western media as mostly Twitter- or Facebook-driven. Many street activists complained of the *abtal al-keyboard* or 'keyboard heroes' who remained safely behind their computer screens, while some militant groups, such as those in Tunisia, even went as far as publishing denouncements of the 'myth of the Twitter revolution'.[203] More soberly, as a team of US-based academics have demonstrated citing the *World Values Survey 6th Wave*, the Internet penetration rates in most of the states which saw uprisings were not very high to begin with. Although about thirty percent of Tunisia's population seemed to have had daily Internet access in 2011, fewer than thirteen percent of Egyptians and under seven percent of Yemenis claimed to have had daily connections.[204]

6

PLAN 'A' – ISLAMISTS VERSUS THE DEEP STATE

THE NEED FOR COUNTER-REVOLUTION

Problematically for ousted elites, the region's surviving monarchies, and their overseas patrons, the task of rolling back the Arab Spring at first seemed difficult, and one that could not so easily be dealt with using the well-honed counter-revolutionary strategies developed by the European empires and then the US throughout the twentieth century. Not only were the scale and scope of the uprisings far too big for a standard counter-insurgency operation, having swept up dozens and perhaps even hundreds of millions, but so too was their diversity. Clearly driven by a mixture of deep-seated socio-economic pressures alongside powerful or at least enabling and emancipatory modernizing forces, they had then been propelled by a vast range of diffuse, cosmopolitan, and ill-defined movements often led by a hotchpotch of liberals, socialists, communists, and secular activists.

The Western powers were particularly wrong-footed, with senior politicians unable to come up with a coherent or convincing response to the fast-moving events. Although they were painfully conscious of their supposed status as representatives of the world's leading democracies, the sight of long-standing local allies being swept aside, and the prospect of the neo-liberal agenda unravelling under more assertive Arab governments, was, as expected, too much to bear. Indeed, a sort of nightmare scenario seemed to be developing, in which the comfortable postcolonial order, which had been allowing Western companies and investors largely unfettered access to Arab assets and resources, could well be replaced by a network of representative and indigenously authentic administrations, not only committed to rebuilding domestic welfare states and promoting social justice, but which would probably be deemed credible diplomatic and economic partners by most of the non-Western world. Expressed another way, centuries of British, French, and then US imperialism in the Arab world, first through the front door and then through the back door, were on the cusp of coming to an end. In the words of Secretary of State Hillary Clinton, speaking on a visit to Qatar in February 2011, 'In too many places, in too many ways, the region's foundations are sinking into the sand.'[1]

Tellingly, despite the amazing scenes of peaceful crowds and pro-democracy banners on Tunisia's streets in early 2011, it took the US government more than ten days following Zine el-Abidine Ben Ali's escape to issue any kind of statement. When it came, it was merely one line in President Barack Obama's State of the Union address: 'The US stands with the people of Tunisia and supports the democratic aspirations of all people.'[2] With much more at stake in Egypt, which was still the second largest recipient of US aid after Israel, most officials did not even attempt neutrality, with many wading in to support the stumbling regime. Notably US special envoy to Egypt Frank Wisner stated at the height of the protests that 'President Mubarak's continued leadership is crucial ... it is his chance to write his own legacy,' while Vice President Joe Biden told *Newshour* viewers: 'Look, Mubarak has been an ally of ours in a number of things and he's been very responsible on, relative to geopolitical interests in the region, Middle East peace efforts, the actions he has taken relative to normalizing the relationship with Israel ... I would not refer to him as a dictator.'[3] Although probably wanting to join Wisner and Biden, Clinton proceeded a little more cautiously, likely because she had already been stung by an earlier leaked diplomatic cable that most Egyptians had already begun to devour. Recorded as having helped distance Hosni Mubarak from a critical Department of State annual report on Egypt, she had also claimed after a visit to Cairo in 2009 that '[she] had a wonderful time with him this morning. I really consider President and Mrs. Mubarak to be friends of my family. So I hope to see him often here in Egypt and in the US.'[4] Nonetheless, on the first 'day of rage' on 25 January 2011 she did plead for the protestors to show restraint on the grounds that 'the Egyptian government is able and is looking for ways to respond to the legitimate needs and interests of the Egyptian people.'[5] Moreover, as late as 7 February, just three days before Mubarak's ouster, she was still advising him to 'retire early', later that year, rather than immediately resign.[6]

Britain and the Western European governments by no means held their tongues either, with the alarm at the prospect of losing such a valued trade partner as Egypt being palpable. Only two years earlier the Egyptian government had listed Britain as the country's biggest foreign investor with 'the direct investments of the top twenty British companies operating in Egypt exceeding $20 billion.'[7] Issuing a joint statement as the crowds thronged into Tahrir Square, the British, French, and German governments duly praised 'the moderating role that President Mubarak has played over many years in the Middle East',[8] while on 1 February Tony Blair stated in his capacity as the envoy for the Middle East Quartet that Mubarak was 'immensely courageous and a force for good'.[9]

While such statements may now seem injudicious blunders, it is likely most officials had been relying on faulty intelligence and poorly informed opinion that had sought to downplay the impact of the Tunisian revolution and the prospects of its contagion to Egypt or elsewhere. The CIA deputy director at the time, Michael Morell, has since described how the agency was stunned by the scale of the Arab Spring. He admitted in his memoirs that 'we failed because to a large extent we were relying on a handful of strong leaders … to help us understand what was going on in the Arab street. We were lax in creating our own windows.'[10] Meanwhile, in a *Foreign Policy* piece, entitled 'Why the Tunisian Revolution Won't Spread', which was published on 16 January 2011 and likely read by Clinton, Biden, and others, the prominent Harvard University political scientist Stephen Walt had stated that 'if you are expecting to see a rapid transformation of the Arab world in the wake of these events, you're likely to be disappointed.' He also reasoned that the Tunisian revolution was likely to make other Arab populations less rather than more likely to challenge their regimes on the basis that 'hey, our government sucks, but it's better than no government at all.'[11]

Similarly influential, the still widely read Bernard Lewis had given an interview in February in which he claimed that '[the Arab people] are simply not ready for free and fair elections' on the grounds that democracy was a 'political concept that has no history, no record whatever in the Arab, Islamic world'.[12] Unsurprisingly Lewis's thoughts were recycled by both Egypt's vice president Omar Suleiman, who declared, 'Egypt is not ready for democracy', and then by Jordan's King Abdullah II, who told the BBC that 'you have to understand that the concept of right, left and centre is not there [for Arabs].'[13] Taking things further, the *Washington Post*'s popular columnist Richard Cohen even tried to portray any prospective Arab democracy as a threat to Israel. With Mubarak still clinging to power he declared: 'My take on [the Arab Spring] is relentlessly gloomy. I care about Israel. I care about Egypt, too, but its survival is hardly at stake.' He explained that 'I care about democratic values, but they are worse than useless in societies that have no tradition of tolerance or respect for minority rights,' and warned that 'those Americans and others who cheer the mobs in the streets of Cairo and other Egyptian cities, who clamor for more robust anti-Mubarak statements from the Obama administration, would be wise to let Washington proceed slowly.'[14]

By March 2011, with two US-backed dictators gone and Yemen's Ali Abdullah Saleh imperilled, there seemed little hope of rescuing the widely hated, ridiculed, and humiliated *ancien régimes*. Moreover, with most of the protestors being exactly the sort of activists that Western policymakers were historically supposed to have been waiting for to emerge and then lead the Arab world to democracy and prosperity, it was also clear that they could not so easily be branded as 'insurgents', 'terrorists', or even agents of foreign powers or transnational plots such as international communism. For one thing, social media made it impossible for anyone to believe such accusations. Instead, it seemed, the best strategy available was to somehow manage or dilute the course of the Arab Spring and ultimately steer it into a more containable format that would at least preserve some of the old postcolonial structures and, likely as top priority, the neo-liberal economic reforms of the previous decade. But given the sensitivities of any direct involvement by the US or other Western powers, not least because they would have been seen as interfering in a democratic process, the counter-revolutions not only needed to be subtle, but they needed to be as indirect as possible and ideally led by reactionary elements within the states themselves.

Making matters more complex given the differing circumstances and weighting of the various power blocs in the revolutionary states, it was soon apparent that each counter-revolution would have to be custom-made so as to allow for the most effective combination of conservative religious groups with historical relations with the West, liberals who could be relied upon to uphold the Washington Consensus, and the military 'deep states' with 'serpentine boundaries' that had been the US's steadfast allies in the 'War on Terror'.[15] As Ibrahim Halawi, the founder of a secular Arab newspaper, noted, the stage had been set for a counter-revolution that was not necessarily going to be violent but which would be based on 'more subtle civil-economic interventions', while as Kings College London's Alex Callinicos has since reflected, 'counter-revolution now haunts the Arab world. But it takes diverse and confusing shapes.'[16]

EGYPT – BACK TO THE BROTHERHOOD

Having jettisoned Hosni Mubarak's civilian regime, and appearing to side with the protestors, or at least not having opened fire on them, by February 2011 Egypt's Supreme Council of the Armed Forces found itself rather unexpectedly in full public control of the state. For both its generals and its Western allies it was imperative that the revolutionary forces on the streets were quickly incorporated into some kind of state-building project before the highly mobilized protestors turned their attention to the military itself and thus attempted to complete the revolutionary process. Probably the most astute observer at the time was Kent State University's Joshua Stacher, who had argued in *Foreign Affairs* just three days before Mubarak's fall that 'Egypt's democratic window has [already] closed' on the basis that the SCAF had proven itself solid and unmoved in the face of the Arab Spring. He also argued that the army's 'aloof neutrality underscored that its role on the side-lines was intentional'.[17] Writing in the *London Review of Books*, Tufts University's Hugh Roberts later made much the same point, arguing that the 'political and repressive core of the Egyptian state – the army – remained intact'.[18]

Although described by political scientist Samer Shehata as having become the 'state within the state', the protests had at least flushed the

SCAF out into the open, which was a position it knew to be a dangerous one.[19] With Omar Suleiman soon discarded as vice president, and Essam Sharaf appointed as transitional prime minister, even the latter admitted that the real power rested with Mubarak's long-serving defence minister, Muhammed Hussein Tantawi, along with younger SCAF members such as military intelligence chief Abdelfattah Sisi.[20] With thousands still congregating in Cairo's public space and pressing on with their demands, the SCAF's vulnerability was increasingly apparent, especially after it issued a fresh communiqué warning that continuing protests were harming national security and 'disrupting the wheels of production'.[21] Trying to break up some of the crowds in early March, over 170 were arrested and allegations of torture were made against the military, prompting the SCAF to order newspaper editors not to publish further stories on Tahrir.[22] Those bloggers who did were often detained while penalties were introduced for activists who continued to mobilize the crowds, including trade union members who fell foul of newly drafted anti-strike legislation.[23] More desperately, the military's eventual forced clearance of Tahrir Square later in the month seemed the final confirmation of its reactionary credentials, especially after Ramy Essam, an activist who had transformed protestors' chants into popular song, was arrested and then reportedly tortured.[24]

Waiting in the wings to replace the SCAF's ineffective transitional ministers and its struggling counter-insurgency were of course the leaders of the Muslim Brotherhood. With the Brotherhood likely to secure at least some sort of popular ballot box legitimacy, it was assumed by both the SCAF and their overseas backers that a Brotherhood-dominated government would still guarantee most of the key structures of the existing regime, including the army's deep state supremacy.[25] Moreover, in addition to the relations it had covertly enjoyed with London and then Washington for several decades, there is evidence that in the years leading up to the Arab Spring a more mature and publicly presentable version of the Brotherhood was being actively cultivated by the Western powers as a potential insurance policy and 'safe pair of hands' in the event that the Cairo presidency collapsed.

Anwar Sadat's earlier rapprochement with the Brotherhood had eventually faltered after many of its members refused to endorse the 1978 Camp David Accords, and Sadat ultimately paid the price with his own life when he was shot by a jihadist infiltrator at a military parade, but the Mubarak regime had nonetheless kept the door at least half open. Despite some Brotherhood activists joining in with protest movements such as the *Kifaya* campaign, the benefits of the organization's substantial presence still seemed to outweigh the costs, not only because it provided basic welfare for potentially restive parts of the country, but also because its members were willing to run as independent candidates in Mubarak's various rigged parliamentary elections.[26] With liberals, Christians, and many others remaining deeply suspicious of political Islam, the Brotherhood's de facto MPs became a useful 'moral safety net' for the government and, as political scientist Holger Albrecht noted, a means to observe and channel societal dissent.[27] In other words, if non-Islamist Egyptians were conditioned to believe that any free and fair election would simply grant the Brotherhood a victory, then they would more willingly acquiesce to Mubarak's authoritarianism.

Having witnessed the Brotherhood effectively win 88 out of the 454 parliamentary seats in the 2005 elections, despite only fielding between 135 and 150 candidates, the US and Britain decided to get much more involved. Described as a 'highly significant' election result by the Congressional Research Service, it had also prompted British Foreign Office officials to write to the foreign secretary urging an increase in contacts with the Brotherhood, albeit with caution given that the organization was still designated a terrorist entity by the Egyptian authorities.[28] Soon after, a Whitehall paper co-authored by a senior British diplomat and a former US assistant secretary of state began to circulate heavily in Washington and London. Clearly referring to Egypt it stated that 'the awkward truth is that the most significant movements which enjoy popular support are those associated with political Islam' before making the case that 'the G8 must enter dialogue with such groups and involve them in US policy for the region.'[29] Despite some criticism from the British ambassador to Egypt at the time who had argued that the West should not confuse engaging with the Islamic world as being the same as engaging with Islamism,[30] the paper's recommendations nonetheless already seemed to have become policy, with Prime Minister Tony Blair stating that 'we want moderate, mainstream Islam to triumph over reactionary Islam,' and, on a separate occasion, remarking that 'a victory for the moderates means an Islam that is open: open to globalization.'[31]

In a written response to parliament in early 2011, and in fact just days before Mubarak's fall, Foreign Secretary William Hague rather reassuringly stated to his nervous colleagues that 'our embassy in Cairo maintains working level contacts with many government and opposition figures, including the Muslim Brotherhood. We have been in contact with members of the Muslim Brotherhood … We will continue to have contacts with those members of the Muslim Brotherhood who are, or who are likely to be, part of the political dialogue process in Egypt.' Driving the point home, he also described the Brotherhood as 'an important part of Egypt's national political mosaic'.[32] Only a few weeks later, with the SCAF's transitional government technically in charge, a number of Foreign Office officials travelled to Egypt to meet with Brotherhood leaders at their headquarters in Alexandria. The discussion focused on 'British efforts' and the sort of role that the Brotherhood could play in the revolutionary aftermath. As Mark Curtis recalls, the meeting was not listed on the Foreign Office's website, nor was it reported by the British media. However, the Brotherhood's website was less discreet, revealing that the British delegation 'desired to open the door for direct political dialogue with the Brothers'.[33] The intended secrecy of the meeting is likely explained by Prime Minister David Cameron's public visit to Cairo only a couple of days later. On this occasion, described as part of his 'push for democracy', he stated that he would be meeting with all political groups except the Brotherhood on the grounds that 'it was not inevitable that open elections in the country would lead to a government dominated by the Brotherhood'.[34]

But it was of course already the plan that the new Egyptian government would be dominated by the revamped Brotherhood thus allowing the SCAF to retreat back to the shadows and for Egypt's foreign partners to get back to business. For this to work, the Brotherhood had to at least be appealing to a majority of Egyptians, and it seems that most of its post-2005 discussions with Western officials had concentrated heavily on the need for modernization. As Jeroen Gunning and Ilan Baron describe, it had been 'refocused on institutional politics, reflecting its ongoing interest in participating in elections'.[35] The aim, most likely, was for the Brotherhood to evolve into the sort of Islamist party that could both win an election and then govern with a reasonable amount of popular support on the basis that it would not go so far as adopting sharia law as the country's legal code or Islam as the state religion. After all, as Columbia University's Alfred Stepan and Yale University's Juan Linz noted, ostensibly similar organizations had recently managed to form fairly stable governments in other Muslim-majority states such as Indonesia, Turkey, Senegal, and Albania. Drawing on examples from Western European history they reasoned that 'a type of secularism that decrees complete separation between religion and the state was [not] empirically necessary for democracy to emerge.'[36]

Unfortunately for the Brotherhood's backers, by 2011 it was still far from the type of pro-democratic and tolerant organization that they had hoped it could become. Seemingly oblivious to the secular and inter-faith masses taking to the streets, its slogan still remained 'Islam is the solution', while its stated aims still included the creation of an Islamic state with sharia law, and many of its senior members remained very much the products of Sayyid Qutb's controversial teachings.[37] Moreover, as Stepan and Linz pointed out, at the time of the revolution part of its website had not been updated since 2007 and included 'nondemocratic features such as a rejection of the idea that a woman or a non-Muslim could ever be president of Egypt, and a recommendation that a high court composed of and appointed by [clerics] should be empowered to review all new legislation to ensure its compliance with sharia'.[38]

Jean-Pierre Filiu has described the Brotherhood as having been just as much caught off guard by the Arab Spring as Mubarak was, and he has argued that the democratic uprisings '[did not] fit with their short-term plans, nor with their long-term visions. They can adapt to it, join it, and even benefit from it, but they certainly cannot pretend that they started it or inspired it.'[39] In fact, there is evidence that at the very beginning of the uprising the Brotherhood's leaders had tried to limit the protests, with media spokesman Essam el-Arian being quoted by the New York Times on 22 January 2011 as recommending non-participation in the revolution. Although el-Arian tried to disown the statement, the crowds in Tahrir Square already seemed to have made up their mind as they chanted 'not for El-Baradei [referring to the liberal politician Muhammad el-Baradei], nor the Brotherhood, but because Egypt is tired'.[40]

By February the Brotherhood's revolutionary credentials seemed further weakened following its leaders' willingness to meet with Omar Suleiman four days before Mubarak's resignation. With most protestors rejecting such negotiation outright, it was deemed a last-ditch attempt by the regime to split the crowds into Islamists and non-Islamists.[41] Importantly there was even division within the Brotherhood's own ranks, with its youth wing staging a conference about the Brotherhood's future. An act of rebellion in itself, a consensus was reached to object to supreme guide Muhammad Badie's order that Brotherhood members must only vote for the Freedom and Justice Party – the organization's political wing – in any forthcoming elections. Moreover, many other members, and especially those that had been participating in the Tahrir Square sit-in, called for internal reform in the Brotherhood, including the need to give women a greater role.[42]

Also critical of the Brotherhood's relations with the SCAF and its apparent willingness to cut deals with the crumbling regime were the more conservative Islamist groups, many of them holding great sway among Cairo's millions of slum dwellers. As described, Salafists had also been taking to the streets in protest and, at least temporarily, had practised some degree of tolerance for other religions and secularists. But after the revolution, and as a Brotherhood-military axis became more likely, they had begun to circulate leaflets condemning *kafir* or 'unbeliever' democracy.[43] Disillusioned Salafists were also blamed for attacks on churches in Imbaba, a poor area of Cairo, which caused the stock market to crash and the new post-Mubarak economy almost immediately to teeter on the brink. Sharing the same concerns, the more hard-line jihadist camp also condemned the Brotherhood's new arrangement. Al-Qaeda's Egyptian-born deputy Ayman al-Zawahiri warned the people it was part of a plot to facilitate foreign intervention and that the sort of political participation advocated by the Brotherhood was illegitimate, while the Syrian ideologue Abu Basir al-Tartusi claimed the organization was 'negotiating with the regime' and thus 'betraying the youth'.[44]

Some, however, have suggested that the Salafist condemnations and the upsurge in violence were nonetheless tolerated by Tantawi as it gave the SCAF greater authority to clear the streets and bring the revolutionary period to an end.[45] Furthermore, if this was the case, it meant that the military deep state was briefly resurrecting an old Mubarak-era strategy that had not only helped justify the continuation of the state of emergency, but had also helped set some limits on the Brotherhood's popularity. Certainly

Mubarak had often been quick to blame violent acts on Salafists, and when he did, the perpetrators were usually described as 'emerging under the cloak of the *Ikhwan* [Muslim Brotherhood]'.[46] As Robin Yassin-Kassab explains, for this purpose Mubarak had always been willing to support some of the 'most retrograde desires of Islamism' in Egypt including the banning of books, imposing restrictions on church-building, and allowing Salafist television stations and other intolerant media networks to flourish.[47] Similarly, as the University of Westminster's Abdelwahab al-Affendi contends, both Sadat and Mubarak had actively 'encouraged [Salafist] traditionalism, and had made a huge body of traditional religious works available to the public'.[48]

EGYPT - AN UNEASY ALLIANCE

The first concrete step for the counter-revolutionary alliance was to be a referendum held on 19 March 2011, which was to introduce several partial amendments to the Mubarak-era constitution. With many protestors demanding a completely new constitution, the referendum was treated with great suspicion, especially after it transpired that the SCAF had appointed an Islamist judge to chair its drafting committee.[49] Moreover, one of the proposed amendments was that a new, hundred-member constitutional committee to formulate a future permanent Egyptian constitution would only be selected after parliamentary elections had taken place, and with its membership to be chosen by the new parliament. With the Brotherhood as the firm favourite to win a majority in such elections given its historical advantage as Mubarak's tolerated opposition and thus its considerable 'head start' over other political parties, the non-Islamists complained this would give it an unfairly prominent role in shaping the new post-2011 state. To allay such fears, the Brotherhood stated that before the parliamentary elections it would be appointing a Christian as vice president of the Freedom and Justice Party, that it would not contest all parliamentary seats, and that it would not be fielding one of its members in any future presidential election. It also promised that it would not be seeking to transform Egypt into a sharia-based Islamic state and instead would be building a *dawla madaniyya* or 'civic state'. But by the time the temporary

231

constitution was published, amendments were already in place to declare sharia as a major source of legislation and, added at the last minute by the SCAF, to grant the military sweeping new powers until a president and parliament could be elected. Furthermore, hinting at the alliance's intended foreign policy and the SCAF's need to maintain the flow of US aid, the Brotherhood also appeared to have relented on its long-standing desire to reshape Egypt's relations with Israel.[50]

Although most of the hardcore Tahrir Square activists voted 'no', the referendum was endorsed by a seventy-seven percent 'yes' vote. Undoubtedly this was a reflection of the Brotherhood's mobilizing capabilities – indeed its website had stated that it was a religious duty to vote – along with a sense of revolutionary fatigue felt by most ordinary Egyptians. As many have suggested, it was also a function of an increased fear that there would either be never-ending military rule or some sort of attempted comeback by Mubarak regime remnants. Either way, with Brotherhood members and other Islamists claiming that the referendum was a 'dramatic victory for Islam over non-Muslim voters', and with the SCAF making no effort to repeal the hated emergency laws, calls for a 'second revolution' began to grow louder. On 8 July the Revolutionary Youth Coalition called for a new government to be forcibly established and on 23 July – Egypt's national day – protestors marched on the SCAF headquarters. With many arrested and sentenced in military courts, or even violently dispersed with live ammunition, the remaining protestors' demands soon changed to 'the people want the fall of the marshal' in reference to field marshal Tantawi.[51]

Despite the obvious intensification of military repression, the Brotherhood unsurprisingly upheld its end of the bargain, with its supreme guide issuing a statement calling on all Egyptians to support the SCAF on the basis that it was 'the defender of the revolution and morally superior to other Arab armies which killed their people'.[52] In October, as preparations for the parliamentary elections gathered pace, this was followed up by both the Freedom and Justice Party and the new, Salafist Nour Party issuing a joint endorsement of the SCAF's measures.[53] Beginning a month later, and finally finishing in January 2012, the elections enjoyed full SCAF approval and, so it seemed, produced the intended results. With the Brotherhood having reneged on its earlier pledge not to contest all seats, it won forty-seven percent of the vote and the right to appoint the speaker of the parliament. With the Nour Party winning twenty-four percent this meant that the two main Islamist parties carried a combined seventy-one percent of the vote and had won 356 out of 498 available seats. Described by the BBC as 'Egypt's complex electoral system', the SCAF clearly enjoyed tight control over the new Islamist parliament and was even confident enough to appoint a secular Mubarak-era politician, Kamal al-Ganzuri, as interim prime minister.[54] Nonetheless, to keep the balance alive it did state it 'would not have the ability to impose anything that the people don't want' and it backed away from a controversial earlier set of recommendations that would have given it the right to review all future legislation relating to the military, would have safeguarded its budget, and would have given it a direct role in drafting the permanent constitution.[55]

As Fouad Ajami remarked on all of this, Hassan al-Banna and the Brotherhood's other founders would have likely looked down upon their descendants with great admiration for their tactical skills as they had managed to 'manoeuvre between the liberals and the SCAF, partaking of the tumult of Tahrir Square but stepping back from the exuberance to underline their commitment to sobriety and public order'.[56] Ajami also predicted that the Brotherhood would eventually strike a more permanent deal with the military in which it would get control over education, social welfare, and justice, while the army generals would get to keep control over foreign policy, including Egypt's relations with Israel and the US.[57] Indeed, as Reem Abou el-Fadl pointed out, during this period the military had effectively entered into a 'a tacit pact with the Brotherhood, whose leaders did not contest the transitional process', while as Filiu observed 'the dynamics of reform witnessed the Islamists moving close to the army'.[58]

By the spring of 2012, however, there were increasing signs of discomfort between the two camps. On the one hand, the military seemed wary of the Brotherhood's substantial popular mandate, while on the other the Brotherhood saw the upcoming presidential elections as the organization's best chance since its creation to realize its long-term goals. In this sense, while recognizing that pushing too far too fast would almost certainly strain its arrangement with the SCAF, the Brotherhood's senior leadership likely deemed it an opportunity that was too good to miss. Using the excuse that it was unable to steer the ongoing constitutional discussions effectively, the Brotherhood duly reneged on another of its post-revolutionary promises by announcing it would after all be entering the May 2012 presidential race. Problematically, however, its first-choice candidate, the charismatic Khayrat al-Shater, was vulnerable to a SCAF veto given that he had served jail time under Mubarak. Meanwhile, the main Salafist contender, Hazem Abu Ismail, who had once publicly stated his respect for Iran's independence from the US, also fell to the wayside after the *New York Times* claimed his dual nationality made him ineligible.[59] Likely leaked to the US media by the SCAF itself, the Egyptian ministry of interior speedily acted upon the story and confirmed Ismail's disqualification.[60] Either way, with the Brotherhood's second-choice candidate, Muhammad Morsi, emerging as the Islamist front runner, the SCAF had ensured that the most appealing Islamist politician was out of the race while the most potentially problematic candidature, at least in terms of foreign relations, was also nipped in the bud.

With Morsi's main rival being the SCAF-approved Ahmad Shafik, the former Egyptian air-force chief and Mubarak's last prime minister, the SCAF had effectively sewn up the election with a win-win outcome for their interests. Regardless of whether it was a Morsi or a Shafiq victory, neither man could legitimately claim any connection to the 2011 revolution and would thus remain just as wary of future protests as the SCAF. Although the still Mubarak-appointed supreme constitutional court sought to tip the balance in favour of Shafik by dismissing the Brotherhood-dominated parliament on the grounds of illegality just two days before the second stage of the presidential election, Morsi's eventual fifty-two percent of the ballot was just enough for the Brotherhood to claim victory.[61] Despite a purported 'show of force', with Morsi supposedly asking for Tantawi's resignation as defence minister, and despite an apparent olive branch offered to non-Islamist parties culminating in Morsi's 'Fairmont Accord' promises, in reality the Brotherhood had strived to keep the SCAF on board, although perhaps this time as its junior partner.[62] Making no issue of well-documented incidents of military violence against protestors, and doing little to unravel the military's control over lucrative state assets such as the Suez Canal, Morsi also appointed several leading SCAF members to key positions. Among them were a number of new presidential advisers and – seemingly symbolic of the up-and-coming younger generation in the SCAF – Sisi as the new defence minister.[63]

Having carefully cultivated an image for himself as something of an Islamist general, Sisi has been accused of 'duping' the international media and deliberately trying to appear to Morsi and the Brotherhood as a potential ally.[64] As Robert Springborg noted in *Foreign Affairs*, Sisi's earlier thesis submitted to the US Army War College 'read like a tract produced by the Brotherhood' and suggested his 'radical political vision ... of how to steer Egyptian society differs markedly from those of the secular-nationalist military rulers who led Egypt for decades.'[65] The *Guardian* similarly homed in on Sisi's thesis, stating: '[It] appears implicitly to endorse the Brotherhood's right to take up political office' and 'describes the concept of the Islamic caliphate as the ideal form of government ... and argues that a government's executive, legislative, and judicial arms should all draw on Islamic beliefs.'[66] Few suggested Sisi had always yearned to be more than a general and, as a shrewd politician-in-the-making, had perhaps been engaging in some Mubarak-era political manoeuvring of his own to make sure he could appeal to as many groups as possible in the event of a revolutionary moment.

EGYPT - MILITARY DICTATORSHIP

Best described as a contest within a counter-revolution, rather than as a counter-revolution in its own right, by early 2013 the SCAF had begun to plot actively against their Brotherhood partners and to prepare for more forceful 'corrective' measures. Seemingly enjoying a false sense of security from his electoral success and having received a personal endorsement from the White House for his role in de-escalating tensions in the Gaza Strip in November 2012, an emboldened Muhammad Morsi had begun to augment the powers of his presidency by trying to push forward a heavily Brotherhood-sponsored draft of a new constitution despite a meagre referendum turnout of less than thirty-three percent.[67] Such a constitution would have placed him, as president, above judicial review.[68]

With Morsi increasingly viewed by non-Islamists as a partisan party leader rather than as a true head of state, the sporadic street protests had become less about the SCAF and more about the Brotherhood, especially after the crowds adopted the slogan 'one hand' to signify their unity with the SCAF, and petitions began circulating calling on the military to step in

and remove Morsi. Although this certainly strengthened the SCAF's position against the Brotherhood, it did mean that the Brotherhood's intended
role of containing revolutionary forces and shielding the military deep
state from the public gaze was failing.[69] As Eva Bellin puts it, Morsi had
'spurned the opposition, refused to practise inclusion, and failed to make
reassuring gestures to non-Islamists. He was strident and had embarked
on a Brotherhood power grab.'[70] Similarly, as Jean-Pierre Filiu contends,
Morsi had put the Brotherhood's internal logic ahead of the national interest, and had wrongly interpreted his election mandate as a 'blank cheque'.[71]

Meeting with a broad range of groups opposed to Morsi, the SCAF's
initial strategy was to form a sort of grand coalition, including even old
regime elites and the Salafist Nour Party. Jointly led by Muhammad
el-Baradei, Hamdeen Sabahi – an old school nationalist who had come
third in the presidential election – and Mubarak's old foreign minister
Amr Moussa, the new National Salvation Front began to press Morsi
to uphold the Fairmont Accord. Although still technically Morsi's subordinate, Abdelfattah Sisi offered to negotiate between the two camps,
but this was rejected by the Brotherhood.[72] With compromise looking
increasingly far-fetched, the plan soon changed to one of coup d'état, or
rather a popular putsch against Morsi that would see the military publicly
rescuing the nation from visibly unpopular Brotherhood rule. As the *Wall
Street Journal* reported, by Spring 2013 the message from the SCAF to the
National Salvation Front and the Nour Party was that if they could put
enough protestors on the streets then the army would forcibly remove the
president. Despite the strong differences between the various opposition
groups, they were described as 'needing each other', with the liberals having
Arab Spring credibility while the former Mubarak officials 'brought deep
pockets and influence over the powerful state bureaucracy'.[73]

Assuming the front-line role was a well-organized grass-roots group
of young activists calling themselves *Tamarod* or 'Rebellion', which was
reportedly receiving logistical support, office space, and financial assistance
from Mubarak-era business elites and members of the National Salvation
Front. Having collected a petition in June, which they claimed had twenty-
two million signatures, but according to the Brotherhood only 170,000
signatures, *Tamarod*'s apparent aim was to surpass the thirteen million
votes Morsi had received in the presidential elections and thus provide

a popular mandate for the intended coup. Keeping a back-seat role, Sisi stated that the military had no intentions of intervening in politics as 'the notion of inviting the army into the country's politics again is extremely dangerous; it could turn Egypt into another Afghanistan or Somalia.'[74] He also pledged that he himself had no personal ambitions beyond his ministerial portfolio. He did, however, warn the media not to criticize the SCAF on the basis that its leaders read everything written about it and would not tolerate anyone offending its officers and soldiers.[75]

By 23 June 2013, with *Tamarod* seeming to gather momentum, and with its petition by then boasting a staggering thirty-three million signatures, Sisi had changed his tune by stating that the army would indeed get involved if it had to, so as to 'prevent civil war'.[76] As some have suggested, the military may have also viewed some of Morsi's recent foreign-policy statements as the final straw. Notably he had claimed that Egypt would keep the Rafah crossing to Gaza open and that Egyptians could go and fight outside the country if they wanted to. The former would have continued to complicate relations between Israel, the SCAF, and the US, while the latter raised the prospect of a new generation of Egyptian jihadists eventually returning home and fighting against the state.[77]

Either way, exactly one week after Sisi's comments Morsi's time was clearly up. In what seems to have been a well-planned operation, *Tamarod's* supporters thronged the central areas of Cairo while military aircraft flew over their heads and painted smoke hearts and Egyptian flags in the sky.[78] *Tamarod's* spokesman Mahmoud Badr duly took to a stage and urged the SCAF to move against the Brotherhood, while the next day Sisi gave Morsi a seemingly impossible forty-eight hours' ultimatum to meet the protestors' demands. The following days saw Morsi and most of the Brotherhood's leadership being rounded up and arrested as the coup apparently followed its scripted course. Within a few more weeks over two thousand mid-level Brotherhood members were detained and then most of the organization's assets were seized after it was declared an illegal organization.[79] Audio conversations leaked from the office of a Sisi aide, and which have since been deemed by a British audio forensics team to have a 'moderately strong chance of being authentic', have also revealed that the SCAF quickly requested the ministry of interior to change Morsi's initial record of arrest to indicate he was being held in a regular prison – as a regular criminal – rather than the reality of being held in a military jail.[80]

In parallel to these arrests was the bloodier step of mopping up those rank-and-file Brotherhood members who had refused to abandon the streets after attempting a counter-protest to *Tamarod*. Having been corralled into two public spaces, one near Cairo University and another in Rabia al-Adawiya in north-east Cairo, they were violently cleared on 14 August. Estimates of the total death count vary, as do the claims over the extent to which the protestors fought back, but it is quite clear that the new Sisi regime had perpetrated a massacre. The Egyptian health ministry claimed 638 had died, including 43 police officers, while Human Rights Watch claimed a minimum of 817 and 'likely 1000' had died and described it as 'one of the world's largest killings of demonstrators in a single day in recent history'.[81] Although Egypt's state media has since portrayed most of the Rabia protestors as having been uneducated or peasants, seemingly as part of an effort to reduce the value of their lives, a recent study by two Oxford University researchers has shown that the majority of those killed hailed from neighborhoods with high rates of literacy.[82] Given the strong similarities, many have since likened the massacre to the Chinese military's attack on the Tiananmen Square crowds in 1989 and even the deployment of Soviet tanks against Alexander Dubček's 'Prague Spring' protests in Czechoslovakia in 1968.[83]

Dealing with *Tamarod* and the opposition parties that had hoped for a temporary 'authoritarian democracy' to see off the Brotherhood but then restore freedoms was a little more complicated as these groups had after all provided the veneer of popular support the SCAF had needed. Moreover, they still seemed useful as they were publicly backing the need for the military to introduce quickly a new constitution that would prevent organizations such as the Brotherhood from ever winning elections again.[84] Appearing in photographs with the *Tamarod* organizers, along with members of the 6 April Movement such as Ahmad Maher, and even Wael Ghonim, Sisi seemed aware of the need to keep them on board until they were expendable.[85] Shortly after the coup, Hugh Roberts described such activists as the 'useful idiots of more sinister and subterranean forces',[86] and indeed they were soon silenced or disposed of. One who had been elected as an MP was told by the security services, 'If you are a patriot you need to shut up and let us do our job, and clean up the mess you made with your revolution.'[87] Meanwhile, Maher of the 6 April Movement was sentenced to three years in prison, with the movement being declared illegal, just like the Brotherhood.[88] Others were less fortunate, either disappearing or in some cases being defenestrated. Apparently having left the country, Ghonim simply fell silent, with his massively followed Twitter feed going dead for several months.

EGYPT – 'SISI MANIA'

With the Mubarak-appointed head of the Supreme Constitutional Court replacing Muhammad Morsi as a place-holding interim president, the SCAF continued to capitalize on the coup's momentum by laying the groundwork for Abdelfattah Sisi's more formal succession.[89] Drafting yet another constitutional charter, but this time one that gave the military and its courts even greater powers, it was put to national referendum in early 2014 and duly passed.[90] Moreover, as 'Sisi mania' took hold, the former defence minister and coup leader was also grandly upgraded to the rank of field marshal.[91]

In something of an echo of the Kremlin's conferral of 'Marshal of the Soviet Union' status on Joseph Stalin, or even Napoleon I's 'marshals of the empire' strategy – both of which aimed to guarantee the allegiance of the state's most senior figures – the Egyptian military was actively encouraging a cult of personality for its new leader.[92] The context of Sisi's ascendancy also fits uncannily well with the described Bonapartism of 1848, not only because of the obvious strong arm tactics and the provision of law and order to a beleaguered population but, as Leon Trotsky explained, because 'the democratic ritual of Bonapartism is the plebiscite. From time to time the question is presented to the citizens: for or against?' As Trotsky observed, in such referendums 'the voter feels the barrel of a revolver between his shoulders ... since the time of Louis Bonaparte, who now seems a provincial dilettante, this technique has received extraordinary development.'[93] The nature of Sisi's new regime also seemed to confirm Vladimir Lenin's once expressed fears that 'officialdom and the standing army are the parasite on the body of bourgeois society' and in many ways demonstrated to the Egyptian people that their revolution had been unable to get as far as Iran in 1979, where the 'coalition of the left and Islamists succeeded in smashing the Shah's army'; Russia in 1917, where 'there arose the necessity to create a new army ... as the bulwark of Soviet power'; or even France in 1789, where brand new battalions were fused into the old royal order of battle.[94]

In any case, as the de facto new emperor or even pharaoh, as *Al-Arabiya* suggested,[95] Sisi was soon confident enough to renege on another of his pre-coup pledges by announcing his candidature for the May 2014 presidential elections. With only Hamdeen Sabahi as a rival and of course with no Islamists standing, the outcome was a foregone conclusion. But even so, it seemed the reality of a military-led government was starting to sink in, with very poor voter turnout reported on the first two days of polling, and with an extra third day of polling having to be hastily added, along with offers of free transport for those who had not yet voted. Thus, although Sisi's eventual victory with ninety-seven percent was portrayed by the state media as a thorough vindication of the military's actions against Morsi in 2013, many considered the circumstances to have tarnished his reputation.[96] Indeed, even the state-owned television cameras had to home in repeatedly on evidently very small numbers of celebrators after the result was announced.

Breathing a collective sigh of relief, the Western governments expectedly moved fast to endorse Sisi's rule. As the SCAF doubtlessly intended, most politicians described the coup as a 'correction' of the revolution and claimed Sisi was keeping alive the 'spirit of Tahrir Square'. Little reference was made on major news networks to the earlier massacres and the purging of most liberal activists, nor to the fact that an elected president had been forcibly removed from office and imprisoned. US secretary of state John Kerry had, after all, already stated that the coup was a 'restoration of democracy' on the basis that the military was asked to intervene by 'millions and millions of people' and that 'the military has not taken over, to the best of our judgement so far.'[97] In her 2014 memoirs Hillary Clinton made much the same case, but also made sure to blame the 'students and activists who had played leading roles in the [2011] demonstrations'. Describing them not as revolutionaries but as a 'disorganized group not prepared to contest or influence anything' she reasoned that 'they would end up handing the country to the Brotherhood or the military by default, which in the end is exactly what happened.'[98] Also firmly embracing Sisi was the British government and former prime minister Tony Blair, the latter having argued that the coup was 'the absolutely necessary rescue of a nation', and shortly after the election having been reported as advising the new Egyptian president on economic reforms.[99] The Pope too was keen to move forward, welcoming Sisi in the Vatican on his first trip to Europe and praising the 'framework of guarantees' enshrined in Egypt's new constitution.[100]

With a powerful mandate for authoritarianism and with most opponents in disarray, whether revolutionary or Islamist, Sisi and the SCAF were well placed to complete the counter-revolution and, so it seemed, accomplish what their short-lived alliance with the Brotherhood had been unable to do. Fearing competition from Egypt's police force, Sisi moved swiftly to subordinate the minister for interior to the military.[101] The government then also began a programme of 're-corporatization' to make sure that the NGOs, universities, and other entities that had played a role in the revolution were more firmly co-opted by the state.[102] In July 2014, a draft law even prohibited scholars from conducting fieldwork or from conducting polls in Egypt without government permission.[103] To prevent future student protests, a private security firm called Falcon was subcontracted to patrol campuses and other public spaces – the name likely derived from the military's insignia. Having helped run Sisi's presidential campaign, the company is understood originally to have been funded by an Egyptian bank in a joint venture with the SCAF. Over three thousand students were arrested and sixteen killed over the course of the next year.[104]

Bringing the religious establishment into lockstep, the government also made sure to police mosques, bar unauthorized preachers, and provide 'unifying' Friday sermon topics. As George Washington University's Nathan Brown recalls, one of the strangest sights was seeing 'Sisi, a military man, giving a lecture at Al-Azhar on what the religious establishment's mission should be'.[105] Boosting his appeal with the old Mubarak business elites and the officer-cum-entrepreneur class in the military, Sisi initiated the 'Long Live Egypt' fund requiring potentially competitive new businesses to make a contribution or, as Robert Springborg puts it 'having a shakedown', in return for the military's blessing and protection. Able to circumvent the national budget and the central bank, the military was also in a position to issue its own bonds, for example for the building of the new Suez Canal, and to resume the former regime's practice of distributing lucrative state contracts to favoured cronies.[106]

Unsurprisingly the new regime also made sure to pick up where Mubarak had left off in terms of monitoring personal and especially electronic communications. Announcing the 'Social Networks Security Hazard Monitoring Operation', the ministry of interior initially described it as a 'public opinion measurement system' before later adding that the operation would be necessary for the 'protection of Egypt', would not require judicial orders, would be never-ending, and would be performed regardless of necessity. A spokesman also explained it would give the ministry new powers to collect data on all Internet users, whether suspects or not. Having bought the sort of deep packet inspection spyware that Mubarak officials had been considering buying from Britain, the Sisi government was understood to have hired a private firm which had a sister company based in the US.[107] Although the latter had ceased to be a publicly listed company in late 2011, the Wall Street Journal reported that over the course of 2014 it had been in talks with 'so-called strategic buyers including [the US] defence contractor Raytheon'.[108]

EGYPT – THE QATAR CONNECTION

With rising debts, damaged infrastructure, and the virtual standstill of major industries such as tourism and manufacturing, no reactionary 'business as usual' Egyptian government was going to survive for long without a substantial infusion of cash. Although having clearly backed the initial Brotherhood-military takeover, the Western powers understandably needed to keep their distance. To plug the gap, wealthy regional proxies were instead encouraged to take the lead and keep things running until the international financial institutions could more smoothly re-engage. In pole position was Qatar, as not only were its gas exports still generating vast surplus revenues, but its popular and Arab Spring-friendly Al-Jazeera network was known to be usefully aligned with, and in some cases even staffed by, Egyptian Islamists. In this sense Qatar's eventual pledges of vast financial support to the Muhammad Morsi government, including promises of $18 billion spread over five years and 'no limits' on future support,[109] are best understood as something of a fusion of the US's long-standing sponsorship of Brotherhood-Wahhabism ties with the new-found 'pro-democracy' and 'pro-revolution' credentials Qatar had managed to garner from its massively influential satellite television channel.

From Doha's perspective the new role was ostensibly a win-win situation. As a small state in a dangerous neighbourhood Qatar was more than ever reliant on the US for its physical protection, and it knew full well that its Egyptian intervention came with the White House's blessing. Moreover, by being able to put its money where its mouth was, Qatar's aid for the first democratically elected Egyptian president helped strengthen even further its glossy new progressive image. Indeed, when asked about the Arab Spring in a *60 Minutes* interview in January 2012, ruler Hamad bin Khalifa al-Thani elusively claimed that Qatar 'had already had its own Qatari Spring a long time ago.'[110] Meanwhile, as Kristian Ulrichsen describes, Hamad's apparent commitment to Al-Jazeera and the 'way it was seen as revolutionizing news reporting across the region' had the desirable effect of 'enhancing the perception that Qatar was somehow different'.[111] Going further, the *Daily Telegraph* even called Al-Jazeera the 'revolutionary force' that was allowing Qatar to 'buck the hierarchical conservatism that has dominated the Arab heartland'.[112]

The Qatari regime's involvement in Egyptian politics also of course helped deflect attention from its own unrepentant authoritarianism. Indeed, just hours after publicly stating how he anticipated working alongside Hamad to 'promote democracy throughout the Middle East', even Barack Obama was quick to point out the hypocrisy of it all. Caught on an open microphone he whispered to a colleague that Hamad was 'a big booster, big promoter of democracy all throughout the Middle East ... [but] now he himself is not reforming significantly ... there's no big move towards democracy in Qatar.'[113] Certainly he had a point as Hamad had been promising for many years that full legislative elections would soon take place and had pledged again in 2011 that they would be held within two years.[114] But with no follow-through, the unelected advisory council's term was instead quietly extended up until 2016 while a huge increase in public sector salaries and pensions costing about $8 billion was announced.[115]

Although some opinion pieces did appear in local newspapers complaining about the lack of public participation in politics, and demanding the right to know the real reason behind the delays in the promised elections, the articles did not, however, appear online.[116] More substantial criticisms from prominent Qataris concerned over the lack of democracy were also made, with veteran activist Ali Khalifa al-Kuwari pointing out that Al-Jazeera's posturing was disingenuous because it never discussed domestic politics, while he and his colleagues went on to publish a manifesto entitled *The people want reform in Qatar too*. Having outlined many of the regime's shortcomings, including the concentration of vast resources in the hands of the ruler, and the state's perpetual reliance on foreign protection, it was duly banned in 2011.[117] Most symbolically, perhaps, a well-known Qatari poet was soon arrested for his own Arab Spring-inspired verses. Held in solitary confinement for a year he was then sentenced to life imprisonment on the very same day that the Egyptian parliamentary elections began in 2012. Uploaded to YouTube, his recitals had proclaimed 'we are all Tunisia' but were rather ironically also deemed to have 'insulted the emir' and 'encouraged the overthrow of [Qatar's] ruling system'.[118]

On a more strategic level for Qatar, bankrolling Morsi also allowed it to deepen greatly its historic links to the Brotherhood which, although nothing comparable to the old Brotherhood-Riyadh nexus, had nonetheless been slowly building. Having acquired a London-based Arabic media outlet in the 1990s at a time when Doha was a relative backwater, some of its pro-Brotherhood employees had come to work in the emirate and their presence provided the ruling family with one of its first significant international relationships.[119] With Al-Jazeera going from strength to strength in the 2000s, more and more Brotherhood members had begun to arrive, and by the time of the Arab Spring, Yusuf al-Qaradawi's *Sharia and Life* show was by far the channel's main event, with viewing figures of more than sixty million every Sunday.[120] Abandoning impartiality, especially when it came to covering Egypt, the Arabic version of Al-Jazeera was soon described as 'breathlessly pro-Brotherhood' with 'obvious bias', while a leaked US diplomatic cable from 2009 revealed how Qatar had been using such coverage to manipulate the Hosni Mubarak regime into various concessions.[121]

Having the Brotherhood and, so it seemed, the Egyptian state much more firmly in its camp by 2012 also helped Qatar hedge better against the more proximate ambitions of Saudi Arabia and Iran. Although reaffirming its Wahhabi credentials in late 2011 by naming its newly opened state mosque after Muhammad Abd al-Wahhab, Qatar had always had a fear of its bigger Wahhabi neighbour's dominance over the region. Not only were there long-standing border disputes, episodes of tribes defecting from one side to another, and a record of failed cooperations over earlier crises on the Arabian Peninsula, but there were also painful memories of how Saudi Arabia along with the UAE had attempted to reinstall former Qatari ruler Khalifa bin Hamad al-Thani after his ouster in 1995 by his son Hamad.[122]

In many ways Qatar's dealings with Iran were no less complicated as most of the emirate's wealth was derived from the massive offshore North Field it shared with the Islamic Republic. Having historically tried to distance itself from Saudi Arabia's rather belligerent and sectarian-based anti-Iran diplomatic campaigns,[123] Doha had already toyed with the idea of rapprochement and had used its temporary membership of the UN Security Council between 2006 and 2007 to vote against resolutions demanding that Iran halt uranium enrichment. Moreover, in 2009, Hamad became one of the first Arab heads of state to congratulate publicly Mahmoud Ahmadinejad on his heavily disputed election victory. Again exposing Qatari hypocrisy, Hamad later even defended the Iranian regime by whitewashing over the Green Revolution and reminding Ahmadinejad's critics that 'Iran has had four presidents since its revolution, while some Arab countries have not changed their leaders at all.'[124]

EGYPT – SAUDI ARABIA TAKES ON THE BROTHERHOOD

In a close parallel to the Egyptian military's increasing dissatisfaction with Muhammad Morsi's presidency, Saudi Arabia was quickly reaching a point of zero tolerance for Qatar's new-found Brotherhood-backed assertiveness. Notwithstanding Riyadh's historic relations with key Egyptian Islamist ideologues and the close integration of its financial sector with Egypt's Islamic banks, by the end of 2012 the Saudi ruling family had come to realize that an empowered Brotherhood was capable of activating chapters across the region and perhaps even prompting something of an 'Islamist Spring'. To put it another way, having enjoyed electoral success in Egypt, and backed by Qatari finance, there was a very real possibility that the Brotherhood and Doha would seek to export their model by sponsoring what seemed to be a vast network of sympathizers in many other Sunni Muslim-majority states, including Saudi Arabia itself.

Having soon entered into direct negotiations with the Supreme Council of the Armed Forces, probably in early 2013, Saudi officials together with counterparts from the equally fearful UAE had effectively promised to replace Qatar as the Egyptian government's main bankrollers following a successful coup d'état. The deal it seemed was for Riyadh and Abu Dhabi to provide $12 billion in aid on the basis that Egypt actually returned $2 billion of remaining Qatari aid to Qatar.[125] Rather prophetically, in 2012, Hamid Dabashi had already warned that Cairo was at risk of a 'fully-fledged military coup' along with an 'American/Saudi ... intervention' and predicted that 'exclusionary and jingoistic nationalism' could destabilize Egypt's nascent civilian government.[126]

Likely having threatened Doha behind the scenes, there is strong evidence to suggest that Saudi Arabia and the UAE had already begun to force Qatar to back off before Morsi's eventual ouster. Exactly a week before *Tamarod* and Abdelfattah Sisi made their move, Qatar had stunned the region by announcing that Hamad bin Khalifa al-Thani would be stepping down in favour of his thirty-three-year-old son Tamim. With some considerable spin, the Qatari regime tried to frame this as some sort of contribution to the Arab Spring on the basis that they were countering the narrative of ancient rulers dying in office and were instead displaying dynamism by ushering in a new and more energetic generation of leaders. In his abdication speech the outgoing Hamad declared that 'the future is ahead of you as you move into a new reign where a young leadership holds up the banner ... [this] puts the ambition of the coming generation as a priority.' He also stated that 'the time has come to open a new page in the journey of our nation that would have a new generation carry the responsibilities with their innovative ideas and active energies.'[127] With the speech having deployed most of the right buzzwords, the Western media largely bought it, and the *Daily Telegraph*, for example, quoted Qatari officials describing the 'power of youth' and how they were 'braced for change', before concluding that the new ruler 'would be hoping his father's gamble on youth is as far-sighted as the decisions that put once-sleepy Qatar on the world stage'.[128] Even more optimistic was the *Economist*, which reasoned that the changeover was due to a combination of Hamad's 'sympathy with the impatience of youth' and his feeling that he needed to 'practise at home what he preached abroad'.[129]

The reality, of course, was that Hamad was only sixty years old, was at the peak of his influence given the situation in Egypt, and neither he nor his son had any intention of introducing any 'innovative ideas' to Qatar. As was pointed out at the time, Tamim had already been entrusted with many key portfolios prior to his succession and many of his father's officials were due to stay on,[130] so the suggestions that Tamim would be undertaking radical reforms or restructuring domestic politics were implausible. Instead the only key policy change was on the Arab Spring, with Qatar's new ruler able to pull away from his father's Egypt policy with at least some shred of dignity.

At first it seemed as though everything had gone to plan, as despite the wobble of Sisi's August 2013 massacres, which had required the Saudi and UAE governments to issue statements of support over the next two days claiming it was '[Egypt's] duty to restore order', the SCAF and the old Mubarak-era elites seemed both grateful and dependent on their new financiers. Released less than two months after the military coup, likely as a Saudi condition, Hosni Mubarak not only quickly endorsed the new dictatorship, explaining to a Kuwaiti journalist that 'the people want Sisi and the people's will shall prevail', but also made repeated references to his gratitude to the late 'Sheikh Zayed of Abu Dhabi and his children'.[131] More visibly, at the height of Sisi's election campaign huge banners depicting the faces of the Saudi and UAE rulers were draped down the walls of the central government's El-Mugamma – the same building that was one of the first focal points of the Arab Spring – while a giant statue of former UAE president and Abu Dhabi ruler Zayed bin Sultan al-Nahyan began to be built outside Cairo.[132] Despite being such an obviously bitter blow to the al-Thani ruling family, the secret deal between Riyadh and Doha also appeared to be holding. Although for a little while Al-Jazeera tried to pursue an anti-Sisi stance and remained loyal to the Brotherhood, Saudi Arabia and the UAE gradually increased their pressure over the course of

247

2014, even removing their ambassadors from Doha at one point, and by the end of the year Qatar agreed to close down its Egypt-specific version of Al-Jazeera and expel a number of Brotherhood exiles.[133]

Some bigger cracks, however, were appearing. With Sisi unable to quell completely Brotherhood protests and, so it seemed, incapable of reaching a position of compromise with the organization's leaders, he was proving unable to emulate Mubarak's strategy of corralling emasculated Islamists into a position of tolerated opposition. With the Brotherhood demanding the release and reinstatement of Morsi as president and refusing to participate in any future elections, the new Egyptian government had little choice but to ramp up repression and escalate the confrontation with its former allies.[134] Blaming Brotherhood elements for a number of terror attacks in Sinai and Cairo in late 2013, but without offering strong supporting evidence, the Sisi administration had upgraded its designation of the Brotherhood from being merely illegal to that of a terror entity.[135] Rather embarrassingly the regime's supposed gratitude to its patrons was also soon called into question with the British-authenticated audio leaks revealing the SCAF's true position on the Gulf monarchies. In one recording seemingly made shortly before the coup, generals discussed the need to transfer money to the '*Tamarod* account' and made it clear that the Saudi and UAE funding needed to be kept exclusively under military control while 'a few pennies' would be put into the Central Bank. In another recording Sisi himself sounded incredulous at the vast sums being transferred from the Gulf, but told another general not to laugh because '[Saudi and the UAE] have money like rice'.[136]

In their own territories the Saudi and UAE leaderships were nonetheless able to capitalize on Sisi's anti-Brotherhood crackdown by mopping up most of their own domestic opposition. Having also designated the Brotherhood a terror entity, they both moved fast to persuade their own populations and their international partners that most of their new inmates had been part of a broader Islamist plot to destabilize the entire region. After all, in Saudi Arabia's case there had been no real Arab Spring to speak of given its extensive police state and its dramatic increase in public spending, with a $10.7 billion package of salary increases and unemployment benefits being announced in February 2011.[137] A 'day of rage' had been announced with twenty-six thousand ostensible 'Saudi liberals' signing up to a Facebook page, but nine days before the protest the page's founder had been found dead, while only one activist actually managed to get through the tight cordons in the centre of Riyadh before then being imprisoned without charge.[138] Two days earlier the grand mufti had also helpfully issued a *fatwa* forbidding protests or petitions and threatening those who ignored this with death by the sword. Reportedly one and a half million copies of the *fatwa* were then printed and distributed across the kingdom.[139]

In this context the harder threat to deal with was always going to come from Saudi Brotherhood members and other Morsi-inspired Saudi Islamists who were feared to be quietly mobilizing elements of the public, and perhaps even the religious establishment, against the ruling family. Having earlier warned the Saudi ruling family that a generation of largely Brotherhood-schooled Saudi religious graduates was on its way, a former US ambassador had been told to 'stop meddling where he wasn't wanted' and that this was 'not his business'.[140] By 2013, however, it seemed such advice was finally being heeded. An 'Islamic Ummah Party' had already been established and had sent a letter to the king telling him that the developments elsewhere in the Islamic world needed to happen in the kingdom, too.[141] Meanwhile, a number of prominent preachers had already started to speak out, including some social media stars with millions of online followers and even international fan bases. Most notably Salman al-Ouda, who had earlier been imprisoned for 'anti-government activities', issued a statement warning all Arab regimes that they were deluded if they thought they were somehow special. He called for a new relationship between rulers and citizens and even a constitutional state.[142] With similarly outspoken clerics beginning to be arrested, protests had begun to take place after Friday sermons outside mosques in Buraidah and other traditionally conservative towns in central Saudi Arabia. In some cases even women took to the streets to demand knowledge of their imprisoned husbands.[143] Introducing new legislation declaring that not only was Brotherhood membership a crime but that showing support for it in any way would constitute a terror offence, Saudi Arabia also began to revisit its old citizenship-stripping practice, with state-backed newspapers calling for its reintroduction on the basis of 'national security threats' from such activists.[144] Soon after, all books penned by Brotherhood-affiliated scholars were removed from the shelves of school and university libraries, including the staple texts by Hassan al-Banna, Sayyed Qutb, and Yusuf al-Qaradawi.[145]

In the UAE the situation was not quite as black and white as in Saudi Arabia because the local Brotherhood-affiliated organization, *Al-Islah*, was only loosely ideologically aligned to the Egyptian movement. For many years it had been tolerated by the UAE's ruling families, with a former ruler of Dubai having even played a role in its 1974 foundation.[146] Although officially dissolved in 1994, it had remained influential in schools, universities, and cultural clubs, with its leader being a nephew of the ruler of Ra's al-Khaimah.[147] After 2004, with Abu Dhabi's new crown prince Muhammad bin Zayed al-Nahyan soon in the driving seat, efforts had been made to roll back *Al-Islah* slowly, with members removed from ministry of education positions and in some cases fired from their jobs as school teachers or university lecturers. But it was in March 2011 when things became much more urgent, as a petition for democratic reforms signed by 133 citizens had been delivered to Muhammad bin Zayed's elder brother, the figurehead ruler.[148] Although some signatories were *Al-Islah* members, many were not, and when a five-man cross-section of the petitioners was imprisoned, including a well-known blogger and a prominent academic, the crown prince's legitimacy was at risk. Released after several months, one of these 'UAE Five' declared that he was glad to be free but that it was a 'sad moment for our homeland, a beginning of a police state that has tarnished the image of the UAE forever'.[149]

The increasing demonization of the Brotherhood in Egypt and then in Saudi Arabia soon provided Muhammad bin Zayed with a much better pretext for further arrests, and in a sort of neo-Bonapartism, the UAE's security services began the process of citizenship-stripping and mass show trials for alleged Brotherhood members. Notably several 'Islamist activists' were deported after their lawyer said they had demanded political reform, while exactly one week after Sisi's 2013 anti-Brotherhood coup, the UAE sentenced 69 out of 94 suspected *Al-Islah* members to prison terms ranging from seven to fifteen years. Among their number were well-known lawyers, academics, student organization members, and even a judge.[150] Most implausibly, the charges laid against them included the setting up of a 'military wing', an accusation earlier denied by *Al-Islah's* spokesman who had asked, 'How is it possible that a group of civilians consisting of university professors, teachers, lawyers and businessmen turn into a military organization?'[151] But as if to underscore their point, the UAE authorities nonetheless also rounded up dozens of Egyptians who had been purportedly 'training Al-Islah in subversion tactics', and at one point even issued an arrest warrant for the Qatar-based al-Qaradawi, who had been increasingly critical of the UAE's actions.[152] Somehow this later translated into an official request by the Egyptian government for an Interpol arrest warrant for al-Qaradawi for 'incitement and assistance to commit intentional murder' and numerous other offences.[153]

The UAE's mass arrests were justified ideologically by its foreign minister, another brother of Muhammad bin Zayed, who argued that 'the Brotherhood does not believe in the nation state' and was 'encroaching on the sovereignty and integrity of nations'.[154] More crudely Dubai's police chief claimed that the Brotherhood had become a greater threat than Iran and that a plot was unfolding which would see them gain power in Kuwait and then take over all the other Gulf monarchies by 2016.[155] Perhaps closer to the truth, and in a distinct echo of Mubarak's frequently expressed fears, Muhammad bin Zayed himself had earlier told US diplomats, 'If an election were held tomorrow, the [UAE] Muslim Brotherhood would win.'[156] As Ziauddin Sardar put it, the UAE had managed to use the label of Islamism to 'scare little children and liberal democrats alike', while as Jean-Pierre Filiu had predicted, the UAE had effectively resorted to authoritarianism as 'the only antidote to an overwhelmingly popular Islamism that would inevitably win any electoral contest'.[157]

Responses from the other Arab monarchies to the anti-Brotherhood campaign have been more mixed, as they have had to balance their need to appease Saudi Arabia and the UAE with their often differing domestic realities. In Kuwait's case, where the local Brotherhood chapter had long since distanced itself from Egypt due to the central organization's unwillingness to confront Saddam Hussein, its members had largely remained on good terms with the government and the ruling family. Similarly in Bahrain, where the regime's main threat had historically been the Shia-dominated opposition, the Sunni Brotherhood had most often served as a sectarian ally and occasionally had even taken part in pro-government demonstrations.[158] Unwilling and perhaps unable to follow the Saudi lead on declaring the

Brotherhood a terror organization, Bahrain nonetheless did try to placate its powerful neighbour by implementing electoral boundary changes that disadvantaged the organization. Moreover, some Bahraini Brotherhood members were dismissed from the cabinet while their long-standing influence in the ministry for education was reportedly reduced.[159]

In Jordan the situation has also been complex, with evidence of careful fence-sitting to please both camps. On the one hand King Abdullah II was the first Arab leader to visit Egypt and congratulate Sisi after the coup, while the director of the government-backed Al-Rai Centre for Strategic Studies later stated that 'the foreign policy of Jordan and Saudi Arabia has always been identical ... always maintaining a high level of cooperation and coordination over many regional and international affairs.' But on the other hand there are signs that Jordan has trodden carefully given that a portion of a $5 billion aid package promised by the Gulf Cooperation Council is supposed to come from Qatar, and given that a substantial number of Jordanian expatriates work in Qatar.[160] Indeed, although Jordan joined Saudi Arabia and the UAE in withdrawing its ambassador from Qatar, it baulked at any form of terror designation, and the consensus in Amman seemed to be that 'Jordan's Brotherhood has never shown a bloody attitude, nor has it ever demanded regime change like in Egypt.'[161]

On the international stage, and especially with the Western powers, the Saudi and UAE Brotherhood policy was far less successful. This was likely because policymakers in the US and Britain were largely indifferent as to exactly which combination of reactionary forces ended up running Egypt, as long as the counter-revolution prevailed in one shape or another. In other words, it did not matter that much to Washington or London whether an Islamist government, a combination of Islamism and military rule, or straightforward military rule was running the show as long as stability was restored. Furthermore, it seems that Saudi Arabia and the UAE had also underestimated the extent of the West's historic relationship and long-standing appreciation of the Brotherhood's role as a conservative counterweight to problematic nationalist, secular, or progressive forces. After all, if Sisi stumbled at some point in the future, the Brotherhood may be needed to step in once again.

Most embarrassingly for the UAE, having viewed the British government as a lower hanging fruit than the US government, a considerable lobbying effort failed to convince London of the need to expel Brotherhood exiles and declare the organization illegal. Launched in early 2014, a British inquiry into the Brotherhood, widely understood to have been requested by the UAE, was heavily criticized and most predicted it was unlikely to lead anywhere. Although former MI6 director Richard Dearlove had once described the Brotherhood as 'at heart a terrorist organization', this did not seem to be a view shared by parliament.[162] Foreign Office minister David Howell had for example already argued that 'the Brotherhood should not be judged as just one lump, or one group of people with more extreme views' and had claimed that 'today's Brotherhood is obviously of a different pattern and the senior people in it have a position that should be understood and discussed.'[163] The view in academia was similarly circumspect, as although there was generally little love lost for the Brotherhood, most agreed that any designation of it as a terror entity would be wrong. Putting it best, Marc Lynch claimed that 'the [British] push to name the Brotherhood a terrorist organization is an analytical step backward, and one which the British government at least reportedly has declined to take.'[164]

By November 2015, and just a few weeks before the inquiry's expectedly inconclusive results were finally published, the *Guardian* revealed details of a number of internal UAE documents written by a senior British expatriate adviser to Abu Dhabi. Dating from summer 2012, one of these indicated that Muhammad bin Zayed was going to complain to the prime minister about Morsi's election victory, and that the UAE was ready to offer a deal in which Britain would be rewarded with lucrative oil concessions and fresh arms deals provided that the BBC reigned in its coverage of the Brotherhood's ascendancy. As the expatriate framed it, the UAE was going to allow 'British Petroleum back in the game' and would 'further deepen the intelligence and military relationship [with Britain]'.[165] Indeed, only a few months later, and with no changes in BBC coverage, BP was temporarily excluded from bidding for an Abu Dhabi concession, while in 2013 BAE's long-running bid to sell Typhoons to the UAE was abruptly dismissed. A second document from 2014, and thus after the inquiry had been launched, was similarly unambiguous as it revealed that Britain's ambassador to the UAE had been warned that Abu Dhabi was still unhappy about Britain's indifference to the Brotherhood and was worried that it did not understand how the organization was 'an existential threat to its ally'.[166]

TUNISIA – UNDER PRESSURE

Given the absence of any Sisi-style 'corrective coups' and the post-2011 state's relative stability, Tunisia soon began to be hailed as the one true Arab Spring success story. On the surface at least it certainly seemed to be passing Samuel Huntington's 'two turnover' test for new democracies, which stipulates that a country passes 'if the party or group that takes power in the initial election at the time of transition loses a subsequent election and turns over power to those election winners, and if those winners then peacefully turn over power to the winners of a later election'.[167]

Seeking to explain this apparent achievement on a more structural level, a compelling argument has been made that Tunisia's relatively weak armed forces were unable or unwilling to play the same sort of post-revolutionary role as Egypt's much stronger military. As Jean-Pierre Filiu notes, much of this can be attributed to the presidential palace's fears of mutiny after Habib Bourguiba's poorly planned attempt in the early 1960s to nationalize French bases by force. This had led to hundreds of deaths in the Tunisian armed forces, described as a 'disastrous gamble with their lives and honour', and the regime's subsequent unearthing of a plot hatched by army officers and a former minister to assassinate Bourguiba.[168] With the military duly downgraded and several of its key commanders executed, the police force had instead become the main organ of state security.[169] As a team of US political scientists has recently demonstrated using quantitative methods, following this period the Tunisian military never became part of a heavily militarized state, and certainly not one comparable to the other North African republics.[170] Furthermore, as others have argued, given that the military under Bourguiba and then Zine el-Abidine Ben Ali was unable to develop any real economic or institutional interests, it actually stood to benefit from a more authentic revolutionary state.[171]

Much attention has also been focused on the country's comparatively rich history of civil society and trade union organizations. As both Eva Bellin and Filiu argue, these were largely responsible for steering the country after 2011, serving as watchdogs over the constitution and, with their memberships of several hundred thousand, offering a balance to religious groups.[172] Moreover, Tunisia's 1956 personal status law, which gave equal rights to men and women and helped to separate religion from the state, has been credited with bringing diverse and ideologically competitive groups to the same table on numerous occasions. As the Brookings Institute's Monica Marks notes, throughout the 2000s a number of civil society and political organizations were able to come together, including the most popular Islamist party, *Ennahda*, and were able to agree on several core principles for the future including the need for a democratic political system to be the sole source of legitimacy.[173]

Taking much the same approach, the University of Washington's Ellis Goldberg makes the case that it was the different factions' willingness to accept each other's ballot box victories and even incorporate former regime members into the political process that has been key. As he describes, former officials were 'neither excluded nor subjected to the threat of political or administrative marginalization.'[174] This stands in contrast with Egypt's Muslim Brotherhood-sponsored 'political exclusion law' which attempted to block Mubarak-era officials such as Omar Suleiman from standing in the presidential elections. Although passed by parliament in April 2012, it was suspended by the still Mubarak-appointed Supreme Constitutional Court.[175] Tunisia's stance also differed markedly with the 2013 'political and administrative isolation law' adopted next door in Libya. Preventing any Gaddafi-era official from serving, it was so strict that even defectors who had fought against the Libyan army in 2011 were made to resign on the basis they were former government members.[176]

In Tunisia's case, the various revolutionary groups had not only allowed former foreign minister Beji Caid Essebsi to serve as the first caretaker prime minister, with *Ennahda* leader Rached Ghannouchi describing him as being 'just dusted off and brought out of the archives', but had even accepted Ben Ali's former parliamentary speaker Fouad Mebazaa as the first interim president. Moreover, as Goldberg notes, the formation of Essebsi's *Nidaa Tounes* or 'Call of Tunisia' party containing other regime remnants would not have been possible if *Ennahda* members had not abstained on a vote for new electoral laws that would have banned former Democratic Constitutional Rally members from engaging in politics.[177] Most symbolic, perhaps, was the ability of several disparate factions, including Islamists and secular liberal groups, to form a compromise coalition – the 'Troika' – to make sure that the first democratic elections in October 2011 would return a parliament with sufficient powers and a long-enough term in office to actually get things done.[178] In practice this meant that although *Ennahda* won a majority and got to form the cabinet and appoint the new prime minister, it did not get control over the presidency or several other key ministries.[179]

Under the hood, but perhaps equally importantly, *Ennahda* had also supported a closed-list proportional representation system for the elections in preference to a first past the post system, even though the former effectively marginalized the party's electoral ambitions and favoured smaller parties.[180] As Marks has estimated, the latter would have given *Ennahda* almost ninety percent of the vote rather than the thirty-seven percent they ended up with. Although some have suggested this was a reflection of *Ennahda* not being as powerful as many had assumed, others have claimed that Ghannouchi's long period of exile in London, where he observed the failings of the Westminster system, had given his party a much 'thicker understanding of democratic politics' and the need for more gradualism than its regional counterparts such as the Brotherhood.[181]

Either way the Troika proved solid enough to survive several early tests of Tunisia's revolutionary integrity. Following the prosecution of a television station director in late 2011 for defamation of Islam, after his channel had broadcast a 'blasphemous' animated film, more than three hundred protestors attacked the station's headquarters while others blamed Islamist parties for exacerbating the situation for their own benefit.[182] In early 2012 further clashes erupted after the death of a pro-Essebsi activist was blamed on 'unofficial networks supporting the ruling *Ennahda* party', and a few months later in March 2012 the coalition survived perhaps its first major challenge after managing to clear the streets of thousands who had begun to demand publicly the creation of an Islamic state.[183] With no apparent rush to push through a potentially divisive new constitution, the Tunisian polity seemed well aware of the need to avoid the sort of 'constitutional cul-de-sacs' repeatedly being foisted on the Egyptian people.[184]

TUNISIA – SLEEPWALKING TO COUNTER-REVOLUTION

Beyond its internal politics, some have suggested Tunisia's post-revolutionary stability was also a function of its geopolitical circumstances.

With the country being on the margins of the region's main ideological and sectarian fault lines, without the vast natural resources of some of its neighbours, and a comfortable distance from the most populous and militarily most powerful Arab states, it is tempting to assume that the outcome of its Arab Spring protests simply did not matter that much for external powers. Sadly, however, many of the same patterns and strategies at play in Cairo were also soon identifiable in Tunis, albeit a little more under the surface. Competition between the region's two main counter-revolutionary camps was certainly not as intense as in the all-important Egyptian arena, but there is nonetheless much evidence of a pitted and potentially destabilizing struggle having begun between the sponsors of Islamism and those that have sought to rejuvenate what remains of the old 'deep state'.

As in Egypt, Qatar effectively fired the first salvos, with its ready-made partner, *Ennahda*, arguably even better placed than the Egyptian Muslim Brotherhood to become the country's dominant political force. Having already proven its ballot box credentials when its independent candidates won fourteen percent of the vote in the 1989 parliamentary elections, but then suffering a crackdown at the hands of Zine el-Abidine Ben Ali's security forces, *Ennahda* never really became besmirched in the way that the Brotherhood did with its decades of 'murky deals' with the Hosni Mubarak regime.[185] Furthermore, after *Ennahda* was wrongly blamed for an al-Qaeda attack on Tunisia in 2002 and labelled by Ben Ali as 'the inextinguishable source of terror', the revolutionary credentials of its then exiled leaders were undoubtedly strengthened further.[186]

Closely tied to *Ennahda*'s electoral success in October 2011, Qatar duly began to announce several financial support packages to buttress the new government and, by extension, to strengthen the hand of its Islamist components. A $2 billion Qatar-funded new oil refinery was announced, along with promises of assistance for the Tunisian central bank to help ameliorate its worsening balance of payments.[187] Less tangibly, as Alfred Stepan and Juan Linz observed, the government also seemed willing to leave the country's mosques wide open to foreign funding, with 'a vacuum that Gulf-financed theocratic extremists rushed to fill amid the new con-ditions of greater religious liberty'. As they argued, '*Ennahda* has not yet been able to effectively create alternative spaces and discourses in many key mosques and neighbourhoods.'[188] As a report commissioned for the European Parliament has detailed, by September 2012 these permissive conditions had allowed more than a thousand lightly armed Islamists, who were ostensibly protesting against an amateurish anti-Islam video that had gone viral on social media, to attack an American school and occupy the periphery of the US embassy. Leading to numerous arrests and four deaths, many Tunisians were reportedly bewildered at the scale of the event.[189] More seriously *Ennahda* was also beginning to be accused of being too conciliatory to veterans of the old al-Qaeda-linked Tunisia Islamic Fighting Group which, like the Libyan Islamic Fighting Group, was formed by jihadists returning from Afghanistan and the Balkans. With the group's leader, Seifallah Ben Hassine, already released from prison, allegations were made that his new cross-border militant organization, *Ansar al-Sharia*, was responsible for the September attacks.[190]

Staging a rally of their own in October 2012, Beji Caid Essebsi's *Nidaa Tounes* took to the streets declaring that the Troika coalition had lost its legitimacy. Although their official grievance was that the government had still not finished drafting a new constitution, there were also powerful anti-Islamist undercurrents given the previous month's violence. Indeed, a video had begun to circulate which featured Rached Ghannouchi stating clearly to an audience that *Ennahda's* rivals were 'the enemies of Islam'. Watched by millions, his statements were difficult if not impossible to defend and were even reported by the international media.[191] By 2013, and in a close parallel to the anti-Brotherhood demonstrations in Cairo, the anti-*Ennahda* rallies were growing in size and frequency. Within days of the Egyptian coup d'état the distinctly *Tamarod*-like 'Bardo protests' had begun, with a mix of leftists, trade union activists, professional associations, and regime remnants all clamouring for a new government and blaming *Ennahda* for its toleration of extremist organizations. Importantly, the catalyst for the Tunisian *Tamarod* had been a number of assassinations of secular activists, including one just days before. Although pinned on Islamists at the time, they have remained unattributed.[192]

Having witnessed Muhammad Morsi's fate, *Ennahda* and most likely its foreign backers sought to avoid confrontation at such a moment of weakness and, so it seemed, opted instead for a more compromise-based strategy for survival. As Eva Bellin argues, 'The Egyptian experience served as a cautionary tale for the *Ennahda* leadership in Tunisia and it persuaded the party's elite to make difficult compromises that they had resisted for the year prior.'[193] Similarly, as Nathan Brown and others have pointed out, the timing really mattered, as *Ennahda* knew there was no point in reproducing the Brotherhood's mistakes.[194] Having already nominally supported the ceding of the 'sovereign ministries', *Ennahda* duly agreed to transfer the prime minister position to an independent caretaker by January 2014.[195] Furthermore, *Ennahda* dropped its original preference for a parliament-only system, as opposed to a mixed-powers parliament-president one, and made it clear it would support a constitution confirming Tunisia as a civil state rather than an Islamic state.[196] Most importantly, perhaps, it also announced it would not be fielding a candidate in the November 2014 presidential elections, leaving the path clear for a straightforward contest between Essebsi and the caretaker president Moncef Marzouki.

Although Marzouki had his own party, the Congress for the Republic, and his Arab Spring qualifications were exemplary given his earlier twenty-year exile due to his human rights activism, he was no match for Essebsi, who stormed to victory with nearly fifty-six percent of the vote.[197] The rise of *Nidaa Tounes* and its ability to mobilize against Islamists, especially in the wake of the Tunisian *Tamarod*, had seemed to more than cancel out Essebsi's Ben Ali era links. As his supporters claimed, his career in the regime was so long ago it should not matter, and in any case he displayed a talent for rallying around him 'reformed Ben Ali-ists' along with 'true revolutionaries nostalgic for Bourguiba's era'.[198] From a different perspective, however, many Tunisians pointed out that despite all the trials and tribulations of the Arab Spring, they had simply ended up with a former regime official as their president. Indeed, on his succession Essebsi was remarkably quick to resume and arguably even intensify Ben Ali's old relations with the Western powers. Spending the remainder of 2014 and most of 2015 building upon his government's 'individual partnership and cooperation programme' with NATO and then being upgraded to holding 'enhanced political dialogue' with the organization, Essebsi seemed well on the way to reprising Tunisia's role as a military and counter-terrorism partner.[199]

Given the obvious opportunity for Saudi Arabia and the UAE to impose their brand of counter-revolution at the expense of the Qatar-Islamist alliance, many have suggested their hidden hand behind *Nidaa Tounes* and have pointed out the remarkable similarities between the Egyptian and Tunisian *Tamarod* movements. While no hard evidence is available to connect Riyadh or Abu Dhabi to the Bardo protests or indeed the political assassinations that were their catalyst, there are nonetheless several indicators that a relationship was being steadily built with Essebsi and the remains of Ben Ali's deep state. According to a leaked Saudi foreign ministry diplomatic cable from early 2012, officials were already discussing their fear of an Islamist government in Tunisia that would inevitably align itself with Turkey and Morsi's Egypt.[200]

Other Saudi leaked cables from April 2012 reveal that at the same time Ghannouchi was undertaking a trip to Riyadh, the Saudi government had begun to consider ways to boost its 'cultural ties' with Tunisia, perhaps by funding new Tunisian media organizations in cooperation with the Saudi embassy in Tunis.[201] A few weeks later the Saudi ministry of culture and information seemed to be in on the act, with its staff discussing how they should go about inviting prominent Tunisian media figures and their wives to perform *hajj* in Mecca later that year.[202] Another leaked cable reports how an unnamed representative of the Tunisian Troika coalition had actually begun to contact the Saudi-based Ben Ali and had offered to enter into reconciliation negotiations. According to the cable's author, Ben Ali accepted the offer to begin such talks.[203] Intriguingly, while these overtures were being made, the Troika's ambassador in Bahrain also reportedly informed Saudi officials of a secret and substantial Tunisian oil discovery, although it seems he was unwilling to then furnish them with any substantial details.[204]

In August 2014, following the leaking of tax documents that suggested the UAE had been gifting luxury bullet-proof cars to Essebsi's campaign team, Rafwan Masmoudi, president of the US-based Center for the Study of Islam and Democracy, and a member of the Georgetown University's Berkeley Center, stated that 'the UAE is doing everything it can to derail and thwart the democratic transition in Tunisia.' He explained that 'this gift to Essebsi and *Nidaa Tounes* is a clear violation of Tunisia's party laws and is an attempt to create havoc just two or three months before the upcoming legislative and presidential elections.'[205] By May 2015 the UAE's links were being more openly criticized, even in Tunisia, with demands being made for an all-party parliamentary inquiry into the relationship that seemed to be developing. In particular, a Tunisian journalist and high-profile author who claimed to be a confidant of the president came forward on national television to state that in 2014 UAE officials had urged Essebsi to 'repeat the Egyptian scenario', and had promised that if he succeeded in sidelining *Ennahda* then the UAE would provide Tunisia with considerable financial aid. An opposition politician argued that 'this intervention of the UAE in Tunisian affairs is extremely dangerous, and represents a clear attack against the country and its people.'[206] By November 2015 Tunisian officials reportedly claimed that their Algerian counterparts had given them a warning and 'were very unambiguous and said that they [the UAE] may try to destabilize Tunisia as it is at the moment.'[207]

YEMEN - OUTMANOEUVRING THE ARAB SPRING

On the doorstep of Saudi Arabia and Oman, and in alarmingly close proximity to the West's other key regional allies, Yemen's Arab Spring and its people's apparent ability to oust a long-serving dictator were inevitably identified as existential threats to the oil-rich Gulf monarchies. Indeed, the need for these states to mount a rapid and effective counter-revolution in Yemen was in some ways just as important as in Egypt, with even Riyadh and Doha initially able to set aside their differences in the interests of working together under a collective Gulf Cooperation Council (GCC) plan.

Best placed to intervene was Saudi Arabia, as for many years it had been distributing funds to political actors and groups in the country, on a largely ad hoc basis through its Special Office for Yemen Affairs. Run by the long-serving Saudi defence minister Sultan bin Abdul-Aziz al-Saud, by the beginning of 2011 the office was thought to have been dispensing about $3 billion a year to thousands of recipients. Although formally closed a few months before Sultan's death in May 2011, the funding flow continued through other princes, albeit in an even more haphazard and erratic manner.[208]

Duly taking the lead in brokering the first agreement with Ali Abdullah Saleh, in April 2011 Riyadh had managed to bring the ruling General People's Congress to the same table as the Joint Meeting Parties – a decade-old alliance of purported opposition groups.[209] Allowing the old dictator to avoid the humiliating fate of Hosni Mubarak and Zine el-Abidine Ben Ali was of course essential, as was the need for the JMP, as Saleh's de facto tolerated opposition, to contain and fit under its umbrella the new Arab Spring activists. Comprising various Islamist factions, including some ideologically linked to the Egyptian Muslim Brotherhood, the JMP was very much a 'safe pair of hands' as far as the Gulf monarchies and, by extension, the Western powers were concerned. As Abdelwahab al-Affendi argues, it had played no significant role in mobilizing or sustaining the street protests and, as with the Brotherhood in Cairo, it had been the first organization to try to find a compromise with the old regime.[210] Moreover, although the JMP had attempted some outreach with the new youth groups and student associations that had led the crowds, its motivations were treated with great suspicion by many of the revolutionaries, most of whom demanded Saleh's unconditional removal.[211]

Dragging his heels in accepting the GCC and JMP's terms and refusing the US's strongly worded advice to fulfil his promise to step down, Saleh's position was nonetheless rapidly weakening as the ongoing protests had begun to morph into a civil war. Badly injured in a rocket attack on the presidential palace in June 2011 he even had to flee to Saudi Arabia. But having installed a son in his absence and eventually returning to Yemen after successful treatment, Saleh was still in a position to push for the best terms he could. Eventually adopted by everyone, the GCC's revised deal was even approved by the UN Security Council, whose October 2011 resolution was suspiciously specific about the centrality of the GCC in Yemen's future affairs.[212] Reaffirming that Saleh would be granted immunity, his sons were to be allowed to remain in their positions, and then within two years full presidential elections would be held.[213]

With Saleh having signed away his powers to Vice President Abd Rabbo Mansour Hadi, the General People's Congress and the JMP were to share power while a placeholding election was quickly held to install Hadi as interim president.[214] As a former senior regime official and the GCC's sole 'consensus' candidate, Hadi's uncontested election and the agreement that underpinned it were, as Stacey Philbrick Yadav describes, far from being a 'template for a substantive democratic transition'. Unsurprisingly therefore, and more or less concurrent with the escalating protests against Egypt's

Brotherhood-dominated parliament, many Yemeni activists turned on the JMP with the slogan 'no tribe, no parties, our revolution is a youth revolution'. Also demanding an end to GCC interference and baulking at the immunity provisions for Saleh, many of the ensuing 'Dignity and Life' marches numbered tens of thousands while workplace sit-ins began to take place in what was called a 'parallel revolution' against ongoing public sector corruption that the GCC plan was blamed for having ignored. Moreover, when the transitional government tried to stage a National Dialogue Conference from March 2013 to January 2014, activists complained and boycotted it on the grounds it was yet another mechanism to 'shoe-horn [them] into partisan or demographic categories which prevented them from representing the broad-based nature of the movement'.[215] Indeed, as with the counter-revolutions in Egypt and Tunisia, it appeared to the crowds that the old regime had somehow slipped back into power, with the General People's Congress having been assigned the most seats, while Yemen's effective Brotherhood franchise held the second highest number.[216]

Equally worryingly, the Hadi administration seemed incapable of holding Saleh to his promises, with the latter's entrenched and often tribal links to the Yemeni military and intelligence services proving hard to sever. As Robert Springborg notes, much like Egypt's military deep state, Saleh's senior commanders had enjoyed years of being shored up by the US, not only as a function of their role in the 'War on Terror', but also because Washington viewed them as part of the only Yemeni institution capable of preventing the country from completely disintegrating.[217] Under pressure from Riyadh, Hadi had managed to remove from their posts one of Saleh's half-brothers and one of his nephews – respectively, the chief of air defence and the head of the presidential guard. Soon after, however, the deposed half-brother launched a retaliatory attack on Sana'a's airport,[218] while a series of other explosions and assassinations were linked to Hadi's efforts to oust one of Saleh's sons as head of the republican guard and one of his other nephews who was the chief of the central security forces.[219]

More seriously, and again in apparent retaliation against Hadi, the Yemeni military had begun to suffer some of their worst losses at the hands of the local al-Qaeda franchise, 'al-Qaeda in the Arabian Peninsula'

(AQAP).[220] Notable massacres included 185 soldiers killed in their sleep during a night-time attack on a base near Zinjibar – the capital of the southern province – only a week after Hadi's succession, while 57 soldiers died in an 'audacious attack' on their base in Abyan province a few months later.[221] In a suicide bombing in May 2012, on the eve of Yemen's national day, another hundred soldiers were then killed as they practised their parade for the celebrations.[222] As some have argued, pointing the finger at Saleh loyalists, it is hard to see how AQAP could have carried out these attacks so successfully without first obtaining detailed inside information from those with 'privileged access to restricted intelligence and facilities'.[223]

If this is true, in many ways it should not have come as a surprise, as there is evidence that during the height of the 2011 protests Saleh had already begun to flirt with an extreme version of Mubarak's February 2011 strategy of opening up prisons to destabilize the Tahrir Square protests. Having withdrawn Yemeni army units from Zinjibar in March, Saleh had effectively allowed nearby AQAP militants and their fellow travellers to enter and proclaim an Islamic state known as the Islamic Emirate of Abyan.[224] Greatly reinvigorating the spectre of Islamic fundamentalism, should Saleh fall to Arab Spring protests, the new Islamic state usefully issued a statement confirming that sharia would be the basis of all of its laws and declared that 'from now on women who go out to the markets need to be accompanied by a relative, who [must] carry a proof by identity cards, or passport'.[225] In a rare direct criticism of Saleh, former Yemeni defence minister Abdullah Ali Eliwa accused him of deliberately ordering the army to 'hand over Zinjibar' to the jihadists in order to 'frighten people that if he goes, Yemen will become Somalia'.[226]

Also of concern for Hadi and the other regime remnants in cahoots with the JMP were the increasing tensions between their GCC patrons, especially in the build-up to the Egyptian coup d'état and during the eventual Riyadh-Doha standoff. Most in Sana'a had clearly hoped that Yemen's location – being too close for comfort for both Saudi Arabia and Qatar – would be enough to prevent any spin-off of the anti-Brotherhood war. After all, the UN Security Council's resolution seemed to indicate that Doha's diplomacy in Yemen had already been 'subsumed within the framework of the GCC's collective role in mediation'.[227] Many, however, remained suspicious, including Saleh himself who grudgingly warned the local media on his way to a meeting in Doha that 'Qatar has so much money they don't know what to do with it, and are setting a financial foundation to become one of the big players in the Middle East by funding all the unrest.'[228] On a separate occasion he even denounced Qatar for having 'blatantly interfered in Yemen's affairs' and once told a rally of his support-ers that 'we reject what comes from Qatar or Al-Jazeera.'[229] Unsurprisingly, perhaps, his fears were later confirmed by a leaked Saudi diplomatic cable indicating that Saudi intelligence was already aware of Qatari efforts to pay $250 million to certain Yemeni tribal and Brotherhood leaders so that together they could 'foment rebellion' and prevent the eventual election of a pro-Saudi president.[230]

Unable to turn to the Yemeni military in the same way they had done in Egypt, and with no Yemeni equivalent of Abdelfattah Sisi to push to the front as the country's hardman saviour, Riyadh and Abu Dhabi had to become more creative in their choice of proxies if their control over the counter-revolution was to be maintained. Although the Zaydi-Shia Houthi tribesmen of northern Yemen maintained religious and cultural relations with Iran, and although Saudi Arabia had militarily intervened against them in 2009, and the UAE had often supplied Saleh with weap-ons to fight them, by 2013 the Houthis were nonetheless still seen as potential allies.[231] Not only had they proved willing to launch repeated insurrections against Yemeni governments, but by the time of the Arab Spring their relations with Qatar were evidently sour, given Doha's earlier failed efforts to mediate in Yemen.[232] Moreover, by this stage the Houthis had not only gained considerable battlefield experience, but they had usefully organized themselves into a potent Hezbollah-like paramilitary force called Ansar Allah or 'Partisans of God'.[233] Having been marginalized by the National Dialogue Conference, just like the Arab Spring activists, there are strong indications that by late 2013 factions within Saudi Arabia had sought to cultivate the Houthis alongside those parts of the army that continued to resist government control so that Riyadh would have a future counterweight against the JMP, and especially its Brotherhood-linked and possibly Qatar-backed constituents. As the Guardian reported, a prominent Houthi was flown to London at this time to meet and reach an agreement with Saudi intelligence chief Bandar bin Sultan al-Saud.[234] Meanwhile, as this rather odd alliance of convenience continued to develop, allegations

were made that the UAE had provided one of Saleh's sons with $1 billion
in funding and had sent a delegation to Sana'a to meet with other Houthi
leaders alongside a group of Saleh loyalist army officers.[235]

BAHRAIN – THE FORGOTTEN REVOLUTION

As arguably the only other Arab state where there was a sufficiently
broad-based protest movement in 2011 that represented the majority of
the population, Bahrain and its prospective revolution was equally if not
even more distressing to the status quo powers than the events in Egypt,
Tunisia, and Yemen. As an island kingdom in the centre of the Persian
Gulf it was not only next to some of the largest oil fields in the world, but
was also still a key Western military outpost, especially since the revival
of the US Navy's Fifth Fleet in the 1990s. Moreover, with Bahrain only
twenty-five kilometres across the King Fahd Causeway from Saudi Arabia's
historically most restive Eastern Province, and not much further from the
coastline of Qatar, the fall of its long-reigning al-Khalifa monarchy would
have sent shock waves across the Gulf states and perhaps even burst the
bubble of invincibility enjoyed by the Western-backed Arab monarchies.

Organized by various youth groups rather than established political
societies, an estimated 150,000 streamed onto the streets of Manama
following an initial 'day of rage' on 14 February 2011.[236] With much the
same demands as their comrades in Tunisia and Egypt, what was looking
like it could become the highest per capita movement of the Arab Spring
was nonetheless not yet revolutionary, with most initially campaigning
for the ruling family to honour its earlier promises of political reform.
Calling for the fulfilment of the 'National Action Charter' signed a decade
earlier, which was supposed to lead to a strengthened parliament and the
release of political prisoners, the first waves of Bahraini protests were in
many ways a pushback against the sort of half-hearted and autocratically
created institutions that had long been used by the ruling family and its
allies as fig leaves to disguise the lack of any real political participation.
Notably, during another period of unrest in the late 1990s, British officials
had claimed Bahrain was still moving forward on the basis that it had
adopted a 'respected and accepted form of constitution ... not perfect but

266

we should not write it off', while after limited elections were held in 2002 amid mass boycotts and widespread accusations of human rights abuses and arbitrary detentions, Britain's Foreign Office argued that 'Bahrain is in many ways providing a lead to show that it is possible to create a more democratic state in the Middle East ... with its head held high.'[237]

In this sense the first few days of Bahrain's Arab Spring represented an attempted escape from the trap of 'liberalized autocracy' earlier described by Georgetown University's Daniel Brumberg and, in John Stuart Mill's terms, a rejection of the sort of 'consensual domination' that had previously allowed small and unaccountable elites to rule and make decisions while the masses were being constantly distracted by carefully managed and ultimately pointless elections.[238] But with the security services opening fire on the protestors on 17 February, resulting in several deaths, hundreds of injuries, and even the arresting of doctors and nurses who had witnessed the atrocities, the protestors' demands soon morphed into 'down down Hamad' and other such calls for the overthrow of King Hamad bin Isa al-Khalifa.[239] As Hamid Dabashi observed, it was evident that when regimes such as Bahrain's were at last faced with real challenges, they almost immediately 'scrapped those [constitution] documents and transformed themselves into killing machines defending garrison states'.[240]

As with most previous uprisings, the Sunni ruling family's knee-jerk response was to try to sectarianize the protests and attempt to re-establish societal divides so that, in Leon Trotsky's terms, the king could quickly re-emerge as Bahrain's 'inviolable super arbiter'.[241] Moreover, with the majority on the streets assumed to be Shia, given their demographic superiority, there was the added purpose of attempting to frame the revolution as part of a broader Iran-sponsored plot to destabilize the region and thus endanger the West's long-standing allies. Having demolished at least thirty well-established Shia mosques along with other religious structures on the spurious grounds that they were operating without licences, senior government officials even began to claim that the red and white Bahraini flags being waved by the protestors had begun to feature twelve triangles rather than the usual five, thus symbolizing the Shia belief in there being twelve imams. However, as was soon pointed out, the flags in the photographs the officials were holding up only had ten triangles and this was because they were evidently just two flags that had been stuck together.[242]

As many have since argued, there is little to suggest that the 2011 movement was ever sectarian in nature, with the *New York Times'* correspondents reporting that there were many Sunni participants, and – according to eyewitnesses – one of the most popular slogans was 'no Sunni, no Shia, just Bahraini'.[243] As Chatham House's Jane Kinninmont explains, there was no evidence of a link to Iran either, not least because most of Bahrain's Shia do not even subscribe to the Iranian doctrine of *wilayet-e-faqih* or 'rule by clerics', and have instead historically looked to Iraqi Shia clerics for their guidance.[244] Putting it best, journalist Shirin Sadeghi explained that 'the so-called sectarian divide of Bahrain is a manipulative simplification of a far greater divide: that of the colonially-installed government that has no connection or compassion for the people of Bahrain.'[245]

With the protests still advancing and having reached Manama's financial district, and predicted to soon reach palaces and government buildings, it was becoming obvious that the Bahraini forces on their own, short of committing a massacre, were in danger of losing control. On 21 February 2011, even the Bahrain Formula One Grand Prix – arguably the centrepiece of Bahrain's economic diversification strategy – had had to be called off.[246] By March rumours were rife that foreign troops had begun to arrive in the kingdom to buttress its already heavily expatriate-dependent security services. Spotted in Pakistani newspapers, adverts aimed at army veterans had started to appear declaring the 'urgent need of the Bahraini National Guard', while eyewitnesses began to report the arrival of other Arab soldiers. In fact, on 14 March approximately fifteen hundred Saudi Arabian national guard troops and over five hundred UAE security personnel had crossed the causeway riding in a convoy of British-manufactured armoured personnel carriers.[247]

Although not without precedent, as small Saudi detachments had also been sent to Bahrain during the 1990s, it was the first official deployment of the Gulf Cooperation Council's Peninsula Shield joint force. Although it was ostensibly there to reduce the threat of 'foreign invasion', presumably from Iran, the Bahraini authorities did little to hide its real purpose, having stated that 'the foreign troops have started arriving to Bahrain in light of the regretful situation the kingdom is currently witnessing', and called upon 'all citizens and residents to co-operate fully with the GCC forces and welcome them warmly'.[248] Furthermore, with the exception of some

Kuwaiti naval patrols there was no evidence that other GCC members had contributed, although according to recently leaked Saudi diplomatic cables Bahrain had requested that Moroccan troops also be sent.[249]

Despite some claims that the Saudi and UAE forces helped their Bahraini counterparts clear the streets, especially as they bulldozed the iconic pearl-shaped monument at Lulu Roundabout that had become a sort of Bahraini version of Tahrir Square, it seems their primary role was to remain in the background and provide a 'reservoir of repression', as a team of US political scientists has recently put it.[250] However, with martial law declared and sporadic violence continuing, there is evidence that the supposedly defensive GCC troops had soon begun to embed themselves with Bahraini national guard units. Indeed, many reported hearing Saudi or UAE accents among the members of the night-time house-raiding squads, while over the next couple of years a number of the policemen killed during riot-control duties, often by improvised explosive devices, were later revealed to be part of the GCC deployment.[251]

Even though it had not contributed to the military intervention, there is little doubt that Qatar was fully on board with the GCC's counter-revolution. Al-Jazeera's English channel admittedly produced a wonderfully evocative documentary on the Bahraini uprising called *Shouting in the Dark*, which should be required viewing for all students of Gulf politics, but it was only broadcast once, while the far more influential Arabic channel barely covered Bahrain at all, or if it did then it attempted to misrepresent it.[252] On one occasion Al-Jazeera even barred a Bahraini human rights activist from appearing on a debate show on the request of the Bahraini government guest.[253] Indeed, for those watching closely, the way Al-Jazeera and Qatari officials handled the obvious inconvenience caused by the Arab Spring reaching their own doorstep provides one of the best clues as to Qatar's underlying disingenuity. Fresh from his personal appearances in Tahrir Square, Yusuf al-Qaradawi began to use the same Al-Jazeera show on which he had earlier lambasted Hosni Mubarak to brand Bahrain's uprising as sectarian, rather than about democracy.[254] Qatari prime minister Hamad bin Jassim al-Thani played it more cautiously, but his demand that the Bahraini protestors 'withdraw from the streets in order for dialogue to succeed' was painfully inconsistent with his rhetoric on revolutionary North Africa.[255]

Optimistic that the Gulf monarchies could sort out the mess in their own neighbourhood, as they were also attempting to do in Yemen, the Western powers seemed relatively relaxed over the situation in Bahrain. As soon became clear, a deal had quickly been struck between the US, Britain, and Saudi Arabia, in which the latter would provide much-needed public Arab backing for a NATO no-fly zone over Libya in exchange for Washington and London trying to 'mute criticism' of whatever was going on in Bahrain.[256] According to two UN diplomats this was understood to require Saudi Arabia making sure that the Arab League delivered a 'yes' vote to support NATO's actions, and then in return the kingdom would privately receive approval for launching an intervention in Bahrain.[257] Giving oral evidence to Britain's Foreign Affairs Committee three days after the GCC deployment began, Foreign Secretary William Hague made no mention of the plan and instead claimed he was 'very concerned about events in Bahrain – and Saudi Arabia has sent forces there'. Moreover, he explained that 'I spoke to Prince Saud, the Saudi foreign minister, about this on Sunday evening and he assured me that these were for the defence of installations and the external defence of Bahrain, while it would be the Bahraini forces and police that tried to restore order in their own country'.[258]

With some semblance of stability restored, by the end of the year the worst seemed to be over, with the path soon smooth enough for the US to remove a temporary block that had been placed on arms supplies to Bahrain, and with the king able to appoint another batch of senior Western expatriates as his latest security consultants.[259] Appointed in December 2011 to advise on police reform, former London Metropolitan Police assistant commissioner John Yates went on to describe Bahraini protestors as 'criminals' on British television, while the British media has since alleged that former Miami police chief John Timoney, also brought in as an adviser, is to blame for the dramatic increase in the use of tear gas in Bahrain.[260] Summing up the situation in a keynote address to the National Democratic Institute, Hillary Clinton was remarkably frank with her explanation of how the US's need for a secure supply of energy meant that the government would 'always have to walk and chew gum at the same time' and that 'this is our challenge in a country like Bahrain, which has been America's close friend and partner for decades'.[261] Similarly blunt, a Congressional Research Service report explained that there was no real alternative naval base for the US as facilities elsewhere, even in the UAE, were just not big enough or would involve inconvenient sharing with commercial operations.[262]

Having advised the Bahraini monarchy to commission an independent inquiry into the handling of the 2011 protests under former UN investigator Cherif Bassiouni, Western officials effectively managed to buy even more time, as although the inquiry published its report towards the end of that year, US and British ministers were able to deflect most subsequent criticism of the Bahraini regime on the basis that the king was demonstrably serious about reform but simply needed more time to implement the inquiry's suggestions. Indeed, only weeks after its publication the king was invited to London to meet with Prime Minister David Cameron. According to the British government's press release, their discussion concluded with an exploration of 'how they could boost trade co-operation between the two countries and the opportunities for British business to invest in Bahrain, particularly in the infrastructure sector'.[263]

Despite overwhelming evidence to indicate that most of the inquiry's suggestions had been ignored, and just weeks after the arrest of prominent opposition leader Ali bin Salman, in January 2015 Britain's foreign secretary Philip Hammond was still stating that '[Bahrain] is a country which is travelling in the right direction ... It is making significant reform.'[264] Two months later, the Bahraini embassy in the US was even confident enough to circulate a letter to the US Congress calling on it to approve pending sales of 'Humvees, rifles, ammunition, and tear gas', despite the latter having already been described by the Congressional Research Service as 'equipment that could be used against protestors [in Bahrain]'. In full support of the letter, John McCain, chairman of the Senate's Armed Services Committee, resumed most of the original counter-revolutionary narrative by stating that 'I'm very concerned about Iranian penetration into Bahrain; that's their next target' and, without substantiation, claiming that 'there's no doubt that Iranian weapons are coming into Bahrain.' Nonetheless, giving a good insight into the sort of contortions that had become necessary to keep portraying the Bahraini regime as a suitable partner, McCain did concede that 'there are several things I'm not happy about that [Bahrain's] government has done, but they need to be able to defend their country.' His views were unsurprisingly shared by the chairman

271

of the Senate's Foreign Relations Near East Subcommittee, Jim Risch, who reasoned that 'yes, I'd like the Bahrainis to do some things differently ... [But] how can you have somebody in a coalition and say, OK, fight, but we're not going to sell you any weapons?'[265]

7

PLAN 'B' – A FAKE ARAB SPRING

CONTAINABLE PROTESTS

B eyond the full-blown revolutions in Tunisia, Egypt, and Yemen, and the thwarted uprising in Bahrain, most of the other protests against Western-backed Arab governments in 2011 were either too small-scale or too narrow in their demands to require an organized counter-revolution or armed intervention. In Morocco, for example, the crowds at demonstrations that had begun on 20 February may have reached hundreds of thousands, but the protests were effectively curtailed by a package of measures including constitutional amendments, the co-option of Islamist parties, and soothing noises from the loyal religious establishment.[1] As Ottawa University's Frédéric Vairel has explained, the authorities managed to maintain a careful balance of 'toleration, repression and containment of street mobilization ... and avoided producing martyrs for the opposition movements to capitalize on'.[2] In Jordan similar protests that had focused on corruption, unemployment, and inflation were likewise appeased after King Abdullah II met with Muslim Brotherhood representatives and dismissed his entire cabinet, including the prime minister.[3]

In both cases the treasuries of these monarchies also soon swelled, courtesy of $5 billion in development aid from the Gulf Cooperation Council.[4] This greatly increased the ability of the Moroccan and Jordanian kings to achieve a rapid reduction in unemployment while also maintaining hefty subsidies. As bizarre as it may sound, the GCC even invited the two struggling monarchies to join it as full members, despite neither being anywhere near the Persian Gulf. Some described this as a mutually beneficial deal, as Morocco and Jordan clearly needed the money, while the Gulf monarchies might some day need the military manpower of their poorer colleagues.[5]

Equally manageable were the short-lived protests in Kuwait and Oman, with neither of their 2011 movements reaching anywhere near the same level of potency or revolutionary fervour as in Bahrain. In the former, the government made an early pre-emptive strike, barely hours after Zine el-Abidine Ben Ali had fled Tunisia, by announcing that each citizen, including children, would receive a $3,500 handout as well as a year's allowance of basic food items including sugar and milk.[6] Officially this was a gift to commemorate Kuwait's February 1991 liberation, but given that it was nearly two months early, most interpreted it as yet another pay-off. Visiting Kuwait a few weeks later, British prime minister David Cameron sought to shore up the monarchy's credentials further, stating in a press conference that the ruling family was overseeing 'the gradual development of a liberal democratic society' and that it was taking 'vital steps ... on its journey to democracy'.[7] Although later in the year there was a major wobble when substantial protests forced the resignation of the unelected Kuwaiti prime minister and demanded an investigation into his alleged corruption, these and various workplace strikes soon subsided after a record-breaking new budget was approved, complete with twenty-five percent salary increases for all public sector workers.[8]

In Oman's case the aging Sultan Qaboos bin Said al-Said still seemed to hold the respect of the majority of the population and this almost certainly helped to keep the protests limited in their scope. Most who took to the streets focused on government corruption, unemployment, and the 'abolition of all taxes', with little evidence of any explicit revolutionary demands. Although some did die in clashes with the police, notably in Sohar in February 2011, the security services mostly seemed to hold back and waited for the government to make some sort of move. Sure enough, by the end of the month, promises of increased subsidies and pay rises for the public sector were made, along with social security benefits for the unemployed and other measures estimated to have cost $2.6 billion. Addressing accusations of corruption, Qaboos followed the king of Jordan's lead by sacking twelve ministers in a further effort to appease the opposition. Although there were repeated flare-ups for the next several months, the situation seemed to have stabilized by the autumn, after promises that the National Consultative Council would be granted more legislative power, and that fifty thousand new jobs would be created.[9]

AXIS AGAINST AXIS – FAKING THE ARAB SPRING

In stark contrast to these fairly tepid and ultimately self-contained Arab kingdom protests, the uprisings that had begun in the republics of Libya and Syria soon escalated into full-blown and brutal civil wars and, in Libya's case, the forceful and bloody toppling of its regime. Now commonly used as examples to reinforce some sort of structural argument that authoritarian republics are inherently weaker than traditional monarchies, the reality of course is that these two states were deliberately targeted in a calculated and sustained manner by external actors who saw a strategic use in supporting and boosting the ambitions of local oppositionists. With Tripoli and Damascus having long proven antagonistic to Western interests and Western allies such as the Gulf monarchies and Israel, a golden opportunity had presented itself in 2011 to oust these administrations once and for all under the pretext of humanitarian and even democratic causes.

In this sense, a sort of rerun of the post-9/11 'War on Terror' was launched. As with the earlier removals of the problematic Taliban and Saddam Hussein regimes packaged under the banner of destroying the spectral al-Qaeda, this time the amorphous Arab Spring was exploited for its strategic silver lining. Although the mass nationwide uprisings in Tunisia, Egypt, and Yemen had clearly knocked out key Western clients, the idea was to give ostensibly similar but evidently much smaller-scale protest movements in Libya and Syria the sort of outside helping hand they needed to become full-blown and state-threatening insurgencies.

Apart from the staunchest of anti-imperialists, few would dispute that the dictatorships of Muammar Gaddafi and Bashar al-Assad were equally if not more venal and repressive than those of Hosni Mubarak, Zine el-Abidine Ben Ali, and Ali Abdullah Saleh. Few also would doubt that the world would be a better place without them, and that their supposed 'resistance' to states like Israel was largely for show and primarily a function of their own legitimacy building. As Hamid Dabashi explains, by then both

Libya and Syria, along with the Arab world's other authoritarian-socialist states and Iran-aligned powers were mostly 'united in hypocrisy' as they 'offered no alternative to domination by imperialism; they are a condition of this domination'.[10] But the fact remained that these two regimes, sitting astride vast natural resources and in command of key ports, rivers, and borders, were still significant obstacles that had long frustrated the ambitions of Western governments and their constituent corporations to gain greater access.

With the Western publics still mindful of the disastrous Afghanistan and Iraq campaigns, and with the stakes too high for Washington, London, or Tel Aviv to get caught directly supporting opposition movements in Libya and especially Syria, which was not only allied to Iran but had also long been home to a Russian naval facility, the solution was once again to use Arab proxy powers. In this sense, the same pro-Western states that had survived the Arab Spring and were already underpinning both the Islamist and militaristic strands of the counter-revolutions in North Africa and Yemen soon took on the concurrent role of funding and weaponizing a fraudulent and more violent Western-sponsored version of the Arab Spring. With Saudi Arabia, the UAE, and Qatar duly working together but separately against the Libyan and Syria governments despite their differences elsewhere on the regional chessboard, a sort of 'alliance of rivals' had formed where, as per state cartel theory, the benefits of cooperation were clearly deemed to outweigh the costs.[11] Sometimes referred to as the 'Axis of Moderation', derived from a speech delivered by Tony Blair to the World Affairs Council in 2006 in which he called for an 'alliance of moderation' in the Middle East to counter the 'arc of extremism', and clearly modelled on Condoleezza Rice's 2007 definition of 'centres of moderation' that could fight those 'on the other side of that divide … that have made their choice to destabilize', these three proxies, along with Kuwait, Jordan, and others, were ready to take on the 'Axis of Resistance'.[12]

LIBYA – GADDAFI'S STRANGE REGIME

Surviving numerous assassination attempts and failed uprisings, including the MI6-organized Libyan Islamic Fighting Group plot in the 1990s,

Muammar Gaddafi was not without enemies. Most Libyans seemed well aware of the glaring inconsistencies and political decay at the top of the regime, with almost all of Gaddafi's revolutionary credentials long since evaporated. Having purged his Revolutionary Command Council in the 1970s for fear of competition, he had already begun to move away from a Nasser-like image to that of a qa'id or 'guide' that would lead the Libyan jamahiriya or 'massocracy'. Based on the ramblings of his Green Book, the anti-imperialist jamahiriya was to be supported by the three pillars of socialism, democracy, and Islam and would ultimately provide Libya with a 'popular stateless government'.[13] The reality of course was very different, with Gaddafi having secretly continued to sell oil, his regime's main source of revenue, to Western Europe, via the same small network of companies that had formerly served King Idris al-Senussi.[14] Moreover, despite professing his resistance to Israel and ostensibly supporting Palestine by funding various militant groups, Gaddafi was in fact the only Arab head of state that Palestinian leader Yasser Arafat refused to visit.[15] Meanwhile the Shia cleric Musa al-Sadr, who headed Lebanon's anti-Israeli Amal movement, simply disappeared after being invited to talks in Tripoli.[16]

Although having claimed that the jamahiriya would oversee the dismantling of tribal authorities, by the 1980s Gaddafi had reneged on this, too, after effectively rehabilitating tribal chiefs and playing them off against each other, so as to strengthen his own grip over Libya. In 1993, he even established the Popular Social Leadership as a new assembly to represent the tribes. Its delegates were reportedly encouraged to monitor their own tribesmen and denounce any who criticized the regime.[17] For those who did speak out, the jamahiriya proved as ruthless as any of the region's dictatorships, with thousands believed to have died over the next decade and even the bodies of executed student activists being hung up for display on university campuses. Human Rights Watch claimed that in 1996 alone more than twelve hundred prisoners were massacred at Abu Salim prison, with a corresponding grave later discovered nearby.[18] By 2010 Gaddafi's feared security services were also understood to have reprised their long-standing cooperation with the Tunisian dictatorship. After all, Zine el-Abidine Ben Ali himself had once been the intelligence chief in the brief 1974 Libya–Tunisia federation.[19]

As far as democracy went, few could dispute that the *jamahiriya* seemed to be badly failing, with Gaddafi's Libya effectively morphing into a sultanistic state with most of its committees proving inseparable from his own personal authority. Moreover, it was also becoming something of a dynastic monarchy, with most of Gaddafi's sons having assumed key positions of control over the security services, economic planning, and even Libya's foreign relations. With jet-setting, yacht parties, and playboy lifestyles, their behaviour was soon indistinguishable from that of the most outrageous young Saudi princes.

Nonetheless, and for all its faults, by the time of the Arab Spring the regime did still seem to enjoy a strong core of support. Blessed with oil wealth, and, much like the Gulf monarchies, having developed at least some mechanisms of wealth distribution, the *jamahiriya* had clearly provided a substantial number of its citizens with a better standard of living than those elsewhere in North Africa. As Durham University's Matteo Capasso contends, 'It is too simple, almost unimaginative, to affirm that Gaddafi has ruled for four decades [solely] through a system of violence and repression, with contempt for institutions.' As he demonstrates, the 'implementation of more socialist-inclined policies definitely allowed Gaddafi to establish a consensus among the Libyan population' which in turn helps us understand why his regime experienced 'several phases of popular consent'.[20]

As the Italian researcher Elvira Diana describes, 'from a social perspective, since 1970 the government increased the minimum wage and redistributed to Libyans the land once owned by Italians or the al-Senussi monarchy. Medical care became free for all and the standard of health became among the highest in Africa.' She also notes how 'public education became free and new schools and universities were opened' and that this led to a Libyan 'literary spring' as a result of 'the strong push [Gaddafi] gave to education'. The *jamahiriya* even set up mobile classrooms and prefabricated school buildings in desert oasis communities on the basis that education was for all.[21] Other accomplishments included several laws to improve the education of women and to encourage mixed gender classes. Moreover, girls were to have compulsory education until the age of sixteen and the legal age of marriage was increased to twenty – the highest in the Arab world.[22]

LIBYA – FLIRTING WITH NEO-LIBERALISM

Despite all of Muammar Gaddafi's rhetoric and the apparent self-sufficiency afforded by its oil wealth, there is considerable evidence that by the mid-2000s Libya had tried to warm to the West and jump on the neo-liberal bandwagon. Having witnessed Saddam Hussein's fate in 2003, and likely assuming the 'War on Terror' would soon reach Libya, some have suggested Gaddafi realized he had to switch sides, or at least had to pretend to do so. Others have pointed out that his increasingly rapacious sons and inner circle members were pressuring him to take advantage of the lifting of the sanctions that had been imposed by the UN on Libya in the early 1990s for suspected terror links.[23] Their aim was to facilitate foreign investment and the denationalization of state assets, much as Hosni Mubarak had been doing in Egypt, so that the assets Gaddafi himself had once nationalized could now be bought up by his cronies. Trying to spin this as an extension of the 'popular control' called for in the *Green Book*, the reality it seemed was that Gaddafi's own relatives were angling for their share of Libya's global value.[24]

Problematically, of course, on top of Gaddafi's earlier intransigent stances on al-Qaeda, Saudi Arabia, and other Western allies, there were a multitude of other obstacles still preventing such a rapprochement between the West and Libya, even if it was strictly for business. With Gaddafi's intelligence services having executed numerous dissidents in Western Europe, they were thought to have been particularly active in London, where the Libyan embassy supposedly had a lengthy list of targets it was working through.[25] Moreover, the history of terrorism seemed difficult to forget, with the Gaddafi regime continuing to be blamed for a 1984 gun attack on demonstrators outside the Libyan embassy in London which led to the death of British policewoman Yvonne Fletcher, and of course the downing of Pan Am Flight 103 over Lockerbie in Scotland in 1988. With the plane now known to have been carrying at least four US officials and their bodyguards including the CIA's Beirut station chief and a Defense Intelligence Agency officer on secondment to the CIA, the mid-air explosion was likely seen by the US government as a direct attack on its secret Middle East operations.[26]

But with money on the table, all soon seemed to be forgiven, with even Gaddafi himself beginning to make qualified apologies. In 2003 his government formally accepted responsibility for Lockerbie, even though no direct role was admitted, and even if most fingers had by then already begun to point elsewhere.[27] In fact only a year earlier the dying Palestinian militant Sabri Khalil al-Banna, also known as Abu Nidal, had told his aides that he – not Libya – had been responsible for Lockerbie, and that 'the reports which link the Lockerbie act to others are false reports. We are behind what happened.'[28] Indeed, Abu Nidal's claims tallied with the US's initial intelligence on Lockerbie, which between December 1988 and October 1990 had indicated involvement of the Palestinian Liberation Organization.[29] Trying to boost the Gaddafi regime's repentant reputation further, reports also began to circulate that Libya had hired the US-based Monitor Group to undertake a public relations 'cleansing campaign'. One of the group's letters sent to a senior Libyan official promised that 'we will create a network map to identify significant figures engaged or interested in Libya today ... We will identify and encourage journalists, academics and contemporary thinkers who will have an interest in publishing papers and articles on Libya.'[30]

From about this time Libya had also begun to cooperate heavily with Western intelligence agencies, including the CIA and MI6. According to the Jamestown Foundation, Gaddafi's intelligence chief Moussa Koussa had begun handing over names of Libyan Islamic Fighting Group members living in exile. Although hailed as a 'major intelligence windfall' by the US, they were of course the same characters that MI6 had been working with during the 1990s. Nonetheless, according to documents later discovered in the former office of Koussa, who had defected to Britain almost immediately after the 2011 uprising and was then safely rehabilitated in Qatar, the Western powers had been deporting such Libyan dissidents back to Libya, where Western intelligence officers would then attend interrogation sessions. Bizarrely the same captured documents detailed how British officials were even helping to draft Gaddafi's speeches, and how MI6 had sought to arrange a public relations stunt for Gaddafi and Tony Blair in 2004. This now infamous 'meeting in the desert' was to take place in a Bedouin tent on the grounds that 'the English are fascinated by tents ... the plain fact is that the journalists would love it.'[31]

On top of renditions, Gaddafi also appeared willing to alleviate the North African refugee crisis in the Mediterranean by offering to prevent forcibly African migrants from leaving Libyan shores, in exchange for $5 billion of Italian investments into Libya and six Italian-manufactured naval patrol boats.[32] Although clearly an act of extortion, with one of Gaddafi's sons warning a Western official that without his father in power Europe would face an 'unprecedented illegal immigration from Africa', and later Gaddafi telephone calls to Blair warning of a jihadist invasion of Europe, the Western intelligence agencies nonetheless sought to portray the regime's cooperation as further evidence of Libya coming in from the cold.[33] As a useful proxy Qatar also had a role to play in smoothing such Libyan-European relations, in 2007 having helped facilitate the extradition of a number of Bulgarian nurses who had earlier been imprisoned in Libya on the charge of infecting children with HIV, and two years later facilitating the release of purported Lockerbie bomber Abdelbaset al-Megrahi from British custody.[34]

With relations improving, at least on paper, the *Financial Times* reported that Western businessmen quickly found 'rich and willing clients' among Libya's new generation of business elites.[35] Rising to the fore was Saif al-Islam Gaddafi, who, as the dictator's second eldest son and a postgraduate at the London School of Economics, was identified in leaked US diplomatic cables as the point man for Libya's pending 'political and economic reforms'.[36] As the Libyan equivalent of Gamal Mubarak, he had become a frequent visitor to the Western capitals as part of his self-proclaimed *infitah* or 'opening' strategy, and was regarded as 'ultra-cool, charming, a modernizer'. Understood to have assumed control over the Libyan Investment Authority – the country's major sovereign wealth fund – he had paid Goldman Sachs $1.3 billion to manage its future investments in currencies and stocks.[37]

Among the first big movers was Royal Dutch Shell, which pushed forward quickly from an initial 2004 agreement with Gaddafi and subsequently held twenty-six meetings over the next few years with British government officials hoping to facilitate a bigger deal. British Petroleum joined in, too, winning a Libyan concession in 2007 worth $15 billion, and by the end of the decade hundreds more British companies were operating in Libya in what had become an annual bilateral trade worth $1.5 billion.[38]

From the US side the optimism was no less palpable, with senator John McCain touring Libya in 2009 and noting the 'hydrocarbon producing potential' and the 'high expectations of international oil companies'.[39]

Unsurprisingly, perhaps, with Gaddafi pictured shaking hands with world leaders and finally beginning to receive some good press in the Western media, Libya was also ripe for arms deals. Ahead of the competition were the British companies, with large quantities of advanced military equipment being sold to Libya from 2007 including all of the usual panoply of offensive crowd control hardware such as armoured personnel carriers, sniper rifles, smoke canisters, stun grenades, and water cannons. A sophisticated communications system for Libyan tanks was also sold after being approved for export by the British government, which had already designated Libya a 'priority market' worthy of 'high-level political interventions'.[40] In 2009 alone approximately $500 million worth of British, French, German, and Italian arms were believed to have shipped, and as late as November 2010, just weeks before the Arab Spring began, more than fifty British companies attended a Libyan arms fair held at an airport in Tripoli. Later interviewed by the *Daily Telegraph*, the spokesman for one of the companies explained why 'it [was] not embarrassing for us ... The Libyans were a favoured regime with our government. Tony Blair was out there and they had become a country we could trade with. Our politicians were more than happy to allow us to export out there.'[41] Indeed, when Libyan regime offices were raided in 2011, a letter was found from Blair addressed to Gaddafi. Dated 2007, it began with 'Dear Mu'ammar', thanked Gaddafi for his 'excellent cooperation', and then ended with 'Best wishes yours ever, Tony'.[42]

LIBYA – NOT SO SUPPLICANT

In parallel to the euphoria surrounding the oil-rich state's apparent reintegration into Western markets there were, however, several early warnings that the Libyan regime was unlikely ever to be as compliant as Egypt and Tunisia. According to leaked US diplomatic cables from 2007, the US government was already becoming frustrated with the speed of Gaddafi's liberalization and complained of his merely 'lukewarm embrace of US corporate interests'.[43] The cables also indicated how US officials were wary of lingering 'Libyan resource nationalism' and had tried to demonstrate the 'downsides' of this approach to the Libyan government.[44]

In many ways the US Department of State was right to be suspicious, even if US politicians were not, as there were soon ample indications that Gaddafi was not so supplicant after all. As soon as they had signed concessions with Libya, both ExxonMobil and Total had been strong-armed into signing up to a new oil-sharing agreement that gave them much less favourable terms and called for $5 billion in upfront payments to the Libyan government. A 2008 US cable warned that a US consortium that included ConocoPhilips would be 'next on the block', despite it having already paid out substantial sums to Tripoli. By 2009 things seemed to be getting even worse, with Gaddafi abruptly threatening to renationalize Libyan oil half-way through a video conference with Georgetown University students.[45]

Behind the scenes this sort of rhetoric was already translating into action, with Libyan ministers having begun to force US oil companies to contribute to a new US-Libya 'claims compensation agreement', which was supposed to support the victims of US and Libyan bombings in both countries. Baulking at such moves, the US ambassador described them as 'red lines', although the Department of State was a bit more realistic, suggesting that 'smaller operators and services might relent and pay', and the New York Times noted that several did indeed begin to pay. European companies seemed to be faring no better, with Italy's hopes of winning development contracts seeming to hang on its government having to pay $200 million a year for twenty-five years as 'compensation for colonial injustices'. Meanwhile, multinational corporations ranging from Caterpillar to Coca-Cola reported similar problems, including requirements that they had to enter into joint ventures with state-owned companies that were in effect owned by Gaddafi family members.[46] With history seeming to come full circle, this was exactly the sort of practice that the former king of Libya had been engaged in, with a declassified CIA document revealing the many scandals that erupted after his relatives and ministers had won contracts to build Libya's new highways.[47]

Equally alarming for the Western governments was Gaddafi's apparent free-for-all approach to Libya's investment opportunities, with Tripoli increasingly beginning to grant oil concessions to Chinese, Indian,

Japanese, and Russian companies. Beyond oil, China was also winning huge multibillion-dollar contracts in construction and infrastructure projects including a $2.6 billion railway contract which could just as easily have been awarded to a Western company. Meanwhile, in 2008, Russia agreed to forgive $4.5 billion of Soviet-era debt in exchange for first pick of various new Libyan development contracts.[48] Ruffling US feathers even further, Gaddafi also seemed to have begun supporting the Kremlin's views on NATO expansionism in Georgia and Ukraine and, along with Nigeria, had publicly voiced his opposition to the expansion of the US's Stuttgart-based AFRICOM onto the African continent.[49]

Likely the final blows, the resistance to such cooperation with the US military was doubtlessly exacerbated by the Libyan National Oil Company's announcement in February 2011 that it would be granting no new oil concessions that year, and by the Libyan Investment Authority's decision a few weeks later to begin divesting its US and British assets on the grounds that it was too exposed to Western economies.[50] Moreover, as the Hillary Clinton emails since released by a special congressional inquiry have revealed, at about this time French intelligence had become aware of Gaddafi's plans to establish a new pan-African currency which was to serve as an alternative to Western currencies. This was to be based on the Libyan golden dinar and it was estimated that the Libyan central bank had amassed 143 tons of gold and a similar quantity of silver to back it up.[51]

LIBYA – THE UPRISING

Less than a week after Hosni Mubarak's ouster, Muammar Gaddafi's vulnerabilities also seemed exposed after an Arab Spring-like 'day of rage' began on 17 February 2011. The protest started ostensibly as a response to the arrest two days earlier of a well-known human rights lawyer, Fethi Tarbel, who had begun to represent the families of victims of the 1996 prison massacre: judges, lawyers, and students assembled outside a police station in Libya's eastern city of Benghazi and demanded his release. As eyewitnesses later described, Tarbel's arrest at this time was 'the regime's big mistake.'[52]

With protests soon spreading across the historically restive city, Gaddafi's old policy of 'keeping the East poor as a means by which to limit the potential political threat' – as described in a leaked US diplomatic cable from 2008 – seemed to be proving a severe miscalculation. As US officials had predicted, a poor Benghazi meant there would be 'many young eastern Libyan men ... [with] nothing to lose by participating in extremist violence at home'.[53] Peaceful at first, the demonstrators carried images of Omar al-Mukhtar – the martyred symbol of Libyan resistance to Italian occupation – and declared themselves 'the grandsons of Omar'.[54] The Benghazi movement quickly appeared to grow into a much bigger insurgency, with mass labour strikes and a number of prominent tribal leaders announcing their support.[55] Making matters worse for Tripoli, and giving the uprising a harder edge, reports began to circulate of army and air force defections in Benghazi and Tobruk, also in the east, with two pilots having even flown their planes to Malta.[56]

In many ways, the nightmare of such a powerful but apparently leaderless movement had been foreseen by Gaddafi, with his catchy 1989 short story *Firaar ila jahannam* or 'Escape to hell' having warned of 'how cruel people can be when they flare up together! What a crushing flood that has no mercy for anyone in its way!' In the book he first declares, 'How I love the liberated masses on the march! They are unfettered, with no master, singing and merry after their terrible ordeals!' But he later confesses that 'on the other hand how I fear and apprehend them! They carry their favourite sons high on their shoulders ... but how cruel they can be when they are angrily excited'.[57]

Still in command of the oil-producing regions, and following Saudi Arabia's example, Gaddafi's first response was to promise a massive $24 billion housing and development fund, most of which was to be spent on regenerating the restive and now rebellious eastern provinces. Fatefully, however, his firebrand personality seemed to be leading him into the same sort of trap as his counterparts in Tunisia and Egypt, especially after he took to the airwaves on 20 February and delivered an 'unrepentant speech' that threatened bloody retribution against the dissenters.[58] Making matters worse, only a day later the once pro-reform Saif al-Islam appeared on television to deliver a disjointed, rambling, and threatening speech in defence of his father's regime. Blaming the Benghazi emergency on drunken or drugged Islamists along with 'coffee drinking Arabs', he tried to whitewash the deaths of any protestors thus far, attributing them to 'planning errors', while at the same time promising 'rivers of blood' for those that continued to resist. Ominously he concluded that the government would 'fight to the last minute and to the last bullet'.[59]

With the uprising soon reaching Tripoli and the state television headquarters being stormed, the collapse of the regime seemed imminent, at least according to international media outlets. As the days went by, however, the capital appeared to remain quite firmly in Gaddafi's hands, with the much-anticipated nationwide revolution simply failing to materialize. Explained away with stories of pro-government thugs being unleashed in residential areas to keep people off the streets, along with busloads of paid Gaddafi supporters arriving in public squares and – according to Al-Jazeera – even aircraft and helicopter gunships overflying and gunning protestors down, the true extent of the violence used by the regime during this crucial period has nonetheless been repeatedly called into question. Notwithstanding the Gaddafi family's incendiary speeches, the *New York Times* hinted nearly a month later that the regime's initial response may not have been as repressive as many had made out. Describing how 'the rebels feel no loyalty to the truth in shaping their propaganda' its correspondents believed the rebels were 'claiming non-existent battlefield victories, asserting they were still fighting in a key city days after it fell to Gaddafi forces, and making vastly inflated claims of his barbaric behaviour'.[60] Even US secretary for defense Robert Gates, by then in his final months in post, along with the Department of Defense's Admiral Michael Mullen, stated in a press conference that they had read the media reports but agreed there was 'no confirmation whatsoever' that the Gaddafi regime had been using airpower to attack civilians.[61] After a lengthy investigation the director of the International Crisis Group's North Africa project concluded that the stories of strafing of protestors were indeed untrue.[62]

Apart from some accounts of Serbian guns being used by the regime's forces, there was little other mention in the media of the weapons its thugs were supposed to be using, and certainly no references to the millions of dollars' worth of British and other European arms and crowd control equipment that had been sold to Libya up until a few months earlier.[63] There were, however, plentiful reports being filed that claimed the regime was clinging to power because it was deploying thousands of dark-skinned mercenaries from Mali, Niger, and Chad. Rebel eyewitnesses, for example, had described to Reuters in detail how French-speaking West Africans had attacked the protestors, while Libya's permanent representative to the UN – who had almost instantly defected in February – soon told the world 'we are expecting a real genocide in Tripoli. The airplanes are still bringing mercenaries to the airports.'[64] The head of the working group on mercenaries for the UN's high commissioner for human rights was only slightly more cautious, stating that the evidence of mercenaries being used was 'not 100 percent but it does seem likely' and it was reported that 'he was aware of accounts describing Eastern European as well as African mercenaries in Libya.'[65]

Others have been much more circumspect, with some suggesting the dark-skinned fighters may have been part of Gaddafi's 'Deterrent Battalion' – a foreign legion set up nearly twenty years earlier to counter future tribal mutinies.[66] Some have been even more critical of the mainstream narrative, contending that the 'real genocides' of the Libyan uprising were in fact the bloody and largely ignored reprisals and revenge attacks perpetrated by rebels against populations of black Libyans and African expatriates accused of fighting for the regime. As Concordia University's Maximilian Forte argues, this was a side to the conflict that the 'white, Western world, and those who dominate the conversation about Libya, have missed ... and not by accident'.[67] On 26 February, for example, an apparently impartial Turkish construction worker told the BBC that 'we had seventy to eighty people from Chad working for our company. They were massacred with pruning shears and axes, accused by the attackers of being Gaddafi's troops.' He also stated: 'The Sudanese people were massacred. We saw it for ourselves.'[68]

Just two days after this, and thus only eleven days after the uprising began, it was reported that 'dozens of workers from sub-Saharan Africa, it is feared, have been killed and hundreds are hiding because angry opponents of the government are hunting down black African mercenaries, witnesses [have said].' Reuters too claimed that 'hundreds of black immigrants from the poorest African countries, who work mainly as low-wage day labourers in Libya, have been wounded by the rebels ... from fear of being killed, some of them have refrained from going to a doctor.' The victims also told Reuters that the rebels were using the pretext of revolution to 'accuse [black Africans] of being murderous mercenaries. But in reality they simply refuse to tolerate us. Our camp was burnt down. Our company and our embassy helped us get to the airport.'[69] In March 2011 the *Los Angeles Times* published an equally disturbing account of how dozens of the rebels' prisoners, mostly black Africans, were being paraded in front of journalists in a clear breach of the Geneva Convention. Although its correspondents were prevented from speaking to the prisoners, they still recalled seeing 'one young man from Ghana bolting from the prisoners' queue'. As they described, he shouted in English at them, 'I'm not a soldier! I work for a construction company in Benghazi! They took me from my house.' A guard had then reportedly shouted that 'he lies ... he's a mercenary.'[70]

A few months later, with a bitter civil war raging, Human Rights Watch observed that 'dark-skinned Libyans and sub-Saharan Africans face particular risks because rebel forces and other armed groups have often considered them pro-Gaddafi mercenaries from other African countries.' Its report noted that 'we've seen violent attacks and killings of these people in areas where the [rebels] took control.' Amnesty International gave much the same warning, noting there was a 'disproportionate detention of black Africans in rebel-controlled Al-Zawiya, as well as the targeting of unarmed, migrant farm workers'.[71] In August 2011 even the African Union warned that '[rebels] seem to confuse black people with mercenaries' and that this meant for 'one-third of the population of Libya, which is black, [they are] mercenaries'. Its chairperson further reported that '[the rebels] are killing people, normal workers, mistreating them', and, making a broader point, complained that 'the [rebels'] attitude has been negative all along. I went to Benghazi. We have treated them equally.'[72]

While some dismissed the African Union's conclusions on the basis that Gaddafi had long been one of its most vociferous supporters, it was harder to ignore an investigative report that appeared a few weeks later in the *Daily Telegraph*. Describing the 'ethnic cleansing' of the predominantly black and slave-descended inhabitants of the Libyan town of Tawergha, it detailed how its population of about ten thousand had been collectively accused of remaining loyal to Gaddafi. The reprisal also led to a 'large number of houses, and virtually every shop, being systematically vandalized, looted or set on fire' and with 'even the local hospital vandalized ... the beds were dragged out of the wards and ripped.' One nearby rebel unit was even described as having painted a slogan on the road leading into Tawergha declaring they were 'the brigade for purging slaves [and] black skin'.[73]

As the war dragged on it was also clear that the majority of the regime's armed forces, mercenaries notwithstanding, seemed to have remained loyal. As Robert Springborg argues, in part this may have been due to the prominent role of the *kataib* or 'special battalions' that either answered directly to Gaddafi or were commanded by one of his sons.[74] Although some Libyan scholars have argued that by 2011 tribalism was only superficial,[75] the loyalty of tribes also seemed to matter. The Zintan, for example, had clearly embraced the rebel movement and had pushed their elders to end relations with Gaddafi, but many others such as the powerful Warfalla had evidently continued to endorse the regime, even if they experienced some high-profile defections and had previously mutinied against Gaddafi.[76] In this sense the mainstream explanations put forward by Al-Jazeera and other outlets for the revolution's marked lack of progress, namely that Libya simply had a better-armed and -financed military than had been expected, were largely bogus.[77] The inconvenient reality that few seemed willing to discuss at the time was that the Gaddafi regime – odious as it may have been – was still regarded by many Libyans as the least worst alternative when faced with the prospect of a rebel-led government.

LIBYA – SUBVERTING THE NATIONAL TRANSITIONAL COUNCIL

Even if it had no truly nationwide revolution behind it, and had little real control over the various rebel militias, the Benghazi-based National Transitional Council (NTC) still seemed to embody most of the values and ambitions of the Arab Spring movements elsewhere in the region. A progressive and wholly indigenous organization, it claimed in its first communiqué to represent the city councils in all liberated areas and to represent no foreign interests.[78] Staffed by a mix of Benghazi activists, tribal leaders, defecting army commanders, lawyers, and judges, it duly began to set up a parallel government complete with its own newspaper and television station. With almost Soviet-like organization, workers' committees were established to manage various parts of the economy and infrastructure. As Simon Assaf describes, 'Many observers, including Western journalists, noted the efficiency and energy of the councils and the relaxed air of freedom in the city.' Moreover, he noted that 'in Benghazi, despite food shortages, the poorest citizens told of how they are eating better now than before the revolution.'[79]

The NTC also seems to have withstood an early counter-revolutionary attempt when Muammar Gaddafi's supposedly defecting former justice minister Mustafa Abdel-Jalil declared himself leader of the 'provisional government' before trying to cut a deal between the old regime and the Western powers.[80] Since then more has come to light about the nature of the deal, with the Hillary Clinton emails having revealed that French intelligence had already begun to 'cultivate … particular clients amongst the rebels', and had held secret meetings with Abdel-Jalil. In return for 'weapons and guidance', along with promises of official French recognition for his government after Gaddafi was defeated, Abdel-Jalil was to ensure the 'favouring of French firms and national interests, particularly regarding the oil industry'. Worryingly, at the time this relationship was secretly being built, the French government's official position was that it 'did not know who to support in Libya'.[81]

Likely aware of Abdel-Jalil's intentions, the core of the NTC declared on 28 February 2011 that it wished for no foreign intervention in Libya and expressed its fears that the West would use elements of the old regime to circumvent the 'real revolution'.[82] Indeed, in a US Department of Defense press conference the next day, the secretary for defense bluntly confirmed that the 'rebel leaders' had made no request for a NATO intervention.[83] Less than a week later, however, in what the British media termed an 'embarrassing episode', six SAS soldiers and two MI6 officers were detained by the NTC after having been dropped by helicopters onto farmland on a mission to establish contact with 'anti-regime forces'. Despite having bags containing 'weapons, reconnaissance equipment, and multiple passports', Britain's foreign secretary referred to them as a 'small British diplomatic team' that had had to leave Libya after 'experiencing difficulties'. The NTC again chose to make its position clear, with its spokesperson criticizing Britain's clandestine intrusion and claiming that the incident had 'fuelled doubts about [British] intentions'.[84] Interestingly the NTC also claimed that the Western powers were doing nothing to block incoming Gaddafi supply flights, were refusing to unfreeze Libyan assets abroad and release the funds to the NTC, and were not allowing the NTC to import weapons on the grounds that they could fall into the hands of terrorists when delivered to Libya.[85]

But with the uprising increasingly under pressure as regime units quickly began to regroup and focus their attention on rebel-held cities, it seemed Washington and London had already reached a decision to intervene on their own terms. The opportunity of removing the problematic Gaddafi leadership under the banner of the Arab Spring was too good to miss, even if it ran the risk of alienating the actual protestors who had first risen up against Gaddafi and whose leaders – so it seemed – were increasingly distrustful of the West. In contrast to his earlier radio silence on Zine el-Abidine Ben Ali and Hosni Mubarak, as early as 3 March 2011 Barack Obama had already begun to call for Gaddafi to go, and just six days later both he and David Cameron were stating that they were preparing for military action.[86] In this sense the prospect of forcibly installing a new and more supplicant post-Gaddafi administration had become a much more attractive proposition to the Western powers than any attempted rescue of their erratic trade partner of the past eight years. Indeed, as the *Independent* reported, Cameron had little interest in a last-minute diplomatic intercession by Tony Blair, who had supposedly been contacted by a Gaddafi aide seeking a 'deal with the British'.[87]

Getting around the NTC and its publicly stated position against intervention required a multipronged strategy. The most obvious need was to frame the impending Western-sponsored military action as being primarily driven by humanitarian concerns. As Gaddafi's forces began to inch closer to Benghazi by the middle of March, they were already being described as on a 'murderous rampage' with the regime having promised 'no mercy'.[88] Meanwhile a sensational *casus belli*-style story was published by Al-Jazeera claiming that the Libyan army was on a Viagra-fuelled raping spree across the country. Picked up and republished by almost every Western outlet, and even referred to by the prosecutor of the International Criminal Court, the US ambassador to Libya then repeated the claim to the UN Security Council.[89]

As the University of Texas' Alan Kuperman and others noted, however, those towns being recaptured by the regime were not actually being subjected to massacres.[90] Moreover, as the *New York Times* made clear, Gaddafi's infamous 'no mercy' warning had in fact been directed specifically at the rebel fighters, with the regime having promised an amnesty for 'those who throw their weapons away'.[91] As for the Viagra mass rape story, US intelligence officials did not quite seem to share the US ambassador's position, with one having admitted to *NBC News* that 'there is no evidence that Libyan military forces are being given Viagra and engaging in systematic rape against women in rebel areas'. Leading a UN human rights inquiry into the situation, Cherif Bassiouni was even more circumspect and claimed that the Viagra story was the product of mass hysteria. Going even further, Amnesty International's spokesperson explained that Amnesty had 'not found cases of rape ... Not only have we not met any victims, but we have not even met any persons who have met victims. As for the boxes of Viagra that Gaddafi is supposed to have had distributed, they were found intact near tanks that were completely burnt out'.[92]

The strategy's second need was that the NTC itself needed to be co-opted and stripped of any genuinely revolutionary sentiments so that the post-intervention government would be suitably pro-Western and ready to get back to business. In some ways the problem took care of itself as Gaddafi's forces appeared to be advancing on Benghazi faster than many had expected. Reaffirming the US's strictly humanitarian motives, Clinton warned that 'Gaddafi would do terrible things ... it's just in his nature ... there are some creatures that are like that,' while the *New York Times* reported that the NTC had little option but to 'mortgage the revolution' in return for formally requesting Western intervention so as to prevent a massacre.[93] As Assaf put it, 'the revolution was forced into an unnecessary compromise with imperialism, and it had been panicked into its call for Western military intervention.' Naturally, such intervention came at a significant price, with Abdel-Jalil emerging as the US's choice to take over the NTC's chairmanship.[94] Tellingly, perhaps, a few weeks later the Italian media described him as a possible successor to Saif al-Islam on the basis that he was committed to the same sort of economic reforms.[95]

Conforming to its Western proxy role, Qatar became the first Arab state to recognize the new Abdel-Jalil-led and pro-Western incarnation of the NTC as Libya's official government. Described as 'instrumental' in engineering the old regime's suspension from the Arab League, Doha also began to campaign publicly and heavily for NATO strikes and an enforced no-fly zone over Libya.[96] In parallel, a new Qatar-based 'Libya TV' was also set up. Funded by 'Libyan expatriate businessmen' it broadcast almost unrelenting criticism of the Gaddafi regime while at the same time throwing its full support behind the NATO-friendly NTC.[97] With Qatar in its corner and rejecting various peace initiatives, including one by the African Union, the new NTC soon made it quite clear that any premature end to the fighting would be unacceptable – a view quickly backed up by both the British foreign secretary and the NATO secretary general, who had argued, respectively, that any ceasefire agreement with Gaddafi would be meaningless and that it would impossible to put monitors on the ground to implement and enforce it.[98] Unsurprisingly given its future *raison d'être*, the NTC promised that it would abide by all international contracts that had earlier been signed by the Libyan government, with one of its spokesmen later confirming that all pre-existing 'contracts in the oil fields are absolutely sacrosanct ... There's no question of revoking any contract.'[99]

LIBYA – NATO TAKES ACTION

Proposed by Britain, France, and temporary member Lebanon, but with far from unanimous support, UN Security Council Resolution 1973 on 17 March 2011 paved the way for the first NATO air strikes on Libya just forty-eight hours later.[100] Premised on an earlier 2009 resolution on the 'responsibility to protect' that had led to no interventions in far bloodier conflicts elsewhere in Africa, Resolution 1973 called for a no-fly zone to be enforced over Libya and authorized 'all necessary means' to protect its civilian population, although without permitting any foreign occupation.[101] As Hamid Dabashi recalls, this was interpreted by most observers at the time as allowing everything 'short of putting troops on the ground'.[102]

With the bulk of 'Operation Unified Protector' air power being delivered by Britain and France, and with the US famously choosing to 'lead from behind' after 'purchasing the involvement' of these allies in return for them receiving public credit, it seemed Muammar Gaddafi's long-held fears of Western plots to unseat him were being realized. As recently as 2009 a US diplomatic cable had recorded his personally expressed suspicions that the real goal behind Western economic re-engagement with Libya was to engineer a regime change.[103] Indeed, the US's 'Operation Odyssey Dawn' – the name for its contributing mission as part of Unified Protector – was being managed exclusively by AFRICOM – the same US military institution that Libya and Nigeria had earlier tried to block from entry to the African continent.[104] Reaching the soundest conclusion, Matteo Capasso and anthropologist Igor Cherstich have since contended that the 2011 uprising was seen as a crucial tipping point for a state on the cusp of entering into a civil war, and one which was exploited by the West and its allies in an effort to 'impose their ideological vision for Libya, which would be easier to pursue if Gaddafi were toppled'.[105]

With the described deal in place with the US and Britain to deflect criticism from its own parallel intervention in Bahrain, the GCC and its members had not only pushed for the Arab League's backing of Unified Protector but also soon began to join the NATO powers in policing Libya's skies. With Qatar providing six fighter jets and two strategic support aircraft, while the UAE provided twelve fighter jets, the GCC's combined contingent was almost as big as France's.[106] Helpfully for the first few waves of NATO strikes, the Qatar-based Libya TV not only provided a thorough whitewashing of the campaign but even began to broadcast purportedly intercepted telephone calls between Gaddafi regime officials that indicated they were deliberately moving the dead bodies of rebels to the sites of strategic NATO strikes so as to claim there were heavy civilian casualties. By then understood to be 'largely based in Doha', Mustafa Abdel-Jalil was given the sole platform on Libya TV to call for national unity and for the regime's remaining military units in Tripoli to stand down.[107]

With the compelling humanitarian and responsibility-to-protect narratives in place and, as Maximilian Forte describes, a 'powerful circle of acclamation' surrounding the intervention, few Western opinion-makers beyond the strongest anti-imperialists were really able to put forward any meaningful condemnation of the NATO–GCC campaign.[108] Influential critics such as Juan Cole argued that Unified Protector was quite safe on the basis that it did not involve boots on the ground and that this meant it was incomparable with the 2003 invasion of Iraq. He also claimed the intervention was being done in a 'legal way' because the UN resolution was something of a 'gold standard', and argued that 'if we just don't care if the people of Benghazi are subjected to murder and repression on a vast scale, we aren't people of the Left.'[109] Meanwhile, although Dabashi recognized the intervention as an 'initially counter-revolutionary development' and understood it was using the pretence of humanitarianism, he saw some positives, as NATO's air strikes would 'challenge the very logic of military intervention in a democratic uprising' on the basis that they would end up destroying the same military equipment that the NATO powers had earlier sold to Gaddafi. Others, it seemed, were simply tricked by the messages of qualified support for NATO from some of the most unusual quarters, with *Hezbollah*'s Hassan Nasrallah himself having declared that 'what is taking place in Libya is war imposed by the regime on a people that was peacefully demanding change ... the revolutionary people of Libya should be helped so as to persevere.'[110] Too few had paused to consider that *Hezbollah* and other such 'Axis of Resistance' powers were equally as anti-Gaddafi as they were anti-Western.

With the strikes rolling on and the Libyan regime steadily eroding, it was perhaps the *New Yorker* that got it most wrong. In a lengthy and widely read essay that struck an overly optimistic tone, it disingenuously claimed that the new Libya's 'emergent institutions were [being] developed above all by Libyans, not by an Ahmed Chalabi [in reference to the Iraqi politician involved in the US's invasion of Iraq in 2003], or the CIA. They are indigenous; they have legitimacy.' Going further, the *New Yorker* also attempted to identify a silver lining to the lengthy and bloody civil war, arguing that 'an unintended consequence of the prolonged conflict was that the ragtag Libyan fighters improved their skills on the battlefield and enabled civil institutions to arise from the rubble of a reign of terror.'[111]

LIBYA – AN INTERNATIONAL CRIME

Almost as soon as the dust had settled after the first NATO strikes, evidence began to mount indicating that the participating air forces had little intention of sticking to their UN mandate of enforcing a no-fly zone and protecting civilians. In particular, a video began to circulate of the aftermath of the inaugural French interdiction on 19 March 2011. Although the target was officially supposed to have been a substantial armoured column advancing on Benghazi, the video instead depicted only a handful of military vehicles on an open highway, clearly heading away from the city, and thus travelling in the same direction as the rebel units that eventually arrived on the scene. Nevertheless, the Reuters report that began to circulate – apparently based on a mixture of official NATO press releases and National Transitional Council statements – described 'about fourteen tanks, twenty armoured personnel carriers, two trucks with multiple rocket launchers and dozens of pick-ups destroyed in the strike'.[112]

Most of the reports on subsequent strikes followed much the same format, even though many seemed to have had nothing to do with protecting civilians, and some had actually led to the deaths of civilians. Certainly there were strikes on key air defence and communications systems, but as the *New York Times* recorded there were also strikes on Libya's state television headquarters, and, as CNN claimed, Apache helicopter gunships had ended up killing civilians in a public square.[113] In this context Matteo Capasso notes that NATO's understanding of the need to protect civilians did not seem to extend to Muammar Gaddafi loyalists. Most obviously, as he points out, when rebel forces began to enter the city of Sirte – Gaddafi's home town and one of the regime's last remaining strongholds – the extent of the atrocities committed against its civilian population would likely have been described as 'genocidal' by the Western media if the circumstances had been different.[114] Sharing much the same view, Princeton University professor emeritus Richard Falk observed that the 'NATO forces were obviously far less committed to their supposed protective role than to ensuring that the balance of forces within Libya would be tipped in the direction of the insurrectionary challenge'.[115] Indeed, NATO went far beyond protecting civilian populations, especially after May 2011 when it effectively 'provided air support for the destruction of the Gaddafi state'.[116]

Unsurprisingly, therefore, even after the regime made its last stand in Sirte its scattered retreat on the afternoon of 20 October was heavily bombed, with US Predator drones and French jet fighters knocking out the last few vehicles.[117] Apparently pulled out of a big pipe after fleeing from his car and very much alive, Gaddafi's capture was videoed and broadcast around the world, despite the obvious barbarity of the crowd and the brutality of the scene. Very soon after, however, he was described as having died, but with no further information being given. According to Human Rights Watch he had been stabbed in the rear with a bayonet causing catastrophic blood loss, but the doctor who performed the post-mortem had been threatened with death in order to keep his findings confidential.[118] In an even stranger twist, according to the disclosed emails of Hillary Clinton, the Department of State had been made aware that just five days before this final episode the investigative reporter Seymour Hersh had been contacted by a 'source who was a former financial beneficiary of the Gaddafi regime' who had offered him an exclusive interview with Gaddafi who, by then, had already escaped to Chad.[119] As numerous Libyan bloggers have since speculated, this may mean that the man mobbed by the crowds was in fact one of Gaddafi's many very realistic body doubles.

But if crimes were being committed from the air, then they were almost certainly being committed on the ground, too, despite the UN's restriction on the use of troops. Although the New York Times later claimed that the CIA only ever had a handful of operatives in Libya at this time, its own correspondents had reported in March 2011 that CIA operatives had been working in Libya 'for several weeks' as part of a 'shadow force of Westerners ... which can help bleed Gaddafi's military'. This of course implied that they had arrived at some point in early or mid-February, long before the UN resolution and possibly even before the first days of the Benghazi uprising. Again without stipulating a date, but stating that it had happened 'several weeks ago', the New York Times also quoted US officials as confirming that 'President Obama signed a secret finding authorizing the CIA to provide arms and other support to Libyan rebels.'[120] This was despite earlier US government statements that had claimed it was ready to honour the UN mandate, that confirmed there would be 'no boots on the ground', and that explained the 'Libyan uprising would evolve organically'.[121]

Quickly recovering from the embarrassment of having its agents captured by the first version of the NTC, Britain seemed equally willing to contravene the UN resolution, with Reuters reporting that SAS units had been deployed to help with target acquisition and had infiltrated Tripoli on behalf of the rebels to plant radio equipment.[122] Although barely mentioned on its own television channels or website, Al-Jazeera footage that clearly showed several armed 'Westerners' on rebel front lines was reported on by other media outlets, including the Guardian.[123] As Clinton's emails have since revealed, in March 2011 both British and French special forces were training Libyan rebels in western Egypt and were present 'to a limited degree in the western suburbs of Benghazi'.[124]

In many ways exemplifying the sort of 'international brigandage' predicted by Leon Trotksy in the 1930s,[125] the illegally deployed Western forces in Libya soon seemed to be joined on the ground by those of their principal regional allies. In particular Qatar, which had earlier insisted it was only providing air support, later admitted in October 2011 that it had been sending hundreds of its special forces to every region of Libya. An NTC spokesman even revealed that the Qataris had planned most of the battles that eventually paved the way to victory. One extensive report described how Qatar had been providing training for rebel fighters in both eastern Libya and the western Nafusa mountains, while some had even been brought to Doha for their instruction. It also claimed that Qatari soldiers were spotted in Tripoli at the same time Gaddafi's Bab al-Aziziya compound was finally overrun.[126] Certainly, images of a big Qatari flag flying from the top of its buildings began to circulate widely, either raised by Qatari special forces or by rebels equipped by Qatar. Seemingly forgetting the terms of the UN resolution, British newspapers freely identified the role that 'British-trained Qatari special forces had played' with some even claiming that Qatari forces were pivotal in winning the final battles in Tripoli.[127]

More mindful of the legal complications such admissions could lead to, the US and British governments were a little more wary, with Barack Obama rather evasively stating that the US needed 'more transparency about what Qatar was doing in Libya'.[128] A number of commentators, meanwhile, seemed willing to buy into this idea that Qatar was somehow a free agent, with arguments being made that Doha had chosen to 'make a stand over Libya', that its successes marked 'a high-watermark of Qatari influence', and that the campaign allowed Qatar to 'demonstrate an alignment of values with the international community'.[129] More likely, of course, was that the home of CENTCOM was simply the proxy of choice to deploy Arab soldiers that would ensure rebel units capitalized quickly on the results of NATO air strikes. Indeed, at one point the Qatari armed forces' chief of staff openly stated that his troops were the 'link' between NATO and the rebels.[130]

LIBYA - THE SCRAMBLE FOR ASSETS

Long before the battle for Sirte, the revamped National Transitional Council under Mustafa Abdel-Jalil had already set about denationalizing state assets that fell under rebel control and had begun to promise lucrative contracts and concessions to the NATO powers and their proxies. Having transferred $400 million to the NTC to help with the war effort, Qatar was especially well placed, with its National Bank Group soon able to take a forty-nine percent stake in Libya's Bank of Commerce and Development.[131] Seemingly also underpinning the deal was an agreement, made only a day before Doha recognized the NTC as Libya's official government, in which Qatar was granted exclusive access to rebel-held oil and was allowed to market and sell it on behalf of the new Libya. As Manouchehr Takin from the Center for Global Energy Studies pointed out, this was a 'landmine, legally speaking'. He also posed the question: 'Is this [NTC] representing the Libyan people? Only two countries have accepted that.'[132]

There is evidence that as early as April 2011 French businesses were also trying to move in. According to Hillary Clinton's emails, supposed French humanitarian flights into Libya were actually carrying 'executives from the French company Total, the large construction firm Vinci and the European Aeronautic Defence and Space Company'. Subsequent flights allegedly carried representatives 'from the conglomerate Thalys and other large French firms, all with close ties to [Sarkozy]'. The US Department of State's understanding was that the French businessmen were holding meetings with the NTC before then leaving discreetly in convoys 'organized and protected by paramilitary officers' to head across the border into Egypt. As a close adviser to Clinton put it in an email, French intelligence agents were describing Sarkozy's interests in Libya as being founded on 'a desire to gain a greater share of oil production, increase French influence in Africa, improve his internal political situation in France, [and] provide the French military with an opportunity to reassert its position.'[133]

With undoubtedly similar ambitions, the British government has since admitted that in May 2011 a secret 'Libyan oil cell' had begun to meet. This comprised Foreign Office officials along with Britain's international development minister, and the *Guardian* made the allegation that the cell sought to control the post-regime Libyan oil market in conjunction with a company that had previously been investigated for supplying oil secretly to the Serbian regime in the 1990s and had then been fined after pleading guilty to providing kickbacks to the Saddam Hussein regime during the sanctions era. As the Libyan conflict dragged on, the secret cell and its commercial partner were described by the *Guardian* as 'helping to enforce the sanctions regime to prevent Muammar Gaddafi importing and exporting oil while allowing oil to reach the rebels in the East'.[134]

Italian energy giant Eni was also unwilling to wait for Gaddafi's ouster, with its executives arriving in Tripoli almost immediately after it fell under rebel control. Reportedly there to discuss the resumption of Libyan gas exports, they were barely hours ahead of visits from David Cameron and Nicolas Sarkozy, who jointly told the Libyan people that this was 'your revolution, not our revolution'.[135] By the time the air strikes came to an end, Western officials had become even more blunt, as the sense of competition between the NATO partners for the spoils of war undoubtedly intensified. The US's ambassador to Libya stated that the war-torn country had a need for US companies 'on a big scale', while Britain's defence minister said that businessmen should start to 'pack their suitcases' for Libya to secure reconstruction contracts. This was interpreted by the British media as 'the starting pistol for British firms to pursue contracts in Libya', as it also was for the leading mercenary network which posted a message confirming there 'will be an uptick of activity as companies scramble to get back to Libya ... follow the money, and find your next job'.[136] The chair of Britain's cross-party parliamentary group on Libya even said that 'Britain should come first when it comes to awarding contracts, which would also pay back some of the cost of some £300 million [we] spent on military action.'[137] Indeed, as Germany's *Der Spiegel* had already reported, both the British and French governments had come up with exact price tags for their interventions, believed to be $425 million in Britain's case and $1 million a day for France.[138]

Certainly France's foreign minister claimed it was only 'fair and logical' that French companies should benefit from the war.[139] According to France's *Liberation* newspaper, this assumption was likely based on a letter the NTC had sent to the French government in April 2011 that had offered France 'control over thirty-five percent of Libya's oil in exchange for French support for the insurgency'.[140] Casting more light on this apparent oil-for-strikes deal, Clinton's emails have since revealed that on a follow-up trip to Libya in September 2011 Sarkozy had urged the NTC to honour the promised 'reservation' of part of its oil industry for French firms.[141]

As Oxford University's David Anderson points out, by this stage France and the rest of Europe were also likely viewing such unprecedented access to Libyan hydrocarbons as a good way of reducing their reliance on Russian gas. As he put it, Libya could 'release Western Europe from the strangle-hold of high-pricing Russian producers who currently dominate their gas supply.'[142] Either way, the NTC seemed to be fully on board. Although it had at one point claimed to the media that NATO's intervention was on a 'purely humanitarian basis' it nonetheless seemed fully aware of its obliga-tions by the end of the campaign, having stated that it intended to reward those who showed support 'with Britain and France likely to lead the way'. Moreover, it also made clear that 'our hero revolutionaries wouldn't have made these achievements without the support of the allies, chiefly France and the United Kingdom.'[143]

LIBYA - A ROLE FOR AL-QAEDA

Despite the National Transitional Council's status as NATO's preferred partner, and notwithstanding its substantial backing from the Gulf monar-chies, it was apparent even before the regime fell that not all of the Libyan opposition shared its vision for their country's future. Having risen up alongside Benghazi, the people of Misrata, for example, declared that even when Tripoli fell they would retain at least some form of independence from the new government, and especially one that contained Gaddafi-era remnants.[144] Crucially, the city's well-organized and pluralistic workers' associations and civil cooperatives, unlike those in Benghazi, made it clear they were unwilling to submit to any emasculation of their new-found powers.

Similarly, a number of key Islamist leaders including even the Qatar-based Libyan cleric Sheikh Ali al-Sallabi, whose brother Ismael had helped in organizing Benghazi Islamist militias, began to denounce the NTC's new leaders for 'stealing the revolution' and for having denied many of the rebel factions posts in the new government.[145] Others raised more general

concerns over the new legislation the NTC and its successor organization – the General National Congress – were introducing. These included
a law entitled *Some procedures for the transitional period*, which effectively
granted immunity for all those involved in serious crimes as long as they
were deemed to have been 'military, security, and civilian acts required by
the 17 February revolution [and] committed with the purpose of leading
the revolution to victory'. Furthermore, additional legislation was being
introduced that would not have been out of place in Joseph Stalin's regime,
including a law 'granting legal weight to interrogation reports collected
by revolutionaries' and another that 'criminalized any speech or gesture
that could damage the achievements and the spirit of the revolution'.[146]

Far more serious for the NTC, however, was the growing realization
that large numbers of heavily armed militias remained far beyond its
control. With many such militias being avowedly extremist but having
also clearly enjoyed considerable material and financial support from
Qatar and other Gulf monarchies, officials in the new government were
becoming increasingly aware that they had only ever been one part of a
much bigger plan in taking down the old regime. Certainly, with so much
at stake in the post-Gaddafi Libya, NATO's proxies had made sure, in
something of a shadow strategy, that many of the same battle-hardened
Islamic extremists they had cooperated with in the past would get to play
just as influential a role in Libya as any self-proclaimed 'revolutionaries'
that might eventually turn their back on their patrons. In this sense, Libyan
al-Qaeda members and any local proponents of an Islamic state could be
relied upon not only to accelerate the demise of the old Libyan regime,
but would also help ensure that any new Libyan state remained as fragile
and dependent as possible on its outside protectors.

There is considerable evidence that, by the time of the initial Benghazi
uprising, Western intelligence services were well aware of the extent of the
jihadists' influence in Libya. As well as remnants of the al-Qaeda-linked
Libyan Islamic Fighting Group, there were believed to be entire towns
and suburbs under the sway of similar such organizations, some of which
were home to Libyan veterans of the 1990s foreign legions that fought in
Bosnia and Kosovo. In 2009, for example, a Canadian intelligence report
had already concluded that Benghazi was an 'epicentre of Islamist extremism' from which 'extremist cells' operated. With the report's contents

leaked in time for the 2011 intervention, the *Ottawa Citizen* newspaper described how this led to Canadian pilots participating in Operation Unified Protector joking privately that they had become 'al-Qaeda's air force' on the basis that 'their bombing runs helped to pave the way for rebel groups aligned with the terrorist group.'[147]

Barely a month into the NATO intervention, the *Wall Street Journal* profiled three prominent Libyan jihadists, one being an earlier Guantanamo detainee and the other two being veterans of the Afghan campaign. Although NATO's supreme allied commander in Europe dismissed these and other such fighters as being a 'minor element among the rebels' and representing only a 'flicker of al-Qaeda' among the Libyan opposition, the *Wall Street Journal*'s correspondents nonetheless described them as 'quickly emerging at the forefront of the fight against Gaddafi' because they were understood to be 'training new recruits for the front and protecting against infiltrators'. Interviewed by the paper, one had replied that 'our view is starting to change of the US … if we hated the Americans 100 percent, today it is less than 50 percent.'[148] In fact the fighter being quoted was none other than LIFG member Abel Hakim al-Hasady who had trained for five years in Afghanistan and had then been captured in Pakistan and handed over to the US before being released. In an interview with Italy's *Il Sole 24 Ore* he even stated that after 2003 he had recruited Libyan fighters to go to Iraq and fight US forces there.[149] But by 2011 he was reportedly leading the training of anti-Gaddafi rebels in Darna, east of Benghazi, alongside another LIFG member who had earlier run an al-Qaeda holding company in Sudan and had worked for an al-Qaeda-linked charity in Afghanistan. As the *Independent* reported, the circumstances surrounding al-Hasady's earlier 'mysterious imprisonment and release' by the US remain secret, with the US deputy secretary of state having told Congress that he would only discuss the matter in a closed session.[150]

Other key resurfacing LIFG figures included Adel Hakim Belhadj, whose 'Ferrari 17 Brigade' was believed to be particularly well resourced.[151] Named after the initial uprising and its access to lavish funding, the militia was understood to be backed by Qatar, with even the Qatari military chief accompanying Belhadj on his triumphant arrival in 'liberated' Tripoli. Of the eighteen shipments of approximately twenty thousand tonnes of Qatari weapons imported into Libya over the course of 2011, the *Wall Street*

Journal's sources estimated that only five shipments were destined for the NTC, with the rest having gone to Belhadj and other such commanders.[152]

Much like al-Hasady, Belhadj had a long history of alleged al-Qaeda links and had briefly spent time in US custody after being captured by the CIA in Bangkok in 2004. Later handed over to Libya as part of the described US rapprochement with Gaddafi, he had been 'rehabilitated by the regime' in 2007 and then released from prison in 2010 as part of Saif al-Islam's short-lived efforts to reconcile with elements of the opposition.[153] By 2011 US officials claimed he had turned into a 'moderate politician', and photographs continue to circulate of him apparently receiving some sort of award from senator John McCain. In an especially painful BBC profile, Belhadj was described as a 'Libyan rebel commander' and as the 'rising star of the Libyan leadership'. Importantly he was also reported as having been part of the same Qatar flag-raising group that had earlier stormed Gaddafi's Bab al-Aziziya compound in Tripoli. When asked about any extremist links, the NTC's spokesman seemed temporarily on board with the US and British narrative, explaining that 'everyone knows who Abdel Hakim Belhadj is. He is a Libyan rebel and a moderate person who commands wide respect.'[154]

Unsurprisingly by this stage it seemed that the LIFG was on the road to full rehabilitation, despite its belated designation as a terror group by the US and Britain a few years after 9/11. Indeed, in 2011, the US's West Point Academy stated that the LIFG had an 'increasingly co-operative relationship' with the US military, while other prominent LIFG members living in Britain had had their Home Office control orders dropped, presumably so that they could travel back to Libya.[155]

Beyond the LIFG there is evidence that Qatar had also been financing the *Rafallah al-Sehati* militia. Named after one of the first martyrs of the 17 February uprising, it was described in a report prepared for the European Parliament and then later by the *New York Times* as having jihadists in its ranks and having helped spawn the aforementioned *Ansar al-Sharia* group. On 11 September 2012, the latter was believed to have played a role, complete with rocket-propelled grenade launchers and other heavy weapons, in an attack on the US diplomatic compound in Benghazi that led to the deaths of the US ambassador to Libya, Christopher Stevens, and three other Americans.[156] Although the attack was initially framed by the Department of State as an unstoppable and 'spontaneous eruption of violence triggered by an offensive anti-Muslim video', a successful Freedom of Information Act lawsuit later led to the release of a Department of Defense email revealing that the US had forces in the vicinity that were ready and waiting for the green light to deploy. Either way, Secretary of State Hillary Clinton fell quiet after the event, with the US ambassador to the UN publicly left to pick up the pieces, and with an email received by Clinton a few weeks later indicating that some sort of Benghazi-related Google and YouTube blocking request had earlier been made and would remain in place until the end of the month.[157]

With the knowledge that such empowered jihadist organizations were growing freely in Libya, it is a little easier to understand why, at the time of Gaddafi's fall, visitors to Benghazi claimed to have seen hundreds of jihadist black flags being waved in celebrations.[158] Other eyewitnesses reported seeing, and provided photographs of, a large al-Qaeda flag mounted on the roof of Benghazi's courthouse, the scene of the initial protests. Benghazi residents have also stated that there were 'Islamists driving brand-new SUVs and waving the black al-Qaeda flag driving the city's streets at night shouting.' As one journalist reporting from the area mused, this helped explain why, only a few days earlier and in an apparent act of appeasement, the NTC had made the out-of-character declaration that Libya was to be an 'Islamic state, and sharia law is the source of all our laws'.[159]

Behind the scenes, however, there is little doubt that the NTC was deeply worried about the deal it had been pushed into. A sixteen-page report in English was prepared and sent to US officials detailing the weapons it believed 'Western allies' were supplying to 'dangerous groups'.[160] By the end of 2011 even Mustafa Abdel-Jalil had begun to criticize publicly what he believed was Qatar's 'dangerous role', claiming that Doha was doing things in Libya that the NTC had no control over. The NTC's acting oil and finance minister, Ali Tarhouni, was soon similarly outspoken, complaining that Qatar had been giving out armaments to 'people that we don't know' and describing how they 'paid money to just about anybody ... they intervened in committees that have control over security issues.'[161] After Tarhouni assumed the role of interim prime minister he then made the demand that 'anyone who wishes to come to our house should knock on the front door first.'[162]

By 2012 the LIFG–Qatar faction nevertheless seemed a fait accompli, with Belhadj's new Islamist *Al-Watan* or 'The Nation' party announcing it would contest GNC elections. Understood to be receiving huge funding from Qatar, even the colours of the party's flag – purple and white – were the same as those of the Qatari flag.[163] Although the international media predicted it would do very well, and it had the resources to establish twenty-seven offices across Libya, *Al-Watan* performed incredibly badly and won only three percent of the eventual vote and no seats in the GNC.[164]

Attempting some necessary public distancing from a plan that the US had clearly been a party to, a few months later US officials told the *New York Times* that Qatar had 'strengthened militant groups in Libya, allowing them to become a destabilizing force since the fall of the Gaddafi government'. A former Department of Defense official was also quoted describing the unpopular Islamists as 'more antidemocratic, more hardline, closer to an extreme version of Islam than the main rebel alliance in Libya'. Moreover, citing the case of an Arizona-based arms merchant who had earlier supplied $200 million of weapons to Qatar for the purpose of running them into Libya, the report claimed his 'pipeline' was eventually blocked on the basis that the Qataris 'imposed no controls on who got the weapons ... they just handed them out like candy'.[165] Almost laughably, a Libya-focused meeting of the US deputies committee – a panel made up of deputies from the various intelligence agencies – had even stated that Qatar was 'supposedly a good ally [of the US], but the Islamists they support are not in our interest'.[166]

LIBYA – SEARCHING FOR A SISI

With the popularity of the Islamists and their allied militias continuing to wane throughout 2013, there seemed a real risk that a secular and nationalist General National Congress could somehow still form. Although cooperative with NATO during the uprising, many of the GNC's increasingly empowered politicians seemed potentially unpredictable and perhaps even obstacles to the billions of dollars' worth of Western and Qatari investment deals that had been signed over the past two years. With hundreds of protestors convening in Tripoli's Algeria Square – which had briefly been renamed 'Qatar Square' but was then switched back again – demands were being made for the Islamists to retreat from the capital, as they were seen to be undermining Libyan values, while mass online petitions were collected to reject any further Qatari involvement in Libyan affairs and to block any future Qatari donations.[167]

Having one more go at the ballot box in summer 2014 with even greater funding behind them, Adel Hakim Belhadj and his associates still won only thirty out of the two hundred available seats.[168] Unwilling to accept a marginal role in the new Libyan state, their still powerful and heavily armed paramilitary brigades duly seized control over Tripoli under the banner of the 'Libya Dawn' and formed their own self-declared GNC.[169] Without the firepower to match the renegade government's forces, the elected congress had little choice but to flee the capital and even Benghazi, eventually re-establishing itself as the House of Representatives in the easternmost city of Tobruk.[170]

Weakened, and evidently unable to defend itself, the retreating government had little choice, it seemed, but to gravitate towards a secular strongman that both it and the National Transitional Council before it had earlier tried to keep at a distance. In many ways mirroring the Egyptian counter-revolution, in which different reactionary forces supported by different Gulf monarchies had wrestled for control over Cairo, it appeared that Qatar and the Islamists were again poised to lose out to an Abdelfattah Sisi-style national saviour who could prove more effective at holding the state together and ensuring business as usual with Libya's new-found foreign partners.

Although General Khalifa Hiftar was likely never viewed by the Western powers as the best solution for post-Gaddafi Libya, with a popular Islamist-dominated and Qatar-financed GNC almost certainly the primary objective, there are nonetheless indications that elements within the US had been backing him all along as an alternative 'safe pair of hands'. With a lengthy history of dealing with US intelligence, in 1987 Hiftar had arranged for himself and 1,700 Libyan troops to defect after their forces were captured by the US- and French-backed Chadian army during what was supposed to be an attempted invasion of Chad. Informing the National Front for the Salvation of Libya – then the main opposition group to Gaddafi – that he was on their side, Hiftar was understood to have been cooperating with the US, with 350 of his men trained by US intelligence agents in Chad so that they could become a commando force capable of bringing down Gaddafi. Unable ever to carry out the operation, Hiftar and his men were reportedly brought to the US, with Hiftar having then settled in a town in Virginia about five miles from the CIA's headquarters.[171] After then receiving little further media coverage for several years, in 1996 the *Washington Post* mentioned Hiftar in one of its reports on Libya and described him as the leader of a 'contra-style group based in the US called the Libyan National Army'. This was confirmed by a subsequent Congressional Research Service briefing which stated that 'Hiftar and the Libyan National Army is in exile in the US'.[172]

Referred to by Britain's *Independent* as one of the 'shady men backed by the West to displace Gaddafi', Hiftar had re-emerged in Libya in April 2011 with the rather presumptuous claim he was the new 'chief rebel army commander'. Before his departure he had reportedly met with the US ambassador to Libya and the CIA, both apparently being 'keen to find out what they could about the opposition'. As the *Washington Post* revealed, Hiftar had requested from them 'cutting edge weapons' including 'missiles, rockets, armoured personnel carriers and reconnaissance vehicles', but was ultimately left frustrated after not having received anything.[173] Unable to assume command of the NTC forces, with key defector Abdul Fatah Younis standing in the way, Hiftar's position nevertheless grew much stronger after the death of Younis and his two deputy commanders in Benghazi in July 2011. Described by the French media as being 'shrouded in mystery', the multiple assassinations were ascribed to rebel infighting and, in particular, an alleged attempt by Younis to organize a ceasefire with Saif al-Islam Gaddafi.[174] According to Hillary Clinton's emails, notably an August 2011 memorandum entitled *Who killed Younis and why*, the US Department of State seemed willing to go along with the media narrative, claiming that Mustafa Abdel-Jalil had given a direct order for the assassination on the basis that Younis was entering into a dialogue with the old regime.[175]

Sensing the NTC's and then the elected GNC's growing weakness, by the end of 2013 Hiftar had begun to plan for a Libyan version of the correctional coup d'état that had worked so well in Cairo. With Hiftar increasingly well equipped, the UAE had clearly stepped in to assume the same sort of US-approved role it had also begun to play in Egypt. Indeed, although Abu Dhabi's initial request to ship US-manufactured weapons to Libya was understood to have been rejected, a former US official described how it was still told that 'it's OK to ship other weapons' in a presumed reference to third-party equipment that could not be traced back to the US. Meanwhile, the *New York Times* reported that NATO air and naval forces patrolling the Libyan coastline had been issued with instructions not to intercept any arms-laden cargo planes or ships originating from the Persian Gulf.[176] In fact an earlier NTC briefing supplied to US officials that had identified 'masses of weapons', including tanks and surface-to-air missiles, arriving in eastern Libya had also noted that 'NATO has given permission to a number of weapons-loaded aircraft to land at Benghazi airport and some Tunisian airports'.[177]

Launched in February 2014, Hiftar's coup failed to gather momentum as did his distinctly NATO-sounding 'Operation Dignity' – an armed campaign his forces had then begun to fight against the Islamist militias.[178] In many ways Hiftar's actions may have swung public opinion further away from such military solutions, especially after stories began to circulate of apartment blocks being indiscriminately shelled and, at one point, even Tripoli's airport being bombarded as passengers were waiting to take off.[179] But with a much better opportunity to take a leading role after the summer 2014 elections, and now able to present himself as the guardian of the exiled Tobruk government, it seems Hiftar and his backers were prepared to escalate in order to see off the Qatar-backed Libya Dawn. Almost certainly seeking and quietly receiving US approval, the UAE along with Saudi Arabia began to provide Hiftar with air cover for his new wave of attacks on the GNC. With details remaining sketchy, it seems the UAE flew several aircraft out of Egyptian bases, perhaps alongside Egyptian aircraft, and had then struck a number of targets across Libya. Although Egypt denied any role, the UAE did not, while the four US officials who confirmed knowledge of the strikes merely added the disclaimers that they had 'caught the US by surprise' and were 'unconstructive'.[180]

Beyond assisting Hiftar himself, the UAE's role also seemed to encompass the financing and mobilizing of a number of tribes to aid Hiftar's cause.[181] According to residents of Tripoli, heavily armed members of the Zintan, the Sawaeq, and the Al-Qaqa began to arrive in the city and attempted to take control over the airport. Accused of all sorts of subversive actions ranging from the stealing of fuel canisters to attempted power cuts, the pro-Hiftar tribes were described as trying to 'create the type of resentment that drove the Egyptians to the streets so that the army took advantage of it'. One resident remarked that 'the UAE was trying the same thing they did in Egypt ... Before Morsi was toppled there were lots and lots of lines in front of gas stations in Cairo.' Another described how Libya Dawn forces had found a camp previously used by the Zintan which had 'a huge operations room containing huge printers and Xerox machines producing [anti-GNC] banners and slogans'.[182] Meanwhile, and unbeknownst to most Libyans at the time, it was alleged by the *Guardian* that the UAE had already offered the UN's special representative in Libya a $50,000 a month job in Abu Dhabi. Although since claiming that there was no conflict of interest, the UN official had nevertheless already made clear he was unwilling to treat the GNC as an 'equal actor' and was 'not working on a political plan that would include everybody'. As the *Guardian* reported, he had also talked of breaking the 'very dangerous alliance' that kept the GNC afloat and of having a strategy to 'completely delegitimize the GNC'.[183]

With neither side able to deliver a quick victory or gain nationwide trust, Libya was soon on the cusp of full-blown civil war. As *Jacobin* magazine put it, it had really become an 'imperial bloodbath' given that both major factions were ultimately the counter-revolutionary arms of competing Western proxies trying to fill a vacuum left behind by the collapsing Libyan state.[184] Indeed, by the beginning of 2015 the UN estimated that somewhere between 100,000 and 300,000 Libyans were bearing weapons. With this thought to be more than ten times the number of combatants there had been prior to the NATO intervention, UN representatives claimed it had become impossible to stem the fighting due to the 'regional powers who really hold the tap of weapons and money'.[185]

SYRIA – PARALLEL PLANS

With little chance to enter Syria's markets or reshape its foreign policy under the long reign of Hafez al-Assad, the Western powers saw great opportunity in the succession of his son Bashar in 2000. An ophthalmologist who had trained and lived in London, his British wife, Asma Akhras, was soon described by the *Sunday Times* as the 'fragrant, London-born first lady of Syria' and later by *Vogue* as the 'rose in the desert' and the 'Lady Diana of the Middle East'.[186] The hope, of course, was that Bashar and his princess-like spouse would try to follow the same sort of path as Muammar Gaddafi's sons, with the rest of the al-Assad dynasty – many of whom were monopolizing entire sectors of Syria's economy – inevitably pressing Bashar to open up the economy from the inside. In this sense, it was anticipated that the young new president would pin his future legitimacy on neo-liberalism and, as Chicago University's Lisa Weeden put it, promote 'the fantasy of upward mobility' for those around him.[187] By 2008 even British foreign secretary David Miliband had paid him a visit, ostensibly as part of a British policy to 'ease Syria back into international respectability'. Declaring in Damascus that 'it's very important that we continue to engage countries like Syria, which wants to be a secular state at the heart of a stable Middle East,' Miliband seemed to be handing out honorary membership of the 'Axis of Moderation'.[188]

Making things easier, and in contrast to Gaddafi's relative isolation during the 1980s and 1990s, was Hafez's long legacy of accepting financial support from the Gulf monarchies. Despite his parallel reliance on Soviet and Iranian aid, and despite Syria having never fired a shot in anger against Israel since the early 1970s, his regime's purported role as a front-line state had certainly helped boost donations from the wealthier Arab states that, publicly at least, were also supposed to be in some sort of confrontation with the 'Zionist entity'. Saudi Arabia, for example, had pledged a massive $350 million to Syria in 1975 and, along with its neighbours, it had helped to bankroll Syria's invasion of Lebanon under the banner of an 'Arab deterrence force' so as to counter the shared threat of the Palestinian Liberation Organization and other leftist groups in Beirut. As Jean-Pierre Filiu notes, even after the Camp David accords Syria may still have received up to $2 billion in Gulf aid and, whenever such aid was slow to arrive, Damascus would issue veiled threats to the monarchies via 'friendly terrorist organizations [such as the Islamic Jihad Movement in Palestine]' within their orbit.[189]

With the least historical baggage in its Syrian relations, Qatar soon emerged as the driving force behind the Gulf–Syria rapprochement of the 2000s. With Bashar and Hamad bin Khalifa al-Thani frequent visitors to each other's capitals, with their high-profile wives reportedly friends and often 'spotted in the high-end fashion boutiques together', and with the al-Assads often holidaying in Qatar, too, it seemed the alliance was getting stronger. Ploughing more than $12 billion into Syria between 2006 and

2010, mostly in joint ventures in tourism projects, state-backed Qatari companies and even the Qatar Investments Authority almost overnight became the principal foreign investors in Bashar's gradually liberalizing economy.[190] Moreover, with the Reach Out To Asia aid organization run by Hamad's wife Moza bint Nasser al-Missnad having launched a number of Syria-based projects, including one to promote environmental education in more than 170 schools, there was also strong evidence of parallel soft power relations being established.[191] Most spectacularly, the al-Thanis even set about building a lavish multibillion-dollar home close to Palmyra. With locals describing its floors as made out of the same marble as in the Grand Mosque in Mecca, the resulting Moza Palace stood briefly as a testament to the Syrian regime's tentative reforms.[192]

As with Libya, however, with so much at stake there needed to be other plans in place in the event that Bashar failed to live up to expectations. According to the *Wall Street Journal*, the US had already established secret communications with elements in the Syrian regime in order to explore ways in which Bashar might relinquish power.[193] Moreover, as with the Libyan Islamic Fighting Group and the Muslim Brotherhood in Egypt, Syria's Islamists were also identified as potential allies-in-waiting. Although the Syrian branch of the Brotherhood had long been considered a terrorist organization by US intelligence agencies, its potential usefulness had not gone unnoticed. After all it had once led the biggest resistance movement to Hafez's regime when its more radical Jordanian- and Israeli-backed breakaway group, *Al-Talia al-Muqatila* or 'Fighting Vanguard', had launched a violent guerrilla campaign in 1982 and quickly managed to take over the northern third of the country. As a former CIA analyst put it, Hafez was 'going down at the time ... he was really in trouble.'[194] With the Vanguard killing all *Ba'ath* officials in the city of Hama and, according to the US ambassador at the time, hundreds of others, the regime eventually managed to counter-attack and put down the uprising after a bombardment that killed over twenty thousand and the eventual capturing of over thirty thousand suspected Brotherhood members.[195]

By 2006, even as Qatar's palace was being built and Bashar's wife was still the toast of London high society, there were strong indications that the Brotherhood was being built up as an insurance policy by the British government. Bashar had, after all, recently publicly insulted the king of Saudi

Arabia over his weak stance on Israel. By the end of the year a Brotherhood contingent had been invited to London, ostensibly as part of a 'National Salvation Front' which was staging a conference that called for regime change in Syria.[196] With their presence by then openly tolerated by the British security services, the Syrian Brotherhood's exiled leader told the *Guardian* newspaper that the organization did not see itself as 'the alternative to forty years of corrupt dictatorship ... but as partners with others in the coming age' and that it sought a 'civil, democratic state, not an Islamist republic'.[197]

By 2007 the US seemed firmly on board, with a former CIA officer recalling how the Brotherhood began to receive US and Saudi financial support, and with former US diplomat David Long explaining that the US Bureau of Intelligence and Research had begun to consider it being merely 'benign but risky'.[198] What seems to have been a covert plan to forge, if need be, a new Islamist state in Syria has now been largely corroborated by former French foreign minister Roland Dumas who recently revealed that during a visit to Britain in 2009 he 'met with top British officials, who confessed to me that they were preparing something in Syria ... Britain was preparing gunmen to invade Syria.'[199]

SYRIA - THE UPRISING BEGINS

Given their respective foundations in neo-liberalism and Islamism, both of the West's Syria strategies were severely interrupted by a series of peaceful, secular, and social-justice-oriented protests in the wake of the region-wide Arab Spring. Although much like Libya's initial uprising, they were somewhat localized and appeared to have much narrower support bases than those in Tunisia or Egypt, they nonetheless placed the al-Assad regime in a defensive and vulnerable position. At first it seemed everything could be easily contained without the need for Gaddafi-like crackdowns. After all, a candlelit vigil held in solidarity with the Egyptian revolution in late January 2011 had been quickly broken up by police, while a Syrian 'day of rage' planned for 5 February saw only a few hundred turn up.[200] On 17 February – the same day as the Benghazi protests began – things seemed more tense following an argument between police and protestors in Damascus holding banners saying, 'The Syrian people

313

will not be humiliated.' But when the interior minister visited the scene in person to assure the crowds that the police officers involved would be investigated, and when Bashar al-Assad announced a range of new social welfare programmes along with the unblocking of social media platforms, it still seemed likely Syria could avoid the fate of Libya.[201]

By March, however, things seemed to be getting more out of control as the increasingly heavy-handed and undoubtedly nervous regime proved unwilling to take many more chances. After fifteen youths were arrested in Daraa for painting on walls 'the people want the regime to fall', much bigger protests started to grow, and by 17 March there were eyewitness reports of civilians being shot while claims began to circulate of horrific torture being used on those who were captured.[202] With the dissidents standing firm, Syria's southernmost city seemed poised to become the epicentre of an urban revolt.[203]

As the Syrian equivalent of Benghazi, Daraa's message soon spread to the historically restive Hama along with Homs and even parts of Damascus. A 'day of dignity' was held on 18 March, with an even bigger protest staged the following Friday.[204] As with Cairo's Tahrir Square, protestors in Homs were heard chanting 'peaceful, Muslims, and Christians' along with other non-sectarian slogans such as 'God, Syria, freedom and nothing else'. Meanwhile, newly formed committees declared that 'the freedom and dignity of our citizenship can only be accessed through peaceful demonstration' and, although there were some reports of public buildings and Ba'ath headquarters being burned down, in many cases the protests remained peaceful, with some even marching without their shirts to prove they held no concealed weapons.[205]

Although Bashar made what seemed a last-ditch attempt to avoid more direct confrontation by pledging to end the forty-eight-year-long state of emergency, increase public sector salaries, and allow new political parties to form, by April it seemed the die was already cast with thousands of troops beginning to lay siege to Daraa, and tanks entering Homs.[206] Galvanized by the martyrdom of Hamza al-Khatib, a thirteen-year-old boy who had been arrested and whose mutilated corpse was afterwards returned to his family, the protests gained a much harder edge and even reached Aleppo which, as Abdel Bari Atwan contends, had long been considered relatively apolitical given its more commercial focus.[207] With dozens being killed every day,[208] and reportedly more than eight thousand arrested in just two months, mobile phone video footage began to go viral of soldiers haphazardly shooting protestors, including women and children.[209] Making matters worse, the regime resorted to temporarily disconnecting the Internet and broadcasting television reports that claimed videos depicting brutal attacks on villages were in fact from Iraq and involved Kurdish militias, even though they clearly contained local landmarks readily identifiable to many Syrians.[210]

Beyond such repression, the regime also engaged in two other strategies in an effort to keep its core constituency as loyal as possible and also, so it hoped, to ward off any attempted external interference. With much the same goal as Ali Abdullah Saleh's encouraging of al-Qaeda militants to take over certain towns, Bashar duly began a 'highly selective' amnesty of prisoners.[211] According to a report prepared for the European Parliament these were known to include numerous prominent jihadists such as Muhammad al-Jowlani, known as Al-Fateh or 'The Conqueror', Abu Khalid al-Suri who had been a courier for al-Qaeda, and perhaps even the infamous Abu Musab al-Suri, who had not only been a member of the 1980s Fighting Vanguard and, as earlier described, a leading light of the 1990s 'Londonistan' scene, but had then gone on to be an administrator for Osama bin Laden. Having been sidelined by al-Qaeda for supposedly trying to poach their recruits, he had begun to work for the Taliban's Mullah Omar while also authoring a lengthy and influential text, *A call to a global Islamic resistance*, which had pushed for jihadism to be more decentralized and without an al-Qaeda-style core organization.[212]

Others released included Awwad al-Makhlaf, who went on to become a governor for the eventual Islamic State in the northern town of Al-Raqqah, and Abu al-Athir al-Absi, who first formed his own jihadist group before becoming an Islamic State governor in Homs.[213] Meanwhile, in Lebanon, with the authorities appearing to act on Syrian instruction, approximately seventy other jihadist prisoners were understood to have been set free, including some that had taken part in a deadly uprising only a few years earlier.[214] Adding further weight to claims that Bashar was trying to radicalize the opposition by emptying extremists into their ranks, there were reports that even before their release such inmates had already been moved to more comfortable prisons so that they could mingle with other political prisoners, including students. According to one jihadist fighter later

315

interviewed by the *Guardian*, this was because the regime 'wanted them
to be radicalized ... if this stayed as a street protest, it would have toppled
[the regime] within months, and they knew it.'²¹⁵ Indeed, within months of
Bashar's spring amnesty, suicide bombings had begun in both Damascus
and Aleppo, and by February 2012 al-Jowlani formally established a Syrian
al-Qaeda franchise known as *Jabhat al-Nusra* or 'The Support Front'.²¹⁶ Now
more easily able to frame opposition attacks as terrorism and marginalize
any remaining peaceful protestors, Bashar likely felt on much safer ground.
Some regime defectors, including Syria's former ambassador to Iraq, even
claimed that during this period elements of Syrian intelligence had been
collaborating with the jihadists to mount even larger-scale terror attacks.²¹⁷

Much like the Gaddafi family's implied threats to Western politicians that they might one day turn a blind eye to refugees crossing the
Mediterranean to Europe, by this stage Bashar and his cronies were clearly
trying to supplement the al-Qaeda spectre with the prospect of another
refugee crisis. With two percent of Syria's entire population being camp-
dwelling Palestinians, in some cases only a few hundred miles from the
Israeli border, one of Syria's top businessmen and a cousin of Bashar stated
in a three-hour interview with the *New York Times*: 'If there is no stability
here, there's no way there will be stability in Israel ... no way, and nobody
can guarantee what will happen after, God forbid, anything happens to
this regime.' When asked if he was making a threat, he replied, 'What I'm
saying is don't let us suffer, don't put a lot of pressure on the president,
don't push Syria to do anything it is not happy to do.'²¹⁸ Seemingly a public
warning to the US Israel lobby, the interview was soon followed up by
action when a few days later, on the anniversary of the creation of the
state of Israel, the Syrian regime transported hundreds of refugees to the
Golan Heights and set them free. Although Israeli border guards killed
several, a few weeks later exactly the same thing happened with a further
twenty-three refugees being killed.²¹⁹

SYRIA – PREPARING FOR INTERVENTION

Although soon outlasting Muammar Gaddafi, the increasingly brutal and
divisive Bashar al-Assad regime's long-term survival prospects seemed little

better. Despite much fragmentation and the growing jihadist menace, what Syrian blogger Shadia Safwan describes as a 'domestic nucleus of opposition' was nonetheless forming.[220] Even if most of the Syrian population remained loyal to the government, as also initially seemed to be the case in Libya, it became increasingly apparent that such a nucleus was to serve as the conduit for external support and perhaps even a full-scale intervention. Certainly with a number of so-called 'moderate' opposition groups coalescing into a 'Free Syrian Army', their new shadow government – known as the Syrian National Council – seemed well placed to assume the same sort of pro-NATO role as the Libyan National Transitional Council had eventually done. Unsurprisingly given their recent US and British dealings and the role they were probably intended to play if the Arab Spring had not begun, even the Syrian Muslim Brotherhood's several fighting brigades – by then known as the Commission of the Shields of the Revolution – had quickly subordinated themselves to the bigger Western-backed FSA despite many of their preachers continuing to call the US the 'world's leader in terrorism.'[221]

With Bashar's family and many of his key military and security commanders being Alawite, a minority Shia sect which accounted for about twelve percent of the Syrian population in 2011, it seemed that the quickest way for the Western powers and their regional allies to boost the prospects of both the FSA and the Brotherhood was by adding a stronger sectarian edge to the conflict. In this sense, regardless of the non-sectarian slogans of the original protests in Daraa, Hama, Homs, and elsewhere, it was reasoned that if the regime could be portrayed as a cadre of Shia overlords then it could more easily be overwhelmed by a full-scale nationwide revolution led by a Syrian Sunni majority. Leading the charge were prominent preachers in the Gulf monarchies, some of whom had online followings in their millions. Kuwait's Nabil al-Audi, Saudi Arabia's Muhammad al-Arifi, and the Saudi-based Syrian cleric Adnan al-Arour all jumped on the bandwagon by repeatedly describing the Syrian uprising as a jihad against the 'polytheist' Alawite regime and, more broadly, as part of an international Sunni struggle against Shia oppression.[222] Although most US officials were naturally too cautious to offer their opinions, a number of key opinion-makers nonetheless seemed firmly on board. As one of the most influential supporters of the US invasion of Iraq in 2003, Stanford

University's Fouad Ajami perhaps unsurprisingly chose to rationalize the Syrian conflict as a 'revolt that fused a sense of economic disinheritance and the wrath of a Sunni majority determined to rid itself of the rule of a godless lot.'²²³ Similarly, as early as August 2011, the University of Vermont's Gregory Gause had already described 'the sectarian element of the Syrian confrontation, with an ostensibly secular and Alawite Shia-dominated regime brutally suppressing the Sunni Muslim majority.'²²⁴

Although European government briefings noted how such efforts to sectarianize the conflict were fuelling the image of a 'regional Shia conspiracy', the problematic reality in Syria was quite a bit different, helping us understand why the Sunni masses did not immediately shift their allegiances away from the regime to the rebels. As one rebel fighter wistfully told the *New York Times*: 'Before the revolution, we never had this feeling toward any sect.'²²⁵ In Ziauddin Sardar's words, for all its faults, the al-Assad regime was 'a bit more inclusive, sharing power between Sunni, Christian, Druze, and Alawite elites'. As he has since reflected, this is 'perhaps why [Bashar] still has support from members of all communities'.²²⁶ As others have pointed out, not only is Bashar's wife's family Sunni but so too have been many high-ranking officials in the Syrian government including Walid Muallem who, as foreign minister, is arguably the second most public face of the regime.²²⁷ Leading Sunni clerics also remained loyal to the regime, although as Edinburgh University's Thomas Pierret has astutely demonstrated, this was mostly a result of the government having earlier co-opted much of the religious establishment into the political fold.²²⁸

Likely hoping NATO air strikes could be avoided, not least given Syria's complicating alliances with Iran and Russia, the Western governments sought at first to keep their support for the opposition as discreet and as limited as possible. While some have accused the Western embassies of having stirred up the original uprisings, there is little hard evidence to support this view, although there is no doubt they had made early expressions of solidarity. In July 2011, for example, the US and French ambassadors had visited the opposition stronghold in Hama which led to a strong condemnation from the Syrian government. According to the interior minister, 'Ambassador Ford's visit to the restive central city of Hama was proof that Washington was inciting unrest'. He also claimed that 'Mr Ford met with saboteurs and incited them to violence, protest, and rejection of dialogue.' Defending the episode, US officials have explained that Robert Ford and his French counterpart, Eric Chevallier, had indeed travelled to Hama to meet with demonstrators but had left shortly before the protests began. They claimed that when the two men entered the city 'their car was immediately surrounded by friendly protestors who were putting flowers on the windshields, they were putting olive branches on the car, they were chanting "down with the regime".[229]

But by 2012, with the Syrian uprising still not having evolved into a fully national revolution or even a sectarian civil war, there was a growing realization that much more direct support was required. At the very least the opposition needed to get more weapons and funding so they could keep fighting, and ideally they needed sufficiently sophisticated battlefield equipment so that they could enjoy a qualitative advantage over the much larger Syrian government forces. According to Seymour Hersh, a CIA- and MI6-sponsored 'rat line' for weapons duly began, with arms that had origi-nally been sent to Libyan rebels, mostly supplied by Qatar and the UAE, then being re-exported to the Syrian conflict. As he explains, Australian front companies earlier set up in post-Gaddafi Libya took care of the logistics, while the CIA's inclusion of MI6 as its partner was designed to enable the agency to classify the operation as a 'liaison activity' and thus allowed it to circumvent the layers of congressional oversight that had been installed in the wake of the Nicaragua campaign.[230] As later reports in the *Washington Post* and *IHS Janes* indicate, by 2013 this had evolved into a more comprehensive CIA operation, while in parallel the White House announced a more public $500 million programme to train and equip 'the right militants' and the 'moderate rebels'; a process which apparently involved some sort of screening for extremist views and then the transfer of heavy weapons including US-manufactured anti-tank missiles.[231]

SYRIA - ENTER THE PROXIES

In an almost carbon copy of the leading role they had undertaken in Libya, so too were the Gulf monarchies encouraged to enmesh themselves in the politics and financing of the Syrian opposition. As far as these and other nearby Western proxies were concerned, there seemed little downside to having Bashar al-Assad ousted even if some, such as Qatar, had to swallow the loss of recent investments. The spoils to be found in a post-*Ba'ath* Syria would, after all, more than make up for this. Moreover, having witnessed the speed and success of NATO's intervention in Libya, it is likely that even if no promises had been made by Washington the Gulf rulers nevertheless expected a similar intervention, at least in the form of a no-fly zone. In this scenario, they could be confident that the conflict would be wrapped up within a few months thus giving Iran and Syria's other allies such as *Hezbollah* as little opportunity as possible to mount a counter-attack.

As they had in Libya with Mustafa Abdel-Jalil's version of the National Transitional Council, the Gulf monarchies began by using the Arab League as a vehicle to endorse the Syrian National Council and expel the Syrian government. Under Qatari chairmanship the organization had already agreed to do this in November 2011, albeit with Lebanon and Yemen voting no, Iraq abstaining, and Algeria raising serious objections on the basis it would complicate future peaceful solutions. In parallel, the Arab League was also used to lobby the UN Security Council to do the same, but with only limited results given the vetoes of both Russia and China. More successful were Saudi Arabia's efforts to use its UN Human Rights Council membership, which the British government had helped it to secure, to call for 'concrete, immediate, and comprehensive reforms' to address the 'deplorable situation of human rights' in Syria.[232]

Writing soon after the Arab League decision, Columbia University's Joseph Massad made it clear that the 'League and imperial powers have taken over the Syrian uprising in order to remove the al-Assad regime'.[233] Taking a similar position, so it seemed, was the UN and Arab League's joint peace envoy who chose to drop his Arab League affiliation on the basis that it was 'backing the opposition at all costs' and preventing key powers such as Iran from participating in negotiations. Nonetheless, by the beginning of 2013 the Arab League had begun inviting the head of the SNC to sit as Syria's representative under the Syrian flag in its meetings, while it succeeded in freezing Syria's assets in most of its member states and blocking further Arab investment in Syria.[234] Co-founded by a grandson of the previously described former military dictator who had been backed by the CIA and MI6 in their attempt to overthrow the Syrian government in 1957, the SNC was by this stage running a de facto shadow government from bases in Qatar, the United Arab Emirates, and Turkey.[235]

On a state-to-state level, the Doha regime certainly began to assume one of the biggest roles, much like in Libya. Suspending all diplomatic relations and trade agreements with Damascus, and thus abruptly reversing the once burgeoning relationship between the al-Thani and al-Assad dynasties, Qatar and Al-Jazeera soon sought to portray the Syrian uprising as yet another instance of the Arab Spring, just as it had done with the Benghazi protests. Described by Bashar loyalists as broadcasting 'exaggerated and dishonest coverage', Al-Jazeera's intensive coverage of Syria was, as Marc Lynch notes, seen by many as an 'energetic media campaign organized outside Syria ... largely divorced from realities on the ground'.[236]

More importantly there is compelling evidence that the US CENTCOM-hosting Qatar also became the principal NATO link to the conflict, being best placed to provide substantial levels of funds and weapons to the Syrian rebels far beyond the cautious and modest assistance provided by the CIA and MI6. As with its similar job in Libya, however, this was initially obscured by attempts to frame Qatar's intervention as a 'natural step-up in the scale of Qatari diplomacy', as an opportunity for Doha to take a stand against 'tyrannical rule', and as a 'convergence of Qatari and Western responses'.[237] Sultan Barakat of the Brookings Doha Center, for example, described it as something of a natural shift to a more interventionist foreign policy due to the opportunities of the Arab Spring, while the *Economist* explained Qatar's actions as part of its 'pursuing an aggressively non-aligned foreign policy'.[238] Others even tried to present Qatar's intervention as part of 'stepping up to play a role' in the context of Mubarak's demise and '[the] US having lost in a way its central diplomatic partner in the [Arab] world'.[239]

Much closer to the truth, however, was the investigative reporter Elizabeth Dickinson who wrote in an extensive *Foreign Policy* essay in 2014 that '[Qatar] had such freedom to run its network for the last three years because Washington was looking the other way.' Putting it more precisely she also stated that 'in fact, in 2011, the US gave Doha de facto free rein to do what it wasn't willing to do in the Middle East: intervene.'[240] In an article for the BBC, King's College London's David Roberts, who had previously been based in Doha, similarly concluded that 'there is no chance that Qatar is doing this alone: the US and British governments will certainly be involved in or at least apprised of Qatar's plans.'[241]

SYRIA – ARMING THE REBELS

Getting money to the rebels was relatively straightforward, with Qatar having set up a number of funding channels for the Syrian National Council and in some cases directly to the Free Syrian Army. In early 2012, for example, it was reported that the Qatar-backed Libyan National Transitional Council had recycled $100 million to 'anti-al-Assad officials' in Syria, ostensibly as Libyan humanitarian aid for Syria. With further donations made, many also originating from Qatar, the SNC promised that they would reduce any confusion by serving as the 'link between those who want to help and the revolutionaries'. Qatar's prime minister gave his public blessing to such assistance on the grounds that the Syrians are 'right to defend themselves ... I think we should help these people by all means.'[242] In late 2012 he further justified his country's support on the basis that Syria was no longer just in a state of civil war, but that the government had begun to carry out genocide.[243]

Naturally, as with its Libya strategy, Qatar was not only backing the formal opposition, but was also making sure funds reached the more extremist groups, including even al-Qaeda's *Jabhat al-Nusra* franchise. As brazen as Qatari officials had been about contravening the UN resolution on Libya, by admitting the deployment of their special forces on the ground, so too were they quite open about the sort of groups they were willing to finance in Syria. Speaking at a conference in late 2012, Qatar's deputy foreign minister explained to the audience that 'I am very much against excluding anyone at this stage, or bracketing them as terrorists, or bracketing them as al-Qaeda given Qatar's perceived necessity of removing al-Assad at all costs.'[244] Indeed, in a 2012 interview with a German correspondent, one *Al-Nusra* member stated bluntly that his organization's evocative name was 'a great name ... we get money from the Gulf with it.'[245]

Designated a terror fundraiser by the US Department of the Treasury, an Iraqi cleric had already appeared on Al-Jazeera praying at the opening ceremony of Qatar's state mosque and standing only a few feet away from the Qatari crown prince.[246] Similarly, Qatar's ministry for Islamic affairs was understood to have invited a Kuwaiti cleric known for his running of a Syrian opposition support network. Allowed to preach in a Qatari mosque, he argued that mere humanitarian assistance to Syria was insufficient and declared that 'the priority is the support for the jihadists and arming them,' or, as the New York Times reported him saying, 'give your money to the ones who will spend it on jihad, not aid.'[247] After he had returned to Kuwait, collections were raised on his behalf by an individual whose Twitter biography described himself as 'loving Sunni jihadists who hate Shia and infidels' and whose Twitter timeline was 'flush with praise for Osama bin Laden'. When particularly big donations were received, such men tweeted them, including pictures of expensive Qatar-bought jewellery. One al-Qaeda-linked brigade even released a video in which the Kuwaiti cleric personally appeared to thank 'the kind people of Qatar, O people of the Gulf, your money has arrived'.[248]

Some Syrian rebels were also reported to have '[deliberately] grown the long, scraggly beards favoured by hardline Salafist Muslims after hearing that Qatar was more inclined to give weapons to Islamists', while others were understood to be using the money to 'buy weapons in large quantities and then burying them in caches, to be used after the collapse of the al-Assad government'.[249] The New York Times also claimed that members of the Qatari funding and tweeting circle had appeared on Al-Jazeera and had received favourable coverage, while perhaps even more remarkably others reported that Al-Nusra's leaders had begun to visit Doha in person and, according to both US officials and those of other Arab governments, had held meetings with senior Qatari officials and key financiers.[250]

As far as the US was concerned, there only seemed to be one limit on what Qatar could help supply. Likely fearful of civilian aircraft being brought down, a request was reportedly made that no heat-seeking shoulder-mounted anti-aircraft missiles be delivered to Syrian rebels. But by 2013 even this seemed to have been ignored, with US intelligence officials claiming to have knowledge of 'Qatar's shadowy arms network', stating to the New York Times that at least two batches of such missiles had been sent to Syria since the beginning of the year, one being Chinese-manufactured, and the other Eastern European and previously part of Libya's arsenal. A few months later some of the videos produced by rebel units, including known extremist groups, rather embarrassingly featured such missiles – none of which were known to have been part of the Syrian government's inventory nor to have appeared in the Syrian conflict before.[251]

According to data supplied by the Stockholm International Peace Research Institute, over the course of late 2012 and the first half of 2013 approximately 160 military cargo flights arrived in Turkey and Jordan laden with a total of 3,500 tons of weapons and equipment destined for Syria. As the SIPRI has stated, by far the largest number of flights, eighty-five, originated from Qatar.[252] Helping explain this, US officials later confirmed that the CIA had been involved in a 'consultative role' and that Qatar's activeness in the 'global grey market for arms' had been greatly enhanced by its acquisition of C-17 military transport planes from Boeing. These aircraft, described as 'capable of intercontinental flight and landing on short, poorly equipped runways' were understood to be being used for both military and humanitarian missions and had been delivered to Qatar in 2009, making it the only Middle Eastern state at the time in possession of durable long-range aircraft.[253]

Going through the motions, as they had done with Qatar's well-known equipping of Libyan militias, a batch of US officials had tried to place some distance between the two countries, stating that the 'US had growing concerns that, just as in Libya, the Qataris are equipping some of the wrong militants'.[254] Other officials told the media that 'the [Syrian] opposition groups that are receiving most of the lethal aid are exactly the ones we don't want to have it' and claimed that the weaponizing of the Syrian opposition was an operation that was 'going awry'. Complaining to the New York Times, they explained that 'hardline Islamists have received the lion's share of the arms shipped to the Syrian opposition through the shadowy pipeline with roots in Qatar, and, to a lesser degree, Saudi Arabia.'[255] More realistically, however, a few months later a White House official explained that 'Syria is [Qatar's] backyard, and they have their own interests they are pursuing.'[256]

Less is known about the extent of arms flowing into Syria from the other Gulf monarchies during this period; however, the SIPRI's data from late 2012 and early 2013 indicates that thirty-seven of the incoming military cargo flights originated from various parts of Saudi Arabia.[257] Jordanian officials also claimed to have seized several lorry loads of arms destined for Syria that had come from Riyadh, indicating a land route had also been established of which they did not entirely approve.[258] Raising funds for such equipment seemed to be no problem, with reports circulating of numerous Saudi clerics soliciting donations. In one case, a Syria-based Saudi preacher who was known to be close to al-Qaeda was discovered to be running a campaign called 'Wage jihad with your money'. As part of this, donors could earn 'silver status' by giving $175 for sniper bullets or 'gold status' for giving $350 to help purchase mortar rounds.[259] In another case a Saudi citizen known as Sanafi al-Nasr was reportedly killed in north-western Syria after having served as an al-Qaeda recruiter and having 'moved funds from the Gulf into Iraq and then to al-Qaeda leaders in Syria'.[260]

According to a *Wall Street Journal* investigation the bulk of Syria-destined Saudi weapons seemed to have been procured from third-party countries. Their correspondents explained that, in line with the CIA's long-held preference for false flag signalling, 'in September and October [2012], the Saudis approached Croatia to procure more Soviet-era weapons. The Saudis got started distributing these in December and soon saw momentum shift toward the rebels in some areas.' Again, as with attempts to establish some distance from Qatar so as to insulate themselves from any possible fallout from such risky moves, US officials were cited as cautioning that 'this has the potential to go badly wrong ... [because of] the risk that weapons will end up in the hands of violent anti-Western Islamists.' It was also claimed that 'not everyone in the Obama administration is comfortable with the new US partnership with the Saudis on Syria,' with some officials apparently baulking at the role being played by Saudi intelligence chief Bandar bin Sultan al-Saud. Notably, there was a 'fear [Syria] carries the same risk of spinning out of control as an earlier project in which [Saudi Arabia] was involved – the 1980s CIA programme of secretly financing the contras in Nicaragua against a leftist government'.[261]

On top of its clerics visiting Qatar, there are also strong indications that Kuwait itself was serving as a logistical and financing hub for Syrian opposition groups, including extremist organizations. Described in one particularly detailed report as the rebels' 'back office' and as one of the main 'back channels' for private weapons transfers,[262] the emirate's reputation was not helped when a Kuwaiti preacher openly bragged on a Saudi-owned television station in 2013 of having personally bought up weapons from the 'Western-backed councils' in Syria. As he put it, 'when the military councils sell the weapons they receive, guess who buys them? It's me'. Later identified by US officials as a leading supporter of *Al-Nusra*, he also usefully confirmed on television that 'all the Gulf intelligence agencies are competing in Syria and everyone is trying to get the lion's share of the Syrian revolution.'[263]

Much of the Kuwaiti funding for such individuals and their networks seems to have come from a mix of informal mosque collections and those held in family-owned *diwan* meeting houses. In 2013, for example, the *New York Times* described how one such Kuwaiti effort raised enough to pay twelve thousand rebel fighters $2,500 each. When interviewed about this, one former Kuwaiti soldier reasoned that 'now we want to get Bashar out of Syria, so why not cooperate with al-Qaeda?'[264] According to Elizabeth Dickinson, social media also played a prominent role in 'touting their cause'. As she explains, in this way 'a deep Rolodex of Kuwaiti business contacts, clerics, and other prominent Kuwaiti Sunnis raised hundreds of millions of dollars for their clients.'[265] As a briefing prepared for the European Parliament alleged, one such preacher was able to raise so much money in this manner that an entire Syrian brigade named itself after him – the *Katibat al-Sheikh Hajaj al-Ajami*.[266]

Beyond the wealth and apparent sympathy for such causes expressed by many of its citizens, others have also pointed to the usefulness of the Kuwait government's still lax counter-terrorism financing laws, and the sense of impunity that extremists continued to enjoy. Numerous accounts exist of Kuwaiti jihadists remaining at large, while reports abound of known al-Qaeda members being released early or given unusually light sentences. In one uncomfortably high-profile case, Kuwait's Muhsin Fadhli – who it had been assumed was dead – was identified by the US Department of State in 2012 as having become al-Qaeda's leader in Iran. Despite a US-issued reward for his capture, he was then known to have travelled to Syria in 2013 to become part of al-Qaeda's purported Khorasan Group.[267] Reportedly killed in a US air strike in 2015, it transpired that the Department of Defense held him responsible for attacks more than a decade earlier on US marines based on the Kuwaiti island of Failaka.[268] In fact, according to the Arabic media, he had also been accused of playing a part in al-Qaeda's USS *Cole* operation and in 2002 had stood trial in

Kuwait along with three of his compatriots. Despite 'substantial evidence' of them having fought in Afghanistan, Chechnya, and Kashmir, they were only charged with having joined a foreign army, not with being members of a terrorist organization. Fadhli was then understood to have had his conviction overturned and his travel ban lifted on the grounds that his crimes had taken place outside Kuwait.[269]

SYRIA - SEARCHING FOR THE 'RED LINE'

By the beginning of 2013, with the Syrian conflict entering into its second year, there was a growing feeling that much more needed to be done in order to deliver a knockout blow against the al-Assad regime. Having substantially regrouped, with seemingly significant portions of its armed forces remaining loyal, and with frequent reports circulating of *Hezbollah* and even Iranian commanders and soldiers taking part in counter-offensives against rebel-held cities, the Syrian government appeared in a much stronger position than before. Heavily exposed given their overt backing for the opposition and with no victory in sight, the Gulf monarchies and in particular Saudi Arabia and Qatar had begun to call much more loudly for a Libya-like NATO intervention. Although well aware of the Western powers' hesitancy given Syria's fairly strong external alliance structures, at least compared to Muammar Gaddafi's relative isolation, Riyadh and its neighbours nevertheless had taken the view that the United States and Britain had to get more involved whether they liked it or not.

Latching on to comments made by White House officials a year earlier that any use of chemical weapons in Syria would represent a 'red line' for the US, it was reported by the *Wall Street Journal* that in late 2012 'the Saudis started trying to convince Western governments that Mr Assad had crossed what President Barack Obama a year ago called a "red line": the use of chemical weapons.' Giving plenty of detail, the report explained that 'Arab diplomats say Saudi agents flew an injured Syrian to Britain, where tests showed sarin gas exposure.' It also stated that 'Prince Bandar's spy service, which concluded that Mr Assad was using chemical weapons, relayed evidence to the US, which reached a similar conclusion four months later.'[270] In April 2013, Qatar made much the same claim, with its prime

SHADOW WARS

minister contending that the Syrian regime had already crossed red lines, including the limited use of chemical weapons in 'small pockets'. He then made the case that 'the US had to do more.'[271] Over the next few months, a number of similar claims and then counterclaims were made, as the Gulf monarchies and Damascus seemed to fight over what had really happened and whether red lines had really been crossed. In many ways this period was eerily analogous to the narrative wars fought between the embattled Afghan government and the US-backed jihadists in the 1980s. Complete with detailed death tolls and photographs of chemical warfare victims, a determined effort had been made to frame and denigrate the still-surviving Soviet-backed state.[272]

On 21 August 2013, the moment of truth seemed to have arrived, with reports emerging of a serious sarin nerve agent attack on the Ghouta suburb of Damascus. With almost all of the international media pointing to the al-Assad regime, given that Ghouta was in rebel hands, some prominent Western newspapers pre-emptively even declared war on Syria. According to a well-placed journalist, NATO strike plans had already been drawn up and militaries were simply waiting for the green light from their governments.[273] With the US again holding back, as it had done over Libya, it appeared that the British government was to take the lead, with parliament holding a vote on 29 August. Despite widespread predictions that Prime Minister David Cameron would win the vote, a substantial number of his own party's members rebelled, leading to what was later described as a 'historic defeat', and incomparable to anything in British politics since the 1855 resignation of Prime Minister George Hamilton over his government's role in the Crimean War.[274]

Apparently unimpressed by Cameron's case and the intelligence made available to them, the dissenting British MPs were not alone, as in the wake of the attacks serious doubts began to emerge from other quarters. Many questioned whether the Syrian regime was really responsible or, if it was, whether there were really sufficient grounds for another Western military intervention. Arriving in Damascus to cover the story, even one of the BBC's most experienced journalists tweeted that it just did not seem to make sense for the regime to have launched such an attack given that there were UN inspectors already in the city, in such close proximity to Ghouta.[275] In fact, just five days after the attack the inspectors had attempted to visit

Ghouta but had to turn back after unidentified snipers opened fire on their convoy.[276] Meanwhile, on the same day of the British vote, the *Washington Post* revealed details of a secret sensor system in Syria that was already in place. Funded from the $52 billion US 'black budget', details of which were earlier leaked by former intelligence contractor Edward Snowden, the advanced system was understood to be monitored by the US National Reconnaissance Office, which is responsible for controlling all US intelligence satellites.[277] Speaking to Seymour Hersh, former US intelligence officers with knowledge of the system explained that the sensors had earlier been 'implanted near all known chemical warfare sites in Syria. They are designed to provide constant monitoring of the movement of chemical warheads stored by the military.' The former officials also claimed that 'far more important, in terms of early warning, is the sensors' ability to alert US and Israeli intelligence when warheads are being loaded with sarin.' According to them, the system was understood not to have detected any unusual activity in the months and days before 21 August.[278]

Handed out to journalists and then subsequently referred to by Secretary of State John Kerry, a White House intelligence assessment report nonetheless claimed that by 18 August the Syrian regime's 'chemical weapons personnel were on the ground, in the area, making preparations'. As Kerry stated, 'We know that regime elements were told to prepare for the attack.' Declining to reveal its methods on the grounds of 'protecting sources', the assessment report provided little substantiation of its findings and made no reference to the sensor system, but did state that it had relied on unverified classified intercepts of communications along with 'thousands of social media reports, journalist reports, and reports from highly credible non-governmental sources'.[279]

Most mainstream media outlets regurgitated the assessment report uncritically, with the *Washington Post* even claiming on its front page that US intelligence had been able to record 'each step' of the Syrian army attack in real time, 'from the extensive preparations to the launching of rockets to the after-action assessments by Syrian officials'. Basing its analysis on the assessment report, it reported that a 'team of Syrian specialists gathered [on 18 August] in the northern suburb of Adra for a task that US officials say had become routine in the third year of the country's civil conflict: filling warheads with deadly chemicals to kill Syrian rebels'. The newspaper also chose to highlight the assessment report's suggested death toll of 1,429, even though this was four times higher than a British casualty estimate released only a few days before. Buried in the article, however, was a concession that while it was 'unusually detailed' the assessment report 'does not include photographs, recordings or other hard evidence to support its claims'. It also admitted that it did not 'offer proof to back up the administration's assertion that top-ranking Syrian officials were complicit in the attack'.[280]

Casting much more light on the situation in Syria at this time than the White House's assessment report were a number of intelligence briefings from earlier in 2013. Surprisingly extensive, they presented a very clear picture in which the Syrian regime by no means had a monopoly over chemical weapons. A May 2013 CIA briefing, for example, had informed the White House about *Jabhat al-Nusra*'s interest in such substances while also claiming that 'another Sunni fundamentalist group active in Syria, al-Qaeda in Iraq, also understood the science of producing sarin.' It further noted that *Al-Nusra* was believed to be operating in areas close to Damascus, including Ghouta. A month later a four-page secret 'talking points' report summarizing *Al-Nusra*'s chemical weapons capabilities was understood to have been forwarded to the deputy director of the Defense Intelligence Agency. Its contents were described as being 'extensive and comprehensive ... it was not a bunch of we believes.' Not only did it confirm that *Al-Nusra* had the ability to acquire and use sarin, but it also revealed that a sample of sarin in *Al-Nusra*'s hands had been recovered by an Israeli agent.[281]

Worryingly, one of the DIA talking points described *Al-Nusra* as having 'one of the most advanced sarin plots since al-Qaeda's pre-9/11 effort' and claimed that 'Turkey and Saudi-based chemical facilitators were attempting to obtain sarin precursors in bulk, tens of kilograms, likely for the anticipated large scale production effort in Syria.' This seemed to tally with a 130-page Turkish legal indictment from May in which ten suspected *Al-Nusra* members arrested in southern Turkey were described by local policemen as having two kilograms of sarin in their possession. Although the prosecutor requested twenty-five years' imprisonment for the ringleader, he was released pending trial while the nine co-accused were freed after only a brief detention. According to Hersh, by this stage US intelligence was already aware that Turkish intelligence along with the militarized Turkish Gendarmerie were helping *Al-Nusra*. As a former US intelligence official described, '[Turkish intelligence] was running the political liaison with the rebels, and the Gendarmerie handled military logistics, on-the-scene advice and training – including training in chemical warfare.'[282]

Question marks also seemed to hang over the extent to which *Al-Nusra* and other such organizations had really sided with the Syrian people. Although in 2012 many of the anti-regime Friday afternoon protests had included 'we are all *Jabhat al-Nusra*' among their slogans, by 2013 the relationship seemed more strained. As the Brookings Doha Center's Charles Lister points out, although *Al-Nusra*'s targets were 'primarily government-linked' it was 'civilians that bore the brunt, making the group unpopular with the Syrian opposition.'[283] According to an extensive McClatchy investigation and the research of Abdel Bari Atwan, it is unclear how close *Al-Nusra* actually was to Ghouta at the time of the August 2013 attacks; however, it was believed that a similar organization – *Liwa al-Islam*, or 'Brigade of Islam' – controlled much of the district. Importantly it was led by Zahran Alloush, one of the released Syrian jihadists who had then gone on to denounce democracy, call for an Islamic state, and threaten the cleansing of Alawites and Shias. With Alloush's father being a Saudi-based cleric, *Liwa al-Islam* was known to be receiving Saudi backing.[284]

Weakening the 'red line' case even further, in December 2013 a team of security and arms experts published an extensive report entitled *Possible implications of faulty US technical intelligence*. Led by former UN weapons inspector Richard Lloyd and Theodore Postol, a multiple award-winning professor at the Massachusetts Institute of Technology, they arrived at the conclusion that the range of the sarin-carrying rocket involved in the largest of the Ghouta attacks was too small for it to have flown from government-held territory in Damascus, as the US government had asserted. As such, although the team did not investigate the smaller attacks and had no interest in assigning blame to specific perpetrators, its findings did strongly contradict the White House's assessment report and a follow-up statement by Kerry in September 2013 in which he claimed: 'We are certain that none of the opposition has the weapons or capacity to effect a strike of this scale – particularly from the heart of regime territory.'[285]

Commenting on the research, MIT's Postol explained that 'my view when I started this process was that it couldn't be anything but the Syrian government behind the attack. But now I'm not sure of anything. The [US] administration narrative was not even close to reality.' Lloyd meanwhile disputed the assumption that opposition groups were less capable of making rockets than the regime, arguing that 'the Syrian rebels most definitely have the ability to make these weapons ... I think they might have more ability than the Syrian government.' The two experts also contended that Kerry's insistence that US satellite images had shown the impact points of the chemical weapons was unlikely to be true as the rocket charges were too small to create detonations big enough to show up on satellite images.[286] Although the publication of the Lloyd–Postol report was covered by the *New York Times*, it was done so in a manner that did not reflect the researchers' aims or even the report's contents. Instead the *New York Times'* correspondents described how there was 'new analysis [that] could point to particular Syrian military units involved, or be used by defenders of the Syrian government and those suspicious of the US to try to shift blame toward rebels'. They also repeated the Kerry and White House claims that 'satellite detections corroborate that attacks from a regime-controlled area struck neighborhoods where the chemical attacks reportedly occurred.'[287]

Lending more weight to the Lloyd–Postol research, in April 2014 the *London Review of Books* published a detailed essay that alleged MI6 had earlier obtained a sample of the sarin used in Ghouta and that Britain's Porton Down laboratory had concluded it did not match with samples of the batches it knew to be in the Syrian regime's possession. This knowledge, it was claimed, was shared with the US and may help explain why, on top of the British government's parliamentary defeat, the White House was reluctant to authorize its own air strikes against the Syrian state. Quoting a former senior US intelligence official who still had access to current intelligence, the essay further contended that there were members of the Turkish government 'who believed they could get al-Assad's nuts in a vice by dabbling with a sarin attack inside Syria – and forcing Obama to make good on his red line threat.'[288] Interestingly, by this stage it appeared that even the BBC was preparing to backtrack on at least some of the original 2013 narrative. Although in August 2014 its flagship *Newsnight* show repeated BBC footage of victims from exactly a year earlier, with its presenter explaining that 'by chance, just as MPs were voting, these images of a chemical attack were shown for the first time', its complaints team had already admitted to a member of the public that the BBC was aware these were victims of incendiary weapons rather than chemical weapons.[289]

By 2015 it was even clearer that multiple groups in Syria had had at least some opportunity to acquire chemical weapons over the past three years. Leaked documents belonging to the Saudi foreign ministry indicated that in early 2012 the Organization for the Prohibition of Chemical Weapons was aware of several hundred artillery projectiles in Libya which, according to hand-held detectors, were filled with chemical agents.[290] Given that this was at the same time the Libya–Syria 'rat line' was being established, and given the hundreds of military cargo planes known to have been flying into Syria, the possibility that at least some of these warheads found their way from Libya to Syria seems high. Indeed, multiple reports have since suggested that the eventual Islamic State and other groups have been using such munitions. In summer 2015, for example, German special forces who had been training the Kurdish *Peshmerga* militia reported that chemical weapons had been fired on Kurdish positions, with many men suffering from severe burns and respiratory problems. An official *Peshmerga* statement claimed that 'forty-five 120 millimeter mortar shells tipped with chemicals led to the injury of a number of *Peshmerga* forces with burns on different parts of their bodies.' Other Kurdish commanders have reported similar earlier attacks, describing projectiles containing unknown chemical agents.[291] In September 2015 anonymous US officials even told the BBC that the Islamic State was making and using chemical weapons and had evidence it had used them at least four times and had set up an 'active chemical weapons research cell.'[292]

SYRIA – BACK TO THE BATTLEFIELD

With formal NATO intervention an increasingly distant prospect, by the end of 2013 the Western powers and their regional proxies returned to the strategy of strengthening the rebels on the ground. With Bashar al-Assad's Iranian allies now clearly playing a pivotal role on the battlefield, and with *Hezbollah* leader Hassan Nasrallah having already declared of Syria that 'This battle is ours ... and I promise you victory,'[293] the United States' fallback option seemed to be a massive and urgent ramping-up of direct backing for those opposition groups it still felt were publicly supportable, alongside turning an even blinder eye to the type of Syrian rebels that the Gulf monarchies were continuing to support.

Greatly reinvigorated and expanded, the US's programme of supplying the 'right militants' spawned a string of statements over the course of 2014 promising further weapons. In February 2015 the US then announced that teams of such rebels would be brought across to Jordan and Turkey for training, and would be supplied with Toyota Hi-Lux trucks. The Toyotas were to be 'outfitted with a machine gun, communications gear and global positioning system trackers enabling them to call in air strikes ... along with mortars.'[294] In October 2015, just days after Russia began to conduct air strikes on behalf of the Syrian government, US officials informed the media that they had begun to make 'air drops of small arms ammunition' to unspecified Syrian rebels in northern Syria. They explained this was part of their 'revamped strategy.'[295]

As well as the US-supported units often turning on each other, including the worryingly named 'Knights of Righteousness' eventually fighting the 'Syrian Democratic Forces', a more serious problem for the US's renewed efforts was that most of the fighters the CIA had chosen to back had already suffered numerous defeats, with many having had their weapons seized by *Jabhat al-Nusra* or other such groups.[296] According to one Arab intelligence officer, '[extremist organizations] say they are always pleased when sophisticated weapons are sent to anti-al-Assad groups of any kind, because they can always get the arms off them by threats of force or cash payments.'[297] Similarly, as per the US's own intelligence assessments from late 2014, funding from the US and its allies that was flowing to anti-regime rebels was still 'consistently ending up in the hands of the most virulent extremists.'[298] As a former Defense Intelligence Agency official described, once US-backed fighters crossed back over the border into Syria, 'you lose a substantial amount of control or ability to control their actions.'[299]

An even bigger issue for the US, however, was whether its favoured 'moderates' were ever really moderate to begin with. Department of Defense officials had reportedly been aware for some time that the 'vast majority of moderate Free Syrian Army rebels were in fact, Islamist mili-tants.'[300] Also critical of the FSA's credentials was Britain's former ambas-sador to Syria, who stated bluntly in television interviews that the 'so-called FSA is just a footnote ... let's be clear here, we're talking about jihadists, most of the opposition groups are jihadists.'[301] Similarly, as a former direc-tor of French intelligence warned, either the intelligence services had been 'given bad information or it was [the government's] policies that, despite the information, wanted to go in a direction that was not the reality'. In particular he worried that 'we will be manipulated into helping people, supposedly rebellious, whereas in reality they have been pushed by al-Qaeda.'[302] Pointing out that well-known FSA commanders had already publicly defected to the Islamic State or 'other, more militarily successful extremist groups', Abdel Bari Atwan was equally suspicious.[303] Published in summer 2013, a report prepared for the European Parliament stated that Al-Nusra's fighters had 'operated many times alongside FSA formations on the battlefield earning public praise from prominent rebel leaders'. It also described how 'many Salafists are believed to fight within FSA units but these rebel formations portray the uprising as a national struggle against an oppressive dictatorship rather than as a Sunni jihad against an Alawite regime.'[304] An International Crisis Group report from 2012 had made much the same suggestion, arguing that 'mainstream rebel groups eager for more effective weapons and tactics likely find that benefits of such collaboration [with extremist groups] outweigh any long-term political and ideological concerns.'[305]

Others also questioned the FSA's ability to police criminality within its own ranks. Writing for *Middle East Policy*, counter-terrorism specialist Ahmad Hashim noted how the 'undisciplined and brutal behaviour of the FSA' stood in contrast to the much more disciplined *Jabhat Al-Nusra*, which often set up efficient food and medicine distribution systems in areas under its control.[306] Similarly a British journalist familiar with the region accused the FSA of engaging in looting and banditry,[307] while Arabic media correspondents reported that former peasants had been enriching themselves through the FSA, allowing them to buy 'huge new homes and expensive cars'.[308] Giving more detail, an extensive *Daily Telegraph* report featured interviewees in Syria describing how FSA commanders had been focused on profiteering, gun-running, and the extracting of tolls from road checkpoints. One interviewee even described how the FSA was taking bribes from the Syrian regime to allow government forces to get supplies to besieged units. The report concluded that in northern Syria at least the FSA 'has now become a largely criminal enterprise'.[309] Disturbingly, in 2015 NBC News even had to revise its official account of the brief 2012 kidnapping of its chief foreign correspondent Richard Engel.[310] Having originally stated that Engel was captured by the pro-regime and predominantly Alawite *Shabiha* or 'Ghosts' militia before then being rescued by 'Sunni rebels', NBC News' position dramatically changed following an investigation by the *New York Times*. Having interviewed NBC News employees and Syrian activists, it was suggested that 'Mr Engel's team was almost certainly taken by a Sunni criminal element affiliated with the FSA, the loose alliance of rebels opposed to Mr Assad.' The *New York Times'* correspondents concluded that Engel was likely misled by his captors so as to discredit the Syrian government.[311]

To make matters worse, there was considerable evidence that known extremist groups in Syria were actively trying to sanitize their images and present themselves alongside the FSA as suitable candidates for US support. In journalist Patrick Cockburn's assessment of such groups, and especially those close to Damascus, those that had earlier given themselves 'Islamic-sounding names to attract Saudi and Gulf financing' had by this stage 'opportunistically switched to more secular-sounding titles in a bid to attract US support'.[312] According to a European Parliament report, one such organization based close to the Lebanese border had changed its name to the 'Rafic Hariri Brigade' in reference to the pro-Western former Lebanese prime minister.[313] Moreover, the Yarmouk Brigade and other such groups, which ended up becoming part of the US- and Saudi-sponsored 'Southern Front' based out of Jordan and eligible to receive advanced weaponry such as anti-aircraft missiles, had frequently been spotted fighting alongside *Al-Nusra*.[314] In 2013 the Yarmouk Brigade was also understood to have repeatedly detained UN peacekeepers in the Golan Heights, and in late 2014 a Lebanese newspaper accused it of having already secretly pledged allegiance to the Islamic State.[315]

The 'Syrian Islamic Liberation Front' seems to have tried to follow the same sort of path, having recognized the FSA and fought with it but then disbanding within a year after many of its ultra-conservative members had joined *Al-Nusra* or the Islamic State.[316] Moreover, in a widely read January 2014 *Foreign Affairs* article a group called *Harakat Ahrar al-Sham al-Islamiyya* or 'The Islamic movement of the free men of the Levant' was openly described as 'an al-Qaeda-linked group worth befriending', with the three US thinktank authors trying to place it temporarily within the US-friendly camp. But although it had cooperated with the FSA in military actions, others have noted how many of its fighters later moved over to the Islamic State and that it was still very much an al-Qaeda-style organization, having been co-founded by Abu Khalid al-Suri. Indeed, US federal prosecutors have since described it as 'frequently fighting alongside *Jabhat Al-Nusra*' and as having the goal of 'installing an Islamic state in Syria'. Nonetheless, as recently as July 2015, *Ahrar al-Sham*'s spokesman wrote on the *Washington Post*'s website that it still favoured 'a moderate future for Syria that preserves the state and institutes reforms that benefit all Syrians', while a few months later Qatar's foreign minister claimed in an Al-Jazeera interview that it was not an extremist organization but rather 'a Syrian group [looking] for their liberation, and they are working with other moderate groups'.[317]

The most remarkable attempt at a volte-face has, however, been the Saudi-backed *Jaysh al-Islam* or 'Army of Islam' – an umbrella for dozens of rebel groups created in late 2013.[318] Giving an interview on its behalf in May 2015, former *Liwa al-Islam* leader Zahran Alloush tried to backtrack completely on his earlier sectarian and anti-democratic statements. As the University of Oklahoma's Joshua Landis observes, this was evidence of Alloush's increasing savviness as 'every major player wants to be acceptable to the West and to the international community'.[319] Not all, however, were convinced, as a few months later the Jordan government reaffirmed its designation of the group as a terrorist organization, while *Al-Hayat* newspaper reported that *Jaysh al-Islam*'s fighters in Ghouta were putting Alawite civilians in iron cages and using them as 'human shields'.[320] Since then Russia has attempted to add *Jaysh al-Islam* along with *Ahrar al-Sham* to the UN terror sanctions blacklist, but its efforts have been blocked by the US, Britain, France, and the Ukraine, with a US spokesman stating that 'now is not the time to shift course, but rather double down on our efforts towards a reduction in violence,' and with an anonymous Western diplomat stating that such a designation would 'provide a pretext for yet more moderate groups to come under target'.[321]

More information is slowly coming to light about Britain's support for such Syrian rebels, as it seems to have followed the same trajectory as the US, with the definition of 'moderate' being stretched extremely widely. Following an investigation by the *Guardian*, it transpired that since 2013 the Foreign Office and the Ministry of Defence had been hiring contractors to 'produce videos, photos, military reports, radio broadcasts, print products, and social media posts branded with the logos of fighting groups'. According to the investigators, which had seen government contracting documents, Britain was 'effectively running a press office for opposition fighters', and the materials it circulated online were 'posted with no indication of British government involvement'. The campaign appears to have been funded by the 'Conflict and Stability Fund' and to have been based in Istanbul under the guise of delivering 'strategic communications and media operations support to the Syrian moderate armed opposition'. Worryingly, the contracts seen by the *Guardian* included references to *Jaysh al-Islam* and a group called *Harakat Hazm* or 'Steadfast Movement', which had disbanded in March 2015 with most of its weapons being seized by *Jabhat al-Nusra*.[322]

Further light has been cast on British involvement by the circumstances surrounding the collapse of the London trial of a Swedish citizen accused of attending terrorist training camps, receiving weapons, and working with 'a group considered to be al-Qaeda in Syria'. With the evidence supplied to the court having reportedly made clear that 'Britain's security and intelligence agencies would have been deeply embarrassed if the trial had gone ahead,' the suspect's lawyer had stated: 'If it is the case that [the British] government was actively involved in supporting armed resistance to the al-Assad regime at a time when the defendant was present in Syria and himself participating in such resistance, it would be unconscionable to allow the prosecution to continue.' Another lawyer involved in the case agreed, arguing: 'Given that there is a reasonable basis for believing that the British were themselves involved in the supply of arms, if that's so, it would be an utter hypocrisy to prosecute someone who has been involved in the armed resistance.'[323]

As for the Gulf monarchies, the pre-Ghouta dual strategy of providing formal support for US-approved groups, while in parallel allowing private citizens to generate informal support for some of the most extremist organizations, seemed to continue unabated, with likely even larger supplies of weapons and funding in the absence of any NATO-led intervention. Formed at the end of 2013, the 'Islamic Front' was an alliance of six or seven existing Sunni Islamist groups that were widely understood to be backed by Saudi Arabia along with NATO member Turkey. Morphing into the Levant Front by the end of 2014, and then the 'Army of Conquest', it not only included the al-Qaeda-aligned *Harakat Ahrar al-Sham al-Islamiyya,* but by 2015 it was understood to have more openly adopted a jihadist position and to have suffered major defections to the Islamic State.[324]

Meanwhile Qatari and Kuwaiti citizens, as before, were also clearly at the forefront of arming such militias. In March 2014, US undersecretary for terrorism and financial intelligence David Cohen stated that 'a number of fundraisers operating in more permissive jurisdictions – particularly in Kuwait and Qatar – are soliciting donations to fund extremist insurgents, not to meet legitimate humanitarian needs.' He described the recipients as being terrorist groups, including *Al-Nusra,* and stated that 'Qatar has become such a permissive terrorist financing environment, that several major Qatar-based fundraisers act as local representatives for larger terrorist fundraising networks that are based in Kuwait.' Speaking to the media, he also took the opportunity to reaffirm the Department of the Treasury's designation of a Qatari national as being a 'Qatar-based financier who secured funds and provided material support for al-Qaeda and its affiliates'. He stated that this man was understood to have supplied 'al-Qaeda in Syria' with $600,000 in 2013 alone.[325] Specific to Kuwait, Cohen claimed that that 'our ally has become the epicentre for fundraising for terrorist groups in Syria'. He even pointed out that Kuwait's minister for justice and Islamic endowments had 'a history of promoting jihad in Syria ... in fact, his image has been featured on fundraising posters for a prominent *Al-Nusra* financier'.[326]

Illustrative of the ongoing culture of impunity for terror financiers in these states, in October 2014 a Department of the Treasury spokesman identified two Qatari citizens as being designated terrorist financiers that had 'not yet been acted against under Qatari law'. Accused of employing Jordanians who had been using fake Qatari identification documents, they were alleged to have been transferring cash to al-Qaeda operatives. In fact one of the Qataris was a former employee of Qatar's central bank who had earlier been sanctioned by the US and the UN for his role in assisting the alleged 9/11 mastermind Khalid Sheikh Muhammad. Although arrested in 2008 he was released after just three months which, according to leaked US diplomatic cables, had caused great concern.[327] By the summer of 2015 Qatar had failed to arrest two more of its citizens whom the US Department of the Treasury had designated as terror financiers following their social media activity in support of *Al-Nusra*. Although a US official claimed that 'the cooperation that we have received from the Qataris on this matter is a testament that our relationship is improving and growing,' he also had to admit that the men were still at large.[328]

Beyond the facilitation of arms and funding channels to Syrian extremists, it is also very clear that Qatar was actively engaged in trying to improve and normalize the public image of *Al-Nusra*, presumably because by then it had cemented its reputation as the most potent anti-regime fighting force. In early 2015, Reuters even reported that *Al-Nusra* was considering switching its formal affiliation from al-Qaeda to Qatar, 'with which it had good relations'. Its correspondents also described how *Al-Nusra* was to merge with a smaller jihadist group composed of local and foreign fighters led by a Chechen commander, and together the new alliance would be 're-branded by Qatar' so that it could receive more money and support than before.[329] A few weeks later the BBC corroborated much of the story, explaining that Qatar was 'bringing *Al-Nusra* in from the cold' and that the 'new *Al-Nusra*' had pledged to fight only al-Assad's forces and thus would have no interest in attacking the 'far enemy' of the US or its allies. Only a day after this remarkable *Al-Nusra* promise, one of its senior commanders was killed in heavily disputed circumstances. While some pointed to a US drone strike, others claimed he was assassinated by the Syrian regime's special forces. In a BBC article, however, speculation was made as to 'whether he was killed because of an internal disagreement about the putative negotiations to eschew *Al-Nusra*'s al-Qaeda affiliation or not.'[330] Writing a few months later, as *Al-Nusra* began to lose its grip over one of its key bases in Idlib, Charles Lister contended that the organization was 'enduring a consequential internal struggle to define its identity'. In this context a contest was taking place within *Al-Nusra* between those committed to a more pragmatic position, allowing it to cooperate more openly with Qatar, and those who sought a return to a harder line al-Qaeda stance.[331]

Apparently also on board with the normalization strategy, even Israel seemed to have seen value in improving its low-level relations with *Al-Nusra*, especially in areas close to their mutual borders. According to a report prepared by the UN Disengagement Observer Force which detailed eighteen months of border activity, sightings were made of uninjured Syrians being allowed through fence openings along with the transfer of unspecified supplies from Israel to rebel units. The UNDOF also noted that Israeli Defence Force soldiers had been holding meetings with Syrians east of the demilitarized Green Zone and that a small 'tent city' had been set up only a few hundred metres from the border for the families of Syrian army deserters. Although claiming that all Syrians entering Israel were 'infiltrators' and that Israel had not given 'one shekel or one bullet to *Al-Nusra* members', a senior IDF officer nonetheless conceded that Israel had been treating injured *Al-Nusra* fighters on Israeli territory.[332]

In a remarkable May 2015 Al-Jazeera interview, *Al-Nusra*'s Muhammad al-Jowlani sat on a lavish jewelled throne with his face shrouded and answered a series of fawning questions from a prominent Qatar-based journalist. Using his platform, al-Jowlani explained that *Al-Nusra*'s primary purpose was to remove the 'grossly oppressive' Syrian regime, while also making the bizarre claim that its al-Qaeda affiliation made it somehow more moderate than other groups fighting in Syria, on the basis that it offered protection to minorities and had little interest in sectarian warfare. He reiterated the organization's earlier purported promises by stating that *Al-Nusra* had no intention of attacking the West 'unless provoked'.[333] In a gross violation of journalistic ethics Al-Jazeera then followed up on its al-Jowlani exclusive by broadcasting an interview with a Syrian pilot held in custody by *Al-Nusra*.[334]

For keener observers, however, the prospect of a more moderate *Al-Nusra* was already known to be something of a scam. Stating in late 2014 that it had entered into a truce with other extremist groups, or at least that it shared the same goals, the organization was still being described by the media in 2015 as having 'launched offensives against Western-backed groups' and having 'pledged common action with other jihadists against the crusaders'.[335] Most embarrassingly for Qatar, less than a month after the al-Jowlani interview *Al-Nusra* broke its silence by publishing a forty-five minute documentary entitled *The heirs of glory*. Repeating several of

Osama bin Laden's statements, it concluded with *Al-Nusra* justifying 9/11 on the basis that 'the choice to respond [to the West] in the same manner was found to be the most effective solution, so the West may know that the Muslims will never remain silent to the crimes committed against them, and that they will resist oppression and tyranny.'[336]

Following much the same format as their attempts to distance the US from Qatar's roles in financing extremists earlier in the conflict, and of course also in Libya, a variety of US officials had already half-heartedly begun to point their fingers at the murky activities taking place in the CENTCOM-hosting nation. In September 2014, a meeting in the US Senate had heard representatives and witnesses suggesting measures to 'dramatically recast' US relations with Qatar, including further terror designations for some of its citizens and charities, and even the possibility of 'disrupting its financial system'. The idea of moving the US's military facilities out of Qatar was also reportedly mooted, along with the possibility of blocking a pending $11 billion US–Qatar arms deal.[337] A few months later the *Wall Street Journal* then broke the story that during Barack Obama's first term in office the National Security Council had supposedly already lobbied the White House to pull the US Air Force out of Qatar in protest against its support for militant groups.[338] Whether the NSC claim was true or not, in summer 2014 the US Army's retired vice chief of staff had in any case made the same sort of suggestion, arguing that 'it is time to confront Qatar' and that 'we have alternatives to our Combined Air and Operations Center in Doha … other bases and prepositioned *materiel*. We should tell Qatar to end its support for terrorism or we leave.'[339]

Sparking a fresh round of debate on Qatar, in February 2015 a letter signed by a group of lawmakers began to circulate in the US Congress. Addressed to the new secretary for defense, Ashton Carter, the letter included calls from a member of the Senate's Armed Services Committee to identify Qatar as 'the world's safe haven for terrorist groups and militia leaders'. It also urged US officials to 'reassess and re-evaluate' the US's multibillion-dollar military alliance with the country and explained that 'US reliance on Qatar's support such as the Al-Udeid base in Qatar has emboldened the Qataris to believe they can undermine and damage US interests and efforts in the region without consequence.' The letter concluded that 'the US's strategic interests should not be undercut or held captive' and that the new secretary for defense must begin a 'serious exploration of positioning some of our military assets with other allies in the region'.[340]

Naturally the latest bout of criticism and grandstanding went nowhere, with Qatar's strategic usefulness to the US in several regional theatres continuing to trump all other concerns. The $11 billion arms deal went on to become one of the US's biggest defence industry successes of the year, with the Department of Defense and Qatar's defence ministry then signing off on the transfer of Apache attack helicopters, Patriot and Javelin air-defence systems, and various other weapons.[341] Justifying the deal and its ongoing relationship with Doha, the Department of Defense argued in February 2015 that 'the regional military command the US maintains [in Qatar] was vital to American operations in the region.' The *Wall Street Journal* further explained that, in any case, 'the issue was [already] decided in late 2013 when the US extended its lease on the base and didn't pull out any planes.'[342]

Just two days after the 2015 deal went through, and on the eve of his scheduled visit to the US, Qatari ruler Tamim bin Hamad al-Thani helped to smooth the situation further by publishing a *New York Times* opinion piece that explained how Qatar was 'united with our partners in the Gulf to combat violent extremism in all its forms'. Al-Thani also argued that in order for the Middle East to move forward, Qatar and its allies must have a 'bold commitment based on a long-term vision of justice, security, and peace for all the people of the region'. He even managed to squeeze in a reference to 'ending the tyrannical rule of the likes of Bashar al-Assad of Syria' and blamed the Syrian regime for 'carrying out genocide against its own people'. Rather ironically, al-Thani concluded that 'we must avoid deepening the sectarian divisions that have weakened governments and nations, and fueled the fires of violent extremism. This should begin with a conscious effort to combat cynical attempts to deepen and exploit the Sunni–Shia divide for political ends.'[343] For those paying close attention this was of course hypocritical, as only three weeks earlier a prominent Saudi preacher had been hosted in Qatar's state mosque and had delivered a Friday sermon that called on God to 'destroy the Jews ... destroy the Christians and Alawites ... and the Shia'. The vicious sermon was understood to have been promoted by Qatar's ministry for religious affairs on both its website and on Twitter.[344]

SYRIA – THE MEDIA WAR

In parallel to the increased funding and weapons supplies for Syrian rebel militias and jihadist organizations, since 2013 there were also renewed and substantial efforts to win the 'media war'. Not necessarily aiming to provoke fresh debate about a NATO intervention, most of the secret information operations conducted by the Western powers and their regional allies were instead focused on further damaging the Syrian regime's international reputation while at the same time deflecting attention away from the identities and behaviour of their more extremist proxies. In this context, the objective was not the establishing of new 'red lines', but rather the weakening of the Bashar al-Assad administration's ability to portray itself as a legitimate guardian of the Syrian state. In turn this would make it easier on moral grounds to prevent the Syrian regime and its partners from participating in peace negotiations or future transitional governments.

In January 2014, with the Syrian army holding its ground on the battle-field and even advancing in some areas, there was a very real danger that impending 'Geneva II' talks would allow Damascus and Tehran to press for favourable terms. Funded by Qatar and prepared by a leading London law firm, a substantial report on torture under the al-Assad regime was released to CNN the day before the talks were due to begin. With graphic and gruesome contents, the report's primary source was an anonymous defector, codenamed 'Caesar', who had been smuggled out of Syria. Endorsed by a team of lawyers, the report sparked international outrage and resulted in the Iranian government having its Geneva invitation withdrawn. It likely also contributed to the eventual Geneva outcome, with the only terms offered to Bashar requiring him to leave power completely, despite the government still controlling thirteen out of Syria's fourteen provincial capitals.[345]

Alluding to the thousands of foreign fighters in the ranks of the opposition, a spokesman for Damascus tried to rationalize the government's brutality on the grounds that 'we have professional killers inside Syria from around the world. We are defending ourselves.'[346] But as a good example of the sort of 'politics of the last atrocity' that had frequently been used at the last minute to derail peace talks in Northern Ireland,[347] the Qatar report naturally made no reference to other extensive investigations that

had described horrific acts of torture and sectarian cleansing being perpetrated by rebel groups. Published the same week, for example, Human
Rights Watch's annual *World Report* had described how 'armed opposition
forces, including a growing number of pro-opposition foreign fighters,
have also carried out serious abuses including indiscriminate attacks on
civilians, executions, kidnapping, and torture.' The report also documented
how an opposition attack in the Latakia countryside in August 2013 had
led to the deaths of 'at least 190 civilians, including 57 women, at least
18 children, and 14 elderly men. Many of them were summarily executed.'[348]
In December 2015, Human Rights Watch published a follow-up investigation on torture and detentions in Syria after reviewing all of the available
Caesar evidence. Although it noted that 28,707 of the photographs were
of those 'understood to have died in government custody', it also stated
that another 24,568 of the photographs were of 'dead government soldiers
and crime scenes including incidents of terrorism, fires, explosions, and
car bombs'.[349]

Pushing the same sort of message as the Qatar report, often with a focus
on regime atrocities, or making sure that most civilian deaths were blamed
on the Syrian air force, a number of bespoke human rights organizations
and media outlets were also set up to gather and disseminate supposedly
seized evidence and on-the-ground eyewitness accounts that the international media could then use as source material. With mixed success and
varying levels of refinement, most of these entities have tried to present
themselves as neutral and objective and thus as credible conduits to a
war-torn region mostly inaccessible to bona fide journalists.

A good example has been the 'Commission for International Justice
and Accountability', which even has a specific 'Regime Crimes Team'.
Comprising sixty investigators, it describes itself as an independent organization that receives funding from Western governments and has had its
staff trained at 'UK funded human rights seminars in Turkey'. With two
of its directors speaking at a Chatham House seminar in May 2015, the
CIJA claimed to have 'recently completed a case file addressing individual
criminal responsibility at the superior level for crimes committed in
Syrian regime-controlled detention'. According to a detailed *Guardian*
investigation, during their training programme the CIJA's employees were
understood to have been staying in small hotels in Istanbul that did not

require guests to show passports, before then being asked to cross the border from Turkey into Syria to find documents implicating the regime. Given the apparent inexperience of the employees, the CIJA's Canadian training organizer explained that his intention was to 'take these activists – young, enthusiastic, self-appointed, social-media-savvy, with considerable personal courage' and then 'sensitize them to the sort of evidence that is required to inform an international criminal case'.[350]

Interviewed by a *Guardian* correspondent in an unnamed Gulf monarchy, one of the CIJA's investigators who claimed to have returned from Syria gives a good insight into the organization's methodology. Describing how in the city of Al-Raqqah the 'leaders of the local Salafist militia offered to help collect what [he] was looking for; over the next few days, they came with plastic bags and cardboard boxes full of papers.' He also explained how the situation in Deir Ezzor was 'more complicated' because *Jabhat al-Nusra* was the dominant force, but thankfully 'one of the group's local commanders – a man of grace and education – agreed to covertly provide assistance.' The investigator's experiences with the Free Syrian Army in Aleppo seem to have been no less haphazard, as after an FSA unit informed him that regime records had already been burned, they then seemed to change their minds after he had explained how useful they would have been. He described how 'a few days later they shamefacedly brought him a few plastic bags full of documents they had salvaged.' From this batch he was then able to 'rescue a few scraps, including a potentially significant series of exchanges between [government] political commissars in the military' before then 'stuffing them in his computer bag, and being driven out of the area in a black FSA Mercedes'.[351]

Of the various websites and social media feeds set up to focus solely on pro-rebel news, most have been rather crude, with little detective work needed to determine their source of financing and mission objectives. 'Syria Direct', for example, has been frequently cited as a source by the Western media, perhaps due to its stated claim that 'as a result of agenda-free funding, our focus is on providing credible, original, relevant and immediate news and analysis of Syria.'[352] But with no advertising on its website, it appears to have been funded entirely or at least partly by the US Department of State, with transactions of $165,720, $226,520, and $237,020 having been made in September 2014, June 2015, and January

2016 under the banner of a US government programme called *Investing in people in the Middle East and North Africa*.[353]

Other news outlets have, however, been much more sophisticated. The 'Syrian Civil Defence', which is also known as the 'White Helmets', is described as being made up of regular Syrian civilian volunteers who serve as emergency service providers in the absence of state control and who, according to its website, are prepared to help people on all sides of the conflict. As with Syria Direct, this has proven enough of a qualification for the organization to be widely used by the international media as an on-the-ground and objective source. However, almost all of its press releases have sought to portray the Syrian regime, rather than any opposition group or even jihadist militias, as the main destabilizing force in the country. In October 2015, for example, its website's first headline claimed that the regime's infamous 'barrel bombs' have been the biggest killer of civilians,[354] while earlier in the year the *New York Times* reported that the organization was campaigning because 'the West is so focused on the Islamic State that it is ignoring the far greater killing by al-Assad.'[355] In another *New York Times* report from 2015 the White Helmets were also described as trying 'to bring evidence of chlorine gas attacks directly to the French, British and US governments for testing. The aim is to give states a solid basis for action against the attacks.'[356] Within hours of the first Russian air strikes in Syria, the White Helmets were again quoted by the *New York Times* stating that one of their volunteers had been killed by such a strike. The White Helmets have, thus far, never claimed that any of their personnel have been harmed by any of the US or rebel-led actions.[357]

In one of the *New York Times*' many other features on the White Helmets, a very brief mention was made that the organization 'survived on modest financing from the US, Britain and private donors',[358] and in January 2016 Britain's Foreign Office published a short video on Twitter featuring the foreign secretary 'visiting the UK-funded @SyriaCivilDef training centre in Turkey.'[359] Other reports have claimed that the US has provided $13 million so far 'in humanitarian aid to civil defence teams like the Syrian Civil Defence', with a senior Department of State official explaining that 'it enables Syrian civilians to do something tangible in the face of the regime's atrocities. There's nothing that brings a community together more than efforts to rescue people.'[360]

YEMEN – A PAINFUL INTERVENTION

Although unlike in Libya or Syria there was no 'Axis of Resistance' regime to remove, by the end of 2013 the situation in Yemen was nevertheless looking bleak for the nearby Gulf monarchies and, in turn, the Western powers. The Gulf Cooperation Council's United Nations-backed political solution was in danger of unravelling, and although some sort of Qatar-sponsored Islamist rebellion had not materialized, the arguably more powerful Houthi movement had ultimately proven unwilling to deal with Saudi Arabia and the United Arab Emirates. To make matters worse, the Houthi leaders and their *Ansar Allah* paramilitary force seemed to be gravitating to regime remnants closer to Ali Abdullah Saleh than those of the interim president Abd Rabbo Mansour Hadi. Thus, despite the escalating emergency in Yemen having very different foundations to the Libyan and Syrian wars, the West's principal regional allies soon seemed to have little alternative than to adopt many of the same interventionist 'Plan B' strategies they were pursuing in North Africa and the Levant, including a rekindling of their relationship with local extremists.

In September 2014, with most of Yemen's armed forces having disintegrated and with military power really resting with tribes and militias, the GCC's worst nightmare seemed finally to come true when the Houthis began to occupy large parts of the capital city of Sana'a, including the airport.[361] Almost uncontested, their advances were smoothed considerably by several large protests demanding that the government lower the price of fuel and restore 'legitimate rights'. With Hadi's retreating forces responding by opening fire on protestors, many expected Abdul Malik al-Houthi's victory speech in Sana'a to be incendiary and divisive, but instead he urged calm and patience, and – in language not dissimilar to that of the Arab Spring – he declared: 'Our people will not back down from their legitimate demands.' Seemingly in tune with Sana'a's streets, he also called for the dissolution of the GCC-backed government, a rebooting of the long-stalled National Dialogue Conference, and – as a populist measure – the return of fuel subsidies.[362]

Even more disturbingly for Hadi and the GCC, the Houthis were clearly not on their own as it soon transpired there were approximately three thousand Saleh loyalists alongside the two thousand *Ansar Allah* who had entered the capital. Indeed, it is thought to have been a nephew of Saleh and members of Saleh's Sanhan Hashid tribe – most of whom were former soldiers in the Yemeni army and the republican guard – who actually led the offensive.[363] Having set up a new 'Presidential Council' to serve as Sana'a's de facto government, and with their forces moving further south, the Houthi–Saleh alliance soon pushed the sidelined 'internationally recognized government' all the way down to Aden.[364] Even though the two winning camps clearly had a shared objective, and even though reports had circulated ever since the Arab Spring claiming that Saleh's relatives had not only tried to meet with the Houthis, as had Saudi Arabia and the UAE, but also with Iranian officials, the apparent strength of the Houthi–Saleh deal nonetheless caught many by surprise.[365]

According to numerous declassified and leaked secret documents, Saleh had earlier attempted to paint the Houthis as 'terrorists' as part of his previously described efforts to position himself as a pro-US ally in the 'War on Terror'. Then, as the US had sought to curtail Iran's influence in the region, Saleh had tried to re-frame the Houthis as an Iran-backed fifth column. Receiving part of a $5.5 billion GCC aid package as reward for this new stance,[366] in 2006 Saleh told the visiting US CENTCOM commander that '[Iran's] recent support for insurgents in Yemen was unacceptable and, along with other activities in the region, constituted proof of Tehran's desire to re-establish the Persian Empire.' As a US diplomatic cable noted, Saleh also warned that if the Houthis became too powerful then they were likely to attack Saudi Arabia's oilfields. He even claimed his government had seized documents indicating that the Houthis were being encouraged by Iran to assault the US embassy in Sana'a and assassinate the ambassador. On this basis the US was requested to launch an air strike on a Saleh-identified Houthi compound.[367] Although the US demurred, a year later Saleh seemed even more determined to embellish the Houthi–Iran threat, with his foreign minister claiming to US diplomats that Tehran had been 'culturally preparing the Houthis since the 1990s' and had become their main source of funding. Keen to connect the Houthis to other infamous US bogeymen, no matter how implausibly, the minister even claimed Muammar Gaddafi was funding the Houthis too.[368] By 2009, in receipt of over $155 million in US security aid and with his forces having launched a full-blown 'scorched earth' offensive on Houthi positions, Saleh's new foreign policy seemed to be working.[369]

Not all US officials were convinced, however, with one US ambassador to Yemen stating he was cautious about taking a 'leap of faith' over Saleh's claims of Iranian involvement and explaining that 'the same holds true for the Yemenis' allegations regarding the Libyans.'[370] His successor was similarly circumspect, arguing in 2009 that 'whether the Houthis are the instrument Iran has chosen to establish a beachhead in the Arabian Peninsula with remains unclear, although the fact that after five years of conflict there is still no compelling evidence of that link must force us to view this claim with some scepticism.' Moreover, in the same cable his embassy staff referred to 'extravagant claims' that had been made by Saleh about an Iranian ship seized off the coast which was supposed to contain weapons but which, according to 'sensitive reporting', contained no weapons whatsoever.[371]

Either way, by the beginning of 2015 Saleh appeared to have manoeuvred himself skilfully back into power, but this time with the help of old foes. Reaffirming their anti-GCC credentials, the Houthis – and by association Saleh – duly accused Riyadh of seeking to split Yemen along sectarian and geographical lines, especially after Saudi Arabia and most of the other Gulf monarchies relocated their embassies to Aden and Hadi then declared it the country's new capital.[372] Noting the close parallels between the beleaguered Hadi administration and the Saudi-backed Libyan government holed up in Tobruk, Abdel-Malik al-Houthi warned the Yemeni people that 'our elder sister, the Saudi kingdom, doesn't respect the Yemenis and wants to impose here in Yemen the sequence of events and divisions that happened in Libya.'[373]

As with their support for the Tobruk administration and Khalifa Hiftar's forces, and as with the backing given to the Free Syrian Army and other 'moderates' fighting against the Bashar al-Assad regime, the Gulf monarchies' first plan was to defeat the Houthi–Saleh alliance by arming and financing what remained of Hadi's forces along with any other local groups that could still somehow be characterized as pro-Western and willing to resume the old GCC-sponsored transitional plan. These included the Southern Movement separatists – still committed to restoring the short-lived Saudi-backed Democratic Republic of Yemen that had been based in Aden in 1994 – and, so it seems, the various tribes and Islamist groups that had earlier accepted the Hadi interim presidency. With Qatari competition having subsided in the wake of the Egyptian coup, Saudi Arabia and the UAE were even willing to push to one side their own domestic demonization of the Muslim Brotherhood in order to do business grudgingly with its potentially useful Yemeni equivalent.[374] Even Tawakkol Karman, the Nobel Peace Prize-winning Yemeni face of the Arab Spring and a former critic of Saudi Arabia, who by 2015 had risen to become a senior member of an Islamist party, soon made clear in an Al-Jazeera interview that she laid the blame for Yemen's instability on the Houthis and, in vague terms, blamed Iran for 'orchestrating their role in the conflict'.[375]

Nonetheless, with considerable territorial losses and the defection of Hadi's special forces commander to Saleh, the situation looked increasingly desperate for the makeshift Aden–Islamist alliance. With a growing realization that only a significant external intervention could save the day, in early March 2015 Hadi met with the US ambassador and various GCC officials and a few days later preparations were underway for Aden to serve as a launch pad for a much more forceful GCC-led and Western-backed response.[376] For external consumption the Saudi ambassador to the US justified the impending campaign on the basis of UN approval and even a Syria-style pro-democracy platform. He explained that Hadi 'has agreed to a process that is supported by the international community, that is enshrined in several UN Security Council resolutions ... [and] would lead them from where they were to a new state with a new constitution and elections and checks and balances and so forth'. Without naming the UN resolutions he was referring to, he also argued that the Houthis were a 'spoiler' for such a process. As historian John Willis notes, the ambassador's remarks were remarkable given that no mention was made of the Yemeni people, and they sidelined the issue that sizeable portions of the population would never be willing to trust a renewed GCC-sponsored political process that likely intended to restore the status quo.[377]

The first step of the GCC intervention was to make sure that the same sort of airborne campaign that had softened up the Libyan regime's forces also took place against the Houthi–Saleh alliance. With Hadi having already fled to Riyadh, on 25 March 2015 the Saudi and UAE air forces began to strike what they claimed were Houthi military targets up and down the country. Dubbed *Asifat al-Hazim* or 'Operation Decisive Edge', the imagery coming out of the Riyadh-based command centre was uncannily similar to that of the US's old 'War on Terror' operations. Moreover, the Saudi statements that the GCC would keep on bombing until some sort of political result was reached were reminiscent of those expressed by Tony Blair during the strikes on Serbia in 1999, when he said: 'We will carry on pounding day after day, until our objectives are secured,' and those of Britain's chief of defence staff, who stated on the eve of the 2001 invasion of Afghanistan that NATO would bomb 'until the people of the country recognize that this is going to go on until they get the leadership changed'.[378]

Promising a 'joint planning cell' to help with intelligence and logistics, the US clearly sought to display solidarity with the intervention, even if it preferred to maintain the same kind of arms-length position as it had done with the British- and French-led NATO strikes on Libya in 2011. Following the Houthis' seizure of Hadi government documents towards the end of March 2015, there was nevertheless some considerable embarrassment as details of Hadi's close cooperation with a CIA drone programme operating from Saudi Arabia were revealed and published.[379] Britain was a little more open with its support, with officials rather unguardedly promising to 'support the Saudi operation in every way it can'. But in many ways London's response was understandable given that many of the missiles being launched by the Saudi air force were British-manufactured. Indeed, a few months later Britain's Ministry of Defence confirmed the supply of precision-made weapons to the Saudi air campaign, while *Defense News* claimed the ministry had even requested Raytheon UK to swap its Paveway IV missile delivery line positions so that the Saudi air force would get priority over Britain's Royal Air Force.[380]

Apart from some GCC personnel who were quickly deployed to Aden to establish a beachhead and prepare for Hadi's return, the bulk of the intervention's ground troops were not supposed to come from the wealthy Gulf monarchies. The intention instead was for Saudi Arabia to invoke the numerous oil-financed regional alliances it had built up over the years to ensure that infantry from 'friendly' but poorer Arab and Muslim-majority states would bear the brunt of any heavy fighting against the Houthis. To this end a coalition was announced that included Egypt, Sudan, Morocco, and Jordan – the common thread being that all were in receipt of Saudi funding.[381] Soon after, Pakistan was added, likely in an effort to portray the operation as a 'Sunni front' against the supposedly Iran-backed Zaydi-Shia

Houthis. But in all cases these fair-weather allies dragged their heels, with Cairo carefully declining its role, Khartoum limiting itself to air strikes despite substantial Saudi deposits being placed in its central bank,[382] and Islamabad stating it was only willing to help defend Saudi Arabia's borders. Reflected in the Pakistani press, there had begun to emerge 'immense public pressure' to block any further entanglement in the kingdom's affairs, despite the long history of Saudi aid and subsidized oil.[383] In many ways Pakistan's perceived betrayal should not have come as a surprise, with Agence France-Presse having described earlier in the year how a 'wave of criticism' of Saudi Arabia had already begun, and, as the *Financial Times* reported in March 2015, how suspicions of the kingdom's role in funding extremists were running high. As one Pakistani official put it, 'Saudi Arabia is both a friend and a source of the continuing problem.'[384]

More willing to serve as mercenaries, it seemed, were soldiers from non-Arab countries, with Senegal's foreign minister putting an end to much speculation in May 2015 by announcing that 2,100 troops were to be sent to join the GCC's coalition. The news was not met with support in Senegal, with many using social media to question their country's involvement. But given recent announcements that Saudi Arabia was intending to 'heavily invest' in a new long-term development plan, the government's hands seemed tied.[385] Hundreds of Latin American fighters were also soon reported to have arrived in Yemen, including Colombians, Panamanians, Chileans, and Salvadoreans. In fact, so many Colombians were involved that the Colombian defence minister complained that his best soldiers were being poached.[386] Most were understood to have been hired by a private security company employed by the UAE and originally co-founded by Blackwater's Erik Prince. Mercenaries from several other countries were also spotted in Yemen, with 1,500 Moroccans understood to have been mobilized 'in coordination with the US', while veteran Australians and New Zealanders arrived as commanders. According to a UN report, even Eritreans had begun to turn up after the UAE 'compensated' the Eritrean government. The *New York Times* reported that the presence of such Eritreans violated UN resolutions restricting Eritrean military activity, but within a few weeks of the criticism the Hadi administration simply declared the UN high commissioner for human rights *persona non grata* in Yemen on the basis he had 'lost professionalism'.[387]

Handing out money, weapons, and even uniforms, the GCC's own ground forces – mostly made up of Saudi and UAE soldiers – seemed primarily focused on strengthening their Yemeni allies, with Hadi's remaining police and security forces being sent in batches of three hundred back to the UAE to receive training, and with thousands of new local fighters recruited by summer 2015. Joining the 'Salman Decisiveness Brigade' – so-called after the Saudi king – many of these, along with other Saudi and UAE-paid 'tribal irregulars', at first seemed sufficient, as alongside the various foreign mercenaries they were strong enough to liberate Aden and then push back the Houthi–Saleh alliance towards Marib in central Yemen.[388]

In tandem with their important organizational roles close to battlefields, it was clear that the Saudi and UAE forces were also busy securing and even building strategic assets for themselves far behind the front lines. In August 2015, for example, the UAE media began to report that the Saudi navy had been shipping across hundreds of Asian workers to build a naval base on the Yemeni island of Socotra, a World Heritage Site nearly four hundred kilometres from the mainland. This development, indicating GCC geo-strategic drivers far beyond the mere restoration of the Hadi government, seemed to tally with the contents of a Saudi foreign ministry document leaked that summer which, in a presumed reference to the Indian Ocean, had called for a 'naval port for Saudi Arabia on the open sea'.[389] Meanwhile, the UAE's soldiers were reported to have been heavily concentrating on establishing a strong presence around the perimeter of Aden's port district in advance of a ministerial visit in October 2015 to discuss the 'restoration of critical marine and trade infrastructure'. Importantly the UAE's delegation also included representatives of Dubai Ports World, the company that had won a lucrative thirty-year contract back in 2008 to manage two of Aden's terminals but had then had its rights revoked three years later on the basis it had not fulfilled its investment obligations.[390]

YEMEN – BRINGING BACK AL-QAEDA

Despite the capture of Marib and Abd Rabbo Mansour Hadi's brief return in September 2015, there were already signs that the ragtag alliance of Gulf Cooperation Council-led ground forces was unlikely to be able to advance on Sana'a and, even with air cover, was in danger of losing its hard-won territory. Of particular concern were the tribal irregulars, many of whom were described as 'barely out of adolescence', and – so it seemed – were not entirely trustworthy. After the shattering loss of forty-five Emirati and ten Saudi soldiers on 4 September to a missile attack on their base in Marib, the GCC forces reportedly began to camp separately from their Yemeni counterparts due to fears of tip-offs being passed on to their enemies. Interviewed by Reuters, one GCC soldier complained that the Yemenis were 'nuts. They fire around indiscriminately – not disciplined fighters. I don't like to fight where they are.' Another from the UAE explained that the irregulars were being paid $100 a month, along with being given new assault rifles and ammunition, but joked that they kept asking for 'more guns, more body armour, and oh, a Toyota Hi-Lux ... but it has to be a 2015 model!'[391]

Of greater concern was the fact that the longer the war went on, the more likely it was that Iran would attempt to supply the Houthis with sophisticated equipment so that Yemen could serve as a second front in the same Tehran–Riyadh proxy war that was fast developing in Syria. At first there was scepticism about the sort of role the Houthis would be willing to play in such a broader conflict, not least given the obvious disinformation Ali Abdullah Saleh had earlier been supplying to the US. Moreover, as many pointed out, there seemed no incentive for the Houthis to fall into Saudi Arabia's and indeed the Western media's sectarian framework given their alliance with the predominantly Sunni Saleh loyalists and given that many of the tribes in 'fiercely Sunni areas' of Yemen were understood to have welcomed their advances earlier in 2015.[392] As the Canada-based Ruba Ali al-Hassani neatly tweeted, 'Within Yemen, the conflict is political, not sectarian. Beyond its borders, the conflict is more sectarian than political.'[393] A recent Saudi defector and former head of air operations at an airbase near Dhahran has largely corroborated this view, arguing this was not about sectarianism but rather 'a war against the Yemeni nation and against Yemen becoming independent'.[394] As anthropologist and Yemen specialist Gabriele vom Bruck has similarly pointed out, the Houthis 'want Yemen to be independent, that's the key idea, they don't want to be controlled by Saudi or the Americans, and they certainly don't want to replace the Saudis with the Iranians.'[395]

Some US officials also seemed reluctant to buy into the Iran–Houthi spectre, with those familiar with the intelligence on the Houthi–Saleh advances in 2014 stating that the Houthis had actually ignored Iranian advice to not go as far as taking control of Sana'a. On this basis they claimed 'it is wrong to think of the Houthis as a proxy force for Iran' and argued that the Houthis cared more about corruption and the distribution of power in Yemen than the spreading of Shia influence across the region. Moreover, as late as April 2015, a spokeswoman for the US National Security Council confirmed that 'it remains our assessment that Iran does not exert command and control over the Houthis in Yemen'.[396]

With regard to the supply of weapons, much of the dispute in the US intelligence community still seemed to be hanging on the story of an 'Iranian dhow' seized off the Yemeni coast in early 2013. Understood to have been carrying Chinese-designed heat-seeking missiles bearing markings indicating their manufacture in either Iran or Pakistan, along with Bulgarian, Russian, and other Iran-manufactured equipment, the dhow was monitored by US satellites as it left Iranian waters and then sailed into the Arabian Sea. Eventually halted by a US destroyer, it was boarded by a Yemeni coastguard team. However, given that the confirmed point of contact near Al-Ghaydah was only just into Yemen's easternmost territorial waters and very far from the Houthis' power base in northern and north-western Yemen, and given that there was no evidence of the dhow's intended destination, the accusations seem weak. Indeed, a subsequent report from the UN Security Council's monitoring group on Somalia and Eritrea indicated that the diesel on board the ship was likely being smuggled to East Africa.[397] Moreover, at that time Iran was still known to have been supplying weapons to Sudan – a supply route that would have likely used the same path as the intercepted dhow – and according to a report published in 2014 by a Swiss weapons tracking organization, these included Chinese-manufactured arms.[398]

As the war progressed into summer 2015, speculation nonetheless persisted that Iran was getting more heavily involved. According to a leaked letter published by a London-based Arabic newspaper, the Iran Martyrs' Foundation had promised its Houthi-controlled equivalent $3.75 million in support after being encouraged to do so by the Iranian Revolutionary Guard Corps.[399] More seriously, in September, the Associated Press reported that another unregistered dhow had been intercepted close to Yemeni waters while carrying arms. With the US Navy claiming it had originated from Iran, the unnamed country that performed the interception was thought to have been Oman, given that it seized the weapons but also freed the sailors – likely in an effort to appease its fellow GCC members while also maintaining good relations with Tehran.[400] With the relationship exposed, less than a week after the incident Iran's state media reported that the vice president and several other members of the Houthi–Saleh installed Sana'a administration had turned up in Tehran to take part in a number of high-profile meetings.[401]

Either way, from the Saudi and UAE perspective, their growing concerns over the loyalty and efficacy of their ground forces, coupled with the heightened risk that Iran might try to turn the Houthis into a sort of Yemeni version of Lebanon's *Hezbollah*, meant there was even greater urgency to wrap up the conflict in their favour. In this context, and very closely following the pattern of the stumbling Free Syrian Army and the Gulf monarchies' resulting need to back ever more radical and battle-hardened groups to accelerate the demise of the Bashar al-Assad regime, Saudi Arabia had clearly begun to reach out to more extremist Sunni elements to get the job done in Yemen. At first it seemed such help might come from outside, as in April 2015 the old Saudi-sponsored jihadist networks in Afghanistan had been quick to pledge their support for the GCC's coalition. Awkwardly for Riyadh, given its supposedly pro-Western plans for Yemen, Gulbuddin Hekmatyar himself issued a statement offering to dispatch thousands of jihadists to 'go to Saudi Arabia to frustrate the Iranian sinister designs in Yemen'.[402] Similarly, the elderly Jalaluddin Haqqani and his son Sirajuddin, who was effectively in operational command, were also believed to have promised to send fighters.[403]

Causing great embarrassment, the leaked Saudi foreign ministry documents in summer 2015 revealed that the Haqqani network's relations with Riyadh had been continuous, despite the US having belatedly designated it a foreign terrorist organization in 2012, and despite it being accused of having sponsored suicide bombings and 'spectacular attacks' on US forces still in Afghanistan.[404] Notably, Haqqani family members had been meeting with the Saudi ambassador to Pakistan, and on one occasion had requested permission for Jalaluddin to visit Saudi Arabia to receive hospital treatment. According to a follow-up Saudi memorandum, the ministry recommended the visit should go ahead. Most interestingly the leaked documents also indicated that Jalaluddin had held a Saudi passport ever since the Afghan jihad in the 1980s and had held on to it even after being placed on the UN sanctions list in 2001. In 2012 his passport was handed to the Saudi ambassador and, as Pakistani analysts reasoned, this was likely so it could be renewed and then returned to him.[405]

More useful to Saudi Arabia than promises from far-flung jihadists, however, was the potent but dangerous al-Qaeda in the Arabian Peninsula franchise. Despite having crossed swords with the kingdom in 2003, when it launched a series of deadly assaults on expatriate compounds and oil installations and, as discussed, having harassed the transitional Yemeni government in 2011 and 2012, perhaps in collusion with Saleh loyalists, by 2015 it was nonetheless one of the most powerful potential counter-weights to the Houthi–Saleh alliance. As one of the biggest beneficiaries of Yemen's slide into chaos, AQAP had been able to take over vast tracks of the eastern part of the country while at the same time strengthening its presence in the suburbs of many cities outside government control. In this sense, it was likely viewed by Riyadh not only as the most important indigenous Sunni paramilitary force capable of playing a part in a broader sectarian war, but also as a necessary ally if the GCC-led coalition hoped to protect its flanks and push further into Houthi-held territory.

Already anticipating such a GCC–AQAP front forming, given the evidence on the ground in Libya and Syria, Abdul-Malik al-Houthi went public with accusations as soon as the air strikes began, claiming that Saudi Arabia was 'financing acts of terror in the Middle East region and beyond', and declaring that his forces' drive to the south of Yemen was in order to 'root out al-Qaeda [and other extremist groups]'. Meanwhile, the *New York Times* described him portraying al-Qaeda as an instrument of 'a broad international conspiracy'.[406] By June 2015 al-Houthi's suspicions seemed confirmed when a Hadi administration delegation sent to take part in UN-brokered negotiations in Geneva included an alleged AQAP financier. In fact, the man had been added to the US Department of the Treasury's blacklist two years earlier with the explanation that he was 'establishing a political party as cover for AQAP'. He was also described in the US designation as being at the 'centre of global support networks that fund and facilitate terrorism' and he was understood to have played a role in a 2012 multiple car bombing in Yemen.[407] According to Saudi foreign ministry documents leaked the same month, Yemeni activists had earlier complained that the Hadi government was 'the one supporting the presence of al-Qaeda in Yemen and using them as a means to receive financial and military aid'.[408]

By July, the *Wall Street Journal* was stating bluntly that 'local militias backed by Saudi Arabia, special forces from the United Arab Emirates and al-Qaeda militants all fought on the same side this week to wrest back control over most of Yemen's second city, Aden'. The report cited senior Western diplomats in the region as agreeing that the 'Saudi-backed militants' were receiving support from al-Qaeda. Although a qualification was added that the GCC's forces and AQAP were not necessarily fighting together in the same areas of the city, the interviewed eyewitnesses painted a murkier picture. One described how he was 'confused over who has captured Aden, seeing al-Qaeda flags flying in some parts [of the city] and on dozens of armored vehicles'. Another explained: 'We were surprised to see some fighters raising al-Qaeda flags and dragging some rebels on the streets of Crater [a district of Aden] tonight.' Other locals claimed that those who were 'ruling the city jointly with al-Qaeda' were receiving Saudi fuel in order to keep the city running.[409]

Arguing that Saudi Arabia and AQAP had become 'strange bedfellows against a common enemy', the nature of the deal was well explained by the Wilson Center's David Ottaway in a report published the following month. Noting that the GCC air forces had been bombing Houthi targets all over the country, he pointed out that the AQAP strongholds in Hadhramaut had been left completely untouched.[410] Interviewed by the US media, the UAE's commander in Aden tried to give things a different twist, stating that 'everywhere in Yemen, you have al-Qaeda ... what I hear is that they are not attacking the UAE forces because they know that we are not here to take their country or do something bad, and because we are popular.' Nevertheless, another GCC coalition commander interviewed at the same time simply argued that 'we cannot afford to have a second front.'[411]

By August 2015 the deal was very much an open secret, with Reuters reporting in the wake of Saudi and UAE forces arriving that residents had been seeing 'dozens of al-Qaeda militants patrolling the streets with their weapons in total freedom'. Moreover, in an eerie parallel to the Libyan Islamic Fighting Group's temporary takeovers of Benghazi buildings a few years earlier, many claimed to have seen the black flag of al-Qaeda hoisted above Aden government buildings.[412] On the very same day this report was filed, the UAE oddly claimed that they had conducted a 'military operation' against AQAP to free a British hostage. Although Abu Dhabi's assertion was repeated by Britain's Foreign Office, Aden residents told journalists that the hostage was not being kept by AQAP at all, but rather by Yemeni tribesmen who had then been paid off by the GCC coalition.[413] This version of events was quickly substantiated after an AQAP spokesman told Al-Jazeera that 'the incident that the UAE government claims took place with its special forces did not happen' and stated that they had not been holding the hostage.[414]

Even so, posting a slick promotional video in November 2015 highlighting its 'capture' of Taiz from the Houthi–Saleh alliance, AQAP seemed more than willing to stick to its end of the bargain, as its assault on the city was exactly concurrent with that of the Saudi and UAE-led forces.[415] By this stage several more districts in Aden were known to have fallen under AQAP control, while Abyan was also soon overrun, despite local officials having earlier requested help after observing 'suspicious al-Qaeda movements'. Following much the same pattern, by the end of the year the city of Azzan was also apparently handed over to the group with no contest, with local residents claiming AQAP had openly set up checkpoints, taken over government buildings, and had begun 'distributing leaflets asking people to abide by Islamic teachings'.[416] Remarkably, by February 2016 the BBC was bluntly reporting that it had 'evidence that troops from the Saudi-led coalition and al-Qaeda militants are both fighting Houthi rebels in a key battle'. It further explained that a documentary maker who had been filming coalition troops including UAE soldiers on a 'key hilltop' had been warned not to film one of the groups because they were members of AQAP and were angered by her presence, as a woman.[417] Facing mounting criticism, efforts were soon made so that the coalition could be seen as doing something about AQAP, with the Saudi state media claiming in April 2016 that a UAE-led advance into the southern port of Mukalla had killed several hundred of the militants. As Reuters reported, however, hardly any shots were fired as AQAP had already negotiated with 'local clerics and tribesmen' so that it could 'exit quietly'.[418]

8

ENTER THE ISLAMIC STATE – A PHANTOM MENACE

AL-QAEDA'S LIMITS

E merging in Libya, Syria, and then Yemen as the most capable if unsavoury proxies on the ground against the remains of resisting nation states or other potential 'Axis of Resistance' forces, al-Qaeda's local affiliates seemed firmly in the driving seat. By the beginning of 2014 *Jabhat al-Nusra* was arguably the most powerful jihadist organization in Syria, while soon after al-Qaeda in the Arabian Peninsula gained control over huge swathes of Yemen and – by any measure – was stronger than it had ever been.

Only a few years earlier, however, prominent analysts had confidently predicted the demise of al-Qaeda, or at least its core leadership, as for multiple reasons it was deemed unfit for purpose, especially after the advent of the Arab Spring. Hamid Dabashi, for example, described how the power of non-violent civil disobedience in 2011 had 'buried Osama bin Laden under Tahrir Square', and that 'pathological entities like al-Qaeda are now entirely dead and discarded figments of imagination that the US had manufactured and in the end destroyed.'[1]

Jean-Pierre Filiu's *The Arab Revolution: Ten Lessons from the Democratic Uprising* devoted a chapter to how the 'jihadists could become obsolete',[2] while Fouad Ajami saw al-Qaeda as merely part of a 'terrorist fringe that hurled itself in frustration'. Published in summer 2011 by the London

361

School of Economics' Fawaz Gerges, *The Rise and Fall of Al-Qaeda* drew much the same conclusion, arguing that 'the democratic revolutions that swept the Middle East show that al-Qaeda today is a non-entity which exercises no influence over Arabs' political life.'[3]

What little data there was at the time seemed to strengthen Gerges' case, with the US National Counterterrorism Center's annual report stating that most indicators pointed to the demise of the 'global jihad phenomenon', while a Pew survey conducted in Jordan showed that support for al-Qaeda had dropped from sixty-one percent in 2005 to just thirteen percent in 2011.[4] In this sense, the 2011 uprisings seemed to have pushed al-Qaeda to the sidelines of regional and international news, effectively undoing years of accumulated influence-building as al-Qaeda websites and forums were upstaged by televised public protests and widespread social media usage by a full spectrum of activists. As Filiu put it, the Arab public's apparent indifference to subsequent al-Qaeda statements was 'devastating for a network as narcissistic as bin Laden's'.[5] Certainly bin Laden seemed to have nothing to say as the revolutions unfolded, even when bitter enemies such as Hosni Mubarak were ousted.[6]

To make matters worse for al-Qaeda, bin Laden's apparent assassination by US special forces in May 2011 suddenly left it with a significant leadership deficit. Although held in high esteem due to earlier imprisonment and torture under the Mubarak regime in the mid-1980s, and despite being considered 'the real brains behind al-Qaeda' after merging his Egyptian Islamic Jihad with al-Qaeda in 1998, bin Laden's long-serving deputy Ayman Zawahiri was far from a consensus candidate. In fact, it took six weeks of heated debate within al-Qaeda's central council before he was finally appointed as the new chief.[7] Most obviously, he lacked the charisma and timing of his illustrious predecessor, either delivering rambling and belated speeches or going silent for several months on end. One Zawahiri statement on Egypt was so out of date it did not even refer to Mubarak's fall, while declarations on Syria that described the nascent conflict as an 'Islamic battle' and as a 'front for jihad and martyrdom' were considered out of touch and irrelevant. As extremism expert J. M. Berger notes, al-Qaeda's 'public media output dropped precipitously'.[8]

More seriously, Zawahiri was also blamed for having allowed too many franchisees to operate under al-Qaeda's banner. As many saw it, this dilution of the brand had led to greater disorganization and confusion, as well as accusations that the core leadership had little idea any more of what was happening on the ground.[9] As something of a final straw, at least for Zawahiri's claims to the mantle of global jihad, al-Qaeda's central council was also soon caught out in a significant lie. Having told its affiliates in summer 2014 to renew allegiances to the Taliban's Mullah Omar as their spiritual leader, and having even dedicated the first edition of a new al-Qaeda magazine to the topic, it soon transpired Omar had actually died in 2013 – a fact almost certainly known to Zawahiri and his lieutenants.[10]

THE NEED FOR 'NATIONAL JIHADISTS'

For those trying to co-opt the jihadists most capable of waging wars against the Syrian state and other such rivals, the post-Osama bin Laden al-Qaeda understandably looked a bad bet, at least initially. To put it another way, despite the eventual successes of some of its affiliates, Ayman Zawahiri's command hub seemed unlikely ever to direct the same sort of battlefield victories its precursors had delivered against the Soviet-backed Afghan government in the 1980s and had contributed to against Serbia in the 1990s. Moreover, given Zawahiri's apparent lack of a coherent political roadmap, al-Qaeda also seemed unable to offer real alternatives to the people of Libya, Syria, Yemen, and elsewhere, thus impeding the formation of more religiously conservative states to replace the regimes of Muammar Gaddafi, Bashar al-Assad, and Ali Abdullah Saleh.

For this purpose, much more useful jihadist organizations would be those that could concentrate better than al-Qaeda on fighting conventional military campaigns against regular armed forces, such as those in Syria and Yemen, and could also commit to making these 'near enemies' a higher priority than 'far enemies' such as the Western powers or their regional allies. In this scenario, the 'Plan B' conflicts could be won, or perhaps victories accelerated, by more nationally focused jihadists that would be less likely, at least in the short term, to perpetrate 9/11-style blowback attacks on the United States or other 'apostate entities'. Furthermore, given the Western powers and the Gulf monarchies' well-documented history of cooperating with the Taliban and equally fundamentalist regimes, if such jihadist organizations ended up holding on to bits and pieces of the uncooperative nations they had helped destroy, then the Islamic states they eventually governed would likely prove just as compliant.

On top of any military and political capabilities, it was increasingly clear that these 'national jihadists' could also usefully be a lot more sectarian in these conflicts than the historically more restrained al-Qaeda was willing to be. Most obviously in Syria, from 2011 onwards the efforts of the Western powers and their regional allies to sectarianize the conflict by pitting the majority Sunni population against a supposedly Alawite-dominated regime had created a golden opportunity for the expansion of, and recruitment to, groups more willing to obligate themselves to the goal of Sunni supremacy. Similarly, by 2014 the Gulf monarchies' efforts to widen the sectarian fault line between the Zaydi-Shia Houthi movement and the rest of the Yemeni population had also created the conditions for a more avowedly Sunni extremist organization to gain a foothold alongside al-Qaeda in the Arabian Peninsula.

The rise and potency of such al-Qaeda alternatives had in many ways already been predicted, with evidence of considerable awareness of the characteristics and policy implications of more sectarian 'national jihadists' among US planners more than three years before the Arab Spring began. In 2008, for example, the RAND Corporation produced an extensive report entitled *Unfolding the future of the long war*. Commissioned by the US Army Training and Doctrine Command's Army Capability Integration Center, the report's ostensible aim was to assess the 'motivations, implications, and prospects' for the US military in its 'long war' against opponents in the Middle East who sought to 'form a unified Islamic world to supplant Western dominance'. In this sense, the US Army was continuing to develop the same concept of the 'long war' that had originally been conceived by the Highlands Forum – a thinktank set up by the Department of Defense in the 1990s and whose members have since been described as 'holding the reins of Obama's military strategy'. Although much of the 2008 report is unexceptional, it is noteworthy that it identified only two events likely to fundamentally reshape the region. The first of these, rather predictably, was a significant improvement or deterioration in the Israel–Palestine situation, but the second was an 'extreme change' resulting from 'the creation of new Islamic states that impose sharia law'.[11]

The report acknowledged that such a 'powerful Sunni Islamic state may prove even more troublesome than Iran', would give 'outright support to terrorism', and warned that 'the more militarily and economically powerful the state, the more potentially dangerous the situation would be'. Intriguingly, however, elsewhere in the report an explicit case was made for the US to actually co-opt 'national jihadists' so as to counterbalance the more dangerous 'global jihadists' which, in a clear reference to al-Qaeda, it described as 'posing a much greater threat to international security than the sum of that posed by local jihadist groups'.[12] With truly remarkable prescience of the jihadist infighting that was soon to rage across the Arab world, the report went on to state that 'the United States and the host nation could even help the nationalist jihadists execute a military campaign to stamp out al-Qaeda elements that are present locally' and, along with other strategies, suggested how the US could help 'national jihadists' as part of a scenario of 'narrowing the threat' and 'divide and rule' against 'global jihadists'.[13]

Most disturbingly, the 2008 report also explained that the US had already begun to provide 'carrots' in the form of weapons and cash to some of the same 'nationalist insurgency groups' in Iraq that its forces had earlier been fighting against, with the justification that the US and these national jihadists now shared the common threat of al-Qaeda, and that the 'divide and rule' strategy might allow the US to 'reduce its efforts in one region to focus on another'.[14] The authors, it seemed, were not willing to heed Robert Dreyfuss's warning from two years earlier that 'CIA officials preferred to see Islamic activists only in relation to the country in which they were stationed', and that 'the truly transnational reality of jihad continued to elude the CIA'.[15] Nor, it seemed, was the British government, with London unsurprisingly quick to match the US's willingness to support such al-Qaeda alternatives. In the context of negotiating with the Taliban as the Afghanistan conflict worsened, its foreign secretary reached the identical conclusion that 'global jihadists' needed to be separated from more benign, nationally focused Islamic states. In 2009, for example, he informed NATO that Britain's strategy involved 'separating those who want Islamic rule locally from those committed to violent jihad globally'. The only British requirement for such local jihadists appeared to be that they 'must be prepared to shut out al-Qaeda'.[16]

IRAQ – THE INCUBATION CHAMBER

By the time the Libyan and Syrian conflicts began, it was already clear that powerful al-Qaeda alternatives existed in the region, especially in Iraq. In many ways, the rise of such a nationally focused and openly sectarian jihadist organization in the country was grimly predictable given the especially deep-rooted tensions between its Sunni and Shia populations that had been repeatedly exacerbated by foreign interventions. Even under Saddam Hussein, a long-standing fear for Iraqi Sunnis and neighbouring Sunni states, including most of the Gulf monarchies, was that any new Iraqi state, and especially one dominated by the Shia majority, would likely gravitate towards Iran and engage in reprisals against the old elite. In this context Washington's indifference to Saddam's brutal response to the 1991 Shia uprisings – despite the US having earlier spent $40 million on flying Iraqi Shia insurgents to Saudi Arabia for training – can be seen as a function of the George H. Bush administration's ultimate unwillingness to pave the way for a new revolutionary regime in Baghdad that might ally with Tehran and place the US's regional Sunni allies at a disadvantage.[17]

Nonetheless, after the 2003 invasion the Sunni fears of such a Shia state seemed to have been realized. Leaked logs of US Army field reports demonstrate how a mass cover-up of torture, rape, and the mistreatment of detainees had taken place and that the new Iraqi government was engaged in the sectarian-motivated killing of both civilians and soldiers. As Muhammad Idrees Ahmad put it, the Saddam regime had simply been replaced by another 'repressive and murderous authoritarian state, albeit under a more representative sectarian set-up'.[18] Lending more weight to the leaked logs, a survey carried out by the UK-based medical journal *Lancet* revealed that of the 650,000 or so Iraqi deaths between 2003 and 2006, only thirty-one percent of deaths were attributable to US-led military actions.[19] Although the survey's methodology has since been disputed, it seems likely that a very substantial number of the total deaths were at the hands of the government's security services.[20]

While the killings may have slowed after the election in 2006 of Prime Minister Nouri Maliki, his policies seemed further confirmation that the new Iraq was still poised to become a sectarian battlefield. According to a classified US National Security Council memorandum from later that year, the US was already blaming Maliki's government for the 'non-delivery of services to Sunni areas', for stopping military action against Shia insurgents, and for removing army commanders on a sectarian basis.[21] The former US soldier and now imprisoned whistle-blower Bradley (Chelsea) Manning seemed to have reached similar conclusions after being asked to investigate fifteen detainees held by the Iraqi federal police force. Discovering that the evidence being used against them – supposed 'anti-Iraqi literature' – was in fact a pamphlet containing a 'benign scholarly critique' of Maliki, he had complained but had been told to 'shut up and explain how to assist the federal police in finding more detainees'.[22]

In parallel to its domestic sectarianism the Maliki administration's apparent efforts to seek support from Tehran seemed further proof to Iraqi Sunnis and the Gulf monarchies that Baghdad was willing to turn into an Iran-backed Shia power. As Seymour Hersh observed in the *New Yorker* in 2007, 'To the distress of the White House, Iran has forged a close relationship with the Shia-dominated government of Nouri Maliki.' As he argued, this was particularly upsetting for US officials as they had assumed that the post-Saddam state, even if Shia-led, would primarily provide 'a pro-American balance to Sunni extremists, since Iraq's Shia majority had been oppressed under Saddam Hussein'.[23] US thinktank analysts even contended, in the context of a US 'redirection' in the Middle East against Iran and its allies, that 'ties between the US and moderate or even radical Sunnis could put fear into the government of Prime Minister Maliki.' In this scenario, seemingly confirmed by the 'carrots' strategy referred to in the 2008 long war report, it was reasoned that a US–Sunni-extremist alliance would 'make [Maliki] worry that the Sunnis could actually win the civil war there', and that this would encourage him to cooperate with the US.[24]

If anything, however, the Baghdad government chose to sectarianize further and move even closer to Iran, indicating its willingness to confront rather than negotiate with any renewed Sunni insurgency. Taking measures to promote Shias to key military and security positions, it also offered legal protection for Shia militias and began to turn against the Sunni 'Sons of Iraq' who had earlier fought alongside government forces against al-Qaeda-linked jihadists. Notably, in 2007, twenty-five out of the thirty-one tribes in the Sunni-majority Anbar province had agreed to help Maliki and had formed the 'Anbar Salvation Council' after the US had promised

their leaders future administrative or security roles in the Iraqi government along with greater economic largesse for Sunni areas.[25] Baghdad
then not only set about stripping them of these positions, often without
compensation, but some were arrested after old charges against them were
resurrected, while surviving Sunni police chiefs claimed repeated assassination attempts. This has since been described as part of a 'campaign of
intimidation by Maliki officials'.[26]

Baghdad also soon moved against the *Mujahideen-e-Khalq* or 'People's
Mujahideen of Iran' – an Iranian opposition movement that had been
operating in exile from Iraq and whose presence had been quietly tolerated by the US. Attacking its main camp in 2009, the Iraqi government's
forces killed and injured many of its members and thus ignored the US's
stated preference for a non-violent solution.[27] Despite his coalition failing
to win an outright majority in the 2010 national elections, Maliki shored
up his position further by appointing himself as defence minister and
began referring to himself as commander-in-chief of the armed forces.
A new militia known as the 'Baghdad Operations Command' was established and, as further evidence of his reaching out to Tehran, within days
of the US withdrawal from Iraq in 2011 Maliki installed a member of the
pro-Iran *Badr* organization as the new interior minister. Remaining Sunni
politicians, or those critical of Iran, came under increasing pressure, with
an arrest warrant issued against Iraqi vice president Tariq Hashimi for
terrorist offences, and with even Maliki's deputy prime minister Saleh
al-Mutlaq warning that Iraq was spiralling into a dictatorship with a 'one
party show and a one man show'.[28]

IRAQ – THE EMERGING ISLAMIC STATE

Of the 'national jihadist' Sunni groups able to form and expand in the
sectarian crucible of post-2003 Iraq, the most significant was that led by
Ahmad Fadhil al-Kalaylah – a Jordanian from Zarqa, near Amman, who
went by the *nom de guerre* of Abu Musab al-Zarqawi.[29] After suffering a
troubled youth involving drugs and crime, his mother had enrolled him
in various religious courses, and he had eventually left Jordan in 1989
to join the final phase of the Afghan jihad.[30] Meeting with Gulbuddin

Hekmatyar and others, including the editors of jihadist magazines, he trained at some of the biggest al-Qaeda camps before returning to Jordan at some point in either 1992 or 1993.[31] Having then met and been inspired by Abu Muhammad al-Maqdisi, the author of a prominent jihadist text entitled *Democracy: A Religion*, he went on to take part in a number of poorly planned terrorist operations that led to the capture and imprisonment of both men.[32]

Released in 1999 following a mass amnesty, al-Zarqawi had gone back to Afghanistan before then being involved in the failed 'Millennium Plot' at the end of the year to blow up a hotel and two Christian sites in Jordan.[33] During this second trip to Afghanistan he met with al-Qaeda's leadership and received a $200,000 'start-up grant' to set up a camp in Herat so that he could train up Jordanian, Syrian, and Palestinian fighters within his network. Importantly even at this stage Osama bin Laden was understood to have expressed reservations about al-Zarqawi due to the latter's apparent closeness to scholars who favoured 'national jihads' for fighters returning home, rather than al-Qaeda's grander vision of the global jihad.[34] Moreover, al-Zarqawi's fast growing organization, by this stage known as *Al-Tawhid wa al-Jihad* or 'Monotheism and Jihad', had reportedly not yet pledged full allegiance to al-Qaeda due to *Al-Tawhid's* 'stricter theology' and more fervent sectarianism. In a letter later written to bin Laden, al-Zarqawi even tried to persuade him that the Shia were the primary enemy, rather than the US, as they were an 'insurmountable obstacle, the lurking snake, the crafty and malicious scorpion, the spying enemy, and the penetrating venom'. Prophesizing the region's future, he also wrote of how sectarian warfare could be a useful mechanism for 'awaking inattentive Sunnis' to the prospect of 'imminent danger and annihilating death' at the hands of Shia governments.[35]

Despite its misgivings over such sectarian rhetoric, with Ayman Zawahiri contending that Shia could be forgiven for their 'theological errors', and bin Laden's mother after all being a Syrian Alawite from Latakia, al-Qaeda continued to recognize al-Zarqawi's group in what was something of a 'marriage of convenience'. As some suggest, this was likely because bin Laden feared that potential rivals such as the 'Londonistan' veteran Abu Musab al-Suri would otherwise be able to recruit from the same pool.[36]

With his men having fought alongside al-Qaeda units after the US invasion of Afghanistan, in early 2003 al-Zarqawi then moved through Iran to
prepare resistance cells in the event of a US invasion of Iraq. Corroborating
much of this, US Department of the Treasury statements and papers
later discovered in bin Laden's Pakistani hideout have described how
al-Zarqawi's forces along with al-Qaeda units led by Syrian jihadist Yasin
al-Suri had been allowed to train in Iran for months.[37] With al-Zarqawi
seemingly able to put a temporary hold on his anti-Shia views, Jordanian
intelligence has described how he even received weapons and equipment
while in Iran before taking these with him to a jihadist Kurdish enclave
in Iraq run by the 'Islamic Movement of Iraqi Kurdistan' and then later
a group called *Ansar al-Islam* or 'Helpers of Islam'.[38] Understood to have
received funding from Saudi Arabia, *Ansar al-Islam* had also been designated as eligible for US covert aid on the basis it was a potential threat
to Saddam. Moreover, its representatives were known to have met with
Britain's minister of state for foreign affairs and it continued to operate
an office in London until the beginning of 2003, despite the BBC having
reported it as commanding 'an armed militia of several hundred men'.[39]

Outgrowing *Ansar al-Islam*, by 2004 al-Zarqawi had renamed his forces
'al-Qaeda in the land of the two rivers', or more simply 'al-Qaeda in Iraq',
and thus appeared to have finally given his full allegiance to bin Laden.[40]
However, this was understood to have needed lengthy negotiations and
may have been as much about al-Zarqawi sending a signal of resistance to
the US – which had stated only two weeks earlier that al-Zarqawi was not
linked to al-Qaeda – as any meaningful rapprochement with al-Qaeda's
core leadership. Certainly, the policy gap on sectarian tactics was as wide
as ever, with AQI apparently more interested in perpetrating mass attacks
on Iraqi Shia and Christians than attacking US forces. Furthermore, AQI
seemed more than willing to kill civilians using suicide attacks – a strategy
that earned al-Zarqawi the nickname 'Sheikh of the Slaughterers' – and
began to pioneer the filming and distribution of beheading videos.[41]
According to the CIA, it was al-Zarqawi himself who chopped off the head
of captured American radio engineer Nicholas Berg.[42]

As the black sheep of al-Qaeda, AQI soon came in for heavy criticism,
with al-Zarqawi's former mentor al-Maqdisi urging his protégé to scale back

attacks on civilians and to stop indiscriminately using *takfir* – a practice that sanctioned the killing of apostates and which had already been censured by bin Laden's mentor, Abdullah Azzam.[43] Intercepted by US forces, a letter supposedly sent by Zawahiri to al-Zarqawi urged AQI to refocus on winning the hearts and minds of the Iraqi population and argued that the fight against the Shia 'could wait'. Zawahiri also warned al-Zarqawi that his reputation for brutality was becoming bad for al-Qaeda's public relations.[44] In 2005 bin Laden himself is thought have issued a 'furious response' after learning of AQI's role in a triple suicide bombing in Jordan in which innocent wedding guests in a hotel were killed.[45] Despite such cleavages, however, the White House was merely framing AQI as a simple subordinate to bin Laden, with George W. Bush referring to declassified intelligence indicating that 'the merger [between the two groups] gave al-Qaeda's senior leadership a foothold in Iraq to extend its geographic presence.' He also claimed that 'the same folks that are bombing innocent people in Iraq are the same ones who attacked us in America on 11 September.' Reporting on these statements the *New York Times* nonetheless acknowledged that 'the White House and intelligence officials declined to provide any detail on the reports Mr Bush cited.'[46]

Notwithstanding bin Laden and Zawahiri's concerns, and despite his divisively gruesome methods, by 2006 al-Zarqawi had managed to succeed where others had failed, by having brought together several previously disparate jihadist groups in Iraq under one umbrella. With the town of Baqubah as its de facto capital, AQI had been able to establish a central council and – mindful of the need to reduce the perceived influence of foreigners in its ranks – made sure that it was under the nominal leadership of Iraqis.[47] Soon after, it released a video message stating that 'we hope to God that within three months from now the environment will be favourable for us to announce an Islamic emirate.'[48] In this sense, although dying just two months later following a US air strike on an AQI safe house in Baghdad, al-Zarqawi had already begun to lay some of the foundations for a more sectarian, national jihadist alternative to al-Qaeda that could commit to fighting near enemies and which seemed willing to form the sort of governmental structures needed to preside over an eventual Islamic state.

IRAQ – THE PROTO-CALIPHATE

Pressing ahead without Abu Musab al-Zarqawi, the new jihadist federation or 'Alliance of the Scented Ones' began to follow through on its promises and established the 'Islamic State in Iraq' by the end of 2006. It also set up a cabinet of ministers and even an official media agency, *Furqan*. Creating further tension with al-Qaeda's core leadership, which still saw state-building as part of a more idealized and long-term vision rather than an immediate goal, the new ISI also declared itself a 'proto-caliphate' on the basis that the territory it governed was comparable in size to the Prophet Muhammad's first Islamic state in Medina. As one of its founders explained, ISI's birth symbolized 'the end of a stage of jihad and the start of a new one, in which we lay the first cornerstone of the Islamic caliphate project and revive the glory of religion.'[49]

Problematically, however, this was a time when the Sunni insurgency in Iraq was losing momentum, not least due to the US's short-lived efforts to realign the Anbari tribes with the Baghdad government, which had temporarily robbed it of at least some of its natural recruitment pool.[50] As Princeton University's Cole Bunzel describes, the Islamic state project soon began to stumble, proving unable to offer Sunni Iraqis the same sort of autonomous powers that the Kurds in northern Iraq or the Shia in southern Iraq already seemed to be enjoying.[51] As Charles Lister puts it, its leaders had become 'overzealous and alienating' and had 'overestimated their capacity to engender Sunni support'.[52] Territorially the proto-caliphate was also contracting, as although it hung on to small enclaves and fiefdoms, including the town of Al-Tarmia, it was clearly having to retreat from some of its bigger strongholds.[53] Moreover, al-Zarqawi's alliance-building seemed to be posthumously unravelling, with major groups withdrawing from ISI or simply refusing to join. The 'Islamic Army of Iraq', for example, even began to appeal directly to Osama bin Laden to 'restrain his affiliate'.

Many of ISI's rank-and-file fighters also started to drift away simply because they had seen the original organization as a vehicle for liberating Iraq from the US and Shia, rather than as a staging post towards building a caliphate. Some of its members entered into talks with the Iraqi government and even publicly denounced ISI, perhaps helping explain why thirty-four of ISI's forty-two senior commanders ended up being killed or captured in a series of successful government raids. Muddying the waters further, elements of ISI were also understood to have had contacts and patrons within the distinctly secular Syrian regime. As journalists Michael Weiss and Hassan Hassan point out, an abundance of testimonies exist indicating how Bashar al-Assad, perhaps fearing the same fate as Saddam Hussein, had done all he could to jeopardize the US occupation of Iraq. This, so it seems, had led to Damascus facilitating the flow of jihadist fighters into Iraq and, at least until 2009, offering AQI and then ISI members sanctuary in Syrian territory.[54] To some extent this relationship has been corroborated by a 2011 US Court of Appeals judgement which confirmed that the Syrian government was liable to be sued for damages by the families of two US contractors beheaded in Iraq some years before. Notably the court proceedings stated that Syrian officials were understood to have provided material support and resources to both AQI and ISI.[55]

THE ISLAMIC STATE - MYSTERIOUS NEW LEADERSHIP

With the Islamic State in Iraq seemingly in tatters, at first glance the prospects for a powerful 'national jihadist' alternative to al-Qaeda in Iraq appeared greatly diminished. Most intelligence analysts forecasted its future as being 'bleak' in 2010, while US officials claimed its leaders were little more than fictional characters and that it had 'lost any semblance of statehood'.[56] Behind the scenes, however, nothing could be further from the truth, with ISI having already begun to recast itself around a much more advanced and better organized new leadership that was carefully and quietly preparing to take the organization far beyond the limited capabilities of the brutish Abu Musab al-Zarqawi or his ineffective successors.

At the heart of this discreet resurgence was an Iraqi man called Ibrahim Awwad Ibrahim al-Badri al-Sammarrai from the town of Samarra on the banks of the river Tigris, north of Baghdad. Little is known of his background other than the information provided by his official ISI biographer,[57] but by piecing together snippets that have appeared in a number of recent studies, a slightly clearer picture has begun to emerge. Apparently the son of a Qur'anic teacher, he eventually moved to Tobchi, a poor area in east Baghdad, and began to serve as a children's prayer leader and then as a stand-in preacher whenever the cleric was away.[58] Later becoming a preacher in his own right back in Samarra, under the name 'Sheikh Ibrahim', and gaining the nickname 'The Believer' given the seriousness of his disposition, he had then begun to study for a master's degree at the Saddam University of Islamic Studies in Baghdad's Adhamiya district.[59] Remaining at the university while taking on another preaching position at a mosque in Diyala province, north of Baghdad, he is understood to have commenced a PhD. Described rather vaguely in his official biography as being in 'Islamic law', others have suggested the doctorate was actually in the rare field of Qur'anic phonetics and Qur'anic recitation.[60]

Ibrahim's politicization seems to have begun at some point during his academic studies, having been encouraged by an influential academic to read Sayyid Qutb's work and then having been persuaded by one of his uncles to join the Iraqi branch of the Muslim Brotherhood. At some point in 2000, however, after having been mentored by a more jihadist-inclined member of the Brotherhood who had served in the Afghan campaign, it seems Ibrahim chose to leave the organization on the grounds that it was only 'about words, not actions'.[61] Moving from Baghdad to the town of Qaim in Anbar province after the US-led invasion in 2003, he became much more involved in militant activities, taking on the *nom de guerre* 'Abu Dua' and likely associating himself with Sunni insurgent groups such as al-Zarqawi's original network and perhaps also a group called *Jaysh Ansar al-Sunna* or 'Army of the Sunni People'.[62]

At some point in 2004 it is widely accepted that Ibrahim was captured, interrogated at Abu Ghraib prison, and then incarcerated at a US camp in southern Iraq named Bucca, so-called after Ronald Bucca who was one of the American fire marshals who had been killed trying to rescue victims of the 9/11 attacks.[63] According to a supposedly senior ISI commander later interviewed by the *Guardian*, this was where he had first met Ibrahim, who was understood to have been arrested by US forces along with a few other suspects who have since been described elsewhere as 'al-Qaeda affiliated friends in Fallujah'.[64] This version of events has largely been corroborated by a widely circulating US detainee personnel record form that seems to match Ibrahim's description and lists his arrest date as February 2004, although it only describes him as a 'civilian detainee' despite him having been arrested alongside known insurgents.[65]

According to the *Guardian*'s interviewee, most prisoners seemed to defer to Ibrahim, even though he had only been there a short while, and he seemed to have a good reputation among the American prison guards on the basis that he was able to calm other prisoners down and resolve disputes. This may explain why he was 'respected very much by the US Army' and seemed to have special privileges, with the interviewee claiming that if Ibrahim 'wanted to visit people in another camp he could, but we couldn't'. Intriguingly, the interviewee also described how Ibrahim was 'the opposite to the other [jihadist leaders] ... he was remote, far from us all' but that at the same time he 'clearly wanted to be the head of the prison, and involved at the centre of every problem'.[66]

Much of this narrative has been backed up by the claims made by another former Bucca prisoner, later interviewed by Abdel Bari Atwan, who explained that Ibrahim was allowed to give classes and lectures to other prisoners.[67] Similarly, the US major general who eventually became responsible for Bucca has since reflected that Ibrahim 'must have been plotting while he was incarcerated – he must have planned the whole rollout of the Islamic State.' He also speculated that Ibrahim was deliberately placed there as some sort of infiltrator to recruit new ISI members, especially from the ranks of the former Iraqi army, and that Bucca had been running as a 'jihadist university', with most new inmates seeming to have 'foreknowledge of how the prison worked', and one of the large cells being openly referred to as 'Camp Caliphate'.[68]

Others have made much the same point, with the *Guardian*'s interviewee claiming that Bucca had become a de facto networking hub, and that everyone wrote the contact details of their new friends on the elastic of their underwear so that they could all reconnect after their release. This inmate explained that it would have been impossible for so many likeminded jihadists and insurgents to have met together safely in Iraq at that time without such a protective environment as Bucca.[69] Another former prisoner has since described how 'Camp Bucca was a great favor the US did to the mujahideen' on the basis that 'they provided us with a secure atmosphere, a bed and food, and also allowed books giving us a great opportunity to feed our knowledge with the ideas of al-Maqdisi and the jihadist ideology.' As he put it, 'this was under the watchful eye of the US soldiers. New recruits were prepared so that when they were freed they were ticking time bombs.'[70]

Details surrounding Ibrahim's release from Bucca are just as hazy as his entry, with Atwan's interviewee suggesting he was held until 2006, while a former US Army officer claims he was there right up to 2009 when the camp was finally shut down and most detainees were transferred to the Iraqi authorities.[71] Much more plausible, however, is the *Guardian* interviewee's claim that Ibrahim was released in December 2004, only ten months after his arrival.[72] Indeed, this version has since been confirmed by both the US Department of Defense and Hisham al-Hashemi, a consultant to the Iraqi government. Rather incongruously, but seemingly in an effort to explain such a light sentence, an anonymous US official later told the *New York Times* that Ibrahim was considered little more than a 'hanger on' and a 'street thug'.[73] This description of Ibrahim as such a low-value target is not only strangely at odds with Ibrahim's known prominence within Bucca, but is also jarring given the accounts of a journalist who managed to interview Ibrahim's former university colleagues and found out that the US had also arrested a number of Ibrahim's relatives, including his in-laws, on the basis of their kinship links to him.[74]

Either way, released from prison Ibrahim was quickly able to resume his rise within Iraqi jihadist circles. Having successfully defended his PhD thesis, he also co-founded his own organization, known as 'Assembly of the Helpers of Sunnah', which was understood to have been active in the insurgencies in Samarra, Diyala, and Baghdad. After al-Zarqawi's demise, it came under the umbrella of the new ISI, with Ibrahim himself being appointed as an ISI judge in 2006 or 2007. Serving on ISI's sharia law committee and then also its powerful coordination committee – which was able to hire and fire ISI commanders – Ibrahim soon emerged as the organization's deputy leader. Legitimized by his time in Bucca, he was well regarded for both his excellent organizational skills and his command of 'exquisite classical Arabic', and was also understood to have played a key role in preparing an influential and future-focused text called the *Strategic plan to improve the political position of the Islamic State in Iraq*.[75]

Tipped for succession, within a few more years Ibrahim's golden opportunity arose following the deaths of ISI's two co-leaders, who were killed in April 2010 after an ISI captive had revealed to the authorities the location of their safe house in the Tharhar region near Tikrit. There are some important inconsistencies concerning the episode given that the two men were reportedly found 'hiding in a secret basement accessible only through a door underneath the kitchen sink' – circumstances which one would expect to have led to arrests rather than assassinations. Moreover, according to former US Department of State senior adviser William McCants, a mole within Iraqi intelligence had already tipped off Ibrahim about the captive's confession, but Ibrahim had 'failed to pass along the warning to his two ISI leaders'.[76]

With Ibrahim far ahead of his rivals to fill the sudden leadership vacuum, former ISI members have since described how by this time his tribal origins had also begun to come into play. With his home Al-Bu Badri tribe claiming descent from the powerful Quraysh tribe that had controlled Mecca at the time of the Prophet Muhammad's birth, Ibrahim could claim lineage from the very clan which, according to tradition, will produce the next Sunni caliph. With many of his followers duly appending al-Qurayshi to his name, and with Ibrahim taking on the new *nom de guerre* of Abu Bakr al-Baghdidi, even though he was not from Baghdad, he seemed to be signalling his intent not only to rule ISI but also to forge a new caliphate based in Baghdad that could then follow in the path of the first caliph, Abu Bakr al-Siddiq.[77] With purportedly much better ancestral credentials for spiritual leadership than al-Qaeda-endorsed clerics such as Mullah Omar, who had first declared himself as commander of the faithful in 1996 after draping himself in the Prophet Muhammad's cloak, al-Baghdadi seemed to have finally emerged as a serious alternative to Osama bin Laden and Ayman Zawahiri. Indeed, nine out of the eleven members of ISI's central council voted for his succession in preference to bin Laden's preferred candidate, and of the two that voted against one was killed very shortly afterwards.[78]

As one of the former Bucca inmates has explained, the networks al-Baghdadi had built in 2004 and then continued to nurture suddenly became important again after his ISI takeover, with 'the roles vacated [by the two abruptly killed leaders] quickly filled by the alumni of Camp Bucca'. As he claimed, '[Al-Baghdadi's] upper echelons had been preparing for this moment since their time behind the wire of their jail.'[79] For those still in prison, al-Baghdadi also had a plan, as many had been moved from Bucca to the former US prisons in Abu Ghraib, Tikrit, and in Taji – all of which by then were being administered by the Iraqi government. Organizing a stunning breakout in September 2012, ISI was able to free more than a hundred from Tikrit, including an estimated fifty ISI members. Several suicide bombers were believed to have been deployed, while hundreds of mortar rounds were fired at the prison defences.[80] Less than a year later, in an operation named 'Breaking the Walls', ISI managed to do it again, launching simultaneous attacks on Abu Ghraib and Taji. This time, according to Reuters and the BBC, a staggering five hundred prisoners were somehow able to flee.[81]

THE ISLAMIC STATE – A PERSUASIVE IDEOLOGY

As well as introducing comprehensive strategic plans and preparing the Islamic State in Iraq for a much more expansionary future, Abu Bakr al-Baghdadi's rise through the ranks also coincided with the organization's transition into an 'ideologically driven entity par excellence'.[82] Having substantially evolved from the simplistic and thuggish concepts that underpinned the Abu Musab al-Zarqawi regime, the new ISI was not only becoming a strategic rival to al-Qaeda and – with the increasing prominence of al-Baghdadi – offering a personal challenge to the authority of al-Qaeda's leaders, but was also turning into a serious theological alternative.

At first glance, ISI seemed little different to other jihadist organizations, albeit with a stronger flair for sectarian violence and, by 2010 at least, a stronger emphasis on building up a new caliphate. As one study put it, 'If ever there was a familiar foe, the Islamic State was it.'[83] As with al-Qaeda, it appeared to subscribe to much the same sort of Salafi-jihadism which is essentially 'an extremist and minoritarian reading of Islamic scripture that is also textually rigorous, deeply rooted in a pre-modern theological tradition'. Moreover, given its focus on tradition, Salafi-jihadism also seeks to halt the idolatrous worship of false gods and the work of those 'seeking to dilute religious law with manmade law, including those promulgated by democratic legislatures'.[84] As Utrecht University's Joas Wagemakers explains, ISI and its comparators essentially offered 'a more extremist and violent interpretation of Salafism, which is often thought of as an emulation of the first three generations of Muslims – known as the *salaf*'.[85]

In many ways ISI's ideology was also not that much different to conservative Sunni states in the region, and especially those such as Saudi

Arabia and Qatar where, as noted, Wahhabi thought continues to influence heavily their religious establishments. Given ISI's origins as a national jihadist organization and its professed aims of conquering and governing territories, this should come as little surprise as the ruling dynasties of both these monarchies first gained and held onto power by co-opting powerful and deeply traditionalist religious forces that were then successfully wielded against battlefield rivals. Certainly many of ISI's statements have been described as simply long quotations from Wahhabi scholars, including Saudi preachers. Even a number of ISI's 'in-house scholars' were thought to be from the Gulf monarchies, with the influential ISI preacher Turki al-Bin'ali hailing from Bahrain and having claimed that ISI is the 'true inheritor of the Wahhabi movement'.[86] As Princeton University's Bernard Haykel argues, 'It's a kind of untamed Wahhabism ... Wahhabism is the closest religious cognate [to ISI].'[87]

Penning a controversial article entitled 'You can't understand the Islamic State if you don't know the history of Saudi Arabia', retired MI6 officer Alastair Crooke also likened the group's ideologically driven foot soldiers in Iraq to the old Saudi-Wahhabi *Ikhwan* militia.[88] Arguing that its jihadists were 'a neo-*Ikhwan* type of violent, fear-inducing vanguard movement', he effectively updated earlier claims made by historian Assem Akram that the previous generation of jihadists who had gone to fight in the Afghan campaign were best understood as '*ikhwahhabis*'.[89] Making much the same point, as ISI seemed to be expanding fast, the *Financial Times'* David Gardner described its fighters as being 'Wahhabis on steroids'.[90] Naturally such accusations were publicly met with horror and indignation by Saudi and Qatari officials; however, the perception of ISI's ideology, if not its methods, among ordinary citizens in these countries is somewhat murkier. Foreign diplomats, for example, reported seeing ISI car stickers in affluent districts of Doha, while according to an online poll published by the London-based *Al-Hayat* newspaper, ninety-two percent of Saudis surveyed on social media expressed the belief that ISI 'conformed to the values of Islam and Islamic law'. Although a Saudi government spokesperson did question the poll's methodology and claimed the findings were 'inaccurate and exaggerated', a number of other Arab news sites continued to report on it.[91] As a recent Brookings Institute 'Islamic State Twitter Census' revealed, by far the largest number of tweets in support of ISI seemed to originate from Saudi Arabia.[92] As Abdel Bari Atwan contends, such an obviously powerful resonance with ISI's extremism in the kingdom is readily understandable given that all Saudi children, even today, are required to study Wahhabi texts that many scholars believe are promoting and justifying jihad and militant Islam.[93]

In an important difference with Wahhabism and, for that matter, al-Qaeda's relatively more pedestrian interpretation of Salafi-jihadism, ISI arguably made itself even more appealing to its fighters and followers by also adopting many of the tenets of a seductive text entitled *Idarat al-Tawahhush* or 'The Management of Savagery'. Penned in 2004 by Abu Bakr Naji – the nom de plume of an Egyptian jihadist – and clearly read and absorbed by al-Baghdadi, al-Bin'ali and other ISI luminaries, the central thesis was that the Muslim world was having to pass through its most dangerous period, and in order for it to survive and form the nucleus of a new caliphate its leaders would have to manipulate local instabilities and vacuums before then setting up a functioning Islamic state. Along the way, Naji foresaw that supporters of the caliphate would have to engage in a certain amount of savagery and public violence so as to disrupt, exhaust, and dehumanize their opponents, while simultaneously boosting recruitment to the cause and eroding any resistance in their own support base to carrying out acts of violence. As recent studies have explained, much of Naji's thinking seems to have been drawn from the work of fourteenth-century scholar Taqi al-Din Ahmad ibn Taymiyyah, who in turn became another mascot for ISI. Predating Muhammad Abd al-Wahhab by hundreds of years, Ibn Taymiyyah had written of the need to revive 'true Islam' in the face of corruption, assassinations, and Mongol invasions.[94] After taking part in expeditions against the Syrian Alawites, who he considered 'more heretical than Jews or Christians', he also advocated both a substantial dose of violence against the Shia along with the suitably ISI-compatible policy of excommunication.[95]

OPPORTUNITIES IN SYRIA

With the Syrian conflict erupting less than a year after Abu Bakr al-Baghdadi's succession, and with the subsequent collapse in state authority across huge sections of the country, the Islamic State in Iraq's first major opportunity to exploit an Abu Bakr Naji-style vacuum and 'manage savagery' had seemingly arisen, even if it was not in Iraq itself. Rebranding itself as 'Islamic State in Iraq and al-Sham' or 'Islamic State in Iraq and the Levant', to reflect its greater reach, from mid-2013 the expansionary ISIS soon made easy cross-border gains, being either welcomed or quickly overwhelming Sunni tribes in lawless eastern Syria. In some cases these tribes wanted to use their ISIS backing to exact revenge on old enemies, while with others al-Baghdadi moved quickly to strike deals with younger leaders when support from elders was not forthcoming.[96] Many of these rural Syrians had more or less been left to their own devices under Bashar al-Assad, and some of the same tribes that had publicly pledged allegiance to him during his last visit to the region in 2011 were among the first to switch to ISIS two years later.[97]

Soon running up against al-Qaeda's *Jabhat al-Nusra* franchise, however, things became more complicated as ISIS was essentially trying to take over the same parts of Syria as its jihadist rivals. Opting to bluff it out, in January 2014 al-Baghdadi ordered ISIS units to enter and take complete control of the northern city of Al-Raqqah. Any remaining *Al-Nusra* forces were to be absorbed into ISIS on the basis that the *Al-Nusra* leader Muhammad al-Jowlani was 'one of the Islamic State's soldiers who had been sent on a secret mission to Syria'. In fact, there was some truth to this, as it seems al-Jowlani had travelled to Iraq after Bashar's 2011 prison amnesty and had briefly served as the ISI governor of Iraq's Nineveh province. Some have claimed he was also a veteran of the earlier Iraq insurgencies and had been incarcerated at Bucca, just like al-Baghdadi, after being misidentified as an Iraqi. Regardless of his true career history, in 2013 al-Jowlani saw himself still on the rise and better able to prosper as a semi-autonomous al-Qaeda chief than as an al-Baghdadi subordinate. Rejecting the encroachment of ISIS into Syria and reaffirming *Al-Nusra*'s allegiance to al-Qaeda's core leadership, al-Jowlani effectively sparked one of the greatest disputes within the jihadist community, with supporters soon dividing themselves into either ISIS loyalists or those objecting to al-Baghdadi's dangerous defiance of Ayman Zawahiri and the Osama bin Laden legacy.[98]

Writing to both protagonists, Zawahiri initially tried to apportion blame equally, but ultimately demanded that ISIS be disbanded and revert back to the old Iraq-focused ISI, while *Al-Nusra* would be left to concentrate on Syria.[99] Refusing this apparently unrealistic solution, al-Baghdadi is understood to have made several key points that not only cemented the status of ISIS as a full-blown al-Qaeda rival but which also, so it seems, helped him to win over enormous popular support. Rather poignantly he argued that Zawahiri's insistence on recognizing the artificial state boundaries between Iraq and Syria, imposed by Britain and France nearly a century earlier, was an affront to Islam.[100] Secondly he argued that because he himself had never pledged allegiance to Zawahiri after bin Laden's death, ISIS was already beyond al-Qaeda's authority and thus not responsible for following its various guidelines.[101] Most provocatively, a few months later one of al-Baghdadi's deputies also accused al-Qaeda of having tolerated and collaborated with Iran and the Shia for many years. Based on a sizeable grain of truth, this third salvo was a pointed reference to an unpopular letter purportedly sent by Zawahiri to Abu Musab al-Zarqawi warning him of 'mutually assured destruction' should Iran ever be attacked.[102] With ISIS's spokesman declaring that 'al-Qaeda today is no longer the true seat of jihad, its leadership has become an axe trying to destroy the project of the Islamic State and the coming caliphate,' and with ISIS's in-house magazine stating that 'Zawahiri has abandoned the true heritage left by Sheikh Osama,' there seemed to be no turning back.[103] Having assassinated Zawahiri's personal emissary to Syria in early 2014, ISIS was soon branded 'seditious', and in a rather desperate audio message the increasingly isolated al-Qaeda leader declared something of an empty war on his powerful new rivals.[104]

With the pushback against Zawahiri proving enough to keep *Al-Nusra* on the back foot, ISIS was largely left to consolidate its hold over Al-Raqqah. Not only a valuable asset, given its status as a provincial capital and its proximity to vast tracts of fertile farmland, the city also held great symbolism for ISIS. Having been an important summer residence for the first Abbasid Caliphate, and sometimes used by its fifth caliph, Harun al-Rashid, its ancient buildings, including some of the old caliphal walls, made it a particularly suitable Syrian base for the organization.[105] Already used to *Al-Nusra*, most residents seemingly welcomed ISIS's commitment to basic law and order, providing much needed stability to urban and peasant communities that had long been marginalized by the Syrian government and whose businesses had suffered greatly from the cheap imports that had previously flooded across the Turkish border.[106]

Given the criminal acts now known to have been committed by the Free Syrian Army and other non-jihadist rebel groups, ISIS was also well placed to expand elsewhere in the country, including areas close to the city of Aleppo. According to one account, the arrival of ISIS in Manbij, a town previously under FSA control, saw 'Syrians flocking in large numbers to join the jihadist group or work with it at a local level ... for the local community the difference was quickly felt: ISIS provided safety and security; its methods of justice were swift, and nobody was exempt from punishment, including its own fighters'. As a resident described, 'The reason why people support the Islamic State is its honesty and practices compared to the corruption of most of the FSA groups.'[107] Meanwhile, an elderly inhabitant of Deir Ezzor, closer to the Iraqi border, described how he had never felt as safe in twenty years, and as Bradford University's Paul Rogers has claimed, there were actually net refugee flows into ISIS's Syrian territory due to 'routine living conditions actually [being] safer in and around Al-Raqqah than in chaotic and violent districts nearby that ISIS does not control'.[108]

Former FSA commanders have added more to the picture, explaining how ISIS vanguards would immediately disarm local communities and forbid the public display of weapons. They also set about dismantling checkpoints or at least making it possible to drive from one city to another again without having to pay bribes.[109] Interviewed by the *Daily Telegraph*, and then later by the author, a seemingly apolitical Syrian businessman who described himself as 'largely secular' freely revealed that he had chosen to trade almost exclusively in ISIS-held areas. Although this meant he had to pay ISIS's 'fastidiously collected taxes', he nonetheless benefited from ISIS's prevention of theft and corruption. Similarly, several other businessmen and residents in the Aleppo region reported that owners of factories were moving their facilities to ISIS-held areas, attracted by lower crime, greater efficiency and, as one explained, because 'you can find everything from cotton to iron and plastics being processed here.'[110] Making much the same point, a Syrian labourer interviewed by the *New York Times* praised ISIS for having 'got rid of the tyranny of the Arab rulers' while a townsman remarked that the arrival of the group's religious teachers had convinced him there was more to life than wanting to be rich.[111]

EXPANSION IN IRAQ

Although far from suffering the sort of security vacuum present in Syria, Iraq by this stage had conditions that were almost equally conducive for the Islamic State in Iraq and al-Sham to push beyond its original strongholds. Convinced of fresh plots against his Iran-leaning administration orchestrated by Sunni states in the region, Nouri Maliki's administration had retreated even further into sectarian politics, arguably raising Sunni–Shia tensions to levels not seen since the Abu Musab al-Zarqawi insurgency. Certainly, worried that Iraq was now firmly in Iran's hands, the Gulf monarchies did little to disguise their opposition to the Baghdad regime. As Fouad Ajami suggested, 'the Gulf autocracies had hunkered down and done their best to thwart the new Iraqi project' and were hoping to turn Maliki's Iraq into a 'cautionary tale of the folly of unseating even the worst of despots'.[112] Firing back at his perceived enemies, and clearly holding them responsible for the resurgence of Sunni extremism, Maliki publicly stated that Saudi Arabia and Qatar were 'the two countries primarily responsible for the sectarian, terrorist, and security crisis in Iraq'. He also claimed, although without substantiation, that along with supplying weapons they were 'providing political, financial, and media support to terrorist fighters'.[113]

In this context ordinary Iraqi Sunnis were effectively caught between a rock and a hard place, with peaceful rallies against social injustice and economic discrimination in 2012 having led nowhere, and with protest encampments in the predominantly Sunni town of Hawija being broken up in mid-2013 by government troops. Black al-Qaeda flags had supposedly been spotted in the town, but the consensus is that dozens or perhaps even hundreds of civilians ended up being killed.[114] Despite calls from the parliamentary speaker for Maliki to resign, government forces followed up on Hawija by shelling the Sunni-majority towns of Ramadi and Fallujah, and by the end of the year Maliki was claiming such operations were part of an 'ancient sectarian war, invoking seventh century characters'.[115]

Making matters worse, the Maliki administration had also resumed the process of squeezing out remaining Sunni ministers, having arrested more than 150 of the staff working for Finance Minister Raif al-Issawi, and, so it seemed, being prepared to draw the *Badr* organization even closer into his circle of power.[116] Appointing Hadi al-Amiri as his new transport minister, a *Badr* member who had once fought on the side of Iran in the Iran–Iraq War, Maliki had effectively given Tehran the green light to use Iraqi infrastructure to channel supplies and fighters through the country to fight in Syria. By its own admission, in 2014 the *Badr* organization was fielding fifteen hundred of its own men in Syria and was helping Shia Afghan militants travel from Iran to the combat zones.[117] Most dangerously, reports also began to circulate of *Badr* and other Shia militia working alongside government troops and, according to a lengthy Amnesty International investigation, even taking part in coordinated or joint operations in the most restive Sunni areas.[118] By summer 2014, with more than sixty worshippers killed by such forces at a Sunni mosque in Diyala, and with leading Sunni clerics who had previously urged non-violent protests instead stating that 'self-defence has become a religious and legal duty, so defend yourselves and he who will be killed defending his money, family, or country will be considered a martyr,' the scene seemed to be set for far more serious confrontation.[119]

With everything in his favour, Abu Bakr al-Baghdadi had naturally already begun to make his move, with ISIS having quickly taken control over Fallujah earlier in the year along with several other smaller towns and villages. But it was the stunning capture of Mosul in June 2014 – Iraq's second largest city and home to over two million – that really announced ISIS's arrival. Exactly how ISIS managed to overwhelm such numerically superior government forces and enter the city so smoothly is still unclear, with some claiming they were 'accidental occupiers' and with even ISIS supporters apparently 'flabbergasted'.[120] But the victory really seems to have been the result of several months of preparations involving numerous diversionary 'feint attacks' on other Iraqi towns, along with a long-running effort – known grimly as 'Operation Soldiers' Harvest' – to degrade Mosul's security services and intimidate or assassinate its officials.[121] Either way, a force of over thirty thousand Iraqi troops comprising two divisions and various police units was swept aside almost effortlessly by two ISIS battalions thought to have been made up of less than thirteen hundred men.[122]

ISIS's task was likely made easier by rampant corruption within the Iraqi military, with as many as two thirds of the city's defenders believed to have been absent from their posts after having paid off commanding officers in return for semi-permanent leave. Moreover, ISIS appeared to have already been operating a shadow government in Mosul, with Turkish contractors working in the city having complained earlier in the year of having to pay taxes to both local officials and a 'local emir', and others reporting taxes being collected by ISIS on everything from mobile phones to vegetables. Also to ISIS's advantage was a sense that a significant proportion of Mosul's population actually welcomed the group's presence, with reports of Sunni civilians overrunning the barracks of predominantly Shia government soldiers, seemingly in tandem with ISIS. Local residents meanwhile described how the situation in Mosul quickly became 'quite calm' as '[ISIS] seem to be courteous with the people and they protect all the government establishments against looters.'[123] Far from invaders, Abdel Bari Atwan even claims that ISIS's vehicles were greeted by cheering crowds as they raced into the city centre.[124]

Consolidating their grip on the city, as they had done over Al-Raqqah, ISIS seemed well aware of the need to avoid the sort of 'asphyxiating mode of jihadist governance' once associated with al-Zarqawi's followers. Telling its fighters to 'accept repentance from those who are sincere ... forgive your Sunni folk, and be gentle with your tribes', the ISIS leadership also instructed them not to wear uniforms or carry arms in central Mosul so as not to alarm residents, and even instructed them to absorb former Iraqi army officers into ISIS's ranks provided that they paid an $850 'repentance fee'.[125] Although a BBC documentary broadcast several months later aimed to portray ISIS's occupation of Mosul as unpopular and responsible for a poorly performing municipality, its strangely wobbly but high-definition video footage of empty classrooms with perfectly arranged chairs, along with scenes of piled-up refuse bags no different to those one might see in almost any other town, was unconvincing at best and dubiously propagandistic at worst.[126] Instead the reality was perhaps that, for the Sunni majority at least, ISIS was a much better alternative than the increasingly sectarian, corrupt, and discriminatory government forces. As a Mosul resident told the *New York Times* only a few days after the suspicious BBC programme came out, 'Now there is more security and freedom, no arrests, no harassment, no concrete barriers and no checkpoints where we used to spend hours to get into the city.'[127]

THE CALIPHATE RESTORED

Firmly in control of major Syrian and Iraqi cities along with thousands of square miles of contiguous territory, governing a population of millions, and claiming allegiance from more than eighty Sunni tribes, by the end of June 2014 Abu Bakr al-Baghdadi was ready for the next step of the plan. With a spokesman declaring on the first day of Ramadan that the caliphate had been restored, a few days later it was announced that the Islamic State in Iraq and al-Sham would henceforth simply be known as 'the Islamic State'. Al-Raqqah would be its capital, as it had briefly been for the Abbasids, and al-Baghdadi would serve as its caliph.[128] Conveniently for the enemies of the Arab Spring, it was also stated that 'if you disbelieve in democracy, secularism, nationalism, as well as all the other garbage and ideas from the West, and rush to your religion and creed, then by Allah you will own the Earth.'[129] To underscore these supposed anti-Western credentials even further, videos soon followed depicting Islamic State units merrily bulldozing the border posts between Iraq and Syria that, in their eyes at least, were remnants of the Anglo-French Sykes–Picot agreement and thus symbolized the infidels' destruction of the last caliphate.[130]

On 4 July 2014 a man professing to be al-Baghdadi appeared in a remarkable televised sermon entitled 'A Message to the Mujahideen and the Muslim Ummah in the Month of Ramadan'. Soon broadcast around the world and delivered in the great mosque of Al-Nuri in Mosul, it was no coincidence that this was the same site where Saladin made his last speech before going off to lead the fight against the Second Crusade.[131] Heavily cloaked and sporting a large beard, the video showed the man walking slowly and seemingly emulating the kind of gestures associated with the Prophet Muhammad, at one point even cleaning his teeth with a *miswak* twig before commencing his speech.[132] Using what many have since described as flawless classical Arabic and with far better oratory skills than most al-Qaeda-supporting clerics, it contained almost every imaginable Salafi-jihadist cliché and, as was widely pointed out, in many ways served as the ultimate counter-revolutionary response to the progressive, emancipatory, and cosmopolitan language of the Arab Spring. Notably it warned Muslims not to be deceived by 'dazzling slogans such as civilization, peace, co-existence, freedom, democracy, secularism ... among other false slogans', and called for the congregation to 'stand up ... and free yourselves from the shackles of weakness, and [against] ... the agents of the crusaders and the atheists, and the guardians of the Jews.'[133] Importantly, and rather predictably for the sharper observers, the speech also made sure to distinguish between 'caliphi jihadists' and the shortcomings of 'non-caliphi jihadists', with the speaker making pointed references to al-Qaeda's 'abandoned obligations' and the need for the new caliphate to offer extraterritorial citizenship to Muslims all over the world.[134]

As expected, the speech drew heavily on the writings of Taqi al-Din Ahmad ibn Taymiyyah and Muhammad Abd al-Wahhab, but, as with other recent Islamic State missives, no mentions were made of Sayyid Qutb or scholars usually associated with the Muslim Brotherhood.[135] As Marc Lynch notes, this was likely due to feelings within the Islamic State and other jihadist organizations that since the Arab Spring the Brotherhood had evolved into something of a 'firewall against recruitment into violent jihadist groups'.[136] As a former jihadist has put it, by this stage both the Brotherhood and even al-Qaeda were seen as 'big refrigerators for the youth – essentially freezing and arresting their energy' and thus reducing the pool of recruits available to the Islamic State.[137]

From Nouri Maliki's perspective, having soon lost his post as prime minister after the disgrace of Mosul, but nonetheless managing to stay on as vice president, the timing and nature of these Islamic State declarations were deeply suspicious. Restating his claims on Iranian television that Saudi Arabia and Qatar were somehow behind everything, he argued that 'racist extremist ideologies such as Wahhabism' were the root cause of the Islamic State's growth, and that the organization's primary aim was not a religious one, but rather to unseat both Bashar al-Assad's government and his own.[138] Indeed, after the Mosul mosque video went viral, Iraqi officials were adamant that the preacher was a trained actor, and certainly not Abu Bakr al-Baghdadi.[139] Undoubtedly they had a point, as underneath all his heavy garb and facial hair it was impossible to say for certain that this was the same man who had earlier been arrested in Fallujah and then served time in Camp Bucca.

Already known as the 'Invisible Sheikh' due to his frequent wearing of masks,[140] it has since proven impossible to track down anyone with a credible claim of having actually met al-Baghdadi. Not one of the author's interviewees in 2014 and 2015 knew anyone who had, and the man featured in the July 2014 video has made no further broadcast appearances, with all subsequent al-Baghdadi speeches being audio-only. In this sense at least, whoever the man really was, the Islamic State's senior leadership seemed to have learned an important lesson from the old al-Qaeda in Iraq and even al-Qaeda's core, both of which suffered great and almost irreparable legitimacy deficits after the slayings of Abu Musab al-Zarqawi and Osama bin Laden. In the Islamic State's case, its reclusive and well-disguised caliph has in many ways been made immortal, with no promises of further, regular videos, and with the organization likely having no difficulties in creating and dressing up a 'new' al-Baghdadi should the need ever arise.

Although nobody remarked upon it at the time, the strange episode in the Mosul mosque should have also triggered memories in the minds of at least some historians. Not only were the contents of the sermon and the method of its delivery wholly in tune with Britain's historical efforts to buttress the Ottoman Caliphate and then its stillborn attempts to recreate one in Mecca, but it also resonated strongly with the White House's plans for Saudi Arabia's Ibn Saud to become 'the great gookety gook of the Muslim world' and a counterweight to Gamal Abdel Nasser. Moreover, the spectre of the big-bearded al-Baghdadi preaching from the pulpit tallied even closer to a less well-known CIA project dating back to the early 1950s to create a 'Muslim Billy Graham'. So-called after a Christian evangelical preacher who had rapidly acquired celebrity status – the CIA's chosen man was to serve as a 'great mystagogue' who could promote caliphal ideas and thus help the US counter the threats to its interests posed by the Levant's rising secular and progressive Arab republics. With a secret committee of specialists having formed to 'advance the idea of promoting [such a man] to mobilize religious fervour in a great move against communism', the memoirs of two CIA officers indicate it got as far as selecting a 'wild-eyed Iraqi holy man to send on a tour of Arab countries'.[141]

THE RESURRECTION OF SADDAM HUSSEIN

Soon after the Islamic State's expansionary surge in 2014 and its eventual caliphate declaration, numerous reports began to circulate claiming that much of its dramatic rise was due to some sort of secret deal that had already been struck between its leadership and the remnants of the old Saddam Hussein regime. On the one hand, this supposed arrangement helped deepen the existing explanations of how the Islamic State's relatively small numbers of fighters had managed to occupy such big cities, but on the other hand it also appeared to undermine the organization's Salafi-jihadist credentials, especially as it was accused of promoting and relying upon men who had earlier risen up the ranks of the ostensibly secular Iraqi *Ba'ath* party which, after all, had Arab nationalist foundations and whose secretary general was a Christian right up until his death in 1989.[142]

Adding weight to this thesis, it was already known that one of Abu Bakr al-Baghdadi's deputies and, according to some, the man who had smoothed his succession in 2010, was himself a former Iraqi Republican Guard officer. With his real name being Samir Abd Muhammad al-Khlifawi but with the *nom de guerre* of Haji Bakr, he was thought to have succeeded in 'purging [the Islamic State] of most of its non-Iraqi leadership', especially in military matters.[143] Meanwhile, a large number of other Saddam-era veterans, most of whom were believed to have been interned in Camp Bucca alongside al-Baghdadi, also seemed to have gained leading roles.[144] Abu Ali al-Anbari, for example, was a major general in the Iraqi army before joining *Ansar al-Islam* and then becoming the head of the Islamic State's Intelligence Council and its governor general for Syria. Similarly, Abu Muslim al-Turkmani was a former special forces officer and a member of Iraqi military intelligence before then serving as the Islamic State's governor general for Iraq. Fitting the same pattern, Abu Ayman al-Iraqi was a lieutenant colonel in Iraqi air defence intelligence before later emerging as head of the Islamic State's military council.[145]

In contrast, when Syrians began to join the Islamic State, many described how they had expected to become part of an Islamic utopia but instead found themselves being supervised and receiving orders primarily 'from shadowy Iraqis who moved in and out of the battlefield in Syria'. Interviewed by the *Washington Post*, one former Islamic State fighter who had fled for Turkey described how when he had disagreed with his Iraqi superiors 'he was placed under arrest on the orders of a masked Iraqi man who had sat silently through the proceedings, listening and taking notes'. He explained that the man, and the other members of the Islamic State's 'shadowy security service' were in fact all members of Saddam's old intelligence service. With regard to military operations, he described how 'the Iraqi officers are in command, and they make the tactics and the battle plans … but the Iraqis themselves don't fight. They put the [others] on the front lines.'[146] To some extent this dominance over the Islamic State's security apparatus has been corroborated by Ahmad Hashim who has shown how al-Baghdadi made sure to move Saddam-era personnel into command positions for almost all of the sensitive aspects of the caliphate, including the all-important fund collecting roles.[147]

More intriguingly, at some point in early 2014, the Islamic State was also understood to have formed an alliance with the militant group *Jaysh Riijal al-Tariqa al-Naqshbandiyya* or 'Army of the Men of the Naqshbandi Order', which claims to represent a well-established Sunni spiritual order that traces itself back to the time of the first caliphs.[148] Having developed a strong presence in eastern Syria and western Iraq, including Mosul, by 2003 its leader seemed to be none other than Izzat Ibrahim al-Douri – the former vice chairman of Saddam's Revolutionary Command Council, and better known to most Westerners as the elusive ginger-moustached 'King of Clubs' in the US-produced list of Iraq's most wanted men.[149] Thought to have hidden across the border in Al-Raqqah after the US invasion, al-Douri had effectively been running a shadow government of his own in Mosul before the Islamic State had come along. Moreover, he and his Naqshbandi colleagues had effectively inherited the old smuggling network they had set up in the 1990s with Saddam's blessing so as to help Iraq evade UN sanctions on imports.[150]

By 2015 such murky Islamic State–*Ba'ath* relations seemed out in the open after *Der Spiegel* gained access to Haji Bakr's papers, who by then was believed to have been killed in a firefight somewhere in northern Syria. Not only did the documents detail the extent of the Islamic State's organization, including the existence of parallel intelligence agencies and carefully balanced hierarchies in regional government, but they also revealed its substantial cooperation with Saddam regime remnants and what even seemed Bakr's connections within Syria's *Ba'ath* regime. In particular, at one point he had established an understanding with Syria's powerful air force intelligence that meant the Syrian air force would refrain from bombing Islamic State positions in return for Islamic State commanders on the ground ordering their fighters not to fire at Syrian army soldiers.[151]

Taken together, these revelations led many to assume that the Islamic State not only needed the assistance of elements in these current and former regimes, at least temporarily, but that it also sought to model itself upon them. As the Carnegie Middle East Center's Yezid Sayigh argues, the Islamic State's leadership had begun to 'mimic Saddam Hussein' and the organization had become, 'in organizational and strategic terms, a clone of the Saddam *mukhabarat* state'.[152] Of course, as Georgetown University's Joseph Sassoon's rigorous history of the Saddam regime has shown, such rapid cloning would not have been easy given that the multilayered *mukhabarat* had taken decades to build, but from the perspective of the former Iraqi officers, most of whom had been removed from their posts in 2003, or were later dismissed by Nouri Maliki, many seemed willing to gravitate to the Islamic State because it offered them a taste of power once again.[153] Going a bit further, Iraqi officials ousted by the Islamic State's advances have also reasoned that many of the former *Ba'ath* members had joined in only because they thought the Islamic State was weak and could easily be sidelined in the future. The former governor for Nineveh province argued that 'maybe after one month the Islamic State would collapse and [the *Ba'ath*] would then govern', while the former Anbar province police chief claimed that 'the plan of the former *Ba'ath* members is to use the Islamic State as a Trojan horse to derail the political process and take over'.[154] Others simply suggested that both groups saw each other as 'useful idiots' in accomplishing their short-term goals.[155]

To a great extent these assumptions seem valid, as there is little doubt that the Islamic State needed the expertise, connections, and resources of Saddam's veterans in order to gain and hold on to territory and to prevent a post-Maliki prime minister from forming another 2007-style Anbar Salvation Council. In Syria it also made considerable sense to maintain at least some regime links and to avoid mutually assured destruction with Bashar al-Assad's army, at least in the immediate term, as the Islamic State's primary goal was to gain supremacy in Sunni areas rather than taking on the government straight away. In this sense the Syrian air force intelligence's secret deal with Haji Bakr was merely a continuation of Bashar's 2011 amnesty for imprisoned jihadists and was entirely compatible with Damascus's 'stay out of our way, and we will stay out of yours' strategy. The emphasis on short-termism and a 'marriage of convenience' also seems valid, as after the Islamic State appeared to be on top of things it duly began to forbid Saddam posters being put up in its territory and reports began to circulate of uncooperative former *Ba'ath* members being executed.[156] Similarly in Syria, after the consolidation of Al-Raqqah and its demonstrations of military superiority over most other rebel groups, whether jihadist or non-jihadist, the Islamic State's arrangements with Damascus also seemed to go up in smoke after its units mounted a sustained and successful attack on Al-Tabqa airbase – one of the regime's remaining footholds in the region – and then executed more than 160 captured Syrian soldiers after filming a video of them marching in their underwear.[157]

To complete the picture, however, it is also important to appreciate that the Saddam regime these former Iraqi officers had been part of had in many ways long since shed itself of any *Ba'ath* credentials. Indeed, a compelling case can be made that Saddam himself had actively been subverting his own party, having recognized the usefulness of militant Islam and the necessity of keeping on board his core Sunni constituencies. As the University of Pennsylvania's Samuel Helfont has argued in a recent study, it was out of necessity rather than any genuine shift in ideological conviction that Saddam had also sought to instrumentalize Islam in Iraq's foreign policy.[158]

The regime, for example, had not only been actively tolerating the described *Ansar al-Islam*'s mini Islamic state close to the border with Iran, and had allowed it to indoctrinate nearby units of the Iraqi army, but had also steadily been building up the *Fedayeen*.[159] This was a Sunni militia complete with its own safe houses and arms caches that had been killing off regime opponents while also acting as something of a moral police. In the latter days of Saddam's rule, it had even been carrying out public beheadings. As some have pointed out, the *Fedayeen* was also intended to serve as a sectarian fallback force in the event of a 'doomsday scenario' such as a successful Shia or Kurdish revolt.[160] As Abdel Bari Atwan notes, it was no surprise that the purported fax sent by Saddam to the London-based *Al-Quds Al-Arabi* newspaper while in hiding in 2003 was laced with Qur'anic verse and jihadist rhetoric.[161] By this stage he also seemed to have Osama bin Laden's de facto support, with an al-Qaeda communiqué from the time not only urging insurgency against the new Baghdad government, but also stating that the 'socialists' of the *Ba'ath* regime were 'worthy accomplices in any fight against the Americans'.[162] In this context it is much easier to understand why, during his dramatic courtroom speech during his summer 2004 trial, the once avowedly secular Saddam twice complained to the judge that the court had ignored prayer time, questioned its Islamic credentials, and reminded everyone that Iraq was a state based on Islam.[163] Moreover, even when it came to light that Saddam had been offered a secret deal to make a televised request to tell the Sunni insurgents to call a ceasefire in exchange for leniency, he seems to have completely refused, forcing the US to deny all knowledge of negotiations.[164] Embarrassingly, however, only a few days later Britain's *Daily Telegraph* reported on such a deal, but with the British officials it cited rather implausibly claiming it was the other way around, with the insurgents wanting Saddam to be released in exchange for them 'returning to the political process'.[165]

How far back the Islamization of Iraq goes is unclear, as during the Iran–Iraq War Baghdad's primary framing of the conflict was as Arab resistance to Persian encroachment, as it needed both Sunni and Shia Iraqis to fight in its armed forces. Nonetheless, by the late 1980s some Iraqi officials had begun referring to the war with Iran as a 'jihad' and had dropped all references to Iraq being a secular state, and when Iraq invaded Kuwait in 1990, many Sunni Arabs celebrated Saddam as 'a modern mixture of Robin Hood and Saladin'.[166] Moreover, during the 1990s al-Douri had not only been tasked with sanctions busting, but had also been asked by Saddam to launch a 'Faith Campaign' to make Islam part of Iraq's national identity. In a far cry from previous *Ba'ath* administrations, clerics were placed on the government payroll and senior army officers were required to convert. As a former US military intelligence officer describes, the strategy involved the sending into mosques of *Ba'ath* members 'who would remain loyal as they established a foothold in the mosques from which the regime could then monitor or manipulate the Islamist movement'. More visibly, *Allahu Akbar*, or 'God is Great', was added to the Iraqi flag while sharia law punishments were introduced, including amputations, and nightclubs and many bars were closed. Already established, the Saddam University of Islamic Studies began to receive lavish funding, and it was during the time of this Faith Campaign that al-Baghdadi is first thought to have enrolled. Indeed, al-Douri is known to have been close to one of al-Baghdadi's academic mentors, and some claim that al-Baghdadi's ambition at the time was simply to join the Saddam regime's ministry for Islamic endowments. By far the most remarkable new institution, however, was the 'Mother of all Battles' mosque which was opened in 2001. Featuring minarets in the shape of AK-47 rifles and Scud missiles, and supposedly containing a copy of the Qur'an written in Saddam's own blood, it was perhaps the most blatant symbol of the direction the regime was preparing to take Iraq.[167]

'REMAINING AND EXPANDING' – SERVICES AND RECRUITMENT

Beyond its correct reading of the political and security landscapes in Syria and Iraq, much of the Islamic State's phenomenal expansionary momentum and, so it seems, the degree of popular support it then managed to enjoy, must also be put down to the organization's impressive ability to deliver services and to keep generating substantial recruitment. In this sense, the Islamic State soon proved it was capable of far more than simply providing better law and order and a fairer tax system than the powers it was supplanting. Adopting for their own ends the Islamic motto *baqiya wa tatamaddad*, or 'remaining and expanding', its leaders soon made clear the new caliphate was going to become much more than yet another guerilla group or even a military power, as in theory at least it intended to cater to the needs of civilians, women, and children just as much as its battle-hardened fighters.

Apparently wealthy, although with the sources of its income very unclear, the Islamic State was soon offering local officials – quickly admitted to the organization as 'supporters' rather than as full-blown members – much higher salaries than those paid by the Iraqi or Syrian governments. Meanwhile, in an investigation published by a British newspaper entitled 'Why business is booming under the Islamic State one year on', doctors and engineers revealed that their salaries had at least doubled. By the time of the capture of Mosul, the Islamic State was reportedly providing free hospital care – at least for its members – along with free vaccinations for children, nursing homes, free bus services, subsidies on basic foodstuffs, fixed fuel prices, and even a rent-capping system. It had also set about repairing infrastructure in the towns it had begun to occupy, with numerous videos depicting its men filling in potholes, painting street signs, and even watering municipal flower beds.[168] Interviewed by the *New York Times*, several residents of Islamic State-held territory described how the group had been 'fixing power cables, digging sewers, and painting sidewalks'. They also mentioned that it had begun to remove expired meat from markets and even claimed that prosthetic limbs had been introduced in clinics.[169]

In terms of justice, new sharia courts were reportedly swiftly set up, while separate police forces were established, including co-opted members of the towns' original police and even traffic officers capable of issuing Islamic State parking tickets. In an effort to 'demonstrate it could be a more egalitarian provider of existing services than the previous government', citizen charters were also launched in newly occupied towns, clarifying the various laws and regulations the Islamic State expected its citizens to abide by.[170] Little different to the rules in Saudi Arabia, with the exception of introducing a total ban on cigarettes, the Islamic State's charters were also notable for their defining of the rights Christians and worshippers of other monotheistic religions could expect, provided they paid the necessary *jizya* or 'levy'. Unsurprisingly, however, it appears that most Christians chose to leave, with their abandoned houses and even furniture and appliances having later been sold off in Islamic State property auctions.[171] In terms of financial organization, the Islamic State also seems to have been busy, having established the Muslim Financial House – a sort of central bank – at some point in 2014, and by the end of the year making the rather grand announcement that it was about to reinstate the ancient Islamic dinar by minting its own gold, silver, and copper coins.[172]

Although somewhat contrary to Abu Bakr al-Baghdadi's apparent play to Saddam Hussein-era remnants, but of course then fully in line with the announced caliphate and the emphasis on citizenship for all, at about this time the Islamic State also began to recruit much more heavily from outside the region. Echoing Abullah Azzam's earlier calls for *hijra* or the obligatory emigration of all Muslims to the land of Islam, al-Baghdadi naturally wanted to increase the number of fighters at his disposal.[173] By January 2015 the US Department of State estimated that eighteen thousand foreign fighters had already arrived in the Islamic State, with about three hundred being Westerners. As a senior US official claimed, 'We haven't been able to stop the flow, but we have created more friction.' Another conceded to the *New York Times* that 'I still don't think we have our hands around it.'[174] Painting much the same picture, a few weeks later the annual Munich Security Report stated that the number of foreigners fighting in Iraq and Syria had begun to exceed the total at the height of the 1980s Afghan jihad. It also noted that 'fighters from France and five hundred to six hundred from Germany have found their way ... and the number of fighters hailing from Central Asia has also risen significantly.'[175] Giving testimony at a US Senate hearing the next month, a US counter-terrorism official stated that at least twenty thousand foreign fighters from more than ninety countries were known to be in Syria. He stated that 3,400 were Westerners of which 150 were thought to be Americans.[176] If anything, by May 2015 the flow seemed to be even higher, with a UN Security Council report warning that the number of fighters arriving in the Islamic State had increased by seventy percent since the previous summer, and that there were perhaps as many as thirty thousand foreigners hailing from more than a hundred different countries.[177]

The majority of course were coming from Sunni Muslim-majority countries, not only from predictable places such as Saudi Arabia and other Gulf monarchies, but from all across North Africa, including Tunisia and Libya. Even Morocco's interior minister, for example, freely confirmed that in one year alone over a thousand Moroccans had gone to Syria.[178] Moneywise, as with the Islamic State's burgeoning civil service, such fighters were clearly being well paid – between $600 and $800 a month, or in the case of commanding officers even more. This compared very favourably with average salaries in the region, which in some cases were just a couple of hundred dollars.[179] Indeed, confessing to interrogators after his capture in Pakistan, a Syrian recruiter for the Islamic State revealed that he and the preacher of a local mosque had been telling Pakistani recruits they would receive $600 a month if they were to travel to Syria and fight.[180]

Giving us more detail on the apparent centrality of such foreign fighters to the Islamic State's military strategy, the testimony of a writer based in Mosul, which has since been translated and to some extent authenticated by research fellow Aymeen Jawad al-Tamimi, reveals that the Islamic State sought to create an elite four-thousand-strong foreign legion. Known as *Jaysh al-Khilafa* or 'Army of the Caliphate', it was to serve as both a special forces division and – much like Heinrich Himmler's *Waffen SS* – as an ideological vanguard. The testimony also indicated that it could be deployed overseas if necessary, and that its members were forbidden from marrying. According to an activist from Al-Raqqah, also cited by al-Tamimi, the bulk of its men were thought to have been drawn from Chechnya, Algeria, and Uzbekistan, with its leader being Abu Omar al-Shishani – known simply as 'The Chechen'.[181] Indeed, just three months after these details were published, Russian news agencies began to report that the Islamic State's 'recruitment professionals' had been found scouring Central Asia. Uzbekistan's national security spokesman claimed that annual salaries of between \$20,000 and \$30,000 were being offered, along with resettlement packages for families.[182]

Going much further than al-Qaeda and Azzam's concept of *hijra*, however, the Islamic State also made it clear that non-combatants were just as welcome to immigrate. Shortly after the caliphate was declared, al-Baghdadi explicitly made a 'special call' for 'judges, doctors, engineers, and people with military and administrative expertise'.[183] Later on, a purported doctor with a British accent appeared in a video to urge Muslim doctors and nurses from all over the world to come and perform their duty.[184] From the Islamic State's perspective such recruitment offered a similar win-win to the importing of fighters, as there was little doubt that the pool of professionals and bureaucrats in its territories, especially in Syria, had been severely depleted by more than two years of conflict.

Reporting in early 2015, the *New York Times* agreed that such immigrants, including women and children, had indeed been making their way to Syria and Iraq, and claimed that even the West was 'struggling to halt the flow of citizens to the war zones'.[185] The *Washington Post*, meanwhile, reported that the Islamic State had been posting pictures of its members holding kittens and jars of Nutella in an effort to 'win the hearts of female recruits with adorable animals and creamy chocolate'.[186] The extent to which ordinary civilians have really managed to travel and join the Islamic State and then successfully integrate remains unclear, although for every story that appears in the international media featuring a Western woman or teenager having changed their mind after arriving and discovering no creature comforts, it seems likely that many more have gone there and have actually wanted to stay. According to documents seen by the author, vibrant women's community groups exist that have not only tried to provide checklists for things newcomers should try to bring along from their home country, but have also been actively compiling Islamic State recipe lists along with hints and tips on how best to please their future jihadist husbands.

'REMAINING AND EXPANDING' - MASTERS OF PROPAGANDA

Well aware of Osama bin Laden and Ayman Zawahiri's rapid marginalization after the Arab Spring began, Abu Bakr al-Baghdadi's organization had already begun to lay the foundations for the Islamic State's much more impressive media apparatus. With its members soon proving their mastery over potentially powerful new propaganda platforms, the Islamic State was soon described as a 'disruptive innovator'.[187] In a far cry from their luddite precursors, with the Saudi *Ikhwan* having shunned modern technology, and the *Taliban* even having smashed up television sets in the 1990s, the Islamic State's now infamous mass media prowess is perhaps best traced to the US-born and then Yemen-based jihadist scholar Anwar al-Awlaki. Having pushed al-Qaeda to go much further than its old system of email lists, heavily moderated forums, and its vague declaration of 'cyber jihad' as one of its *Thirty-nine principles of jihad*, al-Awlaki was to spend much of his time pioneering the use of media.[188]

Extrajudicially killed by a US drone strike in September 2011,[189] al-Awlaki never lived to see the later implementation of many of his ideas by the Islamic State's experts who, so it seems, were keen to cover all bases. Appealing to traditionalists, their *Dabiq* magazine soon began to be distributed extensively online with its English-language context disseminated around the world and featuring much higher production values than anything al-Qaeda had ever produced. Named after a Syrian town near Aleppo, *Dabiq* has special relevance for the Islamic State as it is prophesized in a *Hadith* that in the 'end of days' Jesus will return to Dabiq to lead an army of Muslims to victory against the 'armies of Rome'. Similarly, the Islamic State's technical training magazine – a bi-monthly publication offering tips for would-be fighters – was soon easily accessible online and evidently became widely read.[190] Quickly eclipsing al-Qaeda's more modest audio-visual crew of just three technicians,[191] the Islamic State also began to rejuvenate the old Islamic State in Iraq's *Furqan* television network and then supplemented it with a Syrian equivalent – *Al-Hayat* – after the organization began to gain territory across the border. As with the magazines, both networks were keen to offer English translations, and sometimes original English language content.[192] In some cases, their audio messages were even translated into Russian, most notably Abu Bakr al-Baghdadi's caliphate declaration, and there were soon repeated attempts to deliver satellite television broadcasts.[193]

As Patrick Cockburn observes, by 2014 '[the Islamic State] may have yearned for a return to the norms of early Islam but their skills in using modern communications and the Internet are well ahead of most political movements in the world.'[194] Similarly in summer 2015 FBI assistant director of counter-terrorism Michael Steinbach made clear in a congressional hearing that the Islamic State was making 'full use of strong encryption technology being implanted by social media platforms including Facebook and also favoured by Apple's platform'. Rather ominously he warned that this had created 'dark spaces' and 'a free zone by which to recruit, radicalize, plot and plan.'[195] Certainly by this stage the crude offerings of other jihadist organizations along with propaganda produced by the region's governments were no match for the vast armies of social media users helping to circulate the Islamic State's increasingly catchy content. In this sense, having gone much further than al-Qaeda, even under al-Awlaki, the Islamic State had evidently recognized and tried to harness the potential of viral marketing and branding. This meant that by the time it advanced into Mosul, support for the Islamic State in its target constituencies was already much higher than it had ever been for al-Qaeda.[196]

Most visibly, at least in summer 2014, the Islamic State was arguably making more use of Twitter than any other political organization had done before. In a report produced by the Brookings Institution, a 'well-crafted strategy' was described involving 'dozens of thousands of highly active accounts spreading Islamic State propaganda'. As the report also noted, methods had clearly been developed to evade the closure of loyalist accounts or, if necessary, the means to reopen them quickly using an established system.[197] Indeed, it was proving difficult for Twitter's parent company to determine which accounts were really sympathetic to the Islamic State and which were not. Although Twitter was able to spot and shut down obviously official accounts, satire accounts were often included in the culls, while users with similar names to Islamic State members also found themselves blocked.[198] Strangely, however, some well-known sympathizers were allowed to tweet freely for several months and amass dozens of thousands of followers,[199] while an account named 'Cyber Caliphate' which openly expressed pro-Islamic State views managed to reach 100,000 followers in the run-up to its bizarrely unlikely but much-publicized hijacking of US CENTCOM's Twitter account.[200] Following a detailed investigation, it was revealed that some of these Islamic State accounts were linked to IP addresses belonging to the British government's Department for Work and Pensions. But as a number of reports noted, these were IP addresses that had earlier been sold by Britain to two Saudi telecommunications companies in unpublished transactions.[201] Certainly, since the Islamic State's major growth spurt in 2014 an unusually substantial number of visits to the author's professional website have been from 'UK Government Department for Work and Pensions'.

As well as helping to glorify the organization, the Islamic State's more prolific Twitter users – known as the *al-mujtahidun* or 'the industrious' – were also using the platform to launch 'trial balloons' to gauge public opinion. For example, a hashtag demanding that the Islamic State form a caliphate was launched a few months before the announcement was actually made. The resulting online discussion, almost certainly monitored by the Islamic State's leadership, will have given it a good idea of what sort of caliph was wanted, and – for example – how much things like the correct lineage really mattered.[202] Other platforms seem to have been a bit less useful for the Islamic State, with aborted attempts to create a Facebook clone called 'MuslimBook', and many of its banned Twitter users unsuccessfully trying to migrate to social media sites such as Diaspora, Russia's VK, Frendica, Ask.fm, and justpaste.it.

Rather innovatively, however, the organization proved itself adept at producing third-party applications, or 'apps', for smartphones and tablets. Reminiscent of the US-funded jihad-promoting textbooks exported to Pakistan and Afghanistan in the 1980s, there is evidence that the Islamic State has been behind a number of educational apps designed to target children. Among these has been 'Huroof', which helps to teach youngsters the Arabic alphabet by introducing vocabulary such as 'gun', 'tank', and 'rocket', and features Islamic a cappella *nasheed* singing that is 'littered with jihadist terminology'.[203] Meanwhile, other apps have allowed the Islamic State quickly to snowball messages and propaganda to thousands and even millions via social media 'bots'. Notably, its 'Dawn of Glad Tidings' app – thought to have been designed by a Palestinian sympathizer who had previously been a commercial applications developer – is understood to have played a pivotal role during 2014 as it allowed pro-Islamic State users to allow their social media feeds to be taken over by the organization. With most of the app's postings containing Islamic State news along with hashtags or links to allow new users to download it, at its peak it was generating approximately forty thousand messages a day. As J. M. Berger contends, even if there were no real people behind many of the postings, it was nonetheless part of a 'smart if deceptive social media strategy' that allowed the Islamic State to 'create an appearance of momentum that gradually turned into real momentum and a growing base of support'.[204] In this manner, as political scientist David Faris claims, the Islamic State was able to manipulate social media so as to build up a 'vast imagined community' alongside any real support base.[205]

With its sympathizers' apparent predilection for posting spectacularly gruesome photographs and video snippets, usually involving dismembered Shia, it is important to note that the Islamic State's online campaign was clearly intended to go further than mere branding or indoctrination, as it also helped feed into the 'management of savagery' strategy. With such images soon supplemented by lavishly produced state-of-the art documentaries – notably a series entitled *Salil al-Sawarem* or 'Clanging of the Swords' – and even a video game modelled on the violent but wildly popular *Grand Theft Auto*, the aim was not only to portray the Islamic State as being strong and winning on the battlefield, but also to desensitize its supporters to necessary violence while striking fear into the hearts of soldiers in the towns it was about to attack.[206] As Ahmad Hashim explains, most of this sort of propaganda was aimed at the games-console-playing 'toxic younger generation of jihadists' that ranged from the self-radicalized to those seeking the sort of adventure that groups such as al-Qaeda no longer seemed to offer.[207] Indeed, in most of the videos watched by the author – and seemingly by hundreds of thousands of others given their popularity on YouTube – a seductive and addictive mix of real-time fighting scenes interspersed with high-quality graphics really made the organization's fighters seem invincible. In many instances the videos depict hovering sniper rifle sights – of the kind seen in many arcade games – which would then suddenly switch to the slaying of Iraqi soldiers, while in other scenes the Islamic State would show off its high-definition drone footage of the battlefields it was currently contesting.

9

THE ISLAMIC STATE –
A STRATEGIC ASSET

QUI BONO – TO WHOSE PROFIT?

With the Islamic State's explosive growth and territorial gains, increasingly at the expense of the Syrian and Iraqi states, it was undoubtedly emerging as a powerful on-the-ground ally for those committed to toppling or weakening the Bashar al-Assad and Nouri Maliki regimes. Meanwhile, given its much sharper sectarian edge than al-Qaeda, and its apparent willingness to take on Iran's proxies and fight them as its 'near enemies', the Islamic State was soon also the most viciously capable front-line force in what seemed an escalating Sunni–Shia region-wide conflict.

More broadly, the Islamic State's reactionary mix of religious traditionalism and regressive practices was proving an especially potent counterweight to the sort of ideas that had threatened to spread in the wake of the Arab Spring. Certainly, in ideological terms, the announced restoration of the caliphate in 2014 fitted perfectly with nearly a century of British and US anti-nationalist, anti-communist, and anti-democratic Middle East policies, including multiple documented attempts by planners in London and Washington to actually restore it themselves. Although the new caliphate's savagery may seem unconscionably nihilistic, it has nonetheless served an equally important purpose for those on the outside, as even after the Arab Spring the surviving Western-backed autocracies have been able to reaffirm their status as the Middle East's 'moderates', just as they were during the 'War on Terror' and, before that, against the threat of international communism. After all, as British MP Enoch Powell once observed, 'St George and the dragon is a poor show without a real dragon, the bigger and scalier the better, ideally with flames coming out of its mouth'.[1]

Beyond such dividends for the status quo, the rise of the Islamic State has been spectacularly good for business. By successfully resurrecting a long-feared militant creed thought capable of threatening everyone in the vicinity and perhaps one day even the global order, the Islamic State has done much to distract millions from the inconvenient truth that most of the world was actually becoming a safer place while, at the same time, its fiery statements and bloody actions have helped corral a whole panoply of governments into signing off on some of the biggest defence contracts and arms procurements in history. As the veteran *New York Times* correspondent Stephen Kinzer put it, even in 2015 'this world of threats is an illusion ... the US has no potent enemies. We are not only safe, but safer than any big power has been in all of modern history.' Likening the new-found menace of the Islamic State to the previous round of al-Qaeda-hunting, he argued that 'heart-rending violence in the Middle East has no serious implication for US security. As for domestic terrorism, the risk for Americans is modest: you have more chance of being struck by lightning on your birthday than of dying in a terror attack.'[2]

In this sense, Kinzer makes a strong point, as although the US attorney general once claimed al-Qaeda had '5,000 operatives in the US', while the British Army's chief of staff later called Islamic extremism 'the struggle of our generation – perhaps our Thirty Years War', the reality was quite different.[3] Indeed, a secret FBI report from 2005 'wistfully noted that although the bureau had managed to arrest a few bad guys here and there ... it had been unable to identify a single true al-Qaeda sleeper cell anywhere in the country'.[4]

THE MANUFACTURING OF EVIL – THE NEW BOGEYMAN

Soon identifying the world's new bogeyman, the international media spent much of the second half of 2014 pumping out tales of the Islamic State's thugs and their almost medieval barbarity. While many stories must have had a grain of truth, the majority were poorly sourced, and some were definitely made up. Reminiscent of the fake Viagra-fuelled Libyan raping spree of 2011, one particularly dubious report claimed the Islamic State had issued an order that all women between the ages of eleven and forty-six be circumcised. Although appearing on the front pages of most Western newspapers, including broadsheets, doubts quickly emerged after Mosul residents confirmed they had never even heard about it.[5] While reporting on Islamic State atrocities in 2015 became a little more cautious, the general theme remained much the same, with such stories continuing to appear on a regular basis, often generated by unverifiable social media sources or purported local activist groups sporting websites and logos not dissimilar to those of the Syrian media outlets that had popped up the year before. But with journalists understandably hungry for exclusives on the world's hottest topic, and newspapers unable to dispatch correspondents anywhere near the Islamic State's territories, this was perhaps as inevitable as it was unfortunate.

Unsurprisingly a wave of comparative analysis also began to appear, as writers soon jockeyed with each other to prove just how evil the Islamic State was and how dangerous it had already become. A firm favourite was of course the Soviet Union, even though there were much better comparators to choose from. In an essay for Reuters, for example, a US academic who had worked extensively with the US Agency for International Development and the World Bank on 'providing democracy assistance to fragile states' tried to liken the Islamic State to the Bolsheviks on the basis that both groups were 'extremist radicals ... [with] threatening ideologies' that had managed to 'seize strategically important regions'. He claimed that the Bolsheviks' 'ruthless strategic vision' had allowed them to go on to threaten Western interests for decades, while in much the same way the Islamic State was a 'rising revolutionary power ... [that had] gone from being just another terrorist group to master of a region.'[6]

Even if such authors did not realize it, many of these 'Islamic State is evil' pieces were eerily similar to those written about Moscow nearly a century earlier. As William Blum notes, the net result of these early-twentieth-century reports – published at a time when it also suited the Western powers to have an easily identifiable barbarian enemy – was 'to picture the Soviet Union as a kind of bedlam inhabited by abject slaves completely at the mercy of an organization of homicidal maniacs whose purpose was to destroy all traces of civilization and carry the nation back to barbarism'. In February 1919, for example, even the *Times'* correspondents told their readers that the brutal Bolsheviks were 'stripping women in the streets ... and people of every class except the scum are subjected to violence by the mobs'.[7] In this context Blum describes how 'literally no story about the Bolsheviks was too contrived, too bizarre, too grotesque, or too perverted to be printed and widely believed ... from women being nationalized to babies being eaten'. Although the US Department of State later admitted the stories about women were fraudulent, by then their purpose had already been served.[8]

Islamic State comparisons in Britain have been no less far-fetched than in the US, but have tended to focus more on the Second World War than the Cold War, perhaps reflecting the greater resonance of the conflict that took place on its very doorstep. Certainly by summer 2015 almost all key British ministers had collectively decided that Abu Bakr al-Baghdadi was the new Adolf Hitler and, by extension, that the Islamic State represented some sort of supercharged fascism. The foreign secretary told an audience in June that the rise of the Islamic State had a 'startling parallel' with the war against the Nazis, while a few weeks later, in reference to the iconic summer 1940 campaign against the Luftwaffe, the defence secretary described his belief that any fight against the Islamic State would be 'a new Battle of Britain'.[9]

Either way, the ghastly spectre of the resurgent 'Nazis' or 'Bolsheviks' was making a big impression, as although the US Department of Homeland Security's intelligence chief stated in February 2015 that the US 'remained unaware of any specific, credible imminent threat to the homeland',[10] only three days later polls revealed that Americans considered the Islamic State to be 'the gravest threat to the US over the next decade', with eighty-four percent claiming that the Islamic State was the most critical threat, far ahead of al-Qaeda, North Korea, Iran, and other states and groups.[11] With some considerable cheek, given his organization's substantial history of financing and equipping Islamic extremists, a month later CIA director John Brennan poured further fuel on the fire by claiming that the Islamic State was 'murderous and psychopathic' and that using the term 'Islamic'

THE ISLAMIC STATE – A STRATEGIC ASSET

was wrong because it gave the organization 'the type of legitimacy that they are so desperately seeking, but which they don't deserve at all'.[12] Chipping in, former CIA director Leon Panetta warned that 'Americans should be braced for a long battle against the brutal terrorist group Islamic State that will test US resolve.'[13] Going perhaps the furthest, Britain's prime minister soon declared that the Islamic State had become an 'existential threat' to the West, and that it was actively plotting terrorist attacks in Britain.[14]

THE BUSINESS OF EVIL – A HISTORY OF CASHING IN

Such fearmongering soon began to translate into Western military expenditure, as historically it had always done so. In this context the Islamic State was again much like the Soviet Union, whose military capabilities were repeatedly and deliberately overstated by the architects of US policy during the twentieth century. As a former US National Security Council member describes, 'the sclerotic Soviet Union is made to hum ... to Stalin's horse-drawn army, complete with shoddy equipment, war-torn roads and spurious morale. The Pentagon adds phantom divisions, then attributes invasion scenarios to the new forces for good measure.'[15] Meanwhile, the Western public was continually reminded that the US suffered a 'bomber gap', then a 'missile gap', and then a 'laser gap' with the USSR. In 1980, as the Afghan war began, US senator Bob Dole claimed to Congress there was 'convincing evidence ... that the Soviet Union had developed a chemical capability that extends far beyond our greatest fears ... a gas that is unaffected by ... our gas masks and leaves our military defenceless'. On this basis, he argued, 'to even suggest a levelling off of defence spending for our nation by the Carter administration at such a critical time in our history is unfathomable'.[16]

As Mark Curtis points out, as the Cold War lumbered towards its end the National Security Council very quickly became rational about the old Soviet threat, even retrospectively describing Moscow as 'a generally status quo, risk-averse adversary'.[17] By this stage, of course, any period of 'the West not knowing what to do with itself' was already over, as a number of non-Soviet apparitions had already been successfully generated and then used to justify increased spending. In 1986, for example, the Operation

El-Dorado Canyon Libyan fiasco had also been exploited to push more military aid in the direction of the Nicaraguan contras. As Ronald Reagan warned, just a day before Congress was due to debate the topic, 'I would remind the House voting this week that this arch terrorist Gaddafi has sent $400 million and an arsenal of weapons and advisors to Nicaragua.'[18] Soon after, of course, the US had then set its sights on Saddam Hussein's regime. After Iraqi forces had brazenly marched into Kuwait in August 1990, George H. Bush immediately likened the episode to Hitler's invasion of Poland and even described it as 'World War Tomorrow'.[19] Moreover, as the US and its allies grandly squared up to Baghdad, Bush claimed that 'our jobs, our way of life, our own freedom, and the freedom of friendly countries around the world will suffer if control of the world's greatest oil reserves fell in the hands of that one man, Saddam Hussein.'[20] Soon Saddam was accused of moving chemical weapons to the front lines, and within a few more months his regime was elevated into an 'active nuclear threat'.[21]

In what is now regarded as one of the finest pieces of war propaganda, the US public and lawmakers were further persuaded of both Iraq's evilness and the need for a massive military intervention following the 'Babies in incubators' testimony. Delivered before Congress's Human Rights Caucus in October 1990 by 'Nayirah', a teenage girl who had only provided her first name, her emotive tale of personally witnessing Iraqi soldiers taking babies out of incubators in Kuwaiti hospitals soon went viral, being broadcast on most of the major US television networks. Although denied by the Iraqi authorities, Bush duly referred to the story more than ten times over the following weeks, and seven senators went on to cite it in their speeches backing military intervention, the vote for which was later won by a margin of only five.[22]

With the green light given for action, and the barbarity of the enemy confirmed, the build-up was truly enormous. To take on Iraq's dilapidated armed forces, mostly made up of old Soviet-era weapons and tanks that had managed to survive the debilitating Iran–Iraq War, the US mobilized all five arms of its military with a total of 500,000 troops.[23] A campaign of mass air strikes in January 1991 quickly softened up most of Iraq's defences and an advance led by huge numbers of armoured units – 'Operation Desert Storm' – easily rolled back Iraq's retreating army from Kuwait. In fact, as a *New Yorker* essay later explained, somewhere between several

410

hundred to several thousand Iraqis were mown down on the 'Highway of Death' as they tried to flee. In reports citing US witnesses some of the surrendering troops were even shot dead as they tried to hand themselves in at makeshift checkpoints.[24]

Despite such an obviously one-sided affair, however, the US needed its first major post-Cold War display of strength to have as big an impact as possible. Later concluding that their air strikes had returned Iraq's power generating capacity to '1920s levels', and that Iraq now had a 'broken economy', Department of Defense analysts along with other officials made it clear that non-military targets had deliberately been hit so as to cause maximum political damage. Norman Schwarzkopf, the general in overall charge of the campaign, later admitted that 'the impact of the war on Iraqi civilians was terrifying and certainly saddening.'[25] In this sense he had followed the orders of his masters to the letter, with Secretary of State James Baker having earlier threatened to 'bomb Iraq back to the stone age'.[26] Offering one of the best and most succinct explanations for this, a former US air force planner has since claimed of the campaign's 'big picture' that 'we wanted to let people know ... get rid of this guy and we'll be more than happy to assist in rebuilding ... we're not going to tolerate Saddam Hussein or his regime. Fix that, and we'll fix your electricity.'[27]

Ostensibly to deal with Iraq's nuclear menace, and likely at the demand of Israel and the West's other regional allies, Desert Storm was also important cover for the US's bombing of all four of Iraq's live nuclear reactors, the environs of which remain contaminated today. In this sense, the war was a highly effective mechanism for the circumvention of a December 1990 UN resolution that had called for 'appropriate measures to prohibit future military attacks on nuclear facilities'.[28] Moreover, as with the later 2003 invasion, and in some ways as with the US's nuclear attacks on mainland Japan in 1945, Desert Storm also proved an invaluable opportunity to test out advanced new weaponry on a people unable to fight back. As has since come to light, even shells containing depleted uranium were used, with a secret report produced by Britain's Atomic Energy Authority having warned that if the depleted uranium ever entered the food chain then it could cause serious health problems. It stated that 'it is in Britain and Kuwait's interest that this is not left to rear its head in the years to come.'[29] But it seems no action was taken, as an investigation published in 2010 – the coverage of which has now been removed from the website of the British newspaper that first covered it – noted that the extent of genetic damage suffered by the inhabitants of the city of Fallujah suggests that some form of uranium had been used and had led to cancer rates 'similar to that in the Hiroshima survivors who were exposed to ionizing radiation from the bomb and uranium in the fallout'.[30]

Only with the military phase coming to an end, however, did details of the biggest benefits of Desert Storm begin to surface, as it soon became clear the Iraq threat had been used effectively to protect US defence spending that had earlier been facing reductions following the US Army's withdrawal from Western Europe. Furthermore, plans to freeze production of the US's B-2 stealth bombers were blocked after hawkish senators 'seized on Iraq's invasion of Kuwait to bolster their case for the radar-eluding weapon'. As one claimed, it 'demonstrated the continuing risk of war and the need for advanced weapons', while another remarked: 'If we needed Saddam Hussein to give us a wake-up call at least we can thank him for that.'[31] Later describing Desert Storm as 'the last classic war' and as a 'war of necessity [with] vital US interests at stake', a National Security Council analyst concluded that 'its outcome got the post-Cold War era off to a good start.'[32] Meanwhile, across the Atlantic, the US's main coalition partners in London and Paris seemed similarly aware of the dividends that would continue to accrue. As Margaret Thatcher warned, while trying to promote British arms sales to Saudi Arabia, 'Iraq, although temporarily crushed, remains a long-term enemy and aggressor.'[33]

Within a few more years, however, important truths about Desert Storm were proving harder to contain. The Nayirah testimony, for example, was soon thoroughly debunked after it emerged that the girl was in fact the daughter of Kuwait's ambassador to the US.[34] Moreover, it was reported that a US public relations firm had coached her, and, as claimed in the *Columbia Journalism Review*, it had sent out a video news release of the testimony to over seven hundred television stations.[35] As the *New York Times* stated, 'The incubator story seriously distorted the American debate about whether to support military action' and called into question the integrity of some of the senators who had voted for it.[36]

More seriously, the assumed circumstances that had led Iraq to invade Kuwait were also beginning to be unpicked. Although there had been a consensus at the time that Saddam saw 1990 as his last opportunity to get his hands on Kuwaiti oil, as without a Soviet Union there would be little prospect of Arab powers being able to play one superpower off against another again,[37] in reality it seems there was some considerable US obfuscation. In particular, Saddam is understood to have sent a delegation to the US embassy in Baghdad prior to commencing action in August 1990, the members of which were told by the US ambassador that Washington would not take positions over any 'border disputes'.[38] Furthermore, according to reports appearing soon after in two major US newspapers, there seemed to have been some considerable provocation from the Kuwaiti side, too, as when the Iraqi army reached Kuwait it discovered documents detailing secret meetings between the head of Kuwait's security services and the CIA. In one of these the Kuwaiti had justified his country's increasing oil production and stated that 'we agreed with the American side to take advantage of the deteriorating economic situation in Iraq in order to put pressure on that country's government'. This revelation alone was understood to have been enough to cause Kuwait's exiled foreign minister to faint.[39]

The very sudden portrayal of Iraq by Bush, Thatcher, and others as some sort of permanent enemy of the West and its allies also began to raise the eyebrows of those beginning to learn more about the US and British arms sales to Baghdad over the course of the 1980s. Indeed, with Thatcher having already discussed 'how to exploit Iraq's promising market for arms', it soon emerged that Britain had been exporting night-vision equipment, missile launch platforms, and a host of other highly sophisticated weaponry to the Saddam regime. Giving the nod to private security contractors just as it had for the concurrent Afghan jihad, the British government was also aware of British firms hiring ex-SAS soldiers to serve as bodyguards to the Iraqi government.[40] Most worryingly, even after Iraq was accused of poison gas attacks on Kurds in Halabja in 1988, Britain still exported three tons of sodium cyanide and sodium sulphate, both recognized as nerve gas antidotes, while the US government approved the export of virus cultures and allowed a US company to sign a $1 billion contract to build a chemicals plant which, according to a former senior Defense Intelligence Agency officer, was clearly intended to be used to manufacture mustard gas.'[41]

Just five months after Halabja, a memorandum sent by Britain's foreign secretary to Thatcher observed that the Iran–Iraq ceasefire would lead to 'opportunities for sales of defence equipment to Iran and Iraq that would be considerable', and in this context a Foreign Office minister stated of Iraq only a year before the Kuwait crisis that 'I doubt if there is any future market of such a scale anywhere where Britain is potentially so well-placed'.[42] The Department of Trade and Industry had meanwhile already allowed for the doubling of export credits for Iraq and had argued that 'this substantial increase reflects the confidence of the British government in the long term strength of the Iraqi economy and the opportunities for an increased level of trade between our two countries.' Certainly, even in 1989 Britain allowed several arms companies to attend a Baghdad arms fair, while a British company manufacturing machine tools described in a UN report as 'having the technical characteristics required for producing key components needed in a nuclear program' continued to export them to Iraq until just two weeks before it invaded Kuwait. Even after, British-made ammunition was still able to get to Iraq, with exports to Jordan continuing 'despite the knowledge that it was a diversionary route for exports to Iraq.'[43]

THE BUSINESS OF EVIL – THE ARMS INDUSTRY BONANZA

Fast-forwarding to 2014, the rise of the Islamic State was soon proving every bit as lucrative as the bogeymen threats of Muammar Gaddafi and Saddam Hussein. Passed in 2011, the US Budget Control Act had originally called for a $350 billion reduction in the Department of Defense's spending, and there were even fears of cuts rising to $1 trillion.[44] But three years later such painful measures had naturally faded into memory, with *Bloomberg* reporting that there was now a new 'opening created for the re-stocking of US arsenals'. Moreover, echoing the various new military programmes wheeled out after the Soviet intervention in Afghanistan in 1980, fresh calls were made to restart a mothballed project originally intended to develop warheads capable of intercepting intercontinental ballistic missiles from states such as North Korea and Iran.[45] In Britain's case the benefits have been a little more subtle, although Islamic State scare tactics have certainly played into the hands of those trying to protect the country's commitment to spend the NATO-benchmarked two percent of GDP on defence.[46] Stating that 'I would be lying to you if I did not say that I am very concerned about the GDP investment in the UK,' the army's chief of staff even warned that without such spending any future British deployments would have to be integrated into US forces, rather than working side-by-side.[47] Helpfully, the Islamic State's own propaganda videos also began to point out Britain's limited military capabilities, with one video even mocking the fact that the Royal Air Force only had 'a handful of planes.'[48]

More visibly the new menace has been used to help justify the creation of a new British-led naval task force in the Persian Gulf to combat smuggling and 'counter the poisonous ideology of *Daesh*', and to push through controversial plans for Britain to re-establish a naval base in Bahrain. Announced in December 2014, the foreign secretary revealed that 'this new base is a permanent expansion of the Royal Navy's footprint and will enable Britain to send more and larger ships to reinforce stability in the Gulf.' In accompanying BBC and other British media reports, the base was described as being 'one of the most important Royal Navy bases in the world' and with the rationale behind it being that 'the threat of the Islamic State may have made Gulf monarchies content to invite British forces to set up on their soil so as to support British operations in Iraq against ISIS.'[49]

The real reasons behind such a return to Bahrain in fact had little to do with the Islamic State. Not only did the base's £15 million price tag and the Bahrain government's reported promise to pay for its construction point to something a lot less substantial than what was announced, but its launch was actually conceived several years earlier, likely in an effort to emulate France's previously described establishment of *Camp de la Paix* in Abu Dhabi back in 2009.[50] Subsequently linked to significant France–UAE arms sales, Nicolas Sarkozy's coup was viewed with great envy by Britain's Conservative Party, which quickly announced a new 'Gulf Initiative' to boost Britain's presence in the Gulf after winning office in 2010. Indeed, even after Britain's December 2014 announcement, its minister of state for defence stated in parliament that the new Bahrain base was merely a continuation of facilities Britain had operated there since the 1950s and that 'negotiations to further enhance and improve these existing facilities with the government of Bahrain commenced in September 2012.'[51] As

Britain's ambassador to Bahrain further explained, the base was to be called HMS Juffair, in reference to the old colonial-era base, and its completion in 2016 would help mark the bicentennial of British relations with Bahrain.[52] Causing much embarrassment for the Ministry of Defence, but perfectly illustrating the non-military rationale behind the project, parliamentary questioning later revealed that the base was actually going to be too shallow for Britain's new *Queen Elizabeth*-class aircraft carriers.[53]

Much like Britain, France itself was also very keen to capitalize on the Islamic State threat by trying to protect its military spending and making sure of its share of any future arms sales to the region. After deploying eight hundred personnel to its base in Abu Dhabi, and several aircraft to a facility in Jordan, President François Hollande told the media in January 2015 that France was also going to send its flagship aircraft carrier *Charles de Gaulle* to the Gulf so as to provide 'precious intelligence about the Islamic State in Iraq'. Unsurprisingly he added that 'the government needed to review the rate of cuts to French military personnel planned over the next three years to take account of security needs.'[54]

In close cooperation with the Western governments, almost all of their constituent arms manufacturers have also been making hay while the sun shines. Most obviously the US's biggest firms have been booming, with their stocks reaching historic highs. Raytheon, for example, saw its share price increase from about $75 at the time the Islamic State began to make its gains in Syria, to over $125 by the end of 2015.[55] Similarly Northrop Grumman rose from $95 to a staggering $186.20 over the same period,[56] while in September 2014 it was reported that Lockheed Martin had reached its all-time share price record after a nineteen percent year-on-year rise.[57]

Explaining it best, in early 2015 the CEO of Lockheed Martin informed a Deutsche Bank analyst that any potential reduction in arms sales 'really isn't coming up' on the grounds that there is still 'volatility all around the region' and that this would continue to deliver new business, with the Middle East remaining a 'growth area' for the company.[58] Making a similar point, the chief investment officer for a US bank responsible for handling Northrop Grumman and Boeing's shares described to *Bloomberg* that 'as we ramp up our military muscle in the Middle East, there's a sense that demand for military equipment and weaponry will likely rise.' Equally optimistic, the deputy manager for Lockheed Martin's F-35 Lightning project stated that 'there's no doubt the world is getting to be a more and more dangerous place, and there are countries around the world that could look to buy aircraft and artillery ... there's a sense that there's less stability in the world than there was before.'[59]

Drone sales seemed a particularly promising growth area, with General Atomics announcing in February 2015 that it was about to sell Predators to the UAE, thus constituting the first transfer of US-manufactured armed drones to a non-NATO member.[60] A few days later Lockheed Martin revealed it was 'aggressively pitching' for drone-manufacturing joint ventures with governments such as the UAE and Jordan, while an existing UAE joint venture with a consortium of US, French, and Spanish companies stated that it saw a '$4.5 billion Middle East drone market in the period up to 2023.'[61] The missile business was also doing well, with the 'unnamed country' behind the first purchase of Britain's new Paveway IV missiles in early 2014 – worth £230 million – being revealed a year later as Saudi Arabia.[62] By this stage, of course, the British missiles were being used to bomb Yemen rather than the Islamic State.

In April 2015 US defence industry officials reportedly told Congress that they were expecting even bigger future purchases from the 'Arab allies fighting the Islamic State', and that these governments were going to 'buy thousands of US-made missiles, bombs and other weapons, replenishing an arsenal that has been depleted over the past year'. As one analyst pointed out, the air forces of these states – all of them monarchies – were previously 'a combination of something between symbols of deterrence and national flying clubs' but were now suddenly having to be used. The *New York Times* noted that Lockheed Martin seemed particularly active in pursuing such sales, as, according to its CEO, 'Lockheed Martin needs to increase foreign business – with the goal of global arms sales becoming twenty-five to thirty percent of its revenue – in part to offset the shrinking of the Pentagon budget after the post-9/11 boom.' US intelligence officials were also cited as 'believing that the proxy wars in the Middle East could last for years, which will make countries in the region even more eager for [Lockheed Martin's] F-35s, considered to be the jewel of the US's future arsenal of weapons.'[63] Meanwhile, things were starting to look particularly good for Boeing, with Kuwait announcing in May 2015 it was going to spend $3 billion on the Super Hornet. Part of a massive

$20 billion arms procurement programme financed from the emirate's general reserve fund, the deal was described as just enough to 'keep the [Super Hornet] St. Louis production line running well into 2019'. Boeing executives understandably confirmed the necessity of such 'near term Middle Eastern orders' while Reuters predicted that without the Kuwait contract the St. Louis operation would have had to close down in 2017.[64]

For dozens of other companies and products, the Islamic State has similarly served to speed up major deals, including earlier stalled contracts that had suffered from significant political opposition. In June 2015, for example, the White House felt confident enough to lift restrictions on US arms sales to Bahrain. Having been put in place following the kingdom's handling of its Arab Spring protests, business was finally able to get back to normal on the grounds that Bahrain was a partner against the Islamic State and that, according to the Department of State, it had 'made some meaningful progress on human rights reforms and reconciliation'.[65] A few months later authorization was finally given for the exporting of $1.4 billion of Boeing- and Raytheon-manufactured joint direct attack munitions to the UAE partly on the basis that it needed to 'remain an active member of Operation Inherent Resolve working to defeat the Islamic State'.[66] Meanwhile, a long-running deal between Canada's General Dynamics Land Systems and Saudi Arabia involving the sale of armoured personnel carriers also at last seemed able to move ahead. Originally conceived to 'replace the decline from Canada's withdrawal from Afghanistan' and to mitigate against the company's perceived risk of falling demand for the new vehicles, the deal had been repeatedly attacked in the Canadian media. Seeming to seal it once and for all, however, Prime Minister Steven Harper explicitly invoked the Islamic State in order to quash his critics. He claimed in September 2015 that 'this is a contract with a country that is an ally in fighting against the Islamic State. A contract that any one of our allies would have signed.'[67]

SURPRISE, SURPRISE – THE ISLAMIC STATE CAME FROM NOWHERE

Despite the huge threat to the global order that the Islamic State had supposedly begun to pose, along with the sudden need for multibillion-dollar upgrades of arsenals around the world, the US government claims it did not see it coming. As late as January 2014, with the organization already in possession of significant Syrian territory and, as described, having taken Fallujah and setting in motion meticulous plans for the capture of Mosul and other parts of Iraq, Barack Obama still saw fit to liken the group to a 'junior varsity team trying to put on a Lakers uniform'. In other words, despite having access to all manner of intelligence briefings, the White House continued to see the Islamic State as a minor league player compared to the likes of al-Qaeda.[68]

In part this was due to the CIA's own spectacular underestimations, having put the Islamic State's strength at about three thousand fighters at the beginning of 2014, but then abruptly revising this to between seven thousand and ten thousand by the summer.[69] In September, long before the barrage of third-party foreign fighter estimates began to be published, the CIA had quietly increased the group's total to a staggering 20,000 to 31,500 fighters.[70] As for the Department of Defense, the intelligence failure seems similarly acute, with Martin Dempsey, chairman of the Joint Chiefs of Staff, later admitting that the US had no plans in place for the fall of Mosul because 'there were several things that surprised us about [the Islamic State], the degree to which they were able to form their own coalition ... the military capability they exhibited'. In his words, 'Yeah, in those initial days, there were a few surprises.'[71]

The reality, however, was that the world's best-resourced intelligence agencies were well aware of the potency and plans of the perceived 'national jihadist' rival to al-Qaeda. As The Times reported in 2007, US intelligence officials were already stating that the post-Abu Musab al-Zarqawi organization – even referring to it explicitly by the current name – was planning the creation of 'a 'militant Islamic state within Iraq' as soon as the US withdrew. As they explained, this new state would stretch from Anbar to Nineveh – which is more or less the exact territory it gained in 2014 – and they revealed that its leaders had already published a document entitled Notifying mankind of the birth of the Islamic State.[72] Meanwhile, a former CIA officer warned that the 'Sunni Arabs are preparing for cataclysmic conflict, and we will need somebody to protect the Christians.'[73] Also on the ball, the previously described 2008 report commissioned by the US Army Training and Doctrine Command's Army Capability Integration

Center predicted perfectly the likely rise in these territories of a 'powerful Sunni Islamic state'.[74]

More damningly, in May 2015 a federal lawsuit served by the US public interest law firm Judicial Watch led to the subpoenaing of several documents, including a seven-page Defense Intelligence Agency report. Dating from summer 2012 it had been marked 'secret' but with the disclaimer 'not finally evaluated intelligence', and according to its headers it had also been circulated to the CIA. As well as helping dispel the illusion of the moderate Free Syrian Army by stating that, in their estimation, it was made up of Islamists including jihadists that were 'the major forces driving the insurgency in Syria', it also revealed an awareness that since the beginning of the Syrian conflict Sunni mosques in Iraq had been recruiting Iraqi Sunnis to go and fight in Syria. As with the 2007 statements and the 2008 long war report it also warned that there was the looming prospect of 'a declared or undeclared Salafist principality in eastern Syria', thus including the Islamic State's eventual capital in Al-Raqqah. Most worryingly, and in an apparent reference to Gulf monarchies and other funders of Syrian rebels, it stated that the rise of such a Salafist principality was 'exactly what the supporting powers to the opposition want in order to isolate the Syrian regime'.[75]

With regard to Nouri Maliki's increasingly Iran-tilting Iraq, the DIA report was just as forthcoming about the consequences of this new, strategically useful Salafist principality. It stated its existence would lead to the 'ideal atmosphere [for the Islamic State] to return to its old pockets in Mosul and Ramadi and will provide a renewed momentum under the presumption of unifying the jihad among Sunni Iraq and Syria'. Going even further, and with the same sort of prescience and word-for-word accurate naming as the 2007 statements, the report noted that such gains in Iraq would allow the group to unify 'the rest of the Sunnis in the Arab World against what it considers one enemy, the dissenters', and that '[it] could also declare an Islamic state through its union with other terrorist organizations in Iraq and Syria, which will create grave danger in regards to unifying Iraq and the protection of its territory'. To cap it all, the report also second-guessed the now massive influx of foreign fighters, claiming that the new Salafist principality would see 'renewing facilitation of terrorist elements from all over the Arab world entering into the Iraqi arena'.[76]

420

Within a month of the DIA report's subpoena, several high-ranking former officials from the US including a former National Security Agency executive, former FBI agents, and a former Department of Defense official confirmed its apparent gravity and pressed for the need for a critical understanding of it.[77] Former MI6 agent Alastair Crooke then tried to provide one, writing that it indicated 'new life' had being given to a pre-existing 'group think' in Western intelligence agencies that some sort of 'Sunni wedge' could be driven 'into the landline linking Iran to Syria'. He explained that planning for this had become particularly popular after the 2006 Israel–Hezbollah war and the West's perceived need to separate Iran further from its allies and proxies.[78]

Going a long way to proving Crooke's thesis, former DIA chief Michael Flynn – who had been in the post at the time the report was circulated in 2012 and remained there until 2014 – quite remarkably not only confirmed in a July 2015 Al-Jazeera interview that the report had crossed his desk but also explained that he 'paid very close attention ... the intelligence was very clear.' When asked if the US government's decision to ignore the intelligence was deliberate or accidental he then stated: 'I don't know that they turned a blind eye, I think it was a decision. I think it was a wilful decision.' As if this was not enough, when the incredulous interviewer asked Flynn to clarify whether he meant there was a decision in the US government knowingly to support such extremist groups, the former DIA chief doubled down by confirming 'it was a wilful decision to do what they're doing.' Moreover, when he was then asked why he did not try to stop arms transfers to the Salafist principality while in office he replied: 'I hate to say this ... but it's not my job'.[79]

THE STRANGEST ROAD TO WAR

At taking territory, weakening Bashar al-Assad, and driving sectarian wedges between Iranian allies, the Islamic State was certainly starting to excel. In this sense, on a strategic level, its big gains had made it by far the best battlefield asset to those who sought the permanent dismemberment of Syria and the removal of Nouri Maliki in Iraq. As former US ambassador to the UN John Bolton soon claimed, 'Today's reality is that Iraq and Syria as we have known them are gone. The Islamic State has carved out a new entity from the post-Ottoman Empire settlement, mobilizing Sunni opposition to the regime of President Bashar al-Assad and the Iran-dominated government of Iraq.' Terming his version of MI6's Sunni wedge as 'Sunnistan', he admitted it 'may not be Switzerland', but he argued 'this is not a democracy initiative, but cold power politics.' Imagining how an independent state would one day be able to form, he described how it would provide a bulwark against Damascus and Baghdad and thus be well placed to receive financing from the Gulf monarchies. Moreover, he argued, such a new conservative Sunni nation would give 'Turkey – still a NATO ally, don't forget – greater stability on its southern border'.[80]

But unlike the Free Syrian Army, *Jabhat al-Nusra*, and the various other groups working towards much the same goals, the Islamic State's especially nasty modus operandi – evidently a key driver behind its success – had soon started to go viral. Widely circulating on social media in the form of videos depicting the mass shootings and decapitations of Shia prisoners, its methods were proving truly shocking and repulsive to the international community, even if they were little different to those of Abu Musab al-Zarqawi's thugs or others in the pre-YouTube era.

With growing public pressure on the US and Britain to act, not least given their assumed responsibilities to Iraq in the wake of the 2003 invasion and their officials' sudden portrayal of the Islamic State as the new menace to Western civilization, something had to be done. Problematically, of course, the Islamic State was effectively on the same side as the West, especially in Syria, and in all its other warzones was certainly in the same camp as the West's regional allies. Moreover, the option of simply launching a few 'just for show' retaliatory air strikes against the organization, as the Bill Clinton administration had done against al-Qaeda in 1998, seemed a difficult sell to the critics, especially given the pushback experienced by the Western governments against strikes on Syria in 2013 and the Western public's growing awareness of the chaos in Libya after the 2011 intervention.

Trying to find the right balance between being seen to take action but yet still allowing the Islamic State to prosper, the West's first few manoeuvres in August 2014 were essentially attempts to establish red line perimeters for the organization. Having made no effort to avert any of the large massacres of Shia and Alawite populations in Iraq or Syria, the US and British air forces only swung into action when the non-Islamic Yazidis – an ethno-religious group in Nineveh province – seemed threatened with extinction or, in the case of their women, sexual slavery.[81] Latching on to the story, the international media depicted a substantial airborne mission to provide humanitarian aid to between twenty thousand and thirty thousand Yazidis stranded on Mount Sinjar's hillsides, all the while helping fend off the Islamic State's encroaching forces and paving the way for Kurdish rescue parties.[82] Giving the story even better legs was the Islamic State itself, which soon published media-friendly English-language pieces justifying its fighters taking concubines from pagan populations such as the Yazidis.[83] Not all were convinced by the episode's details, however, with reports in the *New York Times* suggesting that the US's claims of having resolved the situation were far from true, and a *Washington Post* correspondent questioning 'why, with all of the US assets around Iraq, has no one been able to provide a reasonable head count of the Yazidis?' Furthermore, as a drone expert argued, 'there is no technical reason why we couldn't get a solid ballpark estimate of the number of refugees … the US has the ability to find out the number of Yazidis [but] it might not be a high priority for the overall mission.'[84]

Meanwhile, in a parallel 'red line' exercise, the US claimed it had struck a handful of Islamic State targets – including a sole mortar position – near the Kurdish-majority city of Erbil, while simultaneously dropping aid to stranded civilians and helping Kurdish forces take control of the more or less abandoned city of Kirkuk.[85] Receiving much less coverage than the Sinjar mission, these small-scale actions were again interpreted as having been just enough to persuade the world that something was being done, while at the same time also making clear that Iraqi Kurdish heartlands were to be off limits to the Islamic State and, so it seemed, even the Iraqi state. As Jacky Sutton of the Institute for War and Peace Reporting told the Australian media: 'Now [Kurdish forces have] established themselves in Kirkuk, it's going to take quite a lot of negotiating by the Baghdad government to persuade them to leave.'[86]

As the father of current Iraqi Kurdistan president Masoud Barzani once stated, 'he trusted no other major power than the US' and that the Iraqi Kurds were 'ready to become the 51st state of America.'[87] Certainly as a

New Yorker essay noted at the time of the US's Erbil operation, the survival of an independent or at least semi-independent Iraqi Kurdistan remained useful to US interests, even if the rest of the region was disintegrating, as 'Obama's defence of Erbil is effectively the defence of an undeclared Kurdish oil state whose appeal is best not spoken of in polite or naive company'.[88] As Ahmad Hashim explains, however, US support for Barzani required some considerable tact, as 'due to political considerations the US cannot be seen to be focusing on making the *Peshmerga* [Kurdish militia] Islamic State-resistant ahead of the Iraqi government forces'.[89] In this sense it seemed that the US was merely continuing with its 'no win' policy on the Kurds, as per an old US Congress report from the 1970s which had explained of the prospects of Kurdish autonomy that 'neither Iran nor ourselves wish to see the matter resolved one way or the other', but that 'this was not imparted to our [Kurdish] clients, who were encouraged to continue fighting'.[90] Similarly, a later CIA memorandum described the Kurds as a 'uniquely useful tool for weakening Iraq's potential' and as a 'card to play' against the Iraqi state.[91]

By the middle of August 2014, with the US having ostensibly declared some sort of war against the Islamic State, even though it had actually done little to slow its progress, Abu Bakr al-Baghdadi's media machine went into overdrive in its efforts to capitalize on his organization's apparent new struggle against the ultimate apostate enemy. Even slicker than its early efforts, seemingly with access to new equipment, and with its staff having benefited from substantial training, a series of highly polished videos depicting several Western hostages began to be released. In all cases reportedly discovered by a company called SITE Intelligence Group – a US- and Israel-based jihadist monitoring group that has worked on US government assignments – details of the videos often appeared in the international media before links even showed up on the social media feeds of known Islamic State supporters and sympathizers.[92]

Unlike all previous Islamic State productions, none of which had ever shied away from showing prisoners and victims being killed, the new Western hostage videos were strangely sanitized, with nobody actually dying on camera, and with the prisoners – most of whom were captured journalists or aid workers – presented in Guantanamo Bay-style orange jumpsuits, likely for psychological effect. In each case a British-accented black-masked

Islamic State member took centre stage. Soon nicknamed 'Jihadi John' by the tabloid press, he was later revealed to be a Kuwaiti-born Londoner who was previously 'known to British security services'.[93] Holding an unusually small knife in the air while his captives kneeled, he ominously delivered warnings to the US and British governments. After several quick slashes with the knife, but with no blood appearing, the camera would then cut away with no video footage of the heads actually being severed. The final scene in each video was then always a shot of a body lying on the ground with what appeared to be blood around the neck and the severed head placed on top, followed by the masked man briefly introducing the next hostage.

Released ten days after the Yazidi and Erbil operations had begun, the first video featured an American journalist whose reports were being bought by the *Global Post* website. Earlier embedded with USAID-funded development projects in Iraq, he had previously been captured and held in Libya for forty-four days during the 2011 conflict.[94] With the video going viral, an outcry predictably ensued in the US leading to widespread public demands for a firm response to the Islamic State. There were, however, serious questions raised, with a number of commentators pointing to inconsistencies in the video, and conspiracy theories running wild on social media. Some of the author's thoughts about the most obvious anomalies in the video, including the size of the knife and the incongruity of the final scene, were published by *USA Today* following a telephone interview, but were then removed from the online version of the article later the same day, presumably following an official complaint.[95] By that evening Western police forces were even warning the public that simply viewing the video could trigger charges.[96] Within a week, however, more substantial criticism began to emerge, with *The Times* printing a report featuring anonymous experts from an 'international forensic science company which has worked for police forces across Britain' who confirmed that the video was 'probably staged' and that if any murder took place, then it took place off-camera. Among other discrepancies, the experts noted the strange incisions that seemed to have been made by the knife, and noted that 'camera trickery and slick post-production techniques appear to have been used'.[97]

Others, meanwhile, pointed to what seemed to be similarities between the new batch of Islamic State videos, notably their production values and news-ready format, and a known programme of Iraq-focused CIA video sabotage strategies that had been considered and perhaps even implemented over the previous decade by an 'Office of Technical Services'. As detailed in a *Washington Post* investigation published in 2010, these included the use of fake 'crawls' in Arabic – messages that would appear at the bottom of television screens and could be inserted into Iraqi newscasts. Videos were also produced using the CIA's 'darker skinned employees' that depicted an Osama bin Laden imposter and his cronies sitting and talking around a campfire, and in one case a film featuring a Saddam Hussein looka-like having sex with a teenage boy. According to a former CIA official, the latter video was made to 'look like it was taken by a hidden camera ... very grainy, like it was a secret videotaping of a sex session'. Little more is known about the programme, with a discussion broadcast on PRI's well-respected *The World* show just two days after the investigation's publication having since been deleted online. Another former official has however claimed that because the CIA at that time was suffering from a lack of funding and expertise in such matters the Office of Technical Services was eventually taken over by the Department of Defense, which, so he claimed, already had 'assets in psy-war'.[98]

Since 2014 little further has been said about the authenticity of these Islamic State videos, in part perhaps because of the police warnings, but also because they have proven hard to find in their entirety. Even though an abundance of links to other, much more horrific footage published by the group, mostly involving the gruesome deaths of Syrian or Iraqi government soldiers, remained online throughout this period and continue to be hosted on various social media platforms, the Western hostage videos seem to have fallen into a different category. In Twitter's case a new policy on removing the images of dead people had already been introduced about a month before the first video was released, ostensibly in response to the grieving relatives of a famous American actor who had recently committed suicide and whose pictures and videos were circulating widely. As a prominent terrorism analyst has since stated, 'Although news reports attributed the [new Twitter] policy to the [actor] incident, there were hints that Twitter might have known the [hostage] video was in the works. The crackdown on the Islamic State had started prior to the video's release. In the thirty days preceding the [hostage] video, Twitter had suspended at least eighty

Islamic State accounts, including all of its official outlets.' As he also noted, curious journalists who had been asking why the accounts were removed were already being referred to the new family request policy.[99]

Either way, regardless of their authenticity, the controversial video series had important and fairly immediate consequences. From the perspective of the Islamic State, and especially its described efforts to supplant al-Qaeda as the most legitimate and determined jihadist organization, the outpouring of anger in the West and the belligerent noises made by its officials worked wonders for the group's credibility. With the supposedly increased likelihood that the US would undertake serious military action against the Islamic State, this likely boosted the organization's local and foreign recruitment substantially. Indeed, as *The Management of Savagery* itself stated, the aim was to get the US to 'abandon its war against Islam by proxy ... and the media psychological war ... and force it to fight directly'.[100] As analysts noted, such a perceived confrontation was also necessary because it made it harder for al-Qaeda's core leadership and its affiliates to criticize any further Abu Bakr al-Baghdadi and the newly declared caliphate.[101]

From the US government's point of view, the Western world's growing public rage could also be usefully corralled into an effective mandate to initiate a full-scale no-fly zone over the regions of Iraq and Syria that the Islamic State was understood to control. After all, who would be prepared to bring up the thorny issue of Syrian or Iraqi sovereignty if aircraft were primarily being sent to punish the perpetrators of such cold-blooded killings. Not quite able to back the US all the way given the 2013 parliamentary vote against air strikes in Syria, Britain was nonetheless soon able join in with such operations over Iraq, a task made much easier by the fact that the third Western hostage video, published on 13 September 2014, featured a British citizen. Working for a French aid agency, in 2013 the man had been captured in the Syrian town of Atmeh, very close to the Turkish border and nowhere near any Islamic State territory at the time. He was reportedly kidnapped along with an Italian colleague who was later released.[102] Within two weeks of the video's publication British MPs had voted in favour of British participation in anti-Islamic State air strikes in Iraq by a margin of 524 to just 43. The victim himself had, after all, followed the Islamic State's script and warned in his own execution video that parliament's earlier 2013 vote had been 'a selfish decision', while in the debate itself even Britain's opposition leader Ed Miliband argued that Britain could no longer 'stand by'.[103]

Naturally the scale of the new US and British air campaign was not going to be anywhere near comparable to the strikes launched on Muammar Gaddafi's regime in 2011, or indeed Saddam Hussein's regime in 2003. Instead it seemed the dual aims were to satisfy public demands for at least some sort of visible action against the barbarism of the Islamic State, while at the same time making sure that the air forces of rival powers did not begin to take matters into their own hands and actually try to destroy the Islamic State. In this context, if the Western powers had not begun to patrol the skies over the Islamic State's territory when they did, then there would have been the very real risk of states genuinely allied to the embattled Iraqi and Syrian governments – including Iran and perhaps even Russia – being able to fill the vacuum and do the job themselves. In many ways putting it best was the British prime minister himself, who argued on the back of the British hostage video that it was Britain's 'duty' to join the new US campaign on the basis that the Islamic State was a 'direct threat to Britain', and that he was 'not prepared to subcontract the protection of British streets from terrorism to other countries' air forces'.[104]

A CAMPAIGN OF CONTRADICTIONS

Puzzlingly to many, in late September 2014 the first major actions of the still unnamed US-led campaign involved strikes on positions far away from any Islamic State territory. According to officials this was because an even more dangerous and deadly organization than the Islamic State was understood to have emerged and to be operating in parts of Syria. Purportedly answering to Ayman Zawahiri himself and staffed by al-Qaeda veterans of the Afghan jihad, the new 'Khorasan Group' was reportedly using territory in the region to plan and prepare for terrorist attacks in the West.[105] In this sense, freshly identified 'global jihadists' had suddenly pushed the more 'national jihadists', including the Islamic State, into the background once again, with British media reports a little later claiming that, for the West at least, there was 'some crumb of comfort [that] al-Qaeda and the Islamic State are now at each other's throats'.[106]

Appearing in mid-September 2014, a lone Associated Press report had described an 'intelligence gathering' that had taken place in Washington and whose participants had explained that the Khorasan Group's leaders, under instruction from Zawahiri, were known to be recruiting Europeans and Americans whose passports would allow them to board a US-bound airliner. Hosting the event, US director of national intelligence James Clapper had even said that 'in terms of threat to the homeland, Khorasan may pose as much of a danger as the Islamic State.' Shortly after, and just two days before the anti-Islamic State US campaign was due to begin, a follow-up Department of Defense briefing stated that the Khorasan Group was nearing 'the execution phase of an attack either in Europe or the [US] homeland'.[107] Such warnings were later reiterated by a former CIA deputy director who, in trying to shift the narrative slightly, claimed that the Khorasan Group was in fact the 'external operations arm for *Jabhat al-Nusra*' and that 'they are intending to attack Western Europe and the US ... they are a greater threat – direct threat – than is the Islamic State.'[108]

Doubts were understandably raised, not least because nobody seemed to have actually heard of the Khorasan Group before. Moreover, as some analysts pointed out, the existence of such a unit did not seem to fit with al-Qaeda's modus operandi in recent years, not least because most of its affiliates were bogged down with fighting local insurgencies, and with even al-Qaeda in the Arabian Peninsula understood to have only been able to allocate 'meagre resources' to global terrorist plots.[109] Causing much embarrassment, *Al-Nusra*'s Muhammad al-Jowlani later helped confirm these suspicions by telling Al-Jazeera that 'the so-called Khorasan Group, supposedly active within our ranks, doesn't exist.' He also explained that 'it is merely a Western invention to justify the bombings ... the Americans came up with it to deceive the public. They claim that this secret group was set up to target the Americans but this is not right.'[110]

In any case, the new Khorasan spectre was only of limited strategic use, as it seemed difficult to make a case that its influence extended to Iraq. Moreover, rumours that the Baghdad government was preparing to make a formal request for Iranian air strikes continued to intensify,[111] while US officials had already accused the Syrian air force of having launched cross-border strikes against the Islamic State in western Iraq's Anbar province.[112] Finally getting a name – 'Operation Inherent Resolve' – and a mission statement to 'degrade and ultimately destroy the Islamic State', by October 2014 the US and Britain seemed finally ready to turn their campaign to the Islamic State itself, or rather the skies above the Islamic State.[113] As with other recent Western interventions in the region, including the 2011 Libyan operation, standard procedure required a smattering of Arab allies to be co-opted as legitimizing fig leaves. More a public relations stunt than anything else, the UAE media soon filled itself with pictures of a female Emirati jet fighter pilot, while the Saudi press did much the same with one of its princes, smiling from the cockpit.[114] With some helpful fighting talk, Bahrain's foreign minister publicly blasted the Islamic State, arguing that 'if Afghanistan was a primary school for terrorists, then Syria and Iraq are a university for them.' He also announced that yet another new Gulf Cooperation Council joint command centre was being set up so as to help deal with the threat.[115]

Unsurprisingly perhaps, it soon emerged that the Gulf monarchies were not really as involved as everyone had first claimed. Qatar and Kuwait, for example, were later understood to have not participated at all, having only provided 'logistical assistance', while a US general soon admitted that the Saudi and Bahraini sorties were 'down' due to their efforts in Yemen.[116] In fact, by December 2014 the UAE had completely suspended its involvement, just weeks into the campaign,[117] while in 2015 it was revealed that the US had been responsible for ninety-four percent of all sorties and that Saudi Arabia had stopped taking part months before. As a confused Scottish MP complained, 'It is of huge concern that Arab states appear to be more focused on the war in Yemen rather than the fight against the Islamic State.'[118]

The lack of results achieved by the large number of US and British aircraft and, presumably, the drones believed to be criss-crossing the skies of Syria and Iraq has, however, been much harder to explain. Not least given their supposed objective of eradicating an existential threat to Western civilization and given the comparatively limited military capabilities of their foe. Moreover, as numerous former inhabitants of what are now Islamic State-occupied towns have noted, not only is the surrounding terrain of open countryside and rolling hills perfect for air strikes – and thus far less of a challenge than Afghanistan, for example – but the cities themselves provide few hiding places for military convoys or the sort of artillery and other heavy equipment the Islamic State is known to possess. For example, Al-Raqqah, as described by the author's interviewees, is not a place of tightly packed urban alleyways and underground car parks, but rather a fairly open-plan municipality with clearly identifiable public spaces, wide streets, and supply route highways that stretch hundreds of kilometres through vast tracts of mostly agricultural land.

Citing poor intelligence, analysts soon remarked that only a 'tiny fraction' of the campaign's sorties seemed to have led to actual bombings. Meanwhile, an Islamic State member interviewed by the *Wall Street Journal* claimed that the 'air strikes had been lamer than expected', and soon after the same newspaper reported that despite months of supposed air strikes the US had 'failed to prevent the Islamic State from expanding its control in Syria'.[119] Touted as a major victory for the campaign, a series of well-publicized strikes in and around the Syrian Kurdish border town of Kobane in October 2014 had of course led to a temporary Islamic State retreat, but in many ways this was something of a media spectacle, as the international press were safely camped out on a nearby Turkish hillside and were thus able to report on and even film the explosions of US ordnance pounding territory in the near distance. Less clear was how many Islamic State fighters were actually killed in this manner, rather than at the hands of the town's indomitable militia. After one particularly spectacular day of bombing, almost all of the world's front pages were taken up with scenes of a terrifying number of missiles almost simultaneously hitting a small hillock topped by a solitary Islamic State black flag that had been raised only the day before. Although the flag was described as being 'obliterated in a devastating air strike', it seemed unknown if there were actually any casualties, with a circulating video of the attack showing only a single Islamic State fighter managing to run away.[120] Willing as ever to tie in with Operation Inherent Resolve's objectives, the Islamic State made sure to acknowledge this high-profile defeat. After first filming an English-language video in the suburbs of Kobane that falsely claimed its fighters were 'merely mopping up now', its subsequent videos admitted the retreat and vowed future revenge on the town's people before making the usual threats to the US.[121]

By March 2015, some six months into the operation, US military intelligence officials were quoted as saying that despite 'thousands of Islamic

State fighters having been killed', the organization's 'senior leadership and nerve centre remained largely untouched'.[122] By summer 2015 the situation seemed little better and perhaps even worse, with the US Senate's House Homeland Security Committee noting that the Islamic State had seen a 'doubling' in the number of its foreign fighters, more than replacing any that the Department of Defense claimed had already been killed.[123] Indeed, despite Operation Inherent Resolve in the skies above it, the Islamic State was still evidently more than free to roam around most of its claimed caliphate. Indeed, its convoys – some of which stretched to hundreds of vehicles at any one time – had already driven all the way to the Syrian government's outpost in Palmyra in the very centre of Syria, where its fighters had then filmed promotional videos in broad daylight.[124] And in Iraq it was proving equally resilient – in May 2015 it was able to take control of Ramadi, the capital of Anbar province, again by having crossed largely open terrain.[125]

In parallel to the air campaign, the US had also been touting a $500 million programme to retrain Syrian 'moderate' rebels specifically to fight the Islamic State, presumably as a new priority over the earlier efforts to train them to fight the Syrian government. At the beginning of 2015 the Department of Defense stated it would be fielding 5,400 such anti-Islamic State fighters within a year, but by the summer it transpired that a mere sixty had actually materialized. As Secretary of Defense Ashton Carter admitted, 'We know this program is essential. We need a partner on the ground in Syria to assure the Islamic State's defeat … [but] this number is much smaller than we had hoped for at this point'.[126] Nonetheless, still pressing on with the renewed fantasy of US-trained Syrian combatants, and seemingly oblivious to reports that many had been kidnapped by *Jabhat al-Nusra* or had 'betrayed the US', officials continued to claim that their 'Division 30' was in fact fighting the Islamic State at its front lines in north-western Syria and that the US was supporting its advances with air strikes. This, however, was news to the other local rebel groups fighting in the vicinity, as their spokesman told the *Wall Street Journal* that 'we are fighting the Islamic State by ourselves.' He also claimed that the US strikes were 'largely ineffective' and rather worryingly described how 'Islamic State convoys were freely advancing only hours after the air strikes.'[127]

By the end of summer 2015 the incredibly poorly performing Division 30 project seemed to be fizzling out, with the Senate's House Intelligence Committee voting unanimously to slash its budget by up to twenty percent, although the White House had reportedly tried to protect the CIA side of the operation from such cuts.[128] In any case, by September, the chief of CENTCOM admitted to the Senate's Armed Forces Committee that there were only 'four or five' US-trained fighters still operating in Syria.[129] Even more remarkably, in terms of the US's level of commitment to dealing with the Islamic State, it also came to light that after 'several years of service' the US had deactivated its armed drone squadron in Djibouti – its only such base in East Africa – and for the first time since 2007 the US had no aircraft carrier stationed in the Persian Gulf.[130] With a replacement carrier not due to arrive until later in the winter, at the earliest, this meant that the US Navy had almost no means to project any force across Iraq at a time when the Islamic State was continuing to advance and even when it seemed Russia was preparing to enter the fray.[131]

EXPLAINING FAILURE – THE OFFICIAL LINE

The official explanations for such miserable military responses to the rise of the Islamic State have largely centred on convincing the public that the task is not as easy as it seems. Certainly, even though US war veterans observing the campaign have remarked that a few squadrons of 1940s-era Mustangs or Spitfires could have already easily turned the tide against the organization, and while US presidential contender Ted Cruz called for a James Baker-esque 'bombing of the Islamic State back to the stone age',[132] the Department of Defense has instead been sending out a message that nobody should be expecting such quick or decisive results. In January 2015, for example, a Pentagon spokesman told the media that Operation Inherent Resolve was all about a 'drumbeat, a steady building pressure', while a former US official justified the US's limited support for Baghdad's counter-attacks on the grounds it was 'passive tough love: not allowing the US to get drawn into Iraq, but still helping the country defeat the Islamic State'.[133]

A few months later the chairman of the US Joint Chiefs of Staff similarly warned that any escalation in the campaign would be a mistake, even though the Iraqi government was repeatedly asking for it, and that there needed to be 'greater strategic patience'.[134] Speaking from the same script, a few weeks later the CIA's director added his voice by telling an audience at the Council on Foreign Relations that 'defeating the Islamic State's capabilities will take years'.[135] Soon after, when questioned on CBS's *Face the Nation* as to why 'every single Islamic State gain seemed to come as a surprise to the US government' he doubled down by saying that 'this is going to be a long fight. I don't see this being resolved anytime soon. We need to turn back the Islamic State, we will turn [them] back, I have no doubt about it. But I think there is going to be unfortunately a lot of bloodshed between now and then.'[136]

The Department of State was of course very much in step, with its deputy special presidential envoy to the US-led campaign telling CNN a week before Palmyra fell that 'long term we are going to degrade and defeat this organization … but we have been clear from day one – it is going to take years'.[137] By June 2015, even after the loss of Ramadi, a Department of State spokesman was still telling the media that despite the US's air strikes, any saving of Iraq from the Islamic State was 'still going to take three to five years. It's not going to happen overnight.'[138] By late summer, the US's line remained steadfast, with Barack Obama having told a press conference that the war 'would not be quick … this is a long-term campaign. The Islamic State is opportunistic and it is nimble … it will take time to root them out.'[139] At an Aspen summit, senior Department of State official John Allen, himself a retired general, also described how the Islamic State 'emergency … exploded in our faces', while other senior officials at the event tried to frame things in more tactical terms, arguing that the organization had become 'a fast-moving and confounding enemy, immune to some of the counter-terrorism methods that appeared to work more effectively against al-Qaeda'.[140] US Army chief General Ray Odierno soon echoed these sentiments, informing reporters that the US had 'helped blunt the offensive by the Islamic State, but … right now we are kind of in a stalemate'. Similarly, the chairman of the Joint Chiefs of Staff reiterated his earlier statements, revealing in September 2015 that the US campaign had somehow become 'tactically stalemated'.[141] Symbolic of this high-level indifference, or so it seemed, it also emerged that the Department of Defense had been very slow to assign any form of decoration to Operation Inherent Resolve, with a mere Velcro command-style patch only being introduced in October 2015, and a bronze medal finally appearing in March 2016.[142]

From Britain's perspective, it was imperative to back the US's explanation, with senior officials repeatedly stressing the need for patience and thus reducing the public's expectation of meaningful results. In February 2015, for example, Britain's outgoing ambassador to Saudi Arabia, described by the BBC as the Foreign Office's 'foremost Arabist', stated 'I wouldn't be surprised if we were looking at ten to fifteen years of instability and insecurity [due to the] crisis in the Gulf provoked by Islamic State.'[143] A few months later, Britain's foreign secretary again likened the Islamic State to the Nazis, but this time in the context of it taking five years from Britain's evacuation of Dunkirk to finally defeating the enemy.[144] In terms of battlefield strategy, Britain had much less to defend than the US given its substantially smaller contribution to the campaign, so instead its military officials appeared to concentrate their explanations on the time-consuming and painstakingly accurate nature of British targeting. Claiming in mid-2015 that the Royal Air Force had been hitting Islamic State targets using a mixture of precision missiles and Reaper drones, British military officials seemed keen to portray an air of responsibility while also helping British citizens understand why a much larger array of enemy assets had not yet been destroyed.[145] Importantly, such highly individualized strikes, and especially those delivered by unmanned drones, also helped Britain to contribute to the US-led campaign's presence over Syria's skies, regardless of the 2013 parliamentary vote. In this sense, a legal workaround had been found to assassinate British citizens thought to be at large in Syria and who could conceivably be deemed threats to the national interest. In September 2015, for example, it was reported that RAF drones had managed to kill two young British jihadists, one from Cardiff and the other from Aberdeen. As a British 'act of self-defence', the prime minister claimed of one of the extrajudicial killings that 'there was a terrorist directing murder on our streets and no other means to stop him.'[146]

As some commentators pointed out, Britain's keenness to engage in such drone killings was also likely the result of mounting pressure on the government to be seen as a more reliable ally to the US in the wake of the 2013 vote. As a former British ambassador to the US had remarked earlier in 2015, Britain's 'special relationship [with the US] hangs by a thread'.[147] British media reports soon also spoke of the dismissive view of a 'Shrinking Britain' that had already taken hold in the White House, with the BBC noting that any increased British involvement in Syria would help 'supply real additional military muscle' to help counter the derogatory phrase, as the prime minister could then appear a 'firmer first friend' to the US.[148] In any case, by early December 2015, the British government's problem was starting to take care of itself, as in much the same way that the Islamic State's first British hostage video had helped push through a vote on Britain's intervention in Iraq, a recent Islamic State-linked jihadist attack on Paris was soon used as the launch pad for a fresh vote on air strikes against Syria. This time, achieving a strong majority and with few pointing out that the enemy had changed from the Syrian government to the Islamic State, the result was in any case purely symbolic as only six RAF aircraft were deployed, and over the next three months there was less than one British strike every two days on Islamic State territory in Syria.[149]

Taken together, the ongoing manipulations of such an important campaign as Operation Inherent Resolve seem truly shocking, not least given that it was supposed to be putting an end to an enemy senior politicians had already identified as potentially threatening the global order and the Western world's way of life. But in many ways the abundantly manifest inconsistencies underpinning the US-led operation were nothing new, as not only in the aftermath of 9/11 but also in almost all other previous occasions where the West's strategic assets had proven unsavoury, the same sort of contradictions have also very much been in evidence. During the Afghan jihad in the 1980s, for example, Fawaz Gerges points out that the '[US] administration's public statements were exceptionally hostile [but] no corresponding changes marked its actual behaviour towards the new Islamists'.[150] Moreover, and perhaps most disturbingly, the prophetic 2008 long war report seemed to have also predicted quite accurately the sort of illusory campaign that would eventually need to be waged against the Islamic State, including provision for the establishment of certain red lines along with the US's likely need to subcontract at least some of the work to Britain and other allies. In particular, it noted that US military action 'might seek to counter the Salafi-jihadist movement by trying to use just the minimum level of military resources necessary to keep the jihadist movement from spreading. In this vision, the US might turn to some of its allies to conduct a significant portion of the global direct action effort against [the movement].' A few pages later, the report describes this as a 'contain and react' approach that would allow the jihadists to have an area of sanctuary but would also involve 'deploying perimeters around areas where there are concentrations of transnational jihadists and periodically launching air/missile strikes against high-value targets.'[151]

SUSPICIONS MOUNT – CHALLENGING THE NARRATIVE

The first publicly voiced suspicions about the minimalist Operation Inherent Resolve were understandably raised by those actually trying to fight the Islamic State on the ground. By March 2015, the Iraqi government still seemed to have no meaningful US air support, even as it tried to recapture Tikrit, while its earlier requests for Iranian air support were being stymied by Tehran's inability to really fly aircraft into western Iraq due to US claims that it was 'inappropriate for Iran to join the coalition'. According to one Iraqi senior general, 'the Iraqi defence ministry had requested [US] coalition involvement but no air support from foreign allies had yet been provided.' Importantly, such complaints helped undermine the Western media's narrative at the time, which centred on speculation that the US had either chosen to or had been asked to 'sit out' from the Tikrit operation given the awkwardness of having to cooperate with Iran or the Shia militias fighting alongside the Iraqi army. Indeed, the Iraqi general was quite specific on this point, stating that 'with the advanced technology of the [US] aircraft and weapons they have, of course strikes by them are necessary.'[152] Moreover, when US strikes were eventually forthcoming, apparently on the condition that Shia militias withdrew, the *New York Times* reported witnesses saying they saw 'carpet bombing' and claiming that there did not seem to be any sense of urgency to help unseat the couple of hundred Islamic State fighters believed to be holed up in the city centre. Iraqi officials were also quoted stating their belief that the Islamic State's Tikriti stronghold was in the easily targetable former palace of Saddam Hussein.[153]

With the fall of Ramadi in May 2015 the criticism became louder, especially after an adviser to the Iraqi parliamentary speaker stated openly on television that 'the international coalition has played a bad role …people saw the international coalition dropping weapons for the Islamic State … they dropped heavy weaponry to the forces of terrorism in Ramadi … this is an act of treason.'[154] Remarkably the *Washington Post* later reported that 'Iraqi fighters say they have all seen the videos purportedly showing US helicopters airdropping weapons to the militants' and that 'ordinary people also have seen the videos, heard the stories and reached the same conclusion … that the US is supporting the Islamic State for a variety of pernicious reasons.'[155]

While such claims could be dismissed as some kind of collective conspiracy theory, it is noteworthy that even the Iraqi Kurdish media had begun to ask serious questions about Ramadi. Publishing an interview with an Iraqi army officer, who was in command of one of the last units to retreat from the city after holding out in a sports stadium with about sixty other soldiers, the man argued that the 'Americans weren't really that serious in hitting the Islamic State to help us'. He further contended that 'I don't think all the air strikes and attacks on the Islamic State in the past year and half have degraded any of the Islamic State's capacity. In fact, the Islamic State is getting stronger and has weapons that we don't have.'[156]

By June 2015 even Nouri Maliki's successor, Prime Minister Haider al-Abadi, was wading in. Publicly stating that the US-led campaign was not doing enough either to help Iraq on the battlefield or to try to stem the flow of foreign fighters into the Islamic State, he also revealed that Iraq 'had received very few arms or ammunition despite coalition pledges to provide more. Almost none. We are relying on ourselves.'[157] In this sense he was echoing what the Iraqi parliamentary speaker had told Reuters earlier in the year: 'Until now our feeling is that the international support is not convincing … we might see participation here or there, but it is not enough for the tough situation we are passing through.'[158] By the end of the year, al-Abadi's position had hardened even further and he stated that any further deployment of foreign soldiers to Iraq, including those from the US, would be considered 'a hostile act'.[159]

Beyond the Baghdad administration, the feeling among Shia militia leaders was expectedly much the same. Arguably conducting the majority of front-line operations against the Islamic State, by summer 2015 they seemed to have already worked out the rationale and methods underpinning the US's 'contain and react' approach to the jihadist organization. As one Shia commander put it, 'We believe the US does not want to resolve the crisis but rather wants to manage the crisis … it does not want to end the Islamic State. It wants to exploit the Islamic State to achieve its projects in Iraq and in the region.' He also noted that the promised ramping-up of US-led air strikes had still not materialized.[160] Though he may not have realized it, his suspicions may have been spot on, as only a few months earlier former CIA director and CENTCOM commander David Petraeus had told the *Washington Post* that 'the foremost threat to Iraq's long-term stability and the broader regional equilibrium is not the Islamic State, it is Shia militias, many backed by – and some guided by – Iran'. Making the case that it was better for the Islamic State to survive than be defeated by Iran, he even attempted some moral equivalence by claiming that 'neither the Iranians nor the Islamic State are ten feet tall.' Moreover, when asked about pictures that had been circulating of Iranian commander Qasem Soleimani appearing on the battlefield against the Islamic State, Petraeus said, 'I have several thoughts when I see the pictures of him, but most of those thoughts probably aren't suitable for publication in a family newspaper.'[161]

In Syria, those rebels finding themselves bearing the brunt of the Islamic State's assaults quickly drew the same conclusions as the Iraqi government, soon complaining of 'inexplicable absences' of air strikes at key moments. In May 2015, for example, while the world was busy watching the Islamic State's capture of Palmyra from Syrian government forces, the organization's convoys were also quietly making significant advances north of Aleppo, again along highways through open terrain, so as to cut off rebel supply routes from Turkey. As one rebel brigade member told Reuters, 'The Islamic State is heading to the Turkish border … if this happens I don't know who will be able to explain why the coalition is not bombing [them].' He also stated that 'it's one thing that they don't bomb the regime because of some international circumstances they need to take into account. However, failure to bomb the Islamic State on that particular front is not going to go down well with the rebels.'[162] Perhaps unsurprisingly, even the US-backed Free Syrian Army seemed marginalized, with almost throwaway remarks attributed to US officials and FSA members published in a *Bloomberg* report revealing that the FSA had been 'cut out of the process for selecting targets for US air strikes in Syria' and that 'the FSA's leadership has complained that the US has ignored its offers to share intelligence.'[163]

From the point of view of Syrian non-combatants, distrust of Operation Inherent Resolve also seemed to grow over the course of 2015. Having managed to conduct a survey of over 1,300 civilians across all fourteen governorates, a reputable British market research firm revealed that fifty-seven percent believed the situation had worsened since the US-led campaign began, while more than half opposed the air strikes outright. Most worryingly, eighty-two percent of respondents believed that the Islamic State was a 'US and foreign made group'.[164] Meanwhile, a number of Syrian businessmen and local traders had helped the *Financial times* compile a detailed report demonstrating that the Islamic State had actually been expanding its control and operation over Syria's key infrastructure, including five new oil refineries that it had 'bought'.[165]

As for the other actors involved in fighting the Islamic State, or at least trying to support the governments that were, a number of similar complaints have been made, albeit a little more tactfully. Soon after beginning its own air strikes in October 2015 against 'all terrorists' in Syria,[166] Russia's head of the Main Operations Directorate of the General Staff revealed that Moscow's offer to share possible Islamic State targets with the US-led campaign had been rebuffed. As he put it 'This means that either our partners do not have such coordinates, or that they for some reason do not want us to hit these targets. The reason for this remains unclear to us.'[167] At the same time a number of Russian military bloggers and social media users also expressed their surprise that there were even any Islamic State targets still left to hit, given that by that stage there was already supposed to have been a full year of sustained US-led strikes. Adding more to the picture, even officials from NATO member Germany began to express carefully their dissatisfaction. Having deployed a hundred soldiers to a base just thirty kilometres from the Islamic State's front lines in Iraq, the German army had been trying to train up Kurdish *Peshmerga* militiamen. But in June 2015 it reported that its US-supplied intelligence had been frozen and that repeated requests for electronic surveillance assistance had gone unanswered. As German intelligence officers complained, 'Without the technology of the Americans we're blind.' With a slightly different slant to the Russians, Germany's *Bild* newspaper suspected that terminated intelligence cooperation was due to US fears that the CIA and DIA could end up being part of an ongoing German parliamentary inquiry into foreign spying. As it pointed out, 'Britain earlier this year threatened to end all intelligence cooperation with Germany if any details of joint operations were revealed to the inquiry.'[168]

Most seriously, and proving the hardest to brush aside, criticism of the lacklustre Operation Inherent Resolve was also intensifying in the US itself. In May 2015 the straight-talking former secretary of defense Robert Gates rather charitably observed that 'we don't really have a strategy at all. We're basically playing this day by day.'[169] But less than a week later there were hints of something much more sinister, as a number of serving intelligence and military officials told *Bloomberg* on the condition of anonymity that the US had had 'significant intelligence' about the Islamic State's plans to attack Ramadi and that it was an 'open secret' that such an operation was imminent. As *Bloomberg*'s correspondent noted, this meant that the 'US watched Islamic State fighters, vehicles and heavy equipment gather on the outskirts of Ramadi before the group retook the city in mid-May'. In spite of this, 'the US did not order air strikes against the convoys before the battle started. It left the fighting to Iraqi troops, who ultimately abandoned their positions.' The correspondent also stated that 'the US intelligence community had good warning that the Islamic State intended a new and bolder offensive on Ramadi because it was able to identify the convoys of heavy artillery, vehicle bombs and reinforcements through overhead imagery and eavesdropping on chatter from local Islamic State commanders. It surprised no one, one US intelligence official told me.' Quoting a former adviser to Petraeus, the investigation also revealed that Iraqi government forces in Anbar had been forced to purchase weapons and ammunition on the black market ever since the US-led campaign began, as key supplies were simply no longer reaching them.[170]

Substantiating much of this, in summer 2015 a group of DIA analysts based at CENTCOM came forward to explain that they had submitted documentary evidence and a joint written complaint to the Department of Defense's inspector general in support of their claim that their 'Stalinist' superiors were deliberately downplaying any pessimistic or critical reports on the US's efforts to defeat the Islamic State. They also claimed that their intelligence was being manipulated so as to portray a rosier picture of Operation Inherent Resolve. One official remarked that 'the cancer was within the senior levels of the intelligence command' and explained that more than fifty analysts had made formal complaints, some dating back to the very start of the US-led campaign. Some of the complainants had reportedly then been asked to retire while some had voluntarily agreed to leave their positions.[171] In September 2015 a *New York Times* editorial described these attempts 'to alter the conclusions of rank-and-file intelligence officers' as being 'particularly alarming'.[172]

Beyond officialdom, a number of prominent Western analysts have been busily identifying the campaign's other obvious inconsistencies and contradictions. As Charles Lister noted, progress maps produced by the Department of Defense that had tried to demonstrate how the Islamic State was 'no longer able to operate freely in twenty-five to thirty percent of the populated areas of Iraq it once could' had in fact made no effort to account for territory actually gained by the Islamic State since the strikes began, or the other substantial areas in which it was still known to operate easily. Moreover, he observed that 'the Islamic State has been very minimally challenged since August 2014' and that he would 'fairly forcefully debate' any of the Department of Defense's claims that the Islamic State's gains in Syria had been offset by its losses. Making much the same point, the Institute for the Study of War's Jennifer Cafarella reasoned that such maps were deficient as they excluded large sections of western Syria where the Islamic State was known to have been advancing. As she described, these fresh gains were particularly important as 'they are a forward investment for the Islamic State that will create long-term opportunities for further expansion into zones in which coalition air strikes are unlikely, at least in the near term, to penetrate.'[173] Putting it more bluntly, the International Institute for Strategic Studies' Emile Hokayem warned: 'Next time you read some grand statement by US officials on [the] campaign against the Islamic State or see a CENTCOM map about Islamic State reversals, just bin it.'[174]

Using a more quantitative approach to try to evaluate growing criticisms that Operation Inherent Resolve was not doing enough, Council on Foreign Relations senior fellow Micah Zenko set about proving that despite the supposed menace of the Islamic State and the vast territory it controlled, the US-led campaign nonetheless involved substantially fewer strike sorties than other recent US and NATO-led missions. According to his figures, by July 2015 the campaign had seen a daily average of just eleven such sorties. In contrast there had been forty-six a day against the Muammar Gaddafi regime in 2011, while the US had carried out on average nearly six hundred a day over Iraq in 2003 and eighty-six over Afghanistan in 2001. Going back further, he noted that even NATO's strikes on Serbia in 1999 had averaged 183 a day. Although acknowledging that each US air campaign faced changing circumstances, including a supposedly new-found desire to protect civilians, he nonetheless concluded of Operation Inherent Resolve that 'for a military campaign that allegedly intends to inflict a lasting defeat on the dispersed and large militant army that is the Islamic State, there is a relatively limited – though understandable given the concern of civilian casualties – number of bombs being dropped each day'.[175]

Agreeing with Zenko, former US Department of State chief strategist on counter-terrorism David Kilcullen has similarly pointed out that since the campaign began there was only an average of ten daily strikes on Islamic State targets and, as he argued, 'without even going close to putting troops on the ground, we could be doing a very significantly greater amount to deal with the Islamic State'.[176] Nonetheless, despite so few actual strikes, the US-led coalition has managed to hit the Syrian and Iraqi armies by mistake on at least two occasions, with four Syrian soldiers being killed in their crucial Deir Ezzor redoubt while surrounded by the Islamic State, and twenty-two Iraqi soldiers bombed while advancing on the group in Anbar province. The US was also understood to have bombed a Syrian rebel unit that it had itself earlier trained. According to the unit's spokes-man ten of its fighters were killed after 'a US air strike hit brigade members while they were fighting Islamic State militants'.[177]

Helping to illustrate the situation further, it soon transpired that after Russia began its own air strikes it had, as acknowledged by the British media, 'been carrying out more sorties in a day in Syria than the US-led coalition has done in a month'.[178] Given the concentration of Operation Inherent Resolve aircraft over the skies of most Islamic State-held terri-tory, and reports of the US having taken control of an old airstrip in the north-eastern corner of Syria, it seemed, however, that Russia had little choice but to restrict its strikes to the north-west.[179] Rather ominously, US director of national intelligence James Clapper warned that the '[Russian] intervention in Syria ... risked becoming for Russia what the intervention in Afghanistan became for the former Soviet Union in the 1980s'.[180]

Going further than Zenko and Kilcullen, and perhaps getting a bit closer to the truth, has been Abraham Miller – a University of Cincinnati emeritus professor and a fellow of New York University's Salomon Center. Also comparing the strangely low intensity of Operation Inherent Resolve air strikes with earlier US-led campaigns, but trying to link this to the post-Arab Spring landscape and its deepening sectarian fault lines, he made the realistic argument in June 2015 that the US had no intention of destroying the Islamic State, at least for the time being, and that any air strikes were merely pinpricks. In his words, 'The Islamic State exists as a political structure whose function outweighs the political and military costs of defeating it, not just for the US but also for the Sunni sheikhdoms of the Persian Gulf.' He then concluded that 'the Islamic State fights Shia in Iraq and Syria. The threat they pose is tolerated even by the Gulf sheikhdoms as long as the Islamic State is focused on stopping Iranian hegemony.'[181] Although air strikes launched against a retreating Islamic State convoy outside Fallujah in 2016 – which purportedly killed over 250 of the militants – at first seemed to invalidate Miller's theory, with the US quick to give the impression its own aircraft had been behind them, it was soon apparent that the strikes had actually been carried out by the Iraqi air force, with the exact role of 'coalition' aircraft remaining unclear and 'bad weather' and 'protecting civilians' later cited as reasons for their non-involvement.[182]

FOLLOW THE MONEY – THE SELF-FUNDING NARRATIVE

In solving any mystery, at least with regard to an organization as wealthy and capable as the Islamic State, perhaps the second most important question that needs to be asked after *qui bono* is *qui solvit* or 'who pays?' After all, not only has the Islamic State proven itself capable of procuring or buying advanced weaponry that has been more than a match for its adversaries, but, as demonstrated, it was also able to set up very quickly public services for a population of several million along with an extensive network of public sector employment, and, so it would seem, a subsidy system far more generous than that of any of the states or groups it has been supplanting. In this sense almost overnight the new caliphate was able to establish some of the same sort of allocative state structures, albeit more modest, than one might find in the oil-rich 'rentier state' Gulf monarchies.[183] As the School of Oriental and African Studies' Charles Tripp termed it, 'the rentier caliphate with no new ideas'.[184] But puzzlingly, of course, this new Islamic proto-rentier state does not seem to have had the kind of sustained access to the billions of dollars in export revenues it would really need to pay for everything.

Following the Islamic State's major gains in Syria and Iraq in 2013, and especially 2014, it seemed inevitable that fingers would start to point at suspected funders. After all, it was logical that if money supplies could be cut off, then the group would quickly wither from within, thus dramatically improving the prospects of anyone actually trying to defeat it. Naturally, given the Islamic State's ongoing strategic usefulness on multiple levels, this could not be allowed to happen, and it has been imperative that any substantial identification of the Islamic State's most generous and systematic backers does not take place.

To forestall or undermine such an investigation, most efforts through the latter part of 2014, and most of 2015, duly concentrated on building up a 'self-funding' narrative for the Islamic State. In many ways this was a better orchestrated repeat of an earlier attempt to do the same for al-Qaeda in the weeks following 9/11. Back then there had been a well-planned but mostly ineffective campaign to portray al-Qaeda as a self-sufficient criminal enterprise. Repeated references to Osama bin Laden's enormous inherited wealth were made by US officials, despite earlier published findings that most of his fortune was already gone and that his network of businesses in Sudan was failing.[185] Exactly a month after 9/11 a very thinly sourced story on al-Qaeda's supposed finances then appeared in the *New York Times*. Co-written by a journalist whose later articles on Iraq's weapons of mass destruction helped justify the US invasion but were later determined by the newspaper to be inaccurate, the October 2001 report cited unnamed US officials' claims that bin Laden was using an international chain of retail honey shops to generate income and finance the movement of weapons and agents for al-Qaeda.[186] Meanwhile, by simply repeating bits of this report the BBC claimed that the CIA 'had been gathering information about al-Qaeda's ties to the honey trade for several years. But it was not until last May [2001] that a top secret report on the honey shops was distributed within the intelligence community.'[187]

By late 2006, as the US's fears of Nouri Maliki's Baghdad administration gravitating closer to Iran seemed to be coming true, the self-funding narrative was also beginning to be applied to Abu Musab al-Zarqawi's al-Qaeda in Iraq, and then ultimately the same Islamic State in Iraq that Abu Bakr al-Baghdadi was to join and then eventually lead. In particular, a classified US intelligence report from October that year cited by the *New York Times* stated that al-Zarqawi's Sunni insurgency had managed to become 'self-sustaining financially, raising tens of millions of dollars a year from oil smuggling, kidnapping, counterfeiting, connivance by corrupt Islamic charities and other crimes that the Iraqi government and its US patrons have been largely unable to prevent'. The not-so-secret report also made sure to make very clear that 'terrorist and insurgent finances within Iraq – independent of foreign sources – are currently sufficient to sustain the groups' existence and operation.' Putting figures to it, claims were also made that the Islamic State in Iraq was netting $70 million to $200 million a year from such activities, including $36 million from hostage ransom payments. Importantly the report was actually handed to the *New York Times* by officials rather than leaked, on the basis that 'the findings could improve understanding of the challenges the US faces in Iraq.' Incredibly, the officials revealed that it had been compiled by an all-star inter-agency group drawn from the CIA, the DIA, the FBI, the Department of State, the Department of the Treasury, and even CENTCOM.[188]

Declining to take the document at face value, on this occasion the *New York Times* made sure to interview a number of independent analysts, one of whom described the report's findings as 'imprecise and speculative' while another noted 'the absence of documentation of how [the report's] authors had arrived at their estimates'.[189]Since then a former veteran jihadist, whose lengthy testimonies have now been published by Oxford University Press, has helped to expose such facile self-funding narratives. In his description of the Islamic State in Iraq and other such 'post-al-Qaeda' groups at the time, he said that 'the support infrastructure provided by Gulf financiers has been the elephant in the room ... and I think in the emergence and spread ... and its way of thinking'. He has also explained how this network of Gulf private financing behind al-Zarqawi and others led to the 'militarization of jihad without restraint, without responsibility ... funded and directed by the elite for their own purposes ... the jihadist project has become privatized. Jihad is no longer an activity carried out by the [whole Muslim world]; it is jihad led by the rich.'[190]

Similarly pointing to such external wealth streams, another former jihadist has revealed how youths at that time were 'taking up jihad as a profession ... they are funded by the rich merchants ... they think they are fighting for a cause – but really they are fighting for the objectives of others'.[191] Referring again to the apparent privatization of jihad, and also the considerable continuity in funding networks from the original Afghan jihad to the contemporary insurgency, another former fighter featured in the Oxford University Press volume explained how 'the people who funded the earlier generations of Arab-Afghans remain involved in financing activities ... they are more responsible for this Blackwater-ing of the jihad.' He further remarked of the funders that 'it seems they are very active now, with events after the Arab Spring intensifying.'[192]

Adopting much the same template as the 2006 US intelligence document, since the Islamic State's dramatic capture of Mosul in 2014, a slew of analysis pieces and thinktank reports have tried to build up a similar self-funding explanation for the rapid expansion of the latest incarnation of al-Zarqawi's 'national jihadist' organization. Mostly fuelled by titbits of gossip from the intelligence community or heavily recycled factoids only loosely checked at the point of origin, these have collectively, though mostly unwittingly, served to distract attention from the real networks responsible for boosting and then sustaining the Islamic State's coffers.

First out of the starting blocks was the Brooking Institution, with a report published by its Qatar branch in November 2014 practically being a reproduction of the 2006 assessment. It described the Islamic State's funding model as having 'a focus on maintaining financial independence, in comparison to the traditional al-Qaeda model of relying on external donors and financiers'. Of its multiple sources of funding, these were understood to 'include oil, gas, agriculture, taxation, extortion, kidnapping for ransom, black market antique selling, and other illicit trades'.

Driving the point home, it concluded that after the Islamic State's seizure of further territory in 2014 it was 'likely that the group has continued to be financially self-sufficient'.[193] Similarly, in an otherwise excellent article for *Middle East Policy* in which Ahmad Hashim rightly cautioned against 'the many unverified statements about the sources of the Islamic State's finance that continue to be issued uncritically by governments and the media', he nonetheless made no mention of possible external sponsors and instead simply put forward oil, tax, and extortion as the most likely explanations.[194]

With the consensus quickly building, by March 2015 the *Washington Post* was confident enough to sport the lede 'It's all about oil and extortion' for a feature entitled 'Where does the Islamic State get its funding?' Neither the article nor its accompanying video included any discussion of possible donor networks.[195] Similarly in May 2015 the *New York Times* produced what it claimed to be a breakdown of the Islamic State's finances. With extortion, bank looting, and oil representing the lion's share, again no mention whatsoever was made of external sponsorship.[196] In December 2015, the director of the US Department of the Treasury's Office of Terrorism and Financial Intelligence told a British audience that 'the Islamic State has made more than $500 million from black market oil sales. It has looted between $500 million and $1 billion from bank vaults captured in Iraq and Syria.' Worryingly he also stated that 'unlike many other terrorist groups, the Islamic State derives a relatively small share of its funding from donors abroad. Rather [it] generates wealth from economic activity within the territory it controls. This makes it difficult to constrain its funding.'[197] Even as late as January 2016 the defence editor of a British broadsheet newspaper still felt comfortable in concluding that 'at a time when the Islamic State is using the millions of dollars it has seized from looted Arab banks and its lucrative oil-smuggling operations to fund the growth of extreme Islamic ideology, the Saudi initiative to fund moderate Muslim leaders could prove vital in curbing the growth of Islamist-inspired terrorism.'[198]

There is no doubt, of course, that the activities briefly cited in such reports have been generating at least some income for the Islamic State. According to a local activist's account, for example, the organization was understood to have been collecting 2.5 percent of all proceeds from business owners under the guise of *zakat* or obligatory religious charity. The same source did, however, acknowledge that the *zakat* was then being redistributed to pay for services.[199] But most of the more widely circulating claims, including those put forward by US and British officials, that the Islamic State has been enriching itself by running a punishingly tax heavy regime, have simply made no sense, not least given the organization's need to boost its popularity, but also in view of its efforts to provide local businessmen with a fairer and more consistent fiscal system than those found in neighbouring territories.

As regards looting, almost as soon as Mosul was captured dozens of reports began to state that the organization's fighters had been sacking major banks even though, as with heavy taxes, this was contradictory to the group's modus operandi. Likely derived from comments made by Iraqi lawmaker and one-time CIA asset Ahmed Chalabi, Fox News for example had come up with a surprisingly accurate figure of $429 million that had been purportedly hauled from the city's central vaults. This crime alone was described as making 'the Islamic State the wealthiest terrorist organization in the world', while quoted analysts explained this could help the group 'buy a whole lot of jihad'.[200] Quickly going viral, the narrative went mostly unchallenged, and US officials waited nearly a year before acknowledging that the Mosul Central Bank had in fact not been pillaged and that the Islamic State had actually kept it open for several months, while even continuing to pay the salaries of its staff.[201] Indeed, as the *Financial Times* noted, 'Not a single witness account has emerged of the Islamic State making off with any money, and executives and employees from among the twenty private banks and fifteen government bank branches in Mosul say there is no evidence that militants stole any money.'[202] Adding more to the picture, in May 2015 the chairman of Jordan's Capital Bank revealed in an interview that his Mosul branch was still going strong, having been completely unaffected by the Islamic State's presence. He also remarked that everything was 'business as usual' in Mosul and that the 'lifestyle of the people' was also unchanged.[203]

Reminiscent of the Kosovo Liberation Army's trafficking in human organs, the Islamic State was even accused of profiting from the sale of harvested body parts. In February 2015, for example, reports circulated that bodies discovered in mass graves seemed to have missing kidneys and signs of surgical incisions.[204] Although certainly plausible, especially if the bodies were those of executed Shia prisoners, it seems unlikely that such an activity could really have been serving as a major source of income. To date there has been no follow-up investigation or any substantiating evidence apart from documents apparently seized in a US raid indicating that the Islamic State had issued a ruling permitting the removal of organs from apostates in order to save the lives of Muslims.[205]

A bit more credible, it seems, has been the idea that the Islamic State is doing a healthy trade in selling off Iraqi and Syrian antiquities. In summer 2014 a courier was intercepted while in possession of financial records showing how the Islamic State had made $36 million in such sales from just one Syrian province, and by Spring 2015 Interpol estimated that $100 million a year was being made in this way, with its database having logged more than five thousand missing artefacts in Iraq and Syria.[206] Helping the story along, in July 2015 the US ambassador to Iraq described how early Islamic coins and jewellery had been found during a supposed mission to capture a key Islamic State leader is that these represented the 'first tangible evidence that [the Islamic State's militants] is selling artefacts to fund their activities'.[207] Using archives of satellite imagery of archaeological sites to investigate these claims, a Dartmouth College anthropologist determined that antiquities were certainly being stolen in an organized manner from Islamic State-controlled areas, but that the activity was actually more widespread in areas controlled by Syrian rebels and Kurdish groups.[208]

Of all the self-funding explanations, the most convincing has been that the Islamic State operates a lucrative black market oil-smuggling network. After all, in such war-shattered territories, no combination of antiquity sales, *zakat* collections, or other assorted fees and tolls would be enough to explain the several hundred million or even billions of dollars to which the organization seemed to have access. By summer 2014 descriptions began to circulate of the new caliphate being effectively a 'petro state' on the basis it had cut out the oil middlemen and was reaping as much as $25 to $60 a barrel from oilfields in its possession. Others, meanwhile, claimed that the Islamic State was generating between $3 and $5 million a day from an estimated daily production of eighty thousand barrels.[209] For the next six months, more or less every Islamic State-related article that appeared in the Western media recycled at least one of these statistics, but in almost every case offered no further evidence.

There may be some truth behind the oil exporting narrative, as back in 2013 the European Union had relaxed its oil embargo on Syria so as to 'allow opponents of Bashar al-Assad to sell crude ... [and] to help the civilian population'.[210] But as with the other self-funding income streams there seems to have been considerable exaggeration of the scale of such oil revenues and, as a result, a mostly unwitting effort to divert attention away from the Islamic State's primary financial resources. Notably, as with the delay in admitting that Mosul banks had not been looted, only in February 2015 did Department of Defense officials acknowledge that oil was unlikely to be the Islamic State's main income stream.[211] Within a few weeks the G7's intergovernmental Financial Action Task Force managed to reach the same conclusion, stating that although 'the Islamic State has been engaging in energy-related commerce' there was no sound estimate in existence for its revenues and that the trade 'had probably diminished in importance'.[212]

As to the real sources of income, the Department of Defense has now hinted that it knows donations have played a central role, but it has not yet expanded upon this, and some US officials have persisted with claims that oil continues to generate hundreds of millions of dollars in revenue for the Islamic State.[213] Nonetheless, as the secretary general of the Union of Arab Banks has described, a number of banks in the Middle East have been coming under increased scrutiny from the US because, as he put it, the Department of the Treasury knows that the Islamic State 'needs constant funding, unlike al-Qaeda which may require a small amount of money to conduct specific operations'.[214] Certainly by September 2015 the self-funding myth seemed to be coming to an end, with the Department of the Treasury's assistant secretary for terrorist financing admitting that the Islamic State had 'immense wealth' and was a 'sprawling international organization with tentacles across Europe, Asia, and the Middle East'.[215] After describing this latter scenario to them, more than ninety percent of the author's interviewees on this topic agreed it was accurate, although a substantial number pointed out that the tentacles were actually going into the Islamic State rather than coming out of it. Indeed, a detailed *Wall Street Journal* investigation into the Islamic State's 'cash flow' soon revealed that 'hundreds of money exchange houses' in neighbouring countries such as Turkey and Jordan were facilitating the daily flow of millions of dollars' worth of currency into the organization's territory.[216]

Despite such revelations, very little seems to have actually been done about the Islamic State's obviously generous external sponsors, with the Department of the Treasury having sanctioned only four suspected financiers during the first year of the US-led campaign, and since then only sanctioning a further twenty-five.[217] Moreover, as the president of the Centre d'Analyse du Terrorisme in Strasbourg pointed out, one of the latest batch had already been well known as an Islamic State financial chief for more than fifteen months.[218] The British government has been similarly sidetracked, with the chairman of a parliamentary subcommittee on 'ISIL Financing' telling a hearing in March 2016 that the Islamic State's monthly income of $80 million was made up of 'forty percent oil revenues and fifty percent from taxation by various means'. He also stated that 'we are grossly underestimating the return [the Islamic State] gets from interest and making a turn on looted cash', while another committee member claimed this 'central bank issue' may have been generating $20 million a month for the group.[219]

Causing confusion, however, the head of the Foreign Office's 'Counter-Daesh Coalition Communications Cell' told the panel that 'it was certainly a problem in the early days of the organization that there was funding coming in from Gulf countries and other places.' When pressed on this he stated: 'There was funding going from those countries ... but we have no way of knowing who knew about that and what was happening about that.'[220] Further challenging the government's narrative, in written evidence supplied to the subcommittee by Luay al-Khateeb, the director of the Iraq Energy Institute, it was claimed that 'discussions with oil professionals who have worked on Syrian oil fields now under the Islamic State's control indicate the group was never able to achieve refining of any significant quality to sell the oil outside of Syria [above] a maximum of $20 dollars a barrel ... and even this price occurred briefly over the summer of 2014.' Al-Khateeb also wrote that 'my calculations based on sources inside Syria, suggest the Islamic State made no more than $200 million in a year from oil (at best case scenario),' and that 'based on the analysis here of other estimated income, such as tax, the selling of looted antiquities and confiscated property, set against the estimated maximum operational costs of the group, which I believe to be well over $2 billion per year, it would appear that the Islamic State's income from private donors is far larger than previously estimated.'[221]

Notwithstanding its own admission about the Islamic State's oil economy, the Financial Action Task Force seems to have been equally slow at reaching any kind of consensus on what to do next. Although its 2015 report did briefly mention the existence of Islamic State 'donors who abuse non-governmental organizations', it nevertheless tried to extend the life of the self-funding narrative by claiming that 'most of the Islamic State's funding is not currently derived from external donations, but is generated within the territory in Iraq and Syria where it currently operates.' It also confidently stated, but again with no substantiation, that 'the overall quantitative value of external donations to the Islamic State is minimal relative to its other revenue sources.' Indeed, only one sentence in the entire report suggested the possibility that wealthy individuals in nearby Gulf states have played a role, while much more attention was given to small, low-level 'grass roots' donations, including online crowdsourcing and even foreign fighters who were understood to have self-financed their travel to the Islamic State.[222] Most concerning, despite the existence of credible evidence to the contrary, and as with the British parliamentary subcommittee, the Financial Action Task Force still seemed keen to keep peddling the looting explanation. Notably, based on 'press reports' it claimed that the Islamic State's main source of funding was the pillaging of banks and 'sophisticated extortion rackets built by robbing and demanding portions of economic resources in areas where it operates.'[223] On this basis it even argued that the Islamic State had become a 'new type of terrorist organization with unique funding streams that are crucial to its activities.'[224]

FOLLOW THE MONEY – THE ISLAMIC STATE'S FUNDERS

With at least some fingers starting to point to a network of international sponsors being behind the Islamic State, perhaps similar to that which had backed al-Qaeda and weathered 9/11 mostly intact, it seemed likely that the same donor-based system that had helped finance Abu Musab al-Zarqawi's organization several years earlier had not only survived but had managed to rejuvenate itself. Certainly as the veteran jihadists featured in the recent Oxford University Press volume have pointed out, many of the same funding networks originally established during the Afghan jihad under diplomatic cover from the US have since 'expanded and come to dominate Salafi-jihadist yards around the world ... [and have] led to the working mechanisms that continue to allow this jihadist current to dominate today'.[225]

Given their ideological similarities and the demonstrable strategic value of the Islamic State to their foreign policies, some have naturally suggested that the organization is the latest baby of conservative Gulf monarchies such as Saudi Arabia, Qatar, and Kuwait. Indeed, in the context of the well-documented roles of some of their state-backed bodies in having earlier financed al-Qaeda, along with the known permissiveness of their security and judicial institutions towards al-Qaeda operatives, this has been both a reasonable and logical line of inquiry. Getting the ball rolling just a few weeks after the Islamic State arrived in Mosul, former MI6 director Richard Dearlove told an audience that he had no doubt that wealthy Saudis had 'played a central role in the Islamic State's surge into Sunni areas of Iraq and Syria'. Going further, he pointed to a Riyadh-led sectarian plot by noting that in the immediate wake of 9/11 a senior Saudi had once warned him that 'the time is not far off in the Middle East, Richard, when it will literally be God help the Shia'.[226]

A few months later US vice president Joe Biden waded in, perhaps underestimating the viral capabilities of anything so provocative ending up on YouTube. Telling a gathering at Harvard University that 'the biggest problem the US faces in dealing with Syria and the rise of the Islamic State is America's allies in the region,' he went on to answer a student question by explaining that Saudi Arabia and the UAE had been funnelling weapons and other aid to Syrian rebels that had ended up in the hands of extremist groups.[227] Beyond the usual suspects in the Syrian, Iraqi, and Iranian governments, a number of other voices in the region have also since sided with Dearlove and Biden. Abdelfattah Sisi, for example, has been using the opportunity to pin Islamic State funding on Qatar, the backers of his Muslim Brotherhood enemies,[228] while articles have appeared in the Arabic press echoing Dearlove's claim that '[a senior

454

Saudi] channelled generous funds to the Islamic State'.[229] Meanwhile, in Kuwait, despite the government's public efforts that aim to show it is at least trying to do something about the Islamic State,[230] MPs such as Faisal al-Duwaisan have continued to complain that 'parties in Kuwait are contributing to the Islamic State' and have warned that 'if the government does not educate its children ... the Islamic State would be in Kuwait in less than two years.'[231]

Understandably, such high-profile and widely read accusations have greatly unnerved those who still seek to protect the reputation of the Gulf monarchies and in particular the formal alliances and lucrative business relations they continue to enjoy with the Western powers. On behalf of Qatar, for example, a multitude of reports have been published that have either sought to dismiss entirely the emirate's connections with extremist groups such as the Islamic State or, in the BBC's case, have tried to relegate such links to being 'low level, if they even exist'. Some have pointed out that countries such as Qatar which host Western military bases and branches of prestigious US universities could not possibly have 'policies [or] sympathies for the likes of the Islamic State or al-Qaeda'.[232] Similarly, only a few days after the US Department of Defense admitted that donations were key to understanding the Islamic State's finances, Britain's ambassador to Saudi Arabia joined the debate by telling the BBC that any claims that Saudi Arabia was partly to blame for the rise of the Islamic State were 'nonsense'.[233]

In many ways, however, such spirited defences have not been quite as necessary as they were after 9/11. Certainly those hoping for the same sort of high-level links as the Saudi High Commission's backing of al-Qaeda will probably be left sorely disappointed, not least because in the contemporary era such channels would be too heavily exposed to leakable evidence trails. There may, of course, still be some of the suggested 'low-level' connections between the Islamic State and government apparatuses in the Gulf monarchies, but this time around most indicators seem to point to a much more elaborate and multi-layered web of fronts and proxies. Predictably perhaps, these appear more sophisticated than those which earlier channelled sympathizers' wealth to the likes of Osama bin Laden.

As with most things to do with the Islamic State's growth, the 2008 long war report largely foresaw such a system. Referring to potential funders for the emerging and de facto US-blessed 'national jihadists', it noted that 'any assistance would mainly be covert and would imply advanced information operations capabilities.' Moreover, as for the US's continuing need to be seen to be helping the Baghdad government, even if it was known to be gravitating towards Iran, it also hinted that any support for such jihadists would have to flow through secretive third parties so that the US could still continue aiding the 'host nations' that would actually have to fight the Sunni insurgency.[234]

Getting closest to the truth as to the identity of the donors has been former NATO supreme commander and US Navy admiral James Stavridis. Now dean of the Fletcher School of Diplomacy at Tufts University, he explained in September 2014 that groups such as the Islamic State represented a good investment for 'high rollers trying to get seed money to such organizations'. As he put it, 'these rich Arabs are like what angel investors are to tech start-ups, except they are interested in starting up groups who want to stir up hatred'. Alongside a number of current US officials, NBC News even reported Stavridis claiming that 'the biggest share of the individual donations supporting the Islamic State and the most radical groups comes from Qatar.'[235] Agreeing with this, it seemed, only a few weeks later Chairman of the Joint Chiefs of Staff Martin Dempsey stated in a Senate Armed Services Committee hearing that he knew of individuals in 'major Arab allies' funding the Islamic State.[236]

From the front lines of the battle with the Islamic State, a large number of local officials and military commanders have continually been making exactly the same point. In early 2015, for example, a senior Kurdish official bluntly stated that the Islamic State was still receiving financial support from wealthy Arab donors and that any aid given by Gulf donors to other extremist rebel groups in Syria was simply being absorbed into the Islamic State or *Jabhat al-Nusra*.[237] Another prominent Kurdish official argued that it was not only supporters of the Islamic State in the Gulf monarchies that were helping to fund it, but also those who were afraid of it. In his words 'Gulf [donors] give money to the Islamic State so that it promises not to carry out operations on their territory.'[238] Under the headline 'Private donors from Gulf oil states helping to bankroll salaries of up to 100,000 ISIS fighters', Britain's *Independent* newspaper noted that most officials in Baghdad were privately expressing the same view: that the Islamic State's huge territory, military operations, but only limited resources meant that it could not possibly be sustaining itself without outside help.[239]

Although the exact mechanisms for donations reaching the Islamic State are not yet fully clear, it appears that a more evolved version of the shadow banking network that earlier helped underpin al-Qaeda's growth has again been serving as a vital conduit. After all, we know that the Islamic State was keen to keep banks and financial houses in its territory operating for as long as possible and that it boasts of a substantial number of members who were former finance or informational technology professionals. Making the most of new communications platforms, as it has done with its media operations, the Islamic State is also known to have been creating and manipulating mobile phone applications, with the author's interviewees describing how front companies have developed 'apps' for sympathizers to purchase, with the proceeds then eventually reaching the Islamic State.[240]

More crudely, as with earlier al-Qaeda campaigns, there has still been an important role for the simple smuggling of cash, often driven across the Islamic State's long and porous borders in expensive cars – themselves donations to the cause. In late 2014, for example, the US Department of the Treasury stated that an unnamed Qatari businessman was known to have provided an Islamic State commander with $2 million in cash, while another individual was named as a 'Qatar-based Islamic State financial facilitator'.[241] Moreover, according to another Department of the Treasury press release, a Syrian Islamic State member nicknamed 'Emir of the Suicide Bombers' was understood to have been helping European recruits to reach the Islamic State after having been told by his Qatari backers 'to use the funds for military operations only'. He was also reported as having been enlisted to help with further fundraising efforts back in Qatar.[242] Based on interviews with rebels in Syria, the Wall Street Journal similarly claimed in February 2015 that Islamist fighters from Syria were known to have been travelling to Qatar and 'returning with suitcases full of money'. US officials were also cited as saying that the US government had uncovered connections in Qatar's business, religious, and academic communities to groups including both al-Qaeda and the Islamic State.[243]

Along with such direct money transfers to the Islamic State, whether electronic or cash in hand, another significant channel for donations has been ransom payments. Indeed, a substantial narrative has been built around the fact that a number of governments, including European states but excluding the non-negotiating US and British governments, are known to have been getting their citizens released after third parties have paid vast sums on their behalf. In April 2014, for example, a German publication cited 'unnamed sources in NATO' claiming that four French hostages had been freed after a payment of $18 million.[244] Moreover, after being freed in June 2015, another French Islamic State hostage told reporters he was 'extremely happy to be French, because I am very happy with the way the French government handles this type of situation'. Hinting that a substantial ransom had been paid, he stated 'let's not be naive ... I know there has been a compensation given to the group for my release. I just don't know what it was.' He did, however, claim that when he met President François Hollande he was told somewhat enigmatically that 'France did not pay.'[245] In fact, although the French government went on to claim vehemently that it had not paid, Hollande later stated that 'France does not pay ransom ... that doesn't mean other countries don't do it to help us. I concede that ... we did everything we could and we succeeded because other countries helped us.'[246]

With many other hostages being released under very similar circumstances, attention has naturally turned to identifying who the wealthy intermediaries have been, and whether they are states or individuals. As numerous analysts have remarked, several European governments seem to have nurtured various proxies to facilitate ransom payments while ensuring they themselves do not break international protocols.[247] Unsurprisingly, perhaps, Qatar or people in Qatar have been repeatedly mentioned in this context, with a detailed investigative report from summer 2014 citing Western officials who indicated that Qatar plays a 'private role' in meeting ransom demands and arranging swaps of prisoners on behalf of other states.[248]

With no apparent criticism from such officials, and certainly no references made to ransom payments being de facto funding for extremists, it seems likely that Qatar or elements within it have in recent years been actively encouraged to take on this high-risk proxy role. In this sense, as with most other aspects of their recent Middle East policies, the Western governments and their intelligence services have preferred to shield themselves behind regional actors, and especially those with resources of their own. After all, following the 2011 seizure of documents in bin Laden's Abbottabad compound, and the embarrassing revelation that the CIA had been making secret monthly cash payments to the Kabul government so as to help it pay for the release of al-Qaeda-held hostages, there has understandably been a need to avoid a repeat of such incidents.[249]

In 2012 the *Wall Street Journal* reported that Lebanese officials had been tipped off that a prominent Qatari who was the cousin of the foreign minister was in Beirut to pass money to *Al-Nusra* and had already visited the Sunni-majority border town of Arsal so as to distribute funds. Although arrested on terrorism charges, the man was understood to have been quickly released following strong Qatari diplomatic protestations.[250] Importantly, Arsal was the same town that then suddenly sprouted Islamic State checkpoints in 2014; a move that stunned many observers even though the group's flags had been spotted flying freely there before. With enough time before the Lebanese Army managed to mobilize, the Islamic State managed to seize dozens of Lebanese policemen and soldiers before disappearing from the town almost as suddenly as they had arrived.[251] Although the Islamic State shot and beheaded a number of the captives, the rest were held hostage somewhere outside Arsal, with these survivors then becoming part of a proposed agreement in early 2015, which saw the nearby border region being promised to jihadists as a safe haven, and one of Abu Bakr al-Baghdadi's ex-wives being released from custody.[252] According to the Lebanese media there were not only Qatari intermediaries behind the negotiations, but the chief of Lebanon's security services had only been informed of the possible deal after having met the chief of Qatar's security services while in Turkey.[253]

Also noteworthy were the circumstances surrounding the release of nearly fifty Turkish citizens captured in Mosul by the Islamic State in June 2014. Released and returned to Turkey after three months, the Ankara government made it clear that no ransom had been paid and 'no promises had been made'. According to some of the hostages, however, Prime Minister Recep Tayyip Erdoğan had told them that 'there are things we cannot talk about. To run the state is not like running a grocery store. We have to protect sensitive issues, if you don't there would be a price to pay.' Pointing to the same type of arrangement between the Western governments and wealthy proxies, the chairman of the Turkish Centre for Economics and Foreign Policy Studies remarked, 'This sounds a bit too good to be true ... There are some very legitimate and unanswered questions about how this happened.'[254] Indeed, the last time Turkish hostages had arrived home, back in 2013 after having been captured by extremists in Syria, they were even delivered on a private Qatari jet.[255]

While such ransoms and other elements of the Islamic State's money supply may slowly be proving traceable, the tracking of its weapons has been a much harder task. The origin of some of its stock is of course obvious, having been purloined from Iraqi arsenals. Including advanced US weaponry and dozens of Humvee armoured cars, the organization's booty has frequently been paraded in its videos. Similarly, its many old Soviet-era tanks have likely been seized from retreating Syrian government forces, or other Syrian rebel groups that had managed to acquire them back in 2011. But neither of these 'liberated' stockpiles fully explain the vast and seemingly unrivalled firepower of the Islamic State, which almost always seems better resourced than its enemies. Indeed, as several dozens of the author's interviewees have described, the organization has always had access to high-quality and plentiful weapons – more than the number of fighters – and it has always had sufficient ammunition and spare parts. Moreover, many interviewees noted that the highly prized US equipment is rarely if ever used on the battlefield, instead being preserved for propaganda purposes.

Casting at least a little light on one of the sources of these mystery weapons, a New York Times report from February 2015 described how a European investigator in Kobane had spotted a local militiaman on the street with what appeared to be a brand new US-made M16 assault rifle. With the Kurd claiming to have taken it from a fallen Islamic State fighter, the investigator's curiosity was piqued and the weapon was then photographed and identified. Turning out to be a Chinese-made M16 knock-off, it had had its serial number etched away with the rough spot then touched up with paint. Importantly despite this 'two stage effort to obscure the provenance' of the rifle, the Geneva-based Conflict Armament Research and the Small Arms Survey managed to identify both it and its cartridges as coming from a batch that as recently as 2013 had been in the possession of rebel groups in South Sudan.[256]

Although the 2015 *New York Times* report went little further than suggesting that these weapons had probably been supplied to the South Sudanese rebels by the North Sudanese intelligence services, it seemed very probable that the rifle and presumably others like it must have been transferred to Syria at some point in 2013 by an intermediary with interests in both Sudan and Syria. Indeed, an earlier report exists from summer 2013, which not only exactly matches the Geneva organization's information but also states that 'in deals that have not been publicly acknowledged, Western officials and Syrian rebels say Sudan's government sold Sudanese and Chinese-made arms to Qatar, which [then] arranged delivery through Turkey to the rebels.' Getting closer to an Islamic State 'smoking gun', but without realizing it at the time, the 2013 report also stated that 'emerging evidence that Sudan has fed the secret arms pipeline to rebels adds to a growing body of knowledge about where the opposition [to the Syrian government] is getting its military equipment, often paid for by Qatar, the United Arab Emirates, Jordan, Saudi Arabia or other sympathetic donors.' Moreover, it suggested that Sudan's economic crisis had spurred groups within it to sell such weapons to the highest bidder. As a US official familiar with the transfers put it, 'Qatar has been paying a pretty penny for weapons, with few questions asked,' while two other officials described how the weapons had then been airlifted from Khartoum to somewhere in western Turkey by Ukrainian-flagged aircraft.[257]

FUNDERS NEED FACILITATORS – THE ROLE OF TURKEY

Although the expanding Islamic State soon began to share frontiers with several countries, including Jordan and Saudi Arabia, the bulk of the organization's supplies and funds are widely understood to have been flowing in through Turkey. As former NATO supreme allied commander Wesley Clark told a CNN interviewer, 'Let's be very clear: the Islamic State is not just a terrorist organization, it is a Sunni terrorist organization. It means it blocks and targets Shia, and that means it's serving the interests of Turkey and Saudi Arabia … All along there's always been the idea that Turkey was supporting them in some way.'[258] Moreover, as Joe Biden pointed out during his Harvard University session, Turkey was known to have allowed most of the Islamic State's foreign fighters to cross into Syria, while a detailed report published by Columbia University's Institute for Human Rights reached much the same conclusion.[259]

But despite such accusations levelled against Turkey, the tightening up of its borders has not been a priority for the NATO member. Having clearly identified the same strategic benefits to the Islamic State's survival as the US-led coalition behind Operation Inherent Resolve, as recently as January 2016 it was revealed that substantial tracts of Turkish territory still remained open to use by the Islamic State. Indeed, the jihadists were described as 'seeping through', while US secretary for defense Ashton Carter rather weakly stated that 'Turkey must do more to control its often porous border'.[260] According to flight maps, these areas of Turkey were the same ones over which it had downed a slightly straying Russian aircraft a month earlier and which had led to claims from the Kremlin that 'we have every reason to think that the decision to shoot down our plane was dictated by the desire to protect the [Islamic State's] supply lines to Turkey.'[261]

Much like the Gulf monarchies, on a tactical level, Turkey has naturally had little interest in trying to slow the advances of the most capable opponents of the Iran-leaning Syrian and Iraqi governments. Citing senior Iraqi sources Patrick Cockburn even claims that Turkish intelligence played a role in helping some of the Saddam-era army officers join the Islamic State.[262] Moreover, given its shared stance with Qatar on the Muslim Brotherhood in Egypt, and its recently announced intentions to build a military base in Qatar,[263] the Ankara administration has evidently seen long-term advantages in deepening its relations with the Gulf state that seems most familiar with the Islamic State's financial affairs. On an economic level, Turkey has also had little incentive to challenge the Islamic State, as not only must businesses in its border regions be doing a healthy trade but, as Abdel Bari Atwan has pointed out, there would be significant risks to the $20 billion tourism industry if the Islamic State began to expand its influence in Turkey itself.[264]

Closer to home, the arrival of the Islamic State on the doorstep of Kurdish territories in northern Syria and Iraq has likely been welcomed by Ankara, as the loss of Kurdish lands and fighters to such an organization greatly weakens the ability of Kurdish populations – including those in Turkey – to keep pressing for greater autonomy or independence. In this sense the Islamic State's current fight against the Kurds fits almost perfectly into a decades-old Turkish policy of supporting jihadist groups to undermine broader Kurdish ambitions. Certainly there seems to be a resurfacing of memories of the 1990s, when Turkey was accused of airlifting jihadists from the aftermath of the Bosnian campaign so that they could then serve alongside *Ansar al-Islam* as 'shock troops' against the Kurdistan Workers Party. Importantly, when accused of doing this by several European governments in 1996, Turkish diplomats reportedly responded by claiming they had the tacit approval of the Bill Clinton administration.[265] Alongside this, Turkey was understood to have been tolerating a home-grown Kurdish jihadist organization that sought the creation of an Islamic state in south-eastern Turkey and was willing to fight against the Kurdish separatists. In 1993, a Turkish parliamentary commission revealed that one of the group's training camps had been operating with military assistance,[266] while a former Turkish minister has since claimed that some of these jihadists were even receiving training at the security services' headquarters.[267] In 2011, Turkey's role became even clearer when a former military officer testified in court that he had actually set up the jihadist organization. Known as *Hizbul Kontr* or 'Party of the Contras', it had been designed with the intent of creating a 'contra force to fight and kill militants of the Kurdish Workers Party'.[268]

In this context it is easier to understand why many of the Islamic State's fighters that participated in the first attacks on Kobane in summer 2014 were actually Kurdish. In fact, the Islamic State made much of the fact that their operational commander was a Kurd and that the organization was only interested in eradicating secular and apostate forces, not conducting ethnic cleansing.[269] The past policies also help explain the numerous videos that began to appear of Islamic State fighters near to the Kobane border apparently holding relaxed conversations with Turkish soldiers standing barely metres away from them, along with those that clearly depicted Islamic State fighters opening fire on the flanks of the town's defenders after suddenly emerging from behind giant grain silos next to the Turkish border. Indeed, in June 2015, the Kobane militias revealed that they had found a 'half-completed 440-yard tunnel dug by the Islamic State that appeared to be leading into Turkey, and was splitting into two directions'.[270] In fact, just three days after this startling discovery, the Islamic State was reported to have 're-entered Kobane' after detonating car bombs and causing much confusion for the defenders. As the militia's official spokesman explained, 'It's not easy for the Islamic State to have returned back to Kobane ... The primary information and the eyewitnesses say that they entered from Turkey but officially we don't have confirmed information yet.' Similarly, the co-leader of the Kurdish People's Democratic Party claimed there was a 'high probability that the attackers had entered Kobane from Turkey'.[271] Interviewed by the *Daily Telegraph*, a witness also reasoned that the two cars which had been blown up 'most probably came from the Turkish side' on the basis that 'if they had come from the Syrian side they would have first come across many more important targets, such as the main headquarters building'.[272]

By summer 2015 the picture seemed a little clearer after a captured Turkish Islamic State fighter gave a rather unsettling account of how the organization was operating a shadow state in many Turkish border towns, from where it had been able to recruit freely, setting up an all-Turkish unit called *Saif al-Islam* or 'Sword of Islam'.[273] Although many pointed to a brief flurry of Turkish air strikes in Syria as signalling a change of heart from Ankara, this was on the basis they were part of an official response to an Islamic State-linked explosion in the town of Suruç that had killed protestors demanding more Turkish assistance for the people of Kobane. More likely is that the primary targets were actually Kurdish positions. Indeed, Turkey's mini version of Operation Inherent Resolve was concurrent with a much larger number of other air strikes on targets linked to the Kurdistan Workers Party, with the commander of Turkey's air force even admitting that a 'war was being waged' against the group. Meanwhile, a series of raids on supposed Islamic State safe houses in Turkey were described as being cover for the rounding up of hundreds of Kurdish militants, while President Erdoğan even told CNN that 'the Kurdish Workers Party poses a primary threat [to Turkey], whereas the Islamic State is a secondary threat'.[274]

Getting firmer evidence on Turkey's Islamic State connections has proven dangerous, with investigators that have got too close to the story having been killed or severely punished. After all, the three journalists from three different newspapers that broke the original story in 1992 of links between the Turkish military and *Hizbul Kontr* were all assassinated.[275] Fast-forwarding to October 2014, American reporter Serena Shim had filed a report for Iran's Press TV that claimed she had seen Islamic State fighters being smuggled from Turkey into Kobane in the backs of aid convoys. Expressing concerns to her employers that she might be arrested, this proved to be her last report as she was then killed in a car crash the following day.[276] A year later, in October 2015, the aforementioned Jacky Sutton was found dead in Istanbul airport while en route to Iraqi Kurdistan. According to the Turkish authorities she had supposedly 'killed herself after missing a connecting flight to Erbil and not having the money to buy another ticket'. Claiming foul play, her friends and employer demanded not just a local investigation but also an international one, while CCTV footage later obtained by the British media seemed to show her shortly before her death moving quite normally around the airport with duty-free shopping bags.[277]

Numerous others have been arrested and imprisoned, including reporters for Germany's *Die Welt* and *Die Zeit*, and the staff of a Turkish newspaper that has repeatedly stated it has proof that Turkish intelligence has been helping to supply the Islamic State. In June 2015 four Turkish journalists were also detained for having asked a local governor 'tricky questions' about the Islamic State following the Kurdish militia's recapturing of the Syrian border town of Tal Abyad. Most seriously, in January 2016, another newspaper's editor-in-chief, who claimed to have footage of Turkish weapons being smuggled into Syria under boxes of medicine and warned that 'the Turkish government was arming Islamist militants in Syria', was sentenced to life imprisonment for the crime of espionage.[278]

Despite such repression, a clearer picture has nonetheless begun to form with a number of credible reports and leaked documents helping better explain the mechanisms of the relationship. In November 2015 the Turkish Central Bank warned that unregistered cash entering the market had increased by fifty-two percent that year to $13 billion, thus 'raising doubts about the source of the financing as well as its sustainability in the markets'.[279] Meanwhile, a Turkish media outlet managed to find and interview an Islamic State fighter who was being treated in a Turkish hospital. He stated that in addition to 'many Saudi families who believe in jihad assisting us ... Turkey paved the way for us'. Going further he explained that 'had Turkey not shown such understanding for us, the Islamic State would not be in its current place. Turkey showed us affection ... large

SHADOW WARS

numbers of our [fighters] receive medical treatment in Turkey'.²⁸⁰ More damningly, later that year, a number of documents appeared online that were subsequently authenticated and have heavily implicated Turkish intelligence. They revealed that regular police units had stopped trucks belonging to the intelligence services that were ostensibly 'transporting humanitarian assistance for Turkomans in Syria', but which, according to the Gendarmarie general command, were found to be containing weapons and supplies. In particular, three trucks were carrying 'six metallic containers ... in the first container, twenty-five to thirty missiles or rockets and ten to fifteen crates loaded with ammunition ... in the second container, twenty to twenty-five missiles or rockets, twenty to twenty-five crates of mortar ammunition and Douchka anti-aircraft ammunition in five or six sacks ... the boxes had markings in the Cyrillic alphabet'.²⁸¹

The scandal was so great that the Turkish government obtained a court injunction to force a full media ban on covering the story. The public prosecutor who had ordered the trucks to be searched was then removed from his post and all of the thirteen men who had been involved in the search were taken to court on charges of espionage.²⁸² Vindicating at least some of Serena Shim's earlier reporting, the documents seemed to tally with accounts of Turkish intelligence managing safe houses on behalf of the Islamic State and *Jabhat al-Nusra*. Interviewed by the *Daily Telegraph* in November 2014, a former Free Syrian Army fighter who had been a prisoner of the Syrian regime openly described how he 'ran safe houses in Turkey for foreign fighters looking to join [these groups]'. Reasoning that his cooperation with the Turkish authorities was practical, he argued that 'the most important thing now is to remove the [Syrian] regime and the Islamic State are the strongest group. I will do whatever it takes.'²⁸³

To some extent the documents also helped confirm a summer 2012 *New York Times* report in which activists stated that 'Turkish army vehicles delivered anti-tank weaponry to the border, where it was then smuggled into Syria.' Moreover, in a likely reference to a small unit of CIA officers that the *New York Times* had been informed about by Arab and US intelligence officials, the activists claimed this had been done with the blessing of US officials. Indeed, these 'officials' were understood to be operating on the southern border of Turkey for the purpose of 'helping allies decide which

466

Syrian opposition fighters across the border will receive arms to fight the Syrian government.' Described by the *New York Times*' correspondents as using 'a shadowy network of intermediaries', presumably including Turkish intelligence, the operation effectively channelled a range of 'automatic rifles, rocket-propelled grenades, ammunition and some anti-tank weapons, paid for by Turkey, Qatar, Saudi Arabia, across the border'.[284]

Criticism of Turkey's role by Western governments, notwithstanding Biden and Carter's brief remarks, has understandably been muted, and up until recently almost non-existent. Even following the release of the controversial documents and the heavy crackdown on journalists, most Western officials have only commented in very vague terms about Turkey's relationship with the Islamic State, and have mostly focused on fixable, single issue concerns that are unlikely to damage their NATO ally's overall reputation. Nevertheless, since summer 2015 there have been a few exceptions to this, with a number of senior Western intelligence officials beginning to tell newspapers that they suspected an 'undeclared alliance' between Al-Raqqah and individuals in Ankara had hardened and, in one case, citing the contents of seized flash drives which indicated that links between 'some Turkish officials' and Islamic State members were 'undeniable'.[285]

Amusingly for some, in October 2015, it was also reported that US counter-terrorism officials had finally begun to investigate how so many brand-new Toyota four-wheel-drive vehicles had managed to cross borders into the Islamic State. Although promising no action, the officials claimed the organization had hundreds in its inventory, while speculations were made that the cars had been purchased in the Gulf monarchies, shipped to Turkey, and then driven across with the complicity of border guards.[286] For those who had been following the dramatic rise of the Islamic State, this seemed to make sense, as many had already noted that its vehicles often featured all of the latest upgrades, sometimes including features only available to Gulf dealerships. Also implicating Turkey, analysts pointed to a flurry of reports appearing all over the world that indicated large numbers of such Toyotas were going missing. From Australia, for example, Monash University's Greg Baron reasoned that the vehicles were being stolen to order and then shipped in parts in containers to Turkey before then being delivered to the Islamic State.[287]

10

THE ISLAMIC STATE – A GIFT
THAT KEEPS GIVING

THE RETURN OF THE 'WAR ON TERROR'

B eyond the immediate strategic benefits of the Islamic State's expansion in Iraq and Syria, and its broader implications for military spending and arms industries, the Western powers and their regional allies have been actively using the new threat to rekindle at least some of the counter-terrorism language of the 'War on Terror'. Most obviously, in countries like Saudi Arabia large numbers of dissidents of all persuasions have again been easily swept up under a wave of terrorism charges and, as described, their governments have been able to keep positioning themselves as 'moderate' powers and thus credible partners to Washington and London. Meanwhile, in the West itself, the new menace of the Islamic State has given a sizeable boost to the long-running, post-9/11 efforts to extend state powers over citizens and strengthen domestic security apparatuses. As Marc Lynch points out, by 2014 the rise of the Islamic State 'offered unprecedented political cover for heavy-handed security crackdowns on all forms of dissent in the name of combatting extremism and terrorism'.[1]

In Britain, for example, MI5 director Andrew Parker soon warned that the threat from Islamic State-linked 'home-grown' jihadists was so severe it was the highest he had ever seen in his thirty-two-year career, and on this basis MI5 had to update its 'toolbox' to include more types of computer attacks and online operations.² Even more notable has been the reaction of the French government to the November 2015 Islamic State-linked Paris attacks. Despite having launched only two air strikes of its own on Islamic State territory in Syria since Operation Inherent Resolve began, the Élysée Palace was quick to announce a national state of emergency, with lawmakers soon agreeing to extend it for a further three months. Gaining unprecedented authority to raid homes and seize computers, France's security services had arguably become more powerful than they had been in decades. In January 2016 Prime Minister Manuel Valls declared that the state of emergency might have to last indefinitely, or at least until the Islamic State was completely defeated. In his words, this could take 'an entire generation.'³

The same month the Islamic State's latest propaganda video also helped to tip a long-running debate in Western parliaments, described by the *Guardian* as 'dark and dishonest', on the extent to which intelligence services should be able to read the public's emails, and especially those that have been encrypted.⁴ Usefully featuring what seemed to be encrypted emails, the video strongly suggested such methods had been used by the Paris attackers and were likely to be used in the West again by future Islamic State operatives. But making sure to point out that the encryption featured in the video had been fabricated, US whistle-blower Edward Snowden told the public: 'If any official responds as if it's real, push back'. Moreover, with reference to the British prime minister's stance, he asked, 'Does the Islamic State see advantage in [the] West limiting access to strong security? Juxtaposing spooky fake crypto with the anti-crypto Cameron implies yes.'⁵ Meanwhile the threat of the Islamic State has been increasingly deployed in more mainstream Western political debates, with, for example, Cameron suggesting that 'al-Baghdadi' would welcome 'Brexit', in reference to the campaign to remove Britain from the European Union, and with a surge in Islamic State-linked anti-Muslim rhetoric feeding into the US presidential race.⁶

In many ways the global nature of the 'War on Terror' also seems to have been resurrected by the Islamic State and in particular its raft of new international so-called 'affiliates'. As al-Qaeda's supposedly global tentacles once did, these spin-off organizations have dramatically improved the prospects for 'anti-terror' Western or Western proxy interventions across almost the entire Arab and Islamic worlds. Certainly, despite having barely consolidated its heartlands in Iraq and Syria, the Islamic State rapidly produced scary black maps of its future territories and repeatedly stated its intent to conquer all Muslim-majority territories stretching from the Atlantic Ocean to East Asia. Recycling the old claims of a Western civilizational struggle against the agents of al-Qaeda, in October 2014 former CIA director Leon Panetta argued that this meant 'we're looking at a kind of Thirty Years War ... that will have to extend beyond the Islamic State.' With remarkable prescience he further predicted that the forthcoming, more internationalized Islamic State would 'include emerging threats in Nigeria, Somalia, Yemen, Libya and elsewhere'.[7]

THE ISLAMIC STATE IN LIBYA

With an uncooperative government still in control of the capital city, much like in Syria, it was apparent by the end of 2014 that most of the 'moderate' groups, and even the more brazenly al-Qaeda-aligned factions, were still failing to shape war-torn Libya in the interests of the Western powers, or allies such as Qatar and the United Arab Emirates. Just days after the US Department of Defense warned that the Islamic State had begun to use training camps in Libya, a group called *Majlis Shura Shabab al-Islam*, or 'Islamic Youth Consultative Council', was the first to pledge allegiance to the organization. Members of the cross-border *Ansar al-Sharia* militant organization soon joined in and, after declaring their presence in Sirte, Darna, and elsewhere, the new 'Islamic State in Libya' was born. By the beginning of 2015 its leaders had announced that Libya was to be divided into three governorates in the East, West, and South.[8]

As with the Islamic State's core operations in Iraq and Syria, there were soon signs its new Libya affiliate was much better resourced than the local competition, with it quickly setting up welfare services and distributing food to the population.[9] Fitting into the US's 'nationalist jihadist' template, it emerged that veterans of the formerly MI6-sponsored Libyan Islamic Fighting Group were also involved. Indeed, back in 2005 US officials had already described such veterans as 'sharing the aspiration of al-Qaeda ... [but] having a more nationalist stance and preferring

471

to focus on the near enemy as a priority'.[10] Even so, as with the main operation in Al-Raqqah, the new Libyan affiliate also appeared heavily staffed by foreigners, with an estimated twenty percent of its fighters hailing from elsewhere in the region, including Tunisia, Yemen, and the Gulf monarchies. In one of its first videos – featuring the same high production values as earlier Islamic State output – the focus was on a Saudi fighter who explained to the camera how he had chosen to travel to Libya to help build the caliphate there.[11] According to two truck drivers held captive in Sirte, and then interviewed by the *New York times*, all of the city's jihadists 'bowed to a Saudi administrator' and 'the entire Islamic State government is from abroad, they are the ones calling the shots.' A former local government official similarly described how 'the Islamic State periodically rotates in new administrators, who typically are from the Persian Gulf,' while others even claimed the infamous Abu Ali al-Anbari, the governor general of the Islamic State's Syrian territories, had arrived by boat from Syria.[12]

Soon going on the warpath, or so it seemed, the group's first major target was the leader of the Libya Dawn militias and thus a key supporter of the embattled Tripoli administration. Missing him by a matter of minutes, a luxury Tripoli hotel was bombed in January 2015 leading to the deaths of several civilian residents along with an 'American security contractor'. Citing details of 'Islamic State-linked Twitter accounts' supplied to them by the SITE Intelligence Group, the Western media portrayed it as an Islamic State operation, although Libya Dawn's spokesman was adamant it was perpetrated by 'remnants of the Gaddafi regime'.[13]

In any case, a few weeks later the so-called Islamic State in Libya struck again, seizing dozens of Egyptian Coptic Christians in Sirte and then appearing to behead them in another rather dubious propaganda video that terrorism experts, a New York University academic, and even a Hollywood director have since described as being 'faked' with 'several technical mistakes that show it was manipulated'.[14] Even so, with its reputation preceding it, the wealthy new group soon boasted of fresh pledges from other Libyan militias, and by the end of February 2015 *Ansar al-Sharia* was filmed parading a convoy of the now familiar brand-new-looking Toyota vehicles through Benghazi and then being welcomed by crowds making the Islamic State's salute. As Abdel Bari Atwan notes, by this stage the

Islamic State had control of, or at least a strong presence in, four different Libyan cities.[15]

The first and most obvious beneficiaries of the emerging Islamic State in Libya were those still seeking to undermine Libya Dawn and buttress the Western-recognized and Tobruk-based House of Representatives. With their earlier air strikes on Libya proving contentious and, as previously described, requiring considerable secrecy, Egypt and the UAE were now all clear to go public with rebranded 'anti-Islamic State' interventions. Indeed, within just twenty-four hours of the Coptic Christian hostage video, Cairo announced fresh strikes to 'avenge the bloodshed and to seek retribution from the killers' and reported that the '[Libyan] government's air force' had also begun to bomb 'jihadist targets'.[16] Purportedly hitting 'Islamic State strongholds' in Darna and elsewhere, it was nonetheless unclear what the actual targets were, with strong suggestions circulating that the primary objectives were militias still loyal to Tripoli.[17] Not long after, rumours also began to spread that the Western powers might try to join Egypt and the UAE by renewing their 2011 air strikes, but this time avoiding parliamentary debates or the need for a UN mandate, on the basis that they were necessary to thwart the Islamic State. Several months later this seemed to be turning into a reality with the US Department of Defense stating that it stood ready to 'perform the full spectrum of military operations as required', and with revelations that Britain had already begun to carry out 'reconnaissance flights' over Libya, and that British special forces had visited Tobruk so as to 'build up intelligence on the location of Islamic State fighters and draw up potential targets for possible British and coalition air strikes'. As the British press noted, these strikes would be 'so limited that [they] would not warrant Commons authorization'.[18]

Among the other beneficiaries of the Islamic State's Libyan campaign has been the UAE-backed and former US-based Khalifa Hiftar who had remained in Libya, despite his setbacks, but had become an increasingly divisive figure. The Tripoli government had repeatedly rejected any peace settlement involving him, while militia leaders argued he would 'eat any unity government'. Only after the January 2015 hotel bombing, and the apparent threat to all of Libya posed by the Islamic State, did the Tobruk government grudgingly begin to recognize officially Hiftar's presence in the country. Within three weeks of the Coptic Christian beheadings video, and again apparently because of his strongman status, Hiftar was even confirmed as the new commander-in-chief of the Tobruk-controlled armed forces.[19] Soon after, it was also reported that several thousand Libyan fighters loyal to Hiftar, who had 'fled Libya after the revolution', were set to return. As the Libyan media claimed, they were understood to have received training in Egypt, supervised and financed by the UAE.[20] In May 2015 these claims were corroborated by six broadcasts on Turkish television of leaked conversations between Egyptian officials and a UAE general. Part of the same described series of leaks authenticated by British audio forensics experts, they also revealed that the UAE had agreed to send an arms shipment to an Egyptian port, from where it would be transported into Libya. The conversations included mentions of a 'C-17', likely in reference to the UAE's newly acquired fleet of six C-17 heavy transport aircraft.[21] Confirming much of this, subsequently leaked emails from Abu Dhabi published by the *New York Times* demonstrated that UAE diplomats were well aware that their ongoing arms transfers to Libya, which were described as being 'overseen at head of state level', were in violation of a UN embargo. Worried about blowback, one official recommended strategies to avoid 'exposing how deeply we are involved in Libya ... We should try to provide a cover to lessen the damage.'[22]

Either way, by 2015 things were going badly for the Tripoli government. Not only was it still challenged by the pro-US administration in Tobruk and continuing to face air strikes from two of the West's Arab allies, but its leadership was experiencing repeated Islamic State-linked assassination attempts. To make matters worse, the Qatar-backed and former CIA captive Adel Hakim Belhadj had also resurfaced, but this time allegedly as part of the Islamic State in Libya. Making the allegation on mainstream US television that Belhadj was now 'firmly aligned with the Islamic State and supports their training camps in eastern Libya', US intelligence officials told their interviewers that Belhadj and other such Islamic State commanders in Libya could nevertheless not be attacked because '[the US] didn't have targeting authority to take them out'.[23]

Although Tripoli's fortunes began to improve in 2016, with a UN-sponsored 'unity government' arriving in the city, and with its Tobruk and Hiftar rivals seemingly marginalized, the apparently growing menace of the Islamic State continued to undermine its authority.[24] In February

2016, for example, the US rejected any need for local authorization when it claimed to have hit an Islamic State training camp in Sabratha. As a coastal town, on the western doorstep of Tripoli, it was not only hundreds of miles away from Belhadj's men and the group's other well-known strongholds in Sirte,[25] but as senior European politicians have suggested it may not even have been a camp to begin with. Coming forward soon after the strikes, the Serbian prime minister revealed negotiations had already been underway to release two Serbian embassy employees held by a 'criminal group believed to be linked to the Islamic State' and known to be based there. However, as the Serbian foreign minister complained, not only had the hostages lost their lives, but the US's assertions were based on 'information that has to be checked'.[26] As former British ambassador to Libya Oliver Miles observed, 'There was really no Libyan authority in existence that [was] able to invite them [the US], so I think they did it on their own.' Moreover, he argued that most Libyans would have opposed 'very strongly' such an intervention.[27] Even so, by May 2016 US military activity in Libya seemed to have significantly increased, with Italy having given permission for its airspace to be used for 'defensive' US drone flights into Libya, and US officials confirming that two 'outposts' made up of special operations 'contact teams' had been set up in Benghazi and Misrata. Although their mission was described as 'lining up local partners in advance of a possible offensive against the Islamic State', no US teams appeared to have been sent to liaise with Tripoli.[28] Indeed, only a few days later the prime minister of the UN-backed government, Fayez al-Sarraj, condemned the presence of such foreign ground troops on the basis that their intervention was 'contrary to our principles'.[29]

THE ISLAMIC STATE IN YEMEN

With Sana'a falling into the hands of antagonistic and potentially Iran-aligned forces in 2014, and with even a full-blown intervention in 2015, in de facto cooperation with al-Qaeda in the Arabian Peninsula, failing to deliver results on the ground, the situation in Yemen for the Saudi-led coalition was arguably just as bad as it was for the Western proxies in Libya. Following much the same pattern as in Sirte and Darna, however, a new

Islamic State in Yemen had also announced itself and had begun to add a much harder, and in this case more sectarian edge to the conflict. Initially to the advantage of the Sunni-dominated forces in southern Yemen, including those of Saudi Arabia and the UAE, the hitherto unknown group was well placed to stoke further hatred of the Zaydi-Shia Houthi movement. After all, as a member of Saudi Arabia's Council of Senior Scholars had already declared of Yemen's Houthis on state-owned television, 'We are cleansing the land of these rats.'[30]

Claiming responsibility for two synchronized suicide attacks in March 2015 on Zaydi-Shia mosques in Sana'a that killed at least 120 worshippers, including prominent Houthi leaders and clerics, the Islamic State in Yemen published a suitably slick propaganda video a few weeks later declaring a new Al-Raqqah-aligned affiliate in Yemen. Featuring heavily armed men with brand-new weapons and fully covered faces, it made sure to pay homage to earlier Islamic State productions, with two pristine Toyota vehicles visible in the far distance.[31] As with the new Islamic State franchise in Libya, there were initially doubts about its existence. As some pointed out, before these dramatic attacks there had been very few signs of the Islamic State's presence in Yemen, not least given AQAP's deep-rooted presence in the area, reinforced by its historically close links to al-Qaeda's core leadership.[32]

Nevertheless, an AQAP video in November 2014 had warned that its ranks were being infiltrated by the Islamic State, with one of its most prominent clerics condemning Abu Bakr al-Baghdadi for announcing a caliphate, and demanding that the Islamic State steer clear of Yemen.[33] Indeed, a number of earlier reports indicated that Islamic State trainers had been visiting AQAP and that a number of AQAP scholars had begun to express support for the caliphate project. Some had called for 'solidarity with our Muslim brothers in Iraq against the crusade ... Their blood and injuries are ours and we will surely support them,' while a senior figure was understood to have suggested 'the announcement of the Islamic State of Iraq, Syria, and the Arabian Peninsula.'[34]

Even after the first mosque attacks, described by J. M. Berger as a potential 'Franz Ferdinand moment' given its substantial and obviously sectarian implications, suspicions over the group's authenticity and capacity continued to linger. Although the Islamic State's *Dabiq* magazine had quickly reported on the atrocity, it was noted that it did not provide any of the usual 'martyrs' will' images of the bombers, nor indeed any proof that they had been the perpetrators.[35] Others, meanwhile, pointed to a strange admission by the US Department of Defense on the very same day as the attacks that the US military had 'lost track' and was 'unable to account' for $500 million worth of weapons that had been supplied to Yemen's interior ministry in recent years by various Department of Defense and Department of State programmes. Later suggesting the culprits had been 'Iran-backed rebels', though without providing any substantiation, the *Los Angeles Times'* correspondents revealed that the missing cache included Humvees, M4 assault rifles, night-vision goggles, body armour, and hand-launched drones.[36]

Either way, as the conflict continued to worsen, the opportunities for the Islamic State in Yemen continued to grow, with the group going on to perpetrate several other sectarian attacks in Houthi territory as the Saudi coalition inched its way up the country. Most dramatically, in September 2015, it claimed responsibility for another double suicide bombing on the occasion of *Eid al-Ahda*. Involving a man dressed as a woman, the attackers killed more than ten people inside a Houthi-run mosque before a statement was released declaring it had been 'a security operation facilitated by God against rejectionists'.[37] Likened to the deadly assaults on the Shia Al-Askari shrine in 2006 and 2007 by the Islamic State in Iraq, the Islamic State in Yemen's 2015 attacks were seen as provoking fresh waves of retaliatory sectarian violence and the further destabilization of Sana'a.[38]

THE FIGHT FOR MALI

Again in line with Leon Panetta's predictions, by the end of 2014 the Islamic State was poised to make significant inroads into West Africa. As with Libya and Yemen, resource-rich and strategically important countries with sizeable Muslim populations such as Mali and Nigeria were becoming increasingly unstable as powerful Islamic extremists began to move beyond old al-Qaeda templates by laying claim to vast territories and large populations. Adopting the same sort of 'national jihadist' model as Abu Bakr al-Baghdadi's caliphate, their forces soon proved brutally capable of challenging and even unseating incumbent governments. Meanwhile, as with their comparators in Iraq and Syria, their advances once again seemed to play into the hands of those powers actively seeking the replacement of problematic administrations.

In the case of land-locked Mali, Tuareg tribes that had earlier been promised fast-tracked citizenship in Libya, and had then fought for the regime, had little choice but to move back across the border after Muammar Gaddafi's fall. Mounting an insurrection in January 2012 in the northern part of Mali, their 'Azawad National Liberation Movement' quickly seized control of three cities and, in the interests of survival, had merged with *Ansar Dine* or 'Helpers of Religion' – an al-Qaeda-linked and UN-designated terrorist organization. With Bamako's democratically elected government caught off guard, a military coup d'état soon pushed it to the side, with the new army leaders rapidly legitimizing themselves as defenders of the nation.[39] Unable to hold together, the Azawad–*Ansar Dine* alliance soon unravelled and then paved the way for even greater chaos as rival Tuareg factions fought among themselves while fighters from the more powerful transnational al-Qaeda in the Islamic Maghreb organization began to arrive. Understood to be loyal to AQIM's constituent 'Movement for Unity and Jihad in West Africa', which was seeking the creation of an Islamic state stretching across the entire Sahel – the semi-arid belt south of the Sahara – the men were not only from Mali, but from Algeria, Nigeria, and elsewhere.[40] Including the 'Emir of the Sahara' and veterans from previous jihads in other countries, some were believed to have been trained by older jihadists from Saudi Arabia and the Pakistani tribal regions. Indeed, at one point, the mayor of Timbuktu claimed Pakistanis had been spotted in AQIM's ranks.[41]

By the beginning of 2013, AQIM and *Ansar Dine* were not only holding their ground against the new government, but were evidently starting to win. Having pushed further south and taken control over Kidal, they were only held in check by a brief French intervention and subsequent UN mission to protect Timbuktu's UNESCO World Heritage Site.[42] Importantly, and in much the same way as the Islamic State's concurrent expansion in Syria and Iraq, the Mali jihadists seemed to be benefiting from a staggering array of sophisticated new weapons. According to a report prepared for the European Parliament, they not only appeared to have substantial funding but were understood to be sporting sniper rifles, anti-personnel mines, and even surface-to-air missiles capable of downing Mali air force jets. As the BBC described, the Mali armed forces were 'ill-equipped and its divided army was no match for the firepower of the rebels', while the well-resourced jihadists had become a 'multi-ethnic force motivated by religious fervour'.[43]

Since then the jihadists have remained firmly entrenched, with most analysts agreeing that the longer they remain, the less likely Mali is to ever have a democratically elected government again.[44] Moreover, according to French intelligence sources, any division between AQIM and *Ansar Dine* is thought to be narrowing, with both groups having moved closer to Abu Bakr al-Baghdadi, and AQIM's consultative council having already discussed 'defecting' to the Islamic State. As J. M. Berger notes, a senior AQIM figure is understood to have shifted his loyalty from al-Qaeda to the Islamic State, while AQIM's Algeria-based affiliate *Jund al-Khalifah* or 'Soldiers of the Caliphate' declared its allegiance to the Islamic State at the end of 2014.[45] Although no formal announcement has yet been made by AQIM in Mali, the format of the organization's latest videos nonetheless closely resembles that of the Islamic State's videos. Interpreted as 'paying visual homage to [AQIM's] brutal cousin in Syria' some are even reminiscent of 'Jihadi John' as they feature a British-accented fighter introducing South African and Swedish hostages to the camera.[46]

As with al-Baghdadi's caliphate, accounting for AQIM and *Ansar Dine's* considerable and seemingly sudden increase in resources and firepower has proven difficult. Attempting the same sort of self-funding narrative as that applied to their counterparts in Al-Raqqah and Mosul, in 2013 the BBC asserted that 'the Islamists are far richer, earning money in recent years by kidnapping Westerners for ransom and trafficking cocaine, marijuana, and cigarettes.'[47] French intelligence officials similarly contended that the groups were profiting handsomely from hostage taking while also collecting heavy taxes from road traffic in their territory.[48] Much like the initial wave of reports on the Islamic State's wealth, however, these and other claims were mostly based on out-of-date statistics, including investigations conducted in 2010 and 2011 by the Center for the Study of Threat Convergence and the Geneva Centre for Security Policy.[49]

Dissatisfied by such explanations, analysts have increasingly pointed to the role played by wealthy external sponsors. France's *Le Figaro* newspaper, for example, had already tried to blame the French government for the rise of Mali's new 'Islamic state' on the basis that Nicolas Sarkozy's outgoing administration had been supporting the Azawad National Liberation Movement at the same time it was still allied to *Ansar Dine*.[50] Others, such as the School of Oriental and African Studies' Jeremy Keenan, have also pointed to Algeria's intelligence services on the basis they feared an independent Tuareg state on their border and wanted to see the Azawad insurrection fail, even if it meant Islamic extremists gaining the upper hand. Furthermore, as more recent reports have noted, the Algerian government-owned Sonatrach oil company still theoretically holds a concession for exploration in northern Mali and may have been running into difficulties with the Bamako government. Notably, in October 2011 Reuters revealed the company had still not begun drilling in Mali, but intended to do so whenever it could.[51]

While there may be some truth to Algeria's stance, and especially its position on the Tuareg tribes, the likelihood of it having directly equipped jihadists still seems remote. More convincing, and more closely in line with the well-documented funding channels for other jihadist groups across the region, have been assertions that wealthy Gulf monarchies or at least powerful individuals within them have been playing the leading role. As Keenan claims of *Ansar Dine*'s leader, Iyad al-Ghaly, he had been 'spending a lot of time in the wrong mosques' while earlier based in Saudi Arabia.[52] Indeed, as the report prepared for the European Parliament also records, al-Ghaly was known to have been serving as a Malian consular officer in Saudi Arabia between 2007 and 2010 and had used his position to 'build up connections with wealthy Gulf donors.'[53]

As with almost all of the big expansions of other 'national jihadist' groups over the past few years, one of the strongest links seems to be with Qatar. Certainly, despite Doha-based thinktanks continuing to argue that the country's political engagements and humanitarian work in Mali are for the greater good, and that Qatar 'serves as mediator for conversation, cooperation, and the advancement of peace', the reality may be quite different.[54] Cited by the French media, a June 2012 report produced by French intelligence specifically mentioned Qatar's support for Islamist extremists in Mali. In particular, it detailed how '[the] al-Qaeda-linked *Ansar Dine* and [AQIM] have all received cash from Doha' and that '[French intelligence] sent several notes to warn the Élysée Palace of the emirate of Qatar's international activities'.[55]

Going further, a researcher for the Centre for International Studies and Research at the Sciences Po university in Paris stated that 'Qatari special forces are now in northern Mali to ensure the training of recruits who are in place there, especially *Ansar Dine*,'[56] while others agreed that 'Qatar has financed terrorists in northern Mali operations, including *Ansar Dine*.'[57] Trying to ring the same alarm bell, when the mayor of Gao in Mali was asked by France's RTL if outside countries were supporting the Islamists and providing them with weapons, he replied 'but of course there are countries that support … The French government knows who supports the terrorists … There is Qatar for example.'[58] Providing fresh details in late 2014, a *Deutsche Welle* report argued that accusations of Qatari involvement in *Ansar Dine* were 'less controversial [than other accusations]' not least because al-Ghaly had also once lived in Doha.[59] Adding another angle, in a piece for *Foreign Affairs* former US national security adviser Elliot Abrams cited a French analyst's view that Qatar's 'risk-taking' in Mali was being done on the basis that it sought to secure a role in the country's nascent gas industry. By having the ear of the jihadists it was reasoned that Qatar could gain an advantage over rivals in the region and squeeze out any competition. To some extent these allegations were confirmed by the report prepared for the European Parliament, which described 'the determination of the Qatari authorities to take control of the hydrocarbon resources of an emerging [new] state of Azawad on the Malian territory'.[60]

BOKO HARAM – NIGERIA UNDER ATTACK

Having managed to unshackle itself from its colonial past, and long claiming to be the world's fourth largest democracy, Nigeria had held fresh elections in 2011, described by *The Economist* as 'the real thing' and 'more or less fair'. Winning fifty-nine percent of the vote, President Goodluck Jonathan soon saw his re-elected government presiding over one of the continent's fastest growing economies, which in April 2014 managed to overtake South Africa and, courtesy of its oil industry, was worth an estimated $510 billion.[61]

Accruing nearly sixty percent of all oil revenues, the government-owned Nigerian National Petroleum Company continued to hold majority stakes in all joint ventures with foreign concession holders and required that all foreign companies had to transfer portions of any profits back to the Nigerian government given that the country's constitution states that 'all oil, gas, and minerals are the property of the state.'[62] As the former CEO of an oil multinational observed, if the NNPC was 'properly managed, it has the potential to be bigger than ExxonMobil, the world's largest listed oil company, in terms of reserves and production.'[63]

Beyond the NNPC, Nigeria at the time was also understood to be rich in 'energetic indigenous entrepreneurs' and had established giant local manufacturing conglomerates along with smaller private oil companies owned entirely by Nigerians. Of the latter, the *Financial Times* noted in late 2014 that they were 'part of a group of nascent home-grown companies which have expanded exponentially in the past five years by buying up assets from the supermajors.'[64] Summarizing the situation, *The Economist* asked its readers to 'let Nigeria celebrate its new-found status for a moment. And then let it get on with the task of living up to being Africa's number one.'[65]

Continuing to stand its ground on economic nationalism, the increasingly wealthy and assertive Nigerian government had also been taking a more active role in pan-African affairs. Most notably, as with Muammar Gaddafi's Libyan regime, it remained firmly opposed to US plans to establish an AFRICOM headquarters in Africa. In particular, Jonathan made it clear that such a development, along with any similar sort of NATO encroachment, was not in Africa's interests and that he was prepared to honour former president Umaru Yar'Adua's pledge that 'he would not allow his country to host a US base and that he was also opposed to any such bases in West Africa'.[66] In summer 2012 Nigeria seemed to have won, as US officials confirmed that AFRICOM would no longer seek to set up a headquarters in any part of Africa.[67]

As with Mali, however, Nigeria had been experiencing an especially painful thorn in its side, as for several years a jihadist group called Boko Haram had been forcibly attempting to recreate the old Sokoto Islamic state that had previously existed in the north of the country before Britain's takeover in 1903.[68] As the International Institute for Strategic Studies' Virginia Comolli explains, Boko Haram was likely inspired by the 1978 'Nigeria

Association for the Eradication of the Innovation and the Establishment of the Sunna'. Known locally as *Yan Izala*, it had similarly been trying to set up an Islamic state, with its leader Abu Bakr Gumi understood to be 'acting with Saudi Arabian support and adopting a doctrine inspired by Wahhabism'. Indeed, as Comolli notes, *Yan Izala* 'thrived despite its ongoing militant struggle due to financial support from Saudi Arabia and Kuwait'. Moreover, it seems Boko Haram has also sought to model itself on the subsequent *Dawah* or 'Missionary' movement. Although its leader, Aminu al-Din Abu Bakr, had initially taken a pro-Iran stance, he was understood to have then switched to a more pro-Saudi position with 'Wahhabi tendencies'. By the 1990s, this had led to a 'wave of missionaries descending on northern Nigeria to promote Wahhabism', hailing from 'countries such as Libya, Pakistan, Saudi Arabia, and Sudan ... benefitting from Saudi sponsorship'. By 1999 the new governor of Zamfara had even pressed for sharia law to be fully adopted, citing Saudi Arabia as an example. His proposed laws were aimed at implementing all sharia punishments and 'ridding society of social vices and un-Islamic practices, and limiting interaction between unrelated men and women'.[69]

Although repeatedly attacking civilians and security personnel in its favoured territories, until recently Boko Haram was still seen as a containable threat, though admittedly one with a 'grimly familiar modus operandi of spreading panic and spilling blood with murderous raids, bombings and beheadings'.[70] In 2009, however, the group reappeared like never before with what seemed unprecedented capabilities. Launching a huge surprise attack, it simultaneously assaulted government soldiers across several states in northern Nigeria, leaving hundreds killed and injured. Although the catalyst was initially reported as an unpopular new law enforcing motorcycle helmets, Boko Haram's then leader, Muhammad Yusuf, soon told the Nigerian media that Jonathan's government had been targeting his followers and that 'democracy and the current system of education must be changed otherwise this war that is yet to start would continue for long'.[71]

Like his predecessors at the helm of *Dawah* and *Yan Izala*, Yusuf was believed to have been tutored by graduates of the Islamic University of Medina and strongly influenced by Saudi scholars, including Abu Bakar bin Abdullah whose Wahhabi text *The secular, foreign, and colonialist schools: their history and danger* has been described as 'providing theological backing for Yusuf's rejection of evolution theory and Western science'.[72] Somewhat bizarrely Yusuf was even interviewed by the BBC, during which he expressed profoundly anti-modern views, particularly about the harm of Western-style education, Darwinism, and the concept of the Earth being a sphere rather than flat. Even touching on the subject of rain, he stated that 'we believe it is a creation of God rather than an evaporation caused by the sun that condenses and becomes rain.' Describing him as 'something of an enigma', the BBC observed that he was clearly 'highly educated and very wealthy', while a Nigerian academic described him as being 'a graduate, very proficient in English, living lavishly – people say he drives a Mercedes Benz … and he is very well-educated in a Western context'.[73]

Although captured and executed in summer 2009, Yusuf's death in many ways spurred the insurrection even further. Gaining access to two videos of the event, a BBC journalist reported seeing Yusuf making a confession and then scenes of his dead body riddled with bullets. According to the *New York Times*, 'Security officers paraded Yusuf before television cameras and then summarily executed him in front of a crowd outside a police station.' As its correspondent noted, this public spectacle became 'the decisive moment in which [Yusuf's followers] turned to wider violence, thus inflaming Nigeria'.[74] Certainly with a major martyr for their cause, and under the new leadership of Yusuf's former deputy Abu Bakr Shekau, Boko Haram continued to expand rapidly.

Known as a radical preacher with a history of personal violence, Shekau was also thought to be willing to bring Boko Haram closer to al-Qaeda.[75] As the *New York Times* hinted, this may explain why the group seemed to receive very quickly a second major injection of funding and weaponry, as 'with help from al-Qaeda or other sponsors, Boko Haram soon returned to Nigeria far more sophisticated and better equipped' and was then able to stage 'more lethal attacks'.[76] According to Comolli, the new armaments included heavy machine guns mounted on trucks, which the group had never had before, along with 'difficult-to-manufacture' explosive devices. Some of the latter were later described by forensic investigators as using technology that was 'not believed to be within the reach of a local outfit unless it had access to external know-how and resources'.[77] To make matters worse, by 2011 Shekau's incarnation of Boko Haram also seemed to have begun experimenting with suicide bombings, complete with the now familiar 'martyr videos'. Along with a penchant for murdering students in colleges, the 'chainsaw beheadings' of truck drivers, and the blowing up of buses filled with passengers, these new tactics were described as 'unexpected' by security officials on the grounds that they were very 'un-Nigerian' actions.[78]

Adding a nasty sectarian element, Christian churches also came under attack for the first time, including in areas previously assumed to be far beyond Boko Haram's reach. Seemingly an effort to push Christians away from their proto-Islamic state, these attacks were also seen as a significant departure from the pre-Shekau era, as before him Boko Haram had largely concentrated on military barracks and police stations.[79] By this stage, more or less in parallel with Abu Bakr al-Baghdadi's emphasis on prison breaks in Iraq, Shekau had also begun to concentrate on releasing as many extremists as possible from Nigeria's jails. In one attempt, reportedly taking place after a number of Boko Haram members had returned from foreign trips, more than seven hundred inmates were busted out of Bauchi prison. As Comolli explains, this was very much a 'change in trajectory' for the group's leaders and can be put down to 'the by-product of foreign influences namely of the al-Qaeda variety'.[80]

BOKO HARAM – THE SHIFT TO THE ISLAMIC STATE

As with the jihadist advances in Mali, the sudden and repeated surges in Boko Haram's resources and, so it seemed, its fast-evolving leadership have been perplexing. Complicating any understanding, there appear to be significant inconsistencies in the intelligence available on the group, and a number of equally contradictory responses to its dramatic expansion. In June 2009, for example, just seven weeks before Muhammad Yusuf's first big insurrection that caught the Nigerian government unawares, a US daily security cable sent to all embassies in Africa included a very explicit warning with eighteen lines of text dedicated to it claiming that 'extremists are planning a massive terrorist attack in Nigeria.' Without substantiation it further predicted that this would be a 'massive surprise attack' and that it would be aimed at critical infrastructure, government officials, and members of the public that were 'opposed to the attackers' doctrines'. It also stated that the 'attack is reportedly aimed at sparking sectarian clashes'. Strangely, however, despite the apparent certainty that such a big-scale operation was on its way, the author of the warning seemed to have no idea of what group would be behind it, suggesting either 'Nigerian Shia, *Salafiya*, or the Nigerian Taliban'.[81]

A few months later, and after Boko Haram had already swept into several provinces, a secret diplomatic cable was sent from the US embassy in Nigeria to the CIA, the DIA, and the US National Security Council reflecting on the 'surprise attacks'. Interestingly the cable indicated that 'most interlocutors point to outside influences and settlers as the cause of Boko Haram.' It also described the 'rate of arms coming into Borno' as being 'frightening'. With fourteen lines of text on the subject, the cable's author seemed relieved that most of the embassy's informants in Nigeria were 'not bothered' by the inflammatory killing of Yusuf, even if it seemed to be serving as the spark to light a civil war. Rather chillingly, however, the cable did sound a cautionary note about the Jonathan government's stance, stating that it was only the governing People's Democratic Party that regarded Yusuf's killing as a human rights concern.[82]

Even stranger, it was only in November 2013, more than three years after Abu Bakr Shekau's succession, that the US finally designated Boko Haram a terrorist organization.[83] Absurdly this was despite the group having being long known to have links to multiple al-Qaeda-linked organizations.[84] As early as summer 2011, for example, US AFRICOM's General Carter Ham began warning that Boko Haram had likely established links to AQIM and argued this was potentially 'the most dangerous thing to happen not only to the Africans, but to us as well'.[85] On several levels it seems he was completely correct. Boko Haram was understood to rule over a faction called *Ansaru*, also known as the 'Supporters of Muslims in Black Africa', which was made up of fighters who had briefly fled Nigeria after Yusuf's death and had temporarily joined up with AQIM in neighbouring countries including Mali. Having later returned home, *Ansaru* was then renamed *Yan Sahara* or 'Men of the Sahara' and in 2011, while still part of Boko Haram, it released a video stating that it was al-Qaeda's official affiliate in Nigeria and was to be known as 'al-Qaeda in the Land Beyond the Sahel'.[86] A later Reuters report corroborated much of this, explaining that 'for years intelligence officials have tracked visits by small sub-groups of Boko Haram fighters to Mali, when its desert north was overrun by AQIM … [where they met] AQIM fighters for training and weapons'. Citing Jennifer Giroux of the Centre for Security Studies at ETH Zurich, the investigation also noted that there were broader links between Boko Haram and other extremist Islamist movements in the region.[87]

In particular, beyond AQIM, Boko Haram was understood to have established ties with groups as far afield as al-Qaeda in the Arabian Peninsula and the Somalia-based al-Qaeda affiliate *Al-Shabaab* or 'The Youth'. Indeed, in 2011 Boko Haram had already issued a statement declaring that 'we want to make it known that our jihadists have arrived in Nigeria from Somalia where they received training on warfare from our brethren who made that country ungovernable.'[88] Moreover, after Shekau stated several times that he himself aspired to be linked to al-Qaeda, Boko Haram's leadership then reportedly began to consider establishing ties to Abu Bakr al-Baghdadi and was understood to be 'closing in on its dream of establishing an African caliphate.'[89] By summer 2014, and only several months after its official US terrorism designation, Boko Haram conquered Gwoza, prompting Shekau to announce it was 'now part of the Islamic State' and 'had nothing to do with Nigeria.'[90] In March 2015, seemingly dissatisfied with the lack of media coverage he had received, Shekau somewhat surreally repeated his pledge to Al-Raqqah stating that Boko Haram was indeed part of the Islamic State.[91] Driving the point home to the international media, the Islamic State's *Dabiq* magazine soon carried reports that jihadists in Nigeria had begun to issue pledges and that Boko Haram's declaration of allegiance had been officially accepted.[92]

Also puzzling was Boko Haram's considerable surge in firepower shortly before its first proclamations of allegiance to the Islamic State. Even though the Nigerian security services had largely managed to stall Boko Haram's advances during the first half of 2013, with the group being described as a 'largely urban-based insurgency under pressure', by 2014 it had reportedly experienced a 'sudden desire for territory' and was then able to expand massively.[93] Indeed, its capture of Gwoza and then most of the rest of Borno state was more or less in parallel with al-Baghdadi's surprise surge into Mosul, with the *Independent* describing deepening concerns among Nigerian officials that despite promises of assistance they had received from the US and Britain, they would be unable to stop Boko Haram's 'rapid takeover of a large area of its territory reminiscent of the Islamic State's lightning advances in Iraq'.[94]

Observing all of this, a coalition of Nigerian security experts and academics known as the Nigeria Security Network noted that Boko Haram seemed much better organized and equipped than ever before, and was 'beginning to operate more like a conventional army ... with armoured vehicles and artillery'.[95] Making much the same point, a Cameroonian official observed that '[for] the kind of operations that Boko Haram carries out, you need people of proven intelligence. They must be receiving explosives specialists and strategists'.[96] Similarly, local tribal leaders told Western journalists that Boko Haram suddenly appeared to possess 'sophisticated weapons ... [and] a seemingly limitless amount of heavy weaponry, vehicles, bombs and ammunition'. One village chief even witnessed several state-of-the-art Toyota four-wheel-drive vehicles turn up, bearing Boko Haram members.[97] Meanwhile, in a report published by Amnesty International that mostly focused on the Nigerian government's inability to prevent a Boko Haram kidnapping raid on a girls' school, which was described as a 'gross dereliction of duties to protect civilians', there was nonetheless a rather buried explanation that the authorities had been unable to repel the attack 'due to poor resources and a reported fear of engaging with the often better-equipped armed groups'.[98]

Predicting his state's fate, Borno's governor had already warned it was going to be 'absolutely impossible' for Boko Haram to be defeated on the battlefield as '[it] is better armed and better motivated than our own troops', while other officials cited in a Council on Foreign Relations report confirmed that the group was 'gaining strength, acquiring better weapons, and fielding more fighters than ever'.[99] Indeed, according to Virginia Comolli's interviewees, many Boko Haram members by this stage were known to be from other nearby countries or even Sudan, with one interviewee even claiming that the majority of Boko Haram's fighters were not Nigerian.[100] This influx of foreigners was certainly evident in video footage later captured by the Nigerian military in May 2015, which depicts a Boko Haram gathering to administer sharia justice and features what seems to be a large number of non-Nigerians, including many sporting headdresses known to be uncommon in Nigeria. At the centre of the gathering, a prominent man who is either a preacher or a judge has his face completely covered with a white turban and is speaking in Arabic, rather than any of the local languages.[101]

Also analogous to the rise of the Islamic State was the apparent recasting of Shekau as a more caliph-like and ultimately indestructible figure. As with al-Baghdadi's mysterious but unifying presence for the entire Islamic State in Iraq and Syria, Shekau was soon being described as a 'brand' for Boko Haram's various factions, and seemed to have acquired an al-Baghdadi-like reputation for immortality after his lookalikes kept appearing in different videos even after the Nigerian government claimed to have killed him on three different occasions.[102] As Nigerian officials complained, almost every time Shekau did seem to surface, it was actually an imposter 'speaking in different cadences and with varying mannerisms … appearing much heavier or much darker in skin colour, and the posturing [was] different between each man.'[103]

As with AQIM and *Ansar Dine* in Mali, there was also a noticeable improvement in Boko Haram's media and communications efforts, with most of its post-2014 propaganda films carrying all the hallmarks of the Islamic State. As J. M. Berger describes, in the weeks leading up to Boko Haram's formal pledge of allegiance to the Islamic State, its communications apparatus appeared to have been 'significantly upgraded'.[104] Similarly as Reuters noted, the group's earlier videos had usually been 'crude affairs' and had mostly featured Shekau talking about 'local gripes' rather than grander caliphal ambitions, whereas its more recent videos were much more professional, with 'video makers appearing to have had access to more advanced graphics and editing techniques'.[105]

From early 2015 the quality of Boko Haram's audio messages was also improving and they had begun to go multi-lingual, with English, French, Arabic, and Hausa translations. Most also featured Islamic State-like *nasheed* chanting and even included excerpts from speeches delivered by leading members of the Islamic State. Meanwhile, the group was exploding onto social media, with the BBC speculating that the Islamic State's media experts were by this stage actively involved. Its reports further explained that 'one of the strongest signs of Islamic State influence lies in the concerted efforts to promote the new [Boko Haram] Twitter feed by a senior pro-Islamic State media operative, known on Twitter as Abu-Malik

Shaybah al-Hamad, who claimed to have been in contact with the Boko Haram general command.'[106]

In another important similarity with the Islamic State and, so it seems, further proof of Boko Haram's surging funds, there are several indications that the organization had been able to improve substantially its salaries and had begun to offer numerous new financial incentives for its latest recruits. According to researchers who have attended debriefings of Boko Haram prisoners, all 'seemed to emphasize the monetary expectations of being members of the group'. One would-be suicide bomber, for example, explained that 'his superiors had settled all his debts and had given his wife some money' while others revealed they had been promised wives and thus would be able to avoid needing expensive weddings. One inmate even complained that if the Nigerian government had been able to provide him with a loan to set up a small business then he wouldn't have needed to join Boko Haram in the first place. Others, meanwhile, described how Boko Haram members were being sent across the borders with cash and, in the case of villages in Cameroon, were spotted handing out leaflets while 'preachers offered large amounts of money for those willing to embrace their ideas'.[107]

BOKO HARAM – GENEROUS SPONSORS

Before its big victories in 2014, and certainly before the 2009 uprising, few would dispute that Boko Haram's sources of funding were limited. The consensus back then was that the organization was probably a net extractor of wealth from its members, rather than a distributor, as it was known to rely primarily on subscription fees along with some modest revenue from small businesses operating motorcycle and car taxis in northern Nigeria. In some cases, its coffers may also have been supplemented by local politicians who chose to hire Boko Haram thugs to scare off prospective rivals. Certainly there is evidence of this having happened before 2009, with US officials also confirming that local governments were having to pay off Boko Haram in something of a protection racket.[108]

But even after Boko Haram's later and very obvious external injections of wealth and equipment, a number of attempts have still been made to extend the self-funding narrative. More or less interchangeable with the reports on the Mali extremists' sources of funding, and of course those that have sought to explain the Islamic State's vast income, these have usually been poorly substantiated. In some reports, for example, drug smuggling was put forward as a major explanation, while in January 2015 a lengthy BBC article asked, 'Where does Boko Haram get its money from?', before repeating the now familiar theory that 'when Boko Haram raids towns, it often loots banks.' It also cited three-year-old statements by Nigerian officials who back then had claimed that the organization 'extorts money from businessmen, politicians and government officials, and threatens them with abduction if they fail to pay up'. Ransom payments were also highlighted, with references to US estimates that up to a million dollars was being paid for the release of each wealthy Nigerian hostage, and often much more for foreigners. Somewhat incongruously, however, the BBC's overall conclusion was that Boko Haram was running on an annual net income of about $10 million and was, in the words of one quoted analyst, a 'low cost insurgency'.[109]

Much like the Islamic State, there is little doubt that some substantial ransoms have been paid to Boko Haram. In 2013, the 92-year-old Nigerian former head of the Organization for Petroleum Exporting Countries was kidnapped and then released for an undisclosed sum,[110] while at about the same time an estimated $3 million was paid by France – or perhaps its preferred proxy – to secure the freedom of a French family that had earlier been abducted by Boko Haram members in Cameroon. Meanwhile, *Ansaru* and other Boko Haram factions have been described as receiving al-Qaeda training in hostage-taking in the Islamic Maghreb and of having developed a system in which they would always share a portion of their booty with Shekau's leadership whenever they returned to Nigeria. As Virginia Comolli explains, some of this would be used to pay off the families of any dead fighters, while the rest would be used to help finance Boko Haram's main campaign.[111]

As for the other self-funding activities, such as the allegations of bank looting, much less is clear. A captured Boko Haram spokesman has claimed that a portion of such robberies is always channelled back to Shekau for redistribution, but there seems little further evidence available and no firm indications of how much money was being stored in such banks in the first place.[112] With regard to drug trafficking, there has been even less to go on, as although a report was issued on the subject by Nigeria's national drug enforcement agency in 2013, Nigerian commentators have pointed out that it was misinterpreted by the international media at the time, as in fact it established no direct links whatsoever to Boko Haram.[113]

The subject of Boko Haram's foreign sponsors, as with those apparently behind AQIM, *Ansar Dine*, and the Islamic State itself, has naturally proven much more sensitive and has rarely been discussed by the Western media, although the *Wall Street Journal* did once get as far as stating that 'the African militant groups have become increasingly sophisticated, often thanks to expertise and advice shared by their patrons and allies in the Middle East.'[114] Such reporting will eventually have to change, as it has already begun to do for the Islamic State, especially as evidence continues to build up of the sustained wealth and expensive weaponry that has been reaching Boko Haram and has allowed it to mount major military operations and operate its own resource-rich mini caliphate. Estimates vary, but the extent of its capabilities and the sophistication of its arsenal point to the organization having received hundreds of millions of dollars over the last few years. Indeed, as a former US military intelligence officer who is now based in Nigeria has claimed, as early as 2011 Boko Haram had likely already benefited from about $70 million in 'overseas donations'.[115]

Given the well-documented links between Saudi Arabia and Boko Haram's leaders, both past and present, some have reasonably suggested that either state-backed entities in the kingdom or wealthy individuals within it have continued to fund and grow the organization. After all, as with *Ansar Dine*'s Iyad al-Ghaly, it is now known that Shekau travelled to Saudi Arabia on a regular basis, with documents seized in Osama bin Laden's Abbottabad compound revealing that Shekau enjoyed 'easy and repeated entry' to the country.[116] In an interview in early 2012, still more than a year and a half before the US's designation of Boko Haram as a terrorist organization, the group's spokesman had even stated: 'Al-Qaeda are our elder brothers. During the lesser Hajj [August 2011] our leader travelled to Saudi Arabia and met al-Qaeda there. We enjoy financial and technical support from them. Anything we want from them we ask them.'[117]

Trying to bring things into the open, in summer 2012 a Nigerian security services official made the allegation that Boko Haram had been receiving money raised by a London-based charity which in turn was alleged to be associated with the Saudi-backed Muslim World League.[118] Acting on this, Britain's Lord David Alton raised the issue in parliament, calling for a full inquiry and for Boko Haram to be proscribed as a terrorist organization. Although parliament's concerns were passed on to the Foreign Office and the Charity Commission, the former made no response while the latter explained that no police investigation was going to be carried out on the basis that 'there are a number of registered charities with similar names to this organization, so the commission is not able to confirm at this stage whether or not this relates directly to a UK-registered charity'.[119]

Refusing to go away, the allegations were further investigated by a group of US congressmen, who in May 2014 themselves accused the London-based charity of sponsoring Boko Haram, with their total funding estimates more or less tallying with those of the Nigeria-based former US military intelligence officer.[120] While the charity denied any involvement, the accusations put forward by both the British and US lawmakers then became the subject of an extensive refutation document produced by a consultancy firm with dual headquarters in Riyadh and London.[121] Inadvertently helping confirm the link between Saudi Arabia and the suspect charity, the document put forward numerous unusual counter-accusations. It suggested, for example, that alongside Alton there were several other high-profile British politicians and intelligence officials, including the former director of MI6, who held 'Islamophobic views' and were 'infamous hard-core neoconservatives'.[122]

As with the Mali jihadists, there is evidence that such suspected Saudi funding for Boko Haram soon began to be supplemented and perhaps outweighed by donations from other backers using AQIM as their conduit, which, as described, was being increasingly linked to Qatari entities. As early as 2009, following Boko Haram's first big uprising and the death of Muhammad Yusuf, AQIM's spokesman had not only promised his 'Salafist brothers in Nigeria' that his leaders would cooperate with them but also that they would send weapons and ammunition.[123] In summer 2013, the US Department of State corroborated the link, with a press release noting not only training and communications links between AQIM and Boko Haram, but also a flow of weapons.[124] In May 2014, the Jamestown Foundation's Jacob Zenn further noted there was a 'financial ... and weapons transfer relationship' between the two groups and argued that without this 'Boko Haram could not have got so violent.'[125] A month later the findings of a survey of Nigerian academics, journalists, and government officials pointed to 'local and international benefactors, and links to al-Qaeda and other well-funded groups in the Middle East', although the authors did concede that 'the actual source of the funding is as elusive as the militants themselves.'[126] Since then, however, prominent Boko Haram analysts have continued to describe AQIM as the group's primary funder, with reports even beginning to circulate of Boko Haram fighters being found in possession of banknotes bearing the same marks as those known to have earlier been in the hands of AQIM.[127] Putting it best, perhaps, has been the *New York Times*, which has retrospectively explained that 'Boko Haram has been around for two decades. But money and training from AQIM gave its leader Shekau a substantial boost when he assumed control.'[128]

BOKO HARAM – DELIVERING RESULTS

Regardless of the exact balance between its generous benefactors, after its massive growth in 2014 Boko Haram was certainly proving value for money. Having savagely destabilized the northern part of Nigeria, and with its Islamic State-linked proto-caliphate driving a sectarian wedge through communities, the group was placing increasing pressure on the embattled Abuja government and, much like the Mali insurgency, accelerating the demise of West African democracy. Whereas job creation, education, and electricity had previously been the country's main voting issues, polls revealed that the apparently unstoppable tide of Boko Haram aggression was changing this to national security.[129] Indeed, following a particularly brutal attack by the group in January 2015, just weeks before scheduled elections, public outrage seemed at an all-time high. As Freedom House's regional director put it '[the attack] is incontrovertible evidence that the human rights situation in Nigeria is only getting worse ... The Nigerian government needs to take more active steps to protect its citizens and end this ongoing crisis.'[130]

With the elections postponed, and fearing a repeat of the Bamako coup d'état, pro-democracy Nigerians took to the streets in all major cities to protest against the 'conspiracy of the ruling clique' and to help 'prevent a slide into anarchy by taking destiny into their own hands'. Getting it half-right, *The Economist* forecasted that Goodluck Jonathan's administration was on its way out, as the 'Nigerian people faced the prospect of an unelected interim government on a security and counter-terror ticket as the country's security deteriorates rapidly'.[131] Though not quite a coup nor a dictatorship, when the elections were eventually held in March 2015 Jonathan was comfortably defeated by former general Muhammadu Buhari amid almost martial law-like circumstances, tear-gassing, voter complaints, and more than fifty deaths from attacks on polling stations. A former minister for petroleum in the 1970s, Buhari had taken power as a military dictator in the early 1980s with the term 'Buharism' becoming synonymous with military rule in Nigeria.[132] Having later declared himself a 'converted democrat', and known to have good ties with the Western powers, he had then stood in four different elections, but on each occasion seemed unable to escape his past.[133] Getting closest to the truth, Britain's Channel 4 explained that Buhari's eventual victory in 2015 was largely 'down to major support in Nigeria's northern states, where Boko Haram has been waging a campaign of terror including suicide bombings, kidnappings and raiding villages, slaughtering civilians and burning homes'.[134]

Predicting most of this, in summer 2014 Gerald Horne, an endowed chair holder at the University of Houston, had also argued that those behind Boko Haram sought much the same outcome as had the backers of the old Afghan jihad against the People's Democratic Party in Kabul. Pointing out that Jonathan's government was a democracy and sought to protect rights, he also noted that it was trying to redistribute wealth so as to counter Nigeria's existing 'wildly radical mal-distributions', and that the country now represented a substantial prize given its new-found status as Africa's largest economy. Fearing the worst, and likely influenced by the unfolding conflicts in Libya and Syria, he warned that any of the pledges made by the US and Britain to help the Nigerian government against Boko Haram were going to serve as 'pretexts for interfering more aggressively in the internal affairs of African states, particularly oil-rich Nigeria ... in that regard, the regime of Goodluck Jonathan is rather shaky'.[135]

Given the US's primarily proxy-based post-2011 policies, such direct Western intervention did not of course materialize. Although there was a brief deployment in April 2014 of about thirty US advisers and several drones to help the Nigerian military find the hundreds of girls earlier kidnapped by Boko Haram, this highly publicized but rather narrowly focused operation was in many ways analogous to the 'contain and react' Yazidi and Kobane missions in Iraq and Syria. In other words, it was media-friendly proof that the US and its allies were reacting to the Boko Haram threat, but without actually taking any meaningful steps to destroy it. Indeed, with the action not dissimilar to the eventual and unenthusiastic Operation Inherent Resolve, the *New York Times* later reported that 'after seven months the drone flights have dwindled, many of the advisers have gone home and not one of the kidnapped girls has been found.' Moreover, despite several hundred drone flights having apparently taken place, these had 'yielded no results', while cooperation between US and Nigerian military officials was described as being almost non-existent.[136]

Assessing the situation perfectly, Nigeria's ambassador to the US was understood to have 'accused the Obama administration of failing to support the fight against Boko Haram' and to have himself stated that 'we find it difficult to understand how and why in spite of the US presence in Nigeria with their sophisticated military technology, Boko Haram should be expanding and becoming more deadly'. Supporting this view, the *New York Times* revealed that despite Boko Haram's continuing growth, US officials in Nigeria had actually cancelled the last stage of US training for a newly created Nigerian army battalion. Rather laughably, given the US's close relationship with regimes such as Saudi Arabia and its own belated designation of Boko Haram as a terrorist organization, the Department of State tried to justify the US's reduced involvement on the basis that Nigeria's military had a 'dismal human rights record' and that there are 'legal prohibitions against close dealings with foreign militaries that have engaged in human rights abuses'.[137] Adding a little more to the picture, and in a close parallel with the Iraqi armed forces' complaints of poor supplies for its fight against the Islamic State, shortly before his election defeat Jonathan told Voice of America that 'Nigeria had been facing difficulties in acquiring and operating sophisticated weapons.' In an oblique reference to the US, he blamed this on Nigeria not receiving 'the blessing of the weapons' parent country'.[138]

Helping place such calculated indifference to Boko Haram in the broader strategic context, when later interviewed by the author Horne contended that the 'battle against Boko Haram is half-hearted from the US viewpoint because of various constraints ... [namely that] certain nationals of the Gulf states [are] principal backers' of Boko Haram.[139] While there is certainly much truth to this, it is also important to note how the US military itself has been benefiting directly, albeit quietly, since Buhari's succession. In late January 2015, with Jonathan's chances crumbling and only weeks before Boko Haram's second and more public pledge to the Islamic State, US AFRICOM seemed poised for a comeback. Continuing to ignore the Nigerian government's refusal of its presence in the region by having already established a drone base across the border in Niger and having dispatched three hundred special forces troops to the Cameroonian border, AFRICOM's commander called for a large-scale counter-insurgency campaign and an 'across the board response' in at least four West African countries. As he explained, this was to be part of a 'huge international and multinational response aimed at forces affiliated with Boko Haram'.[140] With the more supplicatory Buhari soon meeting with AFRICOM officials and reportedly signing a deal, the Department of State appeared to forget its earlier human rights concerns and on the same day announced it would provide funding to help the new Nigerian government set up an anti-Boko Haram force. But with promises of only $5 million, the Islamic State's latest affiliate seemed just as safe as its home bases in Iraq and Syria.[141]

Beyond AFRICOM's advances, the Boko Haram-assisted removal of Jonathan has also helped open up Nigeria's valuable state assets to the West. Conveniently for oil multinationals, Buhari quickly indicated his willingness either to dismantle completely the Nigerian National Petroleum Company or, as his central bank governor suggested, to reduce its stakes in future joint ventures to just fifteen percent. Certainly there is a sense of pressure, as in a speech delivered to Buhari's party shortly after the election, former British business secretary Peter Mandelson stated that the new government must 'crack the NNPC nut within a hundred days of taking office'. Meanwhile, in addition to repeating allegations of corruption within the NNPC that have since been denied by the outgoing oil minister, the *Financial Times* described how Western diplomats and foreign oil company officials were complaining that 'as much as $100 billion of fresh investment from the likes of Royal Dutch Shell, ExxonMobil and Total is sitting at Nigeria's door'.[142] By July 2015 things were getting even more target-specific, as at the end of a very general speech that affirmed the US's supposed solidarity with the campaign against Boko Haram and the 'insecurity in the North', the US ambassador to Nigeria went on to declare that 'as you improve the business climate, we encourage trade and investment' and then said 'as you continue the privatization of your power grid, we stand ready to help, through President Obama's Power Africa initiative.'[143]

BEYOND PANETTA – OTHER PLEDGES TO THE ISLAMIC STATE

On top of those in Libya, Yemen, and in West Africa, there have since been several other pledges of allegiance to the Islamic State or, in some cases, strong expressions of interest from leaders of existing jihadist groups. Often with long histories of al-Qaeda engagement, these organizations now clearly suit the core strategic interests of the Islamic State's sponsors, along with helping to supply more fighters and resources to the cause. Meanwhile, from their perspective, the new recruits have evidently begun to receive much more tangible benefits than al-Qaeda's leaders were ever able to provide. In this sense the Islamic State's franchising system has been well placed to take advantage of groups that have found themselves struggling, seeking financial support, or simply looking for better battlefield or communications training.[144]

Giving Leon Panetta an almost hundred percent success rate with his prediction of which countries would go on to see internationalized versions of the Islamic State, by 2015 Somalia was also looking likely. Having emerged from the old Union of Islamic Courts back in 2006, *Al-Shabaab* had formally joined al-Qaeda after Osama bin Laden's death and, as earlier mentioned, had then begun to reach out to other groups including Boko Haram.[145] With its leader Ahmad Abdi Godane killed by a US drone strike in September 2014, the path had suddenly become much clearer for members to contact the Islamic State, especially those who had earlier rebelled by themselves trying to push for a caliphate in Somalia.[146] Facilitating the possible switchover, in summer 2015 the Islamic State began to release a series of videos promising Somalians a better deal than Ayman Zawahiri had offered, and by October CNN was reporting that a senior and former London-based *Al-Shabaab* cleric had already changed sides.[147] Although *Al-Shabaab*'s new leadership quickly renewed their allegiance to Zawahiri, many regarded this as a temporary measure, as the group has since faced multiple defections from its senior commanders, many of whom have taken hundreds of their men with them.[148]

Of those in Panetta's 'elsewhere' category, most prominent has been the pledge made by Egypt's *Ansar Bait al-Maqdis* or 'Supporters of the Holy House [of Jerusalem]'. Declaring their founding of the Islamic State in Sinai in November 2014, they have not only kept the Egyptian government thirsty for substantial arms purchases it can ill afford, but have also helped the Abdelfattah Sisi regime maintain and justify a state of emergency over the bulk of the population.[149] Certainly the rise of an Egyptian Islamic State has provided significant cover for Cairene Bonapartism and an extensive crackdown on all manner of opponents in the wake of the failed Muslim Brotherhood strategy. As Nathan Brown along with the Center for American Progress' Moktar Awad have argued, the Brotherhood will find it increasingly hard to remobilize due to the 'ISIS-ification' of Islamist politics in Egypt, especially as frustrated youths continue to turn to the Islamic State as a solution. Although the 'substantial reorientation' of the Brotherhood that they describe does not quite yet seem in evidence, there are nonetheless already alarming examples of Muhammad Morsi-era officials who have now called for assassinations and even suicide bombings. As Brown and Awad put it, this suits Sisi well as he 'seems to revel in the Brotherhood's now visible embrace of popular resistance, seeing it as proof of claims of Brotherhood violence'.[150]

In other parts of the Arab world, the pattern has more closely resembled the emergence of the new affiliates in Libya and Yemen, with the Islamic State having mostly 'come out of nowhere' rather than taking over another group. But usually without the capability to gain territory or wage conventional war, these mini affiliates instead seem to have been focused on keeping pressure on governments or organizations that remain a source of concern to the Islamic State's backers. On 18 March 2015 in Tunisia, for example, at the exact time its parliament was discussing a proposed but heavily disputed new anti-terrorism law that would have given the government significant new security powers, a massive blast at the Bardo Museum killed dozens of civilians, including tourists, while gunmen seized several hostages.[151] Quickly lending a hand to the story, SITE Intelligence Group claimed that 'Twitter users associated with the Islamic State' were 'overjoyed', while a day later the Islamic State officially claimed responsibility for the attack and promised that there would be more.[152] On this basis Beji Caid Essebsi took to the airwaves to state that Tunisia had no choice but to 'enter a mobilization phase' so as to counter future terror threats. By the end of the month, and after Tunisian special forces ambushed and killed the perpetrators, with secret support from US troops, his government claimed it as a 'crowning success for [Tunisia's] new counterterrorism capabilities'. Buoyed by this, Essebsi then began to implement a NATO–Tunisia 'individual partnership cooperation programme' to help with defence reform and 'the fight against terrorism'.[153] A few months later, with the nation again in mourning following another Islamic State-linked attack involving a lone gunman killing nearly forty tourists on a beach, Essebsi doubled down on his message by promising 'painful but necessary measures' in order to restore stability.[154]

In contrast to the rising security states in Egypt and Tunisia, the Jordanian monarchy appears to have experienced no collateral benefits whatsoever from the rise of the Islamic State, not least given the prospects of a massive refugee crisis on its doorstep, and the known sympathies of communities in Maan, Irbid, and the country's other more restive towns.[155] With a mature and well-functioning security apparatus that had already helped Jordan navigate through the Arab Spring and needed little extra justification for its powers, the calculated response, so it seemed, was to simply try to keep the Islamic State at arm's length. But with the organization's substantial expansion and eventual arrival on Jordan's borders in summer 2014, this was proving harder by the day, not least because the Islamic State had begun to accuse Jordanian intelligence of producing propaganda against the caliphate. Indeed, in June 2014 Jordan even released from prison Abu Muhammad al-Maqdisi, the former mentor but then critic of Abu Musab al-Zarqawi and his proto-Islamic state.[156] Choosing perhaps the most potent comeback of all, in February 2015 the Islamic State released an unconvincing but nonetheless uncritically reported-on video that purportedly showed a captured Jordanian pilot being burned to death while he was standing in a cage on the exact middle of a marked cross on the ground. By doing this the Islamic State succeeded in generating enough public outrage to force the Jordanian air force into very publicly launching dozens of air strikes against it and thus helping widen the monarchy's existing cleavages with its more jihadist-inclined opponents.[157]

RUSSIA AND CHINA - SUPERPOWER IMPLICATIONS

Outside of the Middle East and its obvious challenge to the Russian-backed Syrian government, the Islamic State has also usefully been rejuvenating at least some of the spirit of the 1980s Afghan jihad, and especially the US's intended by-product of radicalizing and mobilizing Muslim populations in Russia's Central Asian territories and neighbours. In this sense, in addition to the Islamic State's described recruitment of foreign fighters and even civil servants from such countries, it has also been laying the groundwork for future jihadist resistance movements that can distract Moscow or potentially even destabilize Russia. In Chechnya, for example, by late 2014 the previously al-Qaeda-aligned 'Caucasus Emirate' was understood to be experiencing significant divisions, with many of its returning fighters having pledged their allegiance to the Islamic State after forming their own pro-Islamic State unit in Syria known as *Jaysh al-Mujahireen wa al-Ansar* or 'Army of Emigrants and Partisans'.[158] Indeed, following a series of attacks in the Chechen capital of Grozny, the majority of Russian analysts polled by the *Moscow Times* suggested that it was the work of the Islamic State rather than al-Qaeda.[159]

Meanwhile, a significant increase in Islamic State-related activity was also being reported in the north-western Caucasus republic of Karachaevo-Cherkessia, leading analysts to conclude that 'southern Russia is becoming increasingly radical, as the ideology of the Islamic State spreads.'[160] By early 2016, Russian officials had also begun to complain that the Islamic State was 'resting and replenishing' itself in Georgian territory close to Chechnya's border. Although the Jamestown Foundation reasoned that it was 'hard to imagine that Moscow does not know the actual situation in the [area]', both Georgian officials and the US ambassador to Georgia denied there was any Islamic State presence.[161]

Equally worrying for the Kremlin, following on from Islamic State propaganda focused on stirring up Kazakhstan and other nearby states, in May 2015 the missing chief of Tajikistan's elite paramilitary police force resurfaced alongside other Tajikis claiming he had defected to the Islamic State. Appearing in a professionally produced video, he promised to bring weapons back home and even referenced the Tajiki fighters who had returned in the early 1990s after the Afghan campaign and had tried to establish their own Islamic state. Notably he vowed jihad on the Russia-aligned government and said, 'Listen you dogs, the president and ministers, if only you knew how many boys, our brothers are here, waiting and yearning to return to Tajikistan to re-establish sharia law there.'[162]

Without the same sort of precedent, the mobilization of the Islamic State against China has been more complex, and, thus far, arguably more successful. Although there are, of course, significant Muslim populations in north-western China that the group can appeal to, the aim instead seems to have been to use the spectre of the Islamic State to promote greater military spending and more powerful security states in pro-Western nations in Asia that either border China or can at least help encircle and contain Beijing's military ambitions. For those with Muslim majorities or communities, this has involved new pledges to Abu Bakr al-Baghdadi by existing local groups, or in some cases the formation of smaller Islamic State-aligned cells. In Indonesia, for example, *Jemaah Islamiyah*, or 'Islamic Congregation', was understood to have declared its allegiance at some point in late 2014, with its leader Alim Abu Bakr Bashir having stated from prison in January 2015 that he had joined the Islamic State.[163] Similarly the Bangsamoro Islamic Freedom Fighters along with other jihadist groups in the Philippines were thought to have joined at about the same time, while in May 2015 Singapore's prime minister warned that along with Singaporeans, 'the Islamic State has so many Indonesian and Malaysian fighters that they form a unit by themselves – the Malay Archipelago Combat Unit.'[164]

In Pakistan and India, both of which have featured as future provinces on Islamic State-produced maps, there has similarly been an increase in jihadist activity, with a number of local organizations appearing to have recently benefited from increased resources and then having announced alliances with Al-Raqqah. Among them has been *Tehrik-i-Taliban* or 'Taliban Movement', which, despite reports of divisions within its ranks, has confirmed allegiance to the Islamic State and declared its support for 'those mujahideen who fight for the sake of the survival of the caliphate'.[165] Rather worryingly, following the arrest of an 'Islamic State in Pakistan' commander in January 2015, Islamabad's respected *Express Tribune*, which is co-published with the *International New York Times*, claimed the man had arrived from Syria five months earlier and had confessed to his interrogators, though perhaps under duress, that his organization's funding was being 'routed through the US'.[166]

Helping put things in perspective amid the flurry of South Asian pledges, and just two days before the *Express Tribune*'s exposé, Barack Obama stated during a visit to New Delhi that the US 'saw a role for India in the battle against the Islamic State'. According to an extensive Reuters report, he was there to facilitate a proposed joint US–Indian venture in drone manufacturing but, as their correspondent put it, this was in the broader context of 'the US viewing India as a vast market and potential counterweight in Asia to a more assertive China'. Moreover, as Reuters also noted, by this stage the US had 'frequently been frustrated with the slow pace of New Delhi's economic reforms and unwillingness to side with Washington in international affairs ... [including] Islamic militancy'.[167]

Arguably even more important than the arming and co-opting of India into the US's China policy has been the necessary repositioning of Japan as a new military power capable of offensive operations and policing the Pacific coastlines. Hampered, however, by its pacifistic post-Second World War constitution and widespread popular pushback, the pro-US prime minister Shinzō Abe had been struggling for more than two years to rebrand Japan as a more militaristic nation. Nonetheless, in January 2015 things started to change rapidly, as precisely during Abe's tour of a number of Middle Eastern countries, the Islamic State chose to release a new series of hostage videos, this time featuring two Japanese prisoners in the now familiar orange jumpsuits. Making an absurd and, as most would argue, impossible demand for a $200 million ransom payment, and then distributing a follow-up video that seemed to show one of the men being executed, the Islamic State then strangely ignored the Japanese government's attempts to establish contact. Moreover, even though a British newspaper questioned the authenticity of the video, with its cited experts claiming that Photoshopped images were being used, both the US and British governments were quick to respond, with Obama condemning it as a 'brutal murder ... the US stands shoulder to shoulder with Japan,' and David Cameron stating that 'the reported brutal murder of Haruna Yukawa and the further threats made by the Islamic State are yet another reminder of the murderous barbarity of these terrorists.'[168]

Either way, Japanese pacifism was being sorely tested and was quickly sidelined, with Abe soon promising greater Japanese support for Operation Inherent Resolve and Japan's security cabinet approving legislation that would implement a 'drastic shift in security policy allowing the military to fight abroad for the first time since the Second World War'. Under the bonnet, this of course required a reinterpretation of Japan's constitution and for the country to drop its long-held, self-imposed ban on exercising the right to collective self-defence and the provision of military aid to allied countries elsewhere in the world. As reported, members of the public still seemed 'divided and wary over the changes' and were worried over future 'entanglement in wars through [Japan's] alliance with Washington'. Street protests took place against the new 'war legislation', and a fight even took place inside parliament. As the BBC described, 'The bill is not widely supported by the country at large.'[169] Nonetheless, with the Islamic State at large, the Abe administration managed to pass a record-breaking $28 billion defence budget that included the purchase of F-35 jets, an Aegis destroyer, and drones. A new foreign intelligence agency was also announced, while in May 2015 Japan hosted its first ever arms fair. Run by a British security firm, it was described by *The Economist* as 'another sign that Japan is slipping its pacifist moorings'. Indeed, Britain was well prepared for the new Japan, as announcements were soon made that Tokyo was developing an amphibious assault force modelled on the Royal Marines and that British experts had already begun to advise Japan on its naval strategy.[170]

EPILOGUE – KEEPING THE WHEEL TURNING

GETTING BUSINESS BACK TO USUAL

With the Arab Spring thwarted in its Tunisian and Egyptian heartlands, and leaderships compliant with international financial institutions (IFIs) largely reinstalled, most of the immediate threats to the interests of the Western powers, their constituent corporations, and their regional allies have been reversed. On the one hand this means the same pressures and inequalities that had been building up prior to 2011 will, if anything, keep on increasing. In Raymond Hinnebusch's words, this means the counter-revolutions are making 'the region more vulnerable than ever to the pathologies of neo-liberalism, including crony-capitalism, inequalities, and vulnerabilities to the IFIs'.[1]

But on the other hand the new mix of counter-revolutionary strategies seem just enough to get business back to usual, at least for the time being. In this sense the externally sponsored new blend of authoritarianism in these and other Arab countries over the past few years – capable of quashing progressive ideas, keeping people off the streets, and securing themselves against the new 'national jihadists' – is proving an effective handmaiden for a full-scale rebooting of both the Washington Consensus and Britain's Global New Deal.

In fact, if we cut through the faux support for Arab democracy put forward in early 2011 by wrong-footed Western government officials, we find that the writing was already on the wall. With the dust barely settling on Tahrir Square, in April 2011 a British minister boldly declared that 'the Arab Spring is a timely reminder of the appeal our values and institutions have beyond our borders ... [as such] the transatlantic alliance must rapidly agree a basis for common action: the spread of capitalist democracy.'[2] Even more bluntly, Barak Obama himself then explained that 'America's support for democracy will be based on ensuring financial stability, promoting reform, and integrating competitive markets with each other and the global economy. And we're going to start with Tunisia and Egypt.'[3] Back in Britain, by early May, Foreign Secretary William Hague launched the 'Foreign Office Business Charter' and confirmed that 'commercial diplomacy will be central to all Foreign Office activities ... Economic stability is the foundation for secure and prosperous societies and diplomatic alliances and political influence is often built on strong commercial relations.'[4]

Softening their tone by at least paying homage to the spirit of the Arab Spring, the major US-based IFIs duly promised $40 billion to support the 'democratic transitions' in Tunisia and Egypt along with other 'Arab states in transition' such as Libya and Yemen. Announced at the May 2015 G8 summit in Deauville, France, the IFI-led 'Deauville Partnership' also included the British government and the European Union along with their 'regional partners', eighty percent of which were Gulf monarchies.[5] As Adam Hanieh explains, this was 'part of a broader neo-liberal design to link rhetorical support for democracy and good governance to the opening up of markets and other pillars of economic liberalization'. And, as Francesco Cavatorta describes, it also showed that the IFIs were determined to demonstrate that their neo-liberal policies had always been credible and that it was only poor governance in the Arab world that had hampered them in the past.[6] In Tunisia's case the president of the World Bank claimed the revolution was primarily the result of 'too much red tape', while the organization's strategy briefing for Tunisia's transitional government made sure to mention the need for 'social and economic inclusion, governance, voice, transparency, and accountability'.[7] Similarly recasting itself as Arab Spring-friendly, the IMF soon made sure to state that 'the IMF is different from the past' and that 'it would pay specific attention to the underprivileged, to the poor.'[8]

On the ground, few were convinced by this veneer of popular partici-pation, with even the World Bank admitting that in Egypt the 'attitude of the people at large towards IFIs is uncertain … [there] exist possible negative sentiments … reforms aimed at improving the environment for private investment may be deeply unpopular.' Certainly in Tunisia, activists were already arguing that IFI loans were 'not a secondary ques-tion to the ongoing social struggles confronting the current Tunisian revolution, but at the heart of the struggle'. They also complained that such interference 'raised economic, political, and social questions that relate to popular sovereignty and foreign control, and how we divide the wealth of the country and achieve rights for all Tunisians'. Putting it best, perhaps, were trade union representatives who claimed that 'the IMF is dictating economic policy and people are unhappy because there is no social justice, freedom, or jobs.' MPs, meanwhile, were particularly concerned over a draft law passed down to them that had been part-prepared by the IFIs and the Paris-based Organization for Economic Cooperation and Development. With criticism mounting 'on the grounds that it would open the country's resources up to exploitation by foreign companies and lead to greater indebtedness', ministers had to push back by replying that it was a 'requirement for foreign donations'. Not all in the Tunisian cabinet were happy, however, as even though the World Bank had praised it for its commitment to 'deepening integration into the global economy to boost growth', it had also been warned to 'resist any pressure to increase wage levels' in case it made the country uncompetitive, and had been criticized for introducing a scheme to assist unemployed graduates.[9]

Either way, as the various Islamist-led and then deep-state counter-revolutions began to take hold, the post-Arab Spring governments were soon able to re-embrace the IFIs and help turn the clock back to 2010. In Tunisia's case, loans from the World bank were quickly accepted while agreements with the IMF have since been signed, the latter requiring the country to adopt wage restraint, reduce taxes for corporations, and imple-ment an 'ambitious structural reform agenda that helps to rebuild Tunisia's economic model by promoting private-sector development … and reduces pervasive state intervention'. Although things have moved a little slower in Egypt, not least due to the counter-revolutionary recalibration in summer

2013, the overall trajectory has still been much the same. While the Muslim Brotherhood had postponed its IMF negotiations, this was only due to public pressure and was likely intended as a temporary delay. Indeed, in early 2013 Hillary Clinton warned that future US aid for Egypt would be conditional on its 'completion of the IMF process', and in any case the Brotherhood was understood to have already given assurances to the US and the IFIs that it would 'prevent a true revolution of social justice taking place ... [including] the equitable distribution of national wealth'. Abdelfattah Sisi's coup-installed regime was naturally then quick to pick up the baton, rapidly arranging World Bank loans and reappointing some of the same Mubarak-era officials that had earlier dealt with the IMF.[10] Cairo soon signalled its willingness to resume negotiations and began to implement some of the measures usually considered prerequisites for IMF financing. As the director of a major Egyptian investment bank explained, 'Sooner or later we will have to resort to the IMF ... For credibility first, before its money.'[11]

By 2014, and certainly 2015, things seemed to be returning to normal, at least from the West's perspective, with a strong green light clearly given to the new regimes by the US and British governments. Picking up from where they had left off, multinationals and other Western companies began to flood back into the region, confident the local authorities knew their place and would continue to guarantee the supply of cheap Arab labour and easy access to their countries' natural resources and former state assets. Jumping on the bandwagon, almost as if the events of 2011 never happened, influential *New York Times* columnist Tom Friedman used a survey produced by a UAE-based public relations firm and an interview with a gushing expatriate to argue that it was in fact the example earlier set by Dubai, the epitome of the Arab neo-liberal order, that was the true 'capital of the Arab Spring', as its leaders had motived other Arabs to demand more from their governments.[12] More chillingly, one of Britain's most powerful unelected officials was by this stage even telling the Foreign Affairs Select Committee that human rights no longer had the same 'profile' it had had in the past, that it was secondary to Britain's 'prosperity agenda', and that the Foreign Office's primary purpose was the promotion of British business overseas.[13]

THE EXPLOITATION OF EGYPT

With rumours of a brand new Egyptian capital city beginning to circulate, all seemed to be moving in the right direction. Eventually announced in early 2015, the proposed development was to house the government along with foreign embassies and most of Cairo's elite. It was to take twelve years to build, was to encompass at least seventy thousand acres, and was to be funded and developed almost entirely by foreign companies. Symbolically launched at a London-based investment conference, Egypt's investment minister explained that 'the government would incur zero cost in the city, and it will be totally developed, master-planned, and executed by a private sector company – a developer from the Gulf.' He also described how the new city would prove that 'Egypt is really committed to an open-market economy' and that more than twenty-five projects in support of the city, including a denationalized electricity network, would be launched to attract foreign investments of $35 billion.[14]

Soon after it was confirmed that the UAE-based real estate investment fund, Capital City Partners, would be serving as the regional gateway for global investors, and that the new city would have an airport as big as Heathrow, a building taller than the Eiffel Tower, and would even be named after one of the UAE's sheikhs.[15] Among those leaping onto the bandwagon was Khalaf al-Habtoor, one of Dubai's top tycoons, who declared himself 'ready to jump on investment opportunities in Egypt'.[16] Indeed, Abdelfattah Sisi's new regime was very likely exactly what he had been waiting for, as amid the Arab Spring he had published an opinion piece in *Gulf News* arguing that Mubarak was 'maintaining stability ... [and had] immediately responded to the protestors' demands', and that the uprisings across North Africa were a 'contagion' that had the risk of spreading.[17]

Arguably best placed among the international investors were British companies, as at the March 2015 Egyptian Economic Development Conference it was revealed that they were already responsible for fifty percent of foreign investments in the new Egypt. As Britain's ambassador explained, 'The British are coming in strength and we want to set an example to the world ... Britain's commitment is about having a permanent presence at the heart of Egypt's economy.'[18] Backing him up, Foreign

Secretary Philip Hammond tweeted from the sidelines that a fresh $12 billion British Petroleum deal to exploit Egypt's hydrocarbon resources was poised to become 'the biggest inward investment in Egypt's history, which represented a long-term economic plan'.[19] Surprising many, it soon emerged that the BP agreement was the first of its kind in Egypt, as it involved no form of profit-sharing with the government as the British company would only be responsible for paying taxes and royalties. As one analyst argued, it meant Egypt was 'essentially privatizing its gas sector and handing control of natural resources to private companies', while exiled former MP Hattem Azzam stated that the 'sudden decision' would require 'deep investigation by the Egyptian people, represented by a legitimate parliament'.[20]

Also at the conference was former prime minister Tony Blair, who took to the stage to praise Egypt's recent IFI-friendly measures, including a new investment law, fuel subsidy reforms, and the promotion of the private sector.[21] Whitewashing the new regime's numerous atrocities, Blair also explained that 'I'm absolutely in favour of democracy ... but I think you've also got to be realistic ... for the first time in my memory you have a leadership in Egypt that understands the modern world.'[22] With such public legitimation the path was soon clear for other Western officials to follow suit, with Italy's prime minister telling the media that 'Sisi is a great leader ... Egypt invested in the future on the leadership of Sisi ... in this moment Egypt will be saved only with the leadership of Sisi, this is my personal position and I am proud of my friendship with him.'[23] By summer 2015 the narrative around Sisi was so solid that Britain's secretary for defence even published an opinion piece on the topic for an Egyptian newspaper. Laced with the usual references to the rise of the Islamic State, he claimed that 'we are strengthening Egypt's hands against the terrorists by supporting its vision of a more prosperous, more democratic society' and that 'Egyptians have rejected both extremism and authoritarianism ... [with] a responsible and accountable government founded on rights, freedoms, and the rule of law ... Britain is offering our solidarity in exchange.'[24]

On top of the Western-backed free-for-all and the new plans for Cairo, which academics have described as 'the wrong thing' and likely to leave the old Cairo to fester,[25] other lucrative opportunities appeared to be re-emerging for the old local companies. Having struggled since 2011 given its association with Mubarak-era land deals, the Amer Group seemed particularly bullish again with its spokesman telling the *Financial Times* that 'our sales are higher after [Sisi's installation] … we believe in Egypt … we compare ourselves to Emaar Properties of Dubai.' Indeed, by the time Blair had delivered his resounding endorsement of the new government, Amer was once more reporting net profits and had launched thirteen new luxury gated real estate projects across the country.[26] By the end of 2014 the company claimed its annual profits were up 670 percent and described this as a 'return to a pre-revolution growth trajectory.'[27] Meanwhile, numerous other developers indicated they were again able to buy up cheap land under the umbrella of Egypt's Tourism Development Authority – an entity originally proposed by the US Agency for International Development. As the University of New Hampshire's Jeannie Sowers argues, this new land rush not only benefited the big companies but also 'current and former higher-ups in the military and security services, who then resold land to tourism developers'. In her view this had led to a 'legal regime for selling coastal land cheaply, without … customary use by local communities; without provision for low and moderate income housing'.[28]

In this light it is easier to understand why Egyptian society was not only becoming more unequal than it had been at any point since 2011, but was likely more divided than it had been under Mubarak. As *Forbes* noted, Egyptian billionaires under Sisi had quickly managed to increase their share of the country's GDP to six percent, with the top eight businessmen controlling over $23 billion – an increase of eighty percent over their holdings prior to the Arab Spring. Although some of the increase may be explained by wealth repatriated from abroad, the bulk does seem to have been generated in Egypt itself. Meanwhile, in parallel to these new riches and opportunities, there has been a 'sharp uptick' in poverty, with over twenty million Egyptians now believed to be living in such circumstances compared to sixteen million before the revolution.[29]

WILD CARD NUMBER ONE – OPENING UP IRAN

Beyond the other, more violent counter-revolutionary responses in Libya, Syria, Yemen, and elsewhere, the Western powers were also intent on turning important domestic events in Iran to their advantage. Long-planned of course, and firmly in the pipeline well before the Arab Spring even began, parts of the US and British governments had been pursuing some sort of opening up of the Iranian economy under the pretext of a 'nuclear deal'. If signed and ratified, this was to lead to Iran agreeing to various limits and restrictions on its civilian nuclear energy programme in exchange for sanctions being lifted. Justifying it best was a British minister, who as early as 2007 stated that 'we want Iran to be much more engaged, because Western Europe needs Iranian gas very badly' and 'there are sixty-eight million people in Iran, and it is a market that the Chinese are positively slavering at. I do not think that any of us want to isolate Iran.'[30]

Given the vagaries of Iranian leadership and its troubled history with Washington, not least with the Israel lobby, the White House could not have been sure everything would work out. But with Tehran emerging as a relative pillar of stability in an increasingly destabilized region, and with Hassan Rouhani's more moderate presidency focused on delivering improvements in standards of living and thus preventing a second Green Revolution, a sufficient chunk of the US political and economic elite had begun to see only a 'win-win' situation in bringing Iran in from the cold. In this sense, an important US 'wild card' seemed to be turning up trumps, as long before the deal finally went through and the sanctions began to be removed in January 2016, a veritable gravy train of Western officials and businessmen had already begun to arrive in Iran.[31]

Amid numerous pieces in Western newspapers extolling Iran's distinguished culture and advertising luxury tours of its ancient wonders, as early as Spring 2015 reports also began to circulate that ExxonMobil was engaging lobbying firms to monitor all political activity relating to the nuclear deal and Iran's negotiations with the US government. Soon after, it transpired that several European oil companies had started to send their executives to Tehran, with the CEO of Italy's Eni SpA stating that investments in Iran could begin very soon and that Iran's national oil company had an 'outstanding credit position'. By the summer, Royal Dutch Shell was similarly establishing a presence, while Russia's Lukoil kept quietly meeting with Iran's oil minister on his trips to Europe.[32]

Industry analysts soon reasoned that Iran 'represented an easy path to growing production ... you could get a pretty good bump pretty quickly,' while one Western executive told the *Financial Times* that Iran was like a 'multibillion-dollar candy store ready to open its doors'. Even better, Iranian experts had begun to indicate that Rouhani wanted to make the investment environment as favourable as possible by treat-ing the oil multinationals as 'partners' in long-term thirty-year joint ventures that would 'look and smell like production-sharing deals'. According to Iran's deputy oil minister, there would be as many as fifty such projects worth over $185 billion 'up for grabs' including some in the huge and mostly undeveloped North and South Pars gas fields and others in some of the world's biggest oil fields containing hundreds of billions of barrels of oil.[33]

With the nuclear deal continuing to build momentum, the final months of 2015 saw things really take off, with Royal Dutch Shell and Total announcing they would each build a hundred fuel stations across Iran as soon as the sanctions lifted, and with British Petroleum having dispatched its own fact-finding mission to Tehran.[34] After Iran claimed that $2 billion worth of European investments had already been agreed, France's foreign minister visited in person and promised that hundreds of French business leaders were due to follow in his footsteps to 'cash in on oil and cars', and that Rouhani was going to be invited to Paris for a state visit. Even Japan's deputy trade minister turned up for what the Japanese media described as a mission 'to avoid [Japan] being beaten by European and US companies'.[35]

With the lifting of sanctions almost a certainty, more than five hun-dred European executives arrived in Geneva at the end of September 2015 to meet with delegates from Iran's national oil company, the Tehran stock exchange, and several other entities. As the conference's organizer explained, the event was not just about oil and infrastructure, but was also about 'the biggest prize ... to access Iran's eighty million popula-tion'. As the representative of a Western drilling company remarked, 'the nuclear agreement with Iran has effectively opened up a sleeping giant and the last major untapped emerging market economy ... Iran has the potential to become a G20 country within a short space of time.'[36] This was definitely no exaggeration, as within days of the nuclear agreement going through, Iran began to reveal details of dozens of mouth-wateringly huge contracts that were being prepared, including a massive $25 billion purchase of 118 new Airbus passenger jets to replace its national carrier's aging fleet.[37]

A NEW IRAN, A NEW SECTARIAN WAR

With the deals every bit as good as the ones Western companies had been signing with the Gulf monarchies during their heyday, by 2015 it stood to reason Iran had once again become a sort of favoured partner. With such big investments at stake, and the promise of much more to come, it became essential that the new Iran should never be directly attacked or significantly destabilized by its regional rivals, including Saudi Arabia and its other Western-armed neighbours. For Washington and London, the best way to safeguard against this, it seems, has been to return quietly to an older, tried-and-tested strategy that seeks to ensure that no Middle East hegemon will ever be able to defeat another. In this context, with direct lines to both Riyadh and Tehran, and long before the ink had dried on the nuclear deal, the US and British governments had already begun to try to manage and contain something of a stalemate between the two camps. Ideally neither Saudi Arabia nor Iran would be able to press home advantages in their various proxy wars, while both sides would have to commit indefinitely to heavy military spending and the strengthening of their security apparatuses.

As an important strategic bonus to this new cold war, the increasingly sectarian foreign policies pursued by both powers have also helped reduce the risk of further Arab Spring-style protests occurring in their expanded spheres of influence. After all, not only do Saudi-Arabia and Iran's respective forms of authoritarian theocracy continue to serve as brakes on any prospects for meaningful reform in the wider Middle East, but the highly reactionary stances the two powers have had to adopt in order to keep their local power bases and regional proxies on board have meant both regimes have an equally vested interest in maintaining the counter-revolutionary status quo in the territories they now contest.

In many ways the West's position on the new Saudi–Iran stand-off is reminiscent of Harry Truman's views on Nazi Germany before the US entered the Second World War. After all, as his well-documented remarks

514

on Adolf Hitler's invasion of the Soviet Union reveal, he and others did not really want to see either side winning, while any long-drawn-out fight between the two sides was seen as ultimately suiting US interests.[38] In the Middle East itself, the desire for such similarly balanced conflicts is of course nothing new, with the Iran–Iraq War of the 1980s having helped cancel out the two major powers of the day, while the other Gulf states were left to cower under the West's protection. As described, even though the US had officially banned arms sales to both combatants, Baghdad was being heavily armed by the Western powers, while creative covert mechanisms were developed to ensure that Iran still got what it needed. As William Blum notes, this had the effect of 'enhancing the ability of the two countries to inflict maximum devastation upon each other and stunt their growth as strong Middle East nations.'[39]

The usefulness of encouraging and promoting sectarian divisions in the region also has pedigree, not only to help spur and sustain such conflicts but also to prevent any shared senses of community or common identities forming, in this case between Sunni and Shia.[40] As a British secretary for India once noted, 'This division of religious feeling is greatly to our advantage,' while another British official once observed, 'The better clashes of Muhammadans are already a source to us of strength and not of weakness.'[41] Fast-forwarding to the late twentieth century, as endowed Columbia University professor Mahmood Mamdani explains of the Ronald Reagan administration's Middle East strategy, it was not only about trying to push Sunni extremists into a holy war against the Soviet Union, but was also aimed at turning 'a religious schism inside Islam, between minority Shia and majority Sunni, into a political schism ... thereby it hoped to contain the influence of the Iranian revolution as a minority Shia affair.'[42]

Even in the wake of 9/11, as the US began to launch its Saudi Arabia blame-deflecting strategy, it seems its main backup plan also relied on stoking up sectarianism. Notably, when George W. Bush's first chairman of the Defense Policy Board co-published his memoirs on the 'War on Terror' with a prominent Bush speechwriter, it was revealed that the White House had already identified the Shia of eastern Saudi Arabia as potential agents provocateurs in the event that the US needed to turn publicly against Riyadh. As they put it, 'independence for the eastern

province would obviously be a catastrophic outcome for the Saudi state ...
[and this] might be a very good outcome for the US. Certainly it's an
outcome to ponder. Even more certainly, we would want the Saudis to
know we are pondering it.'[43] Making much the same point, the Hudson
Institute's Max Singer argued that the secession of the Shia in the East
might well accelerate the fall of the Saudi regime, and if that was the case
then 'so be it'.[44]

More recently, the largely beneficial prospects of a worsening sectarian
fault line were also raised in the 2008 report commissioned by the US Army
Training and Doctrine Command's Army Capability Integration Center. In
rather chilling terms the possibility of a 'sustained Sunni–Shia conflict' is
discussed, along with predictions of an 'upsurge in Shia identity and confidence' and the need for the US to walk a 'diplomatic tightrope' between
its Sunni allies and the Iranian front.[45] To a great extent, this future US role
as sectarian arbitrator was also envisaged by Johns Hopkins University's
Vali Nasr, whose influential 2006 volume, *The Shia Revival: How Conflicts
Within Islam Will Shape the Future*, along with several follow-up articles,
argued that 'the character of the region will be decided in the crucible of
Shia revival and the Sunni response to it,' and that this situation would
offer both the US and Iran the opportunity to 'manage future tensions
between Shia and Sunni'.[46]

Writing in 2012, Hamid Dabashi could see things more clearly in the
post-Arab Spring context and demonstrated that the spectre of a 'Shia
crescent' had indeed been brought back to the region with a vengeance,
'especially by the West's allies, most of which are Sunni-led dictatorships'.
In his words, this was going to become a 'manufactured sectarianism ...
which can divert attention from the main issues afflicting the region's
people'.[47] Returning to the issue in early 2016, Nasr got even closer to the
truth, as although he still framed the worsening sectarianism as part of
a 'great power rivalry' between Saudi Arabia and Iran, as opposed to the
external manipulation of these states by the Western powers, he nonetheless astutely observed that the 'manipulation of sectarian interests [had]
divided opposition movements and shattered the hope for cosmopolitan
politics'. Looking into the rather grim future he also warned that 'sectarian
interests are now too tightly interwoven with regional politics, high and
low, to subside any time soon.'[48]

Putting all this into practice, the West's 'diplomatic tightrope' has clearly led to some remarkable U-turns since the opening up of Iran's economy. On the one hand, both Washington and London have softened their stances considerably on Iran's regional allies, including Hezbollah – which has been deemed more of a liberation movement than a terrorist organiza- tion by the CIA – and even Damascus.[49] Indeed, in early 2016 the BBC subtly began to change all references to Bashar al-Assad's administration from 'regime' to 'government', while almost all senior Western politicians dropped their explicit calls for al-Assad's removal with some even hinting at future cooperation and engagement.[50]

On the other hand, the Western powers have done very little to ensure that Saudi Arabia actually wins against the Iran-linked Houthi movement in Yemen, as although British advisers are understood to have been helping with target acquisition, and there have been a 'very small number' of US troops in the country, there is little real evidence of any further assistance.[51] The US, for example, at one point even sponsored a UN Security Council session that drew attention to the 'dire consequences' of the conflict, while in summer 2015 senior US envoys reportedly began to meet secretly with Houthi leaders in discussions brokered by Omani officials. While much of the conversation was likely focused on prisoner swapping, the US envoys admitted that the Houthis were 'acting like a legitimate government' and that possible political transitions were also being explored.[52] As regards Riyadh's ramping up of sectarianism, however, there has of course been very much tacit support, with US and British officials having done noth- ing to prevent the kingdom's beheading of several Shia activists, including the prominent cleric Sheikh Nimr al-Nimr, on 2 January 2016. Moreover, when the gruesome news hit the international media, the US government was among only a handful in the world not to condemn the killings, with the Department of State's spokesperson instead trying to focus attention on the retaliatory burning down of Saudi Arabia's embassy in Tehran.[53]

WILD CARD NUMBER TWO – AMERICAN OIL

As with the lifting of sanctions on Iran, the arrival of new oil production technologies including shale extraction had long been anticipated, but nobody could be quite sure when and how it would begin to impact on the international oil industry, or for that matter the political economy of the major Middle Eastern crude oil exporters. According to leaked US diplomatic cables from 2009, Saudi Arabia was already alarmed 'by the tenor of discussion in the West about shifting away from reliance on oil and gas, and moves to develop energy independence'. As the US embassy put it, Riyadh was 'concerned that the world will turn away from their main source of livelihood before they have a chance to catch up'.[54] A year later the author's interviewees in Texas predicted big changes within just a few years, as did the University of California's Amy Myers Jaffe writing for *Foreign Policy* in 2011.[55] Almost on schedule, in 2013 there were strong signs that US production was beginning to catch up with Saudi Arabia and Russia, and by summer 2014 'Cowboyistan' officially became the world's biggest oil producer.[56] Coupled with declining Chinese demand and the parallel prospects of Iranian oil eventually returning to the market, oil prices quickly began to fall from highs of over $100 a barrel to around $50, and then to just $37 by the end of 2015.[57]

Unable to make temporary production cuts in order to raise prices as they would have done in the past, Saudi Arabia and the other Gulf monarchies, all still dependent on oil exports, instead had little choice but to try to protect their market share and hope that a short period of very low prices would be enough to drive their new competitors out of business. After all, they were entering 2015 with the advantage of sizeable sovereign wealth funds and foreign currency reserves to fall back on, while most of the shale producers had much higher operating costs and wafer-thin profit margins. While the number of US oil rigs undoubtedly did begin to fall, with some companies struggling to refinance, many remained highly active as new efficiencies were found and costs began to drop. Indeed, over the course of the year the overall 'rig count' may have fallen from 1609 to just 536, but overall oil production barely changed.[58]

Threateningly for Saudi Arabia, with most of its described post-Arab Spring countermeasures having relied on ever-increasing public spending, it soon transpired that the state budget's 'break-even' price for oil had reached close to $100 a barrel, some $30 a barrel more than needed by Iran or other competitors, and more than $50 above most long-term oil price predictions.[59] Indeed, even the Organization of Petroleum Exporting

Countries had begun to warn that oil would not reach $100 a barrel again until 2040 at the earliest.[60] With a widening deficit and doubts about Saudi Arabia's ability to reform and reverse the decline any time soon, alarm bells began to sound. Reportedly having run a deficit in 2015 equivalent to more than twenty percent of its GDP, it was understood Riyadh had already withdrawn more than $115 billion from its reserves in order to cover the shortfall.[61] On this basis the IMF warned that Saudi Arabia had only five years of financial assets remaining, while CNBC analysts predicted it would 'go broke' by summer 2018.[62]

While the near-term prospect of a major US ally collapsing was certainly a cause for concern for some in Washington, for others it nonetheless opened up a new set of opportunities. In particular, Western officials and consultants suddenly found themselves much more able to encourage Riyadh to sell off state assets in order to raise funds. Moreover, as the situation continued to worsen it soon became clear that all of the kingdom's assets were potentially on the table, including the oil industry 'crown jewels' that the al-Saud had managed to hang on to for many years.

Importantly, such Western-led advances on Saudi Arabia's core assets were already very much in the pipeline, even if moving slowly. A series of new private-sector-run cities, for example, had long been under construction. Intended to serve as the kingdom's future ports, industrial zones, and even touristic destinations, they were envisaged as the medium- and long-term means of diversifying the economic base. Among them was King Abdullah Economic City, which was expected to serve the needs of two million inhabitants and was being developed by the same companies as Egypt's new capital. As a spokesman for the project described, 'the business model of an entire city being built by the private sector is so unusual that it required adjustments from the beginning'.[63]

Similarly planned a while ago, Saudi Arabia also opened up its stock market, the *Tadawul*, to foreign investors in May 2015. Even though the timing was bad, with it mostly ending up selling debt, it was still further evidence that Riyadh understood what was wanted of it.[64] Indeed, as a British minister had earlier warned, the one area in which Saudi Arabia still needed to change was its investment climate. As he argued, 'It needs modernization ... please do your best to open up as many sectors as possible to foreign investors'.[65] Fast-forwarding to September 2015, with the oil price crash really beginning to bite, Saudi Arabia duly declared that foreign ownership of shares in retail and wholesale companies could increase from seventy-five to a hundred percent. At the same time, US businessmen were informed by Deputy Crown Prince Muhammad bin Salman al-Saud that the state-owned Aramco would 'open a series of new projects in refining, distribution and support services to foreign participation'. Rather vaguely he also hinted at 'new opportunities for foreign banks to enter the kingdom, as most banks already operating were nearing maximum credit limits'.[66]

By early 2016 full capitulation seemed imminent, as oil prices had dipped below $30 a barrel for the first time in fourteen years and it emerged that Saudi foreign assets had fallen by $19 billion in one month alone. Emulating Muhammadu Buhari's new Nigeria, an announcement was soon made that the electricity sector was slated for privatization, and that the Capital Markets Authority – the entity behind the *Tadawul* – had started to seek advice on an initial public offering for 2018. More dramatically, and catching many analysts off guard, Prince Muhammad granted *The Economist* an exclusive interview and used it to drop the bombshell that Aramco itself could begin to float shares.[67] By far the kingdom's greatest asset, and hitherto considered a non-negotiable red line for Riyadh, the veiled message was reportedly met with much 'shock and laughter' in the financial world, while others claimed that 'the one thing that works well in Saudi Arabia is now under threat'.[68] Not everyone, however, will have been concerned or perhaps even surprised by the announcement, as several months earlier, and just two weeks before he joined British Petroleum's board of directors, former MI6 director John Sawers wrote in the *Financial Times* that the young prince was 'injecting professionalism and youth in a kingdom that, while not under immediate threat, faces challenges that need skilful handling'.[69] Either way, it soon emerged that Aramco was going to begin by listing five percent of its shares and would be 'targeting London, New York, and Hong Kong for international listing'. As the vanguard of a new 'Vision 2030' plan for the Saudi economy, as prepared by McKinsey management consultants, the Aramco sell-off would also see foreign oil companies such as British Petroleum and ExxonMobil taking 'strategic stakes offering them access to upstream operations'.[70]

A NEW SAUDI ARABIA, A NEW CHAPTER

Even in the most bearish scenario of a fully mothballed US shale oil industry, a consensus began to emerge that such reversals would only be temporary as even modest future price rallies would soon see idled rigs roaring back to life.[71] Moreover, with such new technologies spreading across the world, shale and other new oil production methods were thought unlikely to remain a US-only phenomenon for much longer. In this sense Saudi Arabia had already lost its long-held status as the world's sole 'swing producer' capable of influencing prices on its own. Further eroding the kingdom's historically privileged position in Western policy circles, the impact of the new oil era on its domestic economy was beginning to undermine rapidly its ability to keep recycling oil revenues back to its Western allies. Certainly even in the most bullish scenarios of oil prices eventually trebling or quadrupling, it became evident that Saudi Arabia would soon have little or no surpluses left to keep financing its historically massive arms purchases or overseas investments.

Already there were signs that Riyadh's difficulties were going to jeopardize its standing as the US's primary Middle Eastern client, with several indications by the end of 2015 that Saudi Arabia had either begun to withdraw or had begun to consider withdrawing some of its holdings in US treasury bonds. In something of a warning shot for Saudi Arabia, within weeks of these rumours the first ever mainstream media coverage of these secretive investments began to appear, with former and current US officials calling for more details on the true extent of the kingdom's investments in the US – an unpalatable prospect for a regime presiding over millions struggling with unemployment and poverty. As a series of unprecedented *Bloomberg* reports described, the bond purchases had been part of a special agreement reached between Saudi Arabia and US after the 1973 oil price shocks, which allowed them to remain above scrutiny and not to be fully included in the Department of the Treasury's otherwise comprehensive breakdown of more than a hundred other sovereign investors. As a former Department of the Treasury assistant secretary argued in January 2016, 'It's mind boggling they haven't undone [the special agreement] ... but it's hard to justify this special treatment at this point.'[72]

With Riyadh on the defensive, a few weeks later Turki bin Faisal al-Saud, a former Saudi ambassador to the US, took to the local media to remind Washington that 'we buy US treasury bonds, with small interest returns, that help [the US's] economy.'[73] By March 2016, following a fresh flurry of 9/11-related accusations about Saudi Arabia in the mainstream Western media, the language had become a little more threatening. Notably, the *New York Times* reported that Saudi officials had begun to tell US lawmakers that if US courts took any further 9/11-related action against the kingdom, then Riyadh would be 'forced to sell up to $750 billion [sic] in treasury securities and other assets in the United States before they could be in danger of being frozen by American courts.'[74] A few weeks later the Saudi foreign minister confirmed his government's position, making clear that it was a 'warning' to the US as such actions could cause 'an erosion of investor confidence [in the US].'[75]

Unfazed, on 17 May 2016 the Senate unanimously passed a bill allowing the families of the 9/11 victims to sue the state of Saudi Arabia for any role it may have had in the attacks, and thus supporting the New York federal court judge's original ruling in 2014.[76] Perhaps co-ordinated, just five days earlier one of the 9/11 Commission members came forward in what was described as the 'first serious public split among the ten commissioners since they issued [their] 2004 report'. Speaking to the media, John F. Lehman claimed 'there was an awful lot of participation by Saudi individuals in supporting the hijackers, and some of those people working in the Saudi government'. He also revealed that the commission had been aware of 'at least five Saudi government officials who were strongly suspected of involvement in the terrorists' support network' and that although 'they may not have been indicted... they were certainly implicated... there was an awful lot of circumstantial evidence'. More cautiously, two other commissioners also stated that 'when it comes to the Saudis, we still haven't gotten to the bottom of what happened on 9/11', and that 'lines of investigation that were pursued by Congress [were] never adequately explored by the commission'.[77] Futhermore, less than twenty-four hours before the Senate's ruling, and this time almost certainly in co-ordination, the Department of the Treasury chose to respond to a *Bloomberg* freedom of information request and finally ended forty-three years of secrecy on

Saudi Arabia's US treasury bonds. Unsurprisingly, Saudi Arabia's holdings had already fallen by 6 percent from January to March in 2016.[78]

Straining the relationship further, the new oil dynamic and mounting pressure on Riyadh was also beginning to raise the prospect that Saudi Arabia might finally have to 'de-peg' its riyal currency from the US dollar. Throughout 2015 speculation grew that the kingdom would eventually have little choice in the matter, as it would inevitably need some fiscal autonomy and a currency devaluation in order to buy some breathing space.[79] Indeed, having run out of options, oil-exporting Kazakhstan and Azerbaijan had already done exactly that, while rumours whirled that other 'petro states' would soon have to follow suit.[80] By January 2016 the riyal was certainly more volatile, hitting an all-time low against the dollar in forward markets and with the Saudi Central Bank then warning all commercial banks in the kingdom against betting on future currency depreciation.[81] Sensing danger, PointState Capital's Zachary Schreiber, who had correctly predicted the timing of the oil price crash in 2014, soon revealed that he was shorting the Saudi riyal. As he saw it, the kingdom's economy would be 'structurally insolvent in two or three years', its central bank asset sheet was 'much lower than expected', and any selling of the Aramco 'golden goose' would be insufficient to meet the deficits.[82] While it still seemed likely that Riyadh would do everything in its power to avoid a de-peg, even if this meant draining all of its reserves, US planners clearly had little choice but to prepare for the eventual demise of the 'petro dollar'.

How exactly Saudi Arabia's dramatically changing fortunes would factor into the US's Middle East policy was not clear, as for some the existence of a functioning Saudi state was undoubtedly still perceived as the best option, not least for the exploitation of its remaining hydrocarbon resources at a time when its stricken economy and major state assets were about to be prized open by foreign investors. Furthermore, for those who saw the Saudi–Iran stalemate and the associated sectarian conflict as the best way to retain regional balance, the survival of Saudi Arabia as a military power was obviously preferable, especially if, as already seemed the case, it could be left to its own devices on the battlefield and corralled into further wars of attrition. Hinting at his support for such a strategy, in an exclusive conversation with the *Atlantic* published in March 2016, Barack Obama agreed with his interviewer that he was less likely than his predecessors 'to axiomatically side with Saudi Arabia in its dispute with its arch rival, Iran'. He also called on Riyadh 'to find an effective way to share the neighborhood and institute some sort of cold peace [with Iran]'. Moreover, he described how 'sectarian conflicts continue to rage and our Gulf partners, our traditional friends, do not have the ability to put out the flames on their own or decisively win on their own,' but made it clear that if this meant the US needed 'to start coming in and using our military power to settle scores' then this would 'be in the interest neither of the US nor of the Middle East'.[83]

Not all, of course, have seen things this way, as the US and other Western powers have long planned for the prospect of the Saudi state's collapse and, of course, how best to benefit from it. Undoubtedly by late 2015 there were stronger signs than ever that influential elements in the West believed the kingdom must soon be framed as a former ally and perhaps even a rogue state. Riding on a relentless media wave of 'Saudi-bashing' articles and even denunciations of the US–Saudi alliance in *New York Times* and *Washington Post* editorials, numerous officials and politicians, including US presidential hopefuls and British opposition leaders, all began to stake out their anti-Saudi positions.[84]

Providing additional indications of this shift of mood, in January 2016 the British government announced it was launching a full investigation into the foreign funding and support of jihadist groups in Britain. As something that had never happened before, even after 9/11 and the July 2005 London bombings, the British press predicted its findings were likely to lead to a stand-off with Saudi Arabia. Beyond Britain, the German government also seemed to be hedging its bets, with Vice Chancellor Sigmar Gabriel telling the media that 'the Saudi regime poses a danger to public security through its support for Wahhabi mosques around the world' and that 'we have to make clear to the Saudis that the time of looking away is over.'[85]

More subtly there is evidence that Western intelligence agencies had also begun to harden up their positions and were more willing to spill the beans on Saudi Arabia. In December 2015, for example, German intelligence uncharacteristically issued a statement declaring that Saudi

Arabia was 'destabilizing the Arab World' and that its deputy crown prince was pursuing an 'impulsive intervention policy'.[86] Starkly different to all previous public Western criticism of Saudi Arabia, it did much to shift opinion further against the kingdom, not least because it likely reflected the views of other European intelligence agencies, and perhaps even MI6. Equally out of place, a few weeks later a lengthy report appeared in the *New York Times* that was ostensibly focused on Saudi Arabia's support for CIA-backed rebels in Syria, but in fact went much deeper. Citing unnamed former diplomats and intelligence officials, it not only reminded readers of the kingdom's role in financing the Afghan jihad but also printed the first ever mainstream media acknowledgement of Saudi intelligence's old 'Safari Club' – an organization that used to run covert and black operations in Africa on behalf of several other countries. Going further, it also made the allegation that a former Saudi ambassador to the US had personally helped fund the Nicaraguan contras and broker the Iran–Contra deal.[87]

If the large body of existing proof of Saudi Arabia's activities does end up being more widely publicized, and Western governments are obliged to take action, there are it seems only limited options available to them beyond publicly chastising the kingdom or perhaps imposing Iran-style sanctions. Destroying it from the outside, or mounting a Henry Kissinger-style 'teaching it a lesson' operation, appear distant prospects, especially given the West's current proxy-based Middle East policy. Much more likely in this scenario is for Saudi Arabia to be manoeuvred into a position in which existing regional forces are more able to degrade it from within and, if necessary, eventually destroy it. Naturally the 2008 long war report had considered such an outcome, with its scenario of a 'major Muslim state going bad' having specified the prospect of jihadists launching a successful 'fundamentalist uprising' in Saudi Arabia.[88]

In this sense, the Islamic State (or its next incarnation) may be poised to serve another important strategic function, as it is undoubtedly one of the best-placed organizations to drive a wedge through Saudi Arabia. As discussed, the Islamic State not only enjoys a significant support base within the kingdom, including elements of the religious establishment, but any Saudi sponsors that it has seem to be much more diffuse and some steps removed from the sort of state-backed institutions that had historically helped finance al-Qaeda. Moreover, in the eyes of many of the country's more restive conservatives, the Islamic State's ideologies and seductive sectarian rhetoric offer something of a purer and more consistent vision of an ultra-conservative Sunni Islamic state than that currently being administered by the financially and militarily struggling al-Saud regime and its McKinsey-advised deputy crown prince.

The divisions certainly run deep, with fifty-two senior Saudi clerics, including associates of the royally appointed Council of Senior Scholars, and some with millions of Twitter followers, jointly issuing a pointedly sectarian statement in October 2015 asking the public to 'answer the call to jihad' and to go to Syria to 'aid the oppressed and the mujahideen'. Although neither the Islamic State nor any other group was mentioned by name, it was still a significant step as it brazenly undermined a 2014 Saudi decree that had designated such entities as terrorist organizations and had criminalized any attempt by Saudi citizens to go and join them.[89] Only a few months later, a former preacher at Mecca's Grand Mosque declared that 'we follow the same thought as the Islamic State … we do not criticize the thought on which it is based.' Reflecting on who had actually started it all, however, he later suggested that 'intelligence agencies and other countries may have helped it to develop, providing them with weapons and ammunition, and directing them.'[90] Soon after this, with the Western media reporting on a 'flurry of new fundraising campaigns in Saudi Arabia' in the wake of an Iraqi army advance on an Islamic State stronghold in Fallujah, even a spokesman for the kingdom's ministry of interior admitted that 'you cannot control the sympathies of people.'[91]

From the Islamic State's perspective, much as al-Qaeda had eventually seen it, the destabilization and then occupation of Saudi Arabia would be a grand prize given its resources and control over the holy cities of Mecca and Medina. Though not a priority in the early days, with Iraq and Syria as the main focus, by 2015 Abu Bakr al-Baghdadi had nonetheless begun to increase the pressure on Riyadh. Most of the Islamic State's early attacks on the kingdom were aimed at the Shia minority in the East or the 'rejectionist Ismailis' in the South in an effort to underscore its better anti-Shia credentials and prove the al-Saud weak.[92] But more worryingly for Riyadh there were soon also a number of attacks on Saudi military and security targets, with a mosque frequented by special forces being blown up in August 2015, and two Saudi generals assassinated separately on the northern and southern borders, along with numerous killings and car-bombings in other cities across the kingdom.[93] By early 2016, the frequency of such attacks had noticeably increased, with repeated gun battles taking place in and around Mecca, Bishah, and even outside the capital.[94]

Unable to mount a convincing response to the Islamic State's challenge and the rather asymmetrical nature of the threat, Riyadh has done little more than make mass arrests of suspects hoping at least some are key Islamic State operatives, along with issuing hollow warnings that the Saudi government will sue those who dare to compare the kingdom to the Islamic State.[95] Meanwhile, the al-Saud regime has been goaded further by the Islamic State, which has issued maps depicting the country as a future governorate – *Wilayat Najd* – and has released numerous propaganda videos laying claim to Mecca. More provocatively, and in something of a departure from its earlier attacks on Houthi targets in Yemen, the Islamic State also began to target the Saudi-liberated Aden.[96] By late 2015 Saudi-led forces were being killed in coordinated suicide bombings while a wave of assassinations commenced, including that of the city governor. In January 2016 the Islamic State even mounted an assault on the presidential palace while President Abd Rabbo Mansour Hadi was still inside it.[97]

In these circumstances Saudi Arabia's riskiest move would be to end up militarily confronting the Islamic State, either in Yemen or even worse by taking the fight to its heartlands in Syria or Iraq. With little chance of overall victory, especially if the Islamic State morphs into a more diffuse insurgency, and with Riyadh having to sustain a concurrent struggle against Iran and its allies, such a campaign would only serve to weaken the kingdom further. Nonetheless, for those who seek the demise or further debilitation of Saudi Arabia, it is certainly possible that Riyadh may buckle under pressure, as many of its concerned citizens have been calling for firmer action, while numerous Western officials and politicians have demanded it takes a more active role in cleaning up its own backyard.[98] As US secretary for defense Ashton Carter contended, the kingdom and its Gulf allies needed to stop complaining and to 'get in the game', while Obama implied Riyadh was a 'free rider' on US foreign policy.[99]

By the beginning of 2016 it seemed at least some senior Saudi officials had begun to think the unthinkable, with cautious statements made that the kingdom would consider deploying thousands of special forces troops to Syria to 'fight the Islamic State'. Although the proviso was made that this would only take place under the banner of an 'international US-led coalition', and even though Washington was already aware that the Syrian and Iraqi armies had managed to begin clawing back at least some territory from the Islamic State, the prospect of a direct Saudi intervention, no matter how potentially calamitous or unnecessary, still seemed to be music to the US's ears. As a Department of State spokesman put it, 'We welcome this proposal by the Saudis to intensify their efforts by introducing some sort of ground elements into Syria ... [but] exactly what that's going to look like and how that's going to play out I just don't think we can say right now.'[100]

Alea iacta est?

NOTES

1. COUNTER-REVOLUTION – A PATTERN EMERGES

1   *Jacobus* being the Renaissance Latin for James. A. I. Macinnes, *Union and Empire: The Making of the United Kingdom in 1707* (Cambridge: Cambridge University Press, 2007), p. 243.

2   William III of the Dutch House of Orange-Nassau.

3   For a good discussion see E. Vallance, *The Glorious Revolution: Britain's Fight for Liberty* (London: Abacus, 2007). BBC Online, 'The Glorious Revolution', 22 November 2007.

4   R. Dupuy, *La République Jacobine: Terreur, Guerre et Gouvernement Révolutionnaire, 1792–94* (Paris: Le Seuil, 2005), pp. 34–40.

5   P. McPhee, *Robespierre: A Revolutionary Life* (Yale: Yale University Press, 2012), p. 271.

6   A. Mathiez, *La Revolution Française* (Paris: Payot, 1954), pp. 190–5; A. Mathiez, *La Vie Chère et le Mouvement Social: Sous la Terreur* (Paris: Payot, 1927), p. 163; Anonymous, *Memoires de Larevellière-Lépeaux* (Paris: Biliolife, 1895), p. 109; C. Tilly, 'The Analysis of a Counter-Revolution', *History and Theory*, Vol. 3, No. 1, 1963, pp. 32–3.

7   L. Dubreuil, *Histoire des Insurrections de L'Ouest* (Paris: Payot, 1929), part 1, pp. 1–95; A. F. Momoro, *Rapport sur L'État Politique de la Vendée* (Paris: Payot, 1793), p. 2.

8   M. Curtis, *Web of Deceit: Britain's Real Role in the World* (London: Vintage, 2003), p. 240, citing A. L. Morton, *A People's History of England* (London: Lawrence and Wishart, 1996).

9   The Parthenopean Republic.

10   See F. Burkle-Young, *Papal Elections in the Age of Transition, 1878–1922* (New York: Lexington, 2000); J. Davis, *Naples and Napoleon: Southern Italy and the European Revolutions, 1780–1860* (Oxford: Oxford University Press, 2006).

11   See H. Acton, *The Bourbons of Naples (1731–1825)* (London: Faber, 1957); J. Sugden, *Nelson: A Dream of Glory* (London: Jonathan Cape, 2004).

12   See E. Holt, *The Carlist Wars in Spain* (London: Dufour, 1967); C. J. Esdaile, *Spain in the Liberal Age* (London: Blackwell, 2000).

13   J. Brownlee, T. Masoud, A. Reynolds (eds), *The Arab Spring: Pathways of Repression and Reform* (New York: Oxford University Press, 2015), p. 5.

14   J. Sperber, *The European Revolutions, 1848–1851* (Cambridge: Cambridge University Press, 1984); M. Rapport, *1848: Year of Revolution* (New York: Basic Books, 2010); Brownlee, *The Arab Spring*, p. 6.

15   *The Cambridge History of Russia: Volume 2, Imperial Russia, 1689–1917* (Cambridge: Cambridge University Press, 2014), p. 374.

16   K. Korsch, 'State and Counter-Revolution', *Modern Quarterly*, Vol. 11, No. 2, 1939, p. 2.

17   W. Blum, *Killing Hope: US Military and CIA Interventions Since World War II* (London: Zed, 2014), pp. 7–8.

18   P. Kenez, 'The Ideology of the White Movement', *Soviet Studies*, No. 32, 1980, p. 90.

19   Z. Y. Gitelman, *A Century of Ambivalence: The Jews of Russia and the Soviet Union, 1881 to the Present* (Bloomington: Indiana University Press, 2001), p. 70; Blum, *Killing Hope*, p. 7.

20   See L. Humphreys, *The Way of the Heavenly Sword: The Japanese Army in the 1920s* (Palo Alto: Stanford University Press, 1995); R. L. Willett, *Russian Sideshow: America's Undeclared War, 1918–1920* (London: Brassey's, 2003).

21   M. Curtis, *Secret Affairs: Britain's Collusion with Radical Islam* (London: Serpent's Tail, 2012), pp. 14–15; R. Lorenz, 'Economic Bases of the Basmachi Movement in the Ferghana Valley', in *Muslim Communities Reemerge: Historical Perspectives on Nationality, Politics, and Opposition in the Former Soviet Union and Yugoslavia*, ed. A. Kappelerm *et al.* (Durham: Duke University Press, 1994), p. 277; S. F. Starr, *Ferghana Valley: The Heart of Central Asia* (London: Routledge, 2011), p. 101.

22   See S. Haffner, *Failure of a Revolution: Germany 1918–1919* (London: Banner, 1986); L. Trotsky, *The Revolution Betrayed* (London: Dover, 2004), see section on 'From World Revolution to Status Quo'.

23   See D. S. Elazar, *The Making of Fascism: Class, State, and Counter-Revolution, Italy 1919–1922* (London: Praeger, 2001); Korsch, 'State and Counter-Revolution'.

24   Korsch, 'State and Counter-Revolution', p. 1; K. Korsch, 'The Fascist Counter-Revolution', *Living Marxism*, Vol. 5, No. 2, 1940, pp. 29–37.

25   Trotsky, *The Revolution Betrayed*, see section on 'The League of Nations and the Communist International'.

26   *Washington Post*, 'David Lloyd George', 3 September 1936.

27   *Daily Express*, 'David Lloyd George', 17 November 1936.

28   F. J. R. Salvado, *Politics and Society in Spain 1898–1998* (London: Palgrave, 1999), p. 69; Blum, *Killing Hope*, p. 10.

29   By this stage Italy and Germany had been joined by the fascist *Estado Novo* of Portugal. See G. Howson, *Arms for Spain* (New York: St. Martin's Press, 1998).

30   Reuters, 'Morocco tackles painful role in Spain's past', 14 January 2009.

31   G. Jackson, *The Spanish Republic and the Civil War, 1931–1939* (Princeton: Princeton University Press, 1965); R. Overy, *The Twilight Years: The Paradox of Britain Between*

the Wars (London: Viking, 2009), pp. 319–40; W. Podmore, *Britain, Italy, Germany and the Spanish Civil War* (New York: Edward Mellin, 1998), p. 7.

32   For a full discussion see A. Beevor, *The Battle for Spain: The Spanish Civil War 1936–1939* (London: Weidenfeld & Nicolson, 2007).

33   H. Thomas, *The Spanish Civil War* (London: Penguin, 2003), p. 338; Beevor, *The Battle for Spain*, p. 138.

34   Trotsky, *The Revolution Betrayed*, see sections on 'The Transitional Regime' and 'Program and Reality'.

35   Korsch, 'State and Counter-Revolution', p. 2.

36   Trotsky, *The Revolution Betrayed*, see section on 'From World Revolution to Status Quo'.

37   *The New Militant*, 'The Stalin-Howard Interview', 4 April 1936; G. Scott, *The Rise and Fall of the League of Nations* (London: Hutchinson, 1973).

38   Trotsky, *The Revolution Betrayed*, see sections on 'Program and Reality', 'The Complete Triumph of Socialism', and 'Reinforcement of the Dictatorship'.

39   Ibid., see section on 'From World Revolution to Status Quo'.

40   Beevor, *The Battle for Spain*, pp. 102–22.

41   Trotsky, *The Revolution Betrayed*, see section on 'The League of Nations and the Communist International'; S. D. Goldman, *Nomonhan, 1939: The Red Army's Victory That Shaped World War II* (Monterey: Naval Institute Press, 2012), pp. 162–4.

42   Curtis, *Web of Deceit*, pp. 234, 335.

43   Lord Ogmore being David Rees-Williams. Hansard, 'The Situation in Malaya', 27 December 1952.

44   Curtis, *Web of Deceit*, p. 336.

45   B. Stewart, *Why Spy?: On the Art of Intelligence* (London: Hurst, 2015), pp. 12, 16.

46   Ibid., pp. 14, 19–20; Curtis, *Web of Deceit*, pp. 336–7.

47   Stewart, *Why Spy?*, p. 20.

48   A. Binda, D. Heppenstall (eds), *Masodja: The History of the Rhodesian African Rifles and its Forerunner the Rhodesian Native Regiment* (Johannesburg: South Publishers, 2007), pp. 127–128; Fiji Government records, 'Documentary to Explore Relationship between Malaysia and Fiji during the Malayan Emergency', retrieved 13 September 2014.

49   Quoting Sir Robert Thompson, head of British Advisory Mission in Vietnam, 1961–5. See F. Halliday, *Mercenaries: Counter-insurgency in the Gulf* (London: Spokesman, 1977), p. 54; Stewart, *Why Spy?*, pp. 15–16.

50   Quoting Brian Stewart. Stewart, *Why Spy?*, p. 15.

51   Ibid., p. 17.

52   Ibid., p. 13. Referring to former secretary of the Joint Intelligence Committee, Brian Stewart.

53   Amnesty International, 'Aden 1963–1966', 11 November 1966, p. 2.

54   Hansard, 'Vote A. Number of Land Forces', 10 March 1949.

55   Stewart, *Why Spy?*, p. 16.

56   Halliday, *Mercenaries*, pp. 40–42.

57   W. Ormsby-Gore *et al.*, *Report of the East Africa Commission* (London: Government Printer, 1925), pp.155–160.

58   C. Elkins, *Imperial Reckoning: The Untold Story of Britain's Gulag in Kenya* (New York: Henry Holt, 2005), p. 32; Curtis, *Web of Deceit*, pp. 317–18.

59   Curtis, *Web of Deceit*, pp. 317–18; D. Maughan-Brown, *Land, Freedom and Fiction: History and Ideology in Kenya* (London: Zed, 1985), pp. 30–50.

60   See for example B. Berman, J. Lonsdale, *Unhappy Valley: Conflict in Kenya and Africa; Book One: State & Class* (Oxford: James Currey, 1992).

61   I. Henderson, *Man Hunt in Kenya* (New York: Doubleday, 1958); CIA Historical Review Program, 'Book review of *Man Hunt in Kenya*', 22 September 1993.

62   *Daily Telegraph*, 'Kenyans were tortured during Mau Mau rebellion, High Court hears', 18 July 2012.

63   *Guardian*, 'It's not just Kenya. Squaring up to the seamier side of empire is long overdue', 25 July 2011; *The Times*, 'Hundreds more top secret files missing in Mau Mau abuse case', 15 April 2011.

64   *Guardian*, 'Mau Mau torture case: Kenyans win ruling against UK', 5 October 2011.

65   P. Seale, *The Struggle for Syria* (New Haven: Yale University Press, 1987), pp. 3–5; J. P. Filiu, *From Deep State to Islamic State: The Arab Counter-Revolution and its Jihadi Legacy* (London: Hurst, 2015), p. 32.

66   Cited by Curtis, *Web of Deceit*, pp. 256–7.

67   As quoted by W. Hiers, A. Wimmer, 'Nationalism: Cause or Consequence of the End of Empire', in *Nationalism and War*, ed. J. Hall *et al.* (Cambridge: Cambridge University Press, 2013), p. 239; Curtis, *Web of Deceit*, pp. 237–8.

68   Cited by Curtis, *Web of Deceit*, p. 256.

69   The dynasty being more formally known as the Alawiyya. Filiu, *From Deep State*, p. 27.

70   S. Amin '2011: An Arab Springtime?', *Monthly Review*, June 2011; M. Hudson, 'The Crisis of the Arab State: Study Group Report', Belfer Center for International Affairs, Harvard University, August 2015, p. 3.

71   *Frontline*, 'Revolution or Restoration?', 20 September 2013.

72   R. Dreyfuss, *Devil's Game: How the United States Helped Unleash Fundamentalist Islam* (New York: Metropolitan, 2006), p. 96.

73   See Amin, '2011: An Arab Springtime?'

74   Dreyfuss, *Devil's Game*, pp. 98–9, 121.

75   Ibid. p. 98.

76   Cited by Curtis, *Web of Deceit*, p. 282.

77   Public Records Office, 'Foreign Office 371/118861', 7 January 1956.

78   Curtis, *Secret Affairs*, p. 61. Quoting Sir Ralph Stevenson's report to Britain's foreign secretary in 1955.

79   J. Gordon, *Nasser's Blessed Movement* (New York: Oxford University Press, 1992), pp. 157–9.

80   Dreyfuss, *Devil's Game*, p. 100.

81   Gordon, *Nasser's Blessed Movement*, pp. 184–5; D. Little, *American Orientalism: The United States and the Middle East Since 1945* (Chapel Hill: North Carolina University Press, 2008), p. 167; Curtis, *Web of Deceit*, p. 283.

82   Dreyfuss, *Devil's Game*, p. 100.

83   A. al Affendi, 'A Trans-Islamic Revolution?', *Critical Muslim*, Vol. 1, No. 1, 2012, p. 76.

84   Dreyfuss, *Devil's Game*, pp. 51–3.

85   Curtis, *Secret Affairs*, p. 3; J. Voll, 'The Sudanese Mahdi: Frontier Fundamentalist', *International Journal of Middle East Studies*, Vol. 10, 1979, pp. 145–65.

86   Dreyfuss, *Devil's Game*, pp. 51–53; R. Mitchell, *The Society of the Muslim Brothers* (Oxford: Oxford University Press, 1969), pp. 27, 40–43.

87   Dreyfuss, *Devil's Game*, pp. 54–5.

88   Ibid., p. 57; Curtis, *Secret Affairs*, pp. 23, 56–7. The Egyptian prime minister being Mahmud al-Nuqrashi.

89   Curtis, *Secret Affairs*, p. 57.

90   Ibid., p. 59; Filiu, *From Deep State*, p. 34.

91   Notably the former mufti of Jerusalem, Haj Amin al-Husseini, who had come to Cairo after taking part in the Arab Revolt in Palestine and was then based in Berlin, where he directed Nazi propaganda efforts in the Arab world. By 1946 he was back in Cairo after being invited by the Brotherhood and purportedly working for an MI6 front called the Arab News Agency. Dreyfuss, *Devil's Game*, pp. 60–62; Curtis, *Secret Affairs*, pp. 19–22.

92   Dreyfuss, *Devil's Game*, p. 101. The telegram was intercepted and published by Nasser's adviser Muhammad Heikal.

93   Ibid., p. 100. Referring to US ambassador Jefferson Caffrey's meeting with Hassan Ismail al-Hudaybi.

94   Ibid., p. 95. Quoting Ed Kane.

95   R. Baer, *Sleeping with the Devil: How Washington Sold Our Soul for Saudi Crude* (New York: Broadway Books, 2003), pp. 97–9.

96   Dreyfuss, *Devil's Game*, pp. 101, 104.

97   Filiu, *From Deep State*, p. 50; Dreyfuss, *Devil's Game*, p. 104; Curtis, *Secret Affairs*, p. 61; Public Records Office, 'Foreign Office 371/108318', 27 October 1954.

98   Dreyfuss, *Devil's Game*, p. 124. Referring to Yusuf Yassub, a close adviser of the Saudi king. For further details, see Curtis, *Secret Affairs*, pp. 69–70.

99   Dreyfuss, *Devil's Game*, pp. 106–7.

100 Author interviews with a former CIA official, October 2014.

101 Dreyfuss, *Devil's Game*, p. 107.

102 Cited by Curtis, *Web of Deceit*, pp. 283–4.

103 Notably Abdel Hakim Amer, who was part of a 'collective resignation of the entire leadership' announced by Nasser in 1967, before Nasser retracted his own resignation and reinstated himself. Filiu, *From Deep State*, p. 53.

104 Ibid., pp. 53–4; Dreyfuss, *Devil's Game*, pp. 56–7, 162; al-Affendi, 'A Trans-Islamic Revolution?', pp. 63–4; R. Yassin-Kassab, 'Tahrir Square', *Critical Muslim*, Vol. 1, No. 1, 2012, p. 30.

105 A. Shamis, 'Gaddafi and Me', *Critical Muslim*, Vol. 1, No. 1, 2012, p. 50; al-Affendi, 'A Trans-Islamic Revolution?', p. 63.

106 Curtis, *Secret Affairs*, pp. 107–8.

107 J. Esposito, *Unholy War: Terror in the name of Islam* (New York: Oxford University Press, 2002), p. 86.

108 Dreyfuss, *Devil's Game*, pp. 151–2; Filiu, *From Deep State*, pp. 34, 54.

109 Dreyfuss, *Devil's Game*, p. 154.

110 Ibid., pp. 148, 151.

111 H. Kissinger, *The White House Years* (London: Weidenfeld & Nicolson, 1979), pp. 1290–95.

112 For a good discussion see Department of State, 'Scene setter: President Mubarak's visit to Washington', 19 May 2009.

113 Halliday, *Mercenaries*, p. 28.

114 See R. Zahlan, *The Making of the Modern Gulf States* (New York: Ithaca, 1998); J. Onley, 'Britain's Native Agents in Arabia and Persia in the Nineteenth Century', *Comparative Studies of South Asia, Africa and the Middle East*, Vol. 24, No. 1, 2004.

115 See J. Kostiner, *The Struggle for South Yemen* (London: Palgrave, 1984); S. Mawby, *British Policy in Aden and the Protectorates 1955–67: Last Outpost of a Middle East Empire* (London: Routledge, 2015); Curtis, *Web of Deceit*, p. 280.

116 R. McNamara, *Britain, Nasser and the Balance of Power in the Middle East, 1952–1977* (London: Routledge, 2004); Curtis, *Secret Affairs*, p. 84; Amnesty International, 'Aden, 1963–1966', 11 November 1966, pp. 2–6, 8, 11.

117 Amnesty International, 'Aden, 1963–1966', 11 November 1966, p. 7.

118 Filiu, *From Deep State*, pp. 71–2.

119 J. Stork, 'Socialist Revolution in Arabia: A Report from the People's Democratic Republic of Yemen', *MERIP*, No. 15, March 1973, pp. 3–5; S. Carapico, 'Yemen between Civility and Civil War', in *Civil Society in the Middle East Volume 2*, ed. A. Norton (Leiden: Brill, 2001), pp. 280–84.

120 Filiu, *From Deep State*, p. 72.

121 Ibid., p. 72; Halliday, *Mercenaries*, p. 27; Dreyfuss, *Devil's Game*, p. 140.

122 Curtis, *Secret Affairs*, p. 91; Dreyfuss, *Devil's Game*, p. 140; *Sunday Times*, 'Why we shot up the Yemen fort', 5 April 1964.

123 Hansard, 'Harib Fort (R.A.F. Attack)', 14 April 1964; *Sunday Times*, 'Why we shot up the Yemen fort', 5 April 1964.

124 Author interviews with Clive Jones, October 2015; *Sunday Times*, 'Why we shot up the Yemen fort', 5 April 1964.

125 J. P. Filiu, *The Arab Revolution: Ten Lessons from the Democratic Uprising* (London: Hurst, 2011), pp. 73–4; Filiu, *From Deep State*, pp. 72–3.

126 Author interviews with Clive Jones, October 2015; D. Hart-Davis, *The War That Never Was* (London: Century, 2011), pp. 175–7.

127 Hart-Davis, *The War That Never Was*, pp. 175–7, 181, 184.

128 Halliday, *Mercenaries*, pp. 16, 19.

129 S. Dorril, *MI6: Fifty Years of Special Operations* (London: Fourth Estate, 2001), pp. 675–95.

130 Dreyfuss, *Devil's Game*, p. 141. Quoting Howard Teicher.

131 Ibid., p. 142. Quoting Charles Freeman.

132 Halliday, *Mercenaries*, p. 28; Filiu, *From Deep State*, pp. 75, 78; D. Hiro, *Inside the Middle East* (London: McGraw-Hill, 1982), p. 37.

133 S. Phillips, *Yemen's Democracy Experiment in Regional Perspective* (London: Palgrave, 2008), p. 44.

134 Halliday, *Mercenaries*, p. 28; Filiu, *From Deep State*, pp. 75, 78.

135 M. Colburn, *The Republic of Yemen: Development Challenges in the Twenty-First Century* (New York: Catholic Institute for International Relations, 2002), p.79; Filiu, *From Deep State*, p. 140.

136 *New York Times*, 'South Yemen Sentences 12 To Death for Sabotage Plot', 8 April 1982; Curtis, *Secret Affairs*, p. 158.

137 Curtis, *Web of Deceit*, pp. 277–8.

138 For a full discussion see F. Halliday, *Arabia without Sultans* (London: Saqi, 2001); Curtis, *Web of Deceit*, p. 277.

139 J. B. Meagher, *The Jebel Akhdar War in Oman, 1954–1959* (New York: Marine Corps Command and Staff College, 1985); author interviews with al-Hinai family members, November 2014.

140 Halliday, *Mercenaries*, p. 44; Curtis, *Web of Deceit*, p. 277.

141 Curtis, *Web of Deceit*, p. 270.

142 Bernard Burrows cited in Public Records Office, 'Foreign Office 371/126876/ EA/1015/59', 21 July 1957.

143 Curtis, *Web of Deceit*, p. 278; UN General Assembly, 'Resolution 1514: Declaration on the Granting of Independence to Colonial Countries and Peoples', 14 December 1960.

144 Cited by Curtis, *Web of Deceit*, p. 278.

145 'Monsoon Revolution' being the title of Abdel Razzaq Takriti's seminal text on the uprising. A. R. Takriti, *Monsoon Revolution: Republicans, Sultans, and Empires in Oman, 1965–1976* (Oxford: Oxford University Press, 2013); Halliday, *Mercenaries*, pp. 24, 29, 58.

146 Halliday, *Mercenaries*, pp. 24, 29, 58.

147 Ibid., pp. 31, 48, 53, 65.

148 Curtis, *Web of Deceit*, p. 279.

149 Ibid., p. 279; Halliday, *Mercenaries*, pp. 47–9.

150 Halliday, *Mercenaries*, pp. 55–7.

151 Ibid., p. 52.

152 J. Lucas replying to the 'Gulf Committee' on 25 March 1975. Cited by Halliday, *Mercenaries*, pp. 74–5.

153 Ibid., p. 61; Curtis, *Web of Deceit*, p. 279.

154 Halliday, *Mercenaries*, p. 18.

155 Michael Rice, the eventual museum designer. *Telegraph*, 'Michael Rice – Obituary', 16 November 2013; Curtis, *Web of Deceit*, p. 279; Halliday, *Mercenaries*, p. 61.

156 R. Kane, *Coup D'État Oman* (London: Amazon, 2014).

157 *Guardian*, 'Obituary: Brigadier Tim Landon', 28 August 2007.

158 Halliday, *Mercenaries*, pp. 52–3, 57.

159 Ibid., p. 52.

160 This despite Saudi Arabia having briefly backed the People's Front on the basis of putting pressure on the sultan with whom they had a long-standing border dispute. Curtis, *Secret Affairs*, p. 84.

161 Halliday, *Mercenaries*, pp. 32–6. The US team was providing instruction to the Omani army in the use of anti-tank missiles. It was also alleged that the US was providing maritime surveillance through a network of US-flagged fishing vessels.

162 J. F. Goode, 'Assisting our Brothers, Defending Ourselves: The Iranian Intervention in Oman, 1972–75', *Iranian Studies*, Vol. 47, No. 3, 2014, p. 441.

163 Halliday, *Mercenaries*, pp. 50–51.

164 Notably movements in Kuwait, Bahrain, and Dubai.

165 For a discussion of the strategies employed by Britain and the ruling family of Dubai to head off indigenous Arab nationalism see C. M. Davidson, *Dubai: The Vulnerability of Success* (New York: Columbia University Press, 2008), pp. 39–57.

166 Ibid., pp. 249–51. Saqr returned to Sharjah in 1972 with a group of armed retainers. Although holding his British-appointed successor hostage for sixteen hours, a combined force from Dubai and Abu Dhabi eventually forced his men into a surrender.

167 C. M. Davidson, *Abu Dhabi: Oil and Beyond* (New York: Columbia University Press, 2009), pp. 38, 42–3, 47–8.

168 Curtis, *Web of Deceit*, p. 271; S. Smith, *Kuwait: 1950–1965: Britain, the al-Sabah and Oil* (Oxford: Oxford University Press, 1999), pp. 79–80. Citing a minuted item from late 1957.

169 Curtis, *Web of Deceit*, p. 271.

170 Public Records Office, 'Foreign Office 371/132545', 8 August 1958.

171 Curtis, *Web of Deceit*, pp. 272–3.

172 R. Mobley, 'Gauging the Iraqi threat to Kuwait in the 1960s', CIA: *Studies in Intelligence*, Winter 2001.

173 Cited by Curtis, *Web of Deceit*, p. 273.

174 As discussed by Mobley, 'Gauging the Iraqi threat to Kuwait in the 1960s'.

175 Cited by Curtis, *Web of Deceit*, p. 274.

176 Quoting John Richmond. See H. Bismarck, *British Policy in the Persian Gulf, 1961–1968: Conceptions of Informal Empire* (London: Palgrave, 2013), pp. 18–19; Curtis, *Web of Deceit*, p. 275.

177 Public Records Office, 'Memorandum by the Lord Privy Seal', 2 October 1961.

2. COLD WAR, OIL WAR – AMERICA TAKES OVER

1 K. Korsch, 'The Fascist Counter-Revolution', *Living Marxism*, Vol. 5, No. 2, 1940.

2 Cited by M. Curtis, *Web of Deceit: Britain's Real Role in the World* (London: Vintage, 2003), p. 239.

3 W. Blum, *Killing Hope: US Military and CIA Interventions Since World War II* (London: Zed, 2014), pp. 84–5.

4 Ibid., p. 85.

5 W. C. Matthews, 'The Kennedy Administration, Counterinsurgency, and Iraq's first Baathist Regime', *International Journal of Middle East Studies*, Vol. 43, No. 4, 2011, pp. 639, 646.

6 Ibid., pp. 638–9, 645.

7 Ibid., pp. 636–637; R. Dreyfuss, *Devil's Game: How the United States Helped Unleash Fundamentalist Islam* (New York: Metropolitan, 2006), p. 2.

8 F. J. Abbott, *The Greek Civil War 1947–1949: Lessons for the Operational Artist in Foreign Internal Defense* (Fort Leavenworth: US School of Advanced Military Studies, 1994), pp. 8–9.

9 W. LaFeber, *Inevitable Revolutions: The United States in Central America* (London: W. W. Norton, 1993), pp. 74–78.

10 See P. Gleijeses, *Shattered Hope: The Guatemalan Revolution and the United States, 1944–1954* (Princeton: Princeton University Press, 1991).

11 T. G. Paterson, *American Foreign Relations: A History, Volume 2: Since 1895* (London: Cengage Learning, 2009), pp. 303–5.

12 Ibid., pp. 303–5; S. J. Kirsch, 'PR Guns for Hire: The Spectre of Edward Bernays in Gadhafi's Libya', *Present Tense*, Vol. 2, No. 1, 2011.

13 Cited by Curtis, *Web of Deceit*, p. 239.

14 N. Cullather, *Secret History: The CIA's classified account of its operations in Guatemala, 1952–1954* (Palo Alto, Stanford University Press, 1999), pp. 16–20.

15 It had been authorized in 1951 by the Harry Truman administration.

16 Paterson, *American Foreign Relations*, pp. 303–5; Al-Jazeera, 'Bottom up Revolution', 17 June 2011.

17   For a full discussion see R. H. Immerman, *The CIA in Guatemala: The Foreign Policy of Intervention* (Austin: Texas University Press, 1992); S. Kinzer, S. Schlesinger, *Bitter Fruit: The Story of the American Coup in Guatemala* (Cambridge, Harvard University Press, 1999).

18   Paterson, *American Foreign Relations*, pp. 303–5; Al-Jazeera, 'Bottom Up revolution', 17 June 2011; *The Nation*, 'Dag Hammarskjöld: Statesman of the Century', 9 September 2013.

19   R. May, 'Surviving All Changes is Your Destiny: Violence and Popular Movements in Guatemala', *Latin American Perspectives*, Vol. 26, No. 2, 1999.

20   *New Yorker*, 'The Redirection', 5 March 2007.

21   L. Coltman, *The Real Fidel Castro* (New Haven: Yale University Press, 2003), pp. 166–7.

22   For a full discussion see J. R. Fernandez, *Playa Giron/Bay of Pigs: Washington's First Military Defeat in the Americas* (New York: Pathfinder, 2001); J. R. Rodriguez, *Bay of Pigs and the CIA* (New York: Ocean Press, 1999); P. Kornbluh, *Bay of Pigs Declassified: The Secret CIA Report on the Invasion of Cuba* (New York: The New Press, 1998).

23   J. L. Anderson, *Che Guevara: A Revolutionary Life* (New York: Grove, 1997), p. 509.

24   J. Savimbi, 'The War against Soviet Colonialism', *Policy Review*, January 1986, pp. 18–30.

25   BBC Online, 'DR Congo's troubled history', 16 January 2001; *New York Times*, 'US Relies Heavily on Saudi Money to Support Syrian Rebels', 23 January 2016. The groups opposing UNITA included the Popular Movement for the Liberation of Angola and the National Liberation Front of Angola.

26   *New York Times*, 'UN Orders Review of 1961 Crash That Killed Dag Hammarskjöld', 16 March 2015. For a discussion of the US struggle to secure uranium from the Congo during the Second World War see S. Williams *Spies in the Congo: America's Atomic Mission in World War II* (London: Hurst, 2016).

27   *Time*, 'Jungle Shipwreck', 25 July 1960.

28   Democracy Now, 'Patrice Lumumba: 50 Years Later, Remembering the US-Backed Assassination of Congo's First Democratically Elected Leader', 21 January 2011; *Guardian*, 'Patrice Lumumba: the most important assassination of the 20th century', 17 January 2011.

29   *New York Times*, 'UN Orders Review of 1961 Crash That Killed Dag Hammarskjöld', 16 March 2015.

30   *Guardian*, 'Britain denies conspiracy to kill UN chief', 20 August 1999.

31   BBC Online, 'DR Congo's troubled history', 16 January 2001.

32   F. Halliday, *Mercenaries: Counter-insurgency in the Gulf* (London: Spokesman, 1977), p. 14.

33   BBC Online, On This Day: 25 April 1974, 'Rebels seize control of Portugal'; L. S. Graham, H. M. Makler, *Contemporary Portugal: The Revolution and its Antecedents*

(Austin: Texas University Press, 1979); R. Chilcote, *The Portuguese Revolution: State and Class in the Transition to Democracy* (London: Rowman, 2012), p. 232.

34   B. Stewart, *Why Spy?: On the Art of Intelligence* (London: Hurst, 2015), pp. 26, 29.

35   S. Tucker (ed.), *The Encyclopedia of the Vietnam War: A Political, Social, and Military History* (Oxford: Oxford University Press, 2000), p. 1071.

36   Stewart, *Why Spy?*, pp. 29, 37; Curtis, *Web of Deceit*, p. 236.

37   For a full discussion see E. E. Moïse, *Tonkin Gulf and the Escalation of the Vietnam War* (Chapel Hill: North Carolina University Press, 1996).

38   US Department of State, 'Text of Lyndon Johnson's speech, Gulf of Tonkin Incident', 4 August 1964; *Consortium News*, 'CIA, Iran, and the Gulf of Tonkin', 12 January 2008. The latter prepared by Raymond McGovern, a former CIA officer and chairman of the National Intelligence Estimates.

39   J. Bamford, *Body of Secrets* (New York: Anchor, 2002); *New York Times*, 'Vietnam War Intelligence Deliberately Skewed, Secret Study Says', 2 December 2005.

40   Halliday, *Mercenaries*, pp. 29, 39.

41   Stewart, *Why Spy?*, p. 34.

42   P. E. Sigmund, *The Overthrow of Allende and the Politics of Chile, 1964–1976* (Pittsburgh: Pittsburgh University Press, 1980), p. 154.

43   US Department of State, 'Foreign Relations of the United States, 1969–1976, Volume XXI, Chile 1969–1973', released 2014.

44   Ibid., pp. 47–9.

45   Ibid., p. 418.

46   Ibid., pp. 420–21.

47   See G. A. Herrera, *Pinochet: The Politics of Power* (Boston: Unwin, 1998).

48   Congressional Reports, *US Covert Actions by the Central Intelligence Agency in Chile, 1963–1973* (Washington DC: Arc Manor, 2008), p. 67.

49   Ibid., p.67.

50   BBC Online, 'In pictures: Sandinista revolution remembered', 20 June 2010.

51   Cited by Curtis, *Web of Deceit*, p. 239.

52   T. D. Gill, *Litigation Strategy at the International Court, A Case Study of the Nicaragua v. United States Dispute* (Dordrecht: M. Nijhoff, 1989), p. 329.

53   See L. Walsh, *Firewall: The Iran-Contra Conspiracy and Cover-Up* (New York, W. W. Norton, 1998).

54   Gill, *Litigation Strategy*, p. 329; *New Yorker*, 'The Redirection', 5 March 2007; *New York Times*, 'US Relies Heavily on Saudi Money to Support Syrian Rebels', 23 January 2016.

55   See Walsh, *Firewall*.

56   Associated Press, 'US Concedes Contras Linked to Drugs, But Denies Leadership Involved', 17 April 1986; National Security Archive, 'The Contras, cocaine, and covert operations: Documentation of official U.S. knowledge of drug trafficking and the Contras', released 1990.

57   US Senate Foreign Relations Committee, 'Kerry Committee Report', 13 April 1989.
58   K. Kyle, *Suez: Britain's End of Empire in the Middle East* (London: I. B. Tauris, 2011), p. 552; M. Curtis, *Secret Affairs: Britain's Collusion with Radical Islam* (London: Serpent's Tail, 2012), p. 62.
59   The Truman Doctrine being issued in 1947 and the Monroe Doctrine in 1823.
60   Blum, *Killing Hope*, p. 89.
61   Dreyfuss, *Devil's Game*, p. 121.
62   Ibid., pp. 67–8; Council on Foreign Relations, 'Oil Dependence and US Foreign Policy', January 2012.
63   Curtis, *Web of Deceit*, pp. 15–16.
64   Dreyfuss, *Devil's Game*, p. 69.
65   Referring to a Department of State communication from 1950. Cited by Curtis, *Web of Deceit*, p. 257.
66   US Department of State, 'Annual Policy Assessment for Saudi Arabia: Part Four', 8 January 1976.
67   US Department of State, 'Post Memorandum for Inspection', 17 September 1978.
68   Curtis, *Secret Affairs*, p. 114; G. Gause, *The International Relations of the Persian Gulf* (Cambridge: Cambridge University Press, 2010), p. 22.
69   Dreyfuss, *Devil's Game*, p. 282. Citing interviews with Herb Meyer in October 2004.
70   P. H. Abelson, 'Transportation Fuels', *Science*, Vol. 250, October 1990.
71   Blum, *Killing Hope*, p. 330.
72   Ibid., p. 65; J. Kincheloe, S. Steinberg (eds), *The Miseducation of the West: How schools and the media distort our understanding of the Islamic world* (Westport: Praeger, 2004), pp. 61–5; C. De Bellaigue, *Patriot of Persia: Muhammad Mossadegh and a Tragic Anglo-American Coup* (London: Harper, 2013).
73   Dreyfuss, *Devil's Game*, p. 109; Curtis, *Web of Deceit*, p. 234.
74   Dreyfuss, *Devil's Game*, p. 114; Curtis, *Web of Deceit*, p. 304.
75   Curtis, *Web of Deceit*, p. 304.
76   S. Dorril, *MI6: Fifty Years of Special Operations* (London: Fourth Estate, 2001), p. 560.
77   Cited by Curtis, *Web of Deceit*, p. 305.
78   Blum, *Killing Hope*, p. 65.
79   Ibid., p. 65; Kincheloe *et al.*, *The Miseducation of the West*, pp. 61–5; De Bellaigue, *Patriot of Persia*.
80   Curtis, *Web of Deceit*, p. 306. Citing Public Records Office, 'Foreign Office 248/1531', 26 January 1952; Public Records Office, 'Foreign Office 371/98688', 16 March 1952; Public Records Office, 'Foreign Office 371/91460', 16 March 1952.
81   Seyyid Zia'eddin Tabatabaee was prime minister for five months in 1921 after participating in a coup d'état. He was later exiled to Palestine but was employed by Britain as a consultant on a number of occasions. R. Cottam, *Iran and the United States: A Cold War Case Study* (Pittsburgh, Pittsburgh University Press, 1989), p. 95.

82   *Guardian*, 'CIA admits role in 1953 Iranian coup', 19 August 2015.

83   Public Records Office, 'Cabinet 129/46/CP(51)212', 25 July 1951.

84   Curtis, *Web of Deceit*, p. 307.

85   Ibid., p. 309. Citing Public Records Office, 'Foreign Office FO371/98684', 26 January 1952.

86   Public Records Office, 'Foreign Office 371/91459', 8 June 1951.

87   Kincheloe *et al.*, *The Miseducation of the West*, pp. 61–5; De Bellaigue, *Patriot of Persia*; Dreyfuss, *Devil's Game*, pp. 113–14.

88   Blum, *Killing Hope*, p. 66. Referencing Kermit Roosevelt's memoirs.

89   Curtis, *Web of Deceit*, p. 312; Curtis, *Secret Affairs*, p. 49.

90   CIA, 'Propaganda Commentary C01384520 Mossadeq's Spy Service', undated.

91   CIA, 'Memo from Kermit Roosevelt to [Excised]', 14 July 1953.

92   CIA, 'Memo from Kermit Roosevelt to [Excised]', 15 July 1953.

93   CIA, 'Memo from Kermit Roosevelt to [Excised]', 16 July 1953. See also Curtis, *Web of Deceit*, p. 309.

94   Known as Operation Boot by MI6. See Curtis, *Secret Affairs*, p. 47; Blum, *Killing Hope*, p. 64.

95   The grandson of President Theodore Roosevelt.

96   Blum, *Killing Hope*, p. 65.

97   Ibid., p. 68.

98   Kincheloe *et al.*, *The Miseducation of the West*, pp. 61–5; De Bellaigue, *Patriot of Persia*; Curtis, *Web of Deceit*, p. 311; Curtis, *Secret Affairs*, pp. 51–2.

99   National Security Archive, 'CIA Confirms Role in 1953 Iran Coup', 19 August 2013.

100   Blum, *Killing Hope*, p. 68. Referencing Richard Cottam, a US academic formerly in the employ of the CIA in Tehran at that time.

101   Ibid., p. 69.

102   Ibid., pp. 68, 70.

103   Churchill had requested the BBC to change its usual World Service sign-off from 'It is now midnight' to 'It is now exactly midnight'. See S. Kinzer, *All the Shah's Men: An American Coup and the Roots of Middle East Terror* (London: Wiley, 2008), p. 42.

104   A. Sreberny, M. Torfeh, 'The BBC World Service from wartime propaganda to public diplomacy', in *Diasporas and Diplomacy: Cosmopolitan contact zones at the BBC World Service*, ed. M. Gillespie *et al.* (London: Routledge, 2012), p. 131.

105   Blum, *Killing Hope*, p. 67; Curtis, *Web of Deceit*, p. 309.

106   Blum, *Killing Hope*, pp. 68–9.

107   Ibid., p. 69. Quoting George Stewart.

108   Ibid., p. 70.

109   Dreyfuss, *Devil's Game*, pp. 110–11; Curtis, *Secret Affairs*, p. 50.

110   See for example S. MacKay, *The Iranians* (New York: Plume, 1998), pp. 195–200; E. Abrahamian, *Khomeinism: Essays on the Islamic Republic* (Los Angeles: California University Press, 1993), pp. 102–9.

111 Dreyfuss, *Devil's Game*, p. 113. For a further discussion on how Kashani seemingly turned on Mosaddegh, see J. Buchan, *Days of God: The Revolution in Iran and its Consequences* (London: Simon and Schuster, 2012), pp. 65–8.
112 The agent being Robert Charles Zaehner. S. Clark, 'From Athens to Jerusalem', Gifford Lectures, Glasgow University, 1981; *Daily Telegraph*, 'Obituary: Professor A. K. S. Lambton', 8 August 2008; J. M. Olin, 'Miss Lambton's Advice', blog post for Institute for Strategic Studies, Harvard University, 20 August 2008.
113 Dreyfuss, *Devil's Game*, p. 114.
114 Ibid., p. 112. Quoting Fereydoun Hoveyda.
115 Ibid., p. 112. Citing Dreyfuss' interview with John Waller, former CIA station chief in Tehran from 1946 to 1953.
116 For a good discussion of the Oudh Bequest see Curtis, *Secret Affairs*, p. 16.
117 M. Pahlavi, *Answer to History* (London: Stein, 1980), pp. 15, 59.
118 Curtis, *Secret Affairs*, p. 55. Citing Princess Ashraf Pahlavi's memoirs.
119 Ibid., p. 52; Curtis, *Web of Deceit*, p. 310.
120 CIA, 'Memo from Kermit Roosevelt to [Excised]', 21 September 1953.
121 Curtis, *Secret Affairs*, p. 54. Citing Public Records Office, 'Foreign Office 371/104571', 1 September 1953.
122 Blum, *Killing Hope*, p. 71.
123 Dreyfuss, *Devil's Game*, p. 69.
124 Blum, *Killing Hope*, p. 71. Referring to Gulf Oil & Co.
125 Ibid., p. 71. Referring to Standard Oil Company of New Jersey.
126 A. McCoy, *A Question of Torture: CIA Interrogation, from the Cold War to the War on Terror* (New York: Metropolitan, 2006), p.74. Quoting former CIA analyst Jesse Leaf. See also Curtis, *Web of Deceit*, p. 314.
127 F. Halliday, *Iran: Dictatorship and Development* (London: Pelican, 1978); Curtis, *Secret Affairs*, p. 123.
128 Margaret Thatcher Speech Archive, 'Margaret Thatcher: Speech to Iran-British Chamber of Commerce', 29 April 1978.
129 National Security Archive, 'CIA Confirms Role in 1953 Iran Coup', 19 August 2013.
130 *New York Times*, 'CIA Destroyed Files on 1953 Iran Coup', 29 May 1997.
131 Public Records Office, 'Foreign Office Summary Record: British-American Planning Talks, Washington, FCO8/3216/333/2', 11 October 1978; Public Records Office, 'Foreign Office: Minute, B. L. Crowe to R. S. Gorham, Anglo-American Planning Talks: Iran, FCO 8/3216', 12 October 1978.
132 Public Records Office, 'British Embassy in Washington, Letter, R. S. Muir to R. S. Gorham, Iran, FCO 8/3216', 22 December 1978.
133 *International Herald Tribune*, 'Show Ignores Essential Questions about Iranian King's Role', 21 February 2009.
134 The military dictatorships had ruled since 1949, when there had been a coup d'état led by the Syrian army's chief of staff.

NOTES

135   D. Nohlen, F. Grotz, C. Hartmann, *Elections in Asia: A data handbook, Volume I* (Oxford: Oxford University Press, 2001), pp. 54–5; J. P. Filiu, *From Deep State to Islamic State: The Arab Counter-Revolution and its Jihadi Legacy* (London: Hurst, 2015), pp. 32–5.

136   D. Nohlen *et al.*, *Elections in Asia*, pp. 54–5; Blum, *Killing Hope*, p. 85.

137   Blum, *Killing Hope*, pp. 85–6.

138   Curtis, *Secret Affairs*, pp. 70–71. Citing Public Records Office, 'Foreign Office 371/121858', 24 February 1956; Public Records Office, 'Foreign Office 371/121858', 19 March 1956.

139   Michail Bey Ilyan.

140   Blum, *Killing Hope*, pp. 86–7. Citing Wilbur Crane Eveland.

141   Curtis, *Secret Affairs*, p. 71. Citing MI6 deputy director George Young.

142   Ibid., p. 71. Citing Public Records Office, 'Foreign Office 371/121858', 14 March 1956.

143   Ibid., p. 71; Blum, *Killing Hope*, pp. 86–7.

144   Blum, *Killing Hope*, pp. 87–8; Curtis, *Secret Affairs*, pp. 72–3.

145   For a full discussion see G. H. Torrey, *Syrian Politics and the Military, 1945–1958* (Columbus: Ohio University Press, 1964).

146   Blum, *Killing Hope*, p. 88; Curtis, *Secret Affairs*, p. 73.

147   Blum, *Killing Hope*, p. 88.

148   Ibid., p. 91.

149   Ibid., p. 94.

150   Ibid., pp. 90–91. Quoting Kennett Love of the *New York Times*.

151   Ibid., p. 91. Citing a 1957 Department of Defense report.

152   Ibid., pp. 91–2; E. J. Hughes, *The Ordeal of Power* (London: Macmillan, 1963), pp. 253–4.

153   Syria had been placed under the governorship of an Egyptian field marshal during the period of its incorporation in the United Arab Republic.

154   Y. Oron (ed.), *Middle East Record Volume 2* (London: Weidenfeld & Nicolson, 1965), pp. 605–7; Filiu, *From Deep State*, p. 51.

155   Filiu, *From Deep State*, pp. 58–9.

156   Blum, *Killing Hope*, p. 89. This meeting took place in 1962.

157   Curtis, *Secret Affairs*, pp. 73–5. Citing Public Records Office, 'Foreign Office 371/127880', 8 May 1957; Blum, *Killing Hope*, p. 90; D. Hiro, *The essential Middle East: a comprehensive guide* (London: Carroll & Graf, 2003), pp. 351–2.

158   Blum, *Killing Hope*, p. 90; Curtis, *Secret Affairs*, pp. 73–4; D. W. Lesch, *The Middle East and the United States: a historical and political reassessment* (Boulder: Westview Press, 2003), pp. 125–6.

159   Blum, *Killing Hope*, p. 90; Curtis, *Secret Affairs*, pp. 73–4.

160   *Washington Post*, 'CIA paid millions to Jordan's King Hussein', 18 February 1977.

161   Curtis, *Secret Affairs*, p. 74. Citing Public Records Office, 'Foreign Office 371/127880', 3 July 1957.

162 Ibid., p. 75. Citing Public Records Office, 'Foreign Office 371/127878', 15 February 1957.

163 Dreyfuss, *Devil's Game*, pp. 193–4.

164 Curtis, *Secret Affairs*, p. 74.

165 Dreyfuss, *Devil's Game*, pp. 193–4.

166 The PLO had been antagonized by Hussein's repeated claims on Palestine's West Bank, despite its earlier loss to Israel. Syria dispatched tanks, but they were not provided with air support, as air force chief Hafez al-Assad sought to undermine his chief rival, Saleh Jadid. Filiu, *From Deep State*, p. 40.

167 A. Shlaim, *Lion of Jordan: The Life of King Hussein in War and Peace* (London: Allen Lane, 2007), pp. 301–2; Curtis, *Secret Affairs*, pp. 101–3; P. Seale, *Abu Nidal: A Gun for Hire* (London: Random House, 1992), pp. 80–82. According to Seale, Syria's intervention was on the basis of preventing a massacre of Palestinians, but this has been contested in most of the literature.

168 Matthews, 'The Kennedy Administration', p. 639; Filiu, *From Deep State*, p. 36.

169 Matthews, 'The Kennedy Administration', p. 646; Blum, *Killing Hope*, p. 98.

170 Halliday, *Mercenaries*, pp. 27–8; G. Hadley, *CENTO: The Forgotten Alliance ISIO* (Brighton: Sussex University Press, 1971); Dreyfuss, *Devil's Game*, p. 10.

171 Matthews, 'The Kennedy Administration', pp. 635–6; B. R. Gibson, 'US Foreign Policy, Iraq, and the Cold War 1958–1975' (PhD dissertation, London School of Economics, 2013).

172 Matthews, 'The Kennedy Administration', pp. 636, 639–42.

173 Ibid., p. 643. Quoting from a document written by B. H. Selcke on 10 March 1964 entitled 'USIS Youth activities – Iraq'.

174 Ibid., pp. 641–2. The other former CIA officer was Eric Pollard. It appears the Department of State's criticism scuppered their visit on the basis it would add further weight to rumours that the US was behind the *Ba'ath* regime.

175 Ibid., p. 639. Quoting Roy Melbourne, US chargé d'affaires in Baghdad.

176 Ibid., p. 645.

177 Ibid., pp. 636, 642.

178 Ibid., p. 642. The exposé was entitled 'The Deviationists among the National Guard in the anti-Arab Nationalist Deluge'.

179 Ibid., p. 644.

180 Blum, *Killing Hope*, pp. 94–5.

181 The voter turnout was about fifty-three percent. D. Nohlen *et al.*, *Elections in Asia*, pp. 183–4.

182 Blum, *Killing Hope*, pp. 94–6.

183 Ibid., pp. 95–8.

184 A. Eden, *Full Circle* (London: Cassell, 1960), pp. 330–35.

185 R. Barnet, *Intervention and Revolution* (London: MacGibbon, 1970), pp. 147–8.

186 Blum, *Killing Hope*, p. 97.

187　The envoy being veteran US diplomat Robert Murphy.

188　W. C. Eveland, *Ropes of Sand: America's Failure in the Middle East* (New York: W. W. Norton, 1981), pp. 295–6.

189　For a full discussion see *The Nation*, 'The CIA in Algeria', 20 May 1961; Blum, *Killing Hope*, pp. 150–51.

190　S. De Gramont, *The Secret War* (New York: Dell, 1963), pp. 29–30.

191　Blum, *Killing Hope*, p. 150.

192　*New York Times*, 'Algiers', 29 April 1961.

193　Ibid.; Blum, *Killing Hope*, p. 151.

194　*The Nation*, 'The CIA in Algeria', 20 May 1961; Blum, *Killing Hope*, pp. 150–51.

195　Blum, *Killing Hope*, pp. 149, 152.

196　F. Forsyth, *The Day of the Jackal* (London: Hutchinson, 1971).

197　*The Nation*, 'The CIA's Secret Armies in Europe', 6 April 1992.

198　*Inquiry*, 'Showdown in the Sahara', 12 April 1982; Blum, *Killing Hope*, p. 278.

199　Blum, *Killing Hope*, p. 278.

200　A. Rami, *Un Vie pour la Liberté* (Paris: Payot, 1986); *Irish Times*, 'Morocco: Officer reveals CIA's role in Murder', 8 August 2001.

201　*Independent*, 'The MoD, the arms deal and a 30–year-old bill for £400 million', 24 April 2010.

202　The GCC's members being Saudi Arabia, Kuwait, Bahrain, Qatar, the United Arab Emirates, and Oman.

203　Dreyfuss, *Devil's Game*, p. 71.

204　By comparison Britain's arms exports to the Gulf monarchies in the 1960s were only £150 million per annum. Halliday, *Mercenaries*, p. 12; G. Gresh, *Gulf Security and the U.S. Military: Regime Survival and the Politics of Basing* (Palo Alto: Stanford University Press, 2015), p. 147.

205　Halliday, *Mercenaries*, p. 12.

206　Curtis, *Web of Deceit*, p. 262; *Daily Telegraph*, 'Margaret Thatcher was admonished by US congress for selling arms to Saudi Arabia, papers show', 16 July 2015.

207　Curtis, *Web of Deceit*, pp. 201, 203, 263.

208　*Daily Telegraph*, 'Margaret Thatcher was admonished by US congress for selling arms to Saudi Arabia, papers show', 16 July 2015; *Guardian*, 'Margaret Thatcher's lobbying of Saudi royals over arms deal revealed', 16 July 2015.

209　*Guardian*, 'Margaret Thatcher "very oily to kings", says note in newly released FCO file', 3 July 2015.

210　Margaret Thatcher Speech Archives, 'Margaret Thatcher Speech to Chatham House Conference on Saudi Arabia', 4 October 1993.

211　*Guardian*, 'BAE and the Saudis: How secret cash payments oiled £43bn arms deal', 5 February 2010; Curtis, *Web of Deceit*, p. 262; BBC Online, 'Saudi prince received arms cash', 7 June 2007; *Guardian*, 'Margaret Thatcher's lobbying of Saudi royals over arms deal revealed', 16 July 2015.

212 A. B. Atwan, *Islamic State: The Digital Caliphate* (London: Saqi, 2015), p. 209.

213 *Guardian*, 'US prepares to approve $60bn arms deal with Saudi Arabia', 13 September 2010.

214 *Financial Times*, 'Ministers cite security in effort to block details of Saudi deal', 28 May 2015; Exaronews, 'Third insider blows whistle on "corrupt" Saudi defence deal', 9 July 2012.

215 *Financial Times*, 'UK-Saudi contract details can stay secret, tribunal rules', 24 July 2015.

216 Dreyfuss, *Devil's Game*, p. 70. The Dhahran base closed in 1960.

217 *Jane's Defence Weekly*, 'US Fifth Fleet reborn for active duty in the Persian Gulf', 27 May 1995; Dreyfuss, *Devil's Game*, p. 142.

218 Globalsecurity, 'Special Report on Al-Udeid Air Base, Qatar', 14 July 2014.

219 *New York Times*, 'US Speeding Up Missile Defenses in Persian Gulf', 31 January 2010.

220 C. M. Davidson, *After the Sheikhs: The Coming Collapse of the Gulf Monarchies* (New York: Oxford University Press, 2013), p. 164.

221 *International Herald Tribune*, 'Al-Dhafrah Base', 22 June 2005.

222 Davidson, *After the Sheikhs*, p. 165; *Express Tribune* (Pakistan), 'Al-Shamsi Mystery', 4 July 2011.

223 Davidson, *After the Sheikhs*, pp. 165–6.

224 House of Commons Select Committee on Defence, 'Thirteenth Report 1999/2000', 26 July 2000, paragraph 7.

225 Ibid., paragraph 60.

226 Ibid., paragraph 66.

227 Ibid., paragraph 64.

228 Ibid., paragraph 68.

229 Reuters, 'UAE to shut down Canadian military camp over flights', 10 October 2010.

230 Zayed had died in 2004.

231 *Washington Post*, 'Camp de la Paix', 27 May 2009.

232 *The National* (Abu Dhabi), 'Nicolas Sarkozy opinion editorial', 25 May 2009 (since deleted).

233 Halliday, *Mercenaries*, pp. 9–10, 60–61.

234 Hansard, 'Angola: British Mercenaries', 10 February 1976; Halliday, *Mercenaries*, p. 10.

235 Referring to Airwork. Curtis, *Secret Affairs*, p. 94.

236 Halliday, *Mercenaries*, pp. 60–61.

237 *New York Times*, 'Bahrain Adviser Quits; Briton Had Become Target of Nationalist Elements', 15 August 1956; B. Page, D. Leitch, P. Knightly, *The Philby Conspiracy* (London: Doubleday, 1968). St. John Philby was the father of Kim Philby, the MI6 agent who defected to the Soviet Union in 1963.

238 Halliday, *Mercenaries*, pp. 18–19, 61–2.

239 Ibid., p. 16. One of these, Ronald Cochrane, converted to Islam and became known as Muhammad Mahdi.
240 Curtis, *Secret Affairs*, p. 317.
241 Halliday, *Mercenaries*, p. 16.
242 Author interviews with Emile Nakleh, October 2015.
243 Curtis, *Web of Deceit*, p. 267.
244 *London Gazette*, 'New Year's Honours', 31 December 1984.
245 Bahrain Watch.
246 Bahrain Watch, 'Judge Orders Further Partial Release of Henderson Files', 17 May 2015.
247 Reuters, 'Classified document on Bahrain rankles Britain decades later', 21 May 2015.
248 Halliday, *Mercenaries*, pp. 18, 60–61.
249 Curtis, *Secret Affairs*, p. 120. The British protection of Yamani began in 1975, after the Carlos the Jackal-led hostage-taking of OPEC ministers in Vienna.
250 Curtis, *Web of Deceit*, p. 261.
251 Halliday, *Mercenaries*, pp. 15–22.
252 Curtis, *Secret Affairs*, pp. 138–140; Dreyfuss, *Devil's Game*, p. 143.
253 Halliday, *Mercenaries*, pp. 17, 33.
254 *Wall Street Journal*, 'White Slaves in the Persian Gulf', 7 January 1991; Blum, *Killing Hope*, p. 333.

3. THE ROAD TO AL-QAEDA – THE CIA'S BABY

1 An expression first used by Russian Tsar Nicholas I. See H. Temperley, *England and the Near East* (London: Longmans, 1936), p. 272.
2 The activists were Jamal Eddine al-Afghani and Muhammad Abduh. For a discussion see R. Dreyfuss, *Devil's Game: How the United States Helped Unleash Fundamentalist Islam* (New York: Metropolitan, 2006), p. 19.
3 Ibid., p. 27.
4 Ibid., pp. 30–31. Referring to Muhammed Abduh.
5 M. Curtis, *Secret Affairs: Britain's Collusion with Radical Islam* (London: Serpent's Tail, 2012), p. 8. Quoting Lord Herbert Kitchener in 1915.
6 Ibid., pp. 6–7. Citing the British government's 1914 proclamation 'to the natives of Arabia, Palestine, Syria, and Mesopotamia'. See also A. B. Atwan, *Islamic State: The Digital Caliphate* (London: Saqi, 2015), p. 191.
7 For a full discussion see N. J. Delong-Bas, *Wahhabi Islam: From Revival and Reform to Global Jihad* (London: I. B. Tauris, 2004); Middle East Online, 'Qatar embraces Wahhabism to strengthen regional influence', 18 December 2011.
8 C. Bunzel, 'From Paper State to Caliphate: The Ideology of the Islamic State', *Brookings Project on US relations with the Islamic World – Analysis Paper*, No. 19, March 2015, p. 9.

9   J. M. Berger, J. Stern, *ISIS: The State of Terror* (London: William Collins, 2015), p. 259; Dreyfuss, *Devil's Game*, p. 37.

10 H. Algar, *Wahhabism: A Critical Essay* (New York: Islamic Publications International, 2002), pp. 23–5.

11 Dreyfuss, *Devil's Game*, pp. 38–9.

12 I. Friedman, *Palestine, a Twice-Promised Land?: The British, the Arabs & Zionism, 1915–1920* (London: Transaction Publishers, 2000), pp. 165–170; S. Aburish, *The Rise, Corruption, and Coming Fall of the House of Saud* (London: Bloomsbury, 1994), p. 13; Dreyfuss, *Devil's Game*, p. 42; Curtis, *Secret Affairs*, p. 11.

13 Curtis, *Secret Affairs*, pp. 9–11.

14 Dreyfuss, *Devil's Game*, p. 43.

15 Curtis, *Secret Affairs*, p. 11.

16 Ibid., pp. 10–11; Dreyfuss, *Devil's Game*, p. 40.

17 *New Statesman*, 'The tragic cycle: Western powers and the Middle East', 21 August 2014; Dreyfuss, *Devil's Game*, p. 43.

18 Atwan, *Islamic State*, p. 192.

19 Curtis, *Secret Affairs*, p. 10; D. Fromkin, *A Peace to End All Peace: Creating the Modern Middle East, 1914–1922* (London: Penguin, 1989), p. 106.

20 *American Spectator*, 'Defeating ISIS the World War One Way', 26 September 2014.

21 Dreyfuss, *Devil's Game*, p. 43; J. Habib, *Ibn Saud's Warriors of Islam* (Leiden: Brill, 1978), pp.26–7; Curtis, *Secret Affairs*, p. 12.

22 M. Gilbert, *Churchill and the Jews* (London: Penguin, 2007), p. 35. Churchill made this statement to the House of Commons in 1921.

23 W. Churchill, *The River War: An Historical Account of the Re-conquest of the Soudan* (London: Longman's, 1899), pp. 248–250.

24 Curtis, *Secret Affairs*, p. 12; Aburish, *The Rise*, p. 13. For a full discussion see Ibn Khaldun's sociological notes in the *Muqaddimah of Ibn Khaldun* on *asabiyyah* and the means by which ruling families can emerge on the periphery of empires.

25 PBS Frontline, 'Interview with Madawi al-Rasheed', 2 April 2003.

26 Bunzel, 'From Paper State', p. 9.

27 J. P. Filiu, *From Deep State to Islamic State: The Arab Counter-Revolution and Its Jihadi Legacy* (London: Hurst, 2015), p. 28.

28 Dreyfuss, *Devil's Game*, p. 44; Curtis, *Secret Affairs*, p. 13; *New York Times*, 'Peace Parley in Arabia; Terms Submitted to Yemen at Taif, London Legation Says', 21 May 1934.

29 'Gookety gook' being a joking, rather rude label for someone deemed to be important. Curtis, *Secret Affairs*, p. 68. Citing Eisenhower's memoirs and former British ambassador to Saudi Arabia Willie Morris. For further context also see *Daily Telegraph*, 'Obituary: Sir Michael Weir', 14 August 2006.

30 For further reading on contemporary parallels with the Mamluks of Egypt and Syria see Filiu, *From Deep State*, pp. x–xi, 46.

31   BBC Online, 'The secret US mission to heal Saudi King Ibn Saud', 8 June 2015.

32   Dreyfuss, *Devil's Game*, pp. 89, 123.

33   Ibid., pp. 88–90. Quoting William Eddy, the US Consul general in Dhahran.

34   Curtis, *Secret Affairs*, p. 57; R. Mitchell, *The Society of the Muslim Brothers* (Oxford: Oxford University Press, 1969), p. 39.

35   Cited by Dreyfuss, *Devil's Game*, p. 108.

36   Ibid., pp. 72–3, 76–7.

37   Ibid., p. 79. Citing ambassador Jefferson Caffrey.

38   Ibid., p. 79; Curtis, *Secret Affairs*, p. 88.

39   *Wall Street Journal*, 'The Beachhead', 12 July 2005.

40   Dreyfuss, *Devil's Game*, pp. 54–5, 127.

41   Ibid., pp. 65–6. Referring to Hermann Eilts, the future US ambassador to both Saudi Arabia and Egypt.

42   Ibid., pp. 142–3; Arab Press Service, 'Wahhabism – a unifier or divisive element', 7 January 2013.

43   R. Bronson, 'Rethinking Religion: The Legacy of the US–Saudi Relationship', *Washington Quarterly*, Vol. 28, No. 4, 2005; *Islam Times*, 'A history of treason – King Faisal bin Abdul-Aziz al-Saud', 22 May 2014.

44   Dreyfuss, *Devil's Game*, pp. 126–37; Curtis, *Secret Affairs*, p. 88; Berger, *ISIS*, p. 267.

45   Dreyfuss, *Devil's Game*, p. 3; K. GhaneaBassiri, *A History of Islam in America: From the New World to the New World Order* (Cambridge: Cambridge University Press, 2010), pp. 262–3; Curtis, *Secret Affairs*, p. 85.

46   Dreyfuss, *Devil's Game*, p. 133; Curtis, *Secret Affairs*, pp. 92, 99. Quoting Willie Morris in 1968 and 1972.

47   Curtis, *Secret Affairs*, p. 87. Citing Public Records Office, 'Foreign Office 371/168868', 18 April 1963.

48   Ibid., p. 87. Citing Public Records Office, 'Foreign Office 371/174671', 16 April 1964.

49   Ibid., pp. 87–8.

50   Ibid., p. 92. Citing Public Records Office, 'Foreign Office 371/185517', 20 February 1966.

51   Department of State, 'Annual policy assessment for Saudi Arabia: part four 1976JIDDA00120_b', 8 January 1976.

52   For a good discussion see M. A. Choudhury, U. A. Malike, *The Foundations of Islamic Political Economy* (London: Macmillan, 1992), p. 104.

53   Dreyfuss, *Devil's Game*, p. 163; Curtis, *Secret Affairs*, p. 107.

54   The Mit Ghamr bank was established in 1963 by Ahmad al-Najjar. Dreyfuss, *Devil's Game*, pp. 178–9.

55   Dreyfuss, *Devil's Game*, pp. 164–5, 168–9, 171.

56   Ibid., p. 172. Citing a 2004 interview with Ibrahim Warde.

57   Ibid., p. 180.

58   W. C. Matthews, 'The Kennedy Administration, Counterinsurgency, and Iraq's first
      Baathist Regime', *International Journal of Middle East Studies*, Vol. 43, No. 4, 2011,
      p. 640.

59   Ibid., p. 641. Quoting Robert Neumann, a political scientist employed by the
      assistant secretary of defense.

60   *Jewish Telegraphic Agency*, 'King Faisal Attacks Jews in Washington; Embarrasses
      US Officials', 23 June 1966. After a media storm and protests by Jewish civil society
      organizations in the US, Faisal attempted to soften his position in an interview with
      Voice of America. See *Chicago Tribune*, 'Didn't Strike at Judaism, Faisal Says', 26
      June 1966.

61   J. Campbell, *The Defence of the Middle East* (New York: Praeger, 1960), p. 299.

62   Curtis, *Secret Affairs*, p. 87, 112. Citing Public Records Office, 'Foreign Office
      93/42', 27 September 1973; Public Records Office, 'Foreign Office 371/174671',
      16 April 1964. Quoting James Craig and Colin Crowe, respectively.

63   Ibid., p. 92. Citing Public Records Office, 'Foreign Office 371/185517', 20 February
      1966.

64   Ibid., p. 121. Citing a report prepared by Harold Walker, Britain's ambassador to
      Jeddah. See Public Records Office, 'Foreign Office 8/2590', 8 February 1975.

65   Under Zulfiqar Bhutto. Dreyfuss, *Devil's Game*, p. 262; M. Curtis, *Web of Deceit:
      Britain's Real Role in the World* (London: Vintage, 2003), pp. 134–5.

66   On 6 May 1978, President Nur Muhammad Taraki stated in a televised address that
      Afghanistan is 'non-aligned and independent'. L. Adamec, *Historical Dictionary of
      Afghanistan* (Toronto: Scarecrow, 2012), pp. xlix–l.

67   W. Blum, *Killing Hope: US Military and CIA Interventions Since World War II*
      (London: Zed, 2014), pp. 339–40; *New York Times*, 'Tough choices for Afghanistan's
      regime and its opponents', 18 May 1979.

68   Blum, *Killing Hope*, p. 341.

69   *New York Times*, 'Afghans resist new rights for women', 9 February 1980.

70   Ibid.

71   Dreyfuss, *Devil's Game*, p. 263.

72   Curtis, *Secret Affairs*, pp. 132–3; Atwan, *Islamic State*, p. 194; Berger, *ISIS*,
      p. 270.

73   Curtis, *Secret Affairs*, pp. 147–8. Citing Public Records Office, 'Ministry of Defence
      35/5154', 1 January 1957.

74   Dreyfuss, *Devil's Game*, p. 275.

75   *New York Times*, 'Afghans resist new rights for women', 9 February 1980.

76   Blum, *Killing Hope*, pp. 346–7. Quoting Selig Harrison. See S. Harrison, 'Afghanistan:
      Soviet Intervention, Afghan resistance, and the American role', in *Low Intensity
      Warfare: Counterinsurgency, Proinsurgency, and Antiterrorism in the Eighties*, ed.
      M. Klare *et al.* (New York: Pantheon, 1988), pp. 188–90.

77   Blum, *Killing Hope*, p. 347; Citing *Los Angeles Times*, 22 April 1989 (no longer available).
78   Dreyfuss, *Devil's Game*, p. 263.
79   Blum, *Killing Hope*, p. 347. Citing a Department of State report from 16 August 1979.
80   C. Johnson, *Dismantling the Empire: America's Last Best Hope* (New York: Metropolitan, 2010), p. 128. Citing a 1998 interview with Zbigniew Brzezinski in *Le Nouvel Observateur*.
81   Blum, Killing Hope, p. 342.
82   Ibid., p. 341; M. Urban, *War in Afghanistan* (London: Macmillan, 1988), p. 56.
83   See D. Crist, *The Twilight War: The Secret History of America's Thirty-Year Conflict with Iran* (London: Penguin, 2013). The plan was drafted by Undersecretary for Defense Robert Komer.
84   R. Gate, *From the Shadows* (New York: Simon & Schuster, 1996), pp. 130–135; Blum, *Killing Hope*, p. 344. Blum citing *Wall Street Journal*, 7 January 1980 (no longer available).
85   Dreyfuss, *Devil's Game*, p. 247.
86   Ibid., p. 248. Citing interviews with James Akins in November 2002 and an unnamed former CIA official in May 2004.
87   Blum, *Killing Hope*, pp. 345–6; Johnson, *Dismantling the Empire*, p. 128.
88   *Washington Post*, 'Anatomy of a Victory: CIA's Covert Afghan War', 19 July 1992.
89   Dreyfuss, *Devil's Game*, p. 254. Citing Z. Khalilzad, 'The return of the great game', California Seminar on International Security and Foreign Policy Discussion Paper, No. 88, 1980.
90   Johnson, *Dismantling the Empire*, p. 128.
91   Dreyfuss, *Devil's Game*, p. 2.
92   The census was undertaken in 1970. *New York Times*, 'Soviet 1970 Census Shows Unexpected 5 percent Decline in Those Listing Themselves as Jews', 17 April 1971.
93   Dreyfuss, *Devil's Game*, pp. 123–4. Referring to Donald Wilber, a CIA agent who had also played a key role in the 1953 Iran coup.
94   Most famously Pipes was appointed to head 'Team B' in the 1970s to study Soviet threats to the US and to offer a counterpoint to the CIA's views. Pipes later published his own account of Team B. See R. Pipes, 'Team B: The Reality Behind the Myth', *Commentary Magazine*, Vol. 82, No. 4, 1986. For background also see R. Pipes, 'Muslims of Soviet Central Asia: Trends and Prospects – part 2', *Middle East Journal*, summer 1955, pp. 307–308.
95   See A. Bennigsen, *Islam in the Soviet Union* (London: Pall Mall, 1967). A sequel, co-authored by his daughter, was published in 1983, A. Bennigsen, M. Broxup, *The Islamic Threat to the Soviet State* (London: Palgrave, 1983), pp. 70–75.
96   N. J. Citino, *From Arab Nationalism to OPEC: Eisenhower, King Saudi, and the Making of US–Saudi Relations* (Bloomington: Indiana University Press, 2002), pp. 94–8.

97 Margaret Thatcher Speech Archive, 'Margaret Thatcher Speech to the Foreign Policy Association on The West in the World Today', 18 December 1979.

98 Margaret Thatcher Speech Archive, 'Margaret Thatcher Speech at refugee camp on Pakistan's Afghan border', 8 October 1981.

99 Hansard, 'East–West Relations', 28 January 1980.

100 D. Cordovez, S. Harrison, *Out of Afghanistan: The Inside Story of the Soviet Withdrawal* (New York: Oxford University Press, 1995), p. 164.

101 Dreyfuss, *Devil's Game*, p. 288. Quoting Stephen Cohen.

102 J. Philips, 'Winning the Endgame in Afghanistan', *Heritage Foundation Backgrounder*, No. 181, 18 May 1992. In a twist of history he eventually led the same 'Northern Alliance' against the Taliban which was supported by the US during its 2001 invasion.

103 P. Bergen, *Holy War, Inc.* (New York: Free Press, 2001), p. 68; T. Weiner, *Blank Check: The Pentagon's Black Budget* (New York: Warner, 1990), pp. 149–51.

104 Curtis, *Secret Affairs*, p. 146; G. Crile, *Charlie Wilson's War: The Extraordinary Story of How the Wildest Man in Congress and a Rogue CIA Agent Changed the History of Our Times* (New York: Grove, 2007), pp. 210–22.

105 Dreyfuss, *Devil's Game*, p. 268.

106 Blum, *Killing Hope*, p. 341.

107 *New York Times*, 'Space Shuttle's Flight Dedicated to Afghans', 10 March 1982; *Atlantic*, 'The Gold Standard: The quest for the Holy Grail of Equivalence', 1 January 2002.

108 Curtis, *Secret Affairs*, p. 336. Citing *Guardian*, 5 March 1986 (no longer available).

109 *New York Times*, 'Supreme Court Dismisses Bhutto Appeal', 24 March 1979.

110 Curtis, *Secret Affairs*, p. 152; J. P. Filiu, *The Arab Revolution: Ten Lessons from the Democratic Uprising* (London: Hurst, 2011), p. 9; S. Wolpert, *Zulfi Bhutto of Pakistan* (Oxford: Oxford University Press, 1993).

111 T. J. Lynch *et al.*, *The Oxford Encyclopedia of American Military and Diplomatic History* (Oxford: Oxford University Press, 2013), p. 219; H. A. Rizvi, 'Pakistan's Foreign Policy: an Overview 1974–2004', PILDAT briefing paper for Pakistan's parliament, 2004, pp. 19–20.

112 Bergen, *Holy War*, p. 68.

113 Dreyfuss, *Devil's Game*, p. 275.

114 Bergen, *Holy War*, p. 66; *New Republic*, 'TRB from Washington, Back to Front', 8 October 2001.

115 *Washington Post*, 'Anatomy of a Victory: CIA's Covert Afghan War', 19 July 1992.

116 Bergen, *Holy War*, p. 68; *Washington Post*, 'Anatomy of a Victory: CIA's Covert Afghan War', 19 July 1992.

117 *Washington Post*, 'Anatomy of a Victory: CIA's Covert Afghan War', 19 July 1992.

118 Dreyfuss, *Devil's Game*, p. 277.

119 *Washington Post*, 'Anatomy of a Victory: CIA's Covert Afghan War', 19 July 1992.

120   S. Hall, S. Neale, *Epics, Spectacles, and Blockbusters: A Hollywood History* (Detroit: Wayne State University Press, 2010), pp. 239–40.

121   IMDB, 'Synopsis: Rambo III', 12 January 2015.

122   *Washington Post*, 'Anatomy of a Victory: CIA's Covert Afghan War', 19 July 1992; Curtis, *Secret Affairs*, p. 139.

123   Curtis, *Web of Deceit*, pp. 64–5. Citing SAS veteran Tom Carew.

124   Blum, *Killing Hope*, p. 351. Citing *New York Times*, 18 June 1986; *Los Angeles Times* 22 August 1993 (no longer available).

125   Curtis, *Secret Affairs*, p. 132; Hansard, 'East–West Relations', 28 January 1980.

126   Curtis, *Secret Affairs*, p. 143.

127   Ibid., p. 120, 141, 143; Curtis, *Web of Deceit*, pp. 62–3; A. Kemp, *The SAS: Savage Wars of Peace: 1947 to the Present* (London: John Murray, 1994), p. 201; Centre for Public Integrity, 'Making a Killing', 8 September 2009.

128   *Guardian*, 'Blowback Chronicles', 15 September 2001.

129   Hansard, 'Tim Sainsbury', 15 December 1988; Hansard, 'Tim Sainsbury', 4 April 1989.

130   Hansard, 'Margaret Thatcher, Saladin Security and Keenie Meenie Services', 1 December 1987.

131   BBC Online, 'Scots link to US terror suspect', 16 September 2001; Curtis, *Secret Affairs*, p. 143.

132   Crile, *Charlie Wilson's War*, p. 201; Curtis, *Secret Affairs*, p. 168. Quoting Gust Avrakotos.

133   Jamestown Foundation, 'From Mujahid to Activist: An Interview with a Libyan Veteran of the Afghan Jihad', *Spotlight on Terror*, Vol. 3, No. 2, 2005. Quoting Noman Benotman, an eventual member of the Libyan Islamic Fighting Group.

134   Blum, *Killing Hope*, p. 344; Curtis, *Secret Affairs*, p. 143.

135   Blum, *Killing Hope*, p. 350. Citing *San Francisco Chronicle*, 16 September 1985 (no longer available). Also see J. Roelofs, *Foundations and Public Policy: The Mask of Pluralism* (New York: State University Press, 2003), p. 167.

136   Blum, *Killing Hope*, p. 349.

137   C. Davis, 'A is for Allah, J is for Jihad', *World Policy Journal*, Vol. 19, No. 1, 2002; Middle East Eye, 'Islamic State is the cancer of modern capitalism', 27 March 2015.

138   After revelations of CIA funding, the Asia Foundation severed its links in 1966. See Dreyfuss, *Devil's Game*, pp. 257–8.

139   Ibid., p. 259.

140   R. Wirsing, *Pakistan's Security Under Zia, 1977–1988* (London: Palgrave Macmillan, 1991), p. 60.

141   Dreyfuss, *Devil's Game*, p. 278.

142   *Socialist Worker*, 'Saudi Arabia's get-out-of-terror-free card', 24 February 2015.

143   Dreyfuss, *Devil's Game*, pp. 279–80. Citing former CIA director Robert Gates.

144 M. Hamid, L. Farrall, *The Arabs at War in Afghanistan* (London: Hurst, 2015), p. 36; Blum, *Killing Hope*, p. 350. Citing *Daily Telegraph*, 5 August 1985 (no longer available).

145 Author interviews with Michael Springmann, February 2016.

146 Dreyfuss, *Devil's Game*, p. 275.

147 Blum, *Killing Hope*, p. 341. Citing *Washington Post*, 11 May 1979; *New York Times*, 13 April 1979 (no longer available).

148 Ibid., p. 341. With reference to Soviet prisoners, citing *Washington Post*, 13 January 1985 (no longer available).

149 Ibid., p. 341. Citing *Los Angeles Times*, 30 April 1990 (no longer available).

150 Hamid, *The Arabs at War*, pp. 294–5.

151 S. Coll, *Ghost Wars* (New York: Penguin, 2004), pp. 132–4.

152 Turki bin Faisal had taken over the post in 1979 from his uncle Kamal Adham. Congressional Research Service, 'Saudi Arabia: Background and US Relations', January 2010, p. 27.

153 Crile, *Charlie Wilson's War*, p. 519; *Washington Post*, 'Anatomy of a Victory: CIA's Covert Afghan War', 19 July 1992; *New York Times*, 'Prince Turki's Resumé', 2 August 2005; Curtis, *Secret Affairs*, p. 138.

154 The definitive account of the Grand Mosque seizure is T. Hegghammer, S. Lacroix, *The Meccan Rebellion: The Story of Juhayman al-Utaybi Revisited* (Beirut: Amal, 2011).

155 Atwan, *Islamic State*, p. 207. For a fuller discussion see S. Lacroix, *Awakening Islam: The Politics of Religious Dissent in Contemporary Saudi Arabia* (Cambridge, Mass: Harvard University Press, 2011).

156 For a discussion of the Abu Dhabi role in BCCI see C. M. Davidson, *Dubai: The Vulnerability of Success* (New York: Columbia University Press, 2008), pp. 246–9; Dreyfuss, *Devil's Game*, p. 167.

157 Senate Committee on Foreign Relations, 'The BCCI Affair: A Report by Senator John Kerry and Senator Hank Brown', December 1992, executive summary sections 1, 7.

158 D. E. Kaplan *et al.*, 'The Saudi Connection', *US News & World Report*, Vol. 135, No. 21, 2003.

159 Ibid.

160 CBS News, 'Al-Qaeda Skimming Charity Money', 7 June 2004. For a broader but more sanitized history of Al-Haramain see Y. Bokhari *et al.*, 'A Good Day to Bury a Bad Charity: Charting the Rise and Fall of the Al-Haramain Islamic Foundation', in *Gulf Charities and Islamic Philanthropy in the Age of Terror and Beyond*, eds. R. Lacey, J. Benthall (Berlin: Gerlach, 2014).

161 Arab News, 'Al-Haramain charity founder cleared of all charges', 2 December 2014.

162 Margaret Thatcher Speeches Archive, 'Margaret Thatcher Speech at refugee camp on Pakistan's Afghan border', 8 October 1981.

163 Kaplan, 'The Saudi Connection'; European Parliament, 'The Involvement of Salafism/Wahhabism in the support and supply of arms to rebel groups around the world', Directorate-General for External Policies, June 2013, p. 5. The IIRO's Canadian head testified in a 1999 court case that 'the Muslim World League, which is the mother of IIRO, is a fully government-funded organization ... in other words, I work for the government of Saudi Arabia.'

164 Abdullah al-Turki was the secretary general.

165 European Parliament, 'The Involvement of Salafism/Wahhabism', p. 9.

166 Ibid., pp. 18–19. *Christian Science Monitor*, 'Morocco struggles to tamp down radical Islam', 15 December 2003.

167 Dreyfuss, *Devil's Game*, p. 280. Citing Muhammad Yousef.

168 R. Bronson, *Thicker Than Oil: America's Uneasy Partnership with Saudi Arabia* (New York: Oxford University Press, 2006), pp. 170, 174.

169 R. Paz, 'The Saudi Fatwa against Suicide terrorism', The Washington Institute Policy Analysis, No. 323, 2 May 2001.

170 D. Weinberg, 'King Salman's Shady History', *Foreign Policy*, 27 January 2015.

171 Ibid.

172 Kaplan, 'The Saudi Connection'.

173 Dreyfuss, *Devil's Game*, p. 131. Quoting Ray Close.

174 Hamid, *The Arabs at War*, p. 259.

175 Bronson, *Thicker Than Oil*, p. 174; Curtis, *Secret Affairs*, p. 140.

176 Dreyfuss, *Devil's Game*, p. 279; B. Riedel, 'The 9/11 Attacks' Spiritual Father', Brookings Institute, 11 September 2011; Middle East Eye, 'Islamic State is the cancer of modern capitalism', 27 March 2015.

177 Berger, *ISIS*, p. 273; M. Weiss, H. Hassan, *ISIS: Inside the Army of Terror* (New York: Regan, 2015), p. 12.

178 Hamid, *The Arabs at War*, pp. 271, 319; Berger, *ISIS*, p. 277.

179 Curtis, *Secret Affairs*, p. 138.

180 National Commission on Terrorist Attacks Upon the United States, 'Monograph on Terrorist Financing – Staff Report to the Commission, 2004', p. 91; Weiss, *ISIS*, p. 12.

181 M. Scheuer, *Through our Enemies' Eyes* (Washington DC: Brassey's, 2002), pp. 40–41; European Parliament, 'The Involvement of Salafism/Wahhabism', p. 5.

182 Hamid, *The Arabs at War*, pp. 2, 27, 30.

183 Ibid. p. 296.

184 Dreyfuss, *Devil's Game*, pp. 279–80. Citing Robert Gates.

185 Al-Faruq training camp. See *Vice*, 'What I learned about Al-Qaeda from analysing the Bin Laden Tapes', 28 September 2015.

186 Julaidan was the president of the Tucson Islamic Center from 1984 to 1986. *Arizona Star*, 'The 9/11 Connection', 24 July 2004; Kaplan, 'The Saudi Connection'.

187 *New York Times*, 'Robin Cook, Former British Foreign Secretary, Dies at 59', 7 August 2005; *Guardian*, 'The struggle against terrorism cannot be won by military means', 8 July 2005.

188 Curtis, *Secret Affairs*, p. 138, citing John Cooley.

189 Curtis, *Secret Affairs*, p. 141; Curtis, *Web of Deceit*, p. 61; *Guardian*, 'Bin Laden may flee in tunnels: underground escape routes funded by CIA', 18 September 2001.

190 Kaplan, 'The Saudi Connection'; *New York Times*, 'Archive: Evidence of Financial Links between Saudi Arabia and Al-Qaeda' (accessed 9 October 2015). A collection of documents including redacted Department of the Treasury reports and witness interview transcripts collected by lawyers representing the families of 9/11 victims.

191 Dreyfuss, *Devil's Game*, p. 4.

192 F. Halliday, *Iran: Dictatorship and Development* (New York: Penguin, 1979); J. Bill, 'Iran and the crisis of '78', *Foreign Affairs*, winter 1978/1979, pp. 340–41.

193 Dreyfuss, *Devil's Game*, pp. 215–17, 229.

194 Ibid., p. 295. Referring to Vladimir Kuzichkin who defected from his position as Tehran station chief in 1982.

195 H. Dabashi, *The Arab Spring: The End of Postcolonialism* (London: Zed, 2012), p. 40.

196 J. Ramsey, 'Being Green in Tehran', *Critical Muslim*, Vol. 1, No. 1, 2012, p. 124.

197 Dreyfuss, *Devil's Game*, p. 219. Citing George Lambrakis, a senior US embassy officer in Tehran.

198 Ibid., pp. 236–8.

199 Documents declassified in 2016 confirm that Carter administration officials had been suggesting to Brzezinski the possibility of brokering an alliance between junior Iranian military commanders and Khomeini. The documents also reveal that the US had established a secret channel of communications to Khomeini and had received assurances from him that Iran would continue to sell oil to the US and would not orientate itself towards the Soviet Union. BBC Online, 'Two weeks in January: America's secret engagement with Khomeini', 3 June 2016; R. Cottam, 'US and Soviet Responses', in *Neither East nor West*, eds. N. Keddie, M. Gasiorowski (New Haven: Yale University Press, 1990), p. 276.

200 Dreyfuss, *Devil's Game*, pp. 175, 300.

201 Curtis, *Secret Affairs*, pp. 124–5. Curtis details reports filed by British ambassador to Tehran Anthony Parsons, Prime Minister James Callaghan, Foreign Secretary David Owen, and Owen's statements made in Cabinet meetings.

202 Ibid., pp. 126–7.

203 *Telegraph*, 'How the BBC helped bring the Ayatollah to power', 22 June 2009; R. Bergman, *The Secret War with Iran* (London: Oneworld, 2013).

204 J. J. Trento, *Prelude to Terror: Edwin P. Wilson and the Legacy of America's Private Intelligence Network* (New York: Carroll and Graf, 2005), p. 209.

205 *Christian Science Monitor*, 'Argo helps Iran's dictatorship, harms democracy', 5 March 2013.

206 For a full discussion of the October Surprise, see B. Honegger, *October Surprise* (New York: Tudor, 1989).

207 *New York Times*, 'The Election Story of the Decade', 15 April 1991; Dreyfuss, *Devil's Game*, p. 294.

208 *New York Times*, 'Washington Talk: Briefing; CIA Secrets', 15 February 1988.

209 Curtis, *Secret Affairs*, pp. 163–4. Citing the affidavit made by the British arms trader Leslie Aspin relating to his contacts in 1984 with the CIA's William Casey. The assistance from Iran proved insufficient, with it later being ascertained that it was the Syrian government controlling the kidnappers.

210 Dreyfuss, *Devil's Game*, p. 293; *New York Times*, 'The Election Story of the Decade', 15 April 1991.

211 Curtis, *Secret Affairs*, p. 128. In April 1980 Thatcher informed parliament that 'about 28 or 30' were still being trained.

212 *Guardian*, 'Jailed go-between on UK–Iran arms deals is freed to keep MI6 secrets out of court', 6 February 1999.

213 Curtis, *Secret Affairs*, p. 161.

214 Ibid., p. 161; Curtis, *Web of Deceit*, p. 187.

215 Curtis, *Secret Affairs*, p. 161.

216 J. Bill, *The Eagle and the Lion* (New Haven, Yale University Press, 1988), pp. 272–3. The defecting KGB agent being Vladimir Kuzichkin; *The Times*, 'When Reagan first helped Khomeini', 21 November 1986.

217 Dreyfuss, *Devil's Game*, pp. 217, 224, 239; National Security Archive, 'The Iran–Contra Affair 20 Years On', 24 November 2006.

218 Atwan, *Islamic State*, p. 195.

219 Blum, *Killing Hope*, pp. 345, 350–51.

4. ALLIED TO JIHAD – USEFUL IDIOTS

1 C. Ganske, 'The Long War in the Middle East and Russian Oil', Discovery Institute, 3 August 2006.

2 M. Curtis, *Web of Deceit: Britain's Real Role in the World* (London: Vintage, 2003), p. 62; M. Curtis, *Secret Affairs: Britain's Collusion with Radical Islam* (London: Serpent's Tail, 2012), p. 16; Middle East Eye, 'Islamic State is the cancer of modern capitalism', 27 March 2015.

3 R. Dreyfuss, *Devil's Game: How the United States Helped Unleash Fundamentalist Islam* (New York: Metropolitan, 2006), p. 289; *Newsweek*, 'The Road to September 11', 1 October 2001.

4 Dreyfuss, *Devil's Game*, pp. 285–6. Quoting ISI agent Muhammad Youssef.

5   G. Crile, *Charlie Wilson's War: The Extraordinary Story of How the Wildest Man in Congress and a Rogue CIA Agent Changed the History of Our Times* (New York: Grove, 2007), p. 519; Curtis, *Web of Deceit*, p. 61.
6   M. Hamid, L. Farrall, *The Arabs at War in Afghanistan* (London: Hurst, 2015), pp. 153, 174, 188. For a full discussion of the Haqqani network see V. Brown, D. Rassler, *Fountainhead of Jihad: The Haqqani Network* (New York: Columbia University Press, 2013).
7   W. Blum, *Killing Hope: US Military and CIA Interventions Since World War II* (London: Zed, 2014), p. 351.
8   *New York Times*, 'Archive: Evidence of Financial Links between Saudi Arabia and Al-Qaeda' (accessed 9 October 2015). A collection of documents including redacted Department of the Treasury reports and witness interview transcripts collected by lawyers representing the families of 9/11 victims.
9   A. U. Jan, *Afghanistan: The Genesis of the Final Crusade* (London: Pragmatic, 2006), p. 164.
10   The Argentinian firm was Bridas. BBC Online, 'Taliban in Texas for talks on gas pipeline', 4 December 1997; N. Ahmed, 'America and the Taliban: From Co-operation to War', *Global Dialogue*, Vol. 4, No. 2, 2002; Curtis, *Web of Deceit*, p. 71.
11   Ahmed, 'America and the Taliban'.
12   Dreyfuss, *Devil's Game*, p. 327. Quoting Zalmay Khalilzad, who served as US ambassador to Afghanistan from 2003 to 2005.
13   Curtis, *Secret Affairs*, pp. 143–4. Referring to Ramatullah Safi of the National Islamic Front of Afghanistan.
14   Ibid., p. 146.
15   Dreyfuss, *Devil's Game*, p. 246.
16   Ahmed, 'America and the Taliban'.
17   *Vice*, 'What I learned about Al-Qaeda from analysing the Bin Laden Tapes', 28 September 2015. For a fuller discussion see F. Miller, *The Audacious Aesthetic* (London: Hurst, 2015).
18   *New York Times*, 'Saudis Strip Citizenship from Backer of Militants', 10 April 1994.
19   Middle East Eye, 'Islamic State is the cancer of modern capitalism', 27 March 2015; Curtis, *Secret Affairs*, pp. 174, 177, 180.
20   *Independent*, 'Anti-Soviet warrior puts his army on the road to peace', 6 December 1993.
21   European Parliament, 'The Involvement of Salafism/Wahhabism in the support and supply of arms to rebel groups around the world', Directorate-General for External Policies, June 2013, p. 2.
22   Margaret Thatcher Speech Archives, 'Margaret Thatcher Speech to Chatham House Conference on Saudi Arabia', 4 October 1993.
23   Curtis, *Secret Affairs*, p. 177. Citing US District Court, Southern District of New York, Complaint 4, Civ. 5970, Paragraph 254. The meeting took place at

the Royal Monceau Hotel. Also see *Vanity Fair*, 'The Kingdom and the Towers', 30 June 2011.

24   European Parliament, 'The Involvement of Salafism/Wahhabism', p. 5.

25   *New York Times*, 'Scrutinizing the Saudi Connection', 27 July 2004.

26   A. B. Atwan, *Islamic State: The Digital Caliphate* (London: Saqi, 2015), p. 209.

27   The 1996 *fatwa*, referred to as the 'Ladenese epistle', was published by the London-based *Al-Quds al-Arabi* newspaper. A full transcript in English was published by PBS. See PBS 'Newshour: Bin Laden's Fatwa', 23 August 1996.

28   *Vanity Fair*, 'The Kingdom and the Towers', 30 June 2011.

29   European Parliament, 'The Involvement of Salafism/Wahhabism', p. 6.

30   The report dates from 1993. Cited by S. Dorril, *MI6: Fifty Years of Special Operations* (London: Fourth Estate, 2001), pp. 770–71; Curtis, *Secret Affairs*, pp. 172–3.

31   Hamid, *The Arabs at War*, p. 195; *Guardian*, 'Bin Laden terror network active in 34 countries', 14 September 2001.

32   US District Court, Southern District of New York, 'US vs Osama bin Laden', indictment S(9) 98 Cr. 1023, 1998.

33   Curtis, *Secret Affairs*, p. 185.

34   Agence France-Presse, 'Bin Laden considered seeking asylum in Britain', 29 September 2005.

35   Atwan, *Islamic State*, p. 196.

36   Curtis, *Web of Deceit*, pp. 66, 153, 155; Blum, *Killing Hope*, p. 388; S. Burg, P. Shoup, *The War in Bosnia-Herzegovina: Ethnic Conflict and International Intervention* (London: Routledge, 2000), p. 56.

37   D. E. Kaplan *et al.*, 'The Saudi Connection', *US News & World Report*, Vol. 135, No. 21, 2003; Burg, *The War in Bosnia*, p. 56.

38   Curtis, *Web of Deceit*, pp. 96, 144. Citing Dorril, *MI6*.

39   R. Holbrooke, *To End a War* (New York: Modern Library, 1999), p. 327; Congressional Research Service, 'Bosnia and the European Union Military Force: Post-NATO Peacekeeping', 5 December 2006.

40   Referring to the 'Scorpions' paramilitary unit and the Bosnian Serb 'Army of Republika Srpska'. *Washington Post*, 'Srebrenica Video Vindicates Long Pursuit by Serb Activist', 25 June 2005.

41   BBC Online, 'UN court dismisses Croatia and Serbia genocide claims', 3 February 2015.

42   For a full discussion see F. Hartmann, *Le sang de la realpolitik: L'affaire Srebrenica* (Paris: Don Quichotte, 2015); *Guardian*, 'Revealed: the role of the West in the run-up to Srebrenica's fall', 4 July 2015.

43   BBC Online, 'Allies and Lies', 22 June 2001.

44   Curtis, *Secret Affairs*, p. 209.

45   BBC Online, 'Allies and Lies', 22 June 2001.

46   E. F. Kohlmann, *Al-Qaeda's Jihad in Europe* (London: Bloomsbury, 2004), pp. 70–75.

47   Curtis, *Secret Affairs*, p. 212.

48   PTC (Radio & Television Serbia), 'Serbians in Chicago suing a US company because of the Storm', 20 August 2010. In 2014 the lawsuit was dropped following the judge's ruling that crimes committed in the Balkans were beyond his jurisdiction, despite the claimants' assertion that a substantial portion of the company's activities took place in Virginia. See PTC (Radio & Television Serbia), 'US federal court dismissed the lawsuit of the Serbs because of the military operation Storm', 27 September 2014.

49   Curtis, *Secret Affairs*, p. 215. Citing Douglas Hogg's reply to parliament on 17 February 1994.

50   *Sunday Times*, 'The British Jackal', 21 April 2002. Referring to Omar Saeed Sheikh who was put on trial in Karachi in 2002 accused of involvement in the kidnapping and murder of US journalist Daniel Pearl.

51   Curtis, *Secret Affairs*, p. 214.

52   *The Times*, 'Abu Hamza video call to arms', 13 January 2006; BBC Online, 'BBC apology to Queen over Abu Hamza disclosure', 25 September 2012.

53   *Los Angeles Times*, 'Mujahedeen units: pact with devil', 15 October 2001; *Guardian*, 'America used Islamists to arm the Bosnian Muslims', 22 April 2002.

54   J. M. Berger, J. Stern, *ISIS: The State of Terror* (London: William Collins, 2015), p. 59; J. M. Berger, *Jihad Joe: Americans Who Go to War in the Name of Islam* (Washington DC: Potomac, 2011), see chapter on 'Project Bosnia: 1992–1995'.

55   Middle East Eye, 'Islamic State is the cancer of modern capitalism', 27 March 2015; BBC Online, 'Our World: Bosnia, Cradle of Modern Jihad?', 4 July 2015; Curtis, *Secret Affairs*, p. 206.

56   Abu Abdul-Aziz.

57   Curtis, *Secret Affairs*, p. 207; Globalsecurity, 'Khalid Sheikh Muhammad', 21 October 2008.

58   *New York Times*, 'Archive: Evidence of Financial Links between Saudi Arabia and Al-Qaeda' (accessed 9 October 2015).

59   Curtis, *Secret Affairs*, pp. 207, 218.

60   Reuters, 'Islamic Group Hits Croatia', 22 October 1995.

61   Aiman Deen.

62   Khalid al-Hajj.

63   BBC Online, 'Our World: Bosnia, Cradle of Modern Jihad?', 4 July 2015.

64   A reference to Operation Gucha Gora.

65   BBC Online, 'Our World: Bosnia, Cradle of Modern Jihad?', 4 July 2015.

66   The war ended following the Dayton Agreements of December 1995 signed by Serbia, Bosnia, Croatia, and the Western powers.

67   Curtis, *Secret Affairs*, pp. 238–9.

68   *Independent*, 'War in The Balkans: KLA engages in fierce fighting with Serb army', 12 April 1999.

69   BBC Online, 'UN says Albania stalling Serb human organs inquiry', 23 February 2010; 3News, 'EU to set up court for Kosovo crimes', 5 April 2014. In 2014 the EU announced it was due to begin a $170 million tribunal to try Kosovans involved in the organ trafficking trade in 1999.

70   Curtis, *Web of Deceit*, p. 21; Curtis, *Secret Affairs*, p. 238.

71   Middle East Eye, 'Islamic State is the cancer of modern capitalism', 27 March 2015.

72   *New York Times*, 'Bosnia Plans to Expel Arabs Who Fought in Its War', 2 August 2007.

73   *Los Angeles Times*, 'Mujahedeen units: pact with devil', 15 October 2001.

74   Curtis, *Secret Affairs*, pp. 240–41. Quoting Yossef Bodansky.

75   *Scotsman*, 'Bin Laden opens European terror base in Albania', 29 November 1998.

76   *Guardian*, 'Britain now faces its own blowback', 10 September 2005.

77   Curtis, *Secret Affairs*, p. 239.

78   Ibid., p. 241; *Independent*, 'War in the Balkans: KLA engages in fierce fighting with Serb army', 12 April 1999.

79   BBC Online, 'UK SAS on ground in Kosovo', 13 April 1999.

80   UN Security Council, 'Resolution 1160', 31 March 1998.

81   *Independent*, 'War in Europe: SAS teams fighting behind Serb lines', 16 May 1999.

82   Curtis, *Secret Affairs*, p. 240. Quoting Foreign Office minister Tony Lloyd.

83   *Independent*, 'War in Europe: SAS teams fighting behind Serb lines', 16 May 1999.

84   Curtis, *Secret Affairs*, pp. 242–3. Citing *Scotsman*, 29 August 1999 (no longer available). It was believed that German intelligence had also been providing weapons and training to the KLA.

85   Curtis, *Web of Deceit*, pp. 144–5. Citing the dossier compiled by Professor Michael Mandel.

86   Ibid., p. 384. Referring to Ramsay Clark who filed his complaint in July 1999.

87   Ibid., pp. 134–5, 151.

88   Human Rights Watch, 'Under Orders: War Crimes in Kosovo in 2001', section on 'Abuses by the KLA'.

89   Curtis, *Web of Deceit*, p. 149. Citing Jan Oberg.

90   Ibid., pp. 21, 135–7.

91   Foreign Affairs Committee, '1998–1999 Fourth Report', paragraphs 82–9 on 'Did the military campaign provoke a humanitarian catastrophe?'

92   Hansard, 'Kosovo quoting Robin Cook in reply to George Galloway', 10 May 1999.

93   Hansard, 'Kosovo quoting Robin Cook in reply to Andrew Rowe', 10 May 1999.

94   *New Statesman*, 'The New Statesman Interview – Robin Cook', 5 July 1999.

95   Curtis, *Web of Deceit*, p. 154. Quoting Baroness Symons speaking in November 2001.

96   Blum, *Killing Hope*, p. 389.

97   Today only about half of UN member states officially recognize Kosovo as a state.

98   Curtis, *Web of Deceit*, p. 208.

99   Curtis, *Secret Affairs*, p. 208; Adnkronos (Italy), 'Bosnia: Senior Al-Qaeda figure granted citizenship, says report', 7 April 2003.

100   Kaplan, 'The Saudi Connection'.

101   D. Weinberg, 'King Salman's Shady History', *Foreign Policy*, 27 January 2015; *New York Times*, 'Archive: Evidence of Financial Links between Saudi Arabia and Al-Qaeda' (accessed 9 October 2015).

102   Kohlmann, *Al-Qaeda's Jihad*, pp. 36–47; Curtis, *Secret Affairs*, pp. 208–9.

103   Weinberg, 'King Salman's Shady History'; *New York Times*, 'Archive: Evidence of Financial Links between Saudi Arabia and Al-Qaeda' (accessed 9 October 2015).

104   R. Gunaratna, *Inside Al-Qaeda: Global Network of Terror* (New York: Columbia University Press, 2002), p. 133.

105   *Koha* (Albania), 'Thirty Days of Detention for all Imams', 19 September 2014.

106   J. Esposito, *Unholy War: Terror in the name of Islam* (New York: Oxford University Press, 2002), p. 108.

107   Kaplan, 'The Saudi Connection'; Curtis, *Secret Affairs*, p. 177. The report was revealed by Kaplan in 2003.

108   Kaplan, 'The Saudi Connection'.

109   Kohlmann, *Al-Qaeda's Jihad*, pp. 36–47. Curtis, *Secret Affairs*, pp. 208–9.

110   J. P. Filiu, *From Deep State to Islamic State: The Arab Counter-Revolution and Its Jihadi Legacy* (London: Hurst, 2015), p. 38.

111   Curtis, *Secret Affairs*, p. 225.

112   Library of Congress, 'A Country Study: Libya', Federal Research Division, 2011. See section on 'Qadhafi and the Revolutionary Command Council'.

113   Blum, *Killing Hope*, p. 287.

114   *New York Times*, 'Target Gaddafi', 22 February 1987.

115   *New Statesman*, 'Tale of Anti-Reagan hit team was fraud', 16 August 1985.

116   *New York Times*, 'Four Guilty in Fatal 1986 Berlin Disco Bombing Linked to Libya', 14 November 2001.

117   Defense Media Network, 'Operation El-Dorado Canyon: Libya Under Air Attack in 1986', 7 April 2011.

118   J. Phinney, *Airpower versus Terrorism: Three Case Studies* (Maxwell Air Force Base: Research Department, 2003), pp. 20–21.

119   Defense Media Network, 'Operation El-Dorado Canyon: Libya Under Air Attack in 1986', 7 April 2011; *Times of Malta*, 'Libya thanks Malta for warning of US bombing', 21 January 2010; Monsters and Critics, 'Italy helped save Gaddafi by warning of US air raid', 30 October 2008.

120   *New York Times*, 'Four Guilty in Fatal 1986 Berlin Disco Bombing Linked to Libya', 14 November 2001.

121   Blum, *Killing Hope*, p. 285. Citing *Sunday Times*, 6 April 1986 (no longer available).

122   Blum, *Killing Hope*, p. 286. Citing *Guardian*, 13 October 1986; *Sunday Telegraph*, 12 October 1986 (no longer available).

123   PBS News, 'Interview: Ronald Noble, Secretary General of Interpol', 16 April 2003.

124 Terrorism Monitor, 'Libya and Al-Qaeda: A Complex Relationship', 24 March 2005.

125 Chirac's adviser was Jean-Charles Brisard. *Observer*, 'MI6 halted bid to arrest bin Laden', 10 November 2002.

126 Curtis, *Secret Affairs*, pp. 229–30. Al-Libi had trained al-Qaeda members in surveillance techniques in Nairobi.

127 Jamestown Foundation, 'From Mujahid to Activist: An Interview with a Libyan Veteran of the Afghan Jihad', *Spotlight on Terror*, Vol. 3, No. 2, 2005.

128 Curtis, *Secret Affairs*, pp. 229–30.

129 Ibid., pp. 229–30; GLORIA Center, 'The Libyan Islamic Fighting Group', *Global Research in International Affairs*, Vol. 3, No. 2, 2005.

130 Hamid, *The Arabs at War*, p. 300; *Daily Telegraph*, 'CIA used Manchester manual to justify water boarding', 28 October 2011; *Observer*, 'MI6 halted bid to arrest bin Laden', 10 November 2002.

131 Curtis, *Secret Affairs*, p. 230.

132 The leader of the assassination team, Abdal Muhaymeen, was reportedly a Libyan veteran of the Afghan campaign. Ibid., pp. 226–8; Dorril, *MI6*, pp. 793–4; *Daily Telegraph*, 'CIA used Manchester manual to justify water boarding', 28 October 2011; *Observer*, 'MI6 halted bid to arrest bin Laden', 10 November 2002.

133 Curtis, *Web of Deceit*, p. 98; BBC Online, 'Shayler: Cook misled over Gaddafi plot', 15 February 2000.

134 BBC Online, 'BBC screens Shayler interview', 8 August 1998.

135 BBC Online, 'Shayler: Cook misled over Gaddafi plot', 15 February 2000; *Independent*, 'Kill Gaddafi plot report posted on net', 13 February 2000.

136 Terrorism Monitor, 'Libya and Al-Qaeda: A Complex Relationship', 24 March 2005; Terrorism Monitor, 'LIFG: An Organization in Eclipse', 3 November 2005; *Daily Telegraph*, 'CIA used Manchester manual to justify water boarding', 28 October 2011; *Observer*, 'MI6 halted bid to arrest bin Laden', 10 November 2002.

137 Terrorism Monitor, 'LIFG: An Organization in Eclipse', 3 November 2005; Curtis, *Secret Affairs*, p. 225. Citing the findings of a 2005 Home Office Special Immigration Appeals Commission.

138 J. Brownlee, T. Masoud, A. Reynolds (eds), *The Arab Spring: Pathways of Repression and Reform* (New York: Oxford University Press, 2015), p. 157.

139 L. Wright, *Looming Tower* (New York: Knopf, 2006), pp. 175–8; *Los Angeles Times*, 'Al-Qaeda operative key to 1998 US embassy bombings killed in Somalia', 12 June 2011.

140 CNN, 'US missiles pound targets in Afghanistan, Sudan', 21 August 1998.

141 *New York Times*, 'To Bomb Sudan Plant, or Not: A Year Later, Debates Rankle', 27 October 1999; *New York Times*, 'Look at the Place! Sudan Says, "Say Sorry," but U.S. Won't', 20 October 2005.

142 Wright, *Looming Tower*, pp. 284–5.

143 *Washington Times*, 'Inside The Ring: Missing bin Laden', 18 September 2008; D. Temple-Raston, *The Jihad Next Door: The Lackawanna Six and Rough Justice in an Age of Terror* (New York: Perseus Books, 2007), pp. 119–21.

144 S. Coll, *Ghost Wars* (New York: Penguin, 2004), pp. 410–11.

145 Kaplan, 'The Saudi Connection'.

146 *Washington Post*, 'Planned January 2000 Attacks Failed or Were Thwarted; Plot Targeted US, Jordan, American Warship, Official Says', 24 December 2000.

147 US Court of Appeals for the Ninth Circuit, 'US vs Ressam', 3 February 2010.

148 BBC Online, 'Suicide bombers attack USS Cole', 12 October 2000; *New York Times*, 'Judge Finds Sudan Is Liable in Cole Case', 15 March 2007; BBC Online, 'Sudan 'must pay USS Cole victims', 25 July 2007.

149 CNN, 'Accused 9/11 plotter Khalid Sheikh Mohammed faces New York trial', 13 November 2009; CNN, 'First video of Pentagon 9/11 attack released', 16 May 2006; *Washington Post*, 'Nine Facts about Terrorism in the United States since 9/11', 11 September 2013; *Newsday*, '9/11 Memorial Honors Unborn Babies', 11 September 2011.

150 9/11 Commission, 'National Commission on Terrorist Attacks Upon the United States', 22 July 2004.

151 According to the CIA's testimony to the Joint Inquiry into Terrorist Attacks against the United States which took place on 18 June 2002. Also see Atwan, *Islamic State*, p. 208.

152 Kaplan, 'The Saudi Connection'.

153 CNN, 'GPS Show: Former ambassador to Saudi Arabia on King Salman', 31 July 2015.

154 *Vanity Fair*, The Kingdom and the Towers, 30 June 2011.

155 *New York Times*, 'Scrutinizing the Saudi Connection', 27 July 2004; *Vanity Fair*, 'The Kingdom and the Towers', 30 June 2011.

156 *Vanity Fair*, 'The Kingdom and the Towers', 30 June 2011.

157 See 9/11 Commission, 'National Commission', pp. 339–53; *New York Times*, '9/11 Congressional Report Faults FBI-CIA Lapses', 24 July 2003.

158 See M. Springmann, *Visas for Al-Qaeda: CIA Handouts that Rocked the World* (New York: Daena, 2015).

159 Author interviews with Michael Springmann, February 2016.

160 *National Review*, 'Open Door for Saudi Terrorists: The Visa Express Scandal', 1 July 2002; ABC, 'State Department Lapses Aided 9/11 Hijackers', 2 July 2002.

161 *Vanity Fair*, 'The Kingdom and the Towers', 30 June 2011.

162 In September 2015 the US court restored Saudi Arabia's sovereign immunity once again, but fresh appeals are expected on the basis that 'evidence central to these claims continues to be treated as classified.' See BBC Online, 'US judge clears Saudi Arabia in 9/11 lawsuit', 30 September 2015; Associated Press, 'Judge drops Saudi Arabia from September 11 lawsuit', 29 September 2015.

163 New York Southern District Court, 'Terrorist Attacks on September 11, 2001', Document 2892, 15 September 2014.

164 *Guardian*, 'Rand Paul leads bipartisan effort to declassify 28 pages of 9/11 report', 2 June 2015.

165 *New Yorker*, 'The Twenty-Eight Pages', 29 September 2014.

166 US Congress, 'H.Res.14 – Urging the president to release information regarding the September 11, 2001, terrorist attacks upon the United States', 114th Congress 2015–2016.

167 US Congress, 'The FBI: Protecting the Homeland in the 21st Century', March 2015, pp. 101–102; 9/11 Commission, 'Memorandum for the Record: MFR04019362', 23 February 2004; Interagency Security Classification Appeals Panel, 'ISCAP Appeal No. 2012-048, Document No. 12', 8 July 2015 (declassified), pp. 1–3, 10, 43, 45–6.

168 *New York Times*, 'Florida Ex-Senator Pursues Claims of Saudi Ties to September 11 Attacks', 13 April 2015; *New York Post*, 'How the FBI is whitewashing the Saudi connection to 9/11', 12 April 2015; *New York Times*, 'Scrutinizing the Saudi Connection', 27 July 2004; *Miami Herald*, 'FBI found direct ties between 9/11 hijackers and Saudis living in Florida; Congress kept in dark', 8 September 2011. To a great extent the new FBI information confirms a claim made by two Irish journalists in 2011 that phone records from the house had been handed over to the FBI along with visitor logs from the gated community's entrance. According to the journalists' anonymous source, a 'counter-terrorism official', these logs showed that hijackers had been making telephone calls to the house and two of them had visited the house in person. See Daily Beast, 'The FBI is keeping 80,000 Secret Files on the Saudis and 9/11', 12 May 2016.

169 The captive being Abu Zubaydah. *New York Times*, 'Scrutinizing the Saudi Connection', 27 July 2004; *Vanity Fair*, 'The Kingdom and the Towers', 30 June 2011.

170 *New York Times*, 'Prince Ahmed bin Salman, Top Horse Owner, Dies at 43', 23 July 2002.

171 *Vanity Fair*, 'The Kingdom and the Towers', 30 June 2011.

172 WND, '9/11: 3,000 Americans for 3 Saudi princes', 9 October 2011. An extensive report by Walid Shoebat based exclusively on Arabic sources.

173 *Washington Post*, 'Screws put on Saudi to tackle al-Qaeda financiers', 27 November 2002.

174 *Washington Post*, 'Report Decries Saudi Laxity', 17 October 2002.

175 Weinberg, 'King Salman's Shady History'.

176 Kaplan, 'The Saudi Connection'.

177 NPR, 'Guantanamo Document: Matrix of Threat Indicators', 27 April 2011.

178 New York Southern District Court, 'Terrorist Attacks on September 11, 2001', Document 2892, 15 September 2014.

179 BBC Online, 'US judge clears Saudi Arabia in 9/11 lawsuit', 30 September 2015.

180 Curtis, *Secret Affairs*, p. 313.

181 L. K. Donohue, *The Cost of Counterterrorism: Power, Politics, and Liberty* (Cambridge: Cambridge University Press, 2008), p. 155; Congressional Research Service, 'Saudi Arabia: Terrorist Financing Issues', 14 September 2007, pp. 4–5. Referring to Adel al-Jubeir.

182 Kaplan, 'The Saudi Connection'. Quoting Adel al-Jubeir.

183 Associated Press, 'Saudis Reportedly Funding Iraqi Sunnis', 8 December 2006.

184 *New Yorker*, 'The Redirection', 5 March 2007.

185 Congressional Research Service, 'Saudi Arabia: Terrorist Financing Issues', 14 September 2007, p. 2.

186 *Los Angeles Times*, 'Saudis faulted for funding terror', 2 April 2008.

187 Department of State, 'Scene-setter for Secretary of Defense Gate's May 5–6 2009 visit to Saudi Arabia 09Riyadh612_a', 26 April 2009 (leaked). Notably in this cable the US embassy also copied in the GCC secretariat.

188 Department of State, 'Subject: Terrorist finance: action request for senior 131801', 30 December 2009 (leaked).

189 *New Yorker*, 'The Redirection', 5 March 2007.

190 *Independent*, 'Saudi Arabia is biggest funder of terrorists', 6 December 2010.

191 Atwan, *Islamic State*, pp. 211–12.

192 European Parliament, 'The Involvement of Salafism/Wahhabism', pp. 5, 30.

193 Abdullah Salih al-Ajmi. See The Long War Journal, 'US questioned Kuwait's ability to deal with Guantanamo detainee for good reason', 9 January 2016.

194 Department of State, 'Subject: Terrorist finance: action request for senior 131801', 30 December 2009 (leaked).

195 Ibid.

196 Department of State, 'Extremist recruitment on the rise in southern Punjab 08LAHORE302_a', 13 November 2008 (leaked).

197 *Financial Times*, 'Gas Status Puts Country at Centre of Global Forces', 17 December 2011.

198 For a good discussion see M. Yamani, 'From fragility to stability: a survival strategy for the Saudi monarchy', *Contemporary Arab Affairs*, Vol. 2, No. 1, 2009.

199 Elizabeth Dickinson, 'The Case Against Qatar', *Foreign Policy*, 30 September 2014.

200 *The Hill*, 'Qatar's not-so-charitable record on terror finance', 24 September 2014.

201 *National Geographic*, 'Qatar: Revolution from the Top Down', March 2003.

202 *The Hill*, 'Qatar's not-so-charitable record on terror finance', 24 September 2014.

203 K. Ulrichsen, *Qatar and the Arab Spring* (London: Hurst, 2014), p. 49.

204 Department of State, 'Subject: Terrorist finance: action request for senior 131801', 30 December 2009 (leaked).

NOTES

205 Ulrichsen, *Qatar*, p. 40; ABC, 'Giuliani's ties to Qatar raise questions for Mr. 9/11', 29 November 2007. The escape of Khalid Sheikh Muhammad from Qatar, where he was an employee, seems to have taken place in 1996.

206 W. Clark, *Don't Wait for the Next War* (New York: Public Affairs, 2014), pp. 37–40.

207 *Inter Press Service*, 'US Taliban Policy Influenced by Oil', 16 November 2001; Ahmed, 'America and the Taliban'.

208 Curtis, *Web of Deceit*, pp. 70–71.

209 Ibid., p. 72. Citing a variety of reports from the *Daily Telegraph* and the *Guardian* in October 2001.

210 Ibid., p. 80.

211 Al-Jazeera, 'Headliner: Former Afghan President Hamid Karzai', 12 November 2015.

212 Curtis, *Secret Affairs*, pp. 338–9; *Dawn* (Pakistan), 'UK holds indirect talks with Taliban', 14 June 2004. Both citing the little-known meeting in 2004 between British foreign secretary Jack Straw and the Taliban-aligned cleric Maulana Fazlur Rahman.

213 Curtis, *Secret Affairs*, pp. 338–9.

214 Dickinson, 'The Case Against Qatar'. The Taliban's 'political office' was required to tone itself down soon after opening in Qatar as Karzai had objected to the plaque.

215 *New York Times*, 'Taliban opening Qatar office, and maybe door to talks', 3 January 2012.

216 Dickinson, 'The Case Against Qatar'; Berger, *ISIS*, p. 135.

217 *Express Tribune* (Pakistan), 'Afghan Taliban to open political office in UAE', 17 January 2015; Associated Press, 'Taliban reaffirms authority of its Qatar political office', 24 January 2016.

218 PBS, 'Newshour: Axis of Evil', 20 January 2002.

219 Y. Bodansky, V. S. Forrest, 'Tehran, Baghdad & Damascus: The New Axis Pact', House Republican Research Committee, 10 August 1992; BBC Online, 'US expands Axis of Evil', 6 May 2002; BBC Online, 'Outposts of Tyranny', 19 January 2005. Rice's list included Iran, North Korea, Cuba, Belarus, Burma, and Zimbabwe.

220 The 'finishing his father's work' explanation had wide traction across the region in 2002. See for example *Daily Telegraph*, 'Bush will finish his father's job, says Kurd leader', 16 August 2002. In late 2000 Iraq announced it was no longer going to sell its oil in dollars as this was 'the currency of the enemy'. See *Guardian*, 'Iraq nets handsome profit by dumping dollar for euro', 16 February 2003.

221 Department of Trade and Industry, 'Our Energy Future – Creating a Low Carbon Economy', Energy White Paper, February 2003, pp. 9, 83; Atwan, *Islamic State*, p. 44.

222 *Guardian*, 'The coup that wasn't', 28 September 2005; S. Ritter, *Iraq Confidential: The Untold Story of America's Intelligence Conspiracy* (London: I. B. Tauris, 2009).

223 Ritter, *Iraq Confidential*; Atwan, *Islamic State*, p. 198. Referring to the involvement of the Iraqi National Accord.

224 *Guardian*, 'The Propaganda War', 14 November 1998; *Guardian*, 'Propaganda drive against Iraq', 24 March 1999.

225 Atwan, *Islamic State*, p. 33; UN Security Council, 'Resolution 687', 3 April 1991.

226 *Guardian*, 'The Propaganda War', 14 November 1998; *Guardian*, 'Propaganda drive against Iraq', 24 March 1999.

227 Curtis, Web of Deceit, pp. 11–12.

228 Ritter, *Iraq Confidential*; Blum, *Killing Hope*, p. 391. Citing *Guardian*, 19 September 2002; *Washington Post*, 21 October 2002 (no longer available).

229 Curveball being Rafid Ahmed Alwan al-Janabi. *Guardian*, 'Colin Powell demands answers over Curveball's WMD lies', 16 February 2011.

230 Curtis, *Web of Deceit*, p. 19.

231 *Guardian*, 'Timeline: Dr David Kelly', 18 July 2003; A. Rawnsley, *The End of the Party* (London: Penguin, 2010), pp. 210–12.

232 *Guardian*, 'David Kelly postmortem reveals injuries were self-inflicted', 22 October 2010; N. Baker, *The Strange Death of David Kelly* (London: Methuen, 2007).

233 *Guardian*, 'Letters: David Kelly: 10 Years On', 15 July 2013; *Guardian*, 'Dr. David Kelly: 10 years on, death of scientist remains unsolved for some', 16 July 2013.

234 Cabinet Office, 'FOI Reference: FOI318026', letter addressed to Andrew Watt, 27 June 2013.

235 Curtis, *Web of Deceit*, p. 19; *The Age*, 'Saddam had no links to al-Qaeda', 10 September 2006. The report was prepared by Jonathan Weisman.

236 CBS News, 'George Tenet: At the Centre of the Storm', 25 April 2007.

237 *Independent*, 'Tony Blair Iraq war memo prompts fresh calls for Chilcot inquiry to be published', 18 October 2015.

238 Curtis, *Web of Deceit*, p. 26.

239 Curtis, *Secret Affairs*, p. 234. Citing Stratfor, 'Global Intelligence Update', 23 March 1999.

240 Curtis, *Web of Deceit*, pp. 25–6.

241 *Guardian*, 'US military builds up huge attack force', 13 September 2002.

242 Curtis, *Web of Deceit*, pp. 44–5.

5. THE ARAB SPRING – A SYSTEM THREATENED

1 As measured by the US-based independent watchdog Freedom House. Freedom House, 'Freedom in the World 2010: Methodology', 30 December 2010.

2 J. P. Filiu, *The Arab Revolution: Ten Lessons from the Democratic Uprising* (London: Hurst, 2011), p. 7.

3   B. Grofman, *Political Science as Puzzle Solving* (Ann Arbor: Michigan University Press, 2007), pp. 84–5; J. Brownlee, T. Masoud, A. Reynolds (eds), *The Arab Spring: Pathways of Repression and Reform* (New York: Oxford University Press, 2015), pp. 18–19.

4   R. Yassin-Kassab, 'Tahrir Square', *Critical Muslim*, Vol. 1, No. 1, 2012, p. 23.

5   J. Gunning, I. Z. Baron, *Why Occupy a Square?: People, Protests and Movements in the Egyptian Revolution* (New York: Oxford University Press, 2013), p. 306; A. al-Affendi, 'A Trans-Islamic Revolution?', *Critical Muslim*, Vol. 1, No. 1, 2012, p. 77.

6   Gunning, *Why Occupy a Square?*, p. 307.

7   Yassin-Kassab, 'Tahrir Square', p. 24; al-Affendi, 'A Trans-Islamic Revolution?', p. 77.

8   R. Abou-el-Fadl (ed.), *Revolutionary Egypt: Connecting Domestic and International Struggles* (London: Routledge, 2015); Gunning, *Why Occupy a Square?*, p. 305.

9   BBC Online, 'Syria sidesteps Lebanon demands', 6 March 2005; *Washington Post*, 'Syrian Intelligence Still in Lebanon', 27 April 2005. Although Syria withdrew its armed forces, Syrian intelligence officials were understood to have remained.

10   H. Dabashi, *The Arab Spring: The End of Postcolonialism* (London: Zed, 2012), pp. 28–9. The Iraqi journalist was Muntadhar al-Zaidi.

11   J. Ramsey, 'Being Green in Tehran', *Critical Muslim*, Vol. 1, No. 1, 2012, pp. 127–8. This poll was financed by the Rockefeller Brothers Foundation and carried out by Terror Free Tomorrow, the Center for Public Opinion, the New America Foundation, and KA Europe SPRL. With a margin of error of 3.1 percent it found that 34 percent would vote for Ahmadinejad, while only 14 percent would vote for Mir-Hossein Mousavi – the main opposition or 'green' candidate.

12   Citing a Chatham House study, Cole believed there was little that could properly explain the 'vast swing to Ahmadinejad'. Ramsey, 'Being Green in Tehran', pp. 128, 132–3. Quoting Karm Sadjadpour and Ervand Abrahamian.

13   Dabashi, *The Arab Spring*, p. 4.

14   Ramsey, 'Being Green in Tehran', p. 126.

15   Referring to the 1861 State Law of Tunisia.

16   Z. Sardar, 'Surprise, Surprise!', *Critical Muslim*, Vol. 1, No. 1, 2012, p. 4.

17   Filiu, *The Arab Revolution*, p. 20; BBC Online, 'Tunisia one year on: New trend of self-immolations', 12 January 2012.

18   Brownlee, *The Arab Spring*, p. 68.

19   Filiu, *The Arab Revolution*, p. 69; Brownlee, *The Arab Spring*, p. 206.

20   Brownlee, *The Arab Spring*, p. 68; Sardar, 'Surprise', p. 4; Filiu, *The Arab Revolution*, p. 79. The presidential guard was blamed for shooting thirty-one protestors on 14 January 2011 along with the murder of a Polish priest. They were also thought to be encouraging mob attacks and the desecration of synagogues.

21   *Washington Post*, 'The Resurgence of Arab Militaries', 5 December 2014.

22   This offer was made by Michèle Alliot-Marie, minister for foreign and European affairs who was only in post for four months. Brownlee, *The Arab Spring*, p. 70.

23   BBC Online, 'Tunisia: Ex-President Ben Ali flees to Saudi Arabia', 15 January 2011.

24   Brownlee, *The Arab Spring*, pp. 128–9, 131. The Democratic Constitutional Rally or *Rassemblement Constitutionnel Démocratique*.

25   Yassin-Kassab, 'Tahrir Square', p. 24.

26   One such self-immolation took place on 17 January 2011 but did not attract as much media attention as the movement behind Khalid Said. Dabashi, *The Arab Spring*, p. 18; BBC Online, 'Egypt: We are all Khalid Said', 17 February 2011.

27   Filiu, *The Arab Revolution*, p. 59; al-Affendi, 'A Trans-Islamic Revolution?', p. 65; J. P. Filiu, *From Deep State to Islamic State: The Arab Counter-Revolution and its Jihadi Legacy* (London: Hurst, 2015), p. 151.

28   F. Ajami, 'The Arab Spring at One: A Year of Living Dangerously', *Foreign Affairs*, March 2012.

29   Filiu, *From Deep State*, p. 151.

30   Department of State, 'Academics see the military in decline, but retaining strong influence 08CAIRO2091', 23 September 2008 (leaked).

31   Brownlee, *The Arab Spring*, p. 72; Gunning, *Why Occupy a Square?*, p. 164. Gunning and Baron provide a good collection of estimates which vary quite substantially, but all point to very high numbers compared to previous protests.

32   Ahmad Nazif was replaced by Lieutenant General Ahmed Shafik. Nazif was one of the first Mubarak-era officials to be charged with corruption, being sentenced to three years' imprisonment in September 2012. Former intelligence chief Omar Suleiman was appointed vice president. BBC Online, 'Egypt: Ex-PM Ahmad Nazif jailed for corruption', 13 September 2012; Reuters, 'Egypt's Mubarak picks vice-president for first time', 29 January 2011.

33   Filiu, *The Arab Revolution*, pp. 23, 25.

34   Alexander, 'Digital Generation', pp. 96–7; Filiu, *The Arab Revolution*, p. 100.

35   Filiu, *The Arab Revolution*, p. 40.

36   Al-Affendi, 'A Trans-Islamic Revolution?', p. 67.

37   Dabashi, *The Arab Spring*, pp. 200–201; Al-Jazeera, 'Visions Collide in a sweltering Tahrir Square', 30 July 2011.

38   Gunning, *Why Occupy a Square?*, pp. 1–2.

39   Dabashi, *The Arab Spring*, pp. 172–3; Daily News Egypt, 'Salafobia', 1 August 2011.

40   Filiu, *The Arab Revolution*, p. 61.

41   Filiu, *The Arab Revolution*, p. 70; Brownlee, *The Arab Spring*, p. 74; Dabashi, *The Arab Spring*, p. 195; Yassin-Kassab, 'Tahrir Square', p, 45.

42   Yassin-Kassab, 'Tahrir Square', pp. 21, 45.

43   Ibid., p. 21.

44   V. Langohr, 'Women's Rights Movements during political transitions: activism against public sexual violence in Egypt', *International Journal of Middle East Studies*, Vol. 47, No. 1, 2015, p. 134.

NOTES

45   Filiu, *The Arab Revolution*, pp. 80, 152; Yassin-Kassab, 'Tahrir Square', p. 20; Brownlee, *The Arab Spring*, p. 74.

46   Yassin-Kassab, 'Tahrir Square', p. 42.

47   Ibid., p. 41.

48   Having been de facto nationalized, Mubarak had the power to authorize all key appointments at Al-Azhar. Al-Affendi, 'A Trans-Islamic Revolution?', p. 74; Filiu, *The Arab Revolution*, p. 25.

49   Filiu, *The Arab Revolution*, p. 27.

50   Sardar, 'Surprise', p. 12; Yassin-Kassab, 'Tahrir Square', p. 19.

51   Dabashi, *The Arab Spring*, p. 97; Gunning, *Why Occupy a Square?*, p. 303.

52   H. Lefebvre, *The Production of Space* (London: Wiley, 1991), pp. 416–20. As Lefebvre argued, without a physical space such ideals would likely remain abstract.

53   Gunning, *Why Occupy a Square?*, p. 164; *New York Review of Books*, 'Hannah Arendt: Reflections on Violence', 27 February 1969.

54   J. Stacher, 'Egypt's Democratic Mirage', *Foreign Affairs*, February 2011; Filiu, *The Arab Revolution*, p. 80.

55   McClatchy, 'Text of Egyptian Military Commniqué Number 1', 12 February 2011; McClatchy, 'Text of Egyptian Military Communiqué Number 2', 12 February 2011; Yassin-Kassab, 'Tahrir Square', p. 28.

56   Habib al-Adly, who was oddly not charged with ordering the killing of protestors. Filiu, *From Deep State*, pp. 153, 155; Brownlee, *The Arab Spring*, p. 104.

57   Brownlee, *The Arab Spring*, p. 105. Referring to Ahmad Ezz.

58   *Guardian*, 'Mubarak put under house arrest', 28 March 2011.

59   Including *Taghir* or 'Change' Square. Brownlee, *The Arab Spring*, p. 76.

60   Ibid., p. 76; Filiu, *From Deep State*, p. 196.

61   S. P. Yadav, 'The Yemen model as a failure of political imagination', *International Journal of Middle East Studies*, Vol. 47, No. 1, 2015, pp. 144–5.

62   *New York Times*, 'In Yemen, a Brief Moment Before Women Were Pushed Aside Again', 7 June 2015.

63   Brownlee, *The Arab Spring*, p. 76.

64   The latter incident taking place on 29 May 2011. Reuters, 'Yemen president Saleh fights to keep grip on power', 4 June 2011; Filiu, *The Arab Revolution*, p. 82; Filiu, *From Deep State*, p. 193; Brownlee, *The Arab Spring*, p. 76.

65   Ajami, 'The Arab Spring at One'.

66   For example, Sadiq al-Ahmar. Brownlee, *The Arab Spring*, p. 149.

67   Ali Mohsen al-Ahmar, like Saleh, is a member of the Sanhan Hashid tribe. Filiu, *From Deep State*, p. 193; Brownlee, *The Arab Spring*, p. 77–8.

68   *Los Angeles Times*, 'Yemen: Deal outlined for President Ali Abdullah Saleh to leave within a month', 18 May 2011.

69   For a discussion of 'social death' see L. M. Cacho, *Social Death: Racialized Rightlessness and the Criminalization of the Unprotected* (New York: New York

University Press, 2012); M. LeVine, 'Theorizing Revolutionary Practice: Agendas for Research on the Arab Uprisings', *Middle East Critique*, Vol. 22, No. 3, 2013, p. 197. As historian Mark LeVine has argued, such a moment is often pivotal as 'from this perspective, the moment of revolutionary transformation – the famous breaking the wall of fear – begins precisely when citizens break free of the condition of exclusion, or social death, and assert direct, or potentially direct, political agency.'

70   F. Cavatorta, 'No Democratic Change… and Yet No Authoritarian Continuity: The Inter-paradigm Debate and North Africa After the Uprisings', *British Journal of Middle Eastern Studies*, Vol. 42, No. 1, 2015, p. 142.

71   Filiu, *The Arab Revolution*, p. 135.

72   Brownlee, *The Arab Spring*, p. 23; Gunning, *Why Occupy a Square?*, p. 7; T. Skocpol, *States and Social Revolutions: A Comparative Analysis of France, Russia and China* (Cambridge: Cambridge University Press, 1979), pp. 4–5.

73   Gunning, *Why Occupy a Square?*, p. 9. Quoting D. D. Porta, M. Diana, *Social Movements: An Introduction* (London: Wiley, 1998), p. 16.

74   C. Zirekzadeh, *Social Movements in Politics: A Comparative Study* (London: Palgrave, 2006), pp. 4–5.

75   Sardar, 'Surprise', p. 12.

76   Gunning, *Why Occupy a Square?*, pp. 2, 11.

77   Jadaliyya, 'Preliminary Historical Observations on the Arab Revolutions of 2011', 21 March 2011.

78   M. Kaldor, 'Civil Society in 1989 and 2011', OpenDemocracy, 7 February 2011.

79   Al-Jazeera, 'The Arab world's 1989 revolution?', 2 February 2011.

80   For a full discussion see S. Huntington, *The Third Wave: Democratization in the Late Twentieth Century* (Norman: Oklahoma University Press, 1991).

81   Al-Monitor, 'Arab World Enters Age of Sectarian Wars', 9 June 2013. Quoting Talal Salman.

82   S. Telhami, *The World Through Arab Eyes: Arab Public Opinion and the Reshaping of the Middle East* (New York: Basic Books, 2013), p. 18.

83   Jadaliyya, 'Preliminary Historical Observations on the Arab Revolutions of 2011', 21 March 2011; Dabashi, *The Arab Spring*, p. 127.

84   For a discussion in the context of Arab Spring, see L. J. Underwood, *Cosmopolitanism and the Arab Spring: Foundations for the Decline of Terrorism* (London: Peter Lang, 2012).

85   Dabashi, *The Arab Spring*, pp. 11, 115–16.

86   To some extent this was predicted by M. Valbjørn, A. Bank, 'Examining the Post in Post-democratization: The Future of Middle Eastern Political Rule through Lenses of the Past', *Middle East Critique*, Vol. 19, No. 3, 2010, pp. 183–200.

87   Dabashi, *The Arab Spring*, pp. 23, 128; Al-Jazeera, 'Bottom-up Revolution', 17 June 2011.

88   Ibid., p. 19; Ramsey, 'Being Green in Tehran', p. 126.
89   The protests were organized using a Facebook protest page and returned again in 2015. *Times of Israel*, 'As tents return to Tel Aviv, protesters hope second time's the charm', 2 March 2015.
90   *Der Spiegel*, 'Tahrir Square in Madrid: Spain's Lost Generation Finds Its Voice', 19 May 2011.
91   *Atlantic*, 'Occupy Wall Street and the Arab Spring', 7 October 2011.
92   Ramsey, 'Being Green in Tehran', p. 133.
93   A. Hanieh, 'Shifting Priorities or Business as Usual? Continuity and Change in the post-2011 IMF and World Bank Engagement with Tunisia, Morocco and Egypt', *British Journal of Middle Eastern Studies*, Vol. 42, No. 1, 2015, p. 122.
94   K. Korsch, 'The Fascist Counter-Revolution', *Living Marxism*, Vol. 5, No. 2, 1940.
95   Gunning, *Why Occupy a Square?*, p. 311.
96   *Washington Post*, 'Arab autocrats are not going back to the future', 4 December 2014.
97   R. Hinnebusch, 'Change and Continuity after the Arab Uprising: The Consequences of State Formation in Arab North African States', *British Journal of Middle Eastern Studies*, Vol. 42, No. 1, 2015, p. 15.
98   'Embedded liberalism' was later coined by US political scientist John Ruggie. See J. Ruggie, 'International Regimes, Transactions, and Change: Embedded Liberalism in the Postwar Economic Order', *International Organization*, Vol. 36, No. 2, 1982. For a good discussion of the post-Second World War conferences see B. Steil, *The Battle of Bretton Woods: John Maynard Keynes, Harry Dexter White, and the Making of a New World Order* (Princeton: Princeton University Press, 2014).
99   M. Dunford, 'Globalization and theories of regulation', in *Global Political Economy: Contemporary Theories*, ed. R. Palan (London: Routledge, 2000), p. 143.
100   S. Heydemann, 'Mass politics and the future of authoritarian governance in the Arab world', POMEPS Study 11, 2015, p. 16.
101   Hinnebusch, 'Change and Continuity', p. 16.
102   L. Trotsky, *The Revolution Betrayed* (London: Dover, 2004). See section on 'Program and Reality'.
103   *Washington Post*, 'Arab autocrats are not going back to the future', 4 December 2014.
104   The term was first used by John Williamson in 1989. See J. Williamson 'What Washington Means by Policy Reform' in *Latin American Readjustment: How Much has Happened*, ed. J. Williamson (Washington DC: Institute for International Economics, 1989).
105   Hinnebusch, 'Change and Continuity', p. 18; Hanieh, 'Shifting Priorities', p. 121.
106   World Bank, 'From Privilege to Competition: Unlocking Private-Led Growth in the Middle-East and North Africa', 3 March 2009.
107   World Bank, 'Trade, Investment, and Development in the Middle East and North Africa: Engaging with the World', 7 May 2003.
108   Hinnebusch, 'Change and Continuity', p. 21.

109   Ibid., pp. 18–19.

110   Ibid., p. 21; P. Moore, 'Fiscal politics of enduring authoritarianism', POMEPS Study 11, 2015, p. 25.

111   Filiu, *From Deep State*, pp. 89, 120–21, 131, 149.

112   K. Korsch, 'State and Counter-Revolution', *Modern Quarterly*, Vol. 11, No. 2, 1939, p. 2.

113   K. Kautsky, 'Imperialism and the War', *International Socialist Review*, Vol. 15, 1914.

114   For a good discussion of the 'semi colony' see J. Woddis, *An Introduction to Neocolonialism* (London: Lawrence & Wishart, 1967); E. Mandel, 'Semicolonial Countries and Semi-Industrialized Dependent Countries, *New International*, No. 5, 1985.

115   I. Wallerstein, 'The West, Capitalism, and the Modern World-System', *Review*, Vol. 15, No. 4, 1992, pp. 561–619; I. Wallerstein, *The Modern World-System III* (San Diego: Academic Press, 1989).

116   See M. Hardt, A. Negri, *Empire* (Cambridge: Harvard University Press, 2000).

117   Yassin-Kassab, 'Tahrir Square', p. 43.

118   See for example P. Armstrong, A. Glyn, J. Harrison, *Capitalism Since World War II: The Making and Breakup of the Great Boom* (New York: Fontana, 1984); J. Habermas, *Legitimation Crisis* (Boston: Beacon, 1973).

119   M. Curtis, *Web of Deceit: Britain's Real Role in the World* (London: Vintage, 2003), pp. 210–11, 224. Citing Gordon Brown's speech to the Federal Reserve Bank, New York, 16 November, 2001; Patricia Hewitt's speech, Washington DC, 24 July 2001; Department of Trade and Industry, 'Patricia Hewitt: Free and fair trade for peace and prosperity', 6 November 2001. For a comparison with Roosevelt's 'New Deal' see J. J. Wallis, P. Fishback, S. Kantor, 'Politics, Relief, and Reform: The Transformation of America's Social Welfare System during the New Deal', National Bureau of Economics, Research Working Paper, No. 11080, January 2005.

120   Curtis, *Web of Deceit*, p. 216. Citing Department for International Development, 'Claire Short: Advancing the World trade debate: beyond Seattle', 30 May 2000.

121   Department of Trade and Industry, 'Our Energy Future – Creating a Low Carbon Economy', Energy White Paper, February 2003, p. 83.

122   Curtis, *Web of Deceit*, p. 212. Citing Peter Sutherland.

123   Ibid., p. 213.

124   Ibid., p. 221. Citing UN Sub-Commission on the Promotion and Protection of Human Rights, 'The realization of economic, social and cultural rights; globalization and its impact on the full enjoyment of human rights', Preliminary report, 52nd session, 15 June 2000, p. 6.

125   K. Bogaert, 'Contextualizing the Arab Revolts: The Politics Behind Three Decades of Neo-liberalism in the Arab World', *Middle East Critique*, Vol. 22, No. 3, 2013, pp. 214–15, 224.

126   Dabashi, *The Arab Spring*, p. 3; Heydemann, 'Mass Politics', p. 17. Citing A. Przeworski, *Democracy and the Market: Political and Economic Reforms in*

NOTES

Eastern Europe and Latin America (New York: Columbia University Press, 1990), pp. 190–91.

127 S. Assaf, 'Libya at the crossroads', *International Socialism*, No. 133, 9 January 2012.

128 RS21, 'Adam Hanieh on the Gulf states, neoliberalism and liberation in the Middle East', 6 October 2014.

129 R. Hinnebusch, 'A historical sociology approach to authoritarian resilience in post-Arab Uprising MENA', POMEPS Study 11, 2015, p. 12.

130 RS21, 'Adam Hanieh on the Gulf states, neoliberalism and liberation in the Middle East', 6 October 2014; *Washington Post*, 'Arab autocrats are not going back to the future', 4 December 2014.

131 LeVine, 'Theorizing Revolutionary Practice', pp. 203–204.

132 Yassin-Kassab, 'Tahrir Square', p. 24.

133 Filiu, *The Arab Revolution*, p. 35.

134 Gunning, *Why Occupy a Square?*, p. 306.

135 J. Sowers, 'Activism and political economy in the new-old Egypt', *International Journal of Middle East Studies*, Vol. 47, No. 1, 2015, pp. 140–41; *Financial Times*, 'Egypt business profile: risk pays off for Amer Group', 18 December 2013.

136 Moore, 'Fiscal Politics', p. 25.

137 Yassin-Kassab, 'Tahrir Square', pp. 20, 44.

138 Middle East Eye, 'The Great Egyptian gas giveaway?', 8 April 2015. Sameh Fahmi was charged and found guilty in 2012 of squandering public funds and selling gas cheap to Israel, but then cleared in 2015.

139 Hinnebusch, 'Change and Continuity', p. 19; RS21, 'Adam Hanieh on the Gulf states, neoliberalism and liberation in the Middle East', 6 October 2014.

140 Filiu, *The Arab Revolution*, p. 77.

141 J. Schwedler, 'Amman Cosmopolitan: Spaces and Practices of Aspiration and Consumption', *Comparative Studies of South Asia, Africa, and the Middle East*, Vol. 30, No. 3, 2010, p. 269.

142 Middle East Eye, 'Morocco's King of the Poor', 12 August 2014.

143 *Financial Times*, 'Bahrain land deals highlight alchemy of making money from sand', 10 December 2014.

144 Department of State, 'Oman Inc.: Business Oligarchs and Government in Oman 09MUSCAT851', 16 August 2009 (leaked).

145 In 2015 the Sovereign Wealth Fund Institute placed four of the Gulf monarchies' sovereign wealth funds in the world's top ten. CNBC, 'The world's biggest sovereign wealth funds', 3 January 2015.

146 Department of State, 'Annual policy assessment for Saudi Arabia: part four 1976JIDDA00120_b', 8 January 1976.

147 Also referred to as 'tribal capitalism'. C. M. Davidson, *Abu Dhabi: Oil and Beyond* (New York: Columbia University Press, 2009), pp. 110–11.

148 Mubadala Corporation, with close ties to Abu Dhabi's crown prince, provides perhaps the best example. With growing interests in aerospace, semiconductors,

and other technology-intensive sectors, in cooperation with Western companies, it also owns plants extracting raw materials across the Middle East, Africa, and Asia. *The National* (UAE), 'Abu Dhabi in $4bn aluminium plant deal', 19 June 2011; Reuters, 'UAE's Mubadala, Guinea sign $5 billion bauxite, alumina deal', 25 November 2013.

149   C. M. Davidson, *Dubai: The Vulnerability of Success* (New York: Columbia University Press, 2008), pp. 114–18; M. Hvidt, 'The Dubai model: an outline of key development-process elements in Dubai', *International Journal of Middle East Studies*, Vol. 41, No. 3, 2009.

150   M. Kardoosh, 'The Aqaba Special Economic Zone, Jordan: A Case Study of Governance', ZEF Bonn, January 2005.

151   RS21, 'Adam Hanieh on the Gulf states, neoliberalism and liberation in the Middle East', 6 October 2014; Bogaert, 'Contextualizing the Arab Revolts', p. 227.

152   Al-Monitor, 'Thriving Gulf Cities Emerge as New Centres of Arab World', 8 October 2013.

153   See A. de Tocqueville, *Democracy in America* (London: Saunders and Otley, 1840).

154   Trotsky, *The Revolution Betrayed*. See section on 'Generalized Want and the Gendarme'.

155   *New York Review of Books*, 'Hannah Arendt: Reflections on Violence', 27 February 1969. Citing Engels.

156   S. M. Lipset, 'Some Social Requisites of Democracy: Economic Development and Political Legitimacy', *American Political Science Review*, Vol. 53, No. 1, 1959; S. M. Lipset, *Political Man: The Social Bases of Politics* (Baltimore: Johns Hopkins University Press, 1960).

157   K. Deutsch, 'Social Mobilization and Political Development', *American Political Science Review*, Vol. 55, No. 3, 1961.

158   S. Huntington, *Political Order in Changing Societies* (New Haven: Yale University Press, 1968); Hinnebusch, 'A historical sociology approach', p. 11.

159   D. Lerner, *The Passing of Traditional Society: Modernizing the Middle East* (New York: Free Press, 1958); L. Sigelman, 'Lerner's Model of Modernization: A Reanalysis', *Journal of Developing Areas*, Vol. 8, July 1974, p. 525.

160   Rostow was special assistant to the National Security Advisor. W. C. Matthews, 'The Kennedy Administration, Counterinsurgency, and Iraq's first Baathist Regime', *International Journal of Middle East Studies*, Vol. 43, No. 4, 2011, pp. 635, 637.

161   Ibid., p. 638.

162   J. Lucas of the Foreign Office replying to the 'Gulf Committee' on 25 March 1975. See F. Halliday, *Mercenaries: Counter-insurgency in the Gulf* (London: Spokesman, 1977), pp. 74–5.

163   D. Rueschmeyer, E. H. Stephens, J. Stephens, *Capitalist Development and Democracy* (Cambridge: Cambridge University Press, 1992), p. 6.

164 Hinnebusch, 'A historical sociology approach', p. 11. Citing G. Mosca, *The Ruling Class* (New York: McGraw-Hill, 1935).

165 E. Bellin, 'Explaining democratic divergence', POMEPS Study 11, 2015, pp. 5, 9.

166 Matthews, 'The Kennedy Administration', pp. 636–7.

167 All statistics relating to 2010 derived from published World Bank and International Monetary Fund data. In 2010 the World Bank estimated Tunisian GDP per capita at $9,500 while the IMF estimated it at $10,300. Egypt's GDP per capita was estimated at $6,600 while its literacy rate was estimated at about eighty percent.

168 B. Rahimi, 'Rethinking digital technologies in the Middle East', *International Journal of Middle East Studies*, Vol. 47, No. 2, 2015, p. 362.

169 Filiu, *The Arab Revolution*, p. 44.

170 A. Alexander, 'Digital Generation', *Critical Muslim*, Vol. 1, No. 1, 2012, p. 87.

171 Associated Press, 'Vodafone: Egypt forced us to send text messages', 3 February 2011; *Christian Science Monitor*, 'In Oman, protests spur timid media to cover the news', 1 March 2011; Filiu, *The Arab Revolution*, p. 54; BBC Online, 'UAE Blackberry update was spyware', 21 July 2009.

172 *Bloomberg*, 'Cyber Attacks on Activists Traced to FinFisher Spyware of Gamma', 25 July 2012.

173 *Guardian*, 'Hacking Team hacked: firm sold spying tools to repressive regimes, documents claim', 6 July 2015; Reporters Without Borders, 'The Enemies of the Internet Special Edition – Surveillance', 3 January 2012.

174 Referring to Bandar bin Sultan al-Saud. The Register, 'Saudi Arabia: They liked Hacking Team so much they tried to buy the company', 28 September 2015.

175 Author interviews with Nadim Shehadi, September 2014; M. Lynch, *Voices of the New Arab Public: Iraq, Al-Jazeera, and Middle East Politics Today* (New York: Columbia University Press, 2006); S. Mann, 'How the Arab League turned against Syria', OpenDemocracy, 9 February 2012.

176 E. Dickinson, 'The Case Against Qatar', *Foreign Policy*, 30 September 2014; Dabashi, *The Arab Spring*, p. 214.

177 Alexander, 'Digital Generation', p. 91.

178 K. Ulrichsen, *Qatar and the Arab Spring* (London: Hurst, 2014), p. 49.

179 *New York Times*, 'Seizing a Moment, Al-Jazeera Galvanizes Arab Frustration', 27 January 2011.

180 P. Norris, R. Inglehart, *Cosmopolitan communications: Cultural diversity in a globalized world* (New York: Columbia University Press, 2009).

181 Mann, 'How the Arab League'; M. Hussain, S. Shaikh, 'Three arenas for interrogating digital policies in the Middle East', *International Journal of Middle East Studies*, Vol. 47, No. 2, 2015, p. 366.

182 Ramsey, 'Being Green in Tehran', p. 129; G. Khiabany, 'Technologies of Liberation and/or otherwise', *International Journal of Middle East Studies*, Vol. 47, No. 2, 2015, p. 350.

183 Reuters, 'US State Department speaks to Twitter over Iran', 16 June 2009.

184 *Daily Telegraph*, 'Revolution 2.0 by Wael Ghonim: review', 13 January 2012.

185 Alexander, 'Digital Generation', pp. 92–3.

186 Slim Amamou. Filiu, *The Arab Revolution*, p. 51.

187 D. Faris, 'Multiplicities of purpose: the auditorium building, the state, and the transformation of Arab digital media', *International Journal of Middle East Studies*, Vol. 47, No. 2, 2015, pp. 344–5.

188 RNN had its principal founder arrested in August 2013 following the military coup. Ibid., p. 34.

189 The Egyptian-American digital theorist Laila Sakr has provided evidence of this. L. Sakr, 'A Digital Humanities Approach: Text, the Internet, and the Egyptian Uprising', *Middle East Critique*, Vol. 22, No. 3, 2013, p. 261.

190 Filiu, *The Arab Revolution*, p. 34.

191 M. Ahmad, 'The Terrible Beauty of Wikileaks', *Critical Muslim*, Vol. 1, No. 1, 2012, p. 216.

192 Ibid., pp. 210–12, 216–17.

193 BBC Online, 'Moldova's Twitter revolutionary speaks out', 25 April 2009; Eurasia Daily Monitor, 'Ten Reasons Why the Communist Party Won Moldova's Elections Again', 7 April 7 2009; Ramsey, 'Being Green in Tehran', p. 129. Quoting the *Guardian*'s Matthew Weaver.

194 Ramsey, 'Being Green in Tehran', p. 129. Referring to reports by Radio Free Europe and Radio Liberty.

195 Ibid., pp. 129–30.

196 See E. Morozov, *The Net Delusion: The Dark Side of Internet Freedom* (New York: Public Affairs 2011); Rahimi, 'Rethinking Digital Technologies', p. 362.

197 Alexander, 'Digital Generation', p. 88.

198 Gunning, *Why Occupy a Square?*, pp. 310–11.

199 Filiu, *The Arab Revolution*, p. 60.

200 Sakr, 'A Digital Humanities Approach', p. 248.

201 Alexander, 'Digital Generation', p. 90.

202 Rahimi, 'Rethinking Digital Technologies', p. 364. Citing Navid Hassanpour.

203 Filiu, *The Arab Revolution*, p. 51.

204 Brownlee, *The Arab Spring*, pp. 36–7. Citing the World Values Survey, 6th Wave.

6. PLAN 'A' – ISLAMISTS VERSUS THE DEEP STATE

1 F. Ajami, 'The Arab Spring at One: A Year of Living Dangerously', *Foreign Affairs*, March 2012.

2 J. Brownlee, T. Masoud, A. Reynolds (eds), *The Arab Spring: Pathways of Repression and Reform* (New York: Oxford University Press, 2015), p. 70.

3   *Telegraph,* 'Most US aid to Egypt goes to military', 29 March 2011; Z. Sardar, 'Surprise, Surprise!', *Critical Muslim,* Vol. 1, No. 1, 2012, p. 14; PBS, 'Newshour: Biden: Mubarak is Not a Dictator, But People Have a Right to Protest', 27 January 2011.

4   ABC, 'Secretary Clinton in 2009: I really consider President and Mrs Mubarak to be friends of my family', 31 January 2011.

5   Brownlee, *The Arab Spring,* p. 73.

6   J. Stacher, 'Egypt's Democratic Mirage', *Foreign Affairs,* February 2011.

7   Egypt State Information Service, 'Egypt and Britain', 22 June 2015.

8   M. Curtis, *Secret Affairs: Britain's Collusion with Radical Islam* (London: Serpent's Tail, 2012), p. 354. Referring to a statement made on 29 January 2011.

9   *Guardian,* 'Tony Blair: Mubarak is immensely courageous and a force for good', 2 February 2011.

10   M. Morell, B. Harlow, *The Great War of Our Time: The CIA's Fight Against Terrorism – From Al-Qaeda to ISIS* (New York: Twelve, 2015).

11   S. Walt, 'Why the Tunisian revolution won't spread', *Foreign Policy,* 16 January 2011.

12   *Jerusalem Post,* 'A mass expression of outrage against injustice', 25 February 2011.

13   CNN, 'White House criticizes Egyptian government and vice president', 9 February 2011; BBC Online, 'Interview with His Majesty King Abdullah II', 14 November 2011. For a good discussion on the recycling of Lewis's comments see H. al-Hasan, 'Arabs are not ready for democracy: the orientalist cravings of Arab ruling elites', OpenDemocracy, 7 May 2012.

14   *Washington Post,* 'A Democratic Egypt or a State of Hate?', 1 February 2011.

15   M. LeVine, 'Theorizing Revolutionary Practice: Agendas for Research on the Arab Uprisings', *Middle East Critique,* Vol. 22, No. 3, 2013, p. 192.

16   Middle East Eye, 'Yes, the Arab Spring was worth it – it heralded the power of the masses', 26 November 2014; A. Callinicos, 'Spectres of counter-revolution', *International Socialism,* No. 140, 7 October 2013.

17   Stacher, 'Egypt's Democratic Mirage'.

18   *London Review of Books,* 'The Revolution That Wasn't', 12 September 2013.

19   Samer Shehata argues that Egypt's military does not have a real ideology in the sense that other 'deep states' in Turkey and elsewhere have. M. Hudson, 'The Crisis of the Arab State: Study Group Report', Belfer Center for International Affairs, Harvard University, August 2015, p. 17.

20   J. P. Filiu, *From Deep State to Islamic State: The Arab Counter-Revolution and Its Jihadi Legacy* (London: Hurst, 2015), pp. 154–6.

21   Brownlee, *The Arab Spring,* p. 107.

22   R. Yassin-Kassab, 'Tahrir Square', *Critical Muslim,* Vol. 1, No. 1, 2012, pp. 31–2.

23   Ibid., p. 31; Filiu, *From Deep State,* pp. 157–8.

24   *New York Times,* 'Out of Protest, an Anthem for Egypt's Revolution', 11 December 2011. Essam had sung *Irhal Irhal* or 'Leave Leave'.

25 Callinicos, 'Spectres'.

26 Filiu, *From Deep State*, pp. 56–7; A. al-Affendi, 'A Trans-Islamic Revolution?', *Critical Muslim*, Vol. 1, No. 1, 2012, pp. 64–5; Yassin-Kassab, 'Tahrir Square', p. 38.

27 Al-Affendi, 'A Trans-Islamic Revolution?', p. 74; H. Albrecht, 'How can opposition support authoritarianism? Lessons from Egypt', *Democratization*, Vol. 12, No. 3, 2005, p. 378.

28 Congressional Research Service, 'Egypt: 2005 Presidential and Parliamentary Elections', 15 January 2006; Curtis, *Secret Affairs*, p. 305.

29 Curtis, *Secret Affairs*, pp. 303–4. Citing a 2006 Whitehall-commissioned paper by former British ambassador to Syria Basil Eastwood and former US assistant secretary of state Richard Murphy.

30 Ibid., p. 304. Quoting Derek Plumbly.

31 A. B. Atwan, *Islamic State: The Digital Caliphate* (London: Saqi, 2015), p. 199.

32 Hansard, 'Egypt and the Muslim Brotherhood', 16 February 2011.

33 Curtis, *Secret Affairs*, pp. 356–7. For details of the meeting also see *Jerusalem Post*, 'British gov't slammed for visit to Muslim Brotherhood', 19 February 2011.

34 *Daily Telegraph*, 'Middle East crisis: David Cameron arrives in Egypt to push for democracy', 21 February 2011; Curtis, *Secret Affairs*, p. 357.

35 J. Gunning, I. Z. Baron, *Why Occupy a Square?: People, Protests and Movements in the Egyptian Revolution* (New York: Oxford University Press, 2013), p. 307.

36 A. Stepan, J. Linz, 'Democratization Theory and the Arab Spring', *Journal of Democracy*, Vol. 24, No. 2, 2013, p. 17.

37 BBC Online, 'Profile: Egypt's Muslim Brotherhood', 20 December 2013; R. Dreyfuss, *Devil's Game: How the United States Helped Unleash Fundamentalist Islam* (New York: Metropolitan, 2006), p. 159.

38 Stepan, 'Democratization Theory', p. 23.

39 J. P. Filiu, *The Arab Revolution: Ten Lessons from the Democratic Uprising* (London: Hurst, 2011), p. 104.

40 Ibid., p. 98; al-Affendi, 'A Trans-Islamic Revolution?', p. 66. El-Baradei was understood to have close relations to the Western powers having been the former director general of the International Atomic Energy Agency and the joint 2005 Nobel Peace Prize winner.

41 Al-Affendi, 'A Trans-Islamic Revolution?', p. 66.

42 Yassin-Kassab, 'Tahrir Square', p. 40.

43 Ibid., p. 40.

44 Filiu, *The Arab Revolution*, pp. 109, 114.

45 Yassin-Kassab, 'Tahrir Square', p. 43.

46 Al-Affendi, 'A Trans-Islamic Revolution?', p. 64.

47 Yassin-Kassab, 'Tahrir Square', pp. 40–41.

48 Al-Affendi, 'A Trans-Islamic Revolution?', p. 63.

49 The Revolutionary Youth Coalition demanded a new constitution.

50 Al-Affendi, 'A Trans-Islamic Revolution?', pp. 78, 80; Filiu, *From Deep State*, pp. 156–7; Brownlee, *The Arab Spring*, p. 108.

51 Yassin-Kassab, 'Tahrir Square', p. 33; Filiu, *From Deep State*, pp. 158–60; Brownlee, *The Arab Spring*, p. 110.

52 Brownlee, *The Arab Spring*, p. 110. Referring to Muhammad Badi's statement in July 2011.

53 Filiu, *From Deep State*, pp. 159–60.

54 BBC Online, 'Egypt's Islamist parties win elections to parliament', 21 January 2012; Filiu, *From Deep State*, p. 161; Brownlee, *The Arab Spring*, p. 115. The parliamentary speaker being Saad el-Katatni.

55 Referring to the so-called 'Silmi document' named after the transitional government's deputy prime minister at the time, Ali al-Silmi. The Brotherhood mobilized protests against the document's recommendations. Stepan, 'Democratization Theory', p. 21; Brownlee, *The Arab Spring*, pp. 110–12; E. Goldberg, 'Arab transitions and the old elite', POMEPS Study 11, 2015, p. 22.

56 Ajami, 'The Arab Spring at One'.

57 Ibid.

58 R. Abou-el-Fadl (ed.), *Revolutionary Egypt: Connecting Domestic and International Struggles* (London: Routledge, 2015); Filiu, *The Arab Revolution*, p. 28.

59 *New York Times*, 'Anti-American Egyptian Candidate May Be Tripped Up by Mother's US Ties', 4 April 2012.

60 *Los Angeles Times*, 'Islamists rally to rescue Salafi candidate's presidential bid', 6 April 2012.

61 Brownlee, *The Arab Spring*, pp. 119–20.

62 The accords were named after the meeting place, the Fairmont Hotel. Brownlee, *The Arab Spring*, pp. 119–20.

63 Stepan, 'Democratization Theory', p. 22; Filiu, *From Deep State*, pp. 164–6; *Guardian*, 'Muslim Brotherhood's Mohamed Morsi declared president of Egypt', 26 June 2012; *Guardian*, 'Egypt's supreme court dissolves parliament and outrages Islamists', 14 June 2012.

64 Filiu, *From Deep State*, pp. 164–6; Brownlee, *The Arab Spring*, p. 121.

65 R. Springborg, 'Sisi's Islamist Agenda for Egypt: The General's Radical Political Vision', *Foreign Affairs*, July 2013.

66 *Guardian*, 'Abdel Fatah al-Sisi: behind the public face of Egypt's soon-to-be president', 25 May 2014.

67 Filiu, *From Deep State*, pp. 168–9.

68 E. Bellin, 'Explaining democratic divergence', POMEPS Study 11, 2015, p. 7.

69 Filiu, *From Deep State*, pp. 170–71.

70 Bellin, 'Explaining democratic divergence', p. 7.

71 Filiu, *From Deep State*, p. xiv.

72 Brownlee, *The Arab Spring*, pp. 122–3.

73 *Wall Street Journal*, 'In Egypt, the Deep State Rises Again', 19 July 2013.

74 Filiu, *From Deep State*, p. v.

75 These statements were posted on Sisi's own Facebook page on 15 May 2013. Cited by Filiu, *From Deep State*, pp. 173–4.

76 *Wall Street Journal*, 'In Egypt, the Deep State Rises Again', 19 July 2013; BBC Online, 'Profile: Egypt's Tamarod protest movement', 1 July 2013; Filiu, *From Deep State*, p. 173.

77 S. Grewal, 'Why Tunisia didn't follow Egypt's path', POMEPS Study 12, 2015, p. 52.

78 Brownlee, *The Arab Spring*, p. 124; Filiu, *The Arab Revolution*, pp. 174–5.

79 Filiu, *From Deep State*, pp. 174–5, 179.

80 The forensics team was led by JP French Associates and included academic staff at York University. *New York Times*, 'Leaks Gain Credibility and Potential to Embarrass Egypt's Leaders', 12 May 2015.

81 The Brotherhood claimed over 2,600 were killed. *Daily News Egypt*, 'Health Ministry raises death toll of Wednesday's clashes to 638', 16 August 2013; Al-Jazeera, 'Egypt's Brotherhood to hold march of anger', 16 August 2013; Human Rights Watch, 'All According to Plan', 17 August 2013; Human Rights Watch, 'Egypt: Security Forces Used Excessive Lethal Force', 19 August 2013.

82 *Washington Post*, 'Who actually died in Egypt's Rabaa massacre', 14 August 2015.

83 For a full discussion see K. William, *The Prague Spring and its Aftermath: Czechoslovak Politics, 1968–1970* (Cambridge: Cambridge University Press, 1997).

84 Stepan, 'Democratization Theory', p. 21.

85 Filiu, *The Arab Revolution*, p. 100.

86 *London Review of Books*, 'The Revolution That Wasn't', 12 September 2013.

87 Filiu, *From Deep State*, p. v. Citing a threat reported by former MP Mostafa al-Nagar.

88 J. Sowers, 'Activism and political economy in the new-old Egypt', *International Journal of Middle East Studies*, Vol. 47, No. 1, 2015, p. 41.

89 Interim president Adli Mansour was also a former adviser to Saudi Arabia. Associated Press, 'Egypt's president makes first trip to Saudi Arabia', 10 October 2013.

90 Al-Jazeera, 'Egypt constitution approved by 98.1 percent', 18 January 2014.

91 Al-Arabiya, 'Egypt's Sisi: From field marshal to pharaoh?', 31 January 2014.

92 Stalin was promoted to this rank in 1943 before being promoted to 'Generalissimus of the Soviet Union' two years later. HistoryInfo, '1943: Stalin Becomes Marshal of the Soviet Union', 7 March 2015; Anonymous, *Napoleon and the Marshals of the Empire* (London: Ulan Press, 2012).

93 L. Trotsky, *The Revolution Betrayed* (London: Dover, 2004). See section on 'Bonapartism and the regime in crisis'.

94 Ibid. See sections on 'Program and Reality' and 'The Red Army and its Doctrines'; *London Review of Books*, 'The Revolution That Wasn't', 12 September 2013.

95 Al-Arabiya, 'Egypt's Sisi: From field marshal to pharaoh?', 31 January 2014.

96 Ibid.; Filiu, *From Deep State*, pp. 181–3. Despite the extension the voter turnout was first reported by state media as thirty-five percent, before being 'upgraded' to forty percent.

97 BBC Online, 'Egypt army restoring democracy says John Kerry', 1 August 2013.

98 H. Clinton, *Hard Choices* (New York: Simon & Schuster, 2014), pp. 345–6.

99 *Guardian*, 'Tony Blair to advise Egypt president Sisi on economic reform', 2 July 2014.

100 *Daily News Egypt*, 'Al-Sisi meets Pope Francis', 25 November 2014.

101 Author interviews with Robert Springborg, November 2014.

102 S. Brooke, 'Brotherhood activism and regime consolidation in Egypt', POMEPS Study 12, 2015, p. 44.

103 Sowers, 'Activism', p. 140.

104 Author interviews with Robert Springborg, November 2014; Filiu, *From Deep State*, p. 190.

105 M. Awad, N. Brown, 'Mutual escalation in Egypt', POMEPS Study 12, 2015, p. 41; Brooke, 'Brotherhood activism', p. 44.

106 Author interviews with Robert Springborg, November 2014.

107 L. Herrera, 'Citizenship under surveillance: dealing with the digital age', *International Journal of Middle East Studies*, Vol. 47, No. 2, 2015, p. 355.

108 *Wall Street Journal*, 'Thoma Bravo Renews Sales Process for Security Software Company Blue Coat', 6 February 2015.

109 The $18 billion was to be divided between power plants, gas, steel, and tourism projects. K. Ulrichsen, *Qatar and the Arab Spring* (London: Hurst, 2014), p. 89.

110 CBS, '60 Minutes: Qatar a tiny country exerts powerful influence', 15 January 2012.

111 Ulrichsen, *Qatar*, p. 3.

112 *Daily Telegraph*, 'Qatar: new emir, new broom?', 25 June 2013.

113 *USA Today*, 'Obama: No big move toward democracy in Qatar', 16 April 2011.

114 Doha News, 'Emir: Qatar to hold first legislative elections in 2013', 1 November 2011.

115 Doha News, 'Advisory Council's term extended until 2016 amid government transition', 2 July 2013; Brownlee, *The Arab Spring*, p. 54; Ulrichsen, *Qatar*, p. 85. Public sector salaries were increased by 60 percent while military officers received 120 percent increases.

116 Ulrichsen, *Qatar*, pp. 164–5.

117 *The Economist*, 'Democracy? That's for other Arabs', 8 August 2013; Ulrichsen, *Qatar*, pp. 160–61.

118 Referring to Muhammad ibn al-Dheeb al-Ajami. A few months later his sentence was reduced to fifteen years' imprisonment. Associated Press, 'Qatari poet jailed for life after writing verse inspired by Arab spring', 29 November 2012; *Daily Telegraph*, 'Qatari poet has sentence reduced', 25 February 2013.

119 Author interviews with Nadim Shehadi, September 2014.

120　*Der Spiegel*, 'Islam's Spiritual Dear Abby: The Voice of Egypt's Muslim Brotherhood', 15 February 2011.

121　*Bloomberg*, 'Why Does Al-Jazeera Love a Hateful Islamic Extremist?', 10 July 2013; Ulrichsen, *Qatar*, p. 50.

122　Middle East Online, 'Qatar embraces Wahhabism to strengthen regional influence', 18 December 2011; Ulrichsen, *Qatar*, p. 69; C. M. Davidson, *After the Sheikhs: The Coming Collapse of the Gulf Monarchies* (New York: Oxford University Press, 2013), p. 30; M. Kamrava, 'Royal Factionalism and Political Liberalization in Qatar', *Middle East Journal*, Vol. 63, No. 3, 2009. The Ghafran tribe defected from Qatar to Saudi Arabia. Qatar did not support Saudi Arabia's position on Yemen in the 1990s.

123　See, for example, Department of State, 'Saudi King Abdullah and senior princes on Saudi policy toward Iraq 08RIYADH649_a', 20 April 2008 (leaked).

124　Ulrichsen, *Qatar*, pp. 69–70, 73.

125　Ibid., p. 90; Reuters, 'Egypt returns $2bn to Qatar in sign of growing tensions', 19 September 2013.

126　H. Dabashi, *The Arab Spring: The End of Postcolonialism* (London: Zed, 2012), p. 175.

127　*The Peninsula*, 'The time has come to open a new page in the journey of our nation', 26 June 2013.

128　*Daily Telegraph*, 'Qatar: new emir, new broom?', 25 June 2013.

129　*The Economist*, 'Qatar's new emir: A hard act to follow', 29 June 2014.

130　BBC Online, 'Profile: Qatar Emir, Sheikh Tamim bin Hamad al-Thani', 25 June 2013.

131　Al-Arabiya, 'Saudi king backs Egypt's military', 17 August 2013; Al-Arabiya, 'In rare interview, Mubarak says Egyptians want Sisi', 6 February 2014.

132　Al-Arabiya, 'Giant statue of UAE founder Sheikh Zayed stands in Cairo suburb', 20 September 2015.

133　Al-Jazeera, 'Saudi, UAE, Bahrain withdraw Qatar envoys', 6 March 2014; Associated Press, 'Al-Jazeera shuts down its Egypt channel', 22 December 2014.

134　Brooke, 'Brotherhood activism', p. 44.

135　The attacks were thought to have been undertaken by *Ansar Bait al-Maqdis* and *Ajnad Misr*. Filiu, *From Deep State*, pp. 181, 184; European Parliament, 'The Involvement of Salafism/Wahhabism in the support and supply of arms to rebel groups around the world', Directorate-General for External Policies, June 2013, p. 22.

136　*New York Times*, 'Leaks Gain Credibility and Potential to Embarrass Egypt's Leaders', 12 May 2015; Reuters, 'Egypt's Sisi reassures Gulf leaders after alleged derisive audio leaks', 9 February 2015.

137　GlobalPost, 'Saudi king announces $10.7 billion in spending on social benefits', 23 February 2011.

138　Atwan, *Islamic State*, p. 206.

139 *Guardian*, 'Saudi Arabia prints 1.5m copies of religious edict banning protests', 29 March 2011.
140 Dreyfuss, *Devil's Game*, p. 129. Quoting James Akins.
141 Al-Basheer News, 'Islamic Ummah Party', 6 February 2011; Davidson, *After the Sheikhs*, p. 213.
142 He made the statement on 11 February 2011. He was imprisoned in 1994. See A. Kapiszewski, 'Saudi Arabia: Steps Toward Democratization or Reconfiguration of Authoritarianism?', *Journal of Asian and African Studies*, Vol. 42, No. 5, 2006, pp. 459–82.
143 CNN, 'Small protests have big impact in Saudi Arabia', 25 March 2013; *New York Times*, 'In Saudi Town, Women Protest Detentions, Leading to Their Own', 26 March 2013.
144 K. Diwan, 'The future of the Muslim Brotherhood in the Gulf', POMEPS Study 12, 2015, p. 54; *Gulf News*, 'Saudi Arabia considers revoking citizenships', 18 August 2014.
145 Middle East Eye, 'Saudi Arabia orders Muslim Brotherhood books removed from schools', 1 December 2015.
146 It was approved by then UAE vice president and ruler of Dubai, Rashid bin Said al-Maktoum. Reuters, 'UAE Islamist group had no desire to topple government: families', 2 July 2013.
147 Ibid. Referring to Sultan bin Kayed al-Qasimi.
148 Khalifa bin Zayed al-Nahyan. CNN, 'UAE citizens petition for direct elections and legislative powers', 9 March 2011.
149 Quoting the economist Nasser bin Ghaith. Al-Jazeera, 'UAE pardons jailed activists', 28 November 2011.
150 Reuters, 'UAE detains 6 Islamists stripped of citizenship: lawyer', 9 April 2012; Huffington Post, 'UAE 94 Verdict: Unfair Trial and Torture Ensure the Story is Just Beginning', 5 July 2013.
151 Reuters, 'UAE Islamist group denies reports it has an armed wing', 23 September 2012.
152 Reuters, 'Egypt's Brotherhood says UAE arrests unfounded', 2 January 2013; Ulrichsen, *Qatar*, p. 156.
153 Interpol, 'Al-Qaradawi, Yousef wanted by the judicial authorities of Egypt for prosecution / to serve a sentence', 7 December 2014.
154 Referring to Abdullah bin Zayed al-Nahyan.
155 Ulrichsen, *Qatar*, pp. 119, 154–5.
156 Referring to a US diplomatic cable from 2006 leaked in 2009. See BBC Online, 'Viewpoint: Wealthy and stable UAE keeps the lid on dissent', 15 April 2014; al-Affendi, 'A Trans-Islamic Revolution?', p. 64.
157 Sardar, 'Surprise, Surprise!', p. 12; Filiu, *The Arab Revolution*, p. 73.

158 Al-Affendi, 'A Trans-Islamic Revolution?', pp. 69–70, 72–3; Diwan, 'The future of the Muslim Brotherhood', pp. 53–4.

159 Diwan, 'The future of the Muslim Brotherhood', p. 54.

160 $1.25 billion of the $5 billion package was to come from Qatar.

161 Quoting political scientist Mohammad Abu Rumman. Al-Arabiya, 'Jordan seen unlikely to withdraw envoy from Qatar', 20 March 2014.

162 Guardian, 'David Cameron orders inquiry into activities of Muslim Brotherhood', 1 April 2014.

163 Hansard, 'Egypt and the Muslim Brotherhood', 11 February 2011.

164 M. Lynch, 'Introduction', POMEPS Study 12, 2015, p. 7.

165 House of Commons, 'Muslim Brotherhood review: main findings', 17 December 2015; Guardian, 'UAE told UK: crack down on Muslim Brotherhood or lose arms deals', 6 November 2015.

166 Referring to Khaldun al-Mubarak and Dominic Jermey. Guardian, 'UAE told UK: crack down on Muslim Brotherhood or lose arms deals', 6 November 2015.

167 S. Huntington, The Third Wave: Democratization in the Late Twentieth Century (Norman: Oklahoma University Press, 1991), pp. 266–7.

168 Filiu, From Deep State, p. 44. Bourguiba's most notable attempt to remove French troops was from a base in the Tunisian port of Bizerte in July 1961.

169 Ibid., p. 42; Tunisia Live, 'Tunisia's Military: Striving to Sidestep Politics as Challenges Mount', 25 June 2013.

170 Brownlee, The Arab Spring, p. 191–2.

171 Grewal, 'Why Tunisia didn't', p. 51.

172 Bellin, 'Explaining democratic divergence', p. 6; Filiu, From Deep State, pp. xiv, 232–3.

173 M. Marks, 'How Egypt's coup really affected Tunisia's Islamists', POMEPS Study 12, 2015, p. 46.

174 Goldberg, 'Arab transitions', pp. 19–21.

175 Brownlee, The Arab Spring, p. 116–17.

176 Notably the General National Congress' chairman was obliged to resign as he had been Libya's ambassador to India before defecting in the 1980s. BBC Online, 'Libya GNC Chairman Muhammad al-Magarief resigns', 28 May 2013.

177 R. Basly, 'The Future of al-Nadha in Tunisia', Carnegie Endowment for International Peace, 20 April 2011; Goldberg, 'Arab transitions', pp. 19–21; Brownlee, The Arab Spring, p. 143.

178 The 23 October Coalition. See Brownlee, The Arab Spring, p. 136–7.

179 Ibid., p. 139.

180 This is in contrast to Egypt's first post-2011 elections in which only two thirds of seats were contested in this manner, with the remainder still majoritarian. Ibid., pp. 134–5, 198.

181   Marks, 'How Egypt's coup', p. 45; Brownlee, *The Arab Spring*, pp. 134–5, 201.
182   The French-Iranian cartoon 'Persepolis'. BBC Online, 'Protesters attack TV station over film Persepolis', 9 October 2011; Brownlee, *The Arab Spring*, p. 137.
183   Brownlee, *The Arab Spring*, p. 141.
184   Filiu, *From Deep State*, p. 235; N. Brown, 'Egypt's Constitutional Cul-De-Sac', Carnegie Endowment for International Peace, 31 March 2014.
185   Filiu, *From Deep State*, pp. xiv, 232–3; Filiu, *The Arab Revolution*, p. 14; Marks, 'How Egypt's coup', p. 45.
186   Filiu, *The Arab Revolution*, p. 95.
187   Ulrichsen, *Qatar*, pp. 88–9.
188   Stepan, 'Democratization Theory', p. 25.
189   European Parliament, 'The Involvement of Salafism/Wahhabism', p. 20.
190   Filiu, *From Deep State*, p. 237.
191   Stepan, 'Democratization Theory', p. 12; *Independent*, 'Rached Ghannouchi says he doesn't want an Islamic state in Tunisia. Can he prove his critics wrong?', 24 October 2012.
192   Notably the assassination of Muhammad Brahimi of the Popular Front. Agence France-Presse, 'Tunisia faces strike after opposition's Brahimi assassinated', 26 July 2013; Marks, 'How Egypt's coup', pp. 45, 47–8; Filiu, *From Deep State*, p. 238; Brownlee, *The Arab Spring*, p. 145.
193   Bellin, 'Explaining democratic divergence', p. 8.
194   A. Boukhars, N. Brown, *et al.*, 'The Egypt Effect', Carnegie Endowment for International Peace, 13 February 2014.
195   Mehdi Jomaa. Stepan, 'Democratization Theory', pp. 25–6.
196   Marks, 'How Egypt's coup', p. 47.
197   BBC Online, 'Tunisia election: Essebsi claims historic victory', 22 December 2014.
198   Filiu, *From Deep State*, p. 230.
199   NATO press release, 'NATO and Tunisia take cooperation forward', 28 May 2015.
200   Saudi Arabia Ministry for Foreign Affairs, '7e2e9913–08e3–4b7f-aff8–8b43321bf12f. tif', (undated, leaked).
201   Saudi Arabia Ministry for Foreign Affairs, '5ae72fdc-0636–4c3a-8c44–d861f2fac1cd. tif', 16 April 2012 (leaked).
202   Saudi Arabia Ministry for Foreign Affairs, 'b89cb9f0–c9d7–46f7–afba-409822b302e6.tif', 11 May 2012 (leaked).
203   Saudi Arabia Ministry for Foreign Affairs, '230a6942–cf6f-47aa-85da-64e5af836a61. tif', 5 May 2012 (leaked).
204   Saudi Arabia Ministry for Foreign Affairs, '85da800b-a683–e111–846d-001aa0248408.tif', 5 April 2012 (leaked).
205   Middle East Eye, 'Luxury cars and a foreign funding scandal in Tunisia', 13 August 2014.
206   The journalist was Soufiane ben Farhat, the national television station was Nessma, and the politician was Anwar Gharbi of the People's Movement for Citizens. Middle

East Eye, 'Row in Tunisia over claims that UAE is buying political influence', 25 May 2015.

207 Middle East Eye, 'UAE threatens to destabilize Tunisia for not acting in Abu Dhabi's interests', 30 November 2015.

208 G. Hill, G. Nonneman, 'Yemen, Saudi Arabia, and the Gulf States: Elite Politics, Street Protests and Regional Diplomacy', Chatham House Middle East and North Africa Programme, May 2011.

209 Brownlee, *The Arab Spring*, p. 78.

210 Al-Affendi, 'A Trans-Islamic Revolution?', p. 70; Filiu, *The Arab Revolution*, p. 68.

211 Brownlee, *The Arab Spring*, p. 148; al-Affendi, 'A Trans-Islamic Revolution?', p. 70.

212 UN Security Council, 'Resolution 2014', 21 October 2011.

213 Filiu, *From Deep State*, p. 197.

214 Ibid., pp. 196–7; Brownlee, *The Arab Spring*, p. 79.

215 S. P. Yadav, 'The Yemen model as a failure of political imagination', *International Journal of Middle East Studies*, Vol. 47, No. 1, 2015, pp. 145–6.

216 Brownlee, *The Arab Spring*, p. 152.

217 *Washington Post*, 'The Resurgence of Arab Militaries', 5 December 2014.

218 Brownlee, *The Arab Spring*, p. 150–51. Referring to Muhammad Saleh al-Ahmar and Tariq Muhammed Abd Allah Saleh.

219 Brownlee, *The Arab Spring*, p. 151.

220 Atwan, *Islamic State*, p. 66.

221 Filiu, *From Deep State*, p. 197; *International Business Times*, '57 Dead as Al-Qaeda Militants Attack Yemen Army Outpost', 9 April 2012.

222 BBC Online, 'Al-Qaeda attack on Yemen army parade causes carnage', 21 May 2012.

223 Filiu, *From Deep State*, pp. 197–9.

224 Many were affiliated to *Ansar al-Sharia* or 'Guardians of Islamic Law'.

225 Filiu, *From Deep State*, p. 196; Brownlee, *The Arab Spring*, p. 147; Al-Bawaba, 'Yemen: Al-Qaeda Declares South province as Islamic Emirate', 31 March 2011.

226 *New York Times*, 'Islamists Seize a Yemeni City, Stoking Fears', 29 May 2011.

227 Ulrichsen, *Qatar*, p. 117.

228 Ibid., p. 91. Citing *Yemen Post*, 'Hadi to arrive in Doha Thursday', 2 August 2012.

229 Ibid., p. 111.

230 Saudi Arabia Ministry for Foreign Affairs, 'Saudi embassy report: Qatar instigated unrest in Yemen', 20 June 2015 (leaked).

231 According to a leaked US diplomatic cable, before it got formally involved Saudi Arabia had initially offered to purchase weapons and ammunition for the Yemeni regime from the Czech Republic and Slovakia, while the UAE had agreed to broker a similar deal with Bulgaria. For a good discussion of the 2009 war between Saudi Arabia and the Houthi movement see *Guardian*, 'Saudi Arabia goes to war', 23 November 2009. For information on the Saudi and UAE offers to secure Eastern

European weapons see Department of State, 'Sa'ada solution requires more thought, fewer weapons 09SANAA2052_a', 11 November 2009 (leaked).

232   BBC Online, 'Deadly blast strikes Yemen mosque', 2 May 2008; Ulrichsen, *Qatar*, p. 91. Citing *Yemen Post*, 'Hadi to arrive in Doha Thursday', 2 August 2012.

233   Filiu, *From Deep State*, p. 199.

234   Yadav, 'The Yemen model', p. 146; *Guardian*, 'Saudi's internal power struggle sends ripples across international borders', 21 November 2013.

235   Middle East Eye, 'Was the UAE behind the Houthi takeover of Sana'a?', 2 October 2014.

236   J. Kinninmont, 'Bahrain: Beyond the Impasse', Chatham House, 2012, p. 3.

237   BBC Online, 'Deadly blast strikes Yemen mosque', 2 May 2008; M. Curtis, *Web of Deceit: Britain's Real Role in the World* (London: Vintage, 2003), p. 267. Quoting Mike O'Brien.

238   D. Brumberg, 'The Trap of Liberalized Autocracy', *Journal of Democracy*, Vol. 12, No. 4, 2002; F. Lovett, 'Mill on consensual domination' in *Mill's On Liberty*, ed. C. L. Ten (Cambridge: Cambridge University Press: 2009), pp. 123–37.

239   According to Human Rights Watch there were six deaths between 14 and 17 February, all from police birdshot having been fired at protests. The doctors were later given prison sentences of between five and fifteen years. Human Rights Watch, 'Bahrain: Investigate Deaths Linked to Crackdown', 29 March 2011. *Guardian*, 'Bahrain doctors jailed for treating injured protesters', 29 September 2011.

240   Dabashi, *The Arab Spring*, p. 175.

241   Trotsky, *The Revolution Betrayed*. See section on 'Bonapartism as a Regime of Crisis'.

242   Kinninmont, 'Bahrain', p. 10. Bahrain's minister for information, Sameera Rajab, later repeated these claims on Al-Jazeera on 26 October 2011.

243   Ibid., p. 9; Dabashi, *The Arab Spring*, p. 219; *New York Times*, 'The Bahrain Uprising', 15 February 2011.

244   Most notably Ali al-Sistani and his predecessor, Abu al-Qasem al-Khoie. Kinninmont, 'Bahrain', p. 2.

245   Al-Jazeera, 'Intricacies of Bahrain's Shia-Sunni Divide', 2 September 2011.

246   BBC Sport, 'Bahrain Grand Prix cancelled', 21 February 2011.

247   Tacitas armoured personnel carriers are manufactured by BAE Systems. Curtis, *Secret Affairs*, p. 373; *Telegraph*, 'Saudi troops sent to crush Bahrain protests had British training', 25 May 2011; Al-Jazeera, 'Pakistani recruits for Bahrain', 30 July 2011; *Express Tribune* (Pakistan), 'Bahrain adverts', 11 March 2011.

248   Ulrichsen, *Qatar*, p. 116; Curtis, *Web of Deceit*, p. 265; *Los Angeles Times*, 'Bahrain intervention', 15 March 2011.

249   Declining to send troops, Morocco instead sent an intelligence delegation from their regional branch in Dubai. Saudi Arabia Ministry for Foreign Affairs, '3f0c526a-53f7–4426–941c-c77a01056fee.tif', 18 June 2012 (leaked).

250   Brownlee, *The Arab Spring*, pp. 86–90.

251 See for example *Guardian*, 'A chilling account of the brutal clampdown sweeping Bahrain', 16 April 2012; Reuters, 'Bahrain blast kills three policemen: Interior Ministry', 3 March 2014.

252 Al-Jazeera, 'Shouting in the Dark', 4 August 2011; *Independent*, 'Al-Jazeera – 15 years in the headlines', 2 November 2011.

253 Jamal Fakhro, the first deputy chairman of the Shura Council, was the Bahrain government guest. The Bahraini human rights activist barred from appearing was Maryam al-Khawaja. The third guest was the author, being allowed on to the show but having overheard the pre-broadcast argument. Al-Jazeera, 'Inside Story: Bahrain: Divided nation, disputed narratives', 12 August 2011.

254 Al-Arabiya, 'Qaradawi says Bahrain's revolution sectarian', 19 March 2015.

255 *Los Angeles Times*, 'Al-Jazeera faces tough questions as Doha backs Saudi troops in Bahrain', 15 March 2011; Ulrichsen, *Qatar*, p. 115.

256 *Telegraph*, 'Bahrain hardliners to put Shia MPs on trial', 30 March 2011.

257 *Asia Times*, 'Exposed: The US-Saudi Libya deal', 2 April 2011.

258 Foreign Affairs Committee, 'Oral evidence, column 38', 16 March 2011.

259 Kinninmont, 'Bahrain', p. 12.

260 Channel 4, 'Police watchdog criticises top Met officers', 12 April 2012; *New York Times*, 'An Activist Stands Her Ground in Bahrain', 1 December 2011; *Guardian*, 'John Timoney: the notorious police chief sent to reform forces in Bahrain', 16 February 2012.

261 Department of State, 'Keynote Address at the National Democratic Institute's 2011 Democracy Awards Dinner', 7 November 2011.

262 Congressional Research Service, 'Bahrain: Reform, Security, and US Policy', 20 February 2015.

263 UK Prime Minister's Office, 'Statement on the PM's meeting with King of Bahrain', 12 December 2011.

264 Most individuals and departments blamed by the commission have not been punished, with only ten junior police officers having stood trial. Kinninmont, 'Bahrain', p. 11; BBC Online, 'Bahrain opposition leader Sheikh Ali Salman arrested', 28 December 2014; *Telegraph*, 'Philip Hammond praises improvements in Bahrain's human rights record', 20 January 2015.

265 Al-Monitor, 'Bahrain asks Congress for help in restoring arms sales', 25 March 2015; Congressional Research Service, 'Bahrain: Reform, Security, and US Policy', 20 February 2015.

7. PLAN 'B' – A FAKE ARAB SPRING

1 R. Hinnebusch, 'Change and Continuity after the Arab Uprising: The Consequences of State Formation in Arab North African States', *British Journal of Middle Eastern Studies*, Vol. 42, No. 1, 2015, p. 25; Middle East Eye, 'Morocco's King of the Poor',

12 August 2014; J. P. Filiu, *The Arab Revolution: Ten Lessons from the Democratic Uprising* (London: Hurst, 2011), p. 68. For example, the word 'sacred' referring to the king, was removed from the Moroccan constitution.

2   F. Vairel, 'Of Regime and Movements: authoritarian reform and the 2011 popular uprisings in Morocco', LSE public lectures, 19 May 2015.

3   Al-Jazeera, 'Rallies held in Jordan and Syria', 4 February 2011; BBC Online, 'Jordan protests: King Abdullah names Marouf Bakhit PM', 1 February 2011.

4   Reuters, 'Gulf states approve $5 billion aid to Morocco, Jordan', 20 December 2011.

5   *New York Times*, 'Gulf Council Reaches Out to Morocco and Jordan', 25 May 2011.

6   J. Brownlee, T. Masoud, A. Reynolds (eds), *The Arab Spring: Pathways of Repression and Reform* (New York: Oxford University Press, 2015), p. 54.

7   UK Prime Minister's Office, 'Press conference with Prime Minister of Kuwait', 22 February 2011.

8   Referring to Prime Minister Nasser bin Muhammad al-Sabah who resigned in November 2011. BBC Online, 'Kuwait's prime minister resigns after protests', 28 November 2011; Reuters, 'Kuwait eyes 13 percent budget rise amid industrial unrest', 19 March 2012.

9   C. M. Davidson, *After the Sheikhs: The Coming Collapse of the Gulf Monarchies* (New York: Oxford University Press, 2013), pp. 209–11; *New York Times*, 'Protests in Oman spread from port city to capital', 28 February 2011.

10 H. Dabashi, *The Arab Spring: The End of Postcolonialism* (London: Zed, 2012), pp. 111, 204.

11 For a good discussion of state cartels see J. A. Hobson, *Imperialism* (London: Longman, 1902), p. 311.

12 BBC Online, 'In full: Tony Blair speech', 1 August 2006; *New Yorker*, 'The Redirection', 5 March 2007.

13 I. Cherstich, 'When tribesmen do not act tribal: Libyan tribalism as ideology', *Middle East Critique*, Vol. 23, No. 4, 2014, p. 408; S. Assaf, 'Libya at the crossroads', *International Socialism*, No. 133, 9 January 2012; J. P. Filiu, *From Deep State to Islamic State: The Arab Counter-Revolution and its Jihadi Legacy* (London: Hurst, 2015), p. 80.

14 Assaf, 'Libya at the crossroads'.

15 W. Otman, E. J. Karlberg, *The Libyan Economy: Economic Diversification and International Repositioning* (London: Springer, 2007), p. 36.

16 Al-Sadr disappeared in Libya in 1978 but Gaddafi had sent an imposter to Italy shortly afterwards to give the impression that al-Sadr's disappearance took place after his visit to Libya. *New York Times*, 'Qaddafi Son Arrested by Lebanon in New Twist on Missing Imam Mystery', 14 December 2015.

17 Cherstich, 'When tribesmen', p. 409.

18 Human Rights Watch, 'Libya: June 1996 Killings at Abu Salim Prison', 27 June 2006; *Guardian*, 'Abu Salim: walls that talk', 30 September 2011. The original Human

Rights Watch report was based on the testimony of a sole former inmate who did not actually see any prisoners being killed.

19   Filiu, *The Arab Revolution*, p. 83.

20   M. Capasso, 'The Libyan Drawers: Stateless society, humanitarian intervention, logic of exception, and traversing the phantasy', *Middle East Critique*, Vol. 23, No. 4, 2014, pp. 391–2.

21   E. Diana, 'Literary springs in Libyan literature: contributions of writers to the country's emancipation', *Middle East Critique*, Vol. 23, No. 4, 2014, p. 442. Citing H. Metz (ed.), *Libya: A Country Study* (Washington DC: Library of Congress, 1987), p. 85.

22   Diana, 'Literary springs', p. 442.

23   These sanctions came to an end in 2003. BBC Online, 'Timeline: Libya Sanctions', 15 October 2004.

24   Filiu, *The Arab Revolution*, p. 13; Assaf, 'Libya at the crossroads'.

25   A. Shamis, 'Gaddafi and Me', *Critical Muslim*, Vol. 1, No. 1, 2012, p. 48.

26   Ibid., p. 54; *Guardian*, 'Flight from the truth', 27 June 2001.

27   W. Blum, *Killing Hope: US Military and CIA Interventions Since World War II* (London: Zed, 2014), p. 289.

28   BBC Online, 'Abu Nidal behind Lockerbie bombing', 23 August 2002.

29   Blum, *Killing Hope*, p. 288.

30   *Guardian*, 'Anthony Giddens' trip to see Gaddafi vetted by Libyan intelligence chief', 5 March 2011.

31   C. Tawil, 'Mapping Gaddafi's Tribal Allegiances in Libya', *Jamestown Foundation Terrorism Monitor*, Vol. 9, No. 17. 2005; Doha News, 'Qaddafi's spymaster takes a walk', 6 February 2012; *Observer*, 'Secret Libyan files claim MI6 and the CIA aided human rights violations', 3 September 2011; Assaf, 'Libya at the crossroads'.

32   Dabashi, *The Arab Spring*, p. 198; B. Yaghmaian, 'The Spectre of Black Europe', *Counterpunch*, 23 February 2011.

33   Dabashi, *The Arab Spring*, p. 56; *Daily Telegraph*, 'Colonel Gaddafi warned Tony Blair of Islamist attacks on Europe, phone conversations reveal', 7 January 2016.

34   K. Ulrichsen, *Qatar and the Arab Spring* (London: Hurst, 2014), pp. 122–3; BBC Online, 'HIV medics released to Bulgaria', 24 July 2007; *Daily Telegraph*, 'Lockerbie bomber Megrahi living in luxury villa six months after being at death's door', 20 February 2010.

35   Assaf, 'Libya at the crossroads'; *Financial Times*, 'West's Policy Exposed as Mad Dog Finds Bite', 21 February 2011.

36   Department of State, 'Source Embassy Tripoli 000208', 9 March 2009 (leaked).

37   Assaf, 'Libya at the crossroads'; Z. Sardar, 'Surprise, Surprise!', *Critical Muslim*, Vol. 1, No. 1, 2012, p. 15.

38   *Guardian*, 'Revealed: how Blair colluded with Gaddafi regime in secret', 23 January 2015.

39   Department of State, 'Source Embassy Tripoli 000208', 9 March 2009 (leaked).

40   M. Curtis, *Secret Affairs: Britain's Collusion with Radical Islam* (London: Serpent's Tail, 2012), p. 367; Assaf, 'Libya at the crossroads'; *Daily Telegraph*, 'UK promoted sale of sniper rifles to Gaddafi just weeks before uprising began', 10 November 2011; CAAT, 'EU arms sales to Libya: fleshing out the figures', 25 February 2011.

41   Assaf, 'Libya at the crossroads'; Curtis, *Secret Affairs*, p. 367; CAAT, 'EU arms sales to Libya: fleshing out the figures', 25 February 2011; *Daily Telegraph*, 'UK promoted sale of sniper rifles to Gaddafi just weeks before uprising began', 10 November 2011.

42   *Guardian*, 'Revealed: how Blair colluded with Gaddafi regime in secret', 23 January 2015.

43   D. Mizner, 'A War for Power', *Jacobin*, 3 October 2014.

44   International Committee of the Fourth International, 'WikiLeaks documents shed light on US-backed intervention in Libya', 27 July 2011; *New York Times*, 'Shady dealings helped Gaddafi build fortune and regime', 24 March 2011.

45   Ibid.

46   Ibid.

47   CIA, 'Intelligence Bulletin: Daily Brief', 18 October 1960 [declassified 2003].

48   International Committee of the Fourth International, 'WikiLeaks documents shed light on US-backed intervention in Libya', 27 July 2011; *New York Times*, 'Shady dealings helped Gaddafi build fortune and regime', 24 March 2011.

49   Ibid.; Mizner, 'A War for Power'; G. Shupak, 'The Disaster in Libya', *Jacobin*, 9 February 2015; *Counterpunch*, 'A Victory for the Libyan People?', 31 August 2011.

50   Shupak, 'The Disaster in Libya'; Curtis, *Secret Affairs*, p. 367.

51   Department of State, 'F-2014–20439 Doc No. C05785522', 2 April 2011.

52   Dabashi, *The Arab Spring*, p. 19; *Guardian*, 'Abu Salim: walls that talk', 30 September 2011.

53   International Committee of the Fourth International, 'WikiLeaks documents shed light on US-backed intervention in Libya', 27 July 2011.

54   Omar al-Mukhtar was captured and hanged by Italian forces in 1931.

55   A. B. Atwan, *Islamic State: The Digital Caliphate* (London: Saqi, 2015), p. 220.

56   Brownlee, *The Arab Spring*, pp. 82–3.

57   Diana, 'Literary springs', p. 449; M. Gaddafi, *Escape to Hell and other stories* (Toronto: Hushion House, 1998), p. 63.

58   Brownlee, *The Arab Spring*, p. 81.

59   Shamis, 'Gaddafi and me', p. 60; Assaf, 'Libya at the crossroads'.

60   Assaf, 'Libya at the crossroads'; Filiu, *The Arab Revolution*, p. 85; Al-Jazeera, 'Fresh violence rages in Libya', 22 February 2011; *New York Times*, 'Hopes for a Qaddafi Exit, and Worries of What Comes Next', 21 March 2011.

61 Department of Defense, 'News Briefing with Secretary Gates and Admiral Mullen from the Pentagon', 1 March 2011.
62 Ulrichsen, *Qatar*, p. 125. Citing Hugh Roberts.
63 For a good background discussion, see G. Stamov, 'New meaning for an old relationship: Serbia's arms deals during Gaddafi's reign', LSE Ideas blog post, 20 December 2011.
64 Reuters, 'Analysis: Is Libya's Gaddafi turning to foreign mercenaries?', 24 February 2011; *Counterpunch*, 'A Victory for the Libyan People?', 31 August 2011. Quoting Ibrahim Dabbashi.
65 Reuters, 'Analysis: Is Libya's Gaddafi turning to foreign mercenaries?', 24 February 2011.
66 Brownlee, *The Arab Spring*, p. 155. Citing George Joffe.
67 *Counterpunch*, 'A Victory for the Libyan People?', 31 August 2011.
68 BBC Online, 'African viewpoint: Colonel's continent?', 26 February 2011.
69 World Socialist Website, 'Libyan rebels massacre black Africans', 31 March 2011.
70 *Los Angeles Times*, 'Libyan rebels appear to take leaf from Kadafi's playbook', 24 March 2011.
71 *Counterpunch*, 'A Victory for the Libyan People?', 31 August 2011.
72 Associated Press, 'AU: Libya rebels killing black workers', 29 August 2011.
73 *Daily Telegraph*, 'Gaddafi's ghost town after the loyalists retreat', 11 September 2011; Capasso, 'The Libyan Drawers', p. 398.
74 *Washington Post*, 'The Resurgence of Arab Militaries', 5 December 2014.
75 For example Ali Ahmida. Cited by Brownlee, *The Arab Spring*, p. 156.
76 Notably Mahmoud Jibril who went on to be the National Transitional Council's interim prime minister. Cherstich, 'When tribesmen', pp. 415–16; Brownlee, *The Arab Spring*, pp. 155–6.
77 This argument was put forward by Marwan Bishara. Al-Jazeera, 'A Rude Arab Awakening', 1 August 2011.
78 Brownlee, *The Arab Spring*, p. 82.
79 Assaf, 'Libya at the crossroads'.
80 Ibid.
81 Al-Monitor, 'Abdel-Jalil and France', 23 June 2015; Department of State, 'F-2014–20439 Doc No. C05785522', 2 April 2011.
82 Al-Jazeera, 'Libya opposition launches council', 27 February 2011; Ulrichsen, *Qatar*, p. 123.
83 Department of Defense, 'News Briefing with Secretary Gates and Admiral Mullen from the Pentagon', 1 March 2011.
84 *Guardian*, 'SAS and MI6 officers released by Libya's rebel commanders', 7 March 2011; *Guardian*, 'Al-Jazeera footage captures western troops on the ground in Libya', 30 May 2011.

85   *Asian Tribune*, 'Libyan rebellion has radical Islamist fervour: Benghazi link to Islamic militancy: US Military Document Reveals', 17 March 2011; *Wall Street Journal*, 'Rebels Fight US for Funds It Seized', 9 April 2011.
86   Dabashi, *The Arab Spring*, p. 19.
87   *Independent*, 'Tony Blair tried to save Colonel Gaddafi just before bombing of Libya', 31 August 2015.
88   Ulrichsen, *Qatar*, p. 2.
89   Al-Jazeera, 'Rape used as a weapon in Libya', 28 March 2011; *Guardian*, 'Libya mass rape claims: using Viagra would be a horrific first', 9 June 2011; *Counterpunch*, 'A Victory for the Libyan People?', 31 August 2011.
90   *Counterpunch*, 'A Victory for the Libyan People?', 31 August 2011.
91   *New York Times*, 'Qaddafi Warns of Assault on Benghazi as UN Vote Nears', 17 March 2011.
92   NBC, 'US Intel: no evidence of Viagra as weapon in Libya', 30 April 2011; *Counterpunch*, 'A Victory for the Libyan People?', 31 August 2011.
93   *New York Times*, 'Qaddafi Warns of Assault on Benghazi as UN Vote Nears', 17 March 2011.
94   Assaf, 'Libya at the crossroads'.
95   *Peace Reporter* (Italy), 'Il possibile successore di Gheddafi', 24 March 2011.
96   Ulrichsen, *Qatar*, p. 124.
97   Author interviews with Tripoli residents, September 2014; B. Hounshell, 'The Revolution Will Soon Be Televised', *Foreign Policy*, 28 March 2011.
98   *Guardian*, 'Libyan revolutionary council rejects African Union's peace initiative', 11 April 2011.
99   Assaf, 'Libya at the crossroads'; Reuters, 'Libya to honour all legal oil deals', 24 August 2011.
100   Russia, India, China, Germany, and Brazil all abstained. UN Security Council, 'Security Council Approves No-Fly Zone over Libya, Authorizing All Necessary Measures to Protect Civilians, by Vote of 10 in Favour with 5 Abstentions', 17 March 2011.
101   UN General Assembly, 'Resolution 1973 adopted by the General Assembly', 17 March 2011.
102   Dabashi, *The Arab Spring*, p. 20.
103   *Guardian*, 'Obama: leading from behind on Libya', 11 August 2011; International Committee of the Fourth International, 'WikiLeaks documents shed light on US-backed intervention in Libya', 27 July 2011; *New York Times*, 'Shady dealings helped Gaddafi build fortune and regime', 24 March 2011; *Atlantic*, 'The Obama Doctrine', April 2016.
104   Department of Defense, 'Coalition Launches Operation Odyssey Dawn', 19 March 2011.
105   M. Capasso, I. Cherstich, 'The Libyan event and the part for the whole', *Middle East Critique*, Vol. 23, No. 4, 2014, p. 381; Capasso, 'The Libyan Drawers', p. 394.

106 Joint Task Force Odyssey Dawn Public Affairs, 'New coalition member flies first sortie enforcing no-fly zone over Libya', 25 March 2011.

107 Libya TV (translated), 'New Libya Satellite channel in Qatar confirms Eman al-Obeidy is released from custody via telephone interview', 3 April 2011; Ulrichsen, *Qatar*, p. 126; Peace Reporter (Italy), '*Il possibile successore di Gheddafi*', 24 March 2011.

108 *Counterpunch*, 'A Victory for the Libyan People?', 31 August 2011.

109 Informed Comment, 'An Open Letter to the Left on Libya', 27 March 2011.

110 Dabashi, *The Arab Spring*, pp. 104, 206.

111 *New Yorker*, 'Behind the Curtain', 5 September 2011.

112 Reuters, 'Wreck of Gaddafi's force smoulders near Benghazi', 20 March 2011.

113 Brownlee, *The Arab Spring*, p. 84; *New York Times*, 'Brother of Libya's information minister reported killed in NATO strike', 30 July 2011.

114 Capasso, 'The Libyan Drawers', p. 393.

115 Al-Jazeera, 'Libya after Gaddafi: A dangerous precedent?', 22 October 11.

116 From May 2011 onwards the NATO air strikes by Britain and France began to escalate by attacking regime command and control centres, tanks, rocket launchers and troop carriers. Ulrichsen, *Qatar*, pp. 126–7.

117 Brownlee, *The Arab Spring*, pp. 84–5.

118 *Telegraph*, 'Colonel Gaddafi died after being stabbed with bayonet, says report', 17 October 2012.

119 Department of State, 'F-2014–20439 Doc No. C05787607', 15 October 2011. The email also noted that Chad's president Idriss Deby had been supported by Gaddafi when he took power in 1990.

120 *New York Times*, 'US-Approved Arms for Libya Rebels Fell into Jihadis' Hands', 5 December 2012; *New York Times*, 'CIA Agents in Libya Aid Airstrikes and Meet Rebels', 30 March 2011.

121 *Los Angeles Times*, 'UN Security Council authorizes action against Moammar Kadafi', 18 March 2011.

122 Reuters, 'Special report: The secret plan to take Tripoli', 6 September 2011.

123 *Guardian*, 'Al-Jazeera footage captures western troops on the ground in Libya', 30 May 2011.

124 Department of State, 'F-2014–20439 Doc No. C05782401', 27 March 2011.

125 L. Trotsky, *The Revolution Betrayed* (London: Dover, 2004). See section on 'The Red Army and Its Doctrines'.

126 *Guardian*, 'Qatar admits sending hundreds of troops to support Libya rebels', 26 October 2011.

127 Ulrichsen, *Qatar*, p. 2; *Guardian*, 'Libya: Battle for Tripoli', 23 August 2011.

128 *New York Times*, 'US-Approved Arms for Libya Rebels Fell Into Jihadis' Hands', 5 December 2012.

129 Ulrichsen, *Qatar*, p. 9.

130   *Guardian,* 'Qatar admits sending hundreds of troops to support Libya rebels', 26 October 2010.

131   Ibid.; Ulrichsen, *Qatar,* p. 89.

132   Al-Jazeera, 'Qatar recognises Libyan rebels after oil deal', 28 March 2011.

133   Department of State, 'F-2014–20439 Doc No. C05785522', 2 April 2011; Department of State, 'F-2014–20439 Doc No. C05783741', 5 May 2011; Al-Monitor, 'Emails to Hillary contradict French tale on Libya war', 23 June 2015.

134   *Guardian,* 'Government admits Alan Duncan's links to company in Libyan oil cell', 1 September 2011.

135   *Christian Science Monitor,* 'Sarkozy, Cameron visit Libya for victory lap, pep talk', 15 September 2011.

136   Shupak, 'The Disaster in Libya'; *Guardian,* 'Britain is at centre of global mercenary industry, says charity', 3 February 2016.

137   *Guardian,* 'British firms urged to pack suitcases in rush for Libya business', 21 October 2011.

138   *Der Spiegel,* 'Sarkozy and Cameron in Libya: Heroes for a Day', 15 September 2011.

139   *Guardian,* 'British firms urged to pack suitcases in rush for Libya business', 21 October 2011.

140   CBS, 'Foreign oil, gas firms returning to Libya', 2 September 2011.

141   Department of State, 'F-2014–20439 Doc No. C05788788', 16 September 2011; Al-Monitor, 'Emails to Hillary contradict French tale on Libya war', 23 June 2015.

142   Middle East Eye, 'Islamic State is the cancer of modern capitalism', 27 March 2015. Citing David Anderson.

143   *Christian Science Monitor,* 'Sarkozy, Cameron visit Libya for victory lap, pep talk', 15 September 2011; *Guardian,* 'British firms urged to pack suitcases in rush for Libya business', 21 October 2011.

144   Assaf, 'Libya at the crossroads'.

145   Ibid.; *Los Angeles Times,* 'Islamists take aim at Libya rebels' secular leaders', 13 September 2011; Ulrichsen, *Qatar,* pp. 78, 127.

146   Capasso, 'The Libyan Drawers', pp. 397–8.

147   *Ottawa Citizen,* 'Canadian military predicted chaos in Libya if NATO helped overthrow Gadhafi', 1 March 2015.

148   *Wall Street Journal,* 'Ex-Mujahedeen Help Lead Libyan Rebels', 2 April 2011.

149   *Daily Telegraph,* 'Libyan rebel commander admits his fighters have al-Qaeda links', 25 March 2011; Curtis, *Secret Affairs,* pp. 362, 364.

150   *Independent,* 'The shady men backed by the West to displace Gaddafi', 3 April 2011; Curtis, *Secret Affairs,* pp. 361–2.

151   Ulrichsen, *Qatar,* p. 127.

152   *Wall Street Journal,* 'Tiny Kingdom's Huge Role in Libya Draws Concern', 17 October 2011.

153 BBC Online, 'Profile: Libyan rebel commander Abdel Hakim Belhadj', 4 July 2012; Brownlee, *The Arab Spring*, p. 157; Ulrichsen, *Qatar*, p. 127.

154 *New York Times*, 'US-Approved Arms for Libya Rebels Fell into Jihadis' Hands', 5 December 2012; BBC Online, 'Profile: Libyan rebel commander Abdel Hakim Belhadj', 4 July 2012.

155 *Daily Telegraph*, 'Libyan rebel commander admits his fighters have al-Qaeda links', 25 March 2011; Curtis, *Secret Affairs*, pp. 362, 364.

156 *New York Times*, 'Qatar's Support of Islamists Alienates Allies Near and Far', 7 September 2014; *Guardian*, 'Benghazi raid leaves cradle of Libyan revolution fearing for its future', 21 September 2012; European Parliament, 'The Involvement of Salafism/Wahhabism in the support and supply of arms to rebel groups around the world', Directorate-General for External Policies, June 2013, p. 22.

157 *New York Times*, 'In Clinton Emails on Benghazi, a Rare Glimpse at Her Concerns', 23 March 2015; Judicial Watch, 'New Benghazi Email Shows DOD Offered State Department Forces that Could Move to Benghazi Immediately – Specifics Blacked Out in New Document', 8 December 2015; Department of State, 'F-2015–04841 Doc No. C05739829', 26 September 2012.

158 Atwan, *Islamic State*, p. 172.

159 *Vice*, 'Al-Qaeda Plants Its Flag in Libya', 28 October 2011. Citing Sherif Elhelwa's analysis.

160 *Washington Times*, 'Secret Benghazi report reveals Hillary's Libya war push armed al-Qaeda-tied terrorists', 1 February 2015.

161 D. Kenner, 'Oil, Guns, and Money: Libya's revolution isn't over', *Foreign Policy*, 21 December 2011.

162 *The Economist*, 'Pygmy with the punch of a giant', 5 November 2011.

163 Brownlee, *The Arab Spring*, p. 157; Ulrichsen, *Qatar*, p. 130.

164 Reuters, 'Libyan Islamist militia leader to run in June poll', 15 May 2012; *Libya Herald*, 'Three-day event in Tripoli to announce Nation Party', 10 April 2012; Agence France-Presse, 'Jibril urges unity as Libya wraps up vote count', 8 July 2012.

165 *New York Times*, 'US-Approved Arms for Libya Rebels Fell Into Jihadis' Hands', 5 December 2012.

166 European Parliament, 'The Involvement of Salafism/Wahhabism', p. 22.

167 See for example *Libya Herald*, 'Hundreds gather in Algeria Square: plan to take on the militias', 7 July 2013; Reuters, 'Libyan protestors call for armed militias to be disbanded', 7 July 2013; *Libya Herald*, 'Online protest as Qatar gives Libyan Red Crescent $10 million', 10 June 2013.

168 BBC Online, 'Libyan elections: Low turnout marks bid to end political crisis', 26 June 2014.

169 Shupak, 'The Disaster in Libya'. This is not to be confused with the General National Congress that the NTC morphed into from August 2012 onwards.

170   Filiu, *From Deep State*, p. 245; *Guardian*, 'Libya supreme court rules anti-Islamist parliament unlawful', 6 November 2014.

171   *New York Times*, '350 Libyans Trained to Oust Qaddafi Are to Come to US', 17 May 1991; Shamis, 'Gaddafi and me', pp. 55–6; Shupak, 'The Disaster in Libya'.

172   Congressional Research Service, 'Libya', 19 December 1996.

173   *Independent*, 'The shady men backed by the West to displace Gaddafi', 3 April 2011; World Socialist Web Site, 'A CIA commander for the Libyan rebels', 28 March 2011; *Washington Post*, 'General Hiftar', 26 March 26 1996; *Washington Post*, 'Rebel military commander wants to be America's man on the ground in Libya', 12 April 2011.

174   France 24, 'Mystery surrounds death of Libyan rebel commander', 29 July 2011.

175   Department of State, 'F-2015–04841 Doc No. C05739727', 8 August 2011; Al-Monitor, 'Emails to Hillary contradict French tale on Libya war', 8 June 2015.

176   *New York Times*, 'US-Approved Arms for Libya Rebels Fell into Jihadis' Hands', 5 December 2012.

177   *Washington Times*, 'Secret Benghazi report reveals Hillary's Libya war push armed al-Qaeda-tied terrorists', 1 February 2015.

178   BBC Online, 'Profile: Libyan ex-General Khalifa Haftar', 16 October 2014.

179   Shupak, 'The Disaster in Libya'.

180   *New York Times*, 'Arab Nations Strike in Libya, Surprising US', 25 August 2014; BBC Online, 'Libya crisis: US caught off-guard by air strikes', 26 August 2014.

181   The 1985 CIA plan to invade Libya was blocked by the Department of State. *Washington Post*, 'Plans for Libya', 20 February 1987.

182   Author interviews with Tripoli residents, September 2014.

183   *Guardian*, 'UN Libya envoy accepts £1,000-a-day job from backer of one side in civil war', 4 November 2015.

184   Shupak, 'The Disaster in Libya'.

185   Reuters, 'UN tells backers of Libya's rival sides to pressure them for peace', 25 March 2015.

186   Sardar, 'Surprise, Surprise!', p. 15; *Vogue*, 'A Rose in the Desert: Asma al-Assad, Lady Diana of the Middle East', 25 February 2011.

187   M. Hudson, 'The Crisis of the Arab State: Study Group Report', Belfer Center for International Affairs, Harvard University, August 2015, p. 28. Citing Lisa Weeden.

188   *Guardian*, 'Miliband plans visit to Syria', 13 November 2008; *Guardian*, 'Miliband's road to Damascus', 17 November 2008; Curtis, *Secret Affairs*, p. 310.

189   Filiu, *From Deep State*, pp. 131–2.

190   Elizabeth Dickinson, 'The Case Against Qatar', *Foreign Policy*, 30 September 2014; Ulrichsen, *Qatar*, pp. 108–9, 132; S. Safwan, 'Rebellion in Syria', *Critical Muslim*, Vol. 1, No. 1, 2012, p. 122.

191   *Guardian*, 'Gaza has exposed the Arab leaders to fury and contempt', 20 January 2009; Ulrichsen, *Qatar*, pp. 109, 132.

192 Al-Bawaba, 'A luxury residence of Qatar's royal family in Palmyra is now a Daesh training site', 26 October 2015.

193 *Wall Street Journal*, 'US Pursued Secret Contacts with Assad Regime for Years', 23 December 2015.

194 Quoting Martha Kessler. Atwan, *Islamic State*, pp. 83–4; R. Dreyfuss, *Devil's Game: How the United States Helped Unleash Fundamentalist Islam* (New York: Metropolitan, 2006), p. 202; E. Hoogland, Durham University lecture, 20 June 2014.

195 Dreyfuss, *Devil's Game*, p. 205; Atwan, *Islamic State*, pp. 84–5; Filiu, *The Arab Revolution*, p. 112; A. al-Affendi, 'A Trans-Islamic Revolution?', *Critical Muslim*, Vol. 1, No. 1, 2012, p. 71. Some estimates claim over 40,000 deaths.

196 Curtis, *Secret Affairs*, p. 310; G. Gause, 'Is Saudi Arabia really counter-revolutionary?', *Foreign Policy*, 9 August 2011.

197 Atwan, *Islamic State*, p. 8. Quoting Ali Sadreddine Bayanouni.

198 *New Yorker*, 'The Redirection', 5 March 2007; Dreyfuss, *Devil's Game*, p. 202.

199 *Guardian*, 'Syria intervention plan fuelled by oil interests, not chemical weapon concern', 30 August 2013.

200 M. Weiss, H. Hassan, *ISIS: Inside the Army of Terror* (New York: Regan, 2015), p. 89.

201 Ibid.; Safwan, 'Rebellion in Syria', pp. 117–18.

202 Weiss, *ISIS*, pp. 89–90; Filiu, *The Arab Revolution*, p. 88; Atwan, *Islamic State*, p. 90; Brownlee, *The Arab Spring*, p. 92.

203 Filiu, *The Arab Revolution*, p. 88; Ulrichsen, *Qatar*, p. 132. For eyewitness reports see S. Starr, *Revolt in Syria: Eye-Witness to the Uprising* (London: Hurst, 2012).

204 Atwan, *Islamic State*, p. 90.

205 Filiu, *The Arab Revolution*, p. 89; Filiu, *From Deep State*, p. 201; Atwan, *Islamic State*, p. 90.

206 Atwan, *Islamic State*, pp. 90–91, Dabashi, *The Arab Spring*, p. 22.

207 Sardar, 'Surprise, Surprise!', p. 11; J. M. Berger, J. Stern, *ISIS: The State of Terror* (London: William Collins, 2015), p. 40; Atwan, *Islamic State*, p. 91.

208 Safwan, 'Rebellion in Syria', p. 117. Giving the example of sixty killed in Hama in one day.

209 Filiu, *The Arab Revolution*, p. 89; Sardar, 'Surprise, Surprise!', p. 8.

210 Berger, *ISIS*, p. 40; Safwan, 'Rebellion in Syria', p. 120. Giving the example of footage from an attack on the village of Beyda.

211 For a good discussion see Filiu, *From Deep State*, p. 201.

212 European Parliament, 'The Involvement of Salafism/Wahhabism', p. 16; Filiu, *From Deep State*, p. 201; *Daily Telegraph*, 'Syria releases the 7/7 mastermind', 2 February 2012; M. Hamid, L. Farrall, *The Arabs at War in Afghanistan* (London: Hurst, 2015), p. 274; Berger, *ISIS*, pp. 24, 60; Long War Journal, 'Al-Nusrah Front celebrates 9/11 attacks in new video', 29 June 2015; *Daily Telegraph*, 'Four jihadists, one prison: all released by Assad and now all dead', 11 May 2016. There is some dispute over

NOTES

Abu Musab al-Suri, as al-Qaeda maintains that he was never released from prison. Moreover, as Michael Weiss and Hassan Hassan argue, he was not necessarily released during the Spring 2011 amnesty. See; Weiss, *ISIS*, p. 99.

213 Weiss, *ISIS*, pp. 97, 106.
214 In reference to the summer 2007 jihadi uprising in Nahr al-Bared Palestinian refugee camp. *Guardian*, 'Why Isis Fight', 17 September 2015.
215 Ibid. Quoting Abu Issa.
216 Filiu, *From Deep State*, p. 202.
217 Weiss, *ISIS*, p. 99.
218 *New York Times*, 'Syrian Elite to Fight Protests to the End', 10 May 2011. Featuring Anthony Shadid interviewing Rami Makhlouf.
219 Filiu, *From Deep State*, p. 216.
220 Safwan, 'Rebellion in Syria', p. 121.
221 R. Lefevre, 'The Syrian Brotherhood's Islamic State challenge', POMEPS Study 12, 2015, pp. 56–7.
222 European Parliament, 'The Involvement of Salafism/Wahhabism', p. 14; Brownlee, *The Arab Spring*, p. 91.
223 F. Ajami, 'The Arab Spring at One: A Year of Living Dangerously', *Foreign Affairs*, March 2012.
224 Gause, 'Is Saudi Arabia really counter-revolutionary?'
225 European Parliament, 'The Involvement of Salafism/Wahhabism', p. 14; *New York Times*, 'One Syrian's Journey from Hometown Rebel to ISIS Bomber', 15 January 2016.
226 Sardar, 'Surprise, Surprise!', p. 7.
227 *USA Today*, 'Sunnis fill rebel ranks, but also prop up Assad regime', 1 August 2013; Weiss, *ISIS*, p. 91.
228 For example, Muhammad al-Bouti and Mufti Ahmad Hassoun. See T. Pierret, *Religion and State in Syria: The Sunni Ulama from Coup to Revolution* (New York: Columbia University Press, 2013); European Parliament, 'The Involvement of Salafism/Wahhabism', p. 11.
229 BBC Online, 'US summons Syrian ambassador over protest filming', 9 July 2011.
230 *London Review of Books*, 'The Red Line and the Rat Line', 17 April 2014.
231 *Washington Post*, 'US-backed Syria rebels routed by fighters linked to al-Qaeda', 2 November 2014; Huffington Post, 'American Anti-Tank Weapons Appear in Syrian Rebel Hands', 11 April 2014; *IHS Janes*, 'Syrian insurgents acquire TOW missiles', 7 April 2014.
232 Atwan, *Islamic State*, p. 96; S. Mann, 'How the Arab League turned against Syria', OpenDemocracy, 9 February 2012; Ulrichsen, *Qatar*, p. 135; *Independent*, 'UK helped Saudi Arabia get UN human rights role through secret deal to exchange votes, leaked documents suggest', 30 September 2015.
233 Al-Jazeera, 'The Struggle for Syria', 15 November 2011.

601

234 Atwan, *Islamic State*, pp. 96–7; Ulrichsen, *Qatar*, p. 134.

235 Adib Shishakli was a co-founder of the SNC and went on to become its chief representative in the UAE. *Times of Israel*, 'Lebanese media fear Syrian intervention', 17 March 2013.

236 M. Lynch, *The Arab Uprising: The Unfinished Revolutions of the New Middle East* (New York: Public Affairs, 2012), p. 181.

237 Ulrichsen puts forward these points of view, made by other commentators. Ulrichsen, *Qatar*, pp. 112, 114.

238 S. Barakat, 'The Qatari Spring: Qatar's emerging role in peace-making', LSE Kuwait working paper 24, 2012, p. 36; *The Economist*, 'Qatar's new emir: a hard act to follow', 29 June 2013. *The Economist*'s description of Qatar being 'aggressively non-aligned' seemed to refer to its apparent active neutrality. In the same report, however, it did acknowledge the 'superpower insurance' that Qatar had bought by inviting the US to set up a military headquarters on its territory.

239 NPR, 'US Wary as Qatar Ramps Up Support of Syrian Rebels', 26 April 2013. Quoting Tamara Wittes, director of the Saban Center for Middle East Policy at the Brookings Institution.

240 Dickinson, 'The Case Against Qatar'.

241 BBC Online, 'Is Qatar bringing the Nusra Front in from the cold?', 6 March 2015.

242 *Guardian*, 'Qatar crosses the Syrian Rubicon: £63m to buy weapons for the rebels', 1 March 2012.

243 Agence France-Presse, 'Qatar PM: Syria war amounts to genocide', 30 October 2012.

244 Dickinson, 'The Case Against Qatar'.

245 Weiss, *ISIS*, p. 100.

246 Referring to an Iraqi sheikh and tribal leader that the US Department of the Treasury alleged was a terrorist fundraiser in 2008. *New York Times*, 'Qatar's Support of Islamists Alienates Allies Near and Far', 7 September 2014.

247 Ibid.; Dickinson, 'The Case Against Qatar'.

248 Dickinson, 'The Case Against Qatar'.

249 *New York Times*, 'Rebel Arms Flow Is Said to Benefit Jihadists in Syria', 14 October 2012.

250 *New York Times*, 'Qatar's Support of Islamists Alienates Allies Near and Far', 7 September 2014; *Wall Street Journal*, 'Qatar's Ties to Militants Strain Alliance' 23 February 2015; *Independent*, 'Senior Jabhat al-Nusra commander Abu Hammam al-Shami killed in Syria air strike', 6 March 2015.

251 *New York Times*, 'Taking Outsize Role in Syria, Qatar Funnels Arms to Rebels', 29 June 2013.

252 *New York Times*, 'An Arms Pipeline to the Syrian', 24 March 2013.

253 *New York Times*, 'Taking Outsize Role in Syria, Qatar Funnels Arms to Rebels', 29 June 2013; Agence France-Presse, 'Boeing Wins Qatar Order for C-17 Military

Aircraft', 22 July 2008; *New York Times*, 'Arms Airlift to Syria Rebels Expands, With Aid from CIA', 24 March 2013.

254 *New York Times*, 'US-Approved Arms for Libya Rebels Fell into Jihadis' Hands', 5 December 2012.

255 *New York Times*, 'Rebel Arms Flow Is Said to Benefit Jihadists in Syria', 14 October 2012.

256 *New York Times*, 'Taking Outsize Role in Syria, Qatar Funnels Arms to Rebels', 29 June 2013.

257 *New York Times*, 'An Arms Pipeline to the Syrian Rebels', 24 March 2013.

258 Atwan, *Islamic State*, p. 102.

259 *New York Times*, 'Private Donors' Funds Add Wild Card to War in Syria', 12 November 2013.

260 Reuters, 'Pentagon says al-Qaeda financier killed in Syria air strike', 18 October 2015.

261 *Wall Street Journal*, 'A Veteran Saudi Power Player Works to Build Support to Topple Assad', 25 August 2013.

262 Ulrichsen, *Qatar*, p. 138–9. Citing *The National* (Abu Dhabi), 'Kuwait, the back office of logistical support for Syria's rebels', 5 February 2013. While a credible report, its sole focus on Kuwait with little reference to Qatar, Saudi, UAE or other Gulf sources of aid to Syrian rebels is problematic.

263 *New York Times*, 'Qatar's Support of Islamists Alienates Allies Near and Far', 7 September 2014.

264 *New York Times*, 'Private Donors' Funds Add Wild Card to War in Syria', 12 November 2013.

265 Dickinson, 'The Case Against Qatar'.

266 European Parliament, 'The Involvement of Salafism/Wahhabism', p. 14.

267 Dickinson, 'The Case Against Qatar'; Long War Journal, 'Former head of al-Qaeda's network in Iran now operates in Syria', 25 March 2014; Department of State, 'Rewards for Justice – al-Qaida Reward Offers', 18 October 2012.

268 *Guardian*, 'Senior al-Qaida figure, Muhsin al-Fadhli, killed in US air strike in Syria, officials say', 22 July 2015.

269 *Arab News*, 'Al-Qaeda suspects in Kuwait trial plead not guilty', 17 December 2002; *Asharq al-Awsat* (translated), 'Published investigations on behalf of the Kuwaiti state security with the accused in the case of the organization Al-Qaeda', 12 December 2002.

270 *Wall Street Journal*, 'A Veteran Saudi Power Player Works to Build Support to Topple Assad', 25 August 2015.

271 NPR, 'US Wary as Qatar Ramps Up Support of Syrian Rebels', 26 April 2013.

272 Blum, *Killing Hope*, p. 350.

273 Author's correspondence with a senior British broadsheet journalist, August 2013.

274 A. Callinicos, 'Spectres of counter-revolution', *International Socialism*, No. 140, 7 October 2013. George Hamilton was also known as Lord Aberdeen.

275 Referring to Jeremy Bowen.

276 BBC Online, 'Syria crisis: UN inspectors' convoy hit by sniper fire', 26 August 2013.

277 *Washington Post*, '"Black budget" summary details US spy network's successes, failures and objectives', 29 August 2013.

278 *London Review of Books*, 'Whose Sarin?', 19 December 2013.

279 Ibid.; White House, 'US Government Assessment of the Syrian Government's Use of Chemical Weapons on August 21 2013', 30 August 2013.

280 *Washington Post*, 'More than 1,400 killed in Syrian chemical weapons attack, US says', 30 August 2013.

281 *London Review of Books*, 'Whose Sarin?', 19 December 2013.

282 *London Review of Books*, 'The Red Line and the Rat Line', 17 April 2014.

283 Weiss, *ISIS*, p. 119; C. Lister, 'Profiling the Islamic State', Brookings Doha Center, Analysis Paper 13, November 2014, p. 12.

284 McClatchy, 'Islamist rebel leader walks back rhetoric in first interview with US media', 20 May 2015; Atwan, *Islamic State*, pp. 107–8. Also see (Arabic) 'Speech of Sheikh Zahran Alloush to the Islamic Nation on the subject of the challenge of the rejectionists', 30 September 2013.

285 McClatchy, 'New analysis of rocket used in Syria chemical attack undercuts US claims', 15 January 2014.

286 Ibid.

287 *New York Times*, 'New Study Refines View of Sarin Attack in Syria', 28 December 2013.

288 *London Review of Books*, 'The Red Line and the Rat Line', 17 April 2014.

289 BBC, *Newsnight*, 29 August 2013; BBC, *Newsnight*, 29 August 2014; BBC, 'Complaints CAS-2348765–90RRYX, letter addressed to Mr Robert Stuart', 2 December 2013.

290 Saudi Arabia Ministry for Foreign Affairs, '6d40e57f-d986–e111–846d-001aa0248408.tif', 7 February 2012 (leaked). Referring to a note by the director general of the OPCW.

291 *Daily Telegraph*, 'ISIL used chemical weapons against Kurds in Iraq, say German troops', 14 August 2015.

292 BBC Online, 'US official: IS making and using chemical weapons in Iraq and Syria', 11 September 2015.

293 BBC Online, 'Hezbollah leader Nasrallah vows victory in Syria', 25 May 2013.

294 *Wall Street Journal*, 'US to Give Some Syria Rebels Ability to Call Airstrikes', 17 February 2015.

295 Reuters, 'US air drops ammunition to Syria rebels', 12 October 2015; Al-Jazeera, 'US drops ammunition to rebels fighting ISIL in Syria', 13 October 2015.

296 Examples of groups having their weapons seized include the Harakat Hazm and the Syrian Revolutionary Movement. See *Washington Post*, 'US-backed Syria

rebels routed by fighters linked to al-Qaeda', 2 November 2014; Huffington Post, 'American Anti-Tank Weapons Appear in Syrian Rebel Hands', 11 April 2014; *IHS Janes*, 'Syrian insurgents acquire TOW missiles', 7 April 2014; *Los Angeles Times*, 'In Syria, militias armed by the Pentagon fight those armed by the CIA', 27 March 2016.

297 P. Cockburn, *The Rise of Islamic State: ISIS and the New Sunni Revolution* (London: Verso, 2015), p. 3.

298 Middle East Eye, 'Islamic State is the cancer of modern capitalism', 27 March 2015.

299 *Los Angeles Times*, 'In Syria, militias armed by the Pentagon fight those armed by the CIA', 27 March 2016. Quoting Jeffrey White.

300 Middle East Eye, 'Islamic State is the cancer of modern capitalism', 27 March 2015.

301 Sky News, 'Interview with David Cameron and former British ambassador to Syria Peter Ford', 5 October 2015.

302 *Paris Match* (translated), 'Alain Juillet: an intelligence service must be neutral', 5 May 2016.

303 Atwan, *Islamic State*, p. 104; Al-Jazeera, 'Syrian fighter defects to Qaeda-linked group', 16 December 2013.

304 European Parliament, 'The Involvement of Salafism/Wahhabism', pp. 16–17.

305 International Crisis Group, 'Tentative Jihad: Syria's Fundamentalist Opposition', 12 October 2012.

306 A. Hashim, 'The Islamic State: from Al-Qaeda affiliate to caliphate', *Middle East Policy*, Vol. 21, No. 4, 2014, p. 7.

307 Cockburn, *The Rise of Islamic State*, p. 85.

308 Atwan, *Islamic State*, p. 105.

309 *Daily Telegraph*, 'Syria dispatch: from band of brothers to princes of war', 30 November 2013.

310 NBC, 'New Details on 2012 Kidnapping of NBC News Team in Syria', 16 April 2015.

311 *New York Times*, 'NBC News Alters Account of Correspondent's Kidnapping in Syria', 15 April 2015.

312 Cockburn, *The Rise of Islamic State*, p. 26.

313 European Parliament, 'The Involvement of Salafism/Wahhabism', p. 13.

314 Cockburn, *The Rise of Islamic State*, p. 53.

315 Atwan, *Islamic State*, p. 109; Al-Jazeera, 'UN peacekeepers kidnapped in Golan released', 12 May 2013; *As-Safir* (translated), 'The first battle between Al-Nusra and Daesh in Daraa', 15 December 2014.

316 Atwan, *Islamic State*, p. 107.

317 M. Doran, W. McCants, C. Watts, 'The Good and Bad of Ahrar al-Sham', *Foreign Affairs*, 23 January 2014; Atwan, *Islamic State*, p. 107; *Washington Post*, 'Naturalized US citizen accused of arming rebel group in Syria', 7 December 2015; Al-Jazeera, 'Upfront: Who is Qatar backing in Syria?', 30 October 2015; *Daily Telegraph*, 'Four jihadists, one prison: all released by Assad and now all dead', 11 May 2016.

318 *Guardian*, 'Syria crisis: Saudi Arabia to spend millions to train new rebel force', 7 November 2013.

319 McClatchy, 'Islamist rebel leader walks back rhetoric in first interview with US media', 20 May 2015.

320 Al-Monitor, 'Jordan's Syria blacklist blasted by key players', 28 December 2015; *Al-Hayat* (translated), 'Army of Islam used detainees as human shields', 1 November 2015.

321 Agence France-Presse, 'Russian bid to blacklist Syrian rebel groups blocked at UN', 10 May 2016.

322 *Guardian*, 'How Britain funds the propaganda war against ISIS in Syria', 3 May 2016; Al-Akhbar (Lebanon), 'Harakat Hazm: America's new favourite jihadist group', 22 May 2014.

323 *Guardian*, 'Terror trial collapses after fears of deep embarrassment to security services', 1 June 2015.

324 Weiss, *ISIS*, p. 107; *Independent*, 'Turkey and Saudi Arabia alarm the West by backing Islamist extremists the Americans had bombed in Syria', 12 May 2015; Daily Beast, 'Syria's Saudi jihadist problem', 16 December 2013; Reuters, 'Six Islamist factions unite in largest Syria rebel merger', 22 November 2013.

325 Department of the Treasury, 'Remarks of Under Secretary for Terrorism and Financial Intelligence David Cohen before the Center for a New American Security on Confronting New Threats in Terrorist Financing', 4 March 2014; Department of the Treasury, 'Treasury Designates Al-Qaeda Supporters in Qatar and Yemen', 18 December 2013. Referring to the Qatari citizen al-Rahman bin Umayr al-Nuaymi.

326 Department of the Treasury, 'Remarks of Under Secretary for Terrorism and Financial Intelligence David Cohen before the Center for a New American Security on Confronting New Threats in Terrorist Financing', 4 March 2014. Referring to Nayef al-Ajmi.

327 Department of the Treasury, 'Treasury Designates Gulf-Based al-Qaeda Financiers', 5 June 2008; *Wall Street Journal*, 'Qatar's Ties to Militants Strain Alliance', 23 February 2015; Politico, 'Qatar Needs Tough Love', 23 February 2015.

328 Middle East Eye, 'US imposes sanctions on two Qatari nationals for terrorism financing', 6 August 2015.

329 Reuters, 'Insight: Syria's Nusra Front may leave Qaeda to form new entity', 4 February 2015; Cockburn, *The Rise of Islamic State*, p. 26.

330 BBC Online, 'Is Qatar bringing the Nusra Front in from the cold?', 6 March 2015.

331 Huffington Post, 'An Internal Struggle: Al-Qaeda's Syrian Affiliate Is Grappling with Its Identity', 31 May 2015.

332 *Haaretz*, 'Israel Halts Medical Treatment for Members of Syria's Nusra Front', 20 July 2015; *Jerusalem Post*, 'New UN report reveals collaboration between Israel and Syrian rebels', 12 July 2014.

333 Al-Jazeera, 'Nusra leader: Our mission is to defeat Syrian regime', 28 May 2015.

334 The interview was conducted by Al-Jazeera anchor Ahmed Mansour. It lasted for approximately fifty minutes and was broadcast on Al-Jazeera Arabic on 8 July 2015.

335 Atwan, *Islamic State*, p. 129; Reuters, 'Insight: Syria's Nusra Front may leave Qaeda to form new entity', 4 February 2015; Cockburn, *The Rise of Islamic State*, p. 26.

336 Long War Journal, 'Al-Nusrah Front celebrates 9/11 attacks in new video', 29 June 2015.

337 Dickinson, 'The Case Against Qatar'.

338 *Wall Street Journal*, 'Qatar's Ties to Militants Strain Alliance', 23 February 2015.

339 *Wall Street Journal*, 'An American-Led Coalition Can Defeat ISIS', 24 August 2014. Referring to Jack Keane.

340 Free Beacon, 'Congress to Obama Admin: US Billions Are Enabling Terror Regimes in Qatar', 23 February 2015.

341 Reuters, 'US signs agreement for $11 billion arms sale to Qatar', 14 July 2014.

342 *Wall Street Journal*, 'Qatar's Ties to Militants Strain Alliance', 23 February 2015.

343 *New York Times*, 'Qatar's message to Obama', 24 February 2015.

344 Referring to a sermon delivered at the Grand Mosque in Doha on 30 January 2015. Politico, 'Qatar Needs Tough Love', 23 February 2015.

345 BBC Online, 'Syria accused of torture and 11,000 executions', 21 January 2014; Cockburn, *The Rise of Islamic State*, p. 9. The British law firm was Carter-Ruck.

346 BBC Online, 'Syria accused of torture and 11,000 executions', 21 January 2014.

347 Cockburn, *The Rise of Islamic State*, p. 93; C. C. O'Brien, *States of Ireland* (Dublin: Faber and Faber, 1972), p. 283. The original author of the phrase was Erskine Holmes, chairman of the Northern Ireland Labour Party.

348 See for example Human Rights Watch, 'World Report 2014 – Events of 2013', January 2014, pp. 605–11.

349 Human Rights Watch, 'If the Dead Could Speak: Mass Deaths and Torture in Syria's Detention Facilities', 16 December 2015.

350 Chatham House seminar entitled 'Pursuing Atrocity Accountability in Syria', 14 May 2015; *Guardian*, 'Syria's truth smugglers', 13 May 2015.

351 *Guardian*, 'Syria's truth smugglers', 13 May 2015.

352 http://syriadirect.org/pages/about-us/ (accessed 21 December 2105).

353 usaspending.gov (an official website of the US government). See https://www.usaspending.gov/transparency/Pages/RecipientProfile.aspx?DUNSNumber=557662856&FiscalYear=2014 ; https://www.usaspending.gov/transparency/Pages/RecipientProfile.aspx?DUNSNumber=557662856&FiscalYear=2015 ; https://www.usaspending.gov/transparency/Pages/RecipientProfile.aspx?DUNSNumber=557662856&FiscalYear=2016 (accessed 7 March 2016).

354 www.whitehelmets.org (accessed 9 October 2015).

355 *New York Times*, 'Unpaid, Unarmed Lifesavers in Syria', 14 February 2015.

356 *New York Times*, 'Syria Is Using Chemical Weapons Again, Rescue Workers Say', 6 May 2015.

357 *New York Times*, 'Airstrikes Kill Rescue Worker and Family of 5 in Syria', 3 October 2015.

358 *New York Times*, 'Unpaid, Unarmed Lifesavers in Syria', 14 February 2015.

359 Tweet: @foreignoffice 'Take a look at the Foreign Secretary's visit to UK funded @SyriaCivilDef training centre in #Turkey. #SupportSyrians', 18 January 2016.

360 *Men's Journal*, 'The Most Dangerous Job in the World: Syria's Elite Rescue Force', 1 December 2014. Quoting Mark Ward.

361 *Washington Post*, 'The Resurgence of Arab Militaries', 5 December 2014.

362 Middle East Eye, 'What is Yemen's Al-Houthi really saying?', 12 September 2014.

363 Filiu, *From Deep State*, p. 199; Brownlee, *The Arab Spring*, p. 77.

364 Agence France-Presse, 'Beleaguered Hadi says Aden Yemen capital', 7 March 2015; CBC, 'Yemeni's Abed Rabbo Mansour Hadi arrives in Saudi capital', 26 March 2015.

365 Filiu, *From Deep State*, p. 199; Middle East Eye, 'The Pentagon plan to divide and rule the Muslim world', 3 April 2015. US officials reportedly understood that a meeting had taken place between Ahmed bin Saleh and Iranian officials in Rome. Citing the views of Abdussalam al-Rubaidi, a lecturer at Sana'a University and chief editor of the Yemen Polling Centre's 'Framing the Yemeni Revolution Project'.

366 It is thought that only about ten percent of the promised GCC aid materialized. Filiu, *From Deep State*, p. 143.

367 Department of State, 'Yemenis tell Gen Abizaid about Iranian interference and regional intentions 06SANAA1833_a', 24 June 2006 (leaked).

368 Department of State, 'Yemenis ask Codel for help in Saada; present weak evidence of Iranian links 07SANAA297_a', 26 February 2007 (leaked).

369 Filiu, *From Deep State*, pp. 143–4.

370 Department of State, 'Yemenis ask Codel for help in Saada; present weak evidence of Iranian links 07SANAA297_a', 26 February 2007 (leaked).

371 Department of State, 'Saada solution requires more thought, fewer weapons 09SANAA2052_a', 11 November 2009 (leaked).

372 The UAE defended its move of embassies on the grounds that it was 'in order to entrench constitutional legitimacy in Yemen, embodied by President Abd-Rabbu Mansour Hadi and his government'. Reuters, 'UAE and Kuwait to reopen embassies in Yemen's south, backing Hadi', 27 February 2015; Agence France-Presse, 'Beleaguered Hadi says Aden Yemen capital', 7 March 2015.

373 Associated Press, 'Yemen Shiite rebel leader: Saudi Arabia seeks Yemen split', 26 February 2015.

374 Filiu, *From Deep State*, p. 94; D. Ottaway, 'Saudi Arabia's Yemeni Quagmire', Wilson Center, 15 December 2015.

375 Al-Jazeera, 'Up Front: Preview: Who is to blame for the war in Yemen?', 17 September 2015.

376 Agence France-Presse, 'Beleaguered Hadi says Aden Yemen 'capital', 7 March 2015; Reuters, 'US ambassador meets Yemen's Hadi in Aden', 2 March 2015.

377 J. Willis, 'Operation Decisive Storm and the Expanding Counter-Revolution', MERIP, 30 March 2015.

378 M. Curtis, *Web of Deceit: Britain's Real Role in the World* (London: Vintage, 2003), p. 93. Quoting Admiral Sir Michael Boyce.

379 *Los Angeles Times*, 'Iran-backed rebels loot Yemen files about US spy operations', 25 March 2015.

380 *Guardian*, 'The US isn't winding down its wars – it's just running them at arm's length', 8 April 2015; *Defense News*, 'RAF Bombs Diverted to Saudis for Yemen Strikes', 16 July 2015.

381 Willis, 'Operation Decisive Storm'; *Sudan Tribune*, 'Saudi Arabia agrees to fund dams, agriculture and electricity projects in Sudan', 3 November 2015. Sudan was believed to have received Saudi aid packages in late 2014 and again in November 2015.

382 $1 billion was eventually transferred in August 2015, and earlier in the year Sudan was understood to have closed down Iran-linked cultural centres and shifted its fundraising efforts from Tehran to Riyadh. As a local academic put it, 'The Iranians, while they can help by giving arms, are not in a position to provide financial support.' *Sudan Tribune*, 'Sudan says it received $1 billion in Forex deposits from Saudi Arabia', 13 August 2015; *Wall Street Journal*, 'Sudan's Split with Iran Boosts Saudi Camp', 13 August 2015.

383 Saudi Arabia provided Pakistan with a $1.5 billion loan as recently as 2014. *Guardian*, 'Pakistan weighs up joining Saudi coalition against Houthi rebels in Yemen', 31 March 2015; *Financial Times*, 'Saudi to press Pakistan for more troops', 4 March 2015.

384 *Financial Times*, 'Saudi to press Pakistan for more troops', 4 March 2015; Agence France-Presse, 'Terror wave in Pakistan sparks rare criticism of Saudi Arabia', 21 February 2015.

385 The development plan being 'Programme Senegal Emergent 2035'. *Washington Post*, 'Why Senegal is sending troops to help Saudi Arabia in Yemen', 5 May 2015; BBC Online, 'Why is Senegal sending troops to Saudi Arabia?', 5 May 2015.

386 *Bloomberg*, 'Recruiting Mercenaries for Middle East Fuels Rancor in Colombia', 31 December 2015.

387 *New York Times*, 'Emirates Secretly Sends Colombian Mercenaries to Yemen Fight', 25 November 2015; *Guardian*, 'Australian mercenary reportedly killed in Yemen clashes', 8 December 2015; Middle East Eye, 'Revealed: The mercenaries commanding UAE forces in Yemen', 23 December 2015; *Bloomberg*, 'Saudi Arabia, UAE Paying Eritrea to Back Yemen Fight, UN Says', 5 November 2015; *The Times*, 'Dozens of foreign mercenaries killed in Yemen war, rebels say', 26 December 2016; Morocco World News, 'Morocco Sends 1,500 Soldiers to Participate in Ground Operations in Yemen', 3 December 2015; Reuters, 'Yemen declares UN human rights representative persona non grata', 7 January 2016.

388 Reuters, 'Heavy fighting in Yemen, Saudi Arabia trains tribal fighters', 29 April 2015; Agence France-Presse, 'Yemen army recruits 4,800 southern fighters: officer', 28 August 2015; *The National*, 'UAE brings stability back to life in Aden', 23 September 2015.

389 Sputnik (Russia), 'Saudi Arabia Constructs Naval Base on Yemeni Island After Its Occupation', 16 August 2015. Citing UAE's *Al-Ittihad* newspaper; The Saudi Cables, 'Special Saudi Commission to find access to Arabian Sea', 30 June 2015.

390 *Financial Times*, 'DP World faces loss of Yemen port deal', 17 December 2012; WAM (UAE government news agency), 'DP World in talks to rebuild Yemen maritime and trade sector', 14 October 2015.

391 BBC Online, 'Yemen crisis: President Hadi returns to Aden from exile', 22 September 2015; Reuters, 'Coalition attacks Yemen capital after UAE, Saudi soldiers killed', 5 September 2015; Reuters, 'Yemeni tribesmen's loyalty crucial as Saudi-led forces push for Sanaa', 18 September 2015.

392 For a representative example of the sectarian narrative in the Western media see BBC Online, 'Sectarian power grab tears Yemen apart', 3 April 2015. The Houthi movement's advances were reportedly welcomed on the basis that they secured areas against possible al-Qaeda and other extremist incursions. See Reuters, 'Iran's leader says Saudi air strikes causing genocide', 9 April 2015.

393 Tweet: Ruba Ali al-Hassani: 'Within Yemen, the conflict is political, not sectarian. Beyond its borders, the conflict is more sectarian than political', 10 April 2015.

394 Quoting Dakheel bin Naser al-Qahtani. *Guardian*, 'Saudi royal calls for regime change in Riyadh', 28 September 2015.

395 *Bloomberg*, 'Saudi Claims on Iran's Role in Yemen Face Scepticism in West', 16 April 2015.

396 Huffington Post, 'Iran Warned Houthis Against Yemen Takeover', 20 April 2015.

397 UN Security Council, 'Report on Somalia of the monitoring group on Somalia and Eritrea, 12 July 2013.

398 *New York Times*, 'Seized Chinese Weapons Raise Concerns on Iran', 2 March 2013; *New York Times*, 'Yemen Seizes Sailboat Filled with Weapons, and US Points to Iran', 28 January 2013; Small Arms Survey, *2014: Women and Guns* (Cambridge: Cambridge University Press, 2014), pp. 229–30.

399 *Asharq al-Awsat* (translated), 'Yemen: Classified document reveals extent of Iranian support for Houthis', 6 July 2015. Although London-based, the newspaper is Saudi-owned.

400 Associated Press, 'Ship halted in Arabian Sea carrying illicit arms believed to be from Iran', 30 September 2015.

401 The Sana'a administration was by this stage called the Supreme Revolutionary Committee, with its vice president being Nayef al-Qanes. IRNA (Iran), 'Supreme

Revolutionary Committee: Yemen's response to Saudi Arabia tough', 8 October 2015.

402 *Express Tribune* (Pakistan), 'Countering Iran: Hekmatyar vows to send fighters to Saudi Arabia', 8 April 2015; BBC Online, 'Afghan warlord aided Bin Laden', 11 January 2007.

403 Author interviews with a former Western intelligence official, March 2015.

404 Curtis, *Secret Affairs*, p. 336; *Express Tribune* (Pakistan), 'No sanctuaries in Pakistan: Haqqani network shifts base to Afghanistan', 18 September 2011; *New York Times*, 'US Backs Blacklisting Militant Organization', 6 September 2012.

405 *Wall Street Journal*, 'Saudi Officials Linked to Jihadist Group in WikiLeaks Cables', 28 June 2015; *Dawn* (Pakistan), 'Cables detail Saudi diplomat's meeting with Haqqani's son', 28 June 2015.

406 *New York Times*, 'Saudi Arabia Leads Air Assault in Yemen', 23 March 2015; Al-Manar (Lebanon, translated), 'Ansarullah Leader: US, Israel behind Yemen Terrorist Attacks', 22 March 2015.

407 Associated Press, 'US blasts Yemen for terror financier's role in peace talks', 18 June 2015.

408 Saudi Arabia Ministry for Foreign Affairs, '7000873876 (271) – 15515', 7 December 2011 (leaked).

409 *Wall Street Journal*, 'Al-Qaeda Fights on Same Side as Saudi-Backed Militias in Yemen', 16 July 2015.

410 D. Ottaway, 'Saudi Arabia's terrorist allies in Yemen', in Wilson Center, Viewpoint 81, August 2015.

411 *Wall Street Journal*, 'Is Al-Qaeda Winning in Saudi-Iran Proxy War in Yemen?', 10 September 2015.

412 See for example Reuters, 'Al-Qaeda deploy in Yemen's Aden, British hostage freed', 23 August 2015.

413 BBC Online, 'British hostage held by al-Qaeda in Yemen released', 23 August 2015; Middle East Eye, 'UAE paid ransom to Yemeni tribesmen to free British hostage', 27 August 2015.

414 Al-Jazeera, 'Al-Qaeda denies holding UK hostage freed in Yemen', 26 August 2015.

415 Referring to the video entitled 'The Taiz Offensive', 11 November 2015.

416 Agence France-Presse, 'Yemen's al-Qaeda branch now in control of several Aden neighbourhoods', 22 October 2015; Xinhua (China), 'Al-Qaeda seizes southern Yemeni town', 1 February 2016; Reuters, 'Al-Qaeda militants take over two South Yemen towns, residents say', 2 December 2015.

417 BBC Online, 'Yemen conflict: Al-Qaeda joins coalition battle for Taiz', 22 February 2016.

418 Reuters, 'Yemeni forces seize main oil terminal from Al-Qaeda – sources', 25 April 2016; Long War Journal, 'Arab coalition enters AQAP stronghold in port city of Mukalla, Yemen', 25 April 2016.

8. ENTER THE ISLAMIC STATE – A PHANTOM MENACE

1   H. Dabashi, *The Arab Spring: The End of Postcolonialism* (London: Zed, 2012), p. 12.

2   J. P. Filiu, *The Arab Revolution: Ten Lessons from the Democratic Uprising* (London: Hurst, 2011), pp. 107-20. In his subsequent book, however, Filiu made a good argument that the possibility of obsolescence was only conditional on the survival of the 2011 democratic movements. See J. P. Filiu, *From Deep State to Islamic State: The Arab Counter-Revolution and its Jihadi Legacy* (London: Hurst, 2015), p. xv.

3   F. Ajami, 'The Arab Spring at One: A Year of Living Dangerously', *Foreign Affairs*, March 2012; F. Gerges, *The Rise and Fall of Al-Qaeda* (Oxford: Oxford University Press, 2011).

4   J. Comolli, *Boko Haram: Nigeria's Islamist Insurgency* (London: Hurst, 2015), pp. 96–9.

5   Filiu, *The Arab Revolution*, p. 117.

6   A. B. Atwan, *Islamic State: The Digital Caliphate* (London: Saqi, 2015), p. 70.

7   *Christian Science Monitor*, 'The "cave man" and Al Qaeda', 31 October 2001; Atwan, *Islamic State*, p. 71; M. Weiss, H. Hassan, *ISIS: Inside the Army of Terror* (New York: Regan, 2015), p. 13.

8   Atwan, *Islamic State*, pp. 99–100, 102; *Daily Telegraph*, 'Al-Qaeda leader backs Syrian revolt against President Assad', 12 February 2012; J. M. Berger, 'The Middle East's Franz Ferdinand Moment', *Foreign Policy*, 8 April 2015.

9   A. Hashim, 'The Islamic State: from Al-Qaeda affiliate to caliphate', *Middle East Policy*, Vol. 21, No. 4, 2014, p. 6.

10 Sky News, 'Mullah Omar's Death Confirmed by Taliban', 30 July 2015; Long War Journal, 'Al-Qaeda renews its oath of allegiance to Taliban leader Mullah Omar', 21 July 2014. The magazine is called *Al-Nafir* or 'Call to Arms'.

11 RAND Corporation, 'Unfolding the Future of the Long War: Motivations, Prospects, and Implications for the US Army', RAND Arroyo Center, 2008, pp. xiii, 48–9; Middle East Eye, 'The Pentagon plan to divide and rule the Muslim world', 3 April 2015.

12 RAND, 'Unfolding the Future', pp. 48–9, 68, 104. Referring, it seems, to the Global Jihad Movement founded in 1998 by Zawahiri and bin Laden. For further discussion, see Atwan, *Islamic State*, p. 118.

13 RAND, 'Unfolding the Future', p. 104.

14 Ibid., p. 113.

15 R. Dreyfuss, *Devil's Game: How the United States Helped Unleash Fundamentalist Islam* (New York: Metropolitan, 2006), see introduction.

16 *New Statesman*, 'David Miliband's speech on Afghanistan: Full text', 27 July 2009.

17 Atwan, *Islamic State*, p. 198; Filiu, *The Arab Revolution*, p. 25; Filiu, *From Deep State*, p. 92. For a good discussion of the US indifference to the 1991 uprisings against Saddam Hussein see M. Curtis, *Secret Affairs: Britain's Collusion with Radical Islam* (London: Serpent's Tail, 2012), p. 176.

18   M. I. Ahmad, 'The Terrible Beauty of Wikileaks', *Critical Muslim*, Vol. 1, No. 1, 2012, p. 215.

19   *Washington Post*, 'Study claims Iraq's Excess death toll has reached 655,000', 11 October 2006.

20   BBC Online, 'Huge gaps between Iraq death estimates', 20 October 2006.

21   Weiss, *ISIS*, p. 47.

22   Ahmad, 'The Terrible Beauty', pp. 212–13.

23   *New Yorker*, 'The Redirection', 5 March 2007.

24   Ibid. Quoting Patrick Clawson, an expert on Iran and the deputy director for research at the Washington Institute for Near East Policy.

25   Long War Journal, 'The Sunni Awakening', 3 May 2007; Hashim, 'The Islamic State', p. 4. Also see J. Rayburn, *Iraq after America: Strongmen, Sectarians, Resistance* (New York: Ithaca, 2014).

26   Atwan, *Islamic State*, p. 53; Weiss, *ISIS*, pp. 64–5.

27   *Washington Post*, 'Iraq Raids Camp of Exiles from Iran', 29 July 2009; *New York Times*, 'Hunger Strikers Press for Iraq's Release of Iranian Exiles', 18 September 2009.

28   J. M. Berger, J. Stern, *ISIS: The State of Terror* (London: William Collins, 2015), pp. 28–9. Citing former US ambassador to Iraq Zalmay Khalilzad. Also see Weiss, *ISIS*, pp. 67–8; Atwan, *Islamic State*, p. 54.

29   Berger, *ISIS*, p. 13; Weiss, *ISIS*, p. 11.

30   Weiss, *ISIS*, pp. 11, 13; Berger, *ISIS*, p. 14.

31   Weiss, *ISIS*, p. 14; M. Hamid, L. Farrall, *The Arabs at War in Afghanistan* (London: Hurst, 2015), p. 183.

32   Berger, *ISIS*, p. 15; Weiss, *ISIS*, pp. 14–15.

33   Berger, *ISIS*, p. 16; Weiss, *ISIS*, p. 16. The Jordanian amnesty was to mark the succession of King Abdullah II. The attacks were to have taken place on 1 January 2000.

34   Referring to the scholars of the 'Jalalabad School'. See Hamid, *The Arabs at War*, pp. 316–17; Berger, *ISIS*, p. 16; Weiss, *ISIS*, p. 17.

35   Hashim, 'The Islamic State', p. 2; Weiss, *ISIS*, pp. 18, 27–8. The letter being intercepted by Kurdish agents in 2004.

36   *Chicago Tribune*, 'Bin Laden's mother tried to stop him, Syrian kin say', 13 November 2001; Weiss, *ISIS*, p. 17; C. Bunzel, 'From Paper State to Caliphate: The Ideology of the Islamic State', Brookings Project on US relations with the Islamic World – Analysis Paper, No. 19, March 2015, pp. 13–14; C. Lister, 'Profiling the Islamic State', Brookings Doha Center, Analysis Paper 13, November 2014, pp. 7–8; Hamid, *The Arabs at War*, pp. 257–8; Berger, *ISIS*, p. 21. Citing Aaron Zelin.

37   *Wall Street Journal*, 'The Bin Laden Papers', 14 September 2015.

38   According to a high-ranking Jordanian intelligence official who stated 'In the beginning [Iran] gave him automatic weapons, uniforms, military equipment, when he was with the army of *Ansar al-Islam*. Now they essentially just turn a blind eye

to his activities.' *Atlantic*, 'The Short, Violent Life of Abu Musab al-Zarqawi', July 2006; Lister, 'Profiling the Islamic State', p. 6; Atwan, *Islamic State*, p. 40.

39 Curtis, *Secret Affairs*, pp. 235–6; BBC Online, 'Profile: Kurdish Islamist movement', 13 January 2003.

40 Hashim, 'The Islamic State', p. 2; Atwan, *Islamic State*, p. 49.

41 Weiss, *ISIS*, pp. 30–31; Hashim, 'The Islamic State', pp. 2–3. The nickname was coined by the Saudi-based al-Qaeda magazine *Voice of Jihad* in 2004.

42 Lister, 'Profiling the Islamic State', p. 8; Atwan, *Islamic State*, p. 48; BBC Online, 'Zarqawi beheaded US man in Iraq', 13 May 2004.

43 Weiss, *ISIS*, p. 13; Berger, *ISIS*, p. 278. Although, as discussed later, al-Maqdisi may at this stage have been manipulated by Jordanian intelligence.

44 Hashim, 'The Islamic State', p. 3.

45 Atwan, *Islamic State*, p. 50; Berger, *ISIS*, p. 277.

46 *New York Times*, 'President Links Qaeda of Iraq to Qaeda of 9/11', 25 July 2007.

47 Firstly Abdullah Rashid al-Baghdadi then Abu Omar al-Baghdadi. However, as Atwan notes, most observers at the time agreed that an Egyptian national, Abu Ayyub al-Masri, was in de facto control. Atwan, *Islamic State*, p. 51.

48 Bunzel, 'From Paper State', p. 16; Weiss, *ISIS*, pp. 40, 47.

49 Bunzel, 'From Paper State', pp. 4–5, 8, 17–19; Lister, 'Profiling the Islamic State', pp. 8–9; Hashim, 'The Islamic State', p. 4.

50 Hashim, 'The Islamic State', p. 4.

51 Bunzel, 'From Paper State', pp. 4–5, 17–19.

52 Lister, 'Profiling the Islamic State', pp. 1, 9.

53 Bunzel, 'From Paper State', pp. 20, 22; Weiss, *ISIS*, p. 50. Al-Tarmia was presided over by an emir called Abu Ghazwan.

54 Weiss, *ISIS*, pp. 49, 58–9, 70–78. An example of a public denouncement being that of Nadhim al-Jibouri who eventually gave interviews on both Iraqi and Jordanian television.

55 US Court of Appeals, District of Columbia Circuit, 'No. 08-7118 Francis Gates, individually and as administrator of the estate of Oil Eugene Armstrong v. Syrian Arab Republic', 20 May 2011. The Syrian government did not deny the accusations, instead responding to the judgement by stating it was not liable as the matter was a 'non-justiciable political question'.

56 *New York Times*, 'US Actions in Iraq Fueled Rise of a Rebel', 10 August 2014; Bunzel, 'From Paper State', pp. 22–3. Referring to Abu Omar al-Baghdadi.

57 A widely distributed 'official biography' supposedly penned by the Bahraini jihadist Turki al-Bin'ali. Berger, *ISIS*, p. 33.

58 Weiss, *ISIS*, p. 81; W. McCants, 'The Believer', Brookings Institute Essay, September 2015.

59 Al-Monitor, 'The many names of Abu Bakr al-Baghdadi', 23 March 2015; Hashim, 'The Islamic State', p. 4; P. Cockburn, *The Rise of Islamic State: ISIS and the New*

Sunni Revolution (London: Verso, 2015), pp. 43–4; Atwan, *Islamic State*, pp 110–11, 115; McCants, 'The Believer'. The Saddam University of Islamic Studies was later renamed 'The Iraqi University' after the regime change in 2003.

60   Cockburn, *The Rise of Islamic State*, p. 45; McCants, 'The Believer'; Al-Monitor, 'The many names of Abu Bakr al-Baghdadi', 23 March 2015.

61   Al-Monitor, 'The many names of Abu Bakr al-Baghdadi', 23 March 2015; Hashim, 'The Islamic State', p. 4; Cockburn, *The Rise of Islamic State*, pp. 43–4; Atwan, *Islamic State*, pp. 110–11, 115; McCants, 'The Believer'.

62   Atwan, *Islamic State*, pp. 114–15; Hashim, 'The Islamic State', p. 4.

63   Al-Monitor, 'The many names of Abu Bakr al-Baghdadi', 23 March 2015; Atwan, *Islamic State*, p. 116.

64   As the *Guardian* describes, 'Abu Ahmad' remains a member of the group and is active in its operations in Iraq and Syria. The *Guardian* claims he portrayed himself as a man reluctant to stay with the group, and yet unwilling to risk any attempt to leave. *Guardian*, 'ISIS: The Inside Story', 11 December 2014. For further discussion of the arrests see Al-Monitor, 'The many names of Abu Bakr al-Baghdadi', 23 March 2015; Weiss, *ISIS*, p. 81; Berger, *ISIS*, p. 34. Berger, however, describes the arrest as taking place at some point in late 2004 or early 2005 and with al-Baghdadi merely being an 'apparent hanger-on' among a group of high-level insurgents.

65   McCants, 'The Believer'.

66   *Guardian*, 'ISIS: The Inside Story', 11 December 2014; Weiss, *ISIS*, pp. 81–2.

67   Atwan, *Islamic State*, p. 116.

68   Berger, *ISIS*, p. 37; Weiss, *ISIS*, pp. 60–62. Both quoting Major General Douglas Stone.

69   *Guardian*, 'ISIS: The Inside Story', 11 December 2014.

70   Bunzel, 'From Paper State', pp. 22–3.

71   Atwan, *Islamic State*, p. 116; *Washington Times*, 'Islamic State leader al-Baghdadi formerly a US captive', 14 July 2014.

72   *Guardian*, 'ISIS: The Inside Story', 11 December 2014.

73   *Washington Times*, 'Islamic State leader al-Baghdadi formerly a US captive', 14 July 2014; Weiss, *ISIS*, p. 81.

74   Weiss, *ISIS*, p. 82. Citing Wael Essam. These arrests may, however, have signified al-Baghdadi's rising infamy after release from Bucca.

75   Bunzel, 'From Paper State', p. 23; McCants, 'The Believer'; Atwan, *Islamic State*, pp. 87, 116–17; Weiss, *ISIS*, p. 82; Hashim, 'The Islamic State', p. 6.

76   The two leaders were Abu Omar al-Baghdadi and Abu Ayyub al-Masri. The ISI captive was the organization's emir of Baghdad, Manaf Abd al-Rahim al-Rawi. Weiss, *ISIS*, p. 79; McCants, 'The Believer'.

77   Berger, *ISIS*, pp. 257–8; Lister, 'Profiling the Islamic State', p. 11; Al-Monitor, 'The many names of Abu Bakr al-Baghdadi', 23 March 2015.

78   Atwan, *Islamic State*, p. 39, 112; Bunzel, 'From Paper State', p. 34; Al-Monitor, 'The many names of Abu Bakr al-Baghdadi', 23 March 2015.

79   *Guardian*, 'ISIS: The Inside Story', 11 December 2014.

80   Cockburn, *The Rise of Islamic State*, p. 74; Lister, 'Profiling the Islamic State', p. 11; Weiss, *ISIS*, p. 68.

81   Reuters, 'Al-Qaeda militants flee Iraq jail in violent mass break-out', 22 July 2013; BBC Online, 'Iraq jailbreaks: Hundreds escape in Taji and Abu Ghraib', 22 July 2013; Hashim, 'The Islamic State', p. 6; Berger, *ISIS*, p. 39.

82   Bunzel, 'From Paper State', p. 7.

83   Weiss, *ISIS*, pp. 8–9.

84   Bunzel, 'From Paper State', p. 8.

85   J. Wagemakers, 'Salafi ideas on state-building before and after the rise of the Islamic State', POMEPS Study 12, 2015, p. 31; Berger, *ISIS*, p. 263.

86   Bunzel, 'From Paper State', pp. 10–11.

87   *New York Times*, 'ISIS Harsh Brand of Islam Is Rooted in Austere Saudi Creed', 24 September 2014.

88   Huffington Post, 'You Can't Understand ISIS If You Don't Know the History of Wahhabism in Saudi Arabia', 27 August 2014.

89   Curtis, *Secret Affairs*, p. 139.

90   *Financial Times*, 'Saudis have lost the right to take Sunni leadership', 7 August 2014.

91   Reuters, 'Qatar pares support for Islamists but careful to preserve ties', 2 November 2014; *Al-Hayat* (translated), 'Poll to determine the position of Saudis on Daesh', 21 July 2014; *Rai Alyoum* (translated), '92 percent of Saudis believe that the organization of the Islamic state agrees with Islam', 21 July 2014.

92   J. M. Berger, J. Morgan, 'The ISIS Twitter Census: Defining and Describing the population of ISIS supporters on Twitter', Brookings Institute, Project on US relations with the Islamic World, Analysis Paper 20, March 2015.

93   Atwan, *Islamic State*, p. 210. Notably Kitab al-Tawhid by al-Wahhab.

94   Naji's real name is understood to be Muhammad Khalil al-Hakaymah, according to a number of reports published by the Al-Arabiya Institute for Studies. *Idarat al-Tawahhush* was translated into English in 2006 by William McCants. See Atwan, *Islamic State*, pp. 153, 156; Weiss, *ISIS*, p. 35; Berger, *ISIS*, pp. 23, 209, 264.

95   C. Hillenbrand, *The Crusades: Islamic Perspectives* (Edinburgh: Edinburgh University Press, 1999), pp. 241–3; Weiss, *ISIS*, p. 32.

96   Weiss, *ISIS*, pp. 132–3. Weiss and Hassan explain that by developing such cleavages within tribes, ISIS was effectively preventing a 2006-style tribal awakening against their movement.

97   K. Mazur, 'The Islamic State identity and legacies of Ba'ath rule in Syria's north-east', POMEPS Study 12, 2015, pp. 35–6.

98   Bunzel, 'From Paper State', pp. 25–6; Lister, 'Profiling the Islamic State', p. 13; Hashim, 'The Islamic State', p. 7; Filiu, *From Deep State*, pp. 202, 204; Weiss, *ISIS*, p. 99.

99   Hashim, 'The Islamic State', p. 7; Weiss, *ISIS*, p. 120.

100 Filiu, *From Deep State*, p. 204.

101 ISIS was understood to have not confirmed its approval of al-Qaeda's 2013 *General Guidelines for the work of a Jihadist* document, which precluded attacks on other sects and on public places. Atwan, *Islamic State*, pp. 61–2, 73; Bunzel, 'From Paper State', p. 29; Hashim, 'The Islamic State', p. 7.

102 Weiss, *ISIS*, pp. 21, 46. Referring to Zawahiri's July 2005 letter to al-Zarqawi.

103 Atwan, *Islamic State*, pp. 74, 228.

104 Weiss, *ISIS*, p. 120; Berger, *ISIS*, p. 43. Referring to Abu Khaled al-Suri. Also see *Guardian*, 'Al-Qaeda cut off and ripped apart by ISIS', 10 June 2015; ABC, 'Al-Qaeda Leader Al-Zawahiri Declares War on ISIS Caliph Al-Baghdadi', 10 September 2015.

105 Author interviews with former Al-Raqqah residents, October 2015.

106 Cockburn, *The Rise of Islamic State*, pp. 85, 141.

107 Weiss, *ISIS*, p. 144.

108 P. Rogers, 'Britain in Syria: A Gift to ISIS', OpenDemocracy, 3 December 2015; Weiss, *ISIS*, p. 145.

109 Weiss, *ISIS*, p. 145.

110 *Telegraph*, 'Why business is booming under Islamic State one year on', 8 June 2015.

111 *New York Times*, 'Offering Services, ISIS Digs in Deeper in Seized Territories', 16 June 2015.

112 Ajami, 'The Arab Spring at One'.

113 Al-Jazeera, 'Maliki: Saudi and Qatar at war against Iraq', 9 March 2014.

114 Cockburn, *The Rise of Islamic State*, pp. 62–3, 69; Berger, *ISIS*, p. 30.

115 Weiss, *ISIS*, pp. 68, 135; Cockburn, *The Rise of Islamic State*, p. 74.

116 *New York Times*, 'Tensions Rise in Baghdad with Raid on Official', 20 December 2012.

117 *New Yorker*, 'The Shadow Commander', 20 September 2013; Weiss, *ISIS*, pp. 94–5.

118 Amnesty International, 'Iraq: Absolute impunity: Militia rule in Iraq', 14 October 2014, p. 4.

119 BBC Online, 'Iraq conflict: Diyala Sunni mosque attack kills dozens', 22 August 2014; *Wall Street Journal*, 'Iraq Raids Protesters' Camp', 23 April 2013.

120 *Guardian*, 'ISIS the accidental occupiers must now weigh Mosul as boon or burden', 11 June 2014; Cockburn, *The Rise of Islamic State*, p. 64.

121 The diversionary attacks were launched on Ramadi, Baqubah, and Samarra – the latter being home to the Al-Askari Shia shrine. As Cockburn argues, the attack on the latter was aimed at eliciting a strong response from Baghdad. Cockburn, *The Rise of Islamic State*, pp. 13–14; Lister, 'Profiling the Islamic State', p. 18; Hashim, 'The Islamic State', p. 6.

122 Hashim, 'The Islamic State', p. 9; Cockburn, *The Rise of Islamic State*, p. 11.

123 Cockburn, *The Rise of Islamic State*, pp. 11–12, 16–17, 49.

124 Atwan, *Islamic State*, p. 58.

125 Cockburn, *The Rise of Islamic State*, p. 76; *New York Times*, 'US Actions in Iraq Fueled Rise of a Rebel', 10 August 2014; Atwan, *Islamic State*, p. 141; Weiss, *ISIS*, p. 37.

126 BBC Online, 'The Fifth Floor: Mosul: One Year On', 6 June 2015.

127 *New York Times*, 'Offering Services, ISIS Digs in Deeper in Seized Territories', 16 June 2015.

128 Berger, *ISIS*, p. 45; Atwan, *Islamic State*, p. 127.

129 Berger, *ISIS*, p. 117.

130 R. Nielsen, 'Does the Islamic State believe in sovereignty?' POMEPS Study 12, 2015, pp. 28–30.

131 Weiss, *ISIS*, p. 20.

132 Atwan, *Islamic State*, p. 111.

133 Al-Hayat Media Centre, 'A Message to the Mujahideen and the Muslim Ummah in the month of Ramadan', 4 July 2014.

134 Q. Mecham, 'How much of a state is the Islamic State?', POMEPS Study 12, 2015, p. 21; Berger, *ISIS*, pp. 118–19; J. Schwedler, 'Why academics can't get beyond moderates and radicals', POMEPS Study 12, 2015, p. 11.

135 Bunzel, 'From Paper State', pp. 9–10. In some cases, Islamic State statements even declared the Brotherhood to be 'traitors'.

136 M. Lynch, 'Introduction', POMEPS Study 12, 2015, p. 7.

137 Hamid, *The Arabs at War*, p. 318.

138 Press TV (Iran), 'Exclusive: Maliki says Iran has important role in territorial integrity of regional countries', 23 November 2014.

139 Mehr News Agency (Iran), 'Iraqi officials say caliph is actor', 7 July 2014.

140 Berger, *ISIS*, p. 257.

141 Dreyfuss, *Devil's Game*, p. 87; C. Swift, T. Powers, *The Man who kept secrets: Richard Helms and the CIA* (New York: Pocket, 1979), p. 72; M. Copeland, *The Game Player: Confessions of the CIA's original political operative* (London, Arum 1989), pp. 121, 134–6.

142 Referring to the Syrian-born Michel Aflaq.

143 Atwan, *Islamic State*, p. 125; McCants, 'The Believer'; Lister, 'Profiling the Islamic State', pp. 19–20.

144 Soufan Group, 'The Islamic State', November 2014, pp. 19–20.

145 Atwan, *Islamic State*, pp. 137–40; Weiss, *ISIS*, p. 85; Berger, *ISIS*, p. 38. Al-Turkmani is thought to have been killed in late 2014.

146 *Washington Post*, 'The hidden hand behind the Islamic State militants? Saddam Hussein's', 4 April 2015.

147 Hashim, 'The Islamic State', p. 5.

148 For a good discussion see M. Hisham, *Classical Islam and the Naqshbandi Sufi Tradition* (New York: Islamic Council of America), pp. 555–8.

149 Dreyfuss, *Devil's Game*, p. 253; Weiss, *ISIS*, p. 25.

150 *USA Today*, 'Saddam's No. 2 seeks help for insurgency', 27 March 2006; Lister, 'Profiling the Islamic State', p. 20; Hashim, 'The Islamic State', p. 7; Atwan, *Islamic State*, pp. 137, 140; Weiss, *ISIS*, pp. 24, 83.

151 *Der Spiegel*, 'The Terror Strategist: Secret Files Reveal the Structure of Islamic State', 18 April 2015.

152 M. Hudson, 'The Crisis of the Arab State: Study Group Report', Belfer Center for International Affairs, Harvard University, August 2015, p. 20.

153 Al-Monitor, 'The many names of Abu Bakr al-Baghdadi', 23 March 2015; J. Sassoon, *Saddam Hussein's Ba'ath party: Inside an Authoritarian Regime* (Cambridge: Cambridge University Press, 2012).

154 *Wall Street Journal*, 'Can Iraq's Ba'athists Become Allies Against Islamic State?', 6 August 2015.

155 For a good discussion see Hashim, 'The Islamic State', p. 9.

156 *Wall Street Journal*, 'Can Iraq's Ba'athists Become Allies Against Islamic State?', 6 August 2015.

157 *Daily Star* (Lebanon), 'ISIS seizes last Syrian regime base in Raqqa province', 25 August 2014; Channel NewsAsia, 'IS executes more than 160 Syria troops in new atrocity', 28 August 2014. Even after such attacks and atrocities a number of Western media outlets have continued to claim that deep and long-standing deals remain in place between the Islamic State and the Syrian government. For example, in May 2016, Sky News claimed that a cache of secret documents pointed to an agreement over the fate of Palmyra and a trade deal involving oil and fertilizer. According to Aymeen Jawad al-Tamimi, however, 'none the documents shown prove the story line'. See Sky News, 'IS files reveal Assad's deals with militants', 3 May 2016; Tweet: @ajaltamimi, 2 May 2016.

158 S. Helfont, 'Saddam and the Islamists: The Ba'athist Regime's Instrumentalization of Religion in Foreign Affairs', *Middle East Journal*, Vol. 68, No. 3, 2014.

159 Atwan, *Islamic State*, pp. 34, 39–40.

160 *Washington Post*, 'The hidden hand behind the Islamic State militants? Saddam Hussein's', 4 April 2015; Weiss, *ISIS*, p. 23.

161 Atwan, *Islamic State*, p. 32.

162 Weiss, *ISIS*, p. 21.

163 The very lively forty-six-minute first hearing, which took place on 1 July 2004, is widely available online, with usually two or three versions available on YouTube at any one time.

164 According to a number of Arabic newspapers, including the London-based *Al-Quds al-Arabi*, and also the Algerian French-language newspaper *Liberté*, Donald Rumsfeld had met secretly with Saddam Hussein and a small number of Iraqi officials. See *Liberté*, 'Rumsfeld l'a rencontré lors de son récent séjour en Irak Saddam rejette l'offre Américaine', 6 May 2005; Ynet (Israel), 'US defense secretary offers Saddam a deal to put an end terror in Iraq, London-based Al-Quds al-Arabi says', 28 April 2005.

165 *Daily Telegraph*, 'Saddam may escape noose in deal to halt insurgency', 11 April 2005.

166 *New York Times*, 'How Saddam Hussein Gave us ISIS', 23 December 2015; Filiu, *The Arab Revolution*, p. 122.

167 Atwan, *Islamic State*, pp. 33–4; Weiss, *ISIS*, pp. 24, 26; McCants, 'The Believer'. Also see A. Baram, *Saddam Husayn and Islam, 1968–2003: Ba'thi Iraq from Secularism to Faith* (Washington DC: Woodrow Wilson Center, 2014).

168 *Daily Telegraph*, 'Why business is booming under Islamic State one year on', 8 June 2015; Lister, 'Profiling the Islamic State', pp. 10, 28; Berger, *ISIS*, pp. 73–4; Weiss, *ISIS*, pp. 147, 149. The various videos of infrastructure repair were widely available on YouTube and other platforms in 2014.

169 *New York Times*, 'Offering Services, ISIS Digs in Deeper in Seized Territories', 16 June 2015.

170 Mecham, 'How much of a state', p. 22; Lister, 'Profiling the Islamic State', p. 26.

171 Reuters, 'Ancient Christian population of Mosul flees Islamic State', 19 July 2014; Lister, 'Profiling the Islamic State', pp. 26–7; AINA (Assyrian news network), 'ISIS Opens Market in Mosul for Stolen Assyrian Property', 2 February 2015.

172 Mecham, 'How much of a state', p. 23; *Daily Telegraph*, 'Islamic State announces its own currency', 14 November 2014.

173 Berger, *ISIS*, p. 86.

174 *New York Times*, 'West Struggles To Halt Flow Of Citizens To War Zones', 13 January 2015.

175 Munich Security Report, 'Annual Report 2014', 26 January 2015.

176 Reuters, 'Foreign fighters still flowing to Syria', 11 February 2015.

177 *Guardian*, 'Islamist fighters drawn from half the world's countries, says UN', 26 May 2015.

178 Cockburn, *The Rise of Islamic State*, p. 37.

179 Atwan, *Islamic State*, p. 150; *Independent*, 'Private donors from Gulf oil states helping to bankroll salaries of up to 100,000 Isis fighters', 22 February 2015; Atwan, *Islamic State*, p. 150.

180 *Express Tribune* (Pakistan), 'Startling revelations: IS operative confesses to getting funds via US', 28 January 2015.

181 A. J. al-Tamimi, 'Islamic State Training Camps and Military Divisions', blog post, 24 June 2015; *International Business Times*, 'Inside the Caliphate Army: ISIS's Special Forces Military Unit of Foreign Fighters', 3 July 2015.

182 TASS (Russia), 'Islamic State recruiting professionals in Uzbekistan', 3 September 2015.

183 BBC Online, 'ISIS leader calls on Muslims to build Islamic state', 1 July 2014.

184 *International Business Times*, 'British sounding doctor calls on others to join Islamic State in new video', 13 June 2015.

185 *New York Times*, 'West Struggles To Halt Flow Of Citizens To War Zones', 13 January 2015.

186 *Washington Post*, 'CNN: Islamic State uses Nutella and kittens to entice female recruits', 18 February 2015.

187 Mecham, 'How much of a state', p. 20.

188 Cockburn, *The Rise of Islamic State*, p. 127; Atwan, *Islamic State*, pp. 16–17; 134; Berger, *ISIS*, p. 65. Al-Qaeda's forum moderators often frowned on attempts to promote viral material.

189 BBC Online, 'Islamist cleric Anwar al-Awlaki killed in Yemen', 30 September 2011.

190 Atwan, *Islamic State*, p. 19, Berger, *ISIS*, pp. 113, 119; Lister, 'Profiling the Islamic State', p. 24; Weiss, *ISIS*, p. 32.

191 Weiss, *ISIS*, p. 29.

192 The architect of *Al-Hayat* is thought to be a Syrian-American who relocated to Syria in 2011. See Atwan, *Islamic State*, p. 21; Berger, *ISIS*, p. 113.

193 Berger, *ISIS*, p. 116; *International Business Times*, 'Islamic State rumoured to launch 24-hour online TV channel', 18 January 2015; *New Europe*, 'Islamic State gets satellite TV channel', 14 January 2016. The latest attempt was understood to have been launched on Egypt's Nilesat network.

194 Cockburn, *The Rise of Islamic State*, p. 127.

195 *Business Insider*, 'The FBI claims technology promoted by Apple and WhatsApp is helping ISIS', 4 June 2015.

196 Atwan, *Islamic State*, pp. xiv, 15.

197 Berger, 'The ISIS Twitter Census', p. 12.

198 Berger, *ISIS*, pp. 153–4; D. Faris, 'Multiplicities of purpose: the auditorium building, the state, and the transformation of Arab digital media', *International Journal of Middle East Studies*, Vol. 47, No. 2, 2015, p. 346. Embarrassingly in late 2015 Twitter closed the account of Arab Spring activist Iyad al-Baghdadi. See BBC Online, 'Twitter confuses Iyad el-Baghdadi with Islamic State leader', 1 January 2016.

199 Most notably the account belonging to 'Shami Witness' whose account was shut down in 2014. The account holder proved to be an executive in Bangalore working for an Indian conglomerate. *Daily Telegraph*, 'The rise of the suburban terrorist', 5 July 2015.

200 Atwan, *Islamic State*, p. 27.

201 See for example *Daily Record* (Scotland), 'Hackers trace ISIS Twitter accounts back to Internet addresses linked to Department of Work and Pensions', 14 December 2015.

202 Berger, *ISIS*, pp. 69, 155, 157.

203 Long War Journal, 'Islamic State launches mobile app for children', 11 May 2016; *Guardian*, 'Islamic State releases children's mobile app to teach Arabic', 11 May 2016.

204 Berger, *ISIS*, pp. 147–51, 157.

205 Faris, 'Multiplicities of purpose', p. 347.

206 Berger, *ISIS*, p. 165; Atwan, *Islamic State*, p. 19.

207 Hashim, 'The Islamic State', p. 6.

9. THE ISLAMIC STATE – A STRATEGIC ASSET

1   W. Blum, *Killing Hope: US Military and CIA Interventions Since World War II* (London: Zed, 2014), p. 19.

2   *Boston Globe*, 'The world of threats to the US is an illusion', 12 April 2015.

3   R. Dreyfuss, *Devil's Game: How the United States Helped Unleash Fundamentalist Islam* (New York: Metropolitan, 2006), p. 12; M. Curtis, *Secret Affairs: Britain's Collusion with Radical Islam* (London: Serpent's Tail, 2012), pp. ix–x. The British chief being Richard Dannatt, speaking in 2009.

4   J. Mueller, 'Is There Still a Terrorist Threat? The Myth of the Omnipresent Enemy', *Foreign Affairs*, September 2006.

5   BBC Online, 'Doubts grow over ISIS FGM edict in Iraq', 24 July 2014.

6   Reuters, 'A strategy for defeating Islamic State from an unlikely source', 11 March 2015.

7   Blum, *Killing Hope*, p. 8. This report was published on 12 February 1919.

8   Ibid., pp. 8–9.

9   *Wall Street Journal*, 'UK Ramping Up Intelligence to Win Battle of Britain Against Islamic State', 16 July 2015; BBC Online, 'No easy way to defeat Islamic State', 5 June 2015.

10   Reuters, 'Foreign fighters still flowing to Syria', 11 February 2015. Referring to Francis Taylor's testimony prepared for a hearing of the House of Representatives Committee on Homeland Security.

11   Middle East Eye, 'Americans see Islamic State as gravest threat to US', 14 February 2015.

12   *Time*, 'CIA Director Says ISIS Not Islamic, But Psychopathic', 13 March 2015.

13   *USA Today*, 'Panetta: 30-year war and a leadership test for Obama', 6 October 2014.

14   Reuters, 'Cameron – IS militants are plotting terrible UK attacks', 29 June 2015.

15   Blum, *Killing Hope*, pp. 18–19. Quoting Roger Morris, who served under both Johnson and Nixon.

16   Ibid., pp. 20, 349–50.

17   M. Curtis, *Web of Deceit: Britain's Real Role in the World* (London: Vintage, 2003), p. 79.

18   *New York Times*, 'News Summary', 16 April 1986; Blum, *Killing Hope*, p. 283; H. Dabashi, *The Arab Spring: The End of Postcolonialism* (London: Zed, 2012), p. 117.

19   *Los Angeles Times*, 6 November 1990 (no longer available). Cited by Blum, *Killing Hope*, p. 283.

20   *New York Review of Books*, 'The True history of the Gulf War', 30 January 1992.

21   Blum, *Killing Hope*, p. 333; Curtis, *Web of Deceit*, p. 24; Global Post, 'The legacy of Iraq's bombed nuclear plant', 12 June 2011; UN Security Council, 'Resolution A/RES/45/52 Establishment of a nuclear-weapon-free zone in the region of the Middle East', 1 December 1990.

22 Reuters, 'Iraq rejects US charges of atrocities', 16 October 1990; D. N. Walton, *Appeal to Pity: Argumentum ad Misericordiam* (New York: State University of New York Press, 1997), p. 771.

23 Blum, *Killing Hope*, p. 328. Quoting former assistant secretary for defense Lawrence Korb.

24 *New Yorker*, 'Overwhelming Force: What happened in the final days of the Gulf War?', 22 May 2000; *Time*, 'Death Highway revisited', 18 March 1991.

25 *Washington Post*, 'Allied air war struck broadly in Iraq', 23 June 1991; Curtis, *Web of Deceit*, p. 15.

26 S. Pelletiere, *Losing Iraq: Insurgency and Politics* (New York: Praeger, 2007), p. 111.

27 *Washington Post*, 'Allied air war struck broadly in Iraq', 23 June 1991.

28 Blum, *Killing Hope*, p. 333; Global Post, 'The legacy of Iraq's bombed nuclear plant', 12 June 2011; UN Security Council, 'Resolution A/RES/45/52 Establishment of a nuclear-weapon-free zone in the region of the Middle East', 1 December 1990.

29 This report was leaked to the *Independent* newspaper, which published parts of it on 10 November 1991. Also see Blum, *Killing Hope*, p. 334.

30 *Independent*, 'Toxic Legacy of US Assault on Fallujah Worse Than Hiroshima', 24 July 2010 (the report has been removed from the website). The original research report was entitled 'Cancer, Infant Mortality and Birth Sex-Ratio in Fallujah, Iraq 2005–2009', and the team of academics that produced it was led by a visiting professor at the University of Ulster.

31 Blum, *Killing Hope*, pp. 325–6. Quoting senator Bob Dole.

32 *Wall Street Journal*, 'Desert Storm, the Last Classic War', 31 July 2015.

33 Margaret Thatcher Speech Archives, 'Margaret Thatcher Speech to Chatham House Conference on Saudi Arabia', 4 October 1993.

34 *New York Times*, 'Remember Nayirah, Witness for Kuwait?', 6 January 1992.

35 *New York Times*, 'PR Firm had no reason to question Kuwaiti's testimony', 17 January 1992; A. Rowse, 'How to build support for war', *Columbia Journalism Review*, September 1992.

36 *New York Times*, 'Remember Nayirah, Witness for Kuwait?', 6 January 1992.

37 P. Cockburn, *The Rise of Islamic State: ISIS and the New Sunni Revolution* (London: Verso, 2015), p. 144.

38 A. B. Atwan, *Islamic State: The Digital Caliphate* (London: Saqi, 2015), p. 36. Referring to ambassador April Glasbie.

39 Blum, *Killing Hope*, pp. 322–3. Citing *Los Angeles Times*, 1 November 1990; *Washington Post*, 19 August 1990 (no longer available).

40 Curtis, *Web of Deceit*, p. 37; Curtis, *Secret Affairs*, p. 161.

41 Curtis, *Web of Deceit*, pp. 34–5; *Guardian*, 'Don't trust Bush or Blair on Iraq', 21 August 2002.

42 Curtis, *Web of Deceit*, pp. 36–7. Quoting William Waldegrave.

43   Ibid., pp. 36–7; Curtis, *Secret Affairs*, p. 161. Citing Graeme Stewart with regard to to the ex-SAS bodyguards.

44   CNN, 'Pentagon's nightmare: $1 trillion in cuts', 20 October 2011.

45   *Bloomberg*, 'Syria-Ukraine Wars send US Defense Stocks to Records', 25 September 2014.

46   *Daily Telegraph*, 'British defence spending to fall below NATO benchmark', 5 September 2014.

47   BBC Online, 'UK defence spending concerns US Army chief Raymond Odierno', 2 March 2015.

48   Reuters, 'Britain denounces Islamic State video showing spies shot', 4 January 2016.

49   Quoting Frank Gardner. Other rationales put forward were anti-piracy measures and aerial surveillance. BBC Online, 'UK to establish £15 million permanent Mid East military base', 6 December 2014. The new naval task force was announced in March 2016. See *Independent*, 'Defence Secretary Michael Fallon pays low-key visit to Saudi Arabia to discuss military cooperation', 29 March 2016.

50   Ibid.; *Washington Post*, 'First French Military Base Opens in the Persian Gulf', 27 May 2009.

51   Hansard, 'Mark Francois the minister of state for defence replying to Vernon Coaker MP', 18 December 2014.

52   Middle East Eye, 'New UK-Bahrain naval base takes colonial-era name', 19 June 2015.

53   *The Courier* (Scotland), 'Naval base in Bahrain not deep enough for aircraft carriers being built in Fife', 19 January 2016.

54   *Sydney Morning Herald*, 'French President Francois Hollande says aircraft carrier could support Iraq operations', 15 January 2015.

55   Data supplied by Morningstar. Raytheon at $75.65 on 2 August 2013 and at $126.20 on 11 December 2015.

56   Data supplied by Morningstar. Northrop Grumman at $94.89 on 2 August 2013 and at $186.20 on 11 December 2015.

57   *Bloomberg*, 'Syria-Ukraine Wars send US Defense Stocks to Records', 25 September 2014.

58   The Intercept, 'Big bank's analyst worries that Iran deal could depress weapons sales', 20 March 2015. Citing an 'earnings call' on 27 January 2015 between Deutsche Bank's Myles Walton and Lockheed Martin CEO Marillyn Hewson.

59   *Bloomberg*, 'Syria-Ukraine Wars send US Defense Stocks to Records', 25 September 2014.

60   *Bloomberg*, 'General Atomics Drone Sale to UAE Poised for US Approval', 23 February 2015.

61   Reuters, 'Firms see drone sales in Gulf surging after US eases export policy', 24 February 2015.

62   *Defense News*, 'RAF Bombs Diverted to Saudis for Yemen Strikes', 16 July 2015.

63   *New York Times*, 'Sale of US Arms Fuels the Wars of Arab States', 18 April 2015.

64   Reuters, 'Exclusive – Boeing poised to clinch $3 billion-plus Kuwait FA-18 order', 6 May 2015; *Arabian Business*, 'Kuwait to boost military spending by $20bn', 23 December 2015.

65   BBC Online, 'US resumes aid to military in Bahrain', 29 June 2015.

66   Defense Security Cooperation Agency, 'News release 15-51', 6 November 2015; Reuters, 'US approves $1.29 billion sale of smart bombs to Saudi Arabia', 16 November 2015.

67   CBC, 'How Saudi Arabia, and a $15B armoured vehicle deal, became an election issue', 26 September 2015.

68   Obama made these comments in an interview with the *New Yorker*. See *New Yorker*, 'Going the Distance', 27 January 2014. In summer 2014 the White House claimed the remarks were not relevant to ISIS, but subsequent fact-checking articles indicated strongly that they were. See *Washington Post*, 'Spinning Obama's reference to Islamic State as a JV team', 3 September 2014; Politifact, 'What Obama said about Islamic State as a JV team', 7 September 2014.

69   Atwan, *Islamic State*, pp. 125, 127.

70   Associated Press, 'IS has 20,000–31,500 fighters in Iraq and Syria: CIA', 12 September 2014.

71   *Washington Post*, 'The US's big intelligence problem', 28 May 2015.

72   *The Times*, 'Al-Qaeda planning militant Islamic state within Iraq', 13 May 2007.

73   *New Yorker*, 'The Redirection', 5 March 2007. Quoting Robert Baer, a former CIA agent in Lebanon.

74   RAND Corporation, 'Unfolding the Future of the Long War: Motivations, Prospects, and Implications for the US Army', RAND Arroyo Center, 2008, pp.48–9, 68, 104.

75   Department of Defense, 'Information Report 14-L-0552/DIA), August 2012 (subpoenaed), pp. 287–93.

76   Ibid.

77   N. Ahmed, 'Ex-intel officials: Pentagon report proves US complicity in ISIS', Insurge Intelligence, 2 June 2015.

78   Quoting Alastair Crooke. See Huffington Post, 'If Syria and Iraq Become Fractured, So Too Will Tripoli and North Lebanon', 1 June 2015.

79   Al-Jazeera, 'Head to Head: Who is to blame for the rise of ISIL?', 29 July 2015.

80   *New York Times*, 'John Bolton: To Defeat ISIS, Create a Sunni State', 24 November 2015.

81   J. M. Berger, J. Stern, *ISIS: The State of Terror* (London: William Collins, 2015), pp. 216–17.

82   *Guardian*, '20,000 Iraqis besieged by ISIL escape from mountain after US air strikes', 10 August 2014.

83   *Daily Telegraph*, 'Thousands of Yazidi women sold as sex slaves for theological reasons, says ISIL', 13 August 2014.

84 *New York Times*, 'Despite US Claims, Yazidis Say Crisis is Not Over', 14 August 2014; *Washington Post*, 'Why can't the US figure out how many Yazidis are on Mount Sinjar?', 15 August 2014.

85 Al-Jazeera, 'US jets bomb Islamic State group in Iraq', 9 August 2014.

86 SBS (Australia), 'Explainer: Who are the Peshmerga?', 1 September 2014.

87 Blum, *Killing Hope*, p. 243. Referring to statements made by Mustafa Barzani.

88 *New Yorker*, 'Oil and Why America is Dropping Bombs to Defend Erbil', 10 August 2014.

89 A. Hashim, 'The Islamic State: from al-Qaeda affiliate to caliphate', *Middle East Policy*, Vol. 21, No. 4, 2014, p. 10.

90 The Pike Report was the staff report of the Select Committee on Intelligence, US House of Representatives, based on hearings held in 1975. The committee's chairman was Otis Pike. For a full discussion see O. Pike, *CIA: The Pike Report* (Spokesman: London, 1977).

91 Blum, *Killing Hope*, p. 243.

92 *New York Times*, 'Even Near Home, a New Front Is Opening in the Terror Battle', 23 September 2014; *New Yorker*, 'Private Jihad: How Rita Katz got into the spying business', 29 May 2009.

93 Atwan, *Islamic State*, pp. 131–2; *Daily Telegraph*, 'FBI identifies Jihadi John', 25 September 2014.

94 BBC Online, 'Profile: James Foley, US journalist beheaded by Islamic State', 20 August 2014; ABC (Australia), 'Islamic State hostage ransom demands often met by European governments, expert says; US, UK no-pay policies under fire', 9 June 2015.

95 *USA Today*, 'Video appears to show Islamic State beheading US journalist', 19 August 2014. The author's full comments remained online, as part of the article, for approximately two hours. The article's title was then changed to 'US says beheading video is authentic'.

96 See, for example, NBC, 'Watching Purported James Foley Video May Trigger Charges in UK', 20 August 2014.

97 *The Times*, 'Foley video with Briton was staged, experts say', 25 August 2014.

98 *Washington Post*, 'CIA unit's wacky idea: depict Saddam as gay', 25 May 2010; PRI, 'The World: Fake Saddam Video Plot', 27 May 2010 (no longer available).

99 Berger, *ISIS*, p. 169.

100 Atwan, *Islamic State*, p. 159.

101 For a good discussion see Berger, *ISIS*, pp. 188–9.

102 BBC Online, 'Profile of British hostage David Haines', 14 September 2014.

103 Ibid.; BBC Online, 'MPs support UK air strikes against IS in Iraq', 26 September 2014.

104 BBC Online, 'MPs support UK air strikes against IS in Iraq', 26 September 2014.

105 The Khorasan Group was named after a region in Central Asia from which it is expected the Mahdi will appear with an army of black flags. See Berger, *ISIS*, p. 220.

106 *Daily Telegraph*, 'Islamic State v al-Qaeda: the battle within jihad', 1 April 2015.

107 Associated Press, 'US officials: Terrorist group was nearing attack', 23 September 2014; Associated Press, 'Syrian extremists may pose more direct threat to US than Islamic State', 13 September 2014.

108 Middle East Eye, 'Eyebrows are raised at Al-Nusra leader's dismissal of Khorasan group', 28 May 2015.

109 For a good discussion see Berger, *ISIS*, pp. 60–61.

110 Middle East Eye, 'Eyebrows are raised at Al-Nusra leader's dismissal of Khorasan group', 28 May 2015; Al-Jazeera, 'Nusra leader: Our mission is to defeat Syrian regime', 28 May 2015.

111 The formal request was eventually made in early December 2014. *Guardian*, 'Iran air strikes against ISIS requested by Iraqi government, says Tehran', 6 December 2014.

112 See, for example, ABC, 'Syrian War Planes Strike ISIS Targets in Iraq, US Says', 24 June 2014.

113 US CENTCOM, 'Iraq and Syria Operations Against ISIL Designated as Operation Inherent Resolve: Release No. 20141018', 15 October 2014.

114 *Daily Telegraph*, 'Saudi prince and Emirate's first female fighter pilot take part in Syria air strikes', 25 September 2014.

115 *Financial Times*, 'Interview: Sheikh Khalid al-Khalifa', 1 December 2014.

116 Al-Jazeera, 'US Senators in Saudi Arabia to discuss Syria', 18 January 2015; Agence France-Presse, 'Gulf air strikes on Islamic State down due to Yemen conflict: US general', 11 November 2015.

117 Voice of America, 'UAE Hints at Rejoining Coalition Airstrikes on IS', 6 February 2015.

118 Quoting Stephen Gethins. *Independent*, 'British air strikes in Syria have helped allow Sunni states to ditch fight against ISIS and focus bombing on Shiites in Yemen', 16 December 2015; *Washington Times*, 'Obama anti-ISIS coalition crumbles as Arab allies focus elsewhere', 30 November 2015.

119 *Wall Street Journal*, 'US-led Airstrikes Disrupt Islamic State, But Extremists Hold Territory', 5 October 2014; *Wall Street Journal*, 'Months of Airstrikes Fail to Slow Islamic State In Syria', 15 January 2015.

120 Daily Caller, 'ISIS Plants Flag On Hill Near Kobane, Coalition Airstrike Takes It Out', 24 October 2014; *Daily Mail*, 'Blitzing the black flag of ISIS: Extraordinary moment as massive US airstrike obliterated jihadis' emblem flying on hill above Kobane while a lone sentry stands his ground', 23 October 2014; Agence France-Presse, 'US military obliterate Islamic State flag planted on Kobane hill', 24 October 2014.

121 For details of the first video see BBC Online, 'John Cantlie: Islamic State hostage in Kobane video', 27 October 2014.

122 *Bloomberg*, 'US Exaggerates Islamic State Casualties', 13 March 2015.

123 *New York Times*, 'Thousands Enter Syria to Join ISIS Despite Global Efforts', 26 September 2015.

124 Palmyra was captured in late May 2015. See BBC Online, 'Islamic State seizes Syria's ancient Palmyra', 21 May 2015.

125 BBC Online, 'Islamic State seizes Iraqi city of Ramadi', 17 May 2015.

126 Agence France-Presse, 'US says only 60 Syrians being trained to fight IS', 7 July 2015.

127 *Daily Telegraph*, 'Al-Qaeda-linked rebels in Syria capture leader of US-trained rebel group in blow to West', 30 July 2015; *Wall Street Journal*, 'Islamic State Advances on Strategic Syrian Border Town', 8 September 2015.

128 *Washington Post*, 'Secret CIA effort in Syria faces large funding cut', 13 June 2015.

129 *Daily Telegraph*, 'US-trained Division 30 rebels "betray" US and hand weapons over to al-Qaeda's affiliate in Syria', 22 September 2015.

130 *Stars and Stripes*, 'As USS Roosevelt exits, US has no carriers in Persian Gulf', 9 October 2015; Defense Web, 'US halting UAV flights from Djibouti?', 30 November 2015.

131 *New York Times*, 'As US Escalates Air War on ISIS, Allies Slip Away', 7 November 2015.

132 Fox News, 'Cruz fires up conservatives, says bomb Islamic State back to the Stone Age', 31 August 2014.

133 Reuters, 'US forces building pressure on Islamic State: military chief', 8 January 2015; Reuters, 'Iraq says US-led coalition not doing enough against Islamic State', 14 January 2015.

134 Agence France-Presse, 'Escalating air war on IS not the answer: US general', 8 March 2015.

135 *Time*, 'CIA Director Says ISIS Not Islamic, But Psychopathic', 13 March 2015.

136 CBS, 'Face the Nation: Transcripts of Jeb Bush, John Brennan', 31 May 2015.

137 Huffington Post, 'State Department Official: It's Going to Take Years to Defeat the Islamic State', 10 May 2015.

138 Associated Press, 'US: Saving Iraq from Islamic State could take three to five years', 9 June 2015.

139 *Washington Post*, 'The US air war against the Islamic State, in numbers', 7 July 2015.

140 *Wall Street Journal*, 'US Security Conference Reveals Islamic State as Confounding Foe', 26 July 2015.

141 Voice of America, 'Top US General: Islamic State Fight Stalemated', 9 September 2015.

142 *Washington Post*, 'This is the patch you'll get for fighting the Islamic State', 24 September 2015; *Military Times*, 'This is the US military's new medal for troops fighting ISIS', 30 March 2016.

143 BBC Online, 'UK ambassador: Gulf crisis could last 10-15 years', 5 February 2015. Quoting John Jenkins, outgoing British ambassador to Saudi Arabia.

144 BBC Online, 'No easy way to defeat Islamic State', 5 June 2015.

145 *Guardian*, 'Scale of UK attacks on Islamic State in Iraq revealed', 11 May 2015.

146 BBC Online, 'Islamic State conflict: Two Britons killed in RAF Syria strike', 7 September 2015.

147 *Daily Telegraph*, 'Our special relationship hangs by a thread', 15 January 2015. Quoting Christopher Meyer.

148 BBC Online, 'No easy way to defeat Islamic State', 5 June 2015.

149 BBC Online, 'RAF uses Brimstone missiles against Islamic State in Syria', 11 January 2016; Reuters, 'Britain joins Syria air war', 4 December 2015; Middle East Eye, 'British action in Syria: 33 strikes in just under three months', 25 February 2016.

150 F. Gerges., *America and Political Islam* (Cambridge: Cambridge University Press, 1999), pp. 70–71.

151 RAND, 'Unfolding the Future', pp. 82, 104.

152 Reuters, 'Iraq wants coalition strikes on Tikrit', 16 March 2015; *The Nation* (Pakistan), 'Iraq wants coalition strikes on Tikrit', 16 March 2015.

153 *New York Times*, 'Iraqi Forces in No Hurry to Expel ISIS from Tikrit', 28 March 2015.

154 Dijlah TV (Iraq), 'Interview with Wahda al-Jumaili', 19 May 2015.

155 *Washington Post*, 'Iraqis think the US is in cahoots with the Islamic State, and it is hurting the war', 1 December 2015.

156 Rudaw (Kurdish), 'The stunning story of the fall of Ramadi', 24 May 2015.

157 Reuters, 'Iraqi Prime Minister Abadi Says Allies Not Doing Enough to Counter ISIS', 2 June 2015.

158 Reuters, 'Iraq says US-led coalition not doing enough against Islamic State', 14 January 2015.

159 Radio Free Europe, 'Iraqi PM: Deploying Foreign Ground Troops in Iraq a Hostile Act', 4 December 2015.

160 Quoting Qais al-Khazali, leader of Iran-backed paramilitary group *Asaib Ahl al-Haq*, originally a splinter of the Mahdi Army. Reuters, 'Iraqi militia leader says US not serious about fighting Islamic State', 28 July 2015.

161 *Washington Post*, 'Five thoughts Petraeus has about the future of the Middle East', 20 March 2015.

162 Reuters, 'Islamic State drives back Syria insurgents near Turkey', 31 May 2015.

163 *Bloomberg*, 'US Exaggerates Islamic State Casualties', 13 March 2015.

164 Citing a poll conducted by ORB International in September 2015. *Washington Post*, 'One in five Syrians say Islamic State is a good thing, poll says', 15 September 2015.

165 *Financial Times*, 'Inside ISIS Inc: the journey of a barrel of oil', 14 October 2015.

166 *Independent*, 'War in Syria: Russia's rustbucket military delivers a hi-tech shock to West and Israel', 30 January 2016.

167 Quoting General Andrei Kartapolov. Sputnik (Russia), 'Update from the Chief of the Main Operational Directorate of the General Staff', 7 October 2015.

168 *Daily Telegraph*, 'US freezes intelligence cooperation with German troops in Iraq', 3 June 2015.

169 *Guardian*, 'Seizure of Palmyra and Ramadi by ISIS reveal gaping holes in US jihadi strategy', 21 May 2015.

170 *Bloomberg*, 'US Saw Islamic State Coming, Let It Take Ramadi', 28 May 2015.

171 *New York Times*, 'Analysts Detail Claims That Reports on ISIS Were Distorted', 15 September 2015; Daily Beast, 'Exclusive: 50 Spies Say ISIS Intelligence Was Cooked', 9 September 2015.

172 *New York Times*, 'The Elusive Truth About War on ISIS', 17 September 2015.

173 Daily Beast, 'Exclusive: Pentagon Map Hides ISIS Gains', 22 April 2015.

174 *Guardian*, 'Seizure of Palmyra and Ramadi by ISIS reveal gaping holes in US jihadi strategy', 21 May 2015.

175 M. Zenko, 'Comparing the Islamic State Air War with History', Council on Foreign Relations, blog post, 6 July 2015.

176 ABC (Australia), 'Islamic State look increasingly like a state warns expert', 18 May 2015.

177 Reuters, 'Four Syrian soldiers die in suspected US coalition strike: group', 7 December 2015; Reuters, 'Iraqi soldiers killed in friendly fire Anbar air strike – sources', 12 March 2015; *Wall Street Journal*, 'US Says Friendly Fire Killed Syrian Allies', 10 June 2016.

178 *Independent*, 'War in Syria: Russia's rustbucket military delivers a hi-tech shock to West and Israel', 30 January 2016.

179 The US took control over and expanded the Rmeilan airstrip in late 2015. See BBC Online, 'Syria conflict: US expanding air strip in Kurdish north', 21 January 2016; Al-Jazeera, 'US takes control of Rmeilan airfield in Syria', 20 January 2016.

180 *Wall Street Journal*, 'US, Allies to Boost Aid to Syria Rebels', 4 November 2015.

181 Daily Caller, 'Understanding The Function Of The Islamic State', 19 June 2015.

182 Department of Defense, 'Recent Strike in Mosul killed ISIL Commanders, Pentagon Officials Says', 1 July 2016; ABC, '250 ISIS Militants Killed in US Airstrikes, Officials Say', 30 June 2016; *Washington Post*, 'Iraqi, US aircraft bomb convoy of Islamic State fighters fleeing Fallujah with their families', 30 June 2016.

183 The 'rentier state' in this context was first described by Hossein Mahdavy. See H. Mahdavy, 'The Pattern and Problems of Economic Development in Rentier States: The Case of Iran', in *Studies in the Economic History of the Middle East*, ed. M. A. Cook (Oxford: Oxford University Press, 1970).

184 *Al-Araby al-Jadeed*, 'IS: The rentier caliphate with no new ideas', 8 February 2015.

185 D. E. Kaplan *et al.*, 'The Saudi Connection', *US News & World Report*, Vol. 135, No. 21, 2003.

186 *New York Times*, 'Al-Qaeda; Honey Trade Said to Provide Funds and Cover to bin Laden', 11 October 2001; *New York Times*, 'The Miller Mess: Lingering Issues Among the Answers', 23 October 2005.

187 BBC Online, 'Bin Laden's honey connection', 11 October 2001.
188 *New York Times*, 'US Finds Iraq Insurgency Has Funds to Sustain Itself', 26 November 2006.
189 Ibid.
190 M. Hamid, L. Farrall, *The Arabs at War in Afghanistan* (London: Hurst, 2015), p. 311. Quoting Mustafa Hamid.
191 Ibid., p. 312. Quoting Abdul-Aziz Ali, an associate of Hamid.
192 Ibid., p. 314.
193 C. Lister, 'Profiling the Islamic State', Brookings Doha Center, Analysis Paper 13, November 2014, pp. 2, 22.
194 Hashim, 'The Islamic State', p. 5.
195 *Washington Post*, 'Where does the Islamic State get its funding?', 12 March 2015.
196 *New York Times*, 'ISIS Finances Are Strong', 19 May 2015.
197 Department of the Treasury, 'Remarks by Acting Under Secretary Adam Szubin at Chatham House', 10 December 2015.
198 *Daily Telegraph*, 'Saudi Arabia funds moderate Muslims, not ISIL', 28 January 2016.
199 Syrian Observatory of Human Rights, 'Islamic State imposes taxes on the rich', 21 December 2014.
200 Fox News, 'Extortion, bank robbery fuel ISIS bloody drive to establish Sharia caliphate', 14 June 2014. For a discussion of the Chalabi comments see *Financial Times*, 'Biggest bank robbery that never happened – $400m ISIS heist', 17 July 2014.
201 *Wall Street Journal*, 'Militants in Iraq Siphon State Pay', 23 March 2015.
202 *Financial Times*, 'Biggest bank robbery that never happened – $400m ISIS heist', 17 July 2014.
203 CNBC, 'Capital Bank says it's business as usual in Mosul', 22 May 2015. Quoting the bank's chairman Bassem al-Salem.
204 See, for example, Sky News, 'Islamic State Accused of Harvesting Organs', 18 February 2015.
205 Reuters, 'Islamic State sanctioned organ harvesting in document taken in US raid', 25 December 2015.
206 Atwan, *Islamic State*, p. 148; Middle East Eye, 'Islamic State pockets $100 million yearly from heritage booty', 28 April 2015.
207 Reuters, 'US delivers Iraqi antiquities seized in raid on Islamic State', 15 July 2015. Quoting Stuart Jones.
208 *Washington Post*, 'The Islamic State isn't the only group looting Syrian archaeological sites', 22 October 2015.
209 For a good summary of the various oil figures being touted at this time see K. Johnson, 'The Islamic State is the newest petrostate', *Foreign Policy*, 28 July 2014; Atwan, *Islamic State*, p. 147.
210 Council of the European Union, 'Presse 155: Council eases sanctions against Syria to support opposition and civilians 8611/13', 22 April 2013.

211 K. Brannen, 'Pentagon: Oil no longer the Islamic State's main source of revenue', *Foreign Policy*, 3 February 2015.

212 Financial Action Task Force, 'Financing of the terrorist organisation Islamic State in Iraq and the Levant', February 2015, pp. 10, 14.

213 Brannen, 'Pentagon: Oil'; Reuters, 'Islamic State yearly oil revenue halved to $250 million: US official', 11 May 2016.

214 *Daily Star* (Lebanon), 'Fattouh: ISIS' finances top priority for US', 21 April 2015.

215 Associated Press, 'New US Sanctions Illustrate Sprawling Islamic State Network', 29 September 2015. Quoting Daniel Glaser.

216 *Wall Street Journal*, 'How Islamic State's Secret Banking Network Prospers', 24 February 2016.

217 Associated Press, 'New US Sanctions Illustrate Sprawling Islamic State Network', 29 September 2015.

218 Tweet: @JcBrisard, 29 September 2015.

219 Foreign Affairs Subcommittee, 'ISIL Financing Inquiry: Oral Evidence', 2 March 2016. Quoting John Baron and Crispin Blunt.

220 Ibid. Quoting Dan Chugg. *Daesh* being a derogatory term for the Islamic State that has been officially adopted by the British government.

221 Foreign Affairs Subcommittee, 'ISIL Financing Inquiry: Written Evidence from Luay al-Khatteeb, Executive Director of Iraq Energy Institute', 8 March 2016.

222 Financial Action Task Force, 'Financing of the terrorist organisation Islamic State in Iraq and the Levant', February 2015, pp. 5, 10, 18, 36, and other references throughout the report.

223 Ibid., pp. 12–13.

224 *Wall Street Journal*, 'Islamic State Mostly Financed Through Extortion Rackets', 27 February 2015.

225 Hamid, *The Arabs at War*, p. 315.

226 *Independent*, 'Iraq crisis: How Saudi Arabia helped ISIS take over the north of the country', 13 July 2014.

227 *New York Times*, 'Saudis Are Next on Biden's Mideast Apology List After Harvard Remarks', 6 October 2014; Cockburn, *The Rise of Islamic State*, pp. xix–xx.

228 *Al-Arabiya*, 'GCC backs Qatar in row with Egypt over Libya', 19 February 2015.

229 Cited by Atwan, *Islamic State*, p. 213.

230 For example, in summer 2015 Kuwait arrested a number of suspects in the wake of a suicide bomb attack on a Shia mosque. *Wall Street Journal*, 'Kuwait arrests several suspected members of the Islamic State', 30 July 2015.

231 *Al-Masalah* (translated), 'Kuwaiti MP Duwaisan: There are Parties in Kuwait Contributing to the Funding of Daesh', 10 March 2016.

232 See, for example, BBC Online, 'Is Qatar bringing the Nusra Front in from the cold?', 6 March 2015.

233 BBC Online, 'UK ambassador: Gulf crisis could last 10-15 years', 5 February 2015. Quoting John Jenkins.

234 RAND, 'Unfolding the Future', p. 105.

235 NBC, 'Who's Funding ISIS? Wealthy Gulf Angel Investors, Officials Say', 21 September 2014.

236 Middle East Eye, 'Islamic State is the cancer of modern capitalism', 27 March 2015.

237 Citing Fuad Hussein, the chief of staff of the Kurdish President.

238 Citing and quoting Mahmoud Othman, a veteran member of the Iraqi Kurdish leadership who recently retired from the Iraqi parliament.

239 *Independent*, 'Private donors from Gulf oil states helping to bankroll salaries of up to 100,000 ISIS fighters', 22 February 2015.

240 Also see C. Duhaime, 'ISIS and the age of the digital terrorist and digital terrorist financing', Antimoneylaunderinglaw.com, 29 March 2015; *Wall Street Journal*, 'Financial Sector Is Key to Combating Islamic State', 16 April 2015.

241 *Wall Street Journal*, 'Qatar's Ties to Militants Strain Alliance', 23 February 2015; Elizabeth Dickinson, 'The Case Against Qatar', *Foreign Policy*, 30 September 2014.

242 Department of the Treasury, 'Treasury Designates Twelve Foreign Terrorist Fighter Facilitators', 29 September 2014.

243 *Wall Street Journal*, 'Qatar's Ties to Militants Strain Alliance', 23 February 2015.

244 Reuters, 'France denies it paid ransom for Syria reporters', 26 April 2014.

245 ABC (Australia), 'Islamic State hostage ransom demands often met by European governments, expert says; US, UK no-pay policies under fire', 9 June 2015.

246 *Irish Times*, 'Hollande faults Europe for Scottish independence drive', 19 September 2014.

247 ABC (Australia), 'Islamic State hostage ransom demands often met by European governments, expert says; US, UK no-pay policies under fire', 9 June 2015.

248 See, for example, *Wall Street Journal*, 'Al Qaeda-Linked Groups Increasingly Funded by Ransom', 29 July 2014.

249 *New York Times*, 'CIA Cash Ended Up in Coffers of Al-Qaeda', 14 March 2015.

250 He was, however, later tried in absentia and given a seven-year sentence that still stands. *Wall Street Journal*, 'Qatar's Ties to Militants Strain Alliance', 23 February 2015.

251 *Daily Telegraph*, 'Islamic State seizes territory inside Lebanon', 4 August 2014.

252 Reuters Arabic (translated), 'Interior minister of Lebanon: Arsal occupied and will not slip in the Syrian war', 4 December 2015; Reuters, 'Prisoner swap deal frees Lebanese soldiers and Islamic State leader Baghdadi's ex-wife', 2 December 2015.

253 Confusingly, however, it was reported that by this stage the hostages were being held by both the Islamic State and *Al-Nusra* and that negotiations were taking place with both groups, but separately. See *Daily Star* (Lebanon), 'Breakthrough in Lebanon hostage case: report', 20 February 2015.

254 CBS, 'Turkey remains cagey about hostages freed by ISIS', 21 September 2014.

255 Reuters, 'Freed Lebanese, Turkish hostages fly home after deal', 20 October 2013.

256 *New York Times*, 'Where the Islamic State Gets Its Weapons', 27 April 2015.

257 *New York Times*, 'Arms Shipments Seen from Sudan to Syria Rebels', 12 August 2015.

258 CNN, 'Wesley Clark: ISIS Serving Interests of Turkey and Saudi Arabia', 25 November 2015.

259 *New York Times*, 'Saudis Are Next on Biden's Mideast Apology List After Harvard Remarks', 6 October 2014; Cockburn, *The Rise of Islamic State*, pp. xix–xx; Columbia University Institute for the Study of Human Rights, 'Research Paper: ISIS-Turkey Links', 29 November 2015.

260 Reuters, 'US offers Turkey technology to block Islamic State at Syria border', 21 January 2016; Al-Monitor, 'How the Islamic State is still seeping through Syria-Turkey border', 1 February 2016.

261 BBC Online, 'Russia says Turkey shot down plane for IS oil', 1 December 2015.

262 Cockburn, *The Rise of Islamic State*, p. 77.

263 Reuters, 'Turkey to set up Qatar military base to face common enemies', 16 December 2015.

264 Atwan, *Islamic State*, p. 222.

265 Curtis, *Secret Affairs*, pp. 219–20. Citing Cees Wiebes.

266 European Court of Human Rights, 'Akkoç v. Turkey, Applications 22947/93 and 22948/93', 10 October 2000.

267 Citing Fikri Sağlar. See F. Bulut, M. Farac, *Kod Adı: Hizbullah* (*Code name: Hizbullah*) (Istanbul: Ozan Publishing, 1999).

268 *Bloomberg*, 'Turkey Officer Says He Created Local Hezbollah Group, Star Says', 18 January 2011.

269 M. Weiss, H. Hassan, *ISIS: Inside the Army of Terror* (New York: Regan, 2015), pp. 104–5. Referring to Abu Khattab al-Kurdi.

270 Associated Press, 'Kurds find ISIS tunnel near Turkish border', 26 June 2015.

271 *Daily Telegraph*, 'Turkey let ISIL cross border to attack Kobane', 25 June 2015.

272 *Daily Telegraph* 'Turkey accused of allowing Islamic State fighters to cross its border in Kobane attack', 25 June 2015.

273 Al-Monitor, 'Video: Captured Islamic State Fighter Speaks', 18 June 2015.

274 *Guardian*, 'Turkey carries out first air strikes as part of anti-ISIS US coalition', 29 August 2015; *Guardian*, 'Two Marxist women open fire at US consulate in Istanbul', 10 August 2015; CNN, 'Dozens dead after terror attack in Turkish border city', 21 July 2015; BBC Online, 'Turkey bombs Islamic State targets in Syria', 24 July 2015; *Hurriyet* (Turkey), 'Top commander says Turkey actually waging war since July', 6 October 2015; CNN, 'Erdogan: Without Russia and Iran, Assad will fall in 24 hours', 7 September 2015.

275 Human Rights Watch, 'What is Turkey's Hizbullah?', 16 February 2000.

276 *Daily Mail*, 'Mystery of American journalist killed in car crash in Turkey… just days after she claimed intelligence services had threatened her over her coverage of siege of Kobane', 20 October 2014.

277 *Independent*, 'Jacky Sutton: British journalist who worked for BBC found dead at Istanbul's Ataturk airport', 19 October 2015; *Independent*, 'Jacky Sutton: "Suicide" of ex-BBC journalist called into question', 19 October 2015; *Daily Mirror*, 'CCTV shows Jacky Sutton's final moments in Turkish airport carrying shopping bag before unexplained death', 20 October 2015.

278 Agence France-Presse, 'Turkey Holds Reporters for Asking Tough Question About Islamic State', 16 June 2015; BBC Online, 'Turkish journalists face life in jail over Syria report', 26 January 2016; *Guardian*, 'I revealed the truth about President Erdogan and Syria. For that, he had me jailed', 28 December 2015.

279 *Zaman* (Turkey), 'Unregistered cash to Turkey up 52 percent in 9 months', 11 November 2015.

280 *Jerusalem Post*, 'Islamic State fighter: Turkey paved the way for us', 30 July 2014. Referring to an interview conducted by journalist Deniz Kahraman from *Aydinlik* newspaper and the OdaTV website.

281 Al-Monitor, 'Turkish military says MIT shipped weapons to al-Qaeda', 15 January 2015; Al-Monitor, 'Syria-bound trucks put spotlight on Turkey', 21 January 2014.

282 Ibid.

283 *Daily Telegraph*, 'Fears that US weapons will fall into al-Qaeda's hands as Syrian rebels defect', 11 November 2014.

284 *New York Times*, 'CIA Said to Aid in Steering Arms to Syrian Opposition', 21 June 2012.

285 *Guardian*, 'Turkey sends in jets as Syria's agony spills over every border', 26 July 2015.

286 ABC, 'US Officials Ask How ISIS Got So Many Toyota Trucks', 6 October 2015.

287 By August 2015 a total of 834 Toyota Hi-Luxes had been reported missing in New South Wales alone. *Australian*, 'Syria: Stolen Sydney utes used as armoured vehicles in fighting, experts say', 17 August 2015; Xinhua (China), 'Most stolen Toyota Hilux in Australia being sent to IS: terror experts', 9 October 2015.

10. THE ISLAMIC STATE – A GIFT THAT KEEPS GIVING

1 M. Lynch, 'Introduction', POMEPS Study 11, 2015, p. 4.

2 *Daily Telegraph*, 'Islamic State planning mass attack on Britain, warns head of MI5', 29 October 2015.

3 *New York Times*, 'As US Escalates Air War on ISIS, Allies Slip Away', 7 November 2015; S. O'Grady, 'Could an Entire French Generation Grow Up in a State of Emergency?', *Foreign Policy*, 22 January 2016.

4 For insights into the debate see *Fortune*, 'No, NSA Has Not Changed Stance on Encryption', 23 January 2016; *Guardian*, 'Paris is being used to justify agendas that had nothing to do with the attack', 20 November 2015.

5 *Independent*, 'Whistleblower Edward Snowden brands encrypted ISIS email as a fake', 25 January 2016; *New York Times*, 'ISIS Video Appears to Show Paris Assailants Earlier in Syria and Iraq', 24 January 2016.

6   *Independent*, 'EU referendum: David Cameron says ISIS and Vladimir Putin might be happy with Brexit', 17 May 2016; *Washington Post*, 'Terrorism fears magnify threats, real or imagined', 20 November 2015; *Guardian*, 'Paris is being used to justify agendas that had nothing to do with the attack', 20 November 2015.

7   *USA Today*, 'Panetta: 30-year war and a leadership test for Obama', 6 October 2014.

8   A. Zelin, 'The Islamic State's model', POMEPS Study 12, 2015, pp. 26–7; *Guardian*, 'Ten killed as gunmen storm luxury hotel in Libyan capital', 27 January 2015.

9   Zelin, 'The Islamic State's model', p. 27.

10   M. Curtis, *Secret Affairs: Britain's Collusion with Radical Islam* (London: Serpent's Tail, 2012), p. 226.

11   Zelin, 'The Islamic State's model', p. 27.

12   *New York Times*, 'ISIS' Grip on Libyan City Gives It a Fallback Option', 28 November 2015.

13   *Wall Street Journal*, 'Gunmen stage deadly attack on Libya Hotel', 28 January 2015; *Daily Telegraph*, 'How Gaddafi's home city in Libya fell under the rule of Islamic State jihadists', 10 March 2015.

14   Quoting Veryan Khan of the Florida-based Terrorism Research and Analysis Consortium and Mary Lambert of New York University. See Fox News, 'ISIS' army of 7-footers? Experts say video of Copt beheadings manipulated', 21 February 2015; BBC Online, 'Islamic State: Egyptian Christians held in Libya killed', 15 February 2015.

15   A. B. Atwan, *Islamic State: The Digital Caliphate* (London: Saqi, 2015), p. 221.

16   *Guardian*, 'Egyptian air strikes in Libya kill dozens of ISIS militants', 17 February 2015.

17   Al-Jazeera, 'ISIL assault halts production at 11 Libya oil fields', 5 March 2011.

18   *Sunday Times*, 'Britain plots bombing of ISIS in Libya', 31 January 2016; *Guardian*, 'UK awaits outcome of Libya talks as it weighs military options', 1 February 2016; Agence France-Press, 'Obama looks to take fight to Islamic State in Libya', 30 January 2016; Middle East Eye, 'Revealed: Britain and Jordan's secret war in Libya', 25 March 2016.

19   *Daily Telegraph*, 'Libya's anti-Islamist Hiftar appointed army chief', 2 March 2015; *New York Times*, 'In Libya, a Coup. Or Perhaps Not', 14 February 2014; *Guardian*, 'Ten killed as gunmen storm luxury hotel in Libyan capital', 27 January 2015; *New York Times*, 'Libyan General's Promotion Could Hinder United Nations Peace Talks', 2 March 2015.

20   *El Khabar* (Libya, translated), 'The Entry of Libyan militants trained in Egypt', 18 March 2015.

21   Middle East Eye, 'New leak alleges plan for Egypt and UAE to arm Libya campaign', 22 May 2015.

22   *New York Times*, 'Leaked Emirati Emails Could Threaten Peace Talks in Libya', 12 November 2015.

23   Fox, 'Herridge: ISIS Has Turned Libya into New Support Base, Safe Haven', 2 March 2015.

24   For a discussion of the Unity Government see *Financial Times*, 'Libya's Unity Government consolidates its hold in Tripoli', 6 April 2016.

25   CNN, '43 killed in US airstrike targeting terrorists in Libya', 20 February 2016.

26   Citing Aleksandar Vucic and Ivica Dacic. Associated Press, 'US airstrikes targeting ISIS in Libya kill Serbian hostages, officials say', 20 February 2016.

27   Russia Today, 'DoD, State Department struggle to explain Libya strike legality with 15-year-old authorization and some international law', 20 February 2016.

28   *Washington Post*, 'US establishes Libyan outposts with eye toward offensive against Islamic State', 12 May 2016.

29   Middle East Eye, 'Libyan PM rules out foreign military intervention', 5 June 2016.

30   *National Interest*, 'Saudi Arabia Honors Its Nastiest Clerical Ideologues', 16 October 2015.

31   J. M. Berger, 'The Middle East's Franz Ferdinand Moment', *Foreign Policy*, 8 April 2015; Stratfor, 'New Training Video Highlights Islamic State's Capabilities in Yemen', 24 April 2015.

32   A. Hashim, 'The Islamic State: from Al-Qaeda affiliate to caliphate', *Middle East Policy*, Vol. 21, No. 4, 2014, p. 6; J. M. Berger, J. Stern, *ISIS: The State of Terror* (London: William Collins, 2015), pp. 59–60; Zelin, 'The Islamic State's model', p. 25; Atwan, *Islamic State*, p. 75. Al-Qaeda in the Arabian Peninsula's leader until his death in summer 2015 had, for example, previously served as Osama bin Laden's private secretary in Afghanistan.

33   Berger, 'The Middle East's Franz Ferdinand Moment'; Berger, *ISIS*, p. 186.

34   Citing Makum Hatim. See Atwan, *Islamic State*, p. 75; C. Bunzel, 'From Paper State to Caliphate: The Ideology of the Islamic State', Brookings Project on US relations with the Islamic World – Analysis Paper, No. 19, March 2015, p. 32; Berger, *ISIS*, p. 181.

35   Berger, 'The Middle East's Franz Ferdinand Moment'.

36   Yemen Online, 'Missing Weapons', 20 March 2015; *Los Angeles Times*, 'Iran-backed rebels loot Yemen files about US spy operations', 25 March 2015.

37   Reuters, 'IS suicide bomber dressed as a woman kills ten at Yemen Houthi mosque', 24 September 2015.

38   Berger, 'The Middle East's Franz Ferdinand Moment'; Berger, *ISIS*, p. 25; M. Weiss, H. Hassan, *ISIS: Inside the Army of Terror* (New York: Regan, 2015), p. 46.

39   I. Kohl, 'Libya's Major Minorities. Berber, Tuareg and Tebu: Multiple Narratives of Citizenship, Language and Border Control', *Middle East Critique*, Vol. 23, No. 4, 2014, p. 431; European Parliament, 'The Involvement of Salafism/Wahhabism in the support and supply of arms to rebel groups around the world', Directorate-General for External Policies, June 2013, pp. 26–7; J. Comolli, *Boko Haram: Nigeria's Islamist Insurgency* (London: Hurst, 2015), p. 101; Associated Press, 'Soldiers loot Mali

presidential palace after ousting leader', 22 March 2012; Agence France-Presse, 'Islamist fighters call for Sharia law in Mali', 13 March 2012; UN Security Council, 'Committee pursuant to resolutions 1267 (1999) and 1989 (2011) concerning Al-Qaeda and associated individuals and entities QE.A.135.13', 21 March 2013.

40   European Parliament, 'The Involvement of Salafism/Wahhabism', p. 25; Comolli, *Boko Haram*, pp. 101–2.

41   Atwan, *Islamic State*, p. 224; European Parliament, 'The Involvement of Salafism/ Wahhabism', pp. 25–6.

42   Comolli, *Boko Haram*, p. 102; European Parliament, 'The Involvement of Salafism/ Wahhabism', p. 23. Referring to France's Operation Serval to protect the Ahmed Baba Institute.

43   BBC Online, 'Mali crisis: Key players', 12 March 2013; European Parliament, 'The Involvement of Salafism/Wahhabism', p. 26.

44   BBC Online, 'Mali crisis: Key players', 12 March 2013.

45   Atwan, *Islamic State*, pp. 76–7; Berger, *ISIS*, pp. 181, 185.

46   E. Groll, 'Is AQIM Parroting the Islamic State in Its Latest Hostage Video?', *Foreign Policy*, 23 June 2015.

47   BBC Online, 'Mali crisis: Key players', 12 March 2013.

48   European Parliament, 'The Involvement of Salafism/Wahhabism', p. 26.

49   M. Mohamedou, 'The many faces of Al-Qaeda in the Islamic Maghreb', GCSP Policy paper 15, 2011; J. Burbank, *Trans-Saharan trafficking: A Growing source of terrorist financing* (Washington DC: Center for the Study of Threat Convergence, 2010).

50   *Le Figaro* (translated), 'Mali: Tuareg rebels proclaimed an Islamic state', 27 May 2012.

51   BBC Online, 'Life in Timbuktu under Islamist rule', 23 May 2012; Middle East Eye, 'Mali: A peace deal to promote conflict', 27 May 2015; Reuters, 'Algeria's Sonatrach vows Mali oil drilling by mid-2012', 26 October 2012.

52   BBC Online, 'Life in Timbuktu under Islamist rule', 23 May 2012.

53   European Parliament, 'The Involvement of Salafism/Wahhabism', p. 25.

54   S. Barakat, 'Qatar Mediation: between ambition and achievement', Brookings Doha Center, Analysis Paper 12, November 2014.

55   *Le Canard enchaîné* (translated), 'Our friend Qatar finances the Islamists in Mali', 6 June 2012; European Parliament, 'The Involvement of Salafism/Wahhabism', p. 28.

56   See *Marianne* (translated), 'In Mali, Qatar invests in jihadism', 6 July 2012. Quoting Roland Marchal.

57   Gatestone Institute, 'Qatar and Terror', 22 November 2014.

58   RTL (translated), 'The French government knows who is supporting the terrorists, it is Qatar', 4 July 2012. Quoting Sadio Diallo.

59   *Deutsche Welle*, 'Ansar Dine: radical Islamists in northern Mali', 18 December 2014. Deutsche Welle also claimed that *Ansar Dine* was likely receiving funding from Saudi Arabia.

60   E. Abrams, 'Pressure Points: Qatar in Mali: Which Side Are They On?', Council on Foreign Relations, 22 January 2013. Quoting French analyst Mehdi Lazar; European Parliament, 'The Involvement of Salafism/Wahhabism', p. 29.

61   Energy Information Administration, 'Nigeria: Country Analysis Brief Overview', 30 December 2013; *The Economist*, 'Nigeria: Africa's New Number One', 12 April 2014; *The Economist*, 'Nigeria's presidential election: the real thing', 20 April 2011.

62   *The Economist*, 'Reforming the Oil Industry', 29 September 2007.

63   *Financial Times*, 'Nigeria: the big oil fix', 26 May 2015. Quoting the anonymous CEO of a multinational oil company.

64   *Financial Times*, 'Seplat and Afren in talks over oil merger', 22 December 2014.

65   *The Economist*, 'Nigeria: Africa's New Number One', 12 April 2014.

66   BBC Online, 'US shifts on AFRICOM base plans', 18 February 2008.

67   *This Day* (Nigeria), 'US Forecloses Setting up AFRICOM Headquarters in Africa', 7 September 2012.

68   Boko Haram's more formal name, translated into English, being 'Group of the People of Sunnah for Preaching and Jihad'. *Independent*, 'Boko Haram closes in on its dream of an African caliphate – and ISIS gives its blessing, and advice on strategy', 8 September 2014; Atwan, *Islamic State*, pp. 69, 224.

69   Comolli, *Boko Haram*, pp. 20–21, 23, 35, 37.

70   *Independent*, 'Boko Haram closes in on its dream of an African caliphate – and ISIS gives its blessing, and advice on strategy', 8 September 2014.

71   Council on Foreign Relations, 'Backgrounders: Boko Haram', 7 October 2014; *Guardian*, 'Join us or die: the birth of Boko Haram', 2 February 2016; *Guardian*, 'Nigerian Taliban offensive leaves 150 dead', 27 July 2009.

72   Comolli, *Boko Haram*, p. 52; *Wall Street Journal*, 'Jihad comes to Africa', 5 February 2016.

73   BBC Online, 'Nigeria's Taliban enigma', 31 July 2009.

74   BBC Online, 'Nigeria sect head dies in custody', 31 July 2009; *New York Times*, 'Abduction of Girls an Act Not Even Al-Qaeda Can Condone', 7 May 2014.

75   Comolli, *Boko Haram*, pp. 60–61.

76   *New York Times*, 'Abduction of Girls an Act Not Even Al-Qaeda Can Condone', 7 May 2014.

77   Comolli, *Boko Haram*, p. 106.

78   Ibid., pp. 64, 69; Council on Foreign Relations, 'Backgrounders: Boko Haram', 7 October 2014.

79   Comolli, *Boko Haram*, pp. 63–5. Citing Andrew Walker's analysis.

80   Comolli, *Boko Haram*, pp. 64–5, 80, 100.

81   Department of State, 'Diplomatic Security Daily 09STATE67105', 9 June 2009 (leaked).

82   Department of State, 'Nigeria: Borno State residents not yet recovered from Boko Haram violence 09ABUJA2014_a', 4 November 2009 (leaked).

83 Department of State, 'Terrorist Designations of Boko Haram and Ansaru', 13 November 2013; Council on Foreign Relations, 'Backgrounders: Boko Haram', 7 October 2014.
84 Council on Foreign Relations, 'Backgrounders: Boko Haram', 7 October 2014.
85 Comolli, *Boko Haram*, p. 98; BBC Online, 'Africa's Islamist militants co-ordinate efforts', 26 June 2012.
86 Comolli, Boko Haram, pp. 67, 103.
87 Reuters, 'Boko Haram too extreme for al-Qaeda in West Africa brand', 28 May 2014.
88 Comolli, *Boko Haram*, p. 105.
89 Ibid., pp. 66, 68; Reuters, 'Boko Haram too extreme for al-Qaeda in West Africa brand', 28 May 2014.
90 *Independent*, 'Boko Haram closes in on its dream of an African caliphate – and ISIS gives its blessing, and advice on strategy', 8 September 2014.
91 BBC Online, 'Nigeria's Boko Haram pledges allegiance to Islamic State', 7 March 2015.
92 BBC Online, 'Is Islamic State shaping Boko Haram media?', 4 March 2015; BBC Online, 'Islamic State "accepts" Boko Haram's allegiance pledge', 13 March 2015.
93 *Washington Post*, 'The Islamic State, Boko Haram and the evolution of international jihad', 27 March 2015.
94 Comolli, *Boko Haram*, p. 97; *Independent*, 'Boko Haram closes in on its dream of an African caliphate – and Isis gives its blessing, and advice on strategy', 8 September 2014.
95 *Independent*, 'Boko Haram closes in on its dream of an African caliphate – and Isis gives its blessing, and advice on strategy', 8 September 2014.
96 *Wall Street Journal*, 'Jihad comes to Africa', 5 February 2016.
97 *Independent*, 'Paying for terrorism: Where does Boko Haram gets its money from?', 6 June 2014.
98 Amnesty International, 'Nigerian authorities failed to act on warnings about Boko Haram raid on school', 9 May 2014. The raid on the school led to the abduction of 240 girls.
99 Council on Foreign Relations, 'Backgrounders: Boko Haram', 7 October 2014.
100 Comolli, *Boko Haram*, p. 94.
101 Reuters, 'Captured video appears to show foreign fighters in Nigeria's Boko Haram', 27 May 2015.
102 Council on Foreign Relations, 'Backgrounders: Boko Haram', 7 October 2014.
103 *Washington Post*, 'The myth of the un-killable Abubakar Shekau: Is the feared Boko Haram leader dead, or was it a double?', 25 September 2014.
104 Berger, 'The Middle East's Franz Ferdinand Moment'.
105 Reuters, 'Nigeria's Boko Haram releases beheading video echoing Islamic State', 3 March 2015.

106 BBC Online, 'Is Islamic State shaping Boko Haram media?', 4 March 2015; BBC Online, 'Nigeria's Boko Haram pledges allegiance to Islamic State', 7 March 2015.

107 Comolli, *Boko Haram*, pp. 76–7, 87.

108 Ibid., pp. 78–80.

109 BBC Online, 'How Islamist militancy threatens Africa', 29 May 2013; BBC Online, 'Boko Haram crisis: How have Nigeria's militants become so strong?', 26 January 2015.

110 Alli Shettima Monguno. See *Premium Times* (Nigeria), 'Abducted 92-Year-Old Ex-Oil Minister, Ali Monguno, released', 6 May 2013; Comolli, *Boko Haram*, p. 82.

111 Comolli, *Boko Haram*, pp. 66–7, 88.

112 Ibid., p. 82.

113 Ibid., p. 83; *The Punch* (Nigeria), 'No Boko Haram links with Drug Barons – NDLEA', 5 January 2014.

114 *Wall Street Journal*, 'Jihad comes to Africa', 5 February 2016.

115 Citing retired US major Chris Moghalu who is now based in Nigeria. *This Day* (Nigeria), 'Nigeria: Report Claims Boko Haram Has Benefited from $70 million Overseas Funding', 5 May 2014.

116 *Guardian*, 'Bin Laden files show al-Qaeda and Taliban leaders in close contact', 29 April 2012; Comolli, *Boko Haram*, p. 101.

117 *Guardian*, 'Boko Haram vows to fight until Nigeria establishes Sharia law', 27 January 2012.

118 J. Davis, *Africa and the War on Terrorism* (London: Ashgate, 2013), p. 4; D. Ottaway, *The King's Messenger: Prince Bandar bin Sultan and America's Tangled Relationship with Saudi Arabia* (New York: Walker, 2008), p. 207.

119 *Guardian*, 'Peer raises fears over UK charity's alleged links to Boko Haram', 9 September 2012.

120 The congressmen were led by Sheila Jackson Lee.

121 www.farisspm.com (accessed 14 October 2015). See section on 'Selected Achievements'.

122 Faris Strategic Political Management, 'International Report: Representative Sheila Jackon Lee's False Allegations linking Al-Muntada to Boko Haram', August 2014, p. 12.

123 Comolli, *Boko Haram*, p. 99.

124 Department of State, 'Rewards for Justice: Abubaker Shekau: Up to $7 million reward', 1 August 2013.

125 Reuters, 'Boko Haram too extreme for al-Qaeda in West Africa brand', 28 May 2014.

126 *Independent*, 'Paying for terrorism: Where does Boko Haram gets its money from?', 6 June 2014.

127 Comolli, *Boko Haram*, pp. 68, 81.

128 *New York Times*, 'Jihadists Deepen Collaboration in North Africa', 1 January 2016.

129 NOI Polls, 'Annual New Year Special Poll', January 2015.

130 Department of State Bureau of Counterterrorism, 'Country Reports on Terrorism 2013', 1 February 2014; Freedom House, 'Stronger Nigerian Action Needed against Boko Haram', 15 January 2015.

131 *Guardian*, 'Nigeria: Pro-Democracy Group Warns Against Interim Government', 26 February 2015.

132 AllAfrica (South Africa), 'Nigeria: The Spontaneous Buharism Explosion in the Polity', 14 September 2014; BBC Online, 'Nigeria election: Muhammadu Buhari close to victory', 31 March 2015.

133 M. Buhari, 'Prospects for Democratic Consolidation in Africa: Nigeria's Transition', speech at Chatham House, 26 February 2015.

134 Channel 4, 'Did Boko Haram win Nigeria's election for Muhammadu Buhari?', 31 March 2015.

135 *Final Call* (Nation of Islam), 'Radical Nigerians or a CIA front?', 2 June 2014.

136 *New York Times*, 'With Schoolgirls Taken by Boko Haram Still Missing, US-Nigeria Ties Falter', 31 December 2014.

137 Ibid.

138 Voice of America, 'Nigeria's President: Boko Haram Trained with Islamic State', 11 March 2015.

139 Author interviews with Gerald Horne, October 2015.

140 *Wall Street Journal*, 'Jihad Comes to Africa', 5 February 2016; *New York Times*, 'Jihadists Deepen Collaboration in North Africa', 1 January 2016; World Socialist Web Site, 'US AFRICOM commander calls for huge military campaign in West Africa', 2 February 2015. Quoting General David Rodriguez's remarks at the Center for Strategic and International Studies in Washington DC, January 2015.

141 Reuters, 'US set to provide $5 million for anti-Boko Haram force', 16 June 2015; *Leak Times* (Nigeria), 'Buhari Seals Deal with US to Establish AFRICOM in Nigeria', 16 June 2015.

142 *Financial Times*, 'Nigeria: the big oil fix', 26 May 2015.

143 Channels Television (Nigeria), 'US Pledges continued support to Nigeria', 6 July 2015.

144 For a good discussion of the Islamic State's franchising criteria see Zelin, 'The Islamic State's model', pp. 24–5.

145 Comolli, *Boko Haram*, p. 104; Berger, *ISIS*, p. 58. Al-Shabaab had been rejected by Osama bin Laden but was accepted by Ayman Zawahiri.

146 Atwan, *Islamic State*, p. 135; Berger, *ISIS*, pp. 63–4.

147 A. Meleagrou-Hitchens, 'ISIS and al-Qaeda Struggle for al-Shabaab's Soul', *Foreign Affairs*, 8 October 2015; CNN, 'Al-Shabaab faction pledges allegiance to ISIS', 23 October 2015; *Washington Post*, '2,000 miles from Syria, ISIS is trying to lure recruits in Somalia', 24 December 2015.

148 Voice of America, 'Al-Qaeda or Islamic State? Issue Simmers Within Al-Shabaab', 30 September 2015; Reuters, 'Small group of Somali al-Shabaab swear allegiance to

Islamic State', 23 October 2015; Associated Press, 'Official: 200 al-Shabaab fighters pledge allegiance to IS', 24 December 2015; Berger, *ISIS*, p. 191.

149 For details of the pledge see *New York Times*, 'Militant Group in Egypt Vows Loyalty to ISIS', 10 November 2014.

150 M. Awad, N. Brown, 'Mutual escalation in Egypt', POMEPS Study 12, 2015, pp. 39–41.

151 Reuters, 'Gunmen storm Tunisian museum, kill 17 foreign tourists', 18 March 2015.

152 Associated Press, 'Museum attack in Tunisian capital kills 19; 2 gunmen slain', 18 March 2015; Associated Press, 'ISIS claims responsibility for Tunisia museum attack in audio message', 19 March 2015.

153 BBC Online, 'As it happened: Tunisia attack', 18 March 2015; For a discussion of the programme as it moved forward see NATO, 'Press release: NATO and Tunisia reaffirm willingness to deepen cooperation', 9 June 2015; *Washington Post*, 'Outside the Wire: How US Special Operations troops secretly help foreign forces target terrorists', 16 April 2016.

154 BBC Online, 'Tunisia attack on Sousse beach kills 39', 26 June 2015.

155 For a discussion of Maan see Associated Press, 'Islamic State group support grows in Jordan town', 6 December 2014.

156 Al-Jazeera, 'Jordan releases anti-ISIL Salafi leader', 14 June 2014; Weiss, *ISIS*, p. 29.

157 BBC Online, 'Jordan pilot hostage Moaz al-Kasasbeh burned alive', 3 February 2015; ABC, 'Islamic State: Jordan launches new air strikes against militants after pilot's murder', 5 February 2015.

158 Berger, *ISIS*, p. 189; Weiss, *ISIS*, pp. 86–7.

159 *Moscow Times*, 'Islamic State Suspected in Chechnya Terrorist Attack', 4 December 2014.

160 M. Vatchagaev, 'Islamic State continues to gain influence in southern Russia', Jamestown Foundation Eurasia Daily Monitor, 29 April 2016.

161 M. Vatchagaev, 'Georgian President, US Ambassador Deny Russian Claim That Terrorists Are in Pankisi Gorge', Jamestown Foundation Eurasia Daily Monitor, 4 February 2016.

162 Reuters, 'Chief of elite Tajik police unit defects to Islamic State, vows jihad against enemies', 28 May 2015; *Daily Telegraph*, 'Missing Tajikistan police chief defects to the Islamic State', 28 May 2015.

163 C. Lister, 'Profiling the Islamic State', Brookings Doha Center, Analysis Paper 13, November 2014, p. 33; Atwan, *Islamic State*, pp. 76, 136. Although his sons have reportedly denounced the pledge. See Berger, *ISIS*, p. 181.

164 Berger, *ISIS*, p. 182; Lister, 'Profiling the Islamic State', p. 33; *Bloomberg*, 'Islamic State Is Rapidly Expanding in South-East Asia', 29 May 2015. Quoting Lee Hsien Loong.

165 Atwan, *Islamic State*, p. 76; Berger, *ISIS*, p. 182. Its spokesman was initially fired after a public pledge of allegiance to ISIS, but other commanders then joined him.

166 *Express Tribune* (Pakistan), 'Startling revelations: IS operative confesses to getting funds via US', 28 January 2015.

167 Reuters, 'US sees role for India in battle against Islamic State', 26 January 2015.

168 *Independent*, 'ISIS Japanese Hostages: video purports to show Haruna Yukawa executed and second hostage Kenji Goto with new terms for his release', 24 January 2015; *Independent*, 'ISIS hostage video: Japanese PM says outrageous execution of Haruna Yukawa is likely to be genuine', 25 January 2015.

169 Reuters, 'Abe's cabinet approves Japan security bills', 14 May 2015; BBC Online, 'Scuffles as Japan security bill approved by committee', 17 September 2015.

170 *The Economist*, 'Defence in Japan: Open Arms', 15 May 2015; BBC Online, 'Japan's cabinet approves record boost in defence spending', 24 December 2015; *Wall Street Journal*, 'Japan to Create New Anti-Terrorism Intelligence Unit', 4 December 2015.

EPILOGUE – KEEPING THE WHEEL TURNING

1 R. Hinnebusch, 'A historical sociology approach to authoritarian resilience in post-Arab Uprising MENA', POMEPS Study 11, 2015, p. 12.

2 Foreign Office, 'Transatlantic relations in the 21st century and the UK's policy toward Europe and NATO, transcript of speech by David Lidington', 5 April 2011.

3 S. Simoni, *Understanding Transatlantic Relations: Whither the West?* (London: Routledge, 2013), p. 94.

4 Foreign Office, 'Foreign Secretary launches Foreign Office Business Charter, transcript of speech by William Hague', 10 May 2011.

5 UK Government Policy Paper, '2010 to 2015 Government Policy: Peace and Stability in the Middle East and North Africa: Appendix 8: The Deauville Partnership with Arab countries in Transition', 8 May 2015.

6 F. Cavatorta, 'No Democratic Change… and Yet No Authoritarian Continuity: The Inter-paradigm Debate and North Africa After the Uprisings', *British Journal of Middle Eastern Studies*, Vol. 42, No. 1, 2015, p. 138.

7 K. Bogaert, 'Contextualising the Arab Revolts: The Politics Behind Three Decades of Neo-liberalism in the Arab World', *Middle East Critique*, Vol. 22, No. 3, 2013, p. 218; A. Hanieh, 'Shifting Priorities or Business as Usual? Continuity and Change in the post-2011 IMF and World Bank Engagement with Tunisia, Morocco and Egypt', *British Journal of Middle Eastern Studies*, Vol. 42, No. 1, 2015, pp. 119, 122; RS21, 'Adam Hanieh on the Gulf states, neoliberalism and liberation in the Middle East', 6 October 2014.

8 Hanieh, 'Shifting Priorities', p. 120. Quoting IMF managing director Christine Lagarde.

9 Ibid., pp. 120, 122–5, 131.

10 Ibid., pp. 121, 124, 130, 133; M. Hamid, L. Farrall, *The Arabs at War in Afghanistan* (London: Hurst, 2015), p. 324.

11   *Bloomberg*, 'Even with Billions in Gulf Aid, Egypt May Still Turn to IMF', 27 May 2015.

12   *New York Times*, 'Did Dubai Do it?', 18 November 2014.

13   Simon McDonald is the permanent undersecretary to the Foreign Office and the head of Britain's Diplomatic Service. *Independent*, 'Human rights are no longer a "top priority" for the Government, says Foreign Office chief', 2 October 2015.

14   *The National* (UAE), 'Egypt close to revealing plan for its New Cairo capital', 25 February 2015; *Al-Ahram* (Egypt), 'Is it time for Egypt's new capital city?', 27 August 2014.

15   *Mada Masr* (Egypt), 'Q&A with Dan Ringelstein of SOM, the urban designers behind The Capital Cairo project', 18 March 2015; *Gulf Business*, 'UAE to Build Egypt's New Capital City', 15 March 2015; Reuters, 'Egypt's stalled $35 billion housing scheme: big dreams to harsh reality', 8 October 2015.

16   *Arabian Business*, 'Top UAE tycoon says ready to jump on new Egypt investments', 21 March 2015.

17   This op-ed originally appeared in *Gulf News* on 6 February 2011 with the title 'Egypt's youth uprising has been hijacked'. The same essay was also published on the Al-Habtoor Group's website. Both versions have since been removed.

18   *Cairo Post*, 'The British are coming in force: UK ambassador John Casson', 13 March 2015.

19   Tweet: @PHammondMP, '#BP's $12bn deal to develop oil and gas in Egypt is the biggest inward investment in Egypt's history. #LongTermEconomicPlan', 13 March 2015.

20   Middle East Eye, 'The Great Egyptian gas giveaway?', 8 April 2015.

21   *Al-Ahram* (Egypt), 'Live updates: Egypt's unveils 2030 economic vision at Sharm el-Sheikh conference', 14 March 2015.

22   Citing eyewitness tweets from the *Guardian*'s Egypt correspondent, Patrick Kingsley. See Tweet: @PatrickKingsley, 'Blair in Sharm: I'm absolutely in favour of democracy .... but I think you've also got to be realistic'; 'Blair on Sisi: For the first time in my memory, you have a leadership in Egypt that understands the modern world', 14 March 2015.

23   Al-Jazeera, 'Q&A with Italian PM: I think Sisi is a great leader', 12 July 2015. Quoting Matteo Renzi.

24   *Al-Ahram* (Egypt), 'As Egypt celebrates the new Suez Canal, Britain stands in solidarity', 6 August 2015. Article written by Michael Fallon.

25   *Mada Masr* (Egypt), 'Q&A with Dan Ringelstein of SOM, the urban designers behind The Capital Cairo project', 18 March 2015; Middle East Eye, 'Doubts raised over achievability of Egypt's new capital', 17 March 2015.

26   *Financial Times*, 'Egypt business profile: risk pays off for Amer Group', 18 December 2013; J. Sowers, 'Activism and political economy in the new-old Egypt', *International Journal of Middle East Studies*, Vol. 47, No. 1, 2015, pp. 141–2.

27   Reuters, 'Egypt's Amer Group says 2014 profit up 70 percent', 16 March 2015.

28 Sowers, 'Activism', p. 142.

29 *Forbes*, 'Egypt's billionaires 80 percent richer than before the revolution', 5 May 2015.

30 M. Curtis, *Secret Affairs: Britain's Collusion with Radical Islam* (London: Serpent's Tail, 2012), p. 298. Quoting Foreign Office minister Kim Howells.

31 *New York Times*, 'Iran's Sanctions Lift, and the West Goes to Talk Business', 25 January 2016.

32 *Financial Times*, 'European Oil Majors hold Iran talks', 24 June 2015; *Financial Times*, 'Iran: The oil and gas multibillion-dollar candy store', 16 July 2015; Reuters, 'Iran eyes $185 billion oil and gas projects after sanctions', 23 July 2015; *Bloomberg*, 'Exxon Deploys More Sanction Watchers as Iran Nuke Deal Looms', 21 May 2015.

33 Ibid.

34 *Guardian*, 'Shell and BP make new inroads in Iran', 2 October 2015.

35 *Guardian*, 'Sanctions against Iran crumble as America wrangles over the nuclear deal', 5 August 2015; Reuters, 'Japan, Iran to discuss investment pact after sanctions end: Nikkei', 19 August 2015.

36 *Bloomberg*, 'Iran Forum Offers Europe's Companies Post-Sanctions Opening', 23 September 2015; *Guardian*, 'Shell and BP make new inroads in Iran', 2 October 2015.

37 BBC Online, 'Airbus signs $25 billion deal to sell 118 planes to Iran', 28 January 2016.

38 BBC Online, 'President Truman and the Origins of the Cold War', 17 February 2011; W. Blum, *Killing Hope: US Military and CIA Interventions Since World War II* (London: Zed, 2014), p. 332.

39 Blum, *Killing Hope*, p. 332.

40 Hinnebusch, 'A historical sociology', p. 12.

41 Curtis, *Secret Affairs*, pp. 4–5. Quoting Secretary of State for India Viscount Cross writing to Viceroy Lord Dufferin and, writing in 1888, civil servant John Strachey.

42 *Socialist Worker*, 'Saudi Arabia's get-out-of-terror-free card', 24 February 2015. Quoting Mahmood Mamdani.

43 See R. Perle, D. Frum, *An End to Evil: How to Win the War on Terror* (New York: Ballatine, 2004).

44 R. Dreyfuss, *Devil's Game: How the United States Helped Unleash Fundamentalist Islam* (New York: Metropolitan, 2006), p. 338. Citing interviews with Max Singer, February 2003.

45 RAND Corporation, 'Unfolding the Future of the Long War: Motivations, Prospects, and Implications for the US Army', RAND Arroyo Center, 2008, p. 85.

46 V. Nasr, *The Shia Revival: How Conflicts within Islam Will Shape the Future* (New York: Norton, 2006); V. Nasr, 'When the Shiites Rise', *Foreign Affairs*, July 2006; *New York Times*, 'Muslim Against Muslim', 13 August 2006.

47 H. Dabashi, *The Arab Spring: The End of Postcolonialism* (London: Zed, 2012), pp. 152–3.

48   V. Nasr, 'The War for Islam', *Foreign Policy*, 22 January 2016.

49   E. Hoogland, Durham University lecture, 20 June 2014.

50   See, for example, BBC Online, 'Syria refugee camps set up as Turkey limits entries', 8 February 2016; BBC Online, 'Syria conflict: Donor nations pledge $10 billion in vital aid', 4 February 2016.

51   In May 2016 the Department of Defense admitted there were US troops in Yemen, but made clear that they were focused on al-Qaeda intelligence gathering, as opposed to assisting the main war effort against the Houthi movement. Agence France-Presse, 'US military admits troops are operating inside Yemen to combat al-Qaeda', 6 May 2016; Sky News, 'British Military Experts Advising Saudi Forces in Yemen', 7 January 2016.

52   *Wall Street Journal*, 'US Met Secretly with Yemen Rebels', 1 June 2015; *New York Times*, 'Saudi-Led War in Yemen Frays Ties with the US', 22 December 2015.

53   Department of State, 'John Kirby Spokesperson Daily Press Briefing', 4 January 2016; BBC Online, 'US warns Saudi execution of Shia cleric Nimr could fuel tensions', 3 January 2016.

54   Department of State, 'Scene setter visit of DOE deputy secretary Poneman to Saudi Arabia 04RIYADH001557', 23 November 2009 (leaked).

55   Author interviews in Houston, Texas, July 2010; A. M. Jaffe, 'The Americas, not the Middle East, will be the world capital of energy', *Foreign Policy*, 15 August 2011.

56   *Bloomberg*, 'US Seen as Biggest Oil Producer After Overtaking Saudi', 4 July 2014; *Forbes*, 'Welcome to Cowboyistan: Fracking King Harold Hamm's Plan for US Domination of Global Oil', 9 March 2015.

57   *Wall Street Journal*, 'US Oil Prices End 2015 Down 30 percent for the Year', 31 December 2015; *New York Times*, 'OPEC Split as Oil Prices Fall Sharply', 13 October 2014; Kune (China), 'China's GCC oil imports decrease in 2014', 20 July 2014.

58   Agence France-Presse, 'US Crude Oil Rig Count Fell by 946 Rigs in 2015', 8 January 2016.

59   *Financial Times*, 'Which Oil Producers Are Breaking Even?', 18 January 2016.

60   *Financial Times*, 'US banks hit by cheap oil as OPEC warns of long-term low', 23 December 2015.

61   *Bloomberg*, 'Saudi December Net Foreign Assets Drop More Than $19 Billion', 28 January 2016.

62   International Monetary Fund, 'World Economic and Financial Surveys: Regional Economic Outlook Middle East and Central Asia', 15 October 2015, pp. 17–27; *Independent*, 'Saudi Arabia could be bankrupt within five years, IMF predicts', 23 October 2015; CNBC, 'Saudi Arabia hangs on with cheap oil – but for how long?', 26 August 2015.

63   See, for example, BBC Online, 'Saudi Arabia's new desert megacity', 20 March 2015; *Mada Masr* (Egypt), 'Q&A with Dan Ringelstein of SOM, the urban designers behind The Capital Cairo project', 18 March 2015; Associated Press, 'A private

company is trying to build a $100 billion city-from-scratch in Saudi Arabia', 22 May 2015. The developer being the UAE's Capital City Partners.

64 CNN, 'Saudi Arabia opens up its stock market ... but not to you', 15 June 2015.

65 M. Curtis, *Web of Deceit: Britain's Real Role in the World* (London: Vintage, 2003), p. 259. Quoting Peter Hain's speech on 20 June 2000 to the Investing in Saudi Arabia conference.

66 Reuters, 'Saudi Arabia to allow full foreign ownership in retail', 6 September 2015.

67 *The Economist*, 'Saudi Arabia is considering an IPO of Aramco, probably the world's most valuable company', 7 January 2016; *Bloomberg*, 'Saudi December Net Foreign Assets Drop More Than $19 Billion', 28 January 2016; *Asharq al-Awsat*, 'Saudi Arabia to privatize electricity sector, shifts towards solar power', 3 March 2016; *Bloomberg*, 'Saudi Arabia's $400 billion bourse said to seek banks for IPO', 23 March 2016.

68 *Bloomberg*, 'Shock, Laughter Greet Plan for Saudi Arabia's Record Oil IPO', 8 January 2016; Reuters, 'The one thing in Saudi Arabia that works well is under threat', 4 February 2016.

69 *Financial Times*, 'The House of Saud's embryonic embrace of meritocracy', 1 May 2015; *Financial Times*, 'Former MI6 chief Sir John Sawers joins BP board', 14 May 2015.

70 *Al-Arabiya*, 'Full text of Saudi Arabia's Vision 2030', 26 April 2016; *City AM*, 'Saudi Aramco targets London, New York, Hong Kong for international listing', 9 May 2016; Daily Telegraph, 'Saudi Aramco plans London listing but doubts grow over $2.5 trillion claim', 8 May 2016.

71 For a good discussion see *Bloomberg*, 'Oil price rally isn't as deep-rooted as it looks at first glance', 3 May 2016. *Bloomberg*'s analyst points out that even as oil began to rally close to $50 a barrel, the five-year forward contracts had continued to fall 'reflecting the view that shale oil production could rebound as prices recover, capping any rally'. Similarly, Société Générale's Michael Wittner has stated that 'we believe sustained front end [oil prices of] $45 to $50 will be self-limiting, as US shale producer spending and drilling would stabilize and perhaps recover.'

72 *Bloomberg*, 'Bloomberg's Wong on Saudi Arabia's US Treasury Holdings', 22 January 2016; *Bloomberg*, 'Saudi Arabia's Secret Holdings of US Debt Are Suddenly a Big Deal', 24 January 2016. Quoting Edwin Truman.

73 *Arab News*, 'Mr Obama, we are not free riders', 14 March 2016.

74 *New York Times*, 'Saudi Arabia warns of economic fallout if Congress passes 9/11 bill', 15 April 2016.

75 Reuters, 'Saudi minister confirms warning on proposed US law on 9/11', 2 May 2016.

76 *New York Times*, 'Senate passes bill exposing Saudi Arabia to 9/11 legal claims', 17 May 2016.

77 The other two commissioners being Tim Roemer and an anonymous member. See *Guardian*, 'Saudi officials were supporting 9/11 hijackers, commission member says', 12 May 2016.

78   Saudi Arabia was reported to be holding only $116 billion in US treasury bonds. Most analysts have assumed that it holds much more than this, most likely using 'custodial accounts' operated by states such as Britain and Belgium. This may help understand the Saudi government's claim that it holds '$750 billion in treasury securities'. *Bloomberg*, 'The 42-year history of Saudi Arabia's treasuries holdings', 16 May 2016; *Bloomberg*, 'US discloses Saudi holdings of treasuries for first time', 16 May 2016.

79   *Financial Times*, 'Oil price drop leads to renewed speculation on Saudi riyal', 25 August 2015.

80   *Financial Times*, 'The manat of the moment: What's next after Azerbaijan's de-peg?', 21 December 2015.

81   Reuters, 'Devaluation fears hit Saudi riyal as oil slides', 20 January 2016.

82   *Wall Street Journal*, 'PointState Capital's Zachary Schreiber says he's short the Saudi riyal', 4 May 2016.

83   *Atlantic*, 'The Obama Doctrine', April 2016.

84   *New York Times*, 'Saudi Arabia's Barbaric Executions', 4 January 2016; *Washington Post*, 'Saudi Arabia's reckless regime', 3 January 2016.

85   *Guardian*, 'Inquiry into foreign backers of UK extremists gets green light', 17 January 2016.

86   *Daily Telegraph*, 'Saudi Arabia destabilizing Arab world, German intelligence warns', 2 December 2016.

87   The report named Bandar bin Sultan al-Saud and alleged he had organized payment of $32 million to the contras via a Cayman Islands account. See *New York Times*, 'US Relies Heavily on Saudi Money to Support Syrian Rebels', 23 January 2016.

88   RAND, 'Unfolding the Future', p. 69.

89   *Al-Arabiya*, '52 Saudi clerics, scholars call to battle Russian forces in Syria', 5 October 2015; Reuters, 'Saudi opposition clerics make sectarian call to jihad in Syria', 5 October 2015; *National Interest*, 'Saudi Arabia Honors Its Nastiest Clerical Ideologues', 16 October 2015.

90   Quoting Sheikh Adel al-Kalbani. See Middle East Eye, 'Leading Saudi cleric says IS and Saudi Arabia follow the same thought', 28 January 2016.

91   *Washington Post*, 'Saudi officials tout the country's efforts to crack down on terror financing', 8 June 2016.

92   See, for example, BBC Online, 'Saudi Arabia attack: Islamic State claims Shia mosque bombing', 22 May 2015; Reuters, 'Islamic State attack on Saudi mosque kills one: ministry', 26 October 2015.

93   *Guardian*, 'Islamic State claims suicide bombing at Saudi Arabian mosque', 6 August 2015; *Daily Telegraph*, 'Saudi general killed in attack on border with ISIL-held Iraq', 5 January 2015; Agence France-Presse, 'Saudi general killed on Yemen border while defending country, army says', 27 September 2015; Agence France-Presse, 'Car bomb explodes in Saudi capital Riyadh', 16 July 2015; *Arabian Business*, 'ISIL claims car bomb blast in Saudi capital', 9 February 2016.

94   See, for example, Agence France-Presse, 'Bomb injures policeman at Saudi patrol station', 29 April 2016; Associated Press, 'Saudi raid targeting Islamic State group near Mecca kills four', 5 May 2016; Al-Jazeera, 'Saudi forces kill suspected ISIL fighters near Mecca', 5 May 2016; Reuters, 'Saudi soldier killed in gunbattle with militants', 8 May 2016.

95   See, for example, BBC Online, 'Saudi Arabia arrests 93 members of Islamic State cells', 28 April 2015; Reuters, 'Saudi Arabia says arrests 431 Islamic State suspects, thwarts bombings', 19 July 2015; BBC Online, 'What happened after one man compared Saudi Arabia to Islamic State', 1 December 2015.

96   Reuters, 'Factbox – Gulf Arabs on the rise in Islamic State', 29 June 2015; Reuters, 'Islamic State kills 22 in attacks on Yemen government, Gulf troops, mosque', 6 October 2015.

97   BBC Online, 'Yemen conflict: Governor of Aden killed in Islamic State attack', 6 December 2015; Reuters, 'Islamic State claims Aden suicide car bombing that kills six', 28 January 2016; Reuters, 'Islamic State kills 22 in attacks on Yemen government, Gulf troops, mosque', 6 October, 2015.

98   Numerous such calls have been made, including from US presidential hopefuls. See *The Hill*, 'Sanders blasts Saudi Arabia for suggesting US troops against ISIS', 6 March 2015.

99   *Atlantic*, 'Ashton Carter: Gulf Arabs Need to Get in the Fight', 6 November 2015; Reuters, 'Senior Saudi prince condemns Obama comments on Middle East', 14 March 2016.

100   Reuters, 'Saudi Arabia says open to sending special forces into Syria', 8 February 2016; *Guardian*, 'Saudi Arabia offers to send ground troops to Syria to fight ISIS', 4 February 2016. By the end of 2015 the rejuvenated Iraqi army, with intensifying Iranian support, had already managed to liberate Ramadi. Meanwhile the Syrian army, backed by Russian air strikes, had also begun to retake strategic towns and villages from the Islamic State. Notably, at the time of the Saudi and US statements, Syrian forces and their allies were already preparing to liberate Palmyra, which they eventually entered a few weeks later. See BBC Online, 'Iraq declares Ramadi liberated from Islamic State', 28 December 2015; *Guardian*, 'Assad hails Syrian regime's capture of Palmyra from Isis', 27 March 2016.

INDEX